THE EUROPEAN REFORMATION

The European Reformation

EUAN CAMERON

CLARENDON PRESS · OXFORD

Oxford University Press, Walton Street, Oxford OX2 6DP

Oxford New York Toronto
Delhi Bombay Calcutta Madras Karachi
Petaling Jaya Singapore Hong Kong Tokyo
Nairobi Dar es Salaam Cape Town
Melbourne Auckland

and associated companies in
Berlin Ibadan

Oxford is a trade mark of Oxford University Press

Published in the United States
by Oxford University Press, New York

© *Euan Cameron 1991*

First published 1991
Reprinted 1992

British Library Cataloguing in Publication Data
Cameron, Euan
The European Reformation.
1. Europe. Christian church. Reformation
I. Title 274
ISBN 0-19-873094-2
ISBN 0-19-873093-4 (Pbk.)

Library of Congress Cataloging in Publication Data
Cameron, Euan.
The European Reformation/Euan Cameron.
Includes bibliographical references and index.
1. Reformation. I. Title.
BR305.2.C35 1991   90–47890
274'.06 dc20

ISBN 0-19-873094-2
ISBN 0-19-873093-4 (Pbk.)

Printed in Great Britain by
Butler & Tanner Ltd, Frome and London

For Alexandra and Sarah

Preface

The responsibility for suggesting that I write this book rests squarely with Dr Ivon Asquith, now managing director of the Arts and Reference Division of Oxford University Press, who proposed the idea to me in 1983 and whose support and encouragement have regularly made up for my own fears and misgivings. To Dr Asquith and to subsequent history editors at the Press, Robert Faber and Tony Morris, I am much indebted. The book was begun in the uniquely favourable circumstances of a Junior Fellowship at All Souls College, Oxford. The Warden and Fellows of All Souls made the first stages of the project possible, and then very kindly received me back for a few weeks' work near its conclusion. To my tutor in undergraduate days and mentor since then, Sir Keith Thomas, and to Robin Briggs, who supervised my doctoral thesis, special debts of thanks are owed for their constructive and helpful interest. Since 1985 colleagues in the department of History at the University of Newcastle upon Tyne have sustained and encouraged my efforts; in particular I must thank Professor Jack Watt and Dr Tony Badger, successive heads of department, for their support. Other elder and vastly better scholars of the Reformation period than myself have responded to my daring to attempt such a work with unfailing kindness. Among many it may perhaps not be invidious to mention Professor Patrick Collinson, Dr R. W. Scribner, and the late Professor Richard Stauffer, who were all established authorities in the field at a time when I had barely heard of the Reformation, and yet did nothing but encourage me with the utmost generosity. It is a rare privilege to have a parent who is also an expert in one's own area of work. My father, Professor James K. Cameron, who has opened a new chapter in his career as a sensitive and sympathetic historian of the Renaissance and Reformation in Scotland and Europe since his recent retirement from the Chair of Ecclesiastical history at St Andrews, has unhesitatingly given of his time and energies to discuss ideas, supply references, and find books; and has in many other ways conferred an obligation of gratitude to which these few words can in no way do justice. To my family, for putting up with me during the whole absorbing and demanding process, I owe infinite thanks as well as apologies.

None of these acknowledgements must be taken as presuming to claim the patronage or approval of better historians than myself for the interpretations and opinions expressed in the book. For good or ill, it is essentially one person's attempt to come to terms with one of the most complex and many-faceted movements of western history; and an effort to provide a conceptual structure within which some of the major themes may be related one to another for the benefit of students. The scale of the task would have thoroughly daunted and discouraged anyone who knew the subject better than I did at the start. Not only does the most basic source material far exceed what can be read in one lifetime; new monographs and studies have been published at a phenomenal rate even in the seven years since this project was begun. If it was evident in 1983 that the available basic textbooks for students had been overtaken by the diversification of historical interest into new areas, and by the emergence of new controversies, it is much more so in 1990.

Bearing in mind the range and scale of the scholarly effort devoted to the European Reformation, some historians would insist that the task of constructing a viable synthesis has now outstripped *any* one historian's capacity (let alone mine). This concern may have prompted the remark made by one authority on late medieval and Reformation religious and intellectual history (for whose learning I have the highest possible respect) when discussing how the history of the south German city Reformations should be written: 'The solo flight through the pages of the past, whether undertaken by theologian or intellectual, social or constitutional historian, no longer merits licensing by historical science.' Given that the general reader needs *something* to introduce the subject in a coherent way, there are only limited alternatives to such a 'solo flight'. Either the place of a textbook must be taken by a collection of essays by writers of roughly equal standing; or a scholar of vast experience and seniority must preside over an array of junior historians assigned to distinct areas, and impose *his* concepts on to the work of his troops. Excellent though many works of the first type are, they tend to lack cohesion, since the editor cannot force a single interpretative scheme upon the independent minds of the contributors. The second option (which has thankfully found favour only rarely in the English-speaking tradition) threatens to distort the process of historical research. The general textbook synthesis based on a single continuous vision of the subject (however partial or inadequate) remains indispensable; and it must be preferable for it to draw upon the rich diversity of published monographic research, rather than presiding over it, regulating its approach, or prejudicing its conclusions. The general book should be the servant and mouthpiece of primary research, not its director or its judge.

This book, therefore, offers only provisional opinions on the works of Reformation scholarship which are cited. It selects topics for attention, because selectivity cannot be avoided. It agrees with some interpretations and disagrees with others, simply because to do otherwise would lead to insufferable blandness as well as incomprehensible confusion. It marshals both the familiar and the newer components of the Reformation story behind a single thesis; but does so principally for the sake of convenience and clarity.

It may be helpful to forewarn readers of some of the choices made. First, this book is not a history of Europe in the Reformation period, but of the Reformation movements themselves. The primary theme is so vast that no justice could hope to be done to wider social, cultural, or intellectual trends. Secondly, it is a history of movements rather than a biography (religious, intellectual, or political) of a small number of important people. Anyone who wishes to understand the individual peculiarities of Luther, Zwingli, or Calvin will find more details in the older books than here. The reason for this shift of emphasis is that many more personalities shaped the Reformation (from council chamber and street as well as pulpit) than the few hero-figures of tradition; and those factors which made them different from each other were not always as important as the (less historically fashionable) attributes which they shared. It makes *theological* sense to point out many subtle distinctions between the thought of Luther and Melanchthon (for example); but for explaining *historically* the course of the early Lutheran Reformation it makes very little sense whatever.

The selection process will probably appear most arbitrary, however, where references are concerned. This is a work of synthesis, not a piece of primary research; to have documented fairly every scholarly contribution made to the themes discussed, even in the last generation, would have made the references longer than the book. The works cited here are those which proved most useful or pertinent when the book was written, or which seemed to offer the most accessible summaries or documents for students. If a book or article is not cited, that is not necessarily because it is unknown to me (though vast amounts of writing on the subject must necessarily be) nor yet that it is deemed in any way unsuitable. References to works in English tend to predominate, for the sake of students (whose options are usually limited nowadays by linguistic ability and consequently by restricted library resources); where there is an English translation available of a work published in another language, it is generally the translation which is cited.

This kind of work is only ever ended, rather than finished. It is impossible not to feel humbled as much by the vastness of the historical endeavour which is here so briefly summarized, as by the intensity of thought and feeling experienced by the movement's sixteenth-century participants. It is hoped that any historian whose work is handled in too brusque a fashion here will remember that this book is meant only to be some of the first words that the student may read on the subject; by no means the last.

Gosforth,   E.K.C.
June 1990

Contents

I. *The Background*

II. *The Reformers and Their Message*

III. *Establishing the Reformed Churches*

IV. *The Coalition of Reformers and People Breaks Down*

List of Figures

List of Maps

Introduction
The Reformation and Europe

What was 'the Reformation'?

The Reformation, the movement which divided European Christianity into catholic and protestant traditions, is unique. No other movement of religious protest or reform since antiquity has been so widespread or lasting in its effects, so deep and searching in its criticism of received wisdom, so destructive in what it abolished or so fertile in what it created. Historians sometimes liken other more limited movements to it; they speak of a tenth-century Reformation in Anglo-Saxon England, or a 'premature' Reformation of the English Wycliffites in the fourteenth century; or call heretic movements like the Waldenses in the twelfth century or the Hussites in the fifteenth 'first' or 'early' reformations. Yet 'the Reformation' always refers to the same episode: the religious transformation which overtook European society in the sixteenth century.

The European Reformation was not a simple revolution, a protest movement with a single leader, a defined set of objectives, or a coherent organization. Yet neither was it a floppy or fragmented mess of anarchic or contradictory ambitions. It was a series of *parallel* movements; within *each* of which various sorts of people with differing perspectives for a crucial period in history combined forces to pursue objectives which they only partly understood.

First of all, the Reformation was a protest by churchmen and scholars, privileged classes in medieval society, against their own superiors. Those superiors, the Roman papacy and its agents, had attacked the teachings of a few sincere, respected academic churchmen which had seemed to threaten the prestige and privilege of clergy and papacy. Martin Luther, the first of those protesting clerics, had attacked 'the Pope's crown and the monks' bellies',[1] and they had fought back, to defend their status. The protesting churchmen—the 'reformers'—responded to the Roman counter-attack not by silence or furtive opposition, but by publicly denouncing their accusers in print. Not only that: they developed their teachings to make their protest more coherent, and to justify their disobedience.

Then the most surprising thing of all, in the context of medieval lay people's usual response to religious dissent, took place. Politically active laymen, not (at first) political rulers with axes to grind, but rather ordinary, moderately prosperous householders, took up the reformers' protests, identified them (perhaps mistakenly) as their own, and pressed them upon their governors. This blending and coalition—of reformers' protests and laymen's political ambitions—is the essence of the Reformation. It turned the reformers' movement into a new form of religious dissent: it became not a 'schism', in which a section of the catholic Church rose in political revolt against authority, without altering beliefs or practices; nor yet a 'heresy', whereby a few people deviated from official belief or worship, but without respect, power, or authority. Rather it promoted a new pattern of worship and belief, publicly preached and acknowledged, which *also* formed the basis of new religious *institutions* for all of society, within the whole community, region, or nation concerned.

The coalition of churchmen's protests and lay peoples' political involvement lasted just long enough to make sweeping and irreversible changes in all sorts of aspects of sixteenth-century life. Eventually—sooner in some areas than others—the coalition broke down. The reforming churchmen wished not only to demolish the privileges and oppressions which they saw in the old order, but also to set up a 'Christian commonwealth' in which *their* priorities would be best served. Most laymen, on the other hand, felt that they had not thrown off one burdensome church institution only to subject themselves to another, and resisted such church 'discipline' energetically.

Plan of the Book

This study tries to explain some of these unique features of the European Reformation in a coherent way. First of all the religious life and institutions of late medieval Europe will be sketched out. This sketch will not try to show, with hindsight, that the Reformation was inevitable; nor yet that it followed as a steady evolution from previous trends. It will rather suggest that the complex texture of late fifteenth-century religion, its piety and its protests, its intellectual sincerity and its gross credulity, made it vulnerable to the *particular* kind of critique to which the reformers, more confidently than anyone before, subjected it.

Secondly, the reformers, their message and their own backgrounds and histories, will be presented. This coverage is based on the provisional assumption that one must understand what the clerics behind the initial protests had to say, *before* one studies how their message was manipulated in the involved political struggles of the period. It is not enough to say that ideas (as opposed, say, to social or economic trends) do not matter, or (at the other extreme) that they can be studied in isolation from their context. One needs a 'social history of belief', in which the role of ideas is neither assumed, nor ignored, but *analysed*.

The third major topic of this book is the peculiarly Reformation type of 'coalition' between reformers and politicians. One must first chart the progress of 'established' reformed churches, including not only those political groups which succeeded in setting up a reformed order, but also those which failed. The 'how' and the 'why' of that process constitute the core of the analysis, as of most recent studies of the Reformation in sixteenth-century society. Once again, the extreme interpretations, namely that lay people pressed for the Reformation for *purely* socio-economic or, conversely, *purely* pious motives, are unlikely to satisfy, given the variety of contexts in which the reformed programme was adopted.

The final chapters will consider some of the problems which emerged as the impetus given by that first 'coalition' ran out, and the Reformation came to terms with its unforeseen achievements. Some 'reformers', frustrated with the compromises and wiles of politicians, abandoned the characteristically 'Reformation' posture of reshaping the political community, in favour of the more archaic aim of setting up sectarian cells of 'perfect' followers at odds with society. These sectarians, usually called 'radicals' or 'anabaptists', form the exception to nearly every general rule which one tries to establish about the Reformation; as such they help, in some sense, to define its mainstream. The new churches had to be defended politically and militarily; this need produced both diplomatic initatives and pamphlets of ideas to justify using force against the embodiments of the old 'Christendom'. The second generation of Reformation movements, which gained a footing after about 1550, require a separate analysis. In these cases it was not a question of the whole community deciding within itself where 'true religion' actually lay, so much as of rival pressure groups urging the case of differing and rival 'confessions' which offered a variety of religious 'packages'. Finally, churchmen sought to consolidate their achievements by establishing respect for their own order, and by educating and disciplining their followers; the reactions which they encountered tell us much about lay people's motives and views of the Reformation as a whole.

Europe in the Early Sixteenth Century

Only a thumbnail sketch of the continent in which the Reformation took place can be accommodated here. When one speaks of the 'European' Reformation, it is Latin Christendom, where the Roman papacy was respected and the Roman alphabet written, that one envisages.[2] It was united by Church structures and customs, and even more by the Latin language and educational traditions. By 1500 the continent was still thinly and unevenly populated. Mass disease had wiped out perhaps as many as one-third of the population in the mid-fourteenth century. Repeated lesser plagues had further depressed the total until about 1460–80. Thereafter modest increases had brought the numbers of people back up to perhaps 60–75 per cent of their previous maxima by 1500, to 75–90 per cent by 1550, and perhaps 100 per cent by 1600. In actual numbers, there may have been sixty to eighty-five million Europeans in 1500, and eighty-five to one hundred million in 1600.[3]

The structure of the population, determined by marriage patterns, nutrition, fertility, and disease, ensured that any rise would be gradual.[4] Of those eighty million or so people, nine out of ten lived in small hamlets or scattered farmsteads, their lives shaped by the agricultural cycle. Of the remainder less than half lived in one of the hundred or so towns which by 1600 exceeded 20,000 inhabitants.[5] Those towns, unhealthy even in good years, steadily soaked up the excess population of the countryside to gain cheap (and short-lived) labour.[6] When Reformation historians dwell—as they do—on large corporate towns, they are emphasizing the role of a tiny proportion of Europe's people in the movement.[7]

The alternate collapse and rise of the population had profound social consequences in most regions of Europe. The collapse made labour scarce and staple foods abundant; subsistence became somewhat easier, but actually making a profit from the land required initiative and diversity of effort. Stock-rearing (including sheep for wool), luxury crops for wine-making, brewing, and dyeing, all grew at the expense of grain in western Europe.[8] When the population multiplied, the cultivation of luxuries did *not* always yield the land back again to staple foods. Although basic grains normally rose faster in price than any other commodity in the 'price revolution', restrictions on their marketing and export often made them unattractive to commercial farmers. Only in Poland and the Baltic coast was there a flourishing export trade in cereals; elsewhere they were generally scarce and costly.[9] Not only did the rural proletariat pay more to eat; their position as tenants or labourers usually deteriorated. Marginal rights and 'fringe benefits' like fishing and wood-gathering were whittled down by landlords, and old exactions and oppressions, overlooked in the late Middle Ages, could be rediscovered.[10] With food and land scarcer and valued higher than labour, wages failed to keep pace with either the cost of living or the rents for most kinds of land.[11]

As a life based solely on agriculture became more insecure, in some areas at least more and more of the rural population turned to small-scale manufacturing for the market, above all in textiles, in the process known as 'putting-out' or 'proto-industrialization'. Although the extent and type of this rural craft-working varied, in some cases it caused yet further worry to the towns, who saw their monopolies in both industry and commerce eroded by competition.[12] In turn the towns, no less than the rural proletariat, became 'problem' areas. Markets and even industries in the smaller towns found themselves circumvented. In the greatest cities, in industrial or trading regions such as The Netherlands, southern and central Germany, or northern Italy, the picture was much more complex, as economic hardships were reflected in constitutional disputes between oligarchies and artisan interest groups.[13]

Even Europe's aristocracies had their problems. The rise in demand for land benefited those resourceful enough and powerful enough to make their lordship pay its way. However, those near the bottom ranks of the nobility could not always exploit their position to make up for rising prices. Fragmentation of estates, and often unprofitable and expensive preoccupations with foreign war or rulers' courts, left some petty nobles, especially in central and southern Germany, France, and the Low Countries, with large debts and larger grudges.[14] At the level of princes and monarchs, two necessary expenditures, ceremonial and warfare, became enormously inflated in scale and cost; this inflation required higher taxes (and their political risks), or extensive borrowing or, more commonly, both of these.

One should not conclude from these various social and economic problems that Europe was in a clearly definable 'crisis', which forms a starting-point for the Reformation. Problems there certainly were, and if one studies only one small region one can often see how local socio-economic strains interacted with the religious movements. However, on a much wider perspective the picture becomes far less clear. All sorts of classes both prospered and suffered in the century—with the possible exception of the rural proletariat, who seem almost everywhere to have lost out.[15] The puzzle for the historian should not so much be to find economic 'explanations' for the Reformation; but rather to explain why, with so many urgent difficulties in the day-to-day sphere, the people of Europe so readily expressed their discontents in terms of religion.

There were, of course, areas of enormous growth and promise in early modern European society, summed up in that broadening of physical and mental horizons known as the Renaissance. The 'humanist' movement in northern Europe enlarged the options for thinking people beyond the ways of thinking, teaching, and explaining the world which had evolved as common property in the Middle Ages.[16] It accompanied other developments: the sheer numbers of universities in Europe grew dramatically;[17] to service this growth industry in ideas, the movable type printing-press expanded book production from the 1460s onwards. The issue of the printing-press and the Reformation is complex. The early reformers turned automatically to the press as soon as they needed widespread support.[18] It is hard to imagine the movement growing as it did without printed propaganda. However, this does not mean that the availability of printing 'caused' the Reformation.[19] The press existed for some sixty years before the protests of Luther and his allies. During that period it mostly produced exactly the same kinds of books—bibles, Church service-books, textbooks, and encyclopaedias—as the old manuscript copying-houses.[20] It simply produced more of them, and at lower cost. Secondly, it was by no means obvious that easier communication of texts would favour dissenters. This century has shown that mass media can as easily prop up a tyranny as undermine one. For the Reformation to achieve its aims through printing, its authors had to have something dramatic to say to a wide public; to say it much more persuasively than their opponents; and to evade or subvert official censorship. Printing was a catalyst, a precondition, but not of itself a cause.[21]

The Reformation can only be understood in terms of the late medieval world from which it grew and against which it rebelled. Whatever the reasons for its political successes, the Reformation message began with the late medieval Church and late medieval religion, which must now be considered.

PART I

The Background

I

The Religion of the People of Europe

It used to be fashionable to begin any discussion of the origins and background to the Reformation with a long dirge on the weakness, corruption, and 'decay' of the European Church and religious life around the year 1500. The argument was more or less as follows: the Reformation was a religious revival; religious revivals presuppose a period of decadence before them; therefore the late middle ages must have been religiously decadent. This argument had *some* logic: the reformers (like everyone else, including most churchmen) *did* criticize 'abuses' (the breaking of accepted rules) within the Church. However, that does not mean that the reformers rebelled against the Church *because* of its failings alone.[1] Indeed, they rebelled just as fiercely against many of its ideals and its successes. One must study the Church's aims and ideals first, before considering its faults and flaws and their role in the Reformation.

What *function* did the Church perform within late medieval society? It existed to fulfil a role; how well did it do so? This chapter discusses the *primary* role of the Church, the provision of a religious 'service' to Europe's diverse peoples. Whatever else the Church was supposed to do—and that 'else' included a great deal—it was expected to provide contact between human beings and the supernatural order of their universe, to explain, direct, and console.

1. *The Masses*

It is no longer adequate to describe Europe's religion solely in terms of what the 'official' Church taught people to believe and to do. The rural masses, remote from the urban academic power-houses of theology, had religious priorities of their own, in which their own priests, born of the same stock as their congregations, took part. 'Popular culture' and 'popular religion' must be taken seriously despite the lack of agreement among experts as to what they mean.[2] We know that such unofficial views of religion existed, largely because, after the Reformation was established, both protestant and catholic priests fought long and hard to domesticate them.[3] Even before the Reformation, however, late medieval clergy copiously documented those popular cults which they called 'superstitions'.[4]

Popular belief was much less concerned with the hereafter than with the present life. Most lay people were less worried about saving their souls, than about everyday security. Hence they took steps to ensure that they and theirs had enough to eat: they performed rites to protect crops from blight, storms, or dearth, and their animals from disease and death. They wished to avoid illness and sudden death, especially in dangerous contexts like a sea voyage or wartime; finally, they used an arsenal of supernatural charms to preserve their looks, to attract a suitable partner, to ensure against infertility and impotence, to protect women in childbirth, and to guard children against disease and demonic possession when they were most vulnerable. Such were the immediate pressing concerns of human survival in an age where all the essentials of life were beyond most people's control or foresight. Charms and rituals were 'ineffective techniques to allay anxiety when effective ones were not available'.[5]

Some of these rites and cults were quite distinct from the Church's own rituals. Children born with the 'caul' or part of the amniotic membrane still around the head were widely believed to have special spiritual attributes.[6] Seventh-born sons were also endowed with them.[7] Books were passed around full of magical charms for protecting crops and curing illnesses, the original meaning of their words confused or forgotten.[8] However, because the seasonal rituals of the Church pervaded every aspect of village life, it was much more common for popular superstition to be woven into the texture of 'official' worship. The medieval Church taught people to stop all manual labour on the feast-days of saints in order to devote themselves to their worship. Late medieval people, seeing that a given day was specially 'holy', believed in doing *more* special tasks on those days, in order to gain supernatural benefits, than at other times. On St John Baptist's day (also, significantly, midsummer), herbs were collected to protect against storms and cure goitre, and horses bled by their farriers to cure illness.[9] Firebrands from St John's day bonfires were regarded as talismans, as were eggs laid on Good Friday.[10] On St Blasius's day German horses and cattle were given Blasius-water to drink; on St Agatha's day 'Agatha-bread' or blessed bread.[11]

The saints and their images themselves attracted a host of parasitic popular beliefs. Peasants in the Navarrese countryside desperate for rain carried an image of St Peter or the body of St Felicia in procession to local rivers and submerged them to bring rain. The people of Pamplona tied bracelets to a tree near San Cristobal's Basilica to prevent headaches, and girls hung locks of hair in front of St Urban's image in a local monastery to stop their hair from falling out.[12] Images were sometimes punished by beating or immersion if they failed to produce the desired effect. In a more general way, saints were regarded as the patrons and protectors of particular places, crafts, or trades, or as protectors in particular states of danger, as St Christopher protected travellers and St Margaret women in childbirth; or as the specialist patrons of those afflicted with particular ailments.[13]

The rituals of the Church could be copied, adapted, or parodied to help with everyday life. Women approaching labour might be brought to church with a cymbal tied to their clothing, which would be struck three times; this copied the religious rite of ringing the church bell three times to call for an Ave Maria to be said to give thanks *after* a safe delivery. Old women would hang pieces of parchment with texts of Scripture or the liturgy written on them around the necks of feverish patients, then insist that the spell only worked if the parchment were previously unused, hung towards the sun by three threads wound by a virgin girl called Mary.[14] Many 'conjurations', Christian prayers uttered sometimes in combination with each other or with, say, a juniper wand, were used for purposes as varied as winning a lawsuit or curing a nosebleed.[15]

Serious-minded churchmen repeatedly complained about the sacrilege, parody, or even sorcery implied in these attempts to manipulate holy things mechanically to gain material benefits. However, 'official' religion suffered in parasitic superstition the fruits of its own success in blending itself into rural life. The powers of saints and their shrines had in the past been advertised to attract pilgrims; those powers came to be attributed to the place, the relic, or the festival day themselves rather than to the saint's memory, holiness, or intercession. The Church insisted that one could multiply acts of prayer or worship as often as one liked and gain benefits from them;[16] so ordinary people used prayers as charms. The precise limits between medicine, prayer, and superstition were ill defined.

The Reformation was to offer little to a people who depended so heavily on manipulating the trappings of Christianity in a sub-Christian way. The early reformers were sometimes the victims of such beliefs: in 1523 a Polish traveller found the Saxon peasants around Wittenberg furious with the city-dwellers who had been eating meat in Lent, thinking they had caused the river Elbe to rise and flood their fields.[17] Much later on, protestant ministers were to struggle long against popular devotion to these means of reassurance. The old Church, on the other hand, usually connived at these crude belief-systems until well after the Reformation era. Such systems and attitudes bound people to the rituals, and implicitly to the institutions, of the old Church; only by either discrediting such beliefs, or offering something more persuasive, or cultivating the allegiance of those least superstitious to begin with, could the Reformation have implanted itself.

2. *The Élites*

In the eyes of Europe's spiritual élites religion was a very different matter, although no less tied to the social needs and concerns of the aristocracy, higher clergy, and upper bourgeoisie. There was no clear dividing line between 'popular' and 'élite' religion; indeed, numerous religious activities shared in by all levels of society will be discussed shortly. However, certain 'élite' priorities and preferences were very different from rural 'popular' religion as just described.

First of all, the Church's religion laid down standards of behaviour and offered some limited means to enforce those standards. To be a 'good Christian' was as important as to be a 'good subject'; the sanctions imposed (especially beyond this life) were, theoretically, very severe. One could tell who was a 'good Christian' by whether or not they: learned the Lord's Prayer and the Apostles' Creed; stopped working on Sundays, and went to church to hear mass; confessed their sins once a year, before receiving the communion at Easter; fasted (abstained from certain foods, especially meat) on the eves of saints' days, the Ember days, and in Lent; stopped work to take part in worship on the festival days of the saints, and venerated them; sought the sacraments of the Church when on the point of death; and left money for masses for their souls.[18] Heavy emphasis was laid upon loyalty to and participation in the rites and calendar of the official Church. To enforce these basic norms of behaviour, and to attempt to exact any higher standards, the religion of the élites employed the confessional, the 'sacrament of penance'. In this ritual context the believer was required to list his faults to the priest and answer questions on them, as a prelude to being 'absolved', that is, forgiven and reintegrated into the religious community.[19] Although most people subjected themselves to the confessional only infrequently and hurriedly, the institution did offer a rare opportunity for Europe's ruling classes to supervise individually the behaviour of their subjects.[20]

On the other hand, penitential discipline was not a cynical means for the powerful to dominate the rest; it was inflicted at least as severely, and usually more so, upon members of the ruling classes themselves. Lay people who could afford to do so maintained 'confessors', resident household priests whose function was to discipline and console their patrons' consciences, and who sometimes wrote spiritual biographies of their patrons after their deaths.[21] Some voluntary societies of lay people, like the Company of San Domenico at Sienna, required regular and rigorous confessional discipline as a condition of membership.[22] A well-conducted confession served, for the educated, to console and guide as much to warn and punish; it aimed as much to prevent morbid and over-scrupulous worry about sin, as to reproach complacency. Moreover, so many confessors, of varying qualifications, were available that the laity could largely choose who was to hear them list their sins.[23]

Late medieval catholicism not only offered a rule for life and means to police that rule, it also, very importantly, offered the services of its clergy to carry out works of piety on behalf of lay people who chose not to do so themselves. The Church, in short, offered the wealthy the opportunity to invest in the health of their souls. In contrast to popular belief, the emphasis here was overwhelmingly on the destiny of the soul after death. Prayer, and especially the sacrifice of the mass—even when offered outside congregational worship—was believed to earn an objective, measurable benefit which could be, so to speak, transferred to the account of a pious founder.

This belief is attested by the enormous proliferation in endowed masses for the souls of the departed, sometimes called 'obits' or 'chantries', towards the end of the Middle Ages. These foundations developed in two ways. First, more and more masses were endowed at one go, as it were. It was officially taught that the value of a Church rite could be increased by multiplication of that rite.[24] Whereas the rural masses seem to have adhered to the traditional system of a mass for the soul on the ninth day after death and the first anniversary, by the fifteenth century everyone from the middling bourgeoisie right up to the apex of society was collecting multiples of masses for their souls, said annually for perhaps thirty years, perhaps (for the very richest) in perpetuity.[25] Secondly, there was believed to be an *extra* spiritual value in a sacrifice offered by a specially pious priest.[26] So those elements in the Church which were believed to be unusually holy enjoyed the favour of wealthy lay investors: the strict or 'observant' congregations of friars, or the Carthusian monks with their long-standing prestige.[27]

In other ways lay people could take advantage of the services offered by the official Church's piety. Relics—physical objects associated with Christ, the saints, or some spectacular miracle—had in earlier times given status and authority to local churches, princes of the Church, even lay rulers.[28] In the decades before the Reformation relic cults grew randomly and spontaneously, prompting lay people to visit them, found shrines for them, and make gifts to their cults; or even, for the very wealthiest, to build up private collections of them. In Germany there was a particularly profitable run of such new shrines: the bleeding Eucharistic hosts at Wilsnack and Sternberg, the robe of Christ exhibited at Trier, and the miraculous images of the Virgin at Grimmenthal and Regensburg.[29] One of the most spectacularly devout rulers of the period was Elector Friedrich of the 'Ernestine' branch of the Wettin rulers of Saxony: in 1493 he spent five days in Jerusalem, then in later life spent a fortune rebuilding the castle church in his capital of Wittenberg to house his collection of more than 19,000 relics, including the body of a holy innocent, Mary's milk, and straw from the stable of the Nativity. He also had eighty-three priests say almost 10,000 masses for him during 1520 alone.[30] Rivalling Friedrich's collection was that of the electoral archbishop of Mainz, Albrecht of Brandenburg, whose relics were estimated to free their beneficiaries from over thirty-nine million years in purgatory.[31]

The purpose, from the educated viewpoint, of all this activity was that it helped the individual soul to progress to a more favoured place in the penitential system. Most shrines had 'indulgences' attached to them: in practical terms, a pilgrim on visiting a shrine could acquire (for money) exemption from carrying out the pious works imposed after his last confession. There were many other ways in which 'indulgence' could be obtained, and indeed other purposes to which it could be applied.[32] The basic aim, however, was to add the *Church's* holiness to the believer's efforts to help his own soul. This marks the divide between the religion of the élites and the rural masses: concern with the soul rather than the body; reassurance in the face of God's judgement and punishment of sin, rather than invoking divine aid against the caprices of nature or demonic forces.

3. *Common Features*

So far, one might caricature late medieval piety by suggesting that those who had less need to worry about their bodily wants could afford to expend additional effort and money on fashionable means to ensure their welfare beyond the grave. However, rich and poor people's piety did not exist in watertight compartments. The richest and most cultured held the crudest superstitions, while almost every level of society took some part in the sacraments, the confessional, and rites for the dead. Most of the growth in masses for the dead represented a 'democratization' of the system, an extension of the Church's services to a wider clientele. The Church of the late Middle Ages, in short, offered a range of services to everyone.

The sacraments themselves were offered to mark and to make holy several crucial points in human life: baptism for birth and entry into Church and society, confirmation for admission to full membership of the Church, marriage for pairing and establishing a household, extreme unction in preparation for death. Of the remaining three, penance cleansed the soul in preparation for receiving communion; ordination defined those people who (in normal circumstances) could administer the other six. However, the sacraments were normally received infrequently if at all: the first four were only given once in a lifetime; penance was normally administered once a year to ordinary lay people; the Eucharist was actually *received* (as opposed to simply being heard and watched) perhaps three times (for the serious-minded).[33] Besides these, the Church more frequently and freely dispensed the so-called 'sacramentals', lesser ministrations which lay people could also use. These included the consecrated candles, of varying size and cost, which accompanied church services; the palms blessed on Palm Sunday, herbs blessed on the feast of the Assumption, and especially the varieties of Holy Water.[34]

The Church gave people a forum and a structure for their social life. Attendance at mass, and even more participation in processions and festivals, were grand social occasions in which the community displayed itself to its members. As the mass was 'heard'—from the other side of the screen of the church—more often than received, the congregation could talk, do business, or show off. Nor was it only or principally in the parish church that mass was heard. The late fifteenth and early sixteenth centuries saw a great vogue in the open-ended 'brotherhoods' or 'confraternities', associations of people joined by their trade, social status, or other common bond, who heard mass in common. Within these societies the rich to some extent looked after the poor, and the living looked after the dead, by supporting the costs of burial and praying for the souls of members. Memberships overlapped; belonging to half a dozen or so confraternities at once was not uncommon.[35] Confraternities held special masses to celebrate their patrons, usually the Virgin or her mother St Anne, an occupational or local saint, or a saint associated with the care of a disease like St Roch.[36] Rural confraternities often overlapped with both the parish and other social bodies such as youth associations, all very loosely tied to the priesthood itself.[37]

It is not too blunt to say that the Church provided a large part of popular theatre and entertainment. There were, of course, religious plays as such, 'mystery plays' which provided a crude but memorable presentation of Bible narratives.[38] However, besides deliberately staged plays, which usually enjoyed only one short season a year, many festivals of the Church had a highly theatrical flavour. During the Good Friday to Easter period it was common in Germany to set up a representation of Christ's tomb, called an *ölberg* and often elaborately ornamented, into which the body of Christ from the church crucifix was interred on Good Friday and from which it was ceremonially raised on Easter morning. Other such performances accompanied the festivals of Palm Sunday, Ascension day, and Whitsun.[39] In 1533, the crucial year of the Reformation in Augsburg, rival protestant and catholic families nearly came to blows over the ceremonial raising of the Christ-figure on Ascension day, a powerful indication of its significance for the people there.[40]

In general, all the most popular activities of late medieval religion were based on *doing* something, on participation, activity, movement, essentially on experiencing an event more than on learning or understanding a message. Religious processions, above all on Corpus Christi day (where the consecrated Eucharistic wafer was carried in state as the 'body of Christ'), attracted great crowds. At the end of the fifteenth century the 'Stations of the Cross', a detailed processional re-enactment within the church of Christ's road to Calvary, offered a kind of substitute pilgrimage.[41] Pilgrimage itself, travelling to places of special sanctity, retained its allure, though more usually to an accessible new shrine within Europe than to Jerusalem. An astonishing number of such sites developed in southern Germany, especially Bavaria, in the later Middle Ages.[42]

The Virgin Mary enjoyed special favour from the pious at this period. Not only were more shrines dedicated to her:[43] confraternities were very frequently named after her, and within these centres grew up special cults, such as the devotion of the Rosary: this settled into the pattern of one Our Father, then ten Hail Marys, repeated fifteen times, and was made popular by Dominican friars such as Alain de la Roche in France and Jakob Sprenger in Germany.[44] The belief grew, fostered especially within the order of Franciscan friars and more rapidly in southern Europe than the north, that Mary had been conceived by her mother St Anne free from the inherited or 'original' sin shared by all other human beings. This doctrine of the 'Immaculate Conception', though espoused by many friars, universities, and zealous laymen at the time, remained controversial. It only became a dogma of the Church as late as 1854; it affords further evidence that religion at this period did not depend only on initiatives from the Church hierarchy.[45] Mary's' mother St Anne also enjoyed popular vogue, shown for instance by the *Treatise* in her praise written by Trithemius of Sponheim in 1494.[46]

In one important respect late medieval piety did not conform to this pattern of participating, non-verbal, non-intellectual acts of worship. The preaching and hearing of sermons was also immensely popular at this period, whether in the case of settled local preachers with special endow= ments to support them, or travelling preachers (usually friars) moving from centre to centre. This enthusiasm for the spoken word probably forms the main difference between town and countryside piety: though it is almost certain that townspeople went to country shrines, and that country folk came to the towns to hear sermons. In any case, numerous cities, especially in Germany, established posts for resident preachers in their parish chur- ches. Forty-two towns in the duchy of Württemberg alone had preach- erships, and the movement expanded as far north as Saxony (Eisenach, Gotha, Weimar, Jena) and the Baltic coast (Lübeck) as well as such central and southern cities as Windsheim, Memmingen, and Augsburg.[47]

Some of these preachers became famous personalities. A resident pre- acher like Johann Geiler von Kaysersberg at Strasbourg, or Johannes Heynlin von Stein (d.1496) at Basle, could clearly exercise enormous influence in his city. Others, in France and Italy no less than Germany, were travellers, extending their influence even further; Olivier Maillard (d.1502) or Michel Menot (d.1522) in France, Vincent Ferreri (d.1419) or Giovanni Capistrano (d.1456) in Italy, and the observant Franciscan Jan Brugman (d.1473) in the Low Countries and the Rhineland.[48] However, one should not form too romantic a picture of late medieval preachers. The best were clearly excellent; but the worst were comical and notorious. A decree of the Fifth Lateran Council in 1516 complained about the verbal extravagance and unreliability of some preachers; while Renaissance figures like Erasmus mocked their absurdities.[49]

There are other reasons not to idealize the spiritual quality of late medieval piety. All levels of society readily believed in various kinds of superstition, magic, prophecy, and other supernatural intrusions into the order of creation. These were not 'deviant', 'perverted', or 'aberrant' forms of thought; they were an integral part of the overall picture.[50] Astrology, occult influences at work in the cosmos, the capacity of the natural order to be subverted by monsters: all these found ready acceptance by various people at all social levels.[51] Throughout the late Middle Ages and the

Reformation period, many people claimed that the end of the world and the Second Coming were imminent; though it might be argued that this expectation did not make most ordinary people change their everyday lives, any more than the fear of mass destruction in nuclear war, so much talked about, has done in the latter part of the present century. The most notorious form of late medieval bad taste—to modern eyes—was its fascination with death and decay, shown alike in tracts preparing the reader for death and copious works of art depicting its most gruesome features.[52] It is very hard to judge how 'macabre' this artistic taste really was. Unexpected or premature death was then always present in western Europe, in disease, starvation in famine years, in warfare, in judicial execution. Fifteenth-century people could hardly have anticipated Europeans of the present century by making death clinical, remote, and aseptic.

In the past these features of fifteenth-century religion have usually been denounced as 'anguished', 'flawed', or in some way unsatisfactory: implying that though people behaved in this way, it must somehow have failed to satisfy their needs.[53] This attitude matches the classic, impressionistic description of the late fifteenth century as an 'autumn' of the Middle Ages, with an overripe, overblown, exhausted quality.[54] Such judgements almost always apply some external standard: they deplore late medieval religion because it seems inferior to the high Middle Ages, to the catholicism of the mid-sixteenth century, or to present-day standards of what 'pure' Christianity ought to mean. The historian, however, does not want to know whether present-day theologians approve of this sort of religion; but rather to analyse what people of that time thought of it. The vast bulk of the evidence suggests that they not only participated in it; they *shaped* it according to their own preferences. One must stop talking about 'decay' or 'flaws' *except* to the extent that they were deplored (and not just by a high-minded clique of late medieval reformers) at the time.[55]

A second criticism is sometimes levelled against the characteristic piety of most fifteenth-century people. It can be portrayed as the result of a capitulation, a surrender of principle, by the clergy to the vulgar materialism of the times. By rushing to provide lay people with the multiplicity of masses and other services (so the argument runs) the Church failed to prevent religion from turning into the 'merchandizing', the 'blessed trans-action', by which spiritual goods were bought with worldly ones.[56] In this way the purchasing of masses and the like can be classed as an 'aberrant' or 'misguided' form of piety; the priestly refusal to prevent it can be ranked alongside the late medieval 'failures' of Church authority and prestige. However, there does not seem to be proof that most of the clergy saw matters in this way. The most detailed survey so far of these practices has found no hostility, rather active and adaptable co-operation, between priests and laymen in developing the 'mathematics of salvation'.[57] Indeed, it was the most efficiently *reformed* bodies of observant friars or secular priests (who should have been the first to resist such materialistic piety if they thought it a 'betrayal' or a 'compromise') who actually did most to service lay demand, and reaped the greatest profits from so doing.[58]

There is a further point. Some historians, consciously or not, have tended to assume a 'flaw' in late medieval religion, because it was so abruptly changed in the mid-sixteenth century. People (the argument goes) must have been unhappy with their religion, because they chose protestantism (or reformed catholicism) to replace it. Therefore the question is put, how does late medieval religion explain the Reformation?, and the issues are read backwards. Two unproven assumptions are hidden in these approaches: (*a*) that people *wanted* the Reformation, in its entirety; (*b*) that the state of late medieval religion *ought* to make understanding the causes of the Reformation easier. In fact, there is growing evidence that, once they saw what it meant, many people did *not* want the Reformation, still less did they want to lose their cults and rituals; in many places they clung to them obstinately.[59]

Secondly, *does* late medieval religion make it easier to explain the Reformation? On the evidence of this chapter, it in fact makes it much harder. The Christianity of the later Middle Ages was a supple, flexible, varied entity, adapted to the needs, concerns, and tastes (with all their undoubted crude, primitive features) of the people who created it. It was not an inflexible tyranny presided over by a remote authority. It left room for personal preference and private or local initiative. It threatened, but it also comforted; it disciplined, but it also entertained. If it were *only* a question of piety and worship, we should be hard put to find signs of real mass dissatisfaction with the Church. It was not its *primary* function, then, which made the Church on the eve of the Reformation so vulnerable. It was rather the tangle of *secondary* roles, duties, responsibilities, and their consequences which caused most of the trouble: these form the next major topic.

2

The Vulnerability of the Church

Whatever the people of Europe may have thought about *religion* around the year 1500, they clearly did not think that all was well with the *Church*. From all directions a barrage of varied (and not always consistent) criticisms attacked the failings of individual churchmen and the institution as a whole. Something (or rather many things) were clearly wrong: but what, and why? One must try to avoid using words like 'decay' or 'corruption' to explain this dissatisfaction, as though the late medieval Church was inevitably declining to its natural end according to some determined historical cycle. Early modern 'science' spoke of dead bodies or plants 'decaying' or 'corrupting' during decomposition; the action of bacteria was not understood, and so it was assumed that all 'bodies'—whether natural organisms, or 'political' bodies like human societies—naturally disintegrated after they had lived out their span.[1] 'Corruption' in this sense *is* only a metaphor; it does not of itself tell us anything about the problems of the Church.

This chapter will suggest that the late medieval Church was vulnerable to criticism, because it took on too great a variety of demanding and mutually inconsistent 'secondary' tasks: jobs over and above its primary role of providing a religious 'service'. Many of these tasks developed because in the early Middle Ages the Church served as the custodian, not just of the religious tradition, but of almost all written records, everything from literature to bureaucracy.[2] As society became more sophisticated, these tasks, instead of being returned to lay control, had stayed within the Church's remit. To support all these activities as they multiplied, the Church had to look ever more closely to its revenues, and to drain money from traditional areas of expense—like the parish priesthood—to serve more fashionable ones. The need for money in turn led churchmen to seek for, defend, and often abuse, their privileges and status. Finally, as running the Church became ever more complex, the people whom it recruited and promoted to high office reflected its needs: lawyers, pen-pushers, and politicians first, spiritual leaders second. At every point these features of the late medieval Church grated against the sensitivities of laymen (for one reason) and certain kinds of churchmen (for quite different reasons).

The stages in this argument must now be developed.

1. *A Conflict of Responsibilities*

Even the 'religious' duties of the Church, as narrowly defined as possible, involved potential conflicts of interest. As was shown earlier, the Church 'served' its faithful not only by ministering to them when alive, but also by employing its services on their behalf, usually though not only after their deaths. Put simply, a priest *might* work face to face with a congregation, the kind of work known as 'cure of souls'; but he might equally well be responsible only for the souls of the dead, in prayer and the saying of masses. Thirdly, the Church offered to those who entered strict monastic orders the chance to strive for a superior level of holiness quite apart from the lay congregation. The ways for those entering the Church to serve it could on one hand mean engrossing pastoral duties; on the other the deliberate avoidance of the world; or a middle position working for the world but not within it.[3]

Yet the potential 'distractions' of the clergy from even these varied activities were enormous. The clerical estate was a European-wide corporate body which serviced many of society's needs in the social, administrative, and political sphere. Clerics and Church institutions maintained a large proportion of Europe's system of education and learning. The universities of the late Middle Ages were permeated by Church influence. Universities were usually founded with authority from a papal bull (though not quite invariably: Wittenberg in Saxony was an exception).[4] Of the three higher faculties, Theology, Law, and Medicine, in which doctorates were awarded, theological studies were regulated and overwhelmingly carried out by churchmen, while canon law—the law of the Roman Church—formed at least half the work of Law faculties. Many religious orders, especially friars but also some monks and canons, maintained establishments in university towns to educate their more gifted recruits. Other new foundations— Corpus Christi and Cardinal Colleges in early sixteenth-century Oxford, for instance—owed their beginnings to senior clerics.[5]

The educational concerns of the clergy spread right down through the system. Orders of mendicant friars maintained *studia* or colleges of less than university status, which sometimes (in Lausanne for example) later gave way to full universities. Examples of all kinds of collegiate foundations, whether cathedral chapters, collegiate churches, monasteries, or friaries, at some time maintained schools for basic education.[6] In canon law it was expected that a parish priest would take some responsibility for having a clerk take elementary lessons, usually as part of teaching young choristers.[7] The Church may well, in certain specialized areas, have been losing its monopoly to lay initiatives, especially with the advent of numerous small-town schools in Germany on the eve of the Reformation; however, Church education remained important both in scale and scope.[8]

In much the same way, laymen's initiatives were nibbling away at the Church's contributions to poor relief, but without seriously reducing the importance of religious charity. On the grandest scale, great civic confraternities like the *scuole grandi* of Venice organized and gave social prestige to the business of charity within a religious framework; lesser confraternities often did the same.[9] Monastic houses were often charged with providing rather sporadic welfare services to the poor or to travellers, especially pilgrims.[10] Most importantly, much charitable giving was done under the Church's auspices by those on the point of death, anxious to benefit their souls by a pious donation.[11]

As governments during the twelfth and thirteenth centuries had grown to depend more on written documents and records, laymen had (perhaps with relief) passed over to clerics many administrative duties which seem to have more to do with government than religion. Or, to put it another way, lay regimes supported their bureaucrats by giving them a priestly education and church posts to support them.[12] This movement left to the late Middle Ages the legacy that churchmen made rather efficient record-keepers, and that certain kinds of records of lay people's lives became the Church's exclusive preserve. The Church exhibited the most sophisticated international bureaucracy and the most elaborately codified system of law in the Europe of the time. That system of law inevitably intersected with the lives of ordinary people at certain crucial stages. Baptism defined one's status as a member of the visible Christian community as well as of the eternal Church. The validity of marriages—and therefore the legitimacy of offspring—rested upon canon law and Church courts. The degrees of close blood-relations within which marriage was unlawful were defined by the Church, and defined very widely so as to encourage a lucrative trade in licences to infringe them. The verifying of a will ('probate') normally rested on a Church court.[13] The Church claimed as of right to employ the services of lay justice in imposing its own sentences, for instance in cases of heresy or moral lapses.[14]

In politics as much as in education, welfare, and administration churchmen were to be found. Most striking of all, the papacy was itself an Italian principality, embroiled in war and peace with its neighbours and (after the northern kingdoms invaded Italy in the 1490s) with the other states of Europe. The papal 'patrimony' or 'lands of St Peter' stretched across the middle of Italy, a network of states governed by often unreliable petty princes as papal vicars and a constant source of worry.[15] The popes' prestige as secular rulers was not helped when the early medieval forgery purporting to show how the Emperor Constantine had given vast worldly lordship to the popes was exposed in the 1440s.[16] Yet the papal states were only the most notorious and contentious of the lands under priestly control. There were other papal enclaves, for instance around Avignon.[17] Other princes of the Church were also princes as such, like the archbishop-electors of the Holy Roman Emperor, or the prince-bishops of northern Germany. 'Knightly orders', which combined the ideals of chivalry with those of monasticism, crusading, and pilgrimage, held great power and estates on the margins of Christendom: the Teutonic knights in the recently Christianized Baltic shores of Lithuania, the Order of St John in the Mediterranean confronted with the Ottomans, and the Castilian orders of Alcantara, Calatrava, and Santiago in the borderlands between Christian and Moorish Spain. Like all lordship, churchmen's lordship extended a long way down the hierarchy. The least grand bishop or abbot might administer estates held as 'temporalities', that is, a landed property held from a sovereign in the same way as a lay lord's land.

Apart from administering their own lands, churchmen played a major role in administering those of other rulers. The early modern period undoubtedly saw a great proliferation of layman officials, especially in the lower ranks of secular government;[18] but clerical appointees long held their ground. In the 1490s the king of England depended on the services of Cardinal Morton, the king of France on Cardinal Georges d'Amboise, and the kings of Castile and Aragon on Cardinal Ximénez de Cisneros; Emperor Maximilian depended on Matthäus Lang, archbishop of Salzburg, and in a different way had to take account of the imperial arch-chancellor, Archbishop Berchtold von Henneberg of Mainz. One should not assume that the clerics who held such posts were priests in name only, with no interest in their priestly status other than for the income and the privileges. Some no doubt were just that. However, Richard Fox, bishop of Winchester, served Henry VII and Henry VIII as Lord Privy Seal until 1516: he appointed a series of able deputies to carry out his diocesan work, then with some remorse retired in old age to take up the reins of his diocese in person and in earnest.[19]

Perhaps the most crippling distraction for the Church was acting as a gigantic clearing-house for its own range of posts and revenues. The popes' residence north of the Alps at Avignon between 1309 and 1377 had made practical the aspirations and claims, in themselves much older, that the papacy could arbitrate over who was appointed to many different kinds of church posts.[20] After the popes' return to Rome, and the division of the papacy between two and then three claimants during the Great Schism from 1378 to 1417, the sheer number of papal appointments probably shrank and never fully recovered, as lay rulers gained in influence.[21] What matters here, though, is that the complex administrative machinery remained to occupy people and consume resources, even when it was simply validating decisions reached by other powers.

2. *Economic Problems*

It was far easier to find people to fill the vastly increased number of Church posts at the end of the Middle Ages, than to find money to pay for them. The medieval Church had acquired its responsibilities haphazardly; society had no coherent plan to pay for the religious services which it required. On the contrary, money was constantly diverted, assigned, reassigned, and otherwise shifted around from one cause to another. Issues of money, its collection, distribution, and expenditure, caused much of the Church's 'vulnerability' at this period.

The revenues of the Church were by this stage an enormously tangled and complex web of rights. By gross simplification one can, however, reduce the Church's sources of money to two broad categories:

(1) Revenues which came *directly* from the Church's spiritual role, were unique to Church institutions and theoretically dedicated to maintaining spiritual services. Such revenues were known as 'spiritual' income.

(2) Revenues which just happened to be held by churchmen, but could equally well have been held by a layman (although once passed to the Church they almost invariably stayed with it). These were known as 'temporal' revenues.

Of the 'spiritual' class the most important were the tithes, the Church's levy on the properties or incomes of its subjects, and fees charged, either for a specific service, such as a priest saying a mass for the dead, or in the court of a Church dignitary. 'Temporal' revenues were most commonly rents from agricultural land, but could also include the proceeds of mines, fisheries, tolls, ports, or whatever.[22]

In theory the tithe ought to have varied with the wealth of the parish or community where it was levied. Certainly, like all taxes, it collapsed if the community was deserted or depleted, as so many were in the fifteenth century. However, it probably did not increase pro rata with the population in those areas, especially towns, where the original establishment had been small. Fees were a more flexible source of income; this is shown by the attempts made by lay legislators to keep them down within reasonable limits.[23] Not only that; it was easier to invent new fees, for instance for new forms of 'indulgences', or for licences to break the Church's own marriage laws, than to institute or restore tithes.

In theory a patron might have endowed a new church foundation with 'temporal' revenues at any time. However, in many countries the secular government had long been worried by the mass of laymen's gifts to the Church eating away at the land available to support the aristocracy. The late Middle Ages had seen repeated, not always successful, attempts to restrict (or regulate) the flow of real property into Church hands.[24] Moreover, once land was acquired, it brought with it duties, costs, risks even. Land had to be governed, administered, taxed, and defended by a prince-bishop no less than by a count or duke. Where estates lay in the jurisdiction of a lay sovereign, the individual ecclesiastic's hold on them was not always secure: money might be demanded to 'restore' temporalities to a newly appointed prelate.[25]

There was an overall problem about acquiring any new money to cope with the steadily increasing scope of the Church's activities. New money was nearly always given for *special* purposes. New endowments might go to chantry priests, to fashionable new or reformed religious orders;[26] new money might be paid for the jubilees, confessional letters, and indulgences marketed with such enthusiasm by the papal court. It might pay for a new preacher. It would almost never go to support the bedrock of the Church's work, providing the sacraments to the mass of the laity. Secondly, it would be much easier for the aristocrats and monarchs of the Church to acquire new money than for the proletariat.

Not only was it excessively hard to generate new revenues for the basic work of the Church among its people. Much of the money originally assigned to support the parish ministry had long before the eve of the Reformation been diverted to other uses. This happened in two ways. First, many institutions where churchmen lived communally and separate from the parish, usually (but not only) cathedral chapters, monasteries, nunneries, friaries, or university colleges, received part of their revenue by the 'appropriation' of most or all of the tithe from a large number of parishes often far distant from them. They then became, in a sense, the absentee parish priest or 'rector', responsible for the saying of services, and therefore for the appointment of substitutes, called either vicars (the fortunate and reasonably permanent) or chaplains (the insecure and poorly paid). The number of *new* appropriations may have been declining before the Reformation, but the overwhelming majority of the old ones remained in effect.[27] 'Diverting' money from one cause to another was widespread: the income of a chantry in Henbury Saltmarsh was diverted to repair sea-walls in the Bristol Channel; by the late fifteenth century many English abbeys were re-endowed with the incomes of *other*, suppressed, priories.[28]

Secondly, individuals appointed to rectories, or indeed to vicarages, could divert the bulk of the parish's money, simply by not living and working within it themselves. It had always been common for priests in parish charges to absent themselves, temporarily or permanently, from their supposed places of work. By the late fifteenth century the system of absenteeism had long been 'regulated' by a more or less effective system of licences. Essentially, any parish with an income suitable to an ambitious careerist was liable to be held by an absentee; while the very poorest parish vicarages yielded such a pittance that a priest could only be found at all on the understanding that he hold several such posts at once. Priests might be absent from their parishes for a number of valid reasons apart from pluralism; the commonest were study at university (parish tithes were a recognized means to support students) or service to a bishop or sovereign.[29]

The churches as a whole suffered at local level not only from the moving around of money *within* a given region, but also from rival claims, made by the popes on one hand and secular rulers on the other, to tax them. Papal taxes, known by various titles such as 'Peter's Pence' and 'Annates', were a regular bone of contention between the papacy and France, Spain, England, and the German princes in the decades before the Reformation. Lay rulers expected at the very least to have a veto on what taxes were imposed; at best to take a share in the profits. In fact the papacy did grant to several monarchs the right to levy taxes on their clergy, often in connection with projects for a crusade; some powers taxed their priests by agreement (like the dukes of Brittany and Burgundy, or the kings of Spain) while others, like the city of Venice, taxed their clergy whether the popes liked it or not.[30]

This monetary tangle harmed the Church's image with lay people: an impoverished local priesthood seemed to offer a poor service for the money which it demanded; much of what was levied effectively 'disappeared' into enclosed monasteries or the arcane areas of higher education or administration. In spite of gifts prodigally given to some sectors of the Church, the institution as a whole managed to appear simultaneously impoverished, grasping, and extravagant. Many of these criticisms could have been made in much the same way of secular government. However, particular consequences of the Church's economic problems aggravated its political 'vulnerability' to a dangerous extent: the seeming abuse of its 'spiritual' privileges; the excessive growth of its bureaucratic machine, and the unedifying qualities of many of its personnel.

3. *Abuse of Priestly Status*

By about 1500 the Church had acquired a wide range of powers and privileges, developed to protect the spiritual work and personnel of the Church just when medieval society was taking shape and the clergy were writing down their own distinctive system of law.[31] The priesthood had the powers to give or withhold the sacraments and carry out moral discipline; it could judge and exclude errant members of the laity (including sovereigns) from the community by 'excommunication'; or cut off an entire local church from the universal communion by suspending all its religious services ('interdict'). The privileges of the 'clergy' were designed to exempt the personnel and property of the Church from the intrusions of secular society, in the belief that only in that way could the activities of the Church be, literally, sacrosanct. Hence clerics were theoretically beyond the jurisdiction of criminal courts, to be judged by their bishop or other superior; indeed they claimed (usually half-heartedly) freedom from arrest or molestation by lay authorities of any kind. Only with difficulty could lay courts deal with clerics in suits between parties ('civil' cases). The clergy claimed complete immunity for Church property: once passed to the Church, property was deemed forever to belong to the Church, never to be alienated and to be taxed only with the Church's consent. Appointments to benefices were also supposedly under clerical control—though this was perhaps the least well vindicated of all the Church's privileges.[32]

These powers and immunities had a fairly obvious rationale: for example, most lay taxes had grown out of a duty to serve the ruler in war, which priests could not do; priests and monks were supposed to live by a stricter code than laymen, requiring a separate penal system. However, the clergy of around 1500 had long since ceased to be just worshippers and pastors, if they ever had been. Popes and bishops were politicians, administrators, and landowners. Only by a superhuman effort of self-discipline, which those recruited into the Church were most unlikely to make, could clerics use their privileges in spiritual cases only, and then abstain from using them in more 'worldly' ones.

Clerical status had become something to be defended for its own sake, and a weapon used in the cause of *all* the Church's diverse activities, not just the narrowly religious ones. The popes took the lead in using their status as a political and even as an economic weapon. In the negotiations leading to the marriages of Anne, duchess of Brittany, successively to Kings Charles VIII and Louis XII of France, the respective popes used their power to 'allow' these marriages (by dispensing from canon law) as a lever to pursue their political aims with the French kings.[33] Conversely, Pope Clement VII was to find after 1527 that he could not afford to displease Emperor Charles V by annulling Henry VIII's marriage to the Emperor's relative.[34] In a quite different area, from about 1460 the papacy grew to depend for a large part of its income on the proceeds of selling alum (used for making cloth) mined at Tolfa in the papal states. The popes tried to keep the price high by creating an artificial cartel or monopoly; some, like Paul II, used excommunication (and in the case of Julius II in 1506, an indulgence) to discourage the import of competing Turkish alum.[35]

The lesser aristocrats of the Church most commonly abused their spiritual powers when enforcing payment of tithes. Non-payers (or even late payers) seem to have been all too regularly subjected to lesser excommunications, with the predictable result that these censures fell into disrepute and were widely ignored.[36] Nevertheless, the claim made in 1529 that 'they [the clerics] look so narrowly on their profits that the poor wives must be countable to them of every tenth egg, or else she ... shall be taken as an heretic'[37] is clearly the product of extremist hyperbole. At the level of the parish clergy, it was likely to be immunities, rather than powers, which gave rise to problems. 'Benefit of clergy' against lay criminal justice has probably been overrated as a problem, despite various attempts made by secular law to restrict it.[38] More odious would have been the freedom to trade in despite of local civic by-laws: the commercial breweries maintained by clerics in the Saxon town of Zwickau were a running grievance to the city fathers, who wished to maintain a monopoly for the municipal beer. Many vicarages were provided with a small area of cultivable land, the 'glebe', on which a parish priest might grow crops or keep animals, and even market a small surplus. Where this occurred lay people might be subjected to the multiple irritation of paying tithes on their own produce to someone who was also their competitor in the market-place.[39]

Medieval laymen were not fools, and presumably knew perfectly well when priestly rights were being abused for political ends. Reforming critics among the clergy themselves had been all too ready to point out where 'spiritual' powers were being abused in pursuit of purely worldly ambitions.[40] By the eve of the Reformation there seem to have been rather fewer serious squabbles over such issues as the arrest of clergy by laymen or the abuse of church sanctuary by rebels than in the past. Lay rulers and ecclesiastical judges sorted out issues on the margins of clerical privilege by agreement and negotiation according to the prevailing circumstances. Relations between Church and State in the century before the Reformation were carried out in an atmosphere, not of continuous hostility, so much as of regular haggling and negotiation.[41] It is perfectly obvious, when one looks at what happened in the next century, that the clergy's special status survived exactly as long as lay rulers were willing to accept and uphold it, and no longer. However, compromises struck between rulers and prelates could not please everyone. The haggling was bound to leave *somebody* dissatisfied, some reservoir of grievances which could be drawn upon when needed. It was harder—though not impossible—for burghers in a town to haggle with their clergy over rights than it was for a king or an emperor. Abuses of status should be viewed not as threats to the Church's position in themselves, but as hostages to fortune if the Church became more generally unpopular, and bargaining counters for its opponents to use in negotiation or in propaganda.

4. *The 'Inflation' of Bureaucracy*

For reasons based on the needs of Christendom as much as on the claims of popes, the central machinery of the Church had grown massively in the decades up to the Western Schism in 1378. After the reunification of the papacy at Constance, fifteenth-century popes such as Martin V (1417–31) and Eugenius IV (1431–47) reasserted the papacy's administrative powers to restore its prestige. By 1500, however, the bureaucratic machine was still growing when its usefulness—at least on such a huge scale—was more and more questionable. Whatever the real needs of the Church, its administration was widely *perceived* as an overgrown, costly, parasitic bureaucracy; that perception was in itself a source of weakness to the Church. More people were 'employed' than ever; and procedures became more complex and elaborate.

When the issuing of grants, licences, and such documents had been concentrated on first Avignon and then Rome, the number of clerical officials had grown substantially to draft, issue, and validate such documents. However, later fifteenth-century popes like Calixtus III (1455–8) and Pius II (1458–64) multiplied officials out of proportion to any similar increase in business. Pius II founded a 'college' of seventy abbreviators in 1463 (later suppressed); in 1482 Sixtus IV created a new college of a hundred solicitors; in 1486 Innocent VIII set up a college of twenty-four secretaries and another of seventy-one collectors of the seal. By 1514 there were over a hundred solicitors and archivists each. The simple explanation was, of course, that the popes (like the kings of France) were borrowing money by selling these offices for a capital sum, repaid by the 'salary' and the division of fees among the office-holders. The money drawn in by the popes was substantial: the sale of 2,000 venal offices by Pope Leo X (1513–21) yielded one-sixth of his ordinary income. However, the cost in salaries paid to these officials was also enormous: 30 per cent of ordinary papal income in the mid-1520s, 50 per cent around 1560.[42] The popes had created all these offices to raise money quickly. This motive, even if it had been understood, would not have satisfied those who saw only a very large number of irreligious bureaucrats integrated into the papal court, anxious to tap the administration for further lucre. When Luther complained in 1520 of 'such a swarm of parasites in that place called Rome, all boasting that they belong to the pope, ... lying in wait for the endowments and benefices of Germany as the wolves lie in wait for the sheep', he was echoing sentiments already expressed by scrupulously orthodox prelates and princes within Germany.[43]

The procedures followed by these officials also, inevitably, became more complex and more expensive. So many different kinds of licences were obtainable to evade the terms of canon law—five kinds of dispensations for marriage, retrospective legitimation of offspring, permission to eat dairy produce in Lent, and a host of others—that the suspicion could easily grow that 'canon law was instituted solely for the purpose of making a great deal of money; whoever would be a Christian has to buy his way out of its provisions.'[44] Both the bulk of such documents and the revenue from them, paid to the office of the Datary, grew significantly between 1480 and 1525.[45] These payments were probably disliked by secular rulers more than other papal levies, because the money went directly to Rome; it was much harder for secular sovereigns to take their share than with other religious taxes. What the petitioners themselves thought of the system is hard to guess;

they certainly sent in their requests, in increasing bulk, and paid up as asked.

Perhaps the most notorious instance of bureaucratic overextension, however, occurred in the business of appointments to benefices.[46] The principle had been enunciated, as long ago as 1335 during the Avignon papacy, that the popes reserved the right to provide to benefices of all kinds.[47] By the late fifteenth century this right of provision was little more than a bargaining counter in most parts of Europe; extensive powers over Church posts had been given to, or simply taken by, secular rulers. However, obtaining papal confirmation of titles to major benefices—bishoprics above all—still entailed cost and effort, regardless of who actually had the say in the choice of candidates. The position on this issue in Germany was particularly complex. By the concordat of Vienna in 1448 the papacy shared the right to appoint to benefices with the customary patrons in alternate months, vacancies occurring in the 'papal months' of January, March, May, July, September, and November being filled by the popes. Other technicalities in the concordat extended the potential for papal intrusion into German benefices; and also increased the likelihood of disputes over titles, which would then have to be resolved at the papal court.[48] German noblemen especially suspected, or claimed to suspect, that the papacy was using German Church posts as a means to reward its Italian 'courtiers'.[49]

The canon law on these questions was riddled with possible confusions and contradictions, so that, when there was no clear agreement with a strong monarchy, the way was open for many disputes and abuses, which only the papal bureaucracy could then resolve. The regulations which had been introduced to restrict pluralism (the holding of several 'incompatible' benefices at once) were circumvented by several legal fictions: 'administration' (receiving the profits of a post but not the title); grants *in commendam* (by which the 'commendator' received the bulk of the revenue of a monastery or collegiate foundation where he did not reside); and 'incorporations' (deeming two or more incompatible posts to be one single post for canonical purposes). Benefices could be granted when they were not yet vacant or, conversely, when they had just been granted to someone else. All these processes were regulated, and priced, by the papal Datary.[50]

It was not only the papal 'courtiers' who profited from this manipulation of the legal machinery of the late medieval Church. All these devices were exploited by senior clergy from all sorts of ranks, including some of the nobility who protested against them in the German imperial assemblies. They served the needs of the petitioners as much as those of the papacy itself. However, in the same way as the other 'abuses' already discussed, they made the Church 'vulnerable' if the sanctity and authority of that institution were ever to come seriously into public doubt.

5. *The Personnel the Church Deserved?*

The Church reflected the society which produced it. It contained a monarch, an aristocracy, and a proletariat; they pursued varied interests and ambitions, and furthered their careers by a range of means, officially approved or not. It was unrealistic to expect the clergy to be uniformly dedicated, pious, abstemious, and self-disciplined; and impossible for them all to live up to the best clerical ideals, when those ideals often contradicted each other. The 'failings' of the clergy were, in fact, really the results of their specialization in certain tasks, and of the division and diversion of wealth already described. This section will cast a brief glance over the popes, some of the bishops, and the secular (non-monastic) priesthood[51] in the fifty or so years just preceding the Reformation. The qualifications, the interests, and the 'failings' of members of each of these classes will be considered in turn.

Renaissance popes came from varied backgrounds. Some, like Sixtus IV (Francesco della Rovere), were of obscure social origins, others from distinguished dynasties like the Venetian Barbo (Paul II) or the Roman Colonna (Martin V). All (save the Borgias, who were Catalans, and the Netherlander Adrian VI in 1522–3) were Italians. Several were relatives of previous popes: there were two Borgias (Calixtus III and Alexander VI), two Piccolomini (Pius II and III), two della Rovere (Sixtus IV and Julius II) and two Medici (Leo X and Clement VII). A sort of reciprocity developed, in that the pope was elected by the cardinals, and as popes tended to elect their relatives and supporters as cardinals, some of those cardinals in due course became popes.[52] What is more, factions developed between the various groups of cardinals, seen most spectacularly in the rift between the adherents of Alexander VI and the future Julius II before the former's death in 1503.[53] Once elected, many popes strove to found dynasties, and not just on the papal throne itself. After 1455 popes regularly made their relatives cardinals, gave them leading offices in the administration, or married them into noble or princely families in Italy. Conversely, Italian noble families like the Gonzaga, Este, Sforza, and above all the Medici were glad to have members of their family in the College of Cardinals; gratifying this wish helped the popes' own diplomacy.[54]

Grandeur could be cultivated in subtler ways than dynastic ambition. Several, though not all, popes were energetic and lavish patrons of the writers of the Italian Renaissance, who could be expected to commemorate their patrons: Nicholas V, Pius II, and the Medici popes all supported writers, while Sixtus IV re-established the Roman 'academy' and continued Nicholas V's projects for the Vatican Library, and Paul II (bitterly hostile to some forms of Renaissance literature) nevertheless presided over the introduction of printing to the abbey of Subiaco in the 1460s.[55] More permanent and more magnificent still were the monuments which popes raised to themselves (and incidentally to those whom they worshipped) in the shape of religious buildings within Rome itself. Nicholas V began a series of discussions and projects to rebuild St Peter's;[56] Julius II inaugurated the demolition of the ancient and crumbling basilica and on 18 April 1506 laid the foundation of the present complex of buildings, largely finished in the mid-sixteenth century when Paul V had his full title inscribed on the façade.[57]

The popes became committed to external aggression and warfare for two purposes. They needed to secure control of the papal states, which had been difficult enough to control in the fourteenth century and by the fifteenth were increasingly vital for revenue. Popes who, like Martin V and Eugenius IV, were not otherwise militaristic or expansionist felt bound to seek help from military adventurers like Francesco Sforza, Ranuccio Farnese, or Ferrante of Naples to re-establish their control. The campaign led by Alexander VI's son Cesare Borgia to carve out a principality from whatever parts of the papal state he could gain by force was only the most notorious example; and was possibly rivalled for brutality by the campaigns of his enemy Julius II.[58] Meanwhile, popes still tried to gather forces for a crusade. The Ottoman conquest of Constantinople in 1453 prompted a half-century or so of intermittent efforts by Popes Calixtus III, Pius II, Paul II, Alexander VI, and Leo X to organize a European campaign to recover part of the Ottoman lands for the Church. Not all of these projects were invented purely to justify further papal taxation of Christendom, although that was often how the wider Church saw them. Pius II died in 1464 at Ancona, where he had gone specifically to see to the gathering of a crusading fleet.[59] In practice the least ineffectual crusader was the Albanian rebel Iskander Bey ('Skanderbeg', 1403–67), hired with papal money to harass the Ottomans' borders in the 1460s.

The 'failings' of the popes were simply the darker side to the personalities of many Italian politicians of the period: nepotism (the policy of favouring one's own family in appointments), ambition, acquisitiveness, self-indulgence, and the absence of those qualities of humility, mortification of the flesh, and rejection of the world's pleasures which monasticism prescribed as the ideal. Even the spectacular vices of a few were partly compensated for by their usefulness. Rodrigo Borgia had already legitimized his numerous family by his principal mistress and established them in prominent positions before his election as Alexander VI; the main objections to him seem to have been not his unchastity but the bribery he certainly used to gain election, and the fact that he was not an Italian. Against that he was reputed to be a skilful administrator and manager of people.[60] The warrior-pope Julius II, whose character was brilliantly assassinated by Erasmus after his death, brought order to the streets of Rome, took steps against shipwreckers, and restored the papacy's weakened grasp of its lands.[61]

In the 1460s an English commentator, Thomas Gascoigne, wrote acidly that 'three things make a bishop in England, the will of the King, the will of the pope or the Roman court, and money in abundance paid to the Roman court'.[62] That observation could probably have held good for several other countries where a strong king could make recommendations which the pope could ill refuse. However, because bishops were often nominees of secular government, it does not follow that they were all ill qualified. In the English case, a typical bishop in the late fifteenth century was of modest social origins, trained in canon law at a university, and experienced as an administrator or functionary in the household of another prince of the Church or of the king himself. In the less wealthy sees one would have found the friars, abbots, theologians, and aspiring noblemen.[63] England was unusual in several ways, notably the wealth and size of its bishoprics, and the relative simplicity of relations between kings and popes. In Germany and Italy the politics were more confused, while some Italian sees were so poor as to attract little interest or prestige. Some German sees, chapters, and great abbeys were the near exclusive preserve of particular noble families, while the Italian ones saw a high proportion of lesser urban gentry, as well as many more friars than elsewhere.[64]

Once elected, bishops, like popes, furthered their own careers and the interests of their families;[65] they patronized scholars, they built buildings. A significant proportion[66] promoted various kinds of Church 'reform'. Unlike the popes, however, great bishops under a monarch owed their appointment to (at least) two powers and quite literally served two masters; a prince-bishop might be pulled between the cause of his princely dynasty and the privileges of his Church. The failings most often criticized in bishops were demonstrably the consequences of their not balancing different claims on their time. Above all they were criticized for absence from their dioceses. Bishops could be absent for many reasons, some more and some less disreputable. The worst (particularly common with small sees, or those held in foreign countries) was treating the diocese as a source of income and acknowledging no pastoral responsibility. If sees were held in plurality absence would be almost inevitable. Absence at a royal court or on missions to Rome was a more plausible excuse.[67] To the people of the diocese, however, what mattered was not the reason for a bishop's absence but the qualities of the substitutes whom he appointed. These went by various titles of 'vicars-general', 'officials principal', and 'suffragan bishops', the last appointed to perform rituals reserved to someone of the rank of bishop. Vicars-general and officials were usually Church careerists on the way up, so it was in their interests to be diligent and methodical. However, their responsibilities were inevitably more concerned with routine admin- istration and revenue-collecting; pastoral work, even if vicars-general had wished to carry it out, was usually forestalled by local privileges.[68]

The other accusation most readily laid against the episcopate was that of worldliness, ambition, arrogance, extravagance, or ostentation. Given the social origins of many bishops, and their involvement in politics, they could hardly escape their class's obsession with marks of status. The preacher Geiler von Kaysersberg told the story of a bishop, out riding with an armed retinue, who met a peasant who asked him whether St Martin travelled around with such pomp when *he* was a bishop. The bishop explained to the peasant that he was both duke and bishop, and was travelling in his secular role; whereat the peasant asked what would happen to the bishop, if the duke's deserts caused him to be sent to hell?[69]

The secular clergy was a vast and heterogeneous body, containing at one extreme the wealthy vicar-general with a fistful of benefices on the brink of appointment to a bishopric, and at the other the impoverished curate or chaplain performing basic priestly services for an insecure stipend barely more than a farm-labourer's wage.[70] Generalizations have to be made very carefully. However, the Church's own legal requirements and qualifications make an interesting contrast to what was later (theoretically) expected of protestant ministers. Ordination had to be carried out by the right person (usually the bishop as 'ordinary' or his deputy) at the correct time. The candidate had to have some means of support, be of acceptable age (25 for a priest), be legitimate, chaste, and respectable, and possess sufficient learning to carry out his ritual tasks.[71] In practice even these modest requirements were often not met. The system depended on the bishop's personal supervision, which was frustrated both by the frequent absence of bishops and the willingness of would-be priests to seek ordination in dioceses far from their homes.[72] Bishops, let alone priests, might be given their offices well below the official age for reasons of property and family ambition: the fifteenth-century French preacher Jean Raulin remarked that souls were being given into hands too young to be trusted with an apple.[73]

Besides this habit of regarding the benefice as property and income like a layman's landed estate, several particular failings were habitually criticized in the secular priesthood. The first was ignorance: an alleged lack of interest in or knowledge of the fundamentals of religion. This accusation should be treated carefully, since levels of 'ignorance' varied according to the critic. The *basic* requirement for a priest was to be able to read, or memorize, the rituals of the Church so as to say them; to know how to administer five of the sacraments correctly; and to know when to send a penitent to higher authority. Probably the majority could have done this much. On the eve of the Reformation 158 of 869 priests, mostly unbeneficed chaplains, in Norwich diocese bequeathed at least one book, whether of services, sermons or homilies, encyclopaedias, or guides to pastoral care.[74] The sheer abundance of advice books on the duties of a pastor, or of advice to confessors, suggests that many priests were willing and able to buy them.[75] In some (rare) cases, candidates are known to have been specifically examined before ordination, though bishops could not practically refuse every unsuitable candidate.[76]

Unchastity or concubinage probably worried later reformers more than contemporary critics. Even the extent of the practice is unclear; some bishops do seem to have made a lucrative income from what were, effectively, fines on their priests to legitimize their offspring.[77] It is likely that semi-permanent liaisons between priests and their mistresses did little to disrupt community life, though they gave scope for lay satire and cynicism.[78] No doubt some of the laity might have agreed with the statement made by a heretic in 1539 that it was 'better that priests should marry, than go after other men's wives'.[79] A more serious fault—because more socially disruptive—was that some priests notoriously discarded any trappings of priestly demeanour, swaggering about in armour or in extravagant laymen's clothes, stirring up brawls with laymen only to retire behind their privileges.[80]

The failing of the secular priesthood which seems to have been most bitterly resented was its avarice, its apparent obsession with pursuing its own material betterment by accumulating as much income as possible, in disregard of the concerns of the tenants and tithe-payers who supported it. This attitude William Melton, chancellor of York Minster, bitterly attacked in a sermon to ordinands in 1510, blaming the greed for income and benefices as the cause of laymen's contempt for the priesthood.[81] Bishop Christoph von Stadion of Augsburg opened a synod in 1517 with a similarly blistering attack on his clergy's avarice and taste for luxuries. That many priests were in fact grindingly poor does not seem to have placated those who paid, or calmed those clerical critics who feared the consequences.[82]

Most of the weaknesses which exposed the Church to such criticism can, then, be easily explained if one remembers that the Church system had grown to a point where it attracted certain types of people, for whom career survival required that they behave in an often unedifying way; while those who *had* no career prospects could only act like the impoverished hirelings they were. Nevertheless, the standards which society—and especially reforming critics amongst the priesthood themselves—applied to the conduct of the majority of the Church had never been more stringent. 'Reform' was on the lips of even the most unlikely Church politicians at this period. Just what it meant is the topic of the next two chapters.

3

'Reform' from Within and its Limits

'Reform' or 'reformation', both equivalents to the Latin term *reformatio*, saturated the language of lawyers and churchmen in the late Middle Ages. The term originally meant the redrafting of a set of laws or statutes: in that sense it was used of civic law codes, university curricula, or canon law: the decrees of the Fifth Lateran Council of 1512–17 contained many paragraphs concerning 'reformatio'.[1] It could also mean a much more dramatic renewal of the world-order, as in the anonymous 'Reformation of Emperor Sigismund' of about 1430.[2] Behind the term, for medieval churchmen, lay a philosophical definition. The 'form' of a thing was the essential, unchanging quality common to all the various ways in which that 'thing' could exist. To 're-form' something was to restore it to its true essence: to recover what it had originally been meant to be. To 're-form' the Church was to restore it to conformity with the hierarchy of heaven. The vision of 'reform' in the Church of the late fifteenth century was basically conservative and idealistic.[3] In that specific sense, nearly everyone in the fifteenth century admitted without reserve that 'reform' of the Church was a necessary and a desirable thing.[4] However, the fragmentation and diversity of the Church raised two difficulties for the concept of 'reform': how was one to define the 'form', or the ideal to be pursued; and how was it to be carried out through the tangle of Church institutions? By 1500 it seemed that all the most promising angles had already been tried.

1. Reform from Above: A Lost Cause?

Since the Church was a monarchy, and a special kind of monarchy at that, it had seemed reasonable for its head, the pope, to give the lead in restoring the Church to its ideal state. The thirteenth and fourteenth centuries had been dominated by the idea that the Church should be reformed in 'head and limbs' (*in capite et membris*) according to the biological analogies so popular at the time. The concept was promoted at the second Council of Lyons (1274), and above all at the Council of Vienne (1311–12).[5] During the Councils of Constance (1414–18), Pavia-Sienna (1423–4), and Basle (1431–49) this desire to 'reform' the Church wholesale was transformed: in the absence either of an agreed pope or a pope willing to accept the councils' claims to authority, reform 'in head and limbs' meant that the 'headship' was supposedly transferred on to the broader shoulders of the council fathers; reform essentially meant collective control and limitation of papal monarchy.[6]

However, a 'centralized' reform movement faced the twin obstacles of the collective self-interest, and mutual suspicion, of the different parts of the hierarchy. Self-interest forced popes, cardinals, bishops, or secular rulers to preserve their rights and revenues, if need be at the cost of reform. Popes could not abandon the complex system of arbitrating over benefices which provided much of their income. Cardinals and other prelates could hardly forgo what to others seemed their excessive rank, status, and wealth. In the papal Curia and elsewhere, those who prospered by the existing system probably outnumbered those who (much more noisily) denounced it. Secondly, even if the head of the Church wished to inaugurate a wholesale reform, privileges and exemptions, zealously guarded by those who held them, would stop him. Monarchs and bishops would haggle over powers granted to papal legates; religious orders would resist the authority of bishops.[7] Councils had attempted to cut through this web of privilege and conflicting jurisdiction; they had failed, become enmeshed in national politics, and been denounced by the popes.[8]

Already before 1450 many observers were despairing of a single, whole-sale, centrally directed reform movement achieving very much within the Church. Bernardino of Sienna (d.1444) preached in 1424 that as the politics of the hierarchy made a general reform impossible, there would have to be individual, piecemeal reforms. Johann Nider's *Formicarius* of 1436 saw reform as the preserve of individual religious orders. At the end of the century, Geiler von Kaysersberg, following Nider, called for each bishop to reform his diocese, each priest his parish, and each abbot his monastery.[9] The keynote, therefore, of this chapter must be the fragmentary, even anarchic, movements of reform which abounded in the decades before the Reformation, but which enjoyed very varying degrees of success in the aims which they chose for themselves.

One should not overstate the case. The Fifth Lateran Council, which assembled in 1512 and dissolved on the very eve of Luther's dispute over indulgences in 1517, heard some very traditional demands for the old type of centralized reform. The Augustinian Egidio (Giles) of Viterbo preached a trenchant call for general reform at the opening session.[10] The Venetian ascetics Vincenzo Quirini and Paolo Giustiniani later presented a memorandum to the pope and council outlining a complete overhaul of the Church's administration to make it work together for spiritual renewal.[11] In 1537 a commission of cardinals was still able to see the source of the troubles of Christendom in terms of the popes' unlimited power to appoint to benefices.[12] Nevertheless, the most effective 'reform' campaigns within the Church were particular, individual initiatives.

2. *Piecemeal Reforms: The Papacy, the Religious Orders*

Even *within* each corporate part of the Church, contrary pressures encouraged reform with one hand and held it back with the other. Two different case-studies within the Church illustrate this play of forces. The papacy itself (improbable as it seems) produced a long-running series of 'reform' programmes in the years after 1449. These proposals, aimed directly at faults in the papal court itself, were 'piecemeal' projects in comparison with the visions of reform of all Christendom discussed above. First, in alternation with regular increases in the number of officials, came proposals to reduce them. Domenico de' Domenichi drafted a proposal for Pius II to cut the numbers, and Paul II did (temporarily) abolish the College of Abbreviators. Under a reform commission appointed in 1497 by Pope Alexander VI—Rodrigo Borgia, no less—serious cardinals like Carafa and Piccolomini denounced venal offices. From June 1513 a commission appointed by Julius II sat to discuss the Curia. These exercises demonstrated the limitations to reform. The drive to create offices was irresistible. Alexander VI's proposals were watered down in committees and then forgotten; Julius II actually appointed members of the threatened bureaucracies to the commissions set up to reform them, with predictable results.

The life-styles and privileges of the cardinals and the pope were also discussed. Sixtus IV drafted a bull to reform the Sacred College, which was not promulgated due to the cardinals' opposition. On his death they drew up a massive list of their privileges which the one whom they were to elect was supposedly bound to preserve.[13] The largest section of the reform bull issued by Leo X in May 1514 concerned the cardinals. In this case the proposal was vitiated from the start by its political background: the recently dead Julius II had wished to punish those cardinals who had co-operated with the king of France in the schismatic Council of Pisa in 1511. Alexander VI acquiesced in his cardinals telling him to live more simply and to restrict the numbers of women with access to the papal court, but changed little.[14]

These discussions also touched on the fees and taxes raised by the papal court, and the whole administrative machine. The pattern usually followed was that an abuse was identified; its abolition was declared desirable; vested interests intervened; the abolition was watered down, and in most cases forgotten about even before a bull was issued. The Curia could not agree *whose* life-style should be sacrificed to moral renewal; moreover, the desire to avoid simony (the mortal sin of selling spiritual 'goods' for money) conflicted with the needs of petitioners in the wider world for the Curia's services.[15]

At the papal court, the problem had been the weight of established interests and outside pressures. While both these restrictions also affected the monks, nuns, canons, and friars to some degree, it was far easier for them to initiate reform in a backwater and later, when it had gained in stature, spread its influence far and wide. In the fifteenth century two trends affected the religious orders: first, many communities were drawn into what became called 'congregations of strict observance'; secondly, various newer splinter groups of old movements grew and spread.[16] 'Strict observance' (of the rule of the order) meant just what it said, and followed a broadly similar pattern in numerous cases. An inspirational founder sought permission to take over a run-down monastery (often by exploiting the very abuses of *commendam* described earlier), but used it to revive the religious spirit there. As the house grew in influence, it inspired imitators in the surrounding region, who might look to the house first reformed for guidance and personnel. In due course reformed houses would be grouped together into a 'congregation', centrally organized to oversee each other. The 'congregation' would then be invited to take over more and more derelict or run-down monasteries, and might have to choose between keeping its original purity and remaining small, or expanding and possibly diluting its energies by absorbing many unwilling and ill-disciplined new members.

Examples of the 'observantine movement', as it is sometimes rather grandiosely called, can be found in all the main types of monasticism. Amongst the Benedictine monks, the Venetian aristocrat Lodovico Barbo acquired control of the abbey of Sa Giustina at Padua; it controlled a congregation of four houses in 1419, sixteen on Barbo's death in 1443, and by 1505 included the historic abbey of Monte Cassino as well as some fifty others. In Germany Johann Rode reformed St Matthias's monastery, whose impact spread to Bursfeld in the north, controlling ninety abbeys by the 1520s. Sa Giustina's influence was felt in France, in the reforms of the Benedictine nuns of Fontevrault (1458–75), in those of the monks of Marmoûtier (1466), and of Chezal-Benoît (1480–91).[17] The Augustinians (variously entitled canons regular, eremites, or friars) experienced several waves of reform. The most famous began with the new foundation in 1387 of Windesheim, in The Netherlands, by Florent Radewijns, a disciple of Geerd Groote of Deventer, himself the inspiration behind the brethren of the Common Life.[18] The Windesheimers spread into France and Germany, acquiring a total of eighty-three houses;[19] in Germany they encountered the indigenous reform of the Augustinian Eremites of strict observance, the congregation to which the houses at Erfurt and Wittenberg, and Martin Luther himself, belonged. The Italian Augustinian Eremite Giles of Viterbo played a major role in the Fifth Lateran Council as well as intervening in the affairs of observant Augustinians elsewhere in Europe.[20] Also in Italy, the Paduan Leone Gherardini built up from 1401 a congregation of Augustinian canons based on the previously derelict house of Sa Maria di Fregionaia near Lucca. It acquired eleven houses by 1421, thirty-nine by 1485, and became known as the 'Lateran canons'.[21]

Amongst the friars the situation was more confused, with both reformed congregations and new orders appearing. The most famous 'observants' of all were the observant Franciscan friars, descended from the 'spiritual' branch of the order which, a mere generation after its foundation, had insisted with pertinacity on preserving the poverty, individual and collective, of the order as the absolute priority. This 'observant' wave gained its form in the early fifteenth century under famous preachers such as Bernardino of Sienna, Giovanni Capistrano, Giacopo della Marche, and Alberto di Sarteano. A long battle with the less rigorous wing of the Franciscans, the 'conventuals', continued bitterly until the two wings were definitively split into separate orders in 1517.[22] Meanwhile two new branches of the Franciscans emerged: the Minims under Francesco di Paola (?1436–1507), whose first house was built at Cosenza in 1454; and the Capuchins, founded by Matteo da Bascio and Lodovico da Fossombrone and authorized as an order in 1528–9.[23] Similar observantine movements affected the Dominicans, though with less dramatically divisive results. Meanwhile, one should note, the order of Carthusian monks, the most recent of the great medieval orders, whose boast was that they had never *needed* a reform of discipline, enjoyed a period of special popularity and respect; by the sixteenth century they counted 200 houses in seventeen provinces throughout Europe.[24]

A careful balance needs to be struck in appraising this kind of 'reform' movement. It certainly shows that the search for traditional holiness through abstinence and discipline had lost neither its allure nor its respect. In some instances observant houses actually outnumbered the unreformed houses of the order concerned. The successes and failures of observance have to be measured against the enormous problems which it faced: the sheer number of religious; the diversion and misappropriation of monastic endowments; the suspicion of secular clerics, the hierarchy, and local bishops. In the diocese of Strasbourg, all these problems contributed to keep observant houses in a minority.[25] Moreover, observants tended to focus on one objective, say, rigorous discipline, pastoral work, or intellectual meditation, rather than a balance. The Cassinese and Augustinians emphasized study, hence these orders later became foyers of crypto-protestantism.[26] The Minims and Capuchins emphasized austerity and mortification, as did the Camaldolese hermits, reformed by Paolo Giustiniani from 1520.[27] Secondly, the *esprit de corps* necessary to sustain a new congregation surrounded by passive or resistant monks generated habits of intolerance and mutual vituperation which made rival orders criticize each other without restraint. The observant Dominicans spent the entire fifteenth century in litigation with the main body of the order over authority; while the Lateran canons spent the latter half of the fifteenth century in a bitter tussle with the unreformed canons of St John Lateran in Rome over control of the basilica.[28] Perhaps the chief defect of the reform of strict observance was that its impact on the wider community tended to be limited. Preachers and confessors were produced by such orders; but the main spiritual beneficiaries of such movements were the monks and friars themselves. The dioceses and parishes offered fifteenth-century reform an even more severe test.

3. The 'Unreformable' Bishops and Secular Clergy

Observant monks or friars could, with patronage and by excluding outside influences, restore strict discipline. The ordinary secular clergy received no firmer disciplinary supervision than its bishop could provide,[29] and was under constant pressure from the laity. To achieve the ideal of 'reform', while the property and personnel of the Church were diverted, distracted, and misused, a serious and well-intentioned prelate had to try to persuade

an ill-equipped and largely untrained body of men to resist temptations—
to acquisitiveness or neglect of duty—which their circumstances made
almost irresistible. Yet, many bishops *did* take their pastoral role moderately
seriously; many visited their dioceses, and issued decrees and exhortations
to their clergy to avoid the most damaging forms of indiscipline. Examples
can be found all over Europe, and right up to the eve of the Reformation.
In 1417 the Carthusian prior of Bologna, Niccolò Albergati, was elected
bishop of the city and forthwith began an eight-year visitation of the
diocese. A figure of severe piety, he reputedly never abandoned the habit
of his order even when made a cardinal.[30] Archbishop Antonino of Florence
(d.1459) sought out moral failings remorselessly amongst his clergy (reputedly even using torture!) as well as writing extensively on moral issues.
Patriarch Lorenzo Giustiniani of Venice (d.1456) supported an unusual
(for Italy) circle of pious enthusiasts.[31]

Many northern European bishops also paid at least lip-service to the
ideal of visiting and supervising the conduct of their clergy. Christoph von
Stadion of Augsburg harangued his clergy at a synod in 1517. Christoph
von Utenheim of Basle knew the reforming circles of Geiler von Kaysersberg and the humanists at Strasbourg, and held a reforming synod at
Basle in 1503. Hugo von Hohenlandenberg of Constance held a reform
synod in 1497 and later printed its decrees; though this bishop's notorious
cohabitation with the wife (or widow) of the local *Bürgermeister* perhaps
spoilt the effect of any moral homilies.[32] Several pre-Reformation bishops
of Strasbourg tried fitfully to encourage observant monasticism and piety
among the seculars.[33] French bishops, like the famous Étienne Poncher,
appointed to Paris in 1503, or the more obscure François d'Estaing of
Rodez or Jean de la Trémoille of Auch, supported reform; as did English
ones like Bishops Atwater and Longland in the sprawling diocese of
Lincoln, or John Fisher of Rochester.[34]

By such activity these prelates were simply performing the minimum
oversight expected of their office: the Fourth Lateran Council of 1215 had
stipulated diocesan synods and episcopal visitations at fixed intervals:
intervals which in practice were too close together for a large see, and
demanded too much of the bishop of a small and poor one.[35] Other
requirements, for instance that there should be a theological college in
every archbishopric, had never begun to be enforced. Many problems
combined to make the whole system of visitations a deeply unsatisfactory
method of reform. Tradition had turned the bishop's enquiries into a more
or less stereotyped questionnaire to be asked, very rapidly, of all clergy; it
covered all aspects of parish life, the fabric of buildings no less than the

state of souls, and barely allowed time to gather information, much less to take effective pastoral action to remedy defects.[36] Moreover, this administrative approach could easily degenerate into a routine, or be corrupted through the purchasing of immunity from inspection or the levying of fines for misdemeanours. It was much better at detecting, say, failure to say the canonical 'hours' of the liturgy, than discovering whether a priest cared more about his revenues than his flock.

One detailed study, of a half-century or so of efforts to reform the priesthood in the diocese of Strasbourg, has revealed the following obstacles to reform. First, the machinery of Church government itself created problems: groups and classes of clerics quarrelled amongst themselves; established interests, like chapters and colleges, resisted discipline; the Roman Curia added to the problem with the demands of its courtiers for benefices and the delays and appeals allowed in its procedures.[37] Secondly, economic problems over benefices, exacerbated by a decline in rents, hampered any restructuring. Finally, the whole system of Church property was enmeshed with the moneyed interests of the wealthier laity.[38]

When administrative regulation failed, would-be reformers were thrown back on the even more pious hope that by preaching to their clergy, and by writing works of advice and exhortation for them, they could somehow inspire them to try better. Again in Strasbourg, this was the particular forte of the preacher Johann Geiler von Kaysersberg, just as it had been for the Parisian academic Jean Gerson in the early years of the fifteenth century, and was for other celebrated preachers.[39] Geiler's critiques bore exclusively upon the moral misconduct of individual priests, rather than on the system which made such misconduct so hard to escape. He saw the visitation as an occasion where the bishop should inspire, comfort, and chasten his subordinates. In turn the priests were expected to aspire to high pastoral standards, and so to renew piety in their congregations.[40]

Just how dismal was the state of the local priesthood? There were enormous variations from place to place. In some parts of Europe pastoral care had broken down altogether, with religious services either abandoned completely, or performed perfunctorily and partially by ignorant priests or unlicensed runaway monks or friars.[41] Although such decay was found in prosperous regions of Europe, such as Flanders or Tuscany, it was normally in country villages, not the towns where the Reformation grew best, that the medieval system failed most dismally. Much more typical, for instance in most English parishes, was a steady mediocrity. If the rector or vicar was absent, a substitute was looked for, and sometimes even hired by the laity if the rector failed in his duty.[42] If a parish was too enormous, one or several 'chapels' would be created, which in areas of growing population sometimes became grander than most parish churches.[43] At the opposite extreme, older cities had a superabundance of tiny parishes, often simplified at the Reformation.[44] The quality of the priests, like that of the buildings and services, would have varied from gross incapacity and unsuitability to a mediocre competence. Few indeed of the truly brilliant would have stayed in a parish rather than entering academic life, diocesan administration, or a monastery. A significant minority of ordinary chaplains in Norwich diocese left some books in their wills on the eve of the Reformation, indicating reasonable literacy and commitment at least.[45] Many, it seems fair to suppose, regarded the visitation as a passing phase of interference to be put up with while it unfolded, and ignored once it was over.[46]

'Reform' for the secular clergy, then, remained largely a slogan and a series of paper programmes rather than a widespread reality, simply because the *system*, the legal and economic paraphernalia of the Church's landed endowment, inhibited whatever real efforts were made for the moral and intellectual improvement of the Church's front-line troops. It had been thoroughly tried and found impractical without impossibly sweeping administrative changes against vested interests. Yet clerical pamphleteers made the same complaints and offered the same unrealistic remedies. By 1500 the call for reform of the priesthood had become not a newly recognized urgent problem, but a well-worn literary cliché.

4. *The Clichés of Reform: Ideals and Decay*

The 'vulnerable' features of the clergy against which reformers struggled were in no way new in the last decades of the middle ages. Extravagant or dissolute priests had been chastised in sermons for at least 150 years before 1500; St Bernard of Clairvaux wrote long and hard as early as 1150 against clerical avarice.[47] Pope Alexander VI was easily outdone in vice and political chicanery by John XII (955–64).[48] If the flaws were ancient, so were the criticisms. Yet the 'reforming' agitators of around 1500 seemed to think that theirs was an age of catastrophic decline after centuries of primeval piety. This myth must be seen as a cliché, and a worn-out one at that.

Because 'reform' was a conservative and idealistic concept, writers urging reform imagined an ideal 'golden age' in the history of the Church; a perfect time, located rather vaguely in the remote past, in which everything which was abused and faulty in the present had been perfect and untarnished.[49] A literary tradition of nostalgia for an 'apostolic age' of primitive simplicity had already been established by the writers of the era of the Great Schism. Dietrich of Niem indulged in damning comparisons between the ancient and the modern Church; Henry of Langenstein celebrated the enthusiasm of the old days for holding councils to preserve the faith. Nicolas de Clamanges dreamed of a paradise state where people were holy, fields and trees fertile and fruitful, life long and peaceful. He remarked that his own time was that of the feet of clay in the biblical statue, the apostolic age that of the head of gold.[50]

In these rhetorical, unhistorical apostrophes the pamphleteers of about 1400 were in no way original. They regularly abstracted large passages from much earlier writers such as Guillaume Lemaire, writing in the 1320s, Guillaume Durand from the mid-thirteenth century, or the *Five Books on Consideration* by St Bernard of Clairvaux (1090–1153). The saying was endlessly quoted that in the old days there were golden priests using wooden chalices, now there were wooden priests using golden chalices. Spiritual wealth had declined as material wealth increased.[51] The same emphases and phrases were copied and repeated in the early sixteenth century. John Colet, Dean of St Paul's, preaching to Canterbury convocation in February 1512, quoted St Bernard's words on the supposed 'decline' of the priesthood. Guillaume Briçonnet, bishop of Meaux, drew in 1523 a contrast between the primitive Church, a strong young vine among untended plants, and the modern equivalent, full-grown but weakly and sour.[52]

In one respect, however, the reformers' clichés in the 1500s were even more emotional and far-fetched, and less practical than their predecessors. In the conciliar period one could challenge (selectively according to the political situation) institutional faults. Papal taxes and appointments, the pomp, extravagance, or chicanery of prelates could be freely criticized at a time when popes and cardinals were at war with each other.[53] By the early sixteenth century, however, major structural changes seemed to be no longer on the Church's agenda. Geiler von Kaysersberg, therefore, while he drew deeply on Jean Gerson, rarely complained about the papacy in his sermons; in general, he criticized none of the existing institutions, only their faulty working.[54] All that was left, therefore, was to criticize the moral performance of the clergy. This was done incessantly, repetitively, and possibly unfairly into the bargain. Colet's portrayal of the English clergy as a horde of negligent and ignorant absentees may have been, in terms of pure statistics, quite ill-founded.[55] Briçonnet criticized a more indefinable failing: clergy and laity had the appearance and trappings of religion, but not the 'spirit'. The Church was like the bed of a dried-up stream in summer: the heat of avarice, ambition, and self-indulgence had made the 'spirit' evaporate.[56]

The rhetoric and clichés of religious 'reform', therefore, were echoed in a conventional way, largely without regard either to the actual state of affairs amongst the working clergy, or to the practical, human limitations to what 'reform' could be expected to achieve. In some respects indeed a return to 'apostolic simplicity' would have been a disaster. Had the London secular clergy given up their tithes and lived off alms (as some Carmelite friars urged in the 1460s), many valuable activities, including education and poor relief, must have suffered.[57] So, did the noisy minority of churchmen who urged reform and castigated their colleagues actually cause unnecessary damage to the image of the clergy amongst the people? Certainly they talked down the modest achievements of fifteenth-century reform by comparing their own day to an ideal golden age which had never existed. The real limitations, and the alleged total failure, of late medieval reform may have supplied more ammunition for the political struggles around the Church, which are to be studied next.

4

Challenges from Outside and their Limits

The late medieval Church was its own sternest critic; however, it was also exposed to external challenges, political, legal, moral, and institutional, from laymen and lay governments, and from churchmen who worked largely outside the traditional structures and hierarchies. These challenges usually confined themselves to *one* aspect of the Church at a time: one group might resist papal monarchy but not the privileges of the priesthood; another would try to limit clerics' immunities but leave the sacraments untouched. Such partial and fragmented challenges to the medieval Church contrast with the critique offered by the Reformation: in that era, *every* claim made by the Roman Church was demolished in one interlinked programme.

1. *Councils of the Church versus Popes?*

'Ecumenical councils' of the Church, gatherings of representatives of all Christendom, originated in the remote past. Those in the medieval West, of which perhaps the most important had been the Fourth Lateran Council of 1215, had laid out basic rules of catholic practice.[1] In the era of the Great Schism (1378–1417), they had grown vastly in their claims, as the representative body of the Church at a time when the papacy, and therefore the government of the Church, was divided and disputed. Enthusiasts for the 'conciliar theory' upheld, in various forms, the principle that councils were the fundamental source of authority in the Church, superior to popes, who could err, and that they should have a permanent place in the life of the Church. The decree *Haec Sancta Synodus*, promulgated at the Council of Constance on 6 April 1415, claimed that the council had power directly from Christ, commanding obedience even from popes. The later decree *Frequens* of 6 October 1417 provided for regular councils to be held at fixed intervals after the Council of Constance closed.[2]

After the schism had been to all intents and purposes resolved in 1417, the theory of a council's supremacy over a pope, and its right to meet regularly, remained to haunt the papacy for another century. The Council of Pavia-Sienna (April 1423–February 1424) achieved little; the one which opened at Basle in July 1431 promptly quarrelled with Pope Eugenius IV over the pope's right to dissolve it. In 1433 the pope allowed it to continue; four years later he tried to transfer the council to Italy, whereat the members remaining at Basle declared him suspended (January 1438) and deposed (June 1439). The rebellion of the Council of Basle and its 'antipope' Felix V (Duke Amadeus VIII of Savoy) lasted until the remaining council 'fathers' submitted amicably to Pope Nicholas V in April 1449.[3]

While the Council of Basle was sitting a variety of authors, from both the conciliarist and the papal standpoints, aired sophisticated views about the nature of government and authority within the Church. The challenge was variously expressed, depending on the disputants' academic training, either in terms of canon law ('how does the Church's law and practice say it should be governed?')[4] or in terms of theology ('what is the ideal, celestial pattern of authority to which the earthly Church should conform?'). The political extremism exhibited at the Council of Basle, especially its deposition of a lawfully elected and undoubted pope, caused many divisions and shifts of emphasis among its members; authors such as John of Segovia and Niccolò de' Tudeschi ('Panormitanus') in different ways upheld the council, while others like Cardinals Cesarini and Nicholas of Cusa, and Andrès de Escobar were progressively alienated by it.[5]

For the century or so before the Reformation, therefore, there survived a reservoir of arguments to justify resistance by councils to the absolute claims of the papacy. In terms of practical politics, those arguments had had their day: they were only revived, somewhat unscrupulously, by rulers who were at odds with the papacy for some other reason. Hence in the 1460s the unruly Archbishop Diether von Isenburg of Mainz used the threat of a council in the middle of a row with Pope Pius II over annates; Duke Sigismund of the Tyrol did the same during a quarrel with the papal legate and archbishop of Brixen Nicholas of Cusa. Perhaps the prime example, however, of this manipulation of conciliar ideas was the council called by some rebel cardinals against Pope Julius II during 1511–12; they received support from Louis XII of France, opposed to Julius over Italian politics. It was not only popes who could abuse Church institutions in a political quarrel.[6]

The literary and ideological residue of these quarrels was more important than their immediate political impact. On each occasion fresh works discussing the constitution of the Church were written, while earlier ones were printed. The German jurists Gregor Heimburg and Martin Mair wrote in support of Pius II's opponents in Germany during the 1460s, combining conciliarism with nationalistic criticism of papal misrule.[7] The schismatic Council of Pisa prompted an outpouring of conciliarist writing on the very eve of the Reformation, most notably from the Parisian academics John Mair (or Major) and Jacques Almain, but also from Italians, even within the papal court itself.[8]

The popes had, of course, several responses to all these tests to their political authority. The unruly and ambivalent behaviour of the rebels in the Council of Basle and the schismatic Council of Pisa was ably exploited by papal propagandists such as Juan de Torquemada, who wrote his *Summa de Ecclesia* in 1449, or supporters such as Tommasso di Vio 'Cajetanus' or Giles of Viterbo in the early sixteenth century. Following an attempt to raise taxes for the crusade at the Congress of Mantua in 1459, Pope Pius II issued the decree *Execrabilis* on 18 January 1460, which forbad those who resisted papal commands from making tactical use of an appeal to a future council. The decree seems not to have been used except in emergencies, as when it was reaffirmed by Julius II in the bull *Suscepti regiminis* against his rebellious cardinals in the 1500s.[9] Finally, the popes were able, when confronted with a hostile or rebellious council, to call a rival one of their own into being, as when Eugenius IV 'transferred' the Council of Basle in 1437 to Ferrara and in 1439 to Florence, or when Julius II responded to the 'little council' (*conciliabulum*) of Pisa with the summons of the Fifth Lateran Council.[10]

By the early sixteenth century neither of the extreme positions, conciliarism or papalism, commanded unequivocal support in Europe. Conciliarism was most commonly a widely but rather weakly held general belief in the authority of councils, diluted by decades of an undoubted (if much criticized) succession of popes; it was no longer the urgent war-cry of a small faction, as in the 1400s.[11] It is extremely interesting, but not conclusive, that much of the support for the Council of Basle originated in those very centres, the free self-governing cities of Switzerland and southern Germany, which were later to be so precocious in establishing the Reformation. This shows only that the communal, 'parliamentary', and federative instincts which existed in such cities 'matched', and indeed contributed to, the conciliar movement on one hand, and the civic Reformations on the other. The Reformation was a cousin to the conciliar movement rather than a direct descendant.[12]

2. *Popes, Sovereigns, and 'National Churches'*

Western 'Christendom' was, theoretically, a single spiritual realm, governed by the pope, embracing all peoples and transcending all national boundaries. Such a universal theory had never, least of all in the later Middle Ages, corresponded to reality. Just as the social structure of the Church corresponded to society around it, so its geography more and more reflected the political map of Europe, as nation-states crystallized (England, France, or the Spanish kingdoms) or, just as importantly, *failed* to crystallize (Germany, Switzerland, or Italy). A nation's church expressed its corporate pride; it required its clergy to be fluent in the vernacular; above all, secular rulers required their prelates to be loyal subjects.

Several late medieval developments strengthened the 'national' character of particular countries' churches. The observance movement required the formation of 'provinces' of religious orders, which often corresponded to national boundaries. Much more important was the crisis of the schism and the Councils of Pisa, Constance, and Basle. During the schism secular rulers took sides with either the Roman Pope Urban VI, or the Avignonese Pope Clement VII; the clergy of each 'nation' followed their ruler either in continued loyalty, changes of allegiance, or neutrality. Only after pressure from monarchs (especially Emperor Sigismund) was the Council of Constance summoned. At that council the delegates were grouped in five 'nations' (French, German, Spanish, Italian, and English). While this division reflected not so much political reality, as the artificial arrangements used for matriculating students in medieval universities, it still encouraged national pride and rivalry.[13] After the Council of Constance had closed Pope Martin V regulated his relations with the nations of Christendom by 'concordats' with each political sovereign individually; his successors continued to do so right up to the Reformation.

There were, then, 'national' churches in the late medieval West, in a very practical and everyday sense. Their reality is further shown by the office of 'cardinal-protector', by which several nations acquired on the eve of the Reformation a permanent go-between in relations with the papal court.[14] Such churches became involved in the unending rivalry of secular rulers and the Church hierarchy (including the papacy) over control of religious affairs and 'spiritual' property. One must not imagine, from the perspective of the Reformation, that lay rulers' interference in their churches was in any way new. Before about 1050 local churches, above all those of Germany, were run at the behest of local princes and lords. Bishops and abbots took their place under kings and emperors in the social order as unquestioningly as their lay counterparts.[15] Lay rulers, equally, were seen as in some way sacred, as more than mere laymen.

The lay ruler had only been spiritually downgraded in the so-called 'Gregorian reform' of the late eleventh century, and the tremendous assertion of the prestige of the priesthood which followed. A point was reached where only on sufferance, it seemed, were laymen allowed to be saved at all.[16] Even in this age of priestly self-assertion, however, a strong king could exert tremendous *practical* authority over his higher clergy.[17] The late Middle Ages saw kings and princes claw their way back to spiritual, even 'priestly', status. The term 'mystical body', traditionally used of the Church, was now also used of nations. The 'most Christian' (and miracle-working) kings of France were once again seen as churchmen of a sort; Louis XI, devoted to Our Lady of the small alpine archbishopric of Embrun, obtained in 1482 an honorary canonry in the chapter for himself and his successors.[18] The 'most catholic' kings of Spain built a religious institution, the Inquisition, into their councils.[19]

In practical terms lay rulers also acquired greater powers in religious affairs. One reason for this change of direction was a reaction against the extravagant and unrealistic claims to universal supremacy made, in the course of a struggle with Philip IV of France, by Pope Boniface VIII in the bulls *Ausculta Fili* of 1301 and *Unam Sanctam* of 1302.[20] A similar reaction was provoked by the growth of papal provisions to benefices in the mid-fourteenth century. Finally, the schism and its aftermath gave monarchs potent bargaining counters with the papacy: first the offer of obedience (and the threat to withdraw it); then the threat of supporting a schismatic council such as Basle or Pisa, or the offer to desert one.

The Church's power to regulate its own affairs, then, increasingly depended on the co-operation of the lay ruler. It is debatable how far this was a challenge to the Church, and how far a political process as natural as the interplay between sovereigns and their aristocracies and representative bodies. In different regions of Europe relations between rulers and the universal Church unfolded in a process of negotiation, sometimes punctuated by statements of extreme mutual antagonism, rarely to be taken seriously or upheld for very long on either side. The issues involved were less theoretical and more practical, above all appointments to senior Church benefices, taxation of the clergy, and the judicial activities of the Roman Curia.

During the Great Schism France suspended allegiance from the Avignonese Pope Benedict XIII in a quarrel over major appointments. Some thirty years later, in July 1438, Charles VII issued the 'Pragmatic Sanction of Bourges' while Eugenius IV was embroiled with the Council of Basle: its chief effect was drastically to curtail the popes' power to appoint to French benefices. Traditional means of appointment or election were theoretically restored, but in practice the king could nominate more or less irresistibly if he chose. Thereafter the sanction was imposed or suspended as Franco-papal diplomacy dictated: it was briefly abolished during the 1460s and 1472–5. Finally, in 1515–16 François I, victorious in Italy, secured the friendship of Leo X by negotiating the concordat of Bologna (published in December 1516), by which the king was to nominate to major benefices (save in special cases) and the pope to appoint.[21]

In England it is sometimes said that the issues between Crown and papacy were 'settled' by the parliamentary statutes of Provisors of 1351 and 1390, and those of Praemunire of 1353 and 1393.[22] Certainly they threatened dire penalties against English clerics availing themselves of papal provision to benefices and papal judgement in cases belonging to royal courts respectively. However, the statutes (absolute in common law) were no more the last word on the subject than the papal condemnations of them (absolute in canon law). The policy of the kings of England throughout 150 years or so before the Reformation seems to have been to apply to the popes for papal provision for their nominees to major posts, and to expect to get it, barring occasional obstinacy or lapses of communication on either side.[23]

In both the English and French cases the play of forces was more complex than a simple tension between pope and king. It was usually the politically active laity (in England, the peers and commons in the Parliament, in France the lawyers and judges of the *Parlement* of Paris) who were keenest to claim national privileges over against the papacy. Monarchs readily dangled an anti-papal laity in front of the popes, and then settled on terms. The trend in the later fifteenth century was to concessions, to 'concordats', by which the papacy granted, but also presided over, arrangements with secular rulers. François I had a far harder battle with the *Parlement* of Paris over the concordat of Bologna than he ever had with the popes.

The position of the German Church was more complex, essentially because there was no unequalled sovereign, as in France or England, to extract terms from the papacy. A concordat issued for Germany (as for other nations) at the end of the Council of Constance made ineffectual promises to alleviate the most offensive intrusions of the papal bureaucracy into the revenues of the German Church.[24] The *Reichstag*, the Estates of the Empire, chose in 1438 to stand neutral between Basle and Eugenius IV.

However, the election of the antipope divided Germany, which gradually swung back to the Roman papacy during the 1440s. By the 'Princes' concordat' of 1447 Eugenius IV received promises of loyalty from many German princes in return for generous concessions over appointments to Church posts within their lands. The concordat of Vienna in the following year established the system of alternating 'papal months' for appointments to benefices. This particularly unsatisfactory compromise survived until the Reformation, and prompted the regular listing of 'grievances' against the Curia.[25]

In other instances the popes readily made agreements. The Church in Scotland operated for most of the fifteenth century in reasonable amity with the papacy, occasionally spoilt by schisms, uncertainty, and sheer distance: informal arrangements of long standing were formalized in a concordat in 1487, allowing the king room to nominate senior clergy.[26] In Aragon and Castile a series of grants from the time of Sixtus IV onwards ended in comprehensive rights being conceded in 1523, as were obtained by the Portuguese monarchs in 1514 over their colonial churches.[27] The emphasis has been laid here on appointments, as the most celebrated bone of contention. However, similar agreements were made over royal rights to tax the clergy: it has been pointed out that papal approval for a tax on the clergy could actually assist a monarch in raising the money.[28] Similar haggling took place over contested areas of jurisdiction on the frontiers between Church and State. In any case, popes and secular rulers were not exact rivals. The spiritual and moral authority which popes could (theoretically!) offer could still be very useful to a secular monarch, who would have nothing to fear from papal political power as such. There was no real contest in terms of actual force, but both parties could gain extra prestige if they co-operated.

The papacy seems 'weakened' by these arrangements only if one compares its standing to the outrageous claims of Boniface VIII, or the immense personal prestige of a medieval pope like Gregory VII or Innocent III. In fact, these 'concordats' show how the papacy protected itself from serious, fundamental challenges by entering into a partnership with monarchs on negotiated terms. The popes seem at this period to have had much less to fear from kings and princes than from the rest of the laity. Yet kings and princes had even less still to fear from the papacy. The sixteenth century shows that, if secure on their thrones and in their minds, lay rulers could abrogate the popes' powers whenever they chose. They did not do so; and seem to have found no more difficulty in handling the papacy than they had with their own nobility, or neighbouring rulers.

3. *Laymen against the Church?*

'Anticlericalism', meaning lay people's resentment of the faults, wealth, excessive *esprit de corps*, and power of their clergy, is one of the most convenient and persistent of historians' labels. Like many terms artificially devised to bring a variety of ideas and attitudes together, it has no agreed meaning; some would deny that it really existed on any scale at all.[29] Informed and influential churchmen certainly *said* that they feared laymen's hatred of the priests. Cardinal Cesarini reported to Pope Eugenius IV in 1431 that unless the German clergy improved their conduct, lay people would kill them. In 1509 Bishop Wilhelm von Honstein of Strasbourg asked parish clergy to denounce parishioners 'thinking ill of the clergy' to his court. 'You others, you lay people, you hate us priests—yes, an ancient hatred divides us', preached Geiler von Kaysersberg in 1508.[30] It is not difficult to heap up such testimonies. A similarly careful selection of present-day political satires could convince one that representative government is moribund, its practitioners widely mocked, denounced, and disbelieved. Literate and articulate people who show contempt for rival social groups *may* intend to do away with them altogether; or they may not. How far were the critics of the clergy willing (and able) to go? It is more useful, therefore, to look at the deeds as well as the words of late medieval 'anticlericals', subjects and rulers alike, above all in the hothouses of the Reformation, the corporate towns.

First of all, laymen could have shown their distrust of the old Church by cutting off the supply of voluntary gifts, endowments, bequests, and offerings which were its life-blood. People do not give money willingly to institutions of which they disapprove.[31] The people of Strasbourg do seem to have reduced their gifts to the religious orders in the seventy years or so before 1520. The friars received steadily less, save for the Carmelites (who offered cheap rates for masses for the poor!), while collegiate churches derived more gifts from other clerics (as opposed to laymen) than before. Some of the money, just how much is unknown, *may* have been diverted to indulgences.[32] On the other hand, the new shrines set up in such profusion in southern Germany received lavish gifts.[33] In England some rich patrons, like Lady Margaret Beaufort, patronized both the old-established monasteries *and* the new centres of fashionable devotion.[34] The evidence is contradictory, and shows that the Church was not homogeneous: one could show disapproval of one part of it by ostentatiously diverting gifts to another part. The most important shift was probably away from gifts to monasteries, whose traditional role was to pray for the souls of the dead, towards yearly 'obit' masses, parochial chantries, and chantry colleges for the same purpose.[35] This attitude suggests not virulent distrust of the clergy as a whole, so much as prudent, selective use of funds by lay people—a pattern found elsewhere.

Another possible 'anticlerical' activity was the writing of abusive or satirical literature against the vices of the priesthood. Such literature existed at all social and intellectual levels. In fourteenth-century England specimens of clerical vice had been ridiculed by Geoffrey Chaucer and William Langland, in a way which sixteenth-century reformers were to appreciate and imitate.[36] The early fifteenth-century *Dispute between a Priest and a Knight* was printed many times from 1473 onwards.[37] Ulrich Wiest's poem 'The arrogance of spiritual princes' lambasted the warlike Archbishop Dieter von Erbach of Mainz in 1450 for spending money given as alms on soldiers, tournaments, display, and luxury; while the dialogue 'Usury' of about 1520 mocked the money-lending of priests and monks.[38] Much of such writing showed sheer disgust and little else. However, the boundary between 'anticlerical' writing and reforming propaganda is sometimes unclear. The 'Reformation of Emperor Sigismund', probably written by a German secular priest about 1438, castigated faults (especially in popes, cardinals, bishops, and monks); it also urged conciliar reform, above all of the regular clergy, pressed for ordination only of qualified priests, who should be allowed marriage (living as laymen, then working as priests on alternate weeks!); it then went on to make similarly stringent proposals for the laity as well.[39] Pious reformers could denounce clerical vices and foibles in the most withering terms, but with the intent to purify, not to humiliate, the Church.[40]

There can be no more drastic display of contempt for the clergy than to assault, injure, or kill one of its members in defiance of clerical privilege and the 'sacral' quality of priesthood alike. Spectacular instances of violence against priests in late medieval Germany, such as the duke of Braunschweig who beheaded one of his clerics for suing an inheritance in a 'foreign' court, or the delegates from the Council of Riga in 1428 who were drowned by some Teutonic knights while going to complain to the pope about those same knights, were presumably unusual. None the less, petty violence against priests kept bishops' courts busy; those found guilty could, amongst other things, have their descendants barred from holy orders.[41] The level of such violence does not seem to have increased up to about 1500; and sometimes the clergy gave as good as they got. Some acts of 'violence' (like storming a nunnery and holding a riotous party there) may not have displeased the 'victims' as much as they did the bishop.[42] Priests might have been attacked as much for their political odiousness as for being priests, like the bishops who were killed by rebellious mobs during Cade's rebellion in England in 1450; though, interestingly, popular talk blamed the bishops for both political *and* religious shortcomings.[43] Their 'vulnerability', their much-vaunted 'failings', perhaps made it easier to justify maltreating clerics; but it is not clear that they fared specially badly from *casual* violence in a generally violent age.

It may be different with concerted, organized violence: popular revolutionaries did sometimes single out bishops and monks for harsh treatment.[44] From the mid-fifteenth century the peasant's laced boot (the *Bundschuh*) was adopted as a symbol of popular conspiracy and revolt. It emerged in a rising at Schliengen in 1443, and in the Hegau in 1460; and was used as an emblem for an abortive rising at Sélestat (Schlettstadt) in Alsace in 1493. In the 1500s a peasant named Joss Fritz made several abortive attempts to stir up such rebellions. In 1502 he gathered a very large force of peasants, townspeople, and disbanded soldiers to protest against the taxes levied by the bishop of Speyer and attack his town of Bruchsal. The conspiracy was revealed in the confessional and broken up. In 1513 Fritz was in the Breisgau, gathering allies at the village of Lehen; this time his plans were betrayed after he had commissioned a *Bundschuh* banner from a painter in Freiburg. In 1517 he appeared in the Rhineland, attempting for several months to stir up the vine-growers of the district, threatened with a collapse in the price of their grapes. Yet again his plans were betrayed. In such plans the clergy figured prominently. The *Bundschuh* rebels' password was 'the priests are to blame'; they intended to pillage clerical lands, alleging their wealth to be gained from usury. The rebels of 1493 intended to cut all priests down to one modest benefice.[45] Similar threats were made by the lay preacher Hans Böhm or Böheim, a cowherd who in 1476 took to preaching the abolition of new dues, renunciation of vanities, and violence against the priests at the Franconian village of Niklashausen. He was speedily arrested and burnt by the bishop of Würzburg.[46]

However, many potentially 'anticlerical' measures were *official* acts by entire communities or states to clarify the respective property and legal rights of laymen and clerics, and to restrain or reverse the Church's accumulation of wealth and privileges. The Church, which never took threats to its status lightly, responded to these measures with some skill. In Germany's complicated network of jurisdictions it could charge a high price for partial or formal concessions; its position was weaker, and the concessions made greater, in unified monarchies. The most urgent worry of secular society was the steady, relentless way in which the Church took over more and more property, especially landed property, which then remained under the 'dead hand' of Church ownership and could no longer be taxed. This erosion of the tax base could be delayed, or if possible stopped, in three ways: laymen's rights to grant money to the Church could be limited; Church property could be subjected to laymen's supervision and guardianship; or, finally, the clergy could be pressured into surrendering some of their obnoxious privileges and exemptions.

Late medieval Strasbourg tried several of these approaches. In 1300 the city fathers imposed a ceiling of 1 per cent on the amount of a layman's estate which could be bequeathed to the Church. In 1471 they decreed that nuns (who were often rich heiresses) could only have a life interest in their inheritances, most of which reverted to the city when they died. One of their attempts backfired, when secular priests bought from the city the right to leave property by will (to prevent it lapsing to the bishop's control) and used the right to leave money to monasteries! Even so, by the 1500s the city was desperately worried about the amount of land mortgaged or sold to the Church.[47] There are many examples of such worries in monarchies, as shown for instance by the English statutes of Mortmain in 1279 and 1391. However, such statutes did not actually stop the accumulation of wealth; they simply gave the sovereign an oversight (and a fee) when he licensed the process.[48]

The best examples of lay 'guardianship' over Church property are found in two other great German cities, Augsburg and Nuremberg. In each case complicated arrangements of 'guardianship' (*Pflegschaft*) were made with all sorts of Church bodies, by which, in theory, lay officers supervised the property of, say, a monastery, a chapter, an almshouse, or whatever, while the clergy saw to the strictly religious aspect. One can imagine that the boundary-line which these arrangements theoretically drew between secular and priestly interests became rather vague.[49] Guardianship could be created in other ways, as when the Strasbourg magistracy offered its chapters protection (*Schirm*), by which it in effect paid the clergy's costs in their lawsuits with the bishop, in return for a modest fee and formal acts of loyalty to the city; all chapters took up the offer by 1464.[50] On a grander scale, the Electors Palatine were regarded as 'protectors' of the dioceses within their lands.[51]

Whittling away at the tax privileges of the priesthood was by far the most difficult of these attempts. In Strasbourg the *Schirm* was negotiated after the clergy had become steadily more reluctant to grant voluntary taxes. Individual clerics could be persuaded to purchase citizens' rights

(*Bürgerrecht*), by which they paid taxes and acknowledged the city's courts, but in return for full citizens' privileges.[52] In territorial monarchies the pressure to assimilate clerics into the lay tax system was even less, as kings could negotiate with the papacy for a share of separate clerical taxes. The notion that clerics should 'bear the same burdens as other citizens' was a persistent call, perhaps just because it proved so hard to enforce. The Cologne guildsmen in 1513 pressed for exactly the same kinds of limits to priestly wealth as their betters;[53] the ambition, so frustrated in the fifteenth century, was very speedily realized in the Reformation.[54]

These measures were seen by citizens and rulers as defensive, as aiming to protect the laity rather than bring down the clergy. However, laymen felt more and more that the Church, especially within a close-knit local community, was *their* church, and wished to control its personnel and behaviour as far as possible. Perhaps the most successful of all imperial cities in directing its priesthood was late medieval Nuremberg, with its fewer than 500 clerics far more under the sway of the 20,000 strong citizenry than the bishop of (comparatively) remote Bamberg. The city gained the right to appoint to its two parish churches for alternate months in 1474, and in 1513–14 for all the year; but it was paying dearly for the privilege right up to the Reformation. Meanwhile it regulated the monasteries within its walls, keeping their numbers down and introducing observant reforms, again with the consent of the papacy.[55] This kind of supervision would not in any way have surprised princes or kings of the time. Princes like the Counts (later Electors) Palatine, or the counts and dukes of Württemberg or Bavaria exerted exactly the same sort of control, including the sponsorship of monastic reform as well as the more mundane business of patronage.[56] In England the right vested in laymen of nominating a parish priest, or even a monastic superior, known as 'advowson' (*advocatio*) had continued unabated throughout the Middle Ages and was freely applied and dispensed in the late fifteenth century.

If one looks at this steady growth of secular power over the Church with pure hindsight, one might see it as a steadily mounting disenchantment and alienation with a hidebound corporation waiting to burst forth in unilateral acts at the Reformation. However, lay rulers seem to have been anything but alienated from the Church. On the contrary, they felt so powerfully that the Church was *their* church that they wished to protect their investments in it, for the good, both spiritual and material, of the 'community'. Paradoxically, the usurpations of Church power bound lay rulers more *closely* than ever to the old Church, which they saw as the soul of their city.[57] Moreover, they had strong reasons not to go beyond the bounds of accepted legality, surrounded by jealous neighbours who might exploit a dispute with the Church to serve political ends. The people, on the other hand, could feel the same exasperation as their rulers but lacked their negotiating power. The Church would be as odious as any other potentially oppressive oligarchy, *and* and be seen to fail to live up to the standards which reforming critics taught lay people to expect from it. Above all, these various threats to the old Church lacked cohesion. Conciliarism, moral reform, the desire to 'nationalize' or 'communalize' the Church were ambitious held by different people to varying extents. A moral reformer like Geiler would denounce the Strasbourg law restricting bequests to the Church; an opponent of the papacy like Wimpfeling could denounce conciliarism. This diffuseness was to be changed—briefly—into a devastating unanimity at the Reformation.

4. A 'Lay Spirit' in Religion?

'Anticlericalism' usually had little to do with religion itself: most 'anticlericals' wanted churchmen to behave just as churchmen, rather than officious, interfering, lordly bureaucrats. Lay people could, however, interfere in the priestly sphere, just as clerics did in the lay sphere. If lay people could relate directly to the divinity, they might implicitly question the Church's special status as the primary means by which Christians received God's grace dispensed through the sacramental system; that would have struck at the heart, rather than the outer appendages, of the medieval Church.

In the late fourteenth century the sacramental and priestly principles *seemed* to be challenged in two distinct ways. First, the monopoly held by the traditional religious orders of professed monks and friars on communal Christian life and piety was infringed by some distinctive new forms created in the Low Countries. Geerd Groote of Deventer (1340–84), a highly trained university scholar, had renounced the ambitions of a careerist cleric to become a preaching deacon. He attracted to him several groups of followers and adherents who copied his ideas of study, education, book-copying, asceticism, and living a 'common life' without vows.[58] The more conventional outgrowth of this movement was the reform of the Augustinian canons of Windesheim.[59] However, the sisterhoods and brotherhoods of the Common Life, developed in parallel by Groote's followers, were more innovative: they kept a common household with physical and mental work and regular brief prayer; they dispensed (at least at first) with the usual apparatus of lifetime vows, and mixed priests and laymen together. The first 'brother-houses' were set up by Florent Radewijns at Deventer and Jan Celle at Zwolle, and in the early fifteenth century produced a series of offshoots to the north at Groningen, to the south at Louvain, and into Germany as far as Cologne and the Rhineland.[60]

For this chapter, one wishes to know just how 'special', and in particular how subversive of traditional piety, the attitudes of the Brethren of the Common Life were. Jan Busch, the Chronicler of Windesheim, christened his order's piety the 'modern devotion' (*devotio moderna*).[61] Their pattern of study, work, and prayer differed from the specialization of some late medieval orders, but rather resembled, for instance, the early Cistercians. Most suspicion centred on their being a new order as such; new orders had been banned (theoretically) in 1215. For this reason the local bishops hesitated in recognizing them, and a neighbouring Dominican was condemned by the Council of Constance for writing an excessively violent tract against them.[62] However, on the eve of the Reformation the brethren were very much better integrated into the monastic system than they were at first. By the later fifteenth century, the friars had changed their initial suspicion of the brethren into a positive partnership. Jan Brugman, the Franciscan preacher, told the Deventer brethren in 1460 that 'I like no order more than yours, except my own, the Franciscan order'.[63] Moreover, as printing shrank the manuscript market, the brother-houses became more exclusively places of education; and their education (in contrast to what used to be believed) seems to have been of a very conventional type.[64] Its members included such prominent theologians as Gabriel Biel and Wendelin Steinbach, while the theologian Wessel Gansfort and the scholar Alexander Hegius both lived long in brother-houses.[65] Most seriously of all, the lay element seems to have declined (as it had done before among the Cistercian lay brethren and Franciscan tertiaries) leaving the brethren ever more like just another religious order.[66]

What of their style of piety? The *Imitation of Christ*, the supreme treatise of the brethren's spirituality, was actually written before 1441 by a brother of Agnetenberg, Thomas van Kempen (often latinized as 'a Kempis'), though often attributed at the time to Jean Gerson. The most *potentially* subversive quality of the *Imitation* genre was its emphasis on private prayer and moral self-renewal, at the expense (so it seemed) of the sacramental means which the Church offered. However, this contrast may have been overdrawn. The *Imitation* was full of praise for existing religious forms and orders: it approved of religious obedience and monastic orders, and ended with a long exhortation to confess readily and receive communion devoutly.[67] The means by which the 'devotion' spread tended even more to assimilate its ideals within the ascetic mainstream of fifteenth-century piety. It is usually reckoned to include more than just the spirituality of the brethren: Jean Gerson, pastoral writer as well as academic, is usually reckoned as teaching a 'modern' piety. Gerson's influence was immense, but of a wholly orthodox 'reforming' type.[68] The *Imitation* itself seems to have spread throughout Europe by appealing first of all to the élite of the pious: which meant strict religious orders such as the Carthusian monks and Bridgettine nuns, these were hardly the channels through which a subversive anti-sacramental lay piety could grow.[69]

There was a second trend in late fourteenth-century piety, more recondite but much more threatening to sacramental religion. This was that body of attitudes known as 'mysticism', which believed, in various ways, that by intense contemplation and prayer the believer could have direct access to God. It is important first of all to distinguish the mystical tradition from the 'modern devotion': most brethren were not mystics in any intense way.[70] Secondly, 'mysticism' embraces a very wide range of different attitudes. It has been divided into two broad categories: 'intellectual' mystics who believed that they could unite their *understanding* with the divine through contemplation (which was suspect of heresy); and secondly 'affective' mystics, who had the more modest (and orthodox) hope of uniting the *will* with God and receiving insights on how to live a devout life.[71] The more modest and pious of them, like Jan van Ruysbroeck, the hermit of Groenendael (1293–1381), remained deeply suspicious of the more extravagant visions of the 'Friends of God' (*Gottesfreunde*), 'beghards', or 'beguines' who proliferated in late fourteenth-century Germany and the Low Countries, and often figured in accusations of heresy or simple hysteria.[72]

The most famous exponents of late medieval mysticism emerged in or before the fourteenth century: alongside Ruysbroeck one can cite *Gottesfreunde* like Heinrich of Nördlingen or Rulman Merswin of Strasbourg; the Rhineland Dominicans Eckhart (*c.*1260–1327), Johann Tauler (1300–61), and Heinrich Suso (1295–1366); or the Englishmen Richard Rolle (d.1349) and Walter Hylton (d.1396), or again the Englishwomen Margery Kempe and Julian of Norwich.[73] It is now doubtful whether these figures ever appealed outside a small circle of élite followers: most were either hermits or advisers of small groups of nuns.[74] Moreover, the mystical tradition never regained its fourteenth-century vigour before the Reformation. The fifteenth-century Franciscan, Heinrich Herp (d.1477), was exceptional in continuing the tradition of Ruysbroeck.[75]

Like the conciliar threats to the unity of the Church, the challenges from the 'lay spirit' to the Church's spiritual monopoly were less threatening around 1520 than a century or so before. Those which were widespread were not radical, and those which were radical were not widespread. A much more fashionable and pervasive challenge to the traditional spiritual priorities of western religion was offered by the eloquent but diverse exponents of the 'northern Renaissance'.

5. *The Northern Renaissance and the Church*

The various intellectual trends known as the 'Renaissance' deeply influenced northern European scholars from the mid-fifteenth century onwards. By the eve of the Reformation, Renaissance 'humanism', the movement's intellectual value-system, was immensely fashionable among the younger academic generation. Renaissance humanism was prevalent precisely because it was ill-defined and infinitely diverse, and could adapt itself to many disciplines and contexts. Such diversity makes defining it very difficult.[76] Originally, it was a movement to revive the prestige of rhetorical eloquence, which rapidly became much more than that: by this period, it was essentially a fashion for writing a classical Latin style, purifying the original source texts of classical and Christian antiquity, and emphasizing individual moral uprightness rather than communal ritual purity.[77] Because the humanists were so concerned with ethics and morality on the one hand, and source texts on the other, they at some point expressed opinions about religious questions. Desiderius Erasmus (*c.*1466–1536), the most influential (though not the most typical) single figure of them all, envisaged a 'restoration' (*restitutio*) of Christianity in parallel to the 'rebirth' (*renascentia*) of literature; to be brought about by presenting the sacred texts to readers, who would be morally improved by them.[78] However, this programme was not without its threats to the existing religious order. 'Much humanism was critical and negative in its orientation.'[79] The northern Renaissance can be included among the 'challenges' to the old religious ways, even though it was extremely seductive to churchmen themselves. It helped to make churchmen and laymen alike receptive to the much more destructive critiques of the protestant reformers.

Humanist writers, like almost anyone else who wrote about religion, deplored the inadequacies and failings of the mass of the clergy. Such entirely conventional criticism, when set in the morosely pessimistic verse of Sebastian Brant's *Ship of Fools* of 1494 or the mordant satire of Erasmus's

Praise of Folly of 1509, could reach a far wider audience than any sermon at any reforming synod.[80] Jakob Wimpfeling (1450–1528), who worked as preacher and priest at Speyer, Strasbourg, and Sélestat, vented his rage by writing against a system which deflected wealthy livings to ill-educated, unchaste manipulators of the Church's machinery.[81] Men as diverse as the Hebrew scholar Johannes Reuchlin (1455–1522) and the unruly poet and imperial knight Ulrich von Hutten (1488–1523) could repeat many of the stock criticisms of 'the clergy' while, incidentally, numbering individual clerics amongst their closest allies.[82] Yet few were as effectively abrasive as Erasmus's Folly declaiming that

[priests] insist that they've properly performed their duty if they reel off perfunctorily their feeble prayers which I'd be greatly surprised if any god could hear or understand ... but when it comes to harvesting their gains they're all on the alert, every one of them an expert in the law ... the priests who call themselves 'secular' push the burden [of piety] on to the 'regulars', and they pass it on to the monks; the less strict monks shift it on to the stricter orders, and the whole lot of them leave it to the mendicants; and from there it goes to the Carthusians, amongst whom alone piety lies hidden and buried, hidden in fact so well that you can scarcely ever get a glimpse of it ...[83]

Some, though not all, humanists went beyond a critique of failings to a critique of ideals as well. For most people the various forms of monasticism, with its obedience, abstinences, mortifications, and deprivations, were still the highest form of piety. Few doubted that taking a vow 'added' something to a pious life; a rare exception had been Johann Pupper von Goch (*c.*1400–75), who, despite acting as a superior of Augustinian nuns, asserted that a vow added nothing to grace, and did not atone for the lack of it; that vows helped the 'weak and unstable' rather than the élite.[84] Renaissance humanists were outspoken but inconsistent on this issue. Jakob Wimpfeling aroused a storm of criticism by claiming that St Augustine had never been a monk; he also criticized monks for their unwarranted claims and for seducing the allegiances of the laity.[85]

Erasmus (himself an irregular Augustinian who was dispensed from his vows after years of wandering) mocked monks and friars more mercilessly. His Folly accused the begging friars of noisy, squalid, persistent harassment of others, and all regulars of taking inordinate pride in the trappings of their particular order ('they aren't interested in being like Christ but in being unlike each other') and their pharisaical ceremonies.[86] In the *Colloquies*, dialogues intended to teach Latin prose to young pupils, Erasmus deplored the immorality of persuading young girls to leave pious parents for a nunnery where 'you must take care while you prepare to wed Christ, that you don't wed lots of others', and where false miracles were used to attract recruits; denounced the absurdity of elaborate ceremonial regulations, for example on monastic diet; and called it a mortal sin to give lavish gifts to monasteries and shrines while 'Christ's living temples', the poor, went in want.[87]

On the other hand, many humanists did not share this extreme distaste for pious ceremonies. The Netherlander Josse Clichtove participated in and urged the ascetic kind of monastic renewal.[88] Willibald Pirckheimer, the patrician scholar of Nuremberg, regularly consulted with his numerous sisters and daughters who were nuns and abbesses on the ideals of their orders, and participated in the city's moral oversight of its nunneries. In the early years of the Reformation he persuaded the city to leave some of the nuns in their houses rather than dissolving them by force.[89]

Two other features of the old Church suffered particularly from humanist satire: at one extreme academic theology, as practised in the scholastic 'ways' or schools; and, at the other, the credulous superstition and fetishism of contemporary popular piety. Both were attacked because they did not make their exponents better (i.e. more virtuous) Christians. Theology suffered, in varying degrees, from the humanists' distaste for the technical logic or 'dialectic' as used in the medieval philosophy *and* theology; 'scholastic' logicians were satirized for fussy and unedifying logical quibbles couched in an obscure and inelegant Latin jargon. In fact, on the academic level, the struggle between 'scholasticism' and 'humanism' varied in intensity, the two sometimes collaborating in their proper spheres quite amicably, and even coexisting in the same person.[90] The facts did not get in the way of a good cliché, which made traditional theologians figures of fun at best, and at worst corrupters of morals.[91] Folly remarked:

Paul could exhibit faith, but ... his definition of it is hardly 'magisterial' ... The apostles knew personally the mother of Jesus, but which of them proved how she had been kept immaculate from Adam's sin with the logic our theologians display? ... The apostles baptized wherever they went, yet nowhere did they teach the formal, material, efficient, and final cause of baptism ... Who could understand all of this unless he has frittered away thirty-six whole years over the physics and metaphysics of Aristotle and Scotus?[92]

Yet Wimpfeling (for instance) could complain about the moral uselessness of scholastic theology in one speech, and in another positively recommend it for the defence of the faith.[95] Stranger still, when Pirckheimer wrote to defend Reuchlin in the great *cause célèbre* of the pre-Reformation era,[94] he presented a list of 'true theologians' to be opposed to the obscurantist Cologne faculty whom he denounced: he included, quite deliberately, several who only partly shared humanist attitudes and practised scholastic techniques as well.[95] Even in controversy the 'humanists' were unclear as to whom they could count on or persuade to their side.

The humanists were more agreed in criticizing vulgar superstition: indeed their snobbery on this issue probably limited their appeal. Conrad Mutianus Rufus (1470–1526), canon of Gotha, typically devalued not only crass superstition, but also those who believed that righteousness lay in simply performing the ritual and sacramental duties prescribed by the Church. He denounced the popular attitude which reduced religion to a trade-off of pious works performed in return for divine favours expected. The tonsure he called 'barbarous', and declared 'only the ignorant seek salvation in fasts'. Virtuous conduct, rather than confession or even prayer, was his ideal.[96] Erasmus's Folly mocked lay people who attributed miraculous powers to images of saints or 'imaginary indulgences for their sins'; 'What is more foolish, or indeed more fortunate, than those people who promise themselves more than supreme bliss for reciting daily the verses of the seven psalms ... so the entire life of all Christians is full of such self-delusions, which the priests are quite happy to encourage for the profit it brings them.' If anyone had suggested to the people that they should repent of sin and change their way of life as well as performing rituals, their souls would be thrown into confusion. In the *Colloquies* the same contempt for materialistic religion without an ethical base was expressed.[97]

Yet Erasmus (as he explained) condemned only the avarice of those who forged miracles and relics or the foolish credulity of those who believed them, not the recognized act of piety. Pirckheimer was devoted to the traditional cults. Von Hutten, for all his contempt for avaricious clerics, wished a friend well on pilgrimage to Jerusalem and nearly undertook such a journey himself.[98] Such reverence for the unity and authority of the Church marked off the older generation of northern Renaissance humanists from the younger figures who drifted in such numbers to the Reformation; that same reverence drew the teeth of their sharper criticisms of the Church even before the storm broke over Luther's head. When Wimpfeling was approached by Maximilian I in 1510 to prepare a unilateral sanction against papal interference in the German Church (such as had been imposed in France), he retreated into loyalty to the Church and advised the Emperor just to petition the pope for redress. Mutianus Rufus was already expressing more and more reverence for the Church for several years before 1517. In a tract written on Mary Magdalene before 1517, Pirckheimer expressed utter obedience to the Church, as well as the desire for truth.[99]

This respect for the 'ideal' Church prevented the subversive potential of the humanists' use of new scholarly techniques on the text of the Bible from being realized. A series of publishing milestones marked the gradual introduction of modern text criticism to the Scriptures: Giovanni Pico della Mirandola's work on the Psalter; Reuchlin's composition of a usable Hebrew manual in 1506; Erasmus's publication of Lorenzo Valla's *Annotationes* in 1505, and of his edition of the New Testament in 1516; the commentaries on St Paul by Jacques Lefèvre d'Étaples (1512); and the compilation of the 'polyglot' Bible at the Spanish University of Alcalà up to 1520.[100] In principle these efforts threatened the monopoly of theologians over dogma (since they handed the source of authority over to the grammarians), and thereby threatened the coherent authority of the Church (by questioning corrupt readings of texts which had been used to support traditional dogmas).[101] However, such challenges had to be widely published in open defiance of established authority to become a threat: which both temperamentally and on principle the pre-Reformation humanists refused to do.

The humanists were not, as a rule, popularizers. They based their piety on education, learning, and moral self-control, all of which were essentially élitist principles, neither appealing nor practical for all the clergy, let alone the people as a whole.[102] Humanism's natural setting was a coterie around an inspirational figure like Wimpfeling or Brant at Strasbourg, Pirckheimer at Nuremberg, or Mutianus Rufus at Gotha. The experiment in preaching and simplifying worship at Meaux, near Paris, from 1516 was probably the only attempt to reform a local church on 'humanist' lines.[103] Erasmus's *Enchiridion* of 1503, his first classic statement of ethical, humane piety, was only a commercial success and widely translated after reprinting in 1518, after the Luther controversy had raised the religious temperature.[104] Mutianus Rufus was *so* devoted to small cliques that he positively discouraged his friends from spreading his ideas or publishing his writings. Although Erasmus wished all sorts of people to read the Bible in their leisure moments, he himself wrote in Latin, and vernacular bibles printed before 1520 (which rarely derived from the humanists anyway) do not seem to have stirred a mass vogue for the simple, ethical, 'philosophy of Christ'.[105]

When heaped together, all these various 'challenges' look as though they were bringing the institutional Church to its knees, and have produced many a chapter entitled something like 'the weakness of the Church on the eve of the Reformation'. When confronted with the undoubted fact that late medieval people were deeply religious (in their way), some historians have then suggested that the laity shaped their religion without any help from the priesthood (from whom they were supposedly alienated).[106] As the last two chapters have shown, such a picture would be grossly over simple. The essential point is that the 'challenges' to the Church, like the Church itself, were fragmented and diverse. Those people (priests *or* laymen) who criticized the 'political' Church were often quite ordinary in their religious outlook; those who held critical or innovative religious views were usually politically obedient. Secondly, there was an almost invariable undercurrent of *basic* obedience to the 'concept' of a unique, ideal Church even while members or groups within it were being bitterly resented or opposed. For all its faults, even the bitterest lay critic seems to have accepted that the Church (in one of its many forms) represented salvation of souls and the spiritual welfare of the community. For the vast majority of Europe's people, there was no real alternative. One wishes to know why this was so: the answer lies, probably, in what the Church taught about its spiritual place and role. Before considering that, however, the few people who *may* have believed they had an alternative to the Church—the heretics—must be examined.

5
Heresy: An Alternative Church?

An eleventh-century document made the sweeping statement: 'One who does not consent to the decrees of the apostolic see is deemed to be a heretic.'[1] Heresy was more technically defined as 'an opinion chosen by human perception, founded on the Scriptures, contrary to the teaching of the Church, publicly avowed and obstinately defended'.[2] Though the medieval Church did not always define just what it *did* stand for, it tabulated, codified, and agreed down the centuries which 'erroneous' beliefs it did *not* accept. Jean Courtecuisse (d.1423), writing about 1375, declared that all possible heresies had already been condemned by the Church, either explicitly or implicitly.[3] In practice one became a 'heretic' in the late Middle Ages *either* as a pugnacious theologian who pressed an argument so far as to threaten orthodoxy (like John Wyclif, Jan Hus, or later Martin Luther); *or* as an ordinary lay person who joined, was born into, or otherwise became entangled with an already known group of popular 'heretics' (variously known for instance as Cathars, Waldenses, 'Free Spirits', Fraticelli, or Lollards). Sometimes the descent from one kind of heresy to the other followed naturally, as with the first English Lollards, who came into being when followers of the disgraced academic Wyclif set about preaching to groups of followers in the countryside, and built up a following among the people. The origins of other popular heresies, especially the Waldenses, are more obscure.

How far did the 'heretics' of the late Middle Ages offer a real alternative to the established Church? How far were they an exception to the consent normally given to the idea (if not all the details) of the Church? This question is made harder to answer by the methods used by hostile ecclesiastical judges or 'inquisitors'. First, inquisitors (depending on their skill and experience) often expected heretics to conform as closely as possible to the literary pattern which they found in their manuals.[4] To show his sorrow for the 'crime' and 'sin' of heresy and be forgiven, a first-offender heretic was required to confess *fully* all his heresies (the inquisitor defined what 'fully' meant), and to reveal the names of his fellow heretics. Therefore, those popular heretics (like *some* later Lollards and Waldenses), who wrote nothing of their own before the Reformation, and have left only their judicial confessions, tend to be recorded chiefly or even exclusively in polished inquisitors' versions, which *may* exaggerate the heretics' coherence in beliefs and separateness from the official Church.[5]

1. *The Hussite Movements in Bohemia*

Bohemia in the fifteenth century broke nearly all the rules of how a kingdom of western Christendom was expected to behave. From 1415 onwards it produced a rebellion by most of the population against the hierarchy of the catholic Church; and spawned a range of movements, diverse in their social settings and teachings, ranging from an ordered, structured 'church' in an ill-defined state of schism with Rome at one extreme, to highly exclusive, intolerant, narrow sectarianism at the other. The 'Hussite' movements took their name from the Prague preacher and theologian Jan Hus (*c*.1372–1415), in whose person a number of trends in late fourteenth-century Bohemian religious life had happened to coalesce. On one hand Hus inherited the tradition of pastoral concern, and vigorous popular preaching against the vices and failings of the contemporary clergy, which had developed in Prague from the 1360s onwards.[6] On the other he also, during the 1400s, came to lead a movement of academic resistance in the University of Prague, in which predominantly Czech theologians resuscitated older schools of thought, technically called 'realism', in opposition to the 'nominalist' school prevailing amongst the Germans in the same university. For many of his 'realist' ideas Hus and his allies drew extensively, if selectively, on the teachings of the Oxford academic John Wyclif (d.1384); in particular they developed (though in a less obviously heretical way) Wyclif's doubts about the right of a priest or bishop in mortal sin to exercise the jurisdictional powers of the Church.[7]

Hus's blend of reformist preaching and philosophical chauvinism, laced with nationalist pride, made his critiques of the existing Church order more destructive and dangerous than those of his predecessors. His doctrine of the Church (most trenchantly expressed in his treatise *On the Church* in 1413) led him to challenge the rights of sinful prelates and friars to keep their positions, status, and landed wealth. First driven out of Prague, Hus was summoned to the Council of Constance which, desperate to prove its own orthodoxy in a shaky legal situation, listened to the accusations of Hus's personal and academic enemies among the Czech delegates. In spite of a safe conduct from the Emperor, the council condemned him to be burnt as a heretic on 6 July 1415. Hus's absence and later execution provoked the Czech nobility to lead a revolution against the clergy, effectively annihilating the authority of catholic bishops, confiscating large tracts of Church lands, and exploiting patronage rights over their local churches to the full. The Eucharist, which had been central to late fourteenth-century reforming piety, became the focus and symbol of membership in these rebel churches. The Hussites adopted the practice, first tried by fervent followers of Hus like Jakoubek of Stříbro, of giving the chalice of wine to the laity, who traditionally had only been given the bread: from this the Hussites became known as 'Utraquists', as receiving Communion 'in both kinds' (*sub utraque specie*).[8] They encapsulated their programme in the four Articles of Prague adopted in 1420, demanding freedom of preaching, the chalice for the laity, an end to worldly power wielded by churchmen, and punishment of grave sins committed by clerics.

However, the Hussites soon fragmented and fought amongst themselves. More proletarian protest movements arose among the Prague guildsmen during 1419–22, while in the countryside, from an exotic variety of anticlerical revolutionaries there eventually emerged the most militant and socially innovative of Hussite revolutionaries, the 'Taborites'.[9] Though they failed to take over the national movement, the Taborites under their military leader Jan Zizka (d.1424) fought off a series of expeditions led against them, and probably saved the Bohemian revolt from suppression in its early years. However, their fervent sense of mission, animated by expectations of a new age of perfection for the elect, doomed Taboritism to a meteoric but rather short existence.[10] In contrast the more conservative, aristocratic wing of the movement proved more politically supple and durable. During 1433–6 Jan Rokycana, representing the moderate 'Utraquist' Hussites, negotiated with the Council of Basle the Compactata, by which the Council Fathers (and later Emperor Sigismund) agreed, in a qualified way, to the demands of the Articles of Prague.[11] In 1434 the Utraquists defeated the Taborites in battle at Lipany and vindicated their claim to be the ruling faction of the Hussites. In 1435 a Czech representative assembly elected Rokycana as Hussite archbishop of Prague, though without papal confirmation. Not only did the Hussites control the greater part of the Church in Bohemia; the reign of the 'Hussite King' George of Podebrady from 1458 to 1471 gave the Utraquists some stability despite the hostile machinations of Pope Pius II.[12] The Kutná Hora agreement of

1485 reaffirmed the 1436 Compactata and gave the Utraquist Church more or less official status until the very eve of the Reformation.[13]

The instinct to escape the world and found communities of the devout resurfaced in other, more peaceful forms. In 1458 Peter Chelcicky (c.1380–c.1467) established a community at Kunvald on the estates of George of Podebrady, with the approval of Archbishop Rokycana and the help of the latter's nephew, known as 'Brother Gregory'. In 1467 Gregory organized his followers into a separate church, the 'Brotherly Unity' (*Jednota Bratrská*), with its own priesthood and lay membership distinct from both Utraquists and catholics. Tensions soon developed between the town- and country-based elements of the Unity, which surfaced in 1490, when the inner council of the Unity allowed members to participate in civic offices and the life of the wider community. Between 1495 and 1500 a rift deepened between the tolerant majority of the brethren and a rural minority who wished to preserve strict, fastidious avoidance of the rest of society. In 1500 this minority under Brother Amos founded a separate priesthood and began recriminations against the major unity, inciting the (catholic) King Vladislav II to persecute their former co-religionaries.[14] Meanwhile the majority faction in the Unity produced an articulate theologian of their own, Lukas of Prague (c.1458–1528), whose works were published in Germany.[15]

How far did the various Hussite movements replace or substitute for the activities of the official Church? Two features are clear. First, the Hussite churches grew at the catholics' expense, unlike heretic movements anywhere else in late medieval western Europe, which usually had no impact on Church wealth and little even on church attendance. They offered a complete religious 'service', which most heretic movements did not. Secondly, their protest was based on an explicit denial that the Roman hierarchy represented the one, authoritative, expression of the Church on earth. The Hussite churches offered the nearest thing, in their attitudes towards church-building at least, to an anticipation of the protestant Reformation in fifteenth-century Europe.

However, the impact and spread of their protests were limited by two other factors. First, Hussitism originated in a denial of the right of sinful priests and prelates to wield jurisdiction and authority in the Church, rather than their right to act as priests and administer the sacraments. The Hussites were always slightly ambivalent, therefore, about the 'priestly' value of the Church's ministry. Even the Unity retained the traditional sacraments, while Rokycana's ideas about the Eucharist went even further than catholicism in praising the powers of the mass. Hussite religion, like catholicism but unlike protestantism, was highly sacramental.[16] Secondly, Hussitism was always an essentially Czech phenomenon. It found its first impetus in a rush of ethnic and national pride and indignation, even though many of its earliest enemies were other Czechs. It barely spread to neighbouring provinces like Moravia or Silesia, let alone further afield. The 'Bohemian heretics' were, accordingly, distrusted and dismissed elsewhere in Europe. It was taken for granted in 1519 that an accusation of Hussite errors would blacken Martin Luther's name; only once the new wave of protests had begun did the Hussites' reputation outside their own borders improve.

2. *Popular Lay Heresies*

Outside Bohemia 'popular heretics' followed a quite different pattern of dissent. They were groups of people, usually only a proportion of several communities in an area, who held beliefs opposed to those of the official Church, and spread them among their allies and followers. Sometimes they cherished an 'alternative' religious literature, and kept intermittent contacts with like-minded people in other areas, as a means of comfort. They always ran the risk of persecution from bishops' officers or papal inquisitors. Either for concealment, or because the 'heresy' did not offer a complete religious 'service', such popular heretics stayed in some contact with, and participated in, the rites of the official Church. Their identity consisted in rejecting majority religious culture; but they were continuously exposed to its threats and blandishments. As voluntary dissenters, lacking any obligatory disciplinary structure, they tended to become inconsistent in their protests, and to merge their ideas with popular religion on the one hand, and 'official' worship on the other.

On the eve of the Reformation, two names were regularly used to describe such dissenters: 'Lollards' in England, and 'Waldenses' (*Vaudois, Valdesi, Waldenser*) in parts of southern France, Italy, and Germany. The English Lollards had a fairly clear late fourteenth-century pedigree. The academic theologian John Wyclif (d. 1384) had by the late 1370s made his name as an outspoken defender of the rights of princes over against the papacy. In 1378 he broke with his academic and political career and began to write very trenchant pieces against the claims made by the Roman hierarchy to represent the 'true' Church. Wyclif thus struck at the crucial support for the official Church, its guaranteed sacramental 'service' for the good of souls.[17] For him the 'Church' was simply the body of those chosen by God to be saved, and the clergy were owed credence and respect only conditionally on their moral conduct. In the last years of his life he also wrote against the Church's teaching on the Eucharist, thus alienating some former supporters.[18]

The English hierarchy allowed Wyclif to die of old age in the obscurity of a country rectory. Unlike Hus thirty years later, he was certainly a heretic, but no martyr; he thus forfeited the vast academic and noble support won posthumously by his Bohemian admirer. Wyclif's academic followers were bloodlessly (though not, at first, completely) purged at Oxford University in 1382, while those parliamentary knights who pressed parts of his programme in 1395 and 1410 lost support after the abortive rebellion of Sir John Oldcastle in 1414.[19] Wyclif's enduring influence was exerted below the levels of the learned or the powerful through the 'poor priests' whom he instructed to travel around the countryside teaching his beliefs to the ordinary laity. From as early as 1387 such followers were known opprobriously as 'Lollards'. By preaching, and by passing from hand to hand a manuscript sermon cycle compiled and copied in the East Midlands in the 1390s, and an English translation of the Bible produced by two of Wyclif's followers about the same period, a heretical undercurrent was set up in English life which continued to trouble the authorities on the eve of the Reformation. In the early decades, while the 'poor priests' were still alive, the counter-culture of Bible-reading and sermon-writing set down strong roots in East Anglia, Kent, the Thames valley, and parts of the Midlands of England.[20] At this stage the thrust of Lollard thought was negative—denial of the value of the sacraments, denial of the spiritual power of the clergy, rejection of images, pilgrimages, and other 'services' commonly taken up by the laity—but quite coherent.[21]

There is a distinct gap in the recorded prosecutions for heresy from about 1440 to about 1460, or maybe 1480 in some areas, even where documents survive which ought to tell of any cases, had they been brought.[22] It is the post-1460 wave of Lollard activity which chiefly interests the Reformation historian. Probably some of the same teachers, and some of the same books, were influential in both waves; certainly many of the same areas were affected as before.[23] However, the 'poor priests' disappeared, as Lollards did not, as a rule, 'ordain' their teachers.[24] Instead laymen, usually artisans, spread their ideas among family and friends; in some districts, as in Kent, the Chilterns, Coventry, or the London area, they built up a substantial, numerous following. A sequence of bishops and their officials investigated them, reaching a peak of activity around 1511–12.[25]

However, these last-generation Lollards did show some of the diffuseness and combining of ideas to be expected of an unofficial body of ideas under pressure. In the first place, most attended church services just like normal believers; and not only to escape detection, which the notorious could hardly have hoped to do.[26] To that extent Lollard cells became pious 'conventicles' in which religious dissent was secondary.[27] Secondly, some combined traditional 'Lollard' beliefs (at least in their confessions) with expectations of an imminent new age or a second coming. Thirdly, some denied beliefs which were shared by all sorts of Christians, such as the immortality of the soul or the Virgin birth; finally, there are cases of 'Lollards' saying the Lord's Prayer backwards or using charms.[28] Naturally enough, therefore, the suspicion arises whether Lollardy was perceived as such a threat in the early 1500s, that bishops trawled indiscriminately for dissenters and caught all kinds of fish in their nets.[29] So great was the fright given to the English Church hierarchy by the late fourteenth-century outbreak of dissent that any disenchantment with the Church, from refusal of tithe to the possession of *any* English Bible without authorization, could be taken as a sign of heresy.[30]

The 'Waldensian' heretics of continental Europe had a longer and more obscure history than the Lollards. They were traditionally believed to originate in the lay-preaching movement begun at Lyons in the late twelfth century by a merchant called 'Valdesius', who had lapsed into heresy after disobeying the Church's prohibition on unlicensed preaching. However, the heretics themselves were vague about their origins, and there is no continuous documentary evidence of their existence in any one location from before the middle of the fourteenth century.[31] From the middle to late fourteenth century onwards, two major areas of Waldensian dissent are known. The first was in the south-western Alps between the Dauphiné and Piedmont, which in the fifteenth century produced offshoots and colonies in Provence, and also in Calabria and Apulia in southern Italy; these groups, based on a handful of villages and numbering a few thousand in each case, survived several attempts at suppression right up to the eve of the Reformation.[32] The second zone of Waldensian activity was in Germany, where persecutions uncovered groups in southern and eastern Germany (in the 1390s) and also the north-east: Saxony, Thuringia, Pomerania, Brandenburg (in the 1390s and again in the 1460s and 1470s).[33] In Germany, unlike Mediterranean Europe, Waldensianism seems to have been declining irreversibly as the fifteenth century ended.

Similar 'heresies' were ascribed to Waldenses in both zones, although this similarity may in part derive from the inquisitors' expectations and methods: inquisitors in Germany copied and adapted manuals produced in France or Italy, and vice versa.[34] In any case, 'Waldensianism' consisted of a series of rejections of official Church dogma and usual religious practice, quite similar, in fact, to popular Lollardy. The value of sinful priests' services was questioned; the reality of purgatory, and the value of prayer for the dead, challenged; the taking of oaths, and of human life for any reason, were supposedly forbidden by the heretics.[35]

In certain respects the Waldenses were more impressive than the later Lollards. They supported a brotherhood of travelling preachers, called 'barbes' in southern Europe and 'brothers' in the north; they heard confessions from, and gave advice to, their followers; they trained up their own successors, and conserved a modest literary tradition (although in the late fifteenth century they apparently wrote nothing new of their own).[36] On the political side, the laity of the Alpine valleys were sufficiently organized to fight an armed campaign against the soldiers called in by the inquisitors; and, when that failed, a protracted legal battle to clear their reputations, which succeeded in 1509.[37] However, the actual *scope* of Waldensian religious protest was rather meagre. Overwhelmingly they seem to have conformed in almost every outward detail to ordinary catholic behaviour: confessing to priests (as well as to heretics!), receiving sacraments, taking judicial oaths.[38] They depended on the Church in practice even while they condemned it in theory. Their distinctive rites mimicked official worship, sometimes with a trivial but ostentatious difference[39] rather than putting forward a radical alternative.

These cases present the most numerically impressive instances of heresy on the eve of the Reformation. There were some others, insignificant as to numbers.[40] Two exaggerated assessments must be avoided. Popular heresy was not just vague, incoherent, uninformed folklore without numbers or importance.[41] In its restricted areas it was a persuasive and persistent attitude which gave its persecutors a great deal of trouble. On the other hand, late medieval heretics were not a sophisticated, articulate, Christian underground church waiting to find new allies as the Reformation approached: this myth the protestants themselves fostered, but only by artificially reviving literary remains of some antiquity.[42] As the Reformation spread, Lollards in Essex and Waldenses in Provence did make contact with the reformers.[43] However, it is hard to prove that their tradition of resistance was sufficient to initiate the Reformation in those districts. It could not be guaranteed that dissenters of one kind would automatically make common cause with new dissenters of another kind; indeed, those who had resisted the pressures from inquisitors *might* resist the pressure from preachers to sacrifice their identity just as resolutely.[44] In any case, neither the quantity, nor the essential character, of late medieval popular heresy allows it to be seen as a comprehensive 'alternative' to catholicism. At most it expressed a natural corrective protest against some of the most outrageous claims made for the ministrations of the Church: some people, at least, *could* not believe all that was claimed for the mass, penance, indulgences, relics, or whatever. The most surprising thing is just how little of such protest was, apparently, articulated and recorded.

6

The Church and the Christian Soul

"There was hardly a period in the second millennium of ecclesiastical history which accepted with less resistance the Catholic Church's absolutist claims in matters of dogma."[1] This comment on Germany was equally valid in most of the rest of Europe. However greedy, vicious, grasping, or arrogant individual churchmen were, the Church was still 'Mother Church' and the means to salvation. This attitude was instilled into Europe's population in every aspect of religious life, where (in spite of the theologians' quibbles) the visible, institutional Church on earth and the Churches triumphant in heaven and suffering in purgatory were seen as indissolubly linked.[2] This chapter suggests that lay people's basic belief in the spiritual power of the pre-Reformation Church balanced their political dissatisfaction with its incidental faults; so the pressures for and against the old Church cancelled each other out. The Church was at once showered with tokens of popular esteem, *and* maligned, restricted, and disliked. So long as the Church was still the route to divine grace, it survived; when people were persuaded to believe in a different way to salvation, its support collapsed.

1. *The Lifelong Cycle of Sin, Absolution, and Penance*

How was the 'spiritual role' of the Church explained to ordinary believers? Only when this is understood need the theologians' subtle explanations be considered. Late medieval religion was, at least officially, about saving souls.[3] Individual souls were saved, not in a once-and-for-all act of redemption, but by a lifelong course through a cycle of sin, absolution, and penance. This cycle was determined by the two great facts of religious life: human sin, that is, repeated breaking of the moral law of God, and the forgiveness of sins, offered through the Church in the sacrament of penance.

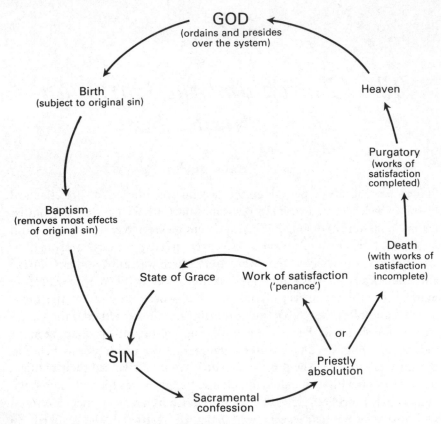

FIG. 1. The Penitential Cycle in Late Medieval Catholicism

The progress can most easily be illustrated in Fig. 1. For most of his or her life, a Christian believer was supposed to pass round the cycle in the lower part of the diagram, from grace to sin, from sin to confession and absolution, and thus back to grace again. The two parts of the sacrament of penance, namely the confession of sins, and the work of satisfaction (commonly called the 'penance') corresponded to the two consequences of sin: 'blame' or 'guilt' was removed by confession and absolution, while a 'penalty', a sort of judicial debt to the Church, was removed by the performing of a penance. If any of this penalty remained unexpiated by pious penance at death, it was atoned for after death, in the excruciating, but temporary, sufferings of purgatory.[4]

For saving souls, therefore, sacramental confession and penance was *the* religious activity in the late Middle Ages: besides the communion (for which it was a precondition), it was the only sacrament normally bestowed more than once in a lifetime. This system had grown steadily down the centuries: first apostasy, then very grave sins, and finally, by a decree of the Fourth Lateran Council of 1215, every individual 'mortal' sin committed since the penitent's last confession was supposed to be confessed in a private hearing with a priest at least once a year.[5] To the subject of confession were devoted some of the most practical priests' manuals of the period. Two of the most popular were published in two dozen or more editions in the first fifty years of printing.[6] The purpose of sacramental confession was to develop and harness the penitent's sorrow for sins committed. How 'perfect' a sorrow was the penitent supposed to bring to his confessor? Opinions varied. The most stringent requirement was that the penitent must be 'contrite', having a complete, perfect sorrow for sin. The preacher Geiler von Kaysersberg, and the theologian Gabriel Biel, whose teachings Geiler largely followed, believed that ordinary believers *could* achieve, if only momentarily, this 'perfect', supreme sorrow for sin and love of God.[7]

However, many theologians, and most writers on confession, took a range of rather less demanding and more reassuring views. According to influential pastoral writers such as Jean Gerson, Johannes Nider, and Antonino of Florence, it could be enough for a penitent to come to confession feeling only an imperfect, inadequate sorrow, technically called 'attrition', for his sins. Divine grace, at work in the sacrament of penance, would then transform the penitent's inadequate sorrow into true 'contrition'.[8] Several popular writers on confession, following Duns Scotus (d.1308), went even further to ease the penitent's mind: 'attrition' was itself a kind of 'meritorious' work to earn grace and forgiveness. Moreover, someone who was only partly, insufficiently attrite, who nevertheless went to confession, because he did not 'put a obstacle' to grace, could be sure of being forgiven.[9] The whole trend of late medieval literature on confession (summed up in the attitude of Silvestro Mazzolini of Priero, whose *Sylvestrina* was published on the very eve of the Reformation, and who was one of the first to write against Luther) was to emphasize the assurance of forgiveness which could be gained by total submission to and acceptance of the sacraments of the Church: 'the absolution of the priest had become a mysterious offering of grace that could counterbalance weakness and doubt.'[10]

Notwithstanding these reassurances, it has been alleged that sacramental confession laid an intolerable 'burden' on medieval people, by tormenting them with doubts and fear as to whether they were sufficiently sorry and truly forgiven, and by imposing an unduly severe, fastidious, fussy concern about every individual little sin.[11] In fact, medieval writers were well aware of the dangers of morbid worry about minor sins (technically, 'scrupulosity'), and gave copious advice on curing such worry.[12] How far were the people of the time morbidly worried by the need to confess their sins? It is clearly naïve to assume that everyone in late medieval Europe swallowed whole the moralists' most grim warnings about sin. Normal practice for lay people, and even for some priests, was to confess once a year, in Lent, and on the point of death.[13] Most conformed, with rare exceptions; Waldensian heretics, who confessed by choice, did so annually to their priests and only once every two, three, five, or more years to heretic pastors.[14] Moreover, confessors were regularly urged to be moderate, lenient, and humane; while those who were *not*, and treated their penitents harshly, found that lay people turned to the many friars and secular penitentiaries who competed for their attention, until they found a congenial one.[15]

Finally, the Church progressively softened the rigours of discipline by offering indulgences with ever more extravagant and inflated claims. An 'indulgence' was, officially, a favour conferred by the Church, which cancelled out the works of satisfaction ('penances') imposed at the recipient's last confession. It presupposed a previous confession. It was based on the belief that the Church held an inexhaustible store of 'surplus' merit accumulated by Christ, the Virgin, and the saints, which the Church could assign to whom it chose.[16] The scope of indulgences was repeatedly enlarged towards the end of the Middle Ages. 'Plenary' indulgences, abolishing *all* penalties, were offered at the increasingly frequent papal 'jubilee' years. Indulgences were applied, 'in the manner of prayers', to souls already presumed to be in purgatory, for the first time in 1476. By the 1500s 'full confessionals' were offered: these allowed the purchaser to choose his own confessor, who could absolve him once in life and on the point of death even for sins normally reserved for the pope to forgive; could grant him a plenary indulgence at any time when he was in danger of death; and could administer the Eucharist to him on demand.[17]

Theologians, though sometimes hesitant, generally acquiesced in this 'inflation', protected as it was by the formidable authority, and even more formidable self-interest, of the papacy. Protests came rarely from such as Johannes Rucherat von Wesel (*c*.1400–81), who for his public opposition was deposed from a preachership and forced to recant in 1479.[18] The situation was muddied still further by bogus bulls like those attributed to Pope Clement VI (1342–52) which circulated in 1500, and claimed to command the angels to transport the souls of pilgrims who died on the way to Rome straight to heaven.[19] In short, lay people could find all sorts of offers from the Church to ease their burdens, if only they would believe in them. The point was not for lay people to despair of their sin: it was for them to depend on, and trust in, the status and powers of the Church.

2. *Explaining How: Theologies of Justification*

The last section probably discussed as much about the saving of souls as the average layman was expected to know. However, one must delve a little into the speculative, as opposed to the practical, areas of theology in this and the following two sections. The reformers were trained in such speculations; they rejected them on one hand, and took over some of their assumptions on the other. The basic principles of the Reformation only make sense if the ideas which they attacked are understood.

Academic theology was practised in the Middle Ages through the exposition of a set of propositions or 'theses'. By the fifteenth century it had diverged into a variety of traditions, known as 'schools' (*scholae*) or 'ways' (*viae*). These 'schools' developed separate identities and traditions, and became associated with particular universities, particular religious orders, particular teachers, or a mixture of all three. The 'strife' between adherents of one or another school was sometimes venomous and bitter. The (basically philosophical) disagreement between the 'ancient way' (*via antiqua*) associated with followers either of Thomas Aquinas (d.1274) or Duns Scotus, and the 'modern way' (*via moderna*) associated with William of Occam (d.1349), Gregory of Rimini (d.1358), Pierre d'Ailly (d.1420), and Jean Gerson (d.1429) gave university theology its structure and party labels.[20]

However, this picture of neatly opposed schools of dogma can be all too easily over-simplified. Several factors diluted the impact of the 'strife of the ways'. First, some universities combined two or more schools amicably, like Tübingen or Wittenberg.[21] Secondly and more important, professional theologians were often more concerned to reconcile apparent opposites, to find the best in any author who suited them, than to preserve the isolated, sectarian purity of their 'school'. Assigning late medieval writers to a 'school' can therefore be dangerous, and allegiances can vary according to the topic at issue.[22] Thirdly and above all (for the historian), most theologians believed strongly that their technical disagreements, especially if they threatened the authority of the Church, should not be aired in public.[23]

Disagreement between the learned was not to be allowed to erode laymen's faith in the Church.

On the question of how souls were saved, there was almost complete agreement on the pastoral side, namely that people should progress through the cycle of sin and absolution as presented above.[24] The issue was not over the cycle itself, but over *who*—God or man—started the believer on his or her way towards eventual salvation; and what precise role was played respectively by God and man in the believer's progress around that cycle. Theologians had somehow to reconcile two opposing dogmas: God's absolute sovereignty over his creation, and man's freedom to respond to the offer of salvation. Of the possible options, one extreme, namely that man purely by his natural abilities could 'deserve' to be saved, was heresy: this was the teaching of the fifth-century British monk Pelagius, and of his follower Julian of Eclanum, which had been condemned in three early Church councils and mercilessly attacked by Augustine of Hippo (354–430), whose writings commanded immense respect in medieval Europe.[25] In the late Middle Ages the term 'Pelagian' might be used to denounce anyone who overrated man's ability to work towards his own salvation.[26]

Acceptable opinion insisted that man needed God's grace to be saved. The question was, at what point was such grace given, and what did it add to human goodness? Scholastic disagreements over this question cut across the lines of debate between 'ancients' and 'moderns': Scotus and his 'ancients' ranged alongside Occam and Gabriel Biel from the 'moderns', but *against* the 'modern' Gregory of Rimini and the followers of the 'ancient' Aquinas. The position of Scotus, Occam, and Biel, especially in its 'modern' forms, was by far the most popular and the most easily applied to preaching and pastoral advice. It ran as follows: God *could*, in principle, save men from their sins by any means which did not contradict his nature. By choice, however, he confined himself to acting within certain rules (known technically as his 'ordained power') which were revealed to the Church; and which were only transgressed in exceptional cases, like (perhaps) the conversion of Paul or the conception of Mary.[27] By an act of pure grace, God had chosen to set up a system by which the attempts of the believer to love God could be rewarded, even though they were not of themselves *actually* sufficient to earn salvation.[28] Man in this world was prey to two conflicting tendencies in his nature. On one hand he possessed an instinct to try to do good and to condemn evil acts in himself, the concept sometimes in jargon called 'synteresis'.[29] On the other, original sin, even after baptism, left a weakness in human nature, known as the 'tinder of sin' (*fomes peccati*), which hindered the workings of the conscience.[30]

The believer's first approach to God was summed up by the Occamists in a much older cliché: 'To those who do what is in them, God will not deny his grace.'[31] Doing 'what was in him' meant a great deal: that a believer should produce, if only momentarily, a spontaneous and utterly unselfish love of God for God's sake, and that with only the 'general assistance' of God himself. That act of unselfish love was said to acquire a kind of 'merit' or 'worthiness' which, though *insufficient* to deserve salvation, was 'of the right type': it was a 'congruent' merit (*meritum de congruo*). The most natural place for this first kind of 'congruent' or 'semi-merit' to be acquired was in the sacrament of penance. Consequently, man became able (or, according to Scotus, actually 'deserved')[32] to be restored to a 'state of grace'. Moreover, he acquired a 'habit of grace' in which, even as he sometimes failed to do 'what was in him', the Holy Spirit dwelt in him and inspired right actions. God, then, in accordance with his 'ordained' position, 'accepted' the combination of the believer's semi-merit and the works flowing from the Holy Spirit in the habit of grace as having truly sufficient or 'condign' merit (*meritum de condigno*) to allow the believer to be 'justly' saved.[33]

Occam and Biel thus solved to their own satisfaction the paradox of God's free grace and man's free will. God freely and graciously set up a system in which 'semi-merit' was rewarded with grace, and in which the workings of grace within the believer were 'accepted' as having merit to be saved. God's free action lay in guaranteeing—reliably—to respond with more favour than justice required to the efforts of the individual soul striving to love him. In practice, though, for the saving of any *one* soul, it was the believer and *his* response to God's offer which set the process of salvation in motion. Biel's position, popular as it was in the early 1500s, was as near to Pelagian heresy as orthodoxy could allow.[34] Yet the Occam–Biel system was extremely popular and widely adopted in various contexts. Bartholomäus Arnoldi von Usingen (d.1532), one of Luther's teachers at Erfurt, taught a version of it;[35] Wendelin Steinbach, Biel's successor at Tübingen University, an assiduous reader of Paul and Augustine, ingeniously interpreted them along very Occamist lines.[36] Geiler von Kaysersberg, despite sympathy for other opinions, thought the ideas of Biel most suitable for preaching to the people.[37]

However, the Occamist position was vigorously challenged by theologians who alleged that it placed far too much emphasis on man's ability to do good and far too little on God's *specific* acts of free grace. Instead of explaining away Augustine's anti-Pelagian invective, as Steinbach did, these writers applied such invective to the Occamists, intensified it, and shaped their ideas around it. Occam's fellow nominalist and critic Gregory of Rimini (d.1358), a Parisian academic and general of the Augustinian order, established one such tradition.[38] Gregory began with a bleaker view of man: without God's *direct* help, man naturally could do nothing but sin. God initiated man's salvation by a first gift of undeserved grace; God then infused into the believer an 'uncreated grace' which dwelt within man and, so to speak, performed good acts on his behalf. Finally, God 'accepted' the goodness infused in man by the Holy Spirit. In no way, and at no stage, did man 'deserve' God's favour.[39]

Gregory's position was taken up by some—though not all—theologians within his order in the late middle ages. Hence some scholars speak of a 'modern Augustinian school' or an 'Augustinian renaissance'.[40] Gregory was followed above all by Italian and Spanish theologians such as Simone Fidati of Cascia (d.1348), Dionysius of Montina, Hugolino of Orvieto (d.1374), Agostino Favaroni of Rome (d.1443), and Jacobus Perez of Valencia (d.1490).[41] It was once argued that a self-conscious 'Augustinian school', associated with the religious order of the same name, was ranked against the Occamist 'school' on justification, and thereby contributed to the Augustinian Eremite Martin Luther's own later condemnation of Occamism. However, this thesis involves dangerous over-simplifications. Medieval theologians cannot be neatly pigeon-holed according to their supposed allegiances. They often cited with approval those with whom, in principle, they should have disagreed; and then failed to cite—or even apparently to be aware of—some of their natural 'allies'.[42]

Very similar to Gregory's critique, but less academically precise, was the teaching of *devotio moderna* religious writers like Johann Pupper von Goch and Wessel Gansfort. Both attacked the 'Pelagianism' which they saw around them. Both insisted that all good acts within man came from the direct action of divine grace. When man had received such grace, according to Gansfort, he became 'the regenerated and purified image of God, ... [enjoying] the most blissful union with him, ... in which neither man nor angel is anything, but only the new creature in Christ'. Such lyrical language was more mystical than technical.[43] True mystics, indeed, obliterated the distinction between God's acts and man's acts: God dwelling in man and man in God were one and the same.[44] The traditions of the 'Augustinian' order, and the mystical tone of the *devotio moderna*, besides quite a lot of Renaissance humanism, merged in the spiritual writer Johannes von Staupitz (c.1460–1524), vicar-general of the observant Augustinians of Germany. Just how far he learned from 'modern' Augustinians of the school of Gregory of Rimini is controversial, and perhaps beside the point. He was not a technical theologian so much as a lyrical prose stylist, counsellor, and confessor, not least to the pious circles of Nuremberg and to Luther himself.[45]

Those scholars who have seen late medieval opposition to Occamist ideas of salvation as 'anticipating' or 'foreshadowing' the Lutheran protests have tended to miss the point.[46] Gregory of Rimini, Staupitz, and their kind argued, often vehemently, over *who*—man or God—propelled the soul of the believer into and through the cycle of contrition and redemption. They did not disrupt the cycle itself. on the contrary, all were committed to the practice of confessing sins, seeking the sacraments, and acquiring 'grace' through penitential exercises. They argued over *whose* 'good works' helped to save a human soul; not really, except in contentious issues like indulgences, over *what* good works mattered. Their debate was neither in its presentation and context, nor in its actual content, a threat to the sacramental, institutional Church. The subtle differences which separated the reformers from their late medieval 'forerunners' made all the difference in the world.[47]

3. *The Church: Holy, Authoritative, Sacrificial?*

Previous chapters showed how the Church drew fire from all quarters. The failings of men and institutions, the exaggerated ideals and modest achievements of 'reform', and the various political and religious 'challenges' all took their toll on the medieval Church's credibility as the 'one, holy, catholic, and apostolic Church' defined in the Nicene creed. To explain why, in spite of everything, the overwhelming majority of Europeans stayed loyal to it in 1500–20, one must look at how the Church portrayed itself. Theologians taught, in various ways, that the Church was indeed 'one, holy, catholic, and apostolic'; the earthly institution was linked, whatever its faults, to the heavenly one. The Church conserved a 'tradition' of belief and practice, either derived from Scripture, or originating separately from it; it determined how Scripture should be interpreted; it supported and maintained the means of communication established between God and man, in the sacramental and sacrificial system. Opinions varied between a careful, thoughtful trust in the Holy Spirit's guidance of the 'true' Church, to a dogmatic insistence falling only just short of teaching papal infallibility. It took no subtle academic education to appreciate the basic gist of such teaching: it was implied, and stated, in everything the old Church said and did. If anything, the less a believer knew, the more likely he was to hear the Church's claims stated in crude, positivist terms.[48] In practice, these claims about the Church fortified and protected the visible institution, warts and all, from some of the dangers inherent in its own self-criticism: they allowed churchmen freely to criticize and to challenge the things they disapproved of, without their criticisms endangering the special status of the Church as a whole. Every traditional epithet applied to the Church, 'one, holy, catholic, and apostolic', had been somehow put in doubt in the fifteenth century: unity by schisms, holiness by moral failings, catholicity by lack of general agreement, apostolicity by doubts about individual popes. In each area the theology of the Church offered reassurance to believers who might doubt that the Church they saw was the 'true' one.

Unity consisted, it was taught, in an 'essential' harmony, even between dissenting elements.[49] Holiness could be redefined, so that even if the *members* of the Church were not actually holy, still, because of its faith, and the sacraments offered within it, the Church itself remained holy.[50] In this way catholic writers responded to the dangerous suggestion that priests in mortal sin might not be true priests at all. Wycliffites and Hussites had revived this suggestion, at least in questioning the *jurisdictional* powers of the Church (though precisely how far their critique extended was not always clear). The 'common priesthood' of the Church could not deviate from Christ's ministry; so even a sinful cleric would still offer true and valid sacraments.[51] However, there was still room for disagreement as to whether, as Giles of Viterbo put it at the Fifth Lateran Council, there were 'times when the bride [the Church] falls asleep and the bridegroom [Christ] returns to heaven', or whether, as for Tommasso di Vio, known as Cajetan, the Church was always *continuously* holy, catholic, and apostolic.[52] It was Cajetan, with his insistence on the Church's *continuous* holiness, who confronted Luther.[53]

The belief in the Communion of Saints was a particularly potent symbol of the Church's links with heaven. The saints interceded in heaven for those on earth; around the Virgin Mary, in particular, a very elaborate theology developed. Theologians like Gabriel Biel, especially in their public sermons rather than their academic treatises, with lyrical extravagance assigned to Mary an enormously important role in the redemption of humanity, to the point where she could be called not only 'mediator' but in a sense 'co-redeemer'.[54] Specific dogmas accrued around Mary, notably that she had been bodily lifted up or 'assumed' into heaven, and that she had been conceived without original sin: such beliefs were widely held in the late medieval Church, though not made articles of faith until long after.[55]

The Church guarded itself against challenges based on the text of Scripture, by the various concepts of 'tradition'. 'Tradition', the handing down of beliefs and practices through the centuries by the Church, was crucial to the relationship between the Scriptures and the Church. Medieval theologians were fond of quoting from Augustine, 'indeed I should not have believed the Gospel, had not the authority of the Catholic Church moved me to do so'.[56] There were roughly three ways in which the Scripture–Church relationship was understood. The oldest version stressed that the truths of Scripture were entirely sufficient to determine all issues of faith and practice, but that they acquired their authority as interpreted in the continuing life of the Church. Scripture and tradition were two stages in the transmission of a *single* source of truth. This 'single-source' theory was, interestingly, stressed by those who, like Bradwardine, Gregory of Rimini and his followers, Johannes von Wesel, and Wessel Gansfort, also opposed Occamist theories of justification.

However, an alternative explanation was developed to protect details of Church practice (like the sacrament of confirmation), which were well-nigh impossible to justify even by 'implicit' references in Scripture. This second view claimed that *besides* the tradition founded on Scripture, there was a 'second source' of equally authoritative truth derived from the unwritten knowledge and conduct of the Church down the ages, which could not be deduced from Scripture alone. This interpretation was popularized by Occam and adopted by most late medieval religious writers, Biel included. It had the important result that a belief called into being to explain *uncontested* practices (like confirmation) could also be used to justify controversial ones (like plenary indulgences). It did not claim to 'create new articles of faith'; but it did allow practices and ideas to 'develop' beyond their old limits. A third concept, advanced by a subtle and influential figure like Gerson, stressed that neither Scripture nor the traditions of the Church were of themselves authoritative. Rather, the voice of the Holy Spirit guiding the Church gave validity to both Scripture *and* Church.[57] From the Reformation perspective, however, the differences between these schemes were less important than the fundamental difference which separated them *all* from the protestant attitude. None of these basically orthodox figures conceived of Scripture and Church actually *conflicting*: Scripture never became a witness *against* agreed beliefs and practices. Always, the two witnesses cohered together, however differently their scope was understood to extend.[58]

What did it mean to say that Scripture was 'interpreted within the tradition of the Church'? Viewed moderately and conscientiously, it might mean that an interpretation of the Bible could become authoritative by the earnest deliberation of the Church, as for instance when a General Council declared something to be an article of faith. However, moderation and subtlety were not equally highly prized by all on the eve of the Reformation. Scripture tended to be conceived of as a species of 'law', and in some cases—heresy above all—dogma and law were intermingled. Hence Ambrosius of Speyer remarked (humorously) about 1485 that one should take the idea that the holy fathers determine matters of interpretation of Scripture, and the pope matters of law with a grain of salt: if it concerned the sacraments or articles of faith, then the pope, not the holy fathers, interpreted doubtful law![59] Or, even more crudely, Silvestro Mazzolini in his early reply to Luther deduced as follows: the Church was represented by the pope; the Church could not err on faith and custom; so, anyone who did not assent to the pope 'as an infallible rule of faith, from whom even Holy Scripture draws its strength and authority', was a heretic.[60]

Perhaps the most potent vindication of the Church, though, was its role in the 'communication of grace': the sacraments in general, and the 'sacrifice' of the mass, with its benefits for the souls of the living and the dead, in particular. Christ offered himself once on the Cross: the Church, in the shape of every priest, both commemorated and in a sense 'repeated' that sacrifice every day when the mass was celebrated. The belief in 'sacrifice' was continued by Occamists like Biel and followers of the 'ancient way' like Cajetan with a very wide range of agreement right up to the Reformation, and in many cases beyond.[61] Such disagreements as did arise, for instance between Cajetan and Gabriel Biel, were over the very technical issue of which kinds of sacrificial 'benefit' were finite or infinite: their basic agreement neatly corresponds to the laity's enthusiasm for the multiplication of masses *ad infinitum*.[62]

Meanwhile, the 'special' quality of the mass was guaranteed by its quality as a 'sacrament' in which the body and blood of Christ were physically present. No one of standing contested the dogma promulgated in 1215 according to which the 'substances' of the bread and wine were at the moment of consecration transformed miraculously into the body and blood of Christ, while the 'species' or 'accidents', that part of the bread and wine which the senses could apprehend, remained unchanged. 'Transubstantiation' thus defined left room for the grosser versions of popular belief, for instance the indestructible or bleeding hosts found at new shrines. Moreover, the belief that the body 'contained' the blood supported the practice of giving the laity only the bread in the communion.[63]

4. Conclusion: A Precarious Equilibrium

Two seemingly contradictory trends may be observed in the religious attitudes of late medieval Europe. On the one hand there is the better informed, more strident, and more aggressive lay involvement in the religious sphere: lay people wished to supervise the 'reform' of the clergy, to select the best clerics to work for them, and to keep the priests strictly within their own legal sphere. On the other there is abundant visible and tangible evidence of extravagant lay devotion to a conventional, ritualized, often materialistic piety: people wished to see, touch, even collect holy things, to engage in 'trade' with the Almighty for the good of their lives on earth and their souls in the next world. The evidence of *both* these tendencies is ample and unlikely to be seriously questioned.

Because 'anticlericalism' and 'popular piety' seem to contradict each other, some historians have been reluctant to take *both* these features of late medieval religion at face value. People (it is alleged) may have been *either* anticlerical *or* pious; but not both. Those who favour one option tend to insist that the other has been overstated.[64] Alternatively, it has been suggested that the piety of pre-1520 Europe was a 'lay piety' which aroused little interest in, and did not depend upon, the allegedly stodgy and apathetic clergy.[65] Such an argument, if taken to extremes, raises the question of how a religion which consisted of confessing and acquiring penitential 'grace', of hearing masses and sermons, of venerating sacraments, of praying to saints in the 'Church triumphant', could exist at all without priests who alone could absolve, dispense the sacraments, and preach. A third suggestion is that the 'pious' and the 'anticlericals' were different people, perhaps from different social brackets. The donors of altar-pieces and builders of shrines would represent the prosperous, privileged classes who were not alienated from the Church, who indeed participated in it and exploited its wealth for their families; the 'anticlericals' the oppressed masses who received only a mediocre and rather costly service in return for their tithes.[66] Against this argument one must cite the many cases of lower-class piety, and upper-class criticism of the Church, which can easily be found.

A much simpler explanation, which takes account of *both* piety *and* 'anticlericalism' among the people of the pre-Reformation era, is surely just as satisfying. Obviously there were then, as at any other time, some people who were utterly apathetic to religion in any shape or form— though perhaps fewer than in modern industrial society, where the vital preconditions of human survival have been made much more controllable and predictable than in the late middle ages. As far as ordinary believers were concerned, it seems entirely reasonable that they should have held both kinds of attitudes at once. They would care, in a largely conventional way, about their religion, and wish to see that it was properly respected. The more pious one was, the more a dissolute priest or materialistic bishop would offend one's sensibilities. Concern for 'the faith', and indeed 'the Church', would be consistent with, even a precondition of, a sense of outrage at those failings which exposed it to criticism or contempt.

However, if sincere piety made for reforming critiques, it also made it very difficult to *do* anything much about the Church's failings. Whenever the question of reform came up, it ran into a mass of obstacles: partly due to the Church itself, with its long-developed tradition of guarding privileges and immunities; but also due to laymen's exploitation of Church property. To cut through the tangle of legal obstacles would have required a unilateral defiance of the Church's rights. Such defiance would have been illegal and (implicitly) impious, because it entailed disobedience to the legal system presided over by Christ's vicar. The feelings which made men like Jakob Wimpfeling or Sebastian Brant call for an improved clergy also made them denounce the political aggression necessary to bring such reforms about. They could not defy 'Holy Mother Church' so long as that Church bulked so large in their system of belief. The dilemma, moreover, was specially acute for the educated classes, who might have high ideals, but also realized just how completely the Church's teaching protected its status. Because they were pious, they wanted a better, purer Church; because they were loyal catholics, they could not *practically* achieve it.

The late medieval Church was set, then, on a precarious and none too comfortable balance between security in principle and vulnerability in practice. It was, moreover, so fragmented by sectional hostilities that it was bound to produce its severest critics from its own ranks. Nevertheless, it had been poised on this balance for the previous century: nothing seems to suggest that it was becoming *more* unstable as the 1510s approached. If anything, one has the impression that the tensions were becoming accepted and routine, however unsatisfactory their results. The point of greatest risk for the Church was its own special, spiritual status which made it the one means of grace and salvation. *If* someone were to come along who could persuade a significant proportion of priests and people that they did *not* depend upon the ministrations of 'the Church' to save their souls, then the 'reforming' challenges could be allowed free rein, unchecked by the principled respect which had so far restrained them within the limits of Church law and belief.

PART II

The Reformers and Their Message

The Reformation fascinates partly because it shows beliefs and ideas interacting with diverse political and social conditions to produce varied results. To make sense of that interaction one must try to understand *both* the ideas *and* the context. Each influenced the other: it would be just as reasonable to study ideas first and society second, or the other way around. This study begins by discussing the beliefs, and how the people who produced those beliefs arrived at them. In so doing, it makes no assumptions about their relative importance.

Certain basic messages distinguished the reformers from all those who had gone before. Many of these messages were articulated by Martin Luther in the period roughly between 1518 and 1521, and adopted, modified, or rediscovered by others during the early 1520s. These beliefs were sharpened to their cutting edge after Luther's theses against indulgences were published late in 1517: the ensuing uproar forced the Wittenberg reformers and their sympathizers to redefine their attitudes to all kinds of authority. To adopt such beliefs, especially after their condemnation by Church and Empire in 1520–1, meant a deliberate and decisive break with the institutional and spiritual continuity of the old Church. So the following chapters will first briefly narrate the early controversies, before the question of establishing a reformed 'Church order' arose; then analyse those particular parts of the reformed religious message which challenged existing belief and practice; and finally consider how 'reformers' reached the stage where they could take part in a religious revolt.

7

The 'Luther-Affair' and its Context

Martin Luther (1483–1546), Augustinian Eremite of the reformed German congregation and Professor of Theology in the 'modern way' at the University of Wittenberg (founded 1502), looms so large over the early history of the Reformation that it is difficult to place him in proper perspective. In his days of notoriety he was one of the most celebrated, written about, and portrayed figures in Europe.[1] He was a formidable intellect and a prolific writer with vast popular appeal. However, he was only one formidable intellect among many even in the 'Lutheran' Reformation; the Church to which he (unintentionally) gave his name is only one church among several in the reformed tradition. He did not set every detail of the standard by which faithfulness to the protestant gospel can be judged; his sometimes peculiar ideas did not even define what all 'Lutherans' felt and believed. He was, first and foremost, an example;[2] a figurehead who showed unheard-of tenacity in a daunting situation. Secondly, he produced a wide range of raw, challenging insights into religious problems. These insights were considered, developed, and rounded off into a complete theology by many hands, not least those of the later Luther himself. They soon had prodigious implications for *everything* about human society which the old Church had touched. This chapter considers how Luther owed notoriety, survival, and popularity at least partly to a set of coincidences.

1. *Martin Luther's Public Career, 1517–22*[3]

In the autumn of 1516 Martin Luther, Professor of Theology, set about changing both the content of his subject and the way in which it was then taught. In September he led his pupil Bartholomäus Bernhardi in a vigorous disputation *against* the very teachings (about man's ability to keep God's law) which Luther, professor in the 'modernist way', was expected to uphold. Luther's colleagues, at first shocked, were soon converted; from the spring of 1517 they reconstructed their syllabus to teach the writings of Augustine and the other Fathers of the early Church, and the Bible as interpreted with humanist techniques. After this academic coup Luther published a short German treatise on the *Seven Penitential Psalms*; for another university occasion on 4 September 1517 he prepared ninety-seven 'theses' against the teachings of Scotus and Occam on man's justification.[4] In these he asserted: 'man is created "a corrupt tree", and can neither will nor do anything but evil'; 'God cannot accept a man unless the grace of God is there justifying him'; 'we are not made righteous by doing righteous deeds; but when we have been made righteous we effect righteous deeds'. Luther published the theses as the *Disputation against Scholastic Theology*; he sent copies to his friends at Nuremberg and to the theologian Johann Maier of Eck (1486–1543) of Ingolstadt.[5]

Ironically, his frontal assault on 'Scholastic Theology' evoked no response whatever. Meanwhile, by the autumn of 1517 Luther, in his capacity as priest and pastor, was concerned that itinerant friars selling letters of 'indulgence'[6] in neighbouring territories were confusing his penitents. On 31 October he wrote respectfully to Albrecht of Brandenburg (1490–1545), archbishop-elector of Mainz (to pay whose debts the indulgences were being sold) warning him that his preachers were misleading and endangering souls, and that Luther as a Doctor of Theology was bound to correct them. At the same time, without fuss or ceremony, he prepared ninety-five 'theses' for disputation on the power of indulgences, and enclosed them with his letter to the archbishop. He *may*, then or later, have also fixed copies to the door of the castle church to initiate an academic disputation; this is disputed.[7] In November Luther circulated his theses privately. The recipients at once, and apparently without Luther's permission, published them; soon printed editions appeared at Leipzig, Magdeburg, Nuremberg, and Basle. The most distinguished object of Luther's critique, the archbishop of Mainz, passed the buck to the papal Curia at Rome. The Dominican friars, however, of whom Albrecht's celebrated indulgence-preacher Johann Tetzel (*c.*1465–1519) was one, literally called for the Augustinian doctor's blood. Tetzel denounced him at their congregation in January 1518, and the order lobbied fellow Dominicans at Rome to have Luther declared a heretic. Luther meanwhile defended his position in the *Resolutions* of his ninety-five theses and in the *Sermon on Indulgence and Grace*, both published in April 1518 and instantaneously popular. For a meeting of the chapter of his order in Heidelberg late that same month he wrote a further forty theses for disputation, with his unique style and message.[8]

In May 1518 the Dominican chapter at Rome secured the nomination of a papal judge, Girolamo Ghinucci, and the theologian Silvestro Mazzolini of Priero (1456–1523) to handle Luther's case. By at best dubious methods the German Dominicans persuaded the papacy that Luther was a dangerous, heretical rebel. In August an initially damning sentence was only suspended because the pope, Leo X (1475–1521; pope 1513–21) was desperate to prevent the election of the future Charles V to the Holy Roman Empire. For that Pope Leo needed the support of Elector Friedrich III 'the Wise' of Saxony (d.1525), in whose lands Wittenberg lay, and who would hardly have welcomed the condemnation of one of his theologians as a heretic. Instead Tommasso di Vio Gaetano ('Cardinal Cajetan', 1469–1534), theologian and general of the Dominicans, was delegated simultaneously to court Friedrich and secure Luther's formal withdrawal or 'recantation' of some of his obnoxious teachings. During 12–14 October 1518 Luther had a series of interviews with Cajetan at Augsburg, at which the two failed to find common ground of any kind: Luther would not simply 'recant', nor yet accept Cajetan's claims for papal power.[9] Elector Friedrich, called on to surrender Luther or exile him, eventually refused. Then a German nobleman and unsuccessful curial bureaucrat, Karl von Miltitz, sent to act under Cajetan, tried to mediate on his own initiative. He met Luther at Altenburg on 4–5 January 1519 and proposed arbitration by the archbishop of Trier. A few days later the Emperor Maximilian I died; papal justice hung fire as Leo X negotiated with Friedrich for several more months.

In March 1518 Eck of Ingolstadt had answered Luther's ninety-five theses in a work called *Obelisks*. Luther's colleague Andreas Bodenstein, known as Karlstadt (*c.*1480–1541), had then provoked Eck with a great list of theses; Luther replied more moderately with his *Asterisks*. This exchange led to the set-piece disputation between Eck, Karlstadt, and Luther, presided over by Duke Georg of 'Albertine' Saxony, which opened on 27 June 1519 at Leipzig. Karlstadt performed badly, and Eck goaded Luther into expressing apparent sympathy for the Bohemian heretic Jan Hus.[10] Eck later exploited the 'Hussite' accusation to have parts of Luther's writings condemned by the Universities of Cologne and Louvain. Those who were not scholastics or papalists, however, became ever more fascinated by and enthusiastic for Luther as a result of such notoriety.

Early in 1520 Luther developed his ideas with typical energy, writing pamphlets at astonishing speed. In March he wrote the treatise *On Good Works* for Friedrich's brother, Duke Johann; in May he responded to a tract by Augustin von Alveld, a Franciscan from Leipzig, with *On the*

Papacy at Rome; in June–August he composed, partly to answer the papal theologian Mazzolini of Priero, the address *To the Christian Nobility of the German Nation*, calling on the lay power to inaugurate Church reform; in August–October he produced his manifesto on Church worship, *The Babylonian Captivity of the Church*. With these major works he developed both a detailed vision of the way in which Christian life ought to be reshaped to accord with his vision of true faith, and a series of practical means to implement the programme.[11]

Von Miltitz's manœuvrings had delayed the papacy, but by January 1520 Luther's case was reopened. In a leisurely way a commission ultimately composed of Eck, Cajetan, and two others prepared Luther's condemnation. The papal bull *Exsurge Domine*, published on 15 June 1520, condemned Luther and forty-one tenets drawn from an out-of-date edition of his works, giving him sixty days to recant or face final anathema. It was so vague and imprecise that some even thought it was forged; Eck, nominated as one of the papal ambassadors or 'nuncios' to Germany in July, added his personal enemies (humanists like Pirckheimer among them) to those condemned in the bull, discrediting it further.[12] The other nuncio, papal librarian Girolamo Aleandro or Aleander (1480–1542) fared better: he had Luther's books burnt at Louvain, Liège, and, through the agency of the Dominican inquisitor Jakob von Hochstraten, at Cologne (though sometimes the books actually burnt were not Luther's but those of his opponents!). By early 1521 Aleander was in no doubt of Luther's popularity in Germany.[13] In October, following another abortive attempt by von Miltitz to conciliate, Luther composed the tract *On Christian Freedom* (or *The Freedom of a Christian*). On 10 December 1520, in response to Aleander's burnings of his books, Luther in a small ceremony at Wittenberg burnt the works of Eck, those of Eck's ally from Leipzig, Jerome Emser (1478–1527), with whom he had already exchanged polemics, and Angelo Carletti of Chivasso's *Summa Angelica* on confession. He surreptitiously added to the bonfire the papal bull of condemnation itself.[14]

The newly elected Emperor Charles V now took a hand. When the imperial representative assembly (the *Reichstag*) met at Worms in January 1521 few members were openly hostile to Luther; the Emperor, zealous for orthodoxy, first forbad him to attend and proposed to submit him to the ban of the Empire. Since Friedrich of Saxony (for one) blocked this move, he was summoned to the *Reichstag* to be asked yet again to recant. On 17 and 18 April, twice asked if he acknowledged his books and would recant his errors, he replied that the books were his, and (finally) refused to recant unless proved wrong by arguments drawn from Scripture. At the end of the second meeting Luther declared: 'Unless I am convinced by the testimony of Scripture or evident reason ... I am bound to the Scriptures which I have adduced and my conscience is captive to the Word of God; I neither can nor will revoke anything, since it is neither safe nor honest to act against conscience.'[15] More arduous, perhaps, than these set-piece sessions were repeated private discussions on 23–5 April where distinguished and reputable churchmen and scholars tried and failed to persuade him to shift his ground.

After Luther had left Worms on 26 April, a portion of the *Reichstag* passed on 26 May an edict condemning him. Meanwhile the pope and Emperor had negotiated an alliance, and a second, unconditional papal bull of condemnation against Luther and his followers, issued on 3 January 1521 but not published, could be made public. Meanwhile Elector Friedrich, leaving the details to others so as to be able to claim ignorance himself, arranged that Luther should be abducted, on the way home, by a group of horsemen in his pay. He was seized near Altenstein on 4 May, just after visiting his relatives at Möhra, and taken into protective custody in the elector's castle of the Wartburg. The plan to stage-manage his abduction was a well-kept secret from all but the conspirators and Nikolaus von Amsdorf, one of his companions on the journey. His disappearance caused a sensation in literate circles: the Nuremberg artist Albrecht Dürer, for example, mourned his loss in his journal.[16] Soon afterwards, however, his colleagues learned of his whereabouts and sent him books; and he composed for the press with renewed vigour. Besides editions of his lectures, he wrote on auricular confession, the Magnificat, a reply to the hostile theologian Jacques Masson ('Latomus', 1475–1544) of Louvain, further polemic with Jerome Emser, a furious attack ('Against the Idol at Halle') on a new indulgence sale by Archbishop Albrecht, and tracts on the mass and on monastic vows; above all, he began to translate the New Testament into German.[17]

2. *Contexts and Catalysts*

In four years the 'Luther-affair' grew from an academic and ecclesiastical feud between two religious orders to set Germany (and much of Europe) by the ears. Luther had not sought such notoriety; nor was it due to his ideas and writings alone. Coincidences, born out of the context, helped to obscure the real issues of the affair, and exaggerate its importance. These same factors gave Luther supporters who would only fully understand his message rather later.

Since around 1500 the Holy Roman Empire, the German *Reich*, had been in a state of political, religious, and cultural agitation. The imperial representative assembly, the *Reichstag*, was in frequent and hectic session during the reigns of Maximilian I (1493–1519) and Charles V (1519–55). Some ten meetings took place in the period 1501–21; membership included the three archbishop-electors (of Mainz, Trier, and Cologne), the three lay electors of Brandenburg, Saxony, and the Palatinate), as well as some 120 prelates, thirty lay princes, and (approximately) sixty-five imperial cities and towns.[18] The chief purpose of these meetings was to try to construct a workable system of government for the whole Empire, comprising a standing executive council for the Empire, a court of arbitration to settle disputes, and an imperial tax to pay for the Emperors' generally inglorious military campaigns in Italy. However, little was accomplished by these plans; the monarchical designs of the Emperors always conflicted with the electors' preference for a loose federal structure, tending to cancel each other out.[19] Meanwhile Germans treated the *Reichstag* as a forum in which to express their grievances against the papacy. In the light of the unsatisfactory concordats of 1447–8,[20] from the Frankfurt *Reichstag* of 1456 onwards lists of complaints were devised against the papal and clerical exploitation of the German Church and people. Maximilian (at odds with the papacy in Italy) instigated the humanist Jakob Wimpfeling to redraft the list for the 1510 *Reichstag*.[21] In 1518 at Augsburg the papal legate, Tommasso di Vio 'Cajetan' pressed for a crusade; the *Reichstag* renewed the protests against the 'grievances' as their price of support. The same Worms *Reichstag* which witnessed Luther's defiance drew up a list of 102 papal 'abuses'. At the Nuremberg meeting of 1522–3, the legate of Pope Adrian IV, Francesco Chieregati, required the enforcement of the Worms edict against Luther. The lay members of the *Reichstag* responded by blaming the 'grievances' (which Luther had echoed in *To the Christian Nobility*) for his popularity, and suggested the holding of a free council of the Church somewhere in Germany. They implied that only attention to these traditional problems could solve the new crisis.[22] Immediately, then, Luther was sheltered behind the Germans' long-standing distrust of Rome and its works.

Meanwhile the publicity over a quite different scholarly row had given Luther's future opponents an evil reputation. In 1509 a converted Jew, Johannes Pfefferkorn, successfully petitioned Maximilian to order all owners of Jewish books to hand them in for him to examine for anti-

Christian opinions. In 1510 the matter was referred to the leading German universities, the inquisitor and prior of the Dominicans of Cologne, Jakob von Hochstraten (d.1527), an ex-Jewish priest, and the German Hebrew scholar Johannes Reuchlin (1455–1522). Reuchlin himself protested against this plan in a private memorandum. In 1511 the Emperor sided with Reuchlin against the others on the commission. Reuchlin engaged in a furious pamphlet controversy with Pfefferkorn, and replied to his denunciations in the German pamphlet *Augenspiegel*, published in 1512. The Cologne theologians then rounded on Reuchlin, and in 1513 the Dominican inquisitor Hochstraten tried to investigate Reuchlin for heresy. In 1514 Pope Leo X appointed the bishop of Speyer to judge the case; the latter upheld Reuchlin and awarded him costs. The Dominicans appealed to Rome, where a committee of cardinals likewise upheld Reuchlin's case, with the exception of Silvestro Mazzolini of Priero. In July 1519 Franz von Sickingen, the most notorious of the imperial 'robber-knights', threatened the Cologne Dominicans with violence unless they paid Reuchlin's legal costs. By May 1520 they had agreed; but Hochstraten meanwhile finally prevailed on the pope (citing the case of Luther as a warning against leniency) to annul his previous interventions and condemn Reuchlin and his pamphlets. Reuchlin submitted to the decree, spurned von Sickingen's offer of further help, and ended his days working with Luther's implacable opponent Eck of Ingolstadt.[23]

The immediate issue (the value of Hebrew literature) would have remained an arcane one but for one crucial, untypical intervention. To help Reuchlin two humanist writers, Johannes Jäger ('Crotus Rubeanus', 1486–1540) and Ulrich von Hutten (1488–1523), published in successive editions from October 1515 to spring 1517 two sets of bogus letters (the *Letters of Obscure Men*) purporting to be written by adversaries of Reuchlin to the Cologne theologian Ortuinus Gratius (Hardouin de Graetz). These satirical letters represented Reuchlin's opponents as idle, ignorant, lecherous pseudo-scholars obsessed with petty arguments and their pursuit of the good life. They tried to polarize the issue into one of conflict between new learning and old ignorance. This attitude simplified and even trivialized the debate. Reuchlin had been attacked primarily as a Judaizer, not as a leader of 'new learning'; many humanists were cool in support of Reuchlin's élitist and obscure Hebraism, and even openly hostile to the tone of the *Letters of Obscure Men*; most of the other polemics had been directed against the Cologne faculty of theology, not scholastic theology as a whole. Nevertheless, such satires pilloried the very people, Dominicans like Hochstraten and Mazzolini, and academic theologians like Gratius, who were soon to be charged with refuting Luther. They entered on the task already subjects of ridicule to the literate of Europe; and remained so for decades.[24]

Luther's case did not immediately awaken widespread interest. To take but one example, in early 1518 von Hutten (a poet and author of fashionable dialogues) regarded the debate as a row between theologians, a class of people he detested. However, in the course of 1518–21 he and his type identified more and more with Luther's anti-scholastic and anti-papal (as opposed to theological) positions. Hutten suspected that Luther's opponent at Augsburg in 1518, Cardinal 'Cajetan', came to the *Reichstag* to preach crusade only to swindle money out of Germany. In his dialogues, entitled *Fever the First, Vadiscus, or the Roman Triad, The Onlookers*, and *Fever the Second*, published between spring 1519 and 1520 (a German translation appeared in time for Luther's appearance at Worms), Hutten popularized anti-papal polemic and sided more and more openly with Luther. He and Crotus saw Luther attacked by their own old enemies and warmed to him.[25] Hutten and von Sickingen joined forces in mid-1520, and associated with other humanists such as Eobanus Hessus, Martin Butzer or Bucer (1491–1551), Johannes Hussgen or Husschin ('Oecolampadius', 1482–1531), and Reuchlin's great-nephew Philipp Schwarzerd ('Melanchthon', 1497–1560) who were later in one form or another to become leading protestant figures. Before the major implications of Luther's highly distinctive message had been fully absorbed, his broader and more familiar protests and proposals had won him a pre-existent party of enthusiasts who thought (wrongly) that his cause was the same one for which they had already been fighting. In due course the older humanists turned against Luther; the younger ones, on the other hand, were mostly converted to views which, in spite of the independence of mind and diverse characters of the formidable minds involved, were in their essence and implications remarkably close to Luther's own.[26]

3. *The Reformation Message Spreads and Diversifies*

If Luther had tried to win sympathy for his ideas by face-to-face conversions, or indeed by political agitation against the condemnations of Church and Crown, spreading his message would have been a slow, laborious, and dangerous process. In the event, he did not even have to try. As Luther himself said early in 1522:

I opposed Indulgences and all the papists, but never with force. I simply taught, preached, and wrote God's word; otherwise I did nothing. And while I slept or drank Wittenberg beer with my friends Philipp [Melanchthon] and [Nikolaus von] Amsdorf, the Word so greatly weakened the Papacy that no prince or emperor ever inflicted such losses on it. I did nothing; the Word did everything . . .[27]

The reputation won by Luther's prolific literary output and his appearances at important public gatherings aroused immense interest and much enthusiastic and often ill-informed partisanship. The familiar aspects of his programme, like the denunciation of vulgar materialism in religion, the public preaching, and the invective against the papacy and scholastic theologians, shielded unfamiliar theological propositions from view, at least at first. However, the essential theological ideas were soon adopted (and adapted) by many others. Both on principle and as a matter of prudence, they chose to represent it as just another form of the 'restoration of Christianity' which the Erasmians had urged.[28] Luther's dogmatic attacks on the foundations of the medieval Church matured like cuckoos' eggs in the humanist nest.[29] Learned coteries in the cities of Franconia, northern Switzerland, Alsace, and Swabia, took up and discussed the ideas of the notorious Augustinian. Civic preachers, often themselves humanists, found audiences receptive if they preached 'the Scriptures' with the same cutting edge that Luther had given them. Within three years or so from the Worms *Reichstag* literate and enthusiastic urban audiences had developed a taste for the primitive forms of Reformation preaching; it proved quite impossible for popes or emperors to wean them from the habit, at least with the unattractive means which they chose to employ.

Luther's message was taken up in a number of cities in central Germany. One of the most interesting was Nuremberg, seat of the *Reichstag*, the imperial council (*Reichsregiment*) and court of justice (*Reichskammergericht*) during the crucial years 1522–4. A small coterie of educated Nurembergers had already followed the teachings of Luther's spiritual mentor and superior Johannes von Staupitz; in 1517–18 they corresponded with Luther through shared acquaintances and gave wide publicity to his early pronouncements. In 1521 the city posted the Worms edict against Luther but made no attempt to enforce its terms. Late that year the city used its patronage to give posts in three of the city's churches to sympathizers of Luther, preacherships to Dominicus Schleupner (d.1547) at St Sebald, Andreas Hosemann ('Osiander', 1498–1552) at St Lorenz, and Thomas Gechauf at the Hospitallers'; and provostships to Hector Pömer (1495–1541) and Georg Bessler (1470–1536). During 1522–4 the city council allowed the preachers to preach their message, as long as they neither stirred up disorder nor changed forms of worship.[30]

Beyond Luther's personal influence and connections, Reformation teachings first acquired followers among the cities and cantons of the Swiss confederation. This league of city-republics and rural territories, known as the *Eidgenossenschaft*, was for practical purposes independent of the German Empire; its sovereign states had diverse constitutions and pursued independent policies within a federal framework. Huldrych Zwingli (1484–1531) arrived in December 1518 in Zürich, one of the largest and most powerful of the cities, to take up the post of 'people's priest' (*Leutpriester*) in the city's main church, the *Grossmünster*. From 1519 his principal task was preaching to the congregation, which he did with verve, abandoning the medieval style of preaching and emphasizing direct contact with the Bible. This approach seems to have been given council approval as early as 1520. As far as one can tell, Zwingli's sermons (whatever their precise content) offered no challenge to existing religious behaviour until Lent 1522. In March, at a gathering at a printer's house, a small quantity of sausage was eaten in pointed defiance of the Lenten fast, Zwingli being present but not partaking. Zwingli none the less preached on the principle of freedom of choice in foods (23 March) and published a tract on the issue (16 April).[31] Meanwhile, early in the year, Zwingli had married secretly. On 2 July he and ten other priests petitioned the bishop of Constance for permission to marry legally (in the full knowledge that it could not be granted); they then published the petition. On 16 July Zwingli confronted the Franciscan friar François Lambert in debate; on 21 July he disputed against the heads of the city's mendicant houses in the presence of the *Bürgermeister* (mayor), and members of the city council. The councillors expressed approval of preaching only from the Bible—Zwingli's method. In August Zwingli defended his actions in the *Apologeticus Architeles*, and in September wrote *The Clarity and Certainty of the Word of God* for the Dominicanesses of Oetenbach.

Early in 1523, the *Bürgermeister* and the smaller council invited the parties in the religious debates to a public hearing to judge who was preaching 'scripturally'. Zwingli apparently envisaged this as an academic disputation, and prepared for the purpose sixty-seven theses, the *Schlussreden*, to be sustained in the academic manner. On 29 January the parties met. The bishop of Constance's delegation refused to debate high theology (and theses which they had barely had time to inspect) before laymen; apart from a brief dispute over prayers to saints, priestly celibacy, and Church authority, Zwingli's articles were ignored. The council then reaffirmed its call for preaching in the city to be based on 'the Word of God'. It is disputed how far this encounter helped to 'establish' the reform. Certainly Zwingli took it as a victory and continued publishing: the 'Exposition' (*Usslegen*) of his January theses, and the tract *On Divine and Human Righteousness*.[32]

Zürich was the first and most celebrated of the northern Swiss cities to hear such a message, but by no means the only one. Joannes Oecolampadius, after a spell as chaplain to Franz von Sickingen at his castle of the Ebernburg in 1521-2, arrived at Basle in November 1522; in June 1523 he and the Franciscan humanist Konrad Kürsner ('Pellicanus', 1478-1556), were made professors of theology in the city's university. In August Oecolampadius offered theses for disputation, and upheld them in spite of qualms on the part of the bishop and the university.[33] The city of St Gallen, site of a venerable and famous abbey, was dominated by Joachim von Watt ('Vadianus', 1484-1551), a native, a cultivated humanist, and an academic with a brilliant literary and medical career at the University of Vienna behind him. In December 1523 another native, Johannes Kessler (1502-74) returned from study at Wittenberg and was urged to pass on what he had learned.[34] At Schaffhausen, there were already in the early 1520s reforming sympathizers in Abbot Michael Eggenstorfer (*c.*1493-1552) and a humanist group around Johann Adelphi. From 1522 reforming sermons were preached there by the friar Sebastian Hofmeister ('Occonomus', 1476-1533) and Sebastian Meyer (?1467-?1545).[35]

In the early 1520s many towns and cities of southern Germany (especially 'free cities of the Empire', subject either directly to the Emperor, or to a strictly limited bishop) attracted and produced their own reforming preachers and ideologues. Pulled between the conflicting forces of Wittenberg and Zürich, they produced their own leaders and networks of alliances: such that it makes more sense to speak of a 'south German' reforming movement than to call one area 'Lutheran' and another 'Zwinglian'. One of the first and most important was the episcopal metropolis of Strasbourg in Alsace. In 1521 the city subscribed the Worms edict. That same year, however, the cathedral preacher Matthäus Zell of Kaisersberg (1477-1548) began to preach reforming sermons on the Epistle to the Romans. His hearers thwarted the cathedral clergy's attempts to stop him, and he soon openly cited Luther with approval. Early in 1523 three churchmen arrived in Strasbourg who were to lead its Reformation: Wolfgang Köpfel ('Capito', 1478-1541), the former secretary of Archbishop Albrecht of Mainz; Martin Bucer, who after his spell with von Sickingen at the Ebernburg had married a nun and taken to preaching reform; and Caspar Heyd ('Hedio', 1494-1552), called to preach against Zell and soon himself converted. Popular enthusiasm for the new preachers forced the city council (with some difficulty) to find posts in the city for all these (and other) reforming preachers.[36]

The second major centre of the south German reformed tradition was the free city of Constance, seat of the council of 1414–18 which ended the Great Schism. Biblical sermons were preached here from 1520 by Jakob Windner (*c*.1480–*c*.1539) and Bartholomäus Metzler (d.1553), joined in March 1522 by Johannes Wanner ('Vannius', *c*.1490–1529), who had been converted after meeting Zwingli at Zürich. The preachers enjoyed the protection of the city secretary Jörg Vögeli and benefited from the city council's desire to protect its preachers against the local bishop.[37] More populous and wealthy was the commercial centre of Augsburg. Oecolampadius preached in the cathedral and taught theology there during 1518–21, where he met influential humanist families like the Peutingers and Adelmanns. Urbanus Rhegius (1489–1541) advocated Lutheranism there from 1521; from 1524 the preacher Michael Keller ('Cellarius', d. 1548) did the same for Zwingli's ideas.[38]

At this stage 'the Reformation' was a movement of ideas and popular preaching, rather than the comprehensive religious and social upheaval that it later became. This first phase, the creation of a favourable climate of opinion, was a crucial precondition of a future 'civic Reformation'. However, in these early stages the only way in which secular authorities helped the Reformation was the strictly negative one, namely that they (or some at least) refused to suppress it.[39] Given that reforming sermons (with the small *r*) had been staple intellectual and spiritual diet for decades, it would have taken strong will, great foresight, and some measure of bigotry even to have tried. The distinctive political establishment of a reformed Church order lay in the future: very soon for Nuremberg or Zürich, rather later for Augsburg and the territorial states. This is therefore a suitable point to consider just what were those ideas and teachings which had aroused such interest.

8

The Reformers' Message
Salvation

This and the next three chapters will suggest how a few of the basic, common themes of the Reformation message justified, indeed required, a clean sweep of the institutions and practices of the old Church. By asserting its corporate monopoly of the 'means of grace' (sacramental absolution and penance, the mass, intercommunion, indulgences, and so on) the old Church had partly counterbalanced the resentment and criticism which its moral and practical shortcomings aroused.[1] In the Reformation that equilibrium was destroyed, because reputable and persuasive figures convinced many people that their souls were really saved *without* the paraphernalia of the sacramental and penitential system. The Church, then, had no excuse for its deficiencies: indeed, its spiritual ministry, which had excused its other faults before, now itself became a blasphemy against Christ. A simple 'anticlerical' attack on the morality and status of the clergy could never have been so destructive. The Reformation destroyed the penitential cycle by the most subtle, roundabout means. Luther and his successors re-examined the theology of salvation itself, by appealing to biblical sources, than which nothing was better calculated to catch the mood of the age. One must follow the reformers' argument through to appreciate the devastating force of their logic on these issues. At every critical point they challenged, redefined, and rearranged the very building-blocks of medieval belief: sin, law, faith, justification, the Church, in explicit defiance not only of the 'Occamist school',[2] but of a much broader medieval consensus.

In this sort of survey anything more than a partial selection from their ideas is obviously impossible. Two themes cannot be adequately treated here: first, the personal stylistic peculiarities of the different reformed writers must be *partly* submerged. An attempt to convey the polyphony of their different characters *and* the broad areas of agreement at the same time could only confuse.[3] Secondly, the development of reformed ideas over time must be compressed somewhat. In fact, this is less of a disadvantage than at first appears: Jean Calvin writing the final edition of his

Institutes in the Geneva of the late 1550s still shared many themes with the young Philip Melanchthon writing in the Wittenberg of the early 1520s.[4] The reformers rounded off their ideas in the middle of the sixteenth century in response to catholic counter-attacks and deviant extremism from their own ranks: the result was often to clarify and crystallize rather than modify their primitive message.

The reformers strove to convince believers that the saving of fallen souls was *not* a process of little lapses and little rituals to correct those lapses. Rather, it was a question of real sin, of a massive, all-corrupting inability to do right, which only God, by utterly gratuitous, self-sacrificing mercy, first covered with his grace, and then gradually, step by step, replaced with his own goodness in the Christian, in a process completed only in death.[5] This vast act of mercy made the piecemeal atonements and 'good works' performed by men, or by the Church for men, seem not only hopelessly inadequate, but treacherously deceptive and blasphemously distracting from the real point. The reformers developed their argument through the themes of sin, the law, Christ, faith, justification, sanctification, and predestination: each of these topics will be examined in turn.

1. *Man, Sin, and the Law*

Man, the reformers agreed, had been created without sin, in the 'image of God', and endowed with reason; that reason he was meant to use to progress towards immortality. Even in his fallen sinful state, Luther admitted, man felt a 'very tiny motion' of the will tending towards moral goodness. For Calvin, moral self-knowledge was there to show man his own moral shortcomings; the 'remnant' of original nature left by God gave to fallen man any intellectual, rational gifts.[6] The concept, then, of so-called *synteresis*[7] did not *wholly* disappear in most of the reformers. However, the sense of sin, the power of sin, and the consequences of 'original' sin in mankind were described by all the major protestant writers in terms far more sweeping and overpowering than in the vast majority of the later scholastics. A heightened and more articulated sense of human inadequacy in the face of God, which the reformers called 'sin', was the starting-point of their theology of salvation.

The first 'original' sin, Adam's disobedience of God in taking the fruit of the forbidden tree (always Adam's, rather than Eve's, disobedience was stressed) was regarded by the reformers as the result of pride, because man persuaded himself that he could become like God; and unbelief, because

Adam did not trust God's word when the fruit was forbidden. Adam's sin was punished by the corrupting of his nature and of the nature of his offspring. After the fall man remained invincibly prone to sin; and that disposition to sin was somehow passed from parents to children, notwithstanding any 'godliness' which the parents might have or seem to have. Sin was, as Melanchthon put it, a 'state of mind contrary to the law of God', in which man 'knows, loves, and seeks nothing but the carnal', and has 'contempt for and ignorance of God'.[8] The late scholastics had variously described original sin either as a 'loss of original righteousness', as a 'void' waiting to be filled, or alternatively as a positive blot, a 'vice in the soul'.[9] The reformers stretched both these views of sin to the uttermost. They insisted that the 'void', the absence of good, implied the presence of evil; they insisted that 'concupiscence' tainted all human nature, not just the lower man.[10]

When writing against Occamists and the like, the reformers emphasized man's 'total depravity' and inadequacy as though that were the whole story: as though man had, in every sense of the word, 'no good in him'. When giving a more balanced picture they could be more subtle. Calvin (following Augustine) made a typically fine distinction when he taught that after the fall man's *natural* gifts (reason, desire for truth, social instincts) were spoilt, but remained in a debased form; only his *supernatural* gifts, that is, any powers relating to understanding or obedience of God, were utterly destroyed. 'Natural' gifts were not a matter for human pride; they were graciously left by God to man after the fall, and fostered by his inspiration.[11] Before God such human lights showed up man's weaknesses, not his strengths. The great classical pagan philosophers, Calvin wrote, were 'blinder than moles' when it came to true religion. Religious truths relating to social behaviour they could only understand fitfully; truths relating to God and his worship men unaided could not understand at all.[12]

Any attempt by sinful man, without special grace, to do good was always fatally flawed, because such good acts were done without faith, and to satisfy the sinner's own pride. Luther insisted that the good works of the unregenerate were actually sins. When trying to do good, or believing themselves to be doing good, fallen men were actually puffing themselves up rather than praising God; or they were setting up their own standards of virtue rather than applying God's standard.[13] Melanchthon said of the 'virtuous pagans' that 'because these characteristics were in impure minds, and further, because these simulated virtues arose from love of self and love of praise, they ought not to be considered real virtues but vices'. Calvin commented of the virtuous pagans that 'because, however excellent anyone has been, his own ambition always pushes him on—a blemish with which all virtues are so sullied that before God they lose all favour—anything in profane men that appears praiseworthy must be considered worthless'.[14]

Because of original sin, man had lost his 'free will', that is (moral) 'free choice' to tell good and evil apart.[15] Fallen man was not (as he was for Biel) balanced between good and evil, free to choose one or the other. There was no longer the least question of the believer 'doing what is in him' to earn the first gift of grace.[16] Although Erasmus made 'free will' the crux of his assault on Luther in his *Diatribe* published in 1525, Luther was unrepentant in his belief that man's sin left him quite unable 'freely' to fulfil the demands of the law. Basing himself on Paul's epistles, he insisted remorselessly that man had freedom only to sin.[17] However, Luther was not alone, even though others, outside the context of bitter polemic, might write in more moderate tones.[18] A pastor and a layman in a remote Alpine valley were heatedly discussing free will. At one point the layman tossed some salt from a pot on the table in front of him on to the floor, and challenged the pastor to prove that he had not been free to throw the salt. The pastor agreed that he was perfectly free to throw away the salt; but was he also 'free' to gather up every grain into the pot again?[19]

If man had no choice but to sin, could he be regarded as 'guilty'? Or should sin rather be regarded as a 'weakness' or a disease in human nature? Luther, Melanchthon, and Calvin stuck to their guns, and insisted (contradicting the early Church Fathers, including even Augustine) that original sin was sin, and conferred guilt.[20] The Zürich reformer Zwingli sometimes preferred to speak of the 'disease' of original sin rather than the 'guilt'. His deviation on this issue derived from his sacramental beliefs, not his teaching on salvation; Bucer defended him on this very point.[21]

It was traditionally believed that the sacrament of baptism 'cleansed' or in some way removed the guilt of original sin. For the reformers, sacraments were not magically effective charms. Therefore, as Calvin made clearer than most, a rite could not simply wash away man's depravity. Original sin remained after baptism, just as sins remained amongst those who had been given grace and 'regenerated'.[22] Sin, therefore, was a far more all-embracing, sweeping concept in the writings of the reformers than it had been for most late medieval religious writers. On the other hand, the social role of reformed teaching on sin may have been very similar to that of their medieval forebears. Scholastics stressed men's need of penance, not to make them despair, but to make them come to confession. Analogously, the reformers told men that they were totally 'depraved', not to crush them, but to show how dazzling was divine mercy revealed in their preaching.

'Sin' was defined by the existence of God's *law*. Ordinary people in the late Middle Ages seem to have regarded Christianity as a set of 'laws' or rules.[23] The reformers, with their stress on sin and guilt, were bound to have a similar concept of 'law'.[24] However, it played a very distinctive role in their system. They interpreted God's moral laws (the Ten Commandments, above all) in their strictest, most all-embracing positive sense, and not as simple prohibitions of specific actions. Since God was concerned with purity of heart as well as outward obedience, the inner state of mind which disposed one to sin was as much forbidden as the act itself. For example, one was forbidden to have other Gods beside the true one: this meant that to trust to any creature, to 'take away even a particle from [God's] glory' was as bad as idolatry. It was not enough not to kill: one must never bear anger against a brother, and strive always to protect his life.[25]

The reformers discarded two ways in which the scholastics softened the moral law. Following Aquinas, the later scholastics had divided the moral law into 'commands', which were obligatory, and 'counsels' ('counsels of perfection', indeed), which were appropriate for monks (for example), but impracticable for the majority. 'Counsels' included the stricter demands of the moral law, like prohibition of sinful thoughts. The reformers heaped scorn on this quibble. A sin either was forbidden or it was not; and if forbidden, was forbidden to all, not just monks. Melanchthon pointed out (mischievously) that the only genuine 'counsel' advised but not insisted upon in the New Testament was celibacy: which had, of course, been rigidly imposed by Church law upon all members of religious orders and all clergy above a certain lowly rank from the eleventh century onwards.[26] Secondly, the Middle Ages differentiated greater and lesser degrees of sin, so-called 'mortal' and 'venial' sins respectively. Venial sins were said to arise out of a brief and involuntary lapse rather than an embedded vice. This subtlety likewise received short shrift. Calvin regarded it as impossible to assert that a disposition to sin did not arise from a deeper spiritual flaw, which amounted to 'mortal' sin. The critical fact, to the protestant mind, was not whether a person sinned more or less grievously, nor yet whether his own piety in any sense 'made up' for his sins. The only thing which mattered was whether a sinner was pardoned by God, having received mercy through faith. As Bucer put it, to the faithful all sins were venial except apostasy; to the faithless all sins were mortal.[27]

These remorseless reinforcements of the moral law implied that it was not just supremely difficult for man in his 'natural state' to fulfil the moral law; it was actually impossible, and impossible even for the holiest of men. So God, in laying down the moral law, must have commanded man to do something which his fallen nature made it quite impossible for him to do. Traditionally minded theologians were shocked, not least because this claim contradicted a statement by St Jerome and a decretal founded on his dictum. Yet Luther insisted mercilessly on the point, mocking the 'so tender decretal' which 'our theological masters are in the habit of considering ... infallible'. If human nature had been enough for man to obey the law, then grace, forgiveness, and Christ himself were unnecessary. If one accepted such a position, one became 'Christian only in name ... Christ [served] no purpose at all except to provide us with an ethic'.[28] Calvin was equally conclusive: 'since the teaching of the law is far above human capacity, a man may indeed view from afar the proffered promises, yet he cannot derive any benefit from them ... horrible threats hang over us, ... and pursue us with inexorable harshness ... the observance of the law is impossible'. The early Zwingli was equally categorical.[29]

So what was the law there for? The work of the law was the first step on the road to salvation. As Melanchthon alleged: 'in the justification of sinners the first work of God is to reveal our sin: to confound our conscience, make us tremble, terrify us, briefly, to condemn us.' Many alarming epithets were applied to the law. Melanchthon cited scriptural passages where the law was called 'the power of anger', 'the power of sin', 'the sceptre of the avenger', 'lightning', 'thunder'; God's revealing of sin was called 'the wrath of God', 'the countenance of wrath', Calvin, likewise, paraphrased Paul to the effect that 'of itself the law can only accuse, condemn, and destroy'; or quoted Augustine to the effect that if grace were absent, 'the law is present only to accuse and condemn us'. Luther, then, was far from unique when (for instance in 1518) he wrote 'the purpose of the law is that a man should despair of himself as it leads him to hell and humbles him, showing him that he is a sinner in all his works'.[30]

In the early years of Lutheran preaching, this 'terrifying', 'negative' role of the law was stressed, with the result that a strong antithesis was made between 'law' and 'Gospel', 'condemnation' and 'justification'.[31] However, in the non-Lutheran reformed tradition 'law' was given more positive connotations as well. Calvin spoke of the law as a purgative, a cure for vanity and hypocrisy. The law revealed God's justice just as Christ's work revealed his love. It moved men to look beyond their works for their salvation, and warned the stubborn. Zwingli, earlier, had disagreed with Luther's negative rhetoric in describing law. The law, he alleged, did not cause despair: it was human weakness in the face of the law which caused despair and condemnation. The law no more condemned a man, than did light shining on a deformed person make that person deformed.[32] Luther himself evaluated the law more positively in the 1530s against so-called 'antinomians', who had suggested that the Ten Commandments did not apply to them.[33]

'Sin', and 'law', then, were two sides of the same coin in the reformers' description of fallen man confronted with the work of God. Sin was revealed by the inexorable demands of the law; law was necessary to draw the sinful to a knowledge of their need of grace, and to restrain those not so drawn. Each of these acted as counterpoint to God's work for man. That work is only feebly captured by the historians' slogan of 'justification by faith', which forms the next topic.

2. *Faith, its Nature and Object*

The early reformers built much of their theology around a highly distinctive redefinition of 'faith'. For the late Middle Ages, there had been several different kinds of faith, 'implicit', 'unformed', 'formed by love', 'infused', 'acquired', and so forth, each kind carrying different implications.[34] In the Reformation there was only *one* kind of 'true' faith, with a series of attributes. Some years into the Reformation these attributes were systematically grouped under the three headings of 'knowledge', 'assent', and 'trust'; but these three components were in fact present from the beginning.

As they shared with the late scholastics the view that 'knowledge' was a part of faith, Luther's or Melanchthon's early controversial writings tended to stress how 'mere' knowledge was not *enough*.[35] Bucer emphasized it rather more, as did Calvin:

Faith rests not upon ignorance, but on knowledge ... by this knowledge, I say, not by submission of our feeling, do we obtain entry into the Kingdom of Heaven ... [Paul] indicates that it is not enough for a man implicitly to believe what he does not understand or even investigate. But he requires explicit recognition of the divine goodness upon which our righteousness rests.[36]

Since 'faith' was offered to those who listened, it was no longer enough for lay Christians to be in 'pious ignorance', obedient and passive, and to rely on the more 'perfect' Christians (priests and monks) to do the rest for them. The believer could not be said to believe 'implicitly', as in the Middle Ages, in things of which he had not heard and which he did not understand. Christians had to listen, be taught, and learn. Secondly, true faith involved assent to and acceptance of things known and things hidden. Melanchthon refused to call faith *without* assent by the traditional term of 'historical faith', insisting that it was only 'opinion concerning beliefs or divine history'. Zwingli echoed the distinction, as did Bucer. It made no sense to speak of the godless, or the devils having a kind of 'faith', since they believed something to be true, but not for them. Calvin amplified the point to the effect that 'assent itself ... is more of the heart than of the brain, and more of the disposition than of the understanding'.[37] As before, this definition rebutted the medieval notion of an 'unformed' faith, acceptance of propositions not yet supported by the commitment of the will: like 'implicit' faith, 'historical faith' was rejected as hypocrisy.

Finally, since Christ's promises contained the offer of free redemption and forgiveness, 'assent' *necessarily* meant placing all trust and absolute confidence solely in the object of faith, Christ's promise. The true believer was to be unshakeably, unreservedly, and permanently convinced that the passion of Christ and his merits applied to himself. For Melanchthon, faith was:

a sure and constant trust in God's goodwill toward us ... nothing else than trust in the divine mercy promised in Christ ... this trust in the goodwill or mercy of God first calms our hearts and then inflames us to give thanks to God ... where there is no sense of the mercy of God, there is either contempt or hatred for God.[38]

For Calvin, the genuine believer's faith would lead to total assurance before God; 'faith' could at times be a synonym for 'confidence'.[39] In this way also the reformers set their faces against one of the most typical of the 'nominalist' scholastics' attitudes to faith. The latter, since they regarded faith as a 'work' of fallible man, thought that the believer's confidence and assurance should always be tempered by a certain humility, by a degree of uncertainty as to whether one really was forgiven. This spiritual state has been memorably described as an 'oscillation between fear and hope'.[40] The classic text of such writers was the Vulgate's mistranslation of Ecclesiastes 9: 1: 'a man does not know whether he is worthy of love or hatred'. Melanchthon, Bucer, and Calvin denounced both the mistranslation and what they saw as the misapplication of the text.[41] There was nothing presumptuous in the believer's assurance, because he was trusting not to his own goodness, but to *God's* goodness. As Luther insisted, God's mercy *deserved* to be trusted utterly; to have such confidence was simply to give God the honour which was his due.[42] Even in the midst of doubt, the believer still called out to God. Despair did not lead to apostasy. By a slightly circular argument, 'true' faith survived temptation, 'counterfeit' faith did not. By insisting that, even when assailed by doubt, the believer was still favoured by God, Calvin attempted (unsuccessfully) to discourage his readers from morbid introspection.[43]

Unlike Biel's act of 'love of God above all else', 'faith' was not an 'achievement', let alone a 'good work'. Rather it was a gift, an unearned blessing, an inspiration from God. Luther denied that people could generate faith inside themselves. If they tried to 'get busy with their own powers and create an idea of faith in their heart . . . nothing comes of it . . . and no improvement follows'; only the faith given by God was strong enough to resist temptation. At times Luther called faith the action of the Word; at others, of the Holy Spirit. This 'inspired' quality was echoed by others. Zwingli called faith 'the pledge and seal with which God seals our hearts' and 'the work of the spirit in the believer'. Bucer stated how God 'gives us this conviction and undoubting confidence of his goodness towards us', and stressed how the Spirit persuaded and illuminated the heart. For Calvin faith was 'the work of God', 'a manifestation of God's power'.[11] Since faith was given and inspired, rather than attained to, God, for inscrutable reasons, chose to give faith to some people and not to others. As Calvin, quoting Augustine, put it: 'Why is it given to one and not to another? I am not ashamed to say: "This is the depth of the cross" . . . I see what I can do; I do not see whence I can do it.'[45]

Although it is generally agreed that Reformation teaching was 'Christ centred', Christ actually took up less space in early protestant theology than one would have expected.[46] There were fewer major conflicts with traditional medieval teaching; anyway, the details of what theologians call 'Christology' and 'atonement theory' were more apt to make the experts disagree than to produce good sermons. Some of the questions, finally, were mysteries regarded as beyond human reason. Just what Christ *was* had been defined for western and most of eastern Christendom by the formulae of the Council of Chalcedon of 451: Christ was at one and the same time truly God and truly man; in his one person were combined two natures, one divine and one human, which were united 'unconfusedly, unchangeably, indivisibly, inseparably'; the two natures made up one person without the attributes of either nature being mingled with the other.[47] The reformers explained such paradoxes in largely traditional ways.[48] Zwingli alone, while accepting the traditional dogmas, tended to make the distinction between Christ's natures more stark: for example, he insisted that it was the human nature of Christ and not the divine which suffered pain, torment, and death on the Cross. This approach reflected partly the different style and manner of his theology, and partly his distinctive understanding of the Eucharist.[49]

On the 'atonement', the explanation of *how* Christ's mediation is effective, there never had been any single authoritative explanation. Luther scattered remarks to the winds without always tying them together. Most commonly, he described Christ's sacrifice as 'satisfaction', echoing the forensic, substitutionary interpretation.[50] He once called this the 'amazing doctrine', that 'one has sinned, another made satisfaction. The one who sins does not make satisfaction; the one who makes satisfaction does not sin.' Luther claimed that the value of Christ's sacrifice was not just sufficient to cover the finite sins of finite men, but actually infinite.[51] However, he also spoke of Christ 'conquering' and 'destroying' sin by his passion, thus harking back to an early patristic approach which suited very well the devil-filled world of his more colourful imagery (though he subtly altered the patristic version to suit his ideas).[52] Calvin spoke of Christ as the mediator who assumed the sins of others. Like Luther, he stressed Christ's actually taking on himself the punishment, and the physical suffering, which others had deserved. He also suggested that Christ's sacrifice was 'exemplary': those who saw Christ taking their sins upon him would be moved to love him the more.[53] Of other reformers, only Oecolampadius gave detailed scrutiny to the atonement.[54]

One polemical point was always in the forefront. The mass, in the common mind of the Middle Ages, was both a sacrament and a sacrifice in itself, with a propitiatory value. From the very first, the protestant reformers insisted that Christ was not just the mediator but the *sole* mediator. Only the work of Christ had 'merit' to save souls; only *his* sacrifice had any power to take away the penalties of sin; his passion had atoned superabundantly for all human sin, past, present, and future. The communion service, then, should be the sign of Christ's passion, not the repetition of it to the point of redundancy. A famous sermon preached in Edward VI's England spoke of the 'diabolical' way in which traditional rites 'took away some part of Christ's passion ... evacuated Christ's cross, and mingled the Lord's supper'.[55] To doctrinal dissent was added outrage. Catholics who believed in their sacrifices were 'insulting' Christ. This mentality was crucial to the temper of religious conflict later in the sixteenth century.

3. Justification

This topic forms the absolute crux of what was shared in the thought of the different reformers. Whatever else Luther and Zwingli disagreed about, or thought they did, they shared this core principle.[56] For Luther this was 'the summary of Christian doctrine' and 'the sun which illuminates God's Holy Church'; for Calvin it was 'the main hinge on which religion turns'.[57] In its broadest sense, 'justification' for the reformers embraced *two* separate processes. First, a sinner was 'justified' in the sense that the guilt of his sins, which deserved God's anger and punishment, was suddenly and unconditionally forgiven. Such guilt ceased to be held against him, or (technically) 'imputed' to him; on the contrary, the merits of Christ's atoning work were credited or 'imputed' to the pardoned sinner instead. Secondly, the believer's soul was renewed from inside by the Holy Spirit, in a gradual breaking-down of 'fleshly' instincts and a step-by-step 'rebirth' which enabled the saved to begin to act rightly. This second process (specifically called 'regeneration' or 'sanctification') is discussed later.[58] For the reformers man was already 'reckoned as justified', already forgiven, *before* inner renewal had taken place, and in no sense *because* of that inner renewal. The first 'justification' occurred as an outward, 'extrinsic', 'alien' process. The second stage, of 'sanctification', was a product, not a cause, of the first.[59]

The crucial logical distinction between 'justification' and 'sanctification' did not spring fully grown from the mind of Luther, or anyone else. Luther seems to have struggled long over his description of the process. Many books have been written trying simply to explain how he reached his mature position.[60] Whatever the answer, his mature view seems to have been established by 1519–20, with the sermon on 'Two Kinds of Righteousness' of 1519, the treatise *The Freedom of a Christian* of 1520, and the tract written against the Louvain theologian Jacobus Latomus (c.1475–1544) in 1521.[61] While in some texts (*The Freedom of a Christian*, for instance) Luther was ecstatic rather than precise, perhaps his clearest description was in the Latomus riposte:

What then? Are we sinners? No, rather we are justified, but by grace. Righteousness is not situated in those qualitative forms, but in the mercy of God. In fact, if you take mercy away from the godly, they are sinners, and really have sin, but it is not imputed to them because they believe and live under the reign of mercy, and because sin is condemned and continually put to death in them ... Surely ... it is almost greater to accept as righteous him who is still infected by sin than him who is entirely pure.[62]

Melanchthon was just as clear:

Why is it that justification is attributed to faith alone? I answer that since we are justified by the mercy of God alone, and faith is clearly the recognition of that mercy by whatever promise you apprehend it, justification is attributed to faith alone. Let those who marvel that justification is attributed only to faith alone marvel also that justification is attributed only to the mercy of God, and not rather to human merits ... wherever you turn, whether to the works preceding justification, or to those which follow, there is no room for our merit. Therefore, justification must be a work of the mercy of God alone.[63]

In Zwingli's *Exposition of the Faith* of 1531, one finds:

We believe that by faith the forgiveness of sins is most assuredly granted to man as often as he prays to God through Christ ... But we say sins are forgiven through faith, by which we mean only that faith makes one sure one's sins are forgiven ... for as it is only the Holy Ghost that can give faith, so only it can give the forgiveness of sins ... none can attain to everlasting life except he whose sins are remitted. Therefore it follows that he who trusts in Christ receives remission of sin.[64]

Bucer paraphrased Paul thus: 'God, on account of the death of Christ undergone on our behalf, forgives us all our sins, absolves us from all guilt, and passes judgment in our favour against Satan and all the ill we may have deserved'; and summarized Melanchthon (approvingly) to the effect that '"we are justified by faith alone" means, "we are pronounced righteous by trusting in mercy alone"'.[65]

Calvin wrote perhaps the definitive formulation of the belief:

Justified by faith is he who, excluded from the righteousness of works, grasps the righteousness of Christ through faith and, clothed in it, appears in God's sight not as a sinner but as a righteous man ... Therefore, we explain justification simply as the acceptance with which God receives us into his favour as righteous men. And we say that it consists in the remission of sins and the imputation of righteousness.[66]

Calvin shared the image of the sinner being 'clothed' in an 'alien' or 'extrinsic' righteousness—a righteousness given to those who were not really righteous—with Melanchthon and Luther.[67] This image conveys the essential novelty of the reformers' position. The sinner might be arrayed with the 'good works' which would impress his fellows, but before God they were rags. The believer, on the other hand, was as it were draped and covered over with Christ's sacrifice, so that divine judgement regarded only the covering of imputed justice, and not the real sins which still clogged and festered underneath.

This teaching overturned the very basis on which the medieval pastoral cycle of sin, confession, and absolution rested. Both the theoretical and the pastoral theology of the late middle ages had assumed that the believer would *alternate* between sin and grace, passing from the former to the latter through the sacraments of penance and communion. By this medieval wisdom, a man was *sometimes* a sinner, *sometimes* righteous—but never both at the same time.[68] For the reformers, on the other hand, the oscillating cycle of sin and 'grace' was meaningless: in Luther's phrase, a believer was at one and the same time a sinner and a righteous man: a sinner in respect of his actual conduct, but justified or 'righteous' inasmuch as God gratuitously attributed Christ's merits to him.[69] The Reformation scheme of salvation could, crudely, be described by the diagram shown in Fig. 2. There was, therefore, no question of the soul becoming 'pure' or 'clean'; the elaborate sacramental means to wash away sin were hopelessly inadequate and fundamentally wrong. Such a paradox—that Christ could accept an essentially 'unclean' soul—profoundly shocked contemporary catholic thought.[70] Moreover, there was no longer any question of the soul attaining to a 'state of grace', acquiring 'habits of grace', or otherwise possessing in itself whatever made it 'righteous'.[71] Melanchthon put this clearly when he redefined 'grace' itself. The Greek and Hebrew words translated by the word 'grace' (*gratia* in the Vulgate Latin) meant simply the 'favour' or 'goodwill' of God towards man. If someone had 'grace', that implied nothing about *them*: it only meant that God had chosen them for special favour. Grace, ultimately, meant nothing more for the protestants than 'forgiveness or remission of sins'.[72]

This teaching was not to be found with such categorical and exclusive precision in Paul, Augustine, or (it is suggested here) any previous writer. This left the reformers with a problem over Augustine, the early Father whom they most revered and quoted. They could either criticize Augustine; or they could tone down their emphases slightly so as to fit him in. Luther and Calvin criticized Augustine. Luther called him 'neither clear nor comprehensive in the matter of imputation'; Calvin rejected his 'view, or at any rate his manner of stating it', because he 'still subsumes grace under sanctification, by which we are reborn in newness of life'.[73] Martin Bucer and Huldrych Zwingli reacted somewhat differently. Bucer, very much influenced by the early Fathers, tended to insist on the strong *link* between justification and regeneration. He agreed that to be 'judged just' and 'made just' were two different things. However, he wanted to repel the accusation that the reformers undermined *all* good works and ethical standards; and felt that an emphasis on 'inner renewal' was the best way to do so. The

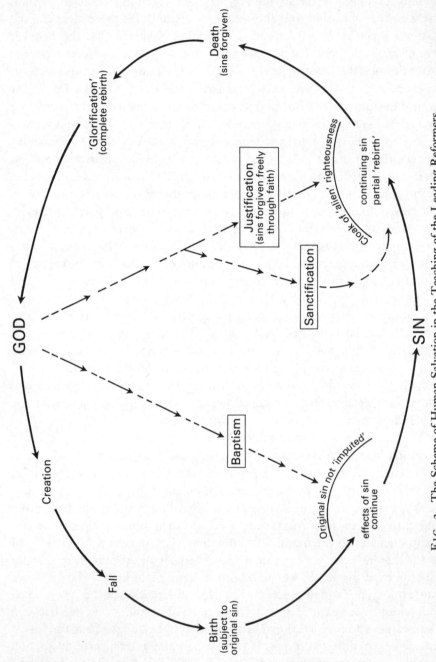

FIG. 2. The Scheme of Human Salvation in the Teaching of the Leading Reformers

Fathers, as he knew, often wrote of justification and regeneration as though they were interchangeable. At times he spoke of a 'twofold' justification (imputed and inner), at others of a 'threefold' (imputed, inner renewal in life, and final glorification after death).[74] Zwingli was grounded in the Fathers, and possibly also reluctant to relinquish the Erasmian stress on 'living' Christ's example which had dominated his early years. Without in any way denying that God alone initiated and sustained the saving process, he did deliberately and persistently emphasize 'renewal' and 'new life'. In so doing he seems to have wished to take the Bible as a whole, and to reconcile apparently opposed passages of Scripture, for example Paul in Romans with the Epistle of James.[75]

4. *Regeneration*

No major reformer—certainly not Luther—taught that believers were 'clothed' with 'alien' righteousness without *also* being inwardly purified and 'sanctified'. The reformers stressed 'renewal of life' without compromising 'imputation' at all. They intended people to be assured of their free salvation; and then to go about their lives cultivating the virtues, but *without* worrying about *either* the balance between sins and 'good works' *or* whether their 'good works' would be 'rewarded'. Such teaching also changed the kind of 'works' which were seen as 'good'.

The early reformers taught that, whereas God's moral law was a source of accusation and despair for fallen man, for the regenerate the law had lost its sting. This was the 'freedom' of which Luther wrote in *The Freedom of a Christian*:

A Christian has all that he needs in faith and needs no works to justify him; and if he has no need of works, he has no need of the law; and if he has no need of the law, surely he is free from the law ... that Christian liberty, our faith ... does not induce us to live in idleness or wickedness but makes the law and works unnecessary for any man's righteousness and salvation.[76]

In very similar ways Melanchthon, Zwingli, Bucer, and Calvin taught that the 'curse of the law' was removed from those who were 'regenerated': instead of trying (and failing) to follow a set of rules in fear and trembling, they were free to do voluntarily what the law used to command.[77]

This teaching challenged received opinion about the 'abrogation' or cancelling of the Old Testament laws. According to tradition, with the coming of Christ the 'judicial' and 'ceremonial' laws of the Old Testament (the specific codes for civil conduct and ritual) had been cancelled or 'abrogated', while the moral law had been retained and made more absolute. For the reformers, even the moral law had in a sense been 'abrogated', because its power to condemn had been taken away. The 'judicial' and 'ceremonial' aspects were 'abrogated' in a similar sense, because they were irrelevant to the spirit. Particular rites or social rules were things neither to cling to nor scrupulously to avoid. The same razor, of course, could be wielded on 'papal' ceremonies.[78] However, unlike the extremists who claimed that God worked two *completely* different dispensations in the Old and New Testaments, and that the Old Testament 'Covenant' was quite meaningless for Christians, the later Luther and Calvin held that the two Testaments, with 'law' and 'Gospel' in each, were complementary, as well as opposed. Calvin even suggested, implausibly, that the Old Testament patriarchs 'so lived under the Old Covenant as not to remain there but ever to aspire to the new', and that in a partial way they understood Christ.[79] In the later decades of the sixteenth century 'law' was given a positive role *alongside* its 'curse' and 'bondage'. It became, not only something to escape from, but a guide for the faithful, a spur to activity. 'Sanctification' was not just an incidental consequence of justification, but its final purpose. Calvin showed this when he described regeneration in several chapters *before* discussing justification by faith.[80]

However, the works of the 'regenerate' still had no actual 'merit' in God's sight. In this life, the 'sanctification' of believers was *always* incomplete and imperfect. Just as those baptized retained original sin, so those who were sanctified remained really sinners. No one, however endowed with grace, was truly 'sinless' before God. Therefore, the saints certainly had no 'surplus' merit, as medieval beliefs surrounding indulgences had claimed.[81] Luther emphasized: 'Everything has been forgiven ... but everything has not yet been made whole.' Likewise Melanchthon: 'the saints have a twofold nature, spirit and flesh ... we are saints insofar as we are spirit ... sin still adheres in the flesh.' Calvin was equally graphic: 'sin ceases only to reign; it does not also cease to dwell in [the regenerate] ... we have not a single work going forth from the saints that ... deserves not shame as its just reward.' Bucer, finally, stated in 1548: 'sin ... is still so powerful that we can possess neither faith, hope nor love ... to the degree of perfection justly enjoined upon us ... all the saints ... must still ask God ... for the remission of their debts.'[82]

What did 'regeneration' entail? First of all, it implied 'repentance', described in terms of the Greek and Hebrew words which stressed a change of heart, rather than the Latin *poenitentia*, with its connotations of ritual 'penance'. So Calvin called it 'the true turning of our life to God, ... that arises from a pure and earnest fear of him'.[83] 'Repentance' was traditionally divided into two parts, 'mortification' and 'vivification', literally 'dying' and 'living again'. In mortification the law 'terrified the conscience' (Melanchthon) or 'killed the soul' (Calvin) by confronting the believer with the awareness of sin. In 'vivification' through the preaching of the Gospel or absolution believers were 'renewed', inspired with confidence to reorient themselves towards faith. Calvin described how God gradually 'wipes out in his elect the corruptions of the flesh, cleanses them of guilt, consecrates them to himself as temples renewing all their minds to true purity'.[84] Like sanctification itself, repentance was always partial and incomplete; it was in no sense the 'cause' of man's acceptance by God. It was a fruit of faith; its presence proved that faith was real and not counterfeit. In contrast to the medieval assumption, contrition never *preceded* faith.[85]

The regenerate not only 'believed'; they lived out the traditional virtues of hope and love of one's neighbour. Luther, Melanchthon, Calvin, and Bucer all listed the social virtues of serving one's neighbour as the fruits of 'new life'.[86] They did not just teach ethical platitudes: they stressed inward attitudes, coming from the heart, not from ritual observance; and secondly, social virtues, addressed to the good of the community, not to an abstract entity such as 'the Church', nor to help the believer's soul. The 'humility' and 'generosity' which they preached might, in some circumstances, have cut across the fissures of rank, hierarchy, or faction which structured sixteenth-century society. Christians were to respect order but not to despise their social inferiors.[87]

Late medieval people had dreaded dying suddenly, with the risk that an unconfessed mortal sin would prevent their eventual entry to heaven. The Church confirmed this fear by the special provisions made for travellers in 'full confessional letters'.[88] The struggle to make 'satisfactions' continued beyond the grave, as believers piled up sacrificial masses for themselves and their relatives in purgatory. Death was feared, prepared for, and guarded against. Luther turned against such a view of death from the very first. In the eighth of the ninety-five theses he wrote that 'according to the [penitential] canons themselves, none applies to the dying'; and in the thirteenth, 'the dying will pay all their debts by their death'. As soon as the doctrine of satisfaction was argued away, the fear of purgatory was removed.[89] For protestants, in death the sanctification of the elect would be completed, and things imperfectly grasped in this life fully apprehended. Calvin taught a balanced attitude: the present life was to be enjoyed with gratitude, as offering a foretaste of the next; but glorification offered the prospect that the tribulations of life would be replaced by the perfection of the divine promises.[90]

Sanctification or 'imparted righteousness' is sometimes seen as a problem for the coherence and consistency of reformed ideas. Did sanctification let good works back in through the back door? Did protestants do good works to 'prove' their justification, where before catholics had done them to acquire it? In what sense did protestants regard good works as 'necessary'?[91] Did Luther so stress justification by imputation *alone*, that others, more imbued with humanist ideas, had to 'correct' his emphases by a new accent on active, 'intrinsic' righteousness?[92] Melanchthon habitually stressed the believer's moral duty: he felt strongly that to preach forgiveness *without* good works would make men spiritually idle. While Luther lived he and Melanchthon worked harmoniously in harness: Luther likened Melanchthon to James, who retained the law, and himself to Paul, who brought it down, adding 'why do you worry? Philipp proceeds in charity and I in faith ... so God achieves the same thing in different ways'.[93] There were, however, bitter and divisive conflicts within Lutheranism after Luther's death in 1546 over this issue. The historian must explain such conflicts—even though he or she may find political, contextual explanations as convincing as causes drawn from pure theology.[94]

'Regeneration' was therefore both an indispensable part of a balanced scheme of salvation and a fatal stumbling-block. As long as the Reformation was a dynamic, polemical, anti-catholic movement of protest and revolt, this doctrine could be left in a minor key. However, once 'protestantism' became a complete system by itself, called upon to defend itself on all sides, a balance had to be struck between the unique message of 'imputation' and the pastoral concern for ethical standards. These debates marked the Reformation's coming of age.

5. *Predestination*

'Predestination', the belief that a sovereign God 'chose' who was to be saved, was a commonplace of medieval thought: the reformers in no way invented it. It featured in their thought for three reasons. First, their God was sovereign, eternal, and independent of any outside agent.[95] Secondly, there was their experience as preachers: why, out of a congregation attending the same sermon, did a few hear, listen, and take note, while the vast majority seemed incapable as well as unwilling?[96] Thirdly, the scheme of justification required it. All the gifts which could redeem man from his otherwise hopeless predicament of sin and condemnation were free gifts which no one could earn or deserve: the only reason for God to give them was his own independent and free grace.

Luther wrote as early as 1517: 'The perfectly infallible preparation for grace, the one and only valid attitude, is the eternal election and predestination of God.' In 1525 he refined his explanation with his classic distinction between 'God revealed' and 'God hidden'. As revealed and preached in the Word, God called all sinners to repentance and offered grace to all. As hidden in the inscrutable mystery of his predestination, he gave to some what he withheld from others. The believer could not hope to investigate, let alone understand, the reason for God's choice.[97] The young Melanchthon (who was later to change his tone) wrote in 1521: 'Since all things that happen, happen necessarily according to divine predestination, our will has no liberty ... If you relate human will to predestination, there is freedom neither in external nor internal acts but all things take place according to divine determination.'[98] Zwingli taught that God was merciful when he chose (elected) certain people; he was just when he applied to them the merit of Christ's sacrifice.[99] Calvin described predestination with progressively greater fullness from 1536, and definitively in the 1559 *Institutes*:

We call predestination God's eternal decree, by which he compacted with himself what he willed to become of each man. For all are not created in equal condition; rather, eternal life is foreordained for some, eternal damnation for others. Therefore, as any man has been created to one or other of these ends, we speak of him as predestined to life or death.[100]

In Calvin's exposition one theme stood out: the unique unbounded sovereignty and majesty of God. God must be allowed to be God, in the fullest possible sense. Like Luther, when puzzled to explain God's hardening of men's hearts to damnation, he tended to speak of the 'incomprehensible mind of God' before which men could only be 'amazed', not curious.[101]

The Occamist theologians, including Biel, had taught that God 'predestined' to be saved those whom he 'foreknew' would respond to his offer of grace by acquiring 'semi-merit'. In this they were contradicted by the followers both of Duns Scotus and of Gregory of Rimini, who taught that God's choice could not be affected by any foreknowledge of man's behaviour.[102] Scotus and Gregory differed over whether God *specifically* saved some and damned others, or whether he saved some and just 'allowed' others to sin and be condemned. Duns Scotus, and von Staupitz, believed that God only predestined those whom he saved, while Gregory insisted that God decreed those whom he damned as much as those whom he saved.[103] The reformers had, then, to take up positions on these issues as part of their academic heritage. On the first question, of election deriving from God's foreknowledge or his will, Luther sometimes seemed unclear, as though he confused foreknowledge and predestination.[104] However, he did so only because he regarded both these qualities as attributes of a supreme God: 'God foreknows nothing contingently, but ... foresees and purposes and does all things by his immutable, eternal, and infallible will ... everything we do, everything that happens, even if it seems to us to happen mutably and contingently, happens in fact nonetheless necessarily and immutably, if you have regard to the will of God.'[105] For Bucer 'foreknowledge, predetermination and election are at this point one and the same thing'; but God in no sense elected men *because* of their 'foreknown' worth.[106] Calvin spelled out just why the Reformation so bitterly opposed traditional and revived catholicism on this point. God 'foreknew' everything, in that all creation was constantly under his view; his decree of election or damnation was quite distinct and separate. Election had nothing to do with 'foreknown' merit, he insisted, citing copious biblical and patristic authorities.[107]

The second question, whether God *explicitly* decreed the damnation of the 'reprobate', those excluded from grace, was perplexing. If so, God had decided that some people, no less and no more sinful than the rest, should be born solely in order to sin and be damned for it. That conclusion seemed to affront Christian belief in God's justice, let alone his mercy; it would be a difficult one to sustain in public preaching. Most medieval writers (except Gregory of Rimini) favoured the 'asymmetrical' answer that God decreed the salvation of the elect but only 'permitted' the rest to continue in sin, then justly damned them.[108] Luther was not technically precise on the subject. On one hand he stressed the absolute power of God in all his creatures. On the other he did not regard God as the cause of evil. God's work in an evil person he likened to a horseman riding a lame horse, or a carpenter using a chipped axe: the good workman could not but produce bad work. To criticize God for not suppressing evil was to 'want God to cease to be God'.[109] There was thus much pastoral advice, but no theoretical resolution of the problem. Zwingli, Oecolampadius, Capito, and Piermartire Vermigli taught that only the elect were truly 'predestined'; the foredoomed were simply 'permitted' to sin, their number was small, and one could not tell who they were.[110]

In contrast, Bucer readily spoke of God 'predestinating' the wicked as much as the elect. Man had no right to answer back to God, or to criticize him for appearing to work evil by hardening men's hearts. Heinrich Bullinger (1504–75), Zwingli's successor at Zürich, similarly described predestination as God's decree either to save or to damn.[111] Calvin put all his authority behind what has since been called 'double predestination': a specific decree both of election and of reprobation. The fall itself could be seen as an outcome of predestination; any attempt to call God 'unjust' for such actions was ignorant as well as rash. Nevertheless, divine predestination still left man responsible for his own sin.[112]

One might *believe* in predestination, but should one preach the belief to the public? This question worried the reformers just as it had done the preachers of the late fifteenth century, and for substantially the same reasons. For some, like the later Melanchthon, Oecolampadius, or Capito, the doctrine was too complex, too easily misunderstood, and too apt to lead to complacency on the one hand or despair on the other.[113] In 1521 Melanchthon had written 'it makes considerable difference that young minds are immediately imbued with this idea that all things come to pass, not according to the plans and efforts of men but according to the will of God'. In the 1530s he became steadily more tentative and unwilling to discuss the issue. In 1555 he stressed that while the saved were indeed 'predestined', one should emphasize that all were 'called', and not speculate over why some remained 'blind'.[114] Calvin censured him, respectfully and without naming names, for advising too much caution in teaching the doctrine.[115]

Luther and Calvin, on the other hand, were quite certain that the dogma could not and should not be suppressed. Erasmus had suggested that some beliefs, even if true, ought not to be made public; Luther retorted that anything in Scripture was fit to publish. What God willed to be taught Erasmus could not suppress on grounds of 'decency' or 'prudence'. Calvin resisted these arguments for silence for almost identical reasons. To disparage the teaching as though it were a dangerous and unwanted piece of baggage was 'to reproach God, as if he had unadvisedly let slip something hurtful to the church'. The doctrine should be taught so far, and only so far, as it was found in Scripture.[116] For Bucer, predestination strengthened one's faith, and to doubt one's election was to doubt God's goodness. One should consider predestination in order to cling to God's promises. This optimistic outlook was echoed in the Thirty-nine Articles issued for the Church of England in 1563: 'the godly consideration of predestination ... is full of sweet, pleasant and unspeakable comfort to godly persons'. Zwingli was perhaps the readiest of all freely to speculate and follow where the argument led; so much so that he incurred the criticism of Calvin for

'curiosity', the 'prying into the secrets of God' which Luther also condemned.[117]

Could the elect *know* that they were indeed predestined to salvation, or
'deduce' from God's good works within them that they were indeed saved?
Calvin and Bucer were cautious: God made the promises, and man should
accept them without doubting that they applied to him. Believers should
look not at their 'maimed and mutilated' righteousness but at the promises
of God; even though the 'seed' (or promise) of election might be seen in
some believers. Zwingli seems occasionally to have been less discreet,
though not systematically.[118] In due course a belief in predestination was
to lead some protestant groups crudely to see themselves as the 'elect
people', 'the saints', 'the godly'. The reformers themselves are not to blame
for this attitude. In the sixteenth century, the doctrine was something
which other ideas (justification above all) led *to*, not something which
beliefs were deduced *from*. It is the consequence of the reformers' revision
of the medieval scheme of salvation, rather than its reason.

6. *Conclusion: An Assault on the 'Penitential Cycle'*

Most medieval people were content to know that they should confess
their sins, do penance, hear mass, and receive the other sacraments as
appropriate, without finding out *why* theologians thought they should do
so. Similarly, many who followed the reformers were neither required nor
able fully to understand the complex reasons for their advice. For lay
people, the point about the Reformation was that it abolished the expensive
and complicated apparatus to which they had resorted so regularly for the
good of their souls. In its place it put preaching, prayer, and acts of moral
piety towards one's neighbour.

Since, even with grace, a sinner could not become sinless or 'clear his
account' with God by pious acts, sacramental penance, the process of
'contrition' (or 'attrition'), confession, and satisfaction was transformed.[119]
Ultimately, private confession of individual sins would be almost completely supplanted in the protestant churches by the general confession
and absolution (already known to the late Middle Ages) in the context of
public prayers.[120] However, the reformers at first wished only to reorganize
and rehabilitate private confession. Luther, Melanchthon, and Calvin each
dissected sacramental penance according to the threefold medieval analysis
of contrition, confession, and satisfaction. Contrition, they held, was
nothing more than the 'mortification' experienced by the regenerate

believer. Confession, they agreed, could and should validly be made in several ways, none of which corresponded to the current catholic rite. People could confess their sins, collectively or individually, before the congregation. Individuals could confess to each other the sins which broke the fellowship of the Church. Thirdly, people could and should (on this all the early reformers were most emphatic) confess their sins to their pastors when they felt the need, to be reassured that the promises of the Gospel applied to *them*. Finally, satisfactions to appease divine justice were a fiction. Christ alone was the propitiation and satisfaction for sin. If sins were forgiven, they were forgiven by a fatherly God, not acknowledged by a judge who then exacted a forensic penalty.[121]

The reformers thus excluded the Roman practice of using penance as a discipline. To list all one's sins individually, to be separately contrite and perform a separate act of satisfaction for each, was patently impossible given the scope and extent of human sin. While being contrite for one sin and doing satisfaction for it, a believer would inevitably commit further sins, so building up a hopeless backlog of penitential obligation. Even to try to list all sins distressed tender consciences: Luther called such requirements an 'instrument for driving souls to despair' and Calvin a 'butchery'.[122] 'Penance', then, asked too much, a sorrow for sin beyond man's ability. Secondly, however, it asked too little, because it replaced faith, repentance, and the renewal of life with an artificial consoling ritual. How, Luther asked, could contrition exist without faith?

How many, I ask, are possessed with the notion that they are in a saved state and are making satisfaction for their sins, if they only mumble over, word for word, the prayers imposed by the priest, even though meanwhile they never give a thought to the amending of their way of life ... no thought is given here to the mortifying of the flesh ... [123]

Melanchthon, while condemning the requirement of 'full contrition' in the penitent, denounced the 'unholy self-satisfied hypocrites who go about without any anguish in their hearts, trusting and building on hypocritical forms of monks, thinking afterward that they are without sin'. Zwingli pointed out that in confession people felt 'a great joy and refreshing', which was just the relaxation of the tension which their own guilt had created: it did not change ways of life.[124] Calvin also thought auricular confession encouraged superstition and complacency:

nothing gives us greater confidence or licence to sin than when, having made confession to a priest, men think themselves able to wipe their mouths and say, 'I have not done it'. And not only are they emboldened throughout the year to sin;

but, freed from the necessity of confession for the rest of the year, they never sigh unto God, they never return to their senses, but heap sins upon sins until they vomit all of them up at once.[125]

Disciplinary sacramental penance was abolished not as an end in itself, but in a greater assault on the notion of 'merit' and 'works-righteousness'. So, all the incidental beliefs attached to the penitential system—works of satisfaction, purgatory, indulgences—were done away with. The arguments used were simple deductions from previous positions. However, the *language* with which Calvin derided purgatory, calling it a 'dreadful blasphemy against Christ', a 'sacrilege', a 'fountain of impiety', foreshadowed the vehemence of confessional hatred later in the century.[126]

The cult of the saints was revised to the point of abolition. For medieval theologians and ordinary people alike, the saints' exceptional 'merit' had given them power to 'intercede' with God for believers who prayed specifically to them. This led to the popular belief that 'patron' saints looked after their own special people, trades, places, or circumstances. Luther redefined the 'Communion of Saints': 'saints' were all true believers; the 'communion' was the spiritual community here on earth. Specially favoured believers were not 'meritorious', nor intercessors, nor even (as for humanists) examples of virtue to be imitated; but instances of God's grace at work through faith. Calvin angrily rejected the various arguments used to support prayers to dead saints (such as that in heaven they were bound to have the same faith and share the same love for humanity as they showed in life) as both unscriptural and as unwarranted speculation about the secrets of the future life. With Zwingli and Oecolampadius, these reformers insisted that the only intercessory prayer a Christian might make was that which one living person made for another.[127]

The saints and their cults had not only shaped the liturgical life of late medieval Christendom; they had also determined the names, structure, and ornaments of most places of worship. The reformers then had a disciplinary and a political problem: how much 'idolatry'—'images' of saints, shrines, relics, and the rest of the paraphernalia—should be removed, how quickly, and how thoroughly? Luther and Zwingli took opposite views, with momentous results for the future of protestantism. Luther argued that education and understanding should precede liturgical change: the people should be instructed inwardly before most of their surroundings were tampered with. Zwingli argued that the outward changes, which embodied the new teaching, should be made as soon as possible. This disagreement belongs primarily to the sphere of Church policy and educational theory rather than beliefs as such. The problem was, however, an unavoidable consequence of reformed teachings; there was no one obvious answer, and varied conclusions were reached by protestant religious leaders of all kinds throughout the sixteenth century.[128]

The sweeping changes demanded in worship and the religious life by the Reformation flowed from a fundamental principle shared by the major figures of the mainstream Reformation movement. Their doctrine stressed the unique mediating work of Christ, apprehended by the elect believer through an undeserved gift of free grace in the experience of 'faith'. It opened up a breach between man's *actual* spiritual and moral state and his *imputed* condition; therefore it ended the nervous 'oscillation' between sin and grace. It thus broke down all the clichés of medieval piety at once; and ended the spiritual justification on which the medieval Church had survived. However, the inner logic of the reformers' critique was evident only to the highly educated. The vast majority of those who enthusiastically supported the reformers' proposals cannot fully have understood the reasoning which lay behind them.[129] No movement in western Europe had hitherto enjoyed such rapid dissemination by the written, printed word; no movement was in its essence *less* easy to impart to the masses. Vital as it was, the reformed theory of salvation did not stand alone. It was accompanied and buttressed by a series of teachings, most importantly on the source of authority for the Church, namely Scripture, its use and interpretation, and on the 'external means', namely the Church, its structures and rituals. These must now be sketched in.

9

The Reformers' Message
Scripture

Luther did not begin with a frontal assault on the spiritual authority of western catholicism, but by challenging a dubious and controversial practice, that of selling indulgences for the dead, in the name of his nascent doctrine of salvation. However, when the Church responded through the views of an extreme papalist school,[1] and Luther defended himself tenaciously against them, traditional concepts of 'authority' came into question. The reformers had to find a source of authority more impressive, more credible, and more venerable than 'the Church' as then perceived. They found one by setting up the authority of 'the Word' *against* that of an institutional church which they later denounced as hopelessly corrupt and antichristian. They borrowed from the Renaissance humanists by identifying that 'Word' with the source, the original text, the canonical Scripture. This 'scriptural principle' is sometimes seen as a second fundamental pillar of the Reformation, alongside the theology of salvation.[2]

1. *The Church and Scripture*

In the later Middle Ages the Church had conserved Scripture, and Scripture had validated the Church. The reformers broke this coherence when they set up Scripture, the 'Word of God', *against* the words of the Church, a mere invention of men. They insisted that Scripture was the rule by which to judge the Church; and that, inverting this proper order, the Roman Church had set itself up as the *master* of Scripture. It had arrogated to itself the power to control, limit, alter, or augment the corpus which it had the right only to preserve and to obey. Whether the accusation was just or fair does not for the moment matter; the leading reformers emphasized it repeatedly.

Luther did not begin by opposing Scripture to *all* human agents. In the early months of the indulgence crisis he thought he was opposed only to a corrupt minority within the Church: hence his initial courteous letter to Albrecht of Mainz, his appeal first to Pope Leo X and then to a General Council, before he insisted at the Worms *Reichstag* that, since popes and councils had often erred and contradicted each other, only the authority of the Bible itself could convince him that he should recant.[3] Before that point, however, he had already set scriptural authority against the opinions of Aristotle, scholastic theologians, or specific decretals which he regarded as erroneous.[4] Soon he asserted categorically that no one could judge or validate Scripture: 'The Pope, Luther, Augustine, Paul, or even an angel from heaven—these should not be masters, judges, or arbiters but only witnesses, disciples, and confessors of Scripture'. Likewise Zwingli, as early as 1522, protested that 'those who make themselves, that is, men, the arbiters of Scripture, make a mockery of trust in the Spirit of God by their design and pretension, seeking to wrest and force the Scriptures according to their own folly'. Bucer drew some complex analogies with messengers of a prince carrying letters with his mandate: did the envoys validate the prince's letter, or vice versa? On this basis he ridiculed the notion that 'the Church gives Scripture its authority, has power over Scripture, can change Scripture'.[5] As for the scholastics' favourite text from Augustine, that he 'would not have believed the Gospel had not the authority of the catholic church moved [him]', Luther, Bucer, and Calvin removed this obstacle by pointing out the context of the statement (so often ignored in medieval study of Augustine). Augustine had written to confute Manichean abuse of Scripture, and was saying that unbelievers could not be convinced by Scripture unless they credited the Church with conserving it; he was not suggesting that Scripture needed the Church to give it its authority for Christians.[6]

All doctrines, then, had to be tested in the light of Scripture, and rejected if they were inconsistent with it. Yet *something* was needed to decide what was proper use of Scripture: Scripture allowed interpretations as diverse as human ingenuity. If an authority in the visible, tangible sense of a pope or a council was unacceptable, what was the alternative? For Luther, the answer (apparently) was a principle. The Scriptures, despite their various characteristics and the combination of 'law' and 'Gospel' in each of the two Testaments, had one subject: Christ. For Luther, 'Christ' meant not miracles, nor yet ethical advice, but the promises contained in Christ's mission and atonement. In other words, the whole Bible was about God's drawing men to himself through Christ. Now the way God did so, for Luther, was by the promise of justification through free grace, as we have seen. Put very baldly, this seems to have meant that Luther interpreted

Scripture, and validated its pronouncements, according to whether they illuminated and confirmed his primary doctrine of salvation.

This (logically rather circular) principle led Luther to make value-judgements about particular books of the Bible. In his early prefaces to the translated New Testament in 1522, he wrote that some books of the New Testament bore specially faithful witness to the message of Christ: St John's Gospel and first Epistle, Paul's Epistles to the Romans, Galatians, and Ephesians, and 1 Peter. On the other hand, some either worked against the essential message (such as the Epistle of James, the 'very strawy Epistle' as he called it) or at least contributed nothing to it, like the Book of Revelation. Subsequently Luther tried to find some good to say even about those writings which he regarded as 'less apostolic'; but the order of priorities remained.[7] Luther was not unique in making value-judgments. All the major reformers rejected the Old Testament Apocrypha; several described how some books of the New Testament period had similarly been omitted from the canon. Zwingli shared Luther's doubts about the authority of the Book of Revelation.[8]

However, other reformers preferred not to set up one intellectual principle, or a 'special list' of approved books, as the key to the Bible. It became standard to appeal to the Holy Spirit as the guide and interpreter. Just as the first writers of the Scriptures were believed to have been 'inspired',[9] so it took an element of inspiration to preach and teach their meaning correctly. They were not like a secular text, to be understood by mere intellectual virtuosity. As Zwingli put it:

When the Word of God shines on the human understanding, it enlightens it in such a way that it understands and confesses the Word and knows the certainty of it ... Before I say anything or listen to the teaching of man, I will first consult the mind of the Spirit of God ... then you should reverently ask God for his grace, that he may give you his mind and Spirit, so that you will not lay hold of your own opinion but of his ... and then go to the written word of the Gospel.[10]

The Bible could not be understood 'in cold blood', so to speak. If 'historical faith' was not faith, so uninspired exegesis was no exegesis. Paul (said Bucer) advised believers to look for understanding not from the Church but from those specifically endowed with 'the gift of interpretation'. Calvin explained that the meaning of Scripture was made clear by God's direct action. To try to build faith by intellectual exercises was to 'do things backwards'; 'the testimony of the Spirit is more excellent than all reason ... God alone is a fit witness of himself in his Word.'[11] Biblical interpretation was more like an act of prayer[12] than a philosophical exercise, let alone a process of human legislation, as the reformers alleged it had become for the Roman Church.[13] Soon the protestants had to defend themselves from the other flank, against those who seemed to formulate their doctrine all from the Spirit and none, or hardly any, from the Word. Such 'Spiritualists' committed the sin of despising the letter of Scripture, just as the catholics were held to have reduced interpretation to formalism.[14]

This vision of Scripture as the inspired Word, validated and interpreted by inspiration, transformed the question of 'Scripture and the Church's traditions'. It destroyed the coinherence of 'the Word' and the continuing 'tradition' of the Church (in any of the forms in which it was understood).[15] Nevertheless, not *all* previous authorities and writers were insignificant or without weight. The early Fathers had a persuasive force: Augustine, above all, was cited to support the reformers' views and to defend them from the accusation of novelty. They could however be disregarded if inconvenient; even Augustine could on occasion be criticized. To give the entire authority of the Church to the sayings of any one of the saints was an error; the Church was not infallible, and indeed was often self-contradictory; the notion of an 'overflow' of extra-scriptural truths was an unnecessary fiction.[16]

Evidently, the historians' slogan of 'Scripture alone' is by itself an insufficient and misleading way to describe the reformers' response to the Bible. Everyone who approached the Bible in the early modern period brought to it some set of presuppositions: traditional scholastics looked for propositions to handle according to set academic rules; humanists extracted a fund of ethical examples to follow; and protestant theologians found a powerful message of man's inadequacy and God's grace which they used to reinforce their primary insights. They also used Scripture as a witness against that Church within which they had begun their lives, with unheard-of thoroughness.

2. Reading and Understanding the Bible

If 'Scripture alone' was to bear such a weight of authority, it had to be interpreted; its text had to be conserved and purified; and it had to be presented to the people. 'Scripture alone' is a more complex topic than at first appears. Most reformers spent a phenomenal amount of time expounding and commenting on the Scriptures. Luther lectured on the Bible every academic year from 1513 until the eve of his death. Melanchthon (by profession a classicist) none the less published commentaries on Corinthians, John's Gospel, Colossians, and Romans. Bucer published his first commentaries on the Psalms in 1526, and lectured and commented on the Gospels, Romans, Ephesians, Zephaniah, and Judges throughout the rest of his career. Bullinger published his commentaries on the New Testament Epistles in 1537. Calvin issued from 1540 a stream of commentaries, soon translated and often reissued, on the greater part of the Old as well as the New Testaments. For the reformers scriptural interpretation or 'exegesis' was *the* theological activity.[17]

Luther, as noted earlier, regarded Christ as the sole content of all Scripture; both parts of the Bible contained both law and Gospel, though in differing measures and forms. So he interpreted the Bible according to the 'twofold literal' approach made popular by Lefèvre d'Étaples and Erasmus in the 1510s,[18] regularly interpreting the prophets and the psalmist as 'prophetically' proclaiming Christ. The early Luther distinguished between 'letter' and 'Spirit', between the cold, formal words and the living essence of the message, related to God's plan and Christ's work.[19] From 1519 onwards he simplified matters: the literal sense was the true one, and the literal sense *truly* had a spiritual meaning for Christians.[20] Zwingli contrasted 'letter' and 'Spirit' in various ways, but meant the 'bare letter' of Scripture to be interpreted both with the aid of, and in the light of, the 'Spirit' behind it. Bucer similarly combined an insistence on the role of the 'Spirit' in interpretation with a very strongly expressed preference for the literal meaning. In practice this would have meant, as it did for Bullinger, reading the biblical texts so as to make their message consistent and coherent with the contents of faith.[21] Calvin, perhaps the most serious and scholarly of all protestant commentators, insisted that the historical sense of a passage was vital to correct interpretation, but was convinced that the messages of the Old Testament applied to the dispensation of the New.[22]

By insisting on a literal interpretation with a prophetic message the reformers, like the humanist exegetes, largely abandoned the far-fetched seeking for 'fourfold allegories' which had been fashionable amongst preachers but distrusted by theologians in the Middle Ages.[23] However, they were not consistent or agreed in this attitude.[24] Apart from old-fashioned allegory, Zwingli, and even more Calvin, developed the notion of Old Testament figures being 'types' or 'pre-figurings' of New Testament personalities or ideas. Calvin often spoke of God 'accommodating' himself to human understanding by teaching spiritual things in earthly language. Hence, the Old Testament described spiritual goals and benefits in terms of earthly 'prefigurings' (the 'Promised Land', for example); in the new

Gospel, these had been replaced by an undisguised, direct spiritual message.[25]

Once one had decided how Scripture was to be used, the definitive text was still needed. The humanists bequeathed to the Reformation the conviction that the Bible had to be studied with the full panoply of textual skills, hitherto chiefly used to retrieve the texts of classical authors. Valla and Erasmus had shown that the Bible could not be studied in the Vulgate (up till that time the standard text) or indeed in any Latin translation whatever, without the risk of serious misunderstandings.[26] So the theologian needed to know the language of the original Scriptures, and to correct its text. Concepts such as 'grace' or 'penance', defined and expressed in Latin, had carried much weight in the past. By showing that the resonances of a Latin word were absent from its Greek or Hebrew equivalent, much theological tradition could be pared away. Textual corrections could be used both to question particular passages of accepted texts, or the traditionally received date or authorship of an entire book of the Bible. Luther thus doubted the apostolicity of some of the later Epistles in the New Testament; most reformers denied that Paul wrote the Epistle to the Hebrews.[27]

The reformers' translations of the Bible were also shaped by their scholarship. There had been vernacular Bibles in the late Middle Ages in plenty, but the translations had often been inaccurate and heavily overlaid with commentary. The reformers prided themselves on producing versions as close to what they conceived to be the spirit of the author as possible, with reference to Greek and Hebrew originals. However, the reformers did not translate for the sake of pure detached scholarship, as the humanists may have. Defending his translating methods in 1530, Luther justified adding the word 'alone' to his translation of Romans 3: 28 ('we conclude that a man is justified by faith *alone*') partly with reference to native German idioms; but also in terms of his principal dogma.[28] In other words, the reformer arrived at his beliefs (through Scripture) and then interpreted and translated Scripture as it best conformed to those beliefs. Since the reformers believed so intensely that their dogmas contained the essential Gospel, they could not have been expected to handle the text in isolation from their message.

Once the Bible had been corrected, translated, and interpreted, then (and only then, one might say!) it was offered to the people. Since the reformers appealed to Scripture as their source of authority, they represented themselves to their audience as proclaiming the 'truths' of Scripture, instead of the inventions and fictions of the Roman Church.[29] Such remarks cannot be taken exactly at face value. The call from laymen for the 'truths of Scripture' as opposed to the 'fables of men' was a chestnut dating from long before the Reformation which the protestants were only too glad to latch on to.[30] The reading of the Bible had never actually been *forbidden* to laymen, whether in Latin or in translation, by the Church as a whole in the Middle Ages.[31] In any case, it was not the Bible unadorned which the reformers offered, but the Bible as understood in the light of a particular insight.

There was always a risk that unlearned people who read only a small part of the Bible would fly off into realms of fantasy, and devise exotic new ideas for themselves on the basis of their reading. The scholastics dealt with this problem by teaching that 'implicit faith' absolved the believer of need to know and understand every detail of the Church's teaching; obedience and assent to the institutional Church would guarantee eventual salvation.[32] Renaissance humanists, on the contrary, had assumed that the Bible could safely be handled by those only barely literate, because they would extract from it only moral exhortations and examples of virtues to follow: in other words, that they would react to the Bible as the northern humanists did. Erasmus, therefore, wrote in the preface to his 1516 New Testament that it was desirable for the uneducated to read the (simple) truths of Scripture in their own language.[33]

In the controversy over 'free will' between Erasmus and Luther the boot was firmly on the other foot: Erasmus professed that he would subscribe to what the Church taught 'whether I grasp what it prescribes or not'; that one should not 'through irreverent inquisitiveness rush into those things which are hidden, not to say superfluous', such as God's foreknowledge or man's ability to work for his own salvation, but concentrate on those moral injunctions which were plain to all; and that some truths, even if theologically acceptable, ought not to be proclaimed to the world at large for fear of giving offence to the multitude. Luther insisted that those issues which Erasmus called 'superfluous' were on the contrary essential for any believer who wished to worship God truly. God might in certain respects be hidden and inscrutable, but Scripture was, to the inspired reader, perfectly plain in every detail. 'Those things which are either contained in *or proved by* Holy Writ are not only plain, but also salutary, and can therefore safely be published, learned, and known, as indeed they ought to be.'[34]

However, it was one thing for a qualified theologian to publish his expositions of Scripture to the world; quite another for the people to read Scripture for themselves *without* the help of a specialized interpreter. The

Reformation, while appearing to set the Scriptures before everyone, in fact imposed a number of 'filters' designed to protect them from inexpert handling. First of all, Scripture revealed itself *by* the Spirit, but *through* the Word. The Bible, the authoritative source of all doctrine, could only be understood correctly with the aid of linguistic, historical, and other scholarly skills, which were the specialist's privilege.[35] Secondly, preaching the Word was the common, not the individual, property of Christians. Handling the Bible was the proper task of the specialist appointed by the community to equip himself for that job.[36] Thirdly, the vast didactic output of the reforming writers themselves—from simple, short catechisms and primers for children to vast treatises like the *Institutes* for theological students and expert ministers—was consciously intended to prepare, orientate, and, one might say, prejudice the believer before he tackled the text of Scripture himself.[37]

In the very beginning, Luther may have believed that ordinary fathers of households could both instruct their families, read the Bible to them, and exercise moral discipline over them. If this was so, he also believed that such ordinary laymen needed to be thoroughly instructed first. His reaction to what he felt was the premature reform of worship at Wittenberg in 1522[38] shows how much he wished to convince by *teaching* before altering outward structures. He pressed for the setting up of sufficient schools to broaden knowledge of the biblical languages. He later realized that even *with* such teaching, the common people could barely cope with such intellectual demands.[39] Later reformers insisted that ordinary people needed to have the Bible elucidated for them by experts—that is, protestant ministers. Heinrich Bullinger of Zürich insisted on this in a sermon published in 1549. Those people who claimed 'that the Scriptures ought indeed to be read of all men ... so that every man may lawfully invent and choose to himself such sense as every one shall be persuaded in himself to be most convenient ... altogether condemn the order received of the churches, whereby the minister of the church doth expound the scriptures to the congregation'. Scripture was 'difficult or obscure to the unlearned, unskilful, unexercised, and malicious or corrupted wills'. Christ himself expounded the Scriptures in the synagogue. 'We therefore, the interpreters of God's holy word, and faithful ministers of the church of Christ, must have a diligent regard to keep the scriptures sound and perfect, and to teach the people of Christ the word of God sincerely.'[40] When the Reformation settled down, students—never mind ordinary laymen—were commonly taught the various formal catechisms (such as those produced by Luther in 1529, or Calvin in 1545, and by innumerable other protestant writers) for several years *before* they were let loose on the Bible. Indeed, in some cases only the more able students who proved competent in Greek would be allowed to read the Bible for themselves.[41]

'Scripture alone' needs to be understood in a particular, technical light. Protestantism was neither crudely fundamentalist, nor radically democratic in offering the Scriptures to the people without restraint. 'Scripture alone' only makes sense if one bears in mind that (*a*) the phrase connoted a conscious desire to *oppose* parts of a 'tradition' which was seen as pernicious; and (*b*) that 'Scripture' for the protestants meant 'Christ', and 'Christ' meant their version of the Gospel message. 'Scripture alone' was handmaiden both to their polemic and to their theory of salvation.

10

The Reformers' Message
The Church

The reformers stabilized their movement by replacing the authority of the old Church with the authority of self-interpreting Scripture. For basically the same reasons of self-preservation, they had to find an alternative to the organic community of the western Church consistent with their principles. Their vision of the Church evolved and became more sophisticated as time went by. On the theoretical level, three groups of major questions had to be addressed. First, if 'the Church' was not the unity of Roman Christendom, then what was it, and how could one be sure that one was within it? Secondly, what kind of 'ministers' should the Church have? Thirdly, how should the Christian community relate to the secular state?

1. *The 'Community of the Faithful'*

Since the reformers believed in the 'Holy Catholic Church' of the creeds, they had somehow to define a 'Church' which remained universal and holy even while they condemned Rome, its hierarchy, and its priests with ever greater ferocity. All the leading protestant theologians taught that the true, universal 'Church' was essentially the aggregate of all those Christians who *truly* believed; all those, separated by time and place, who had received the gift of faith and were integrated into God's scheme of salvation. The 'true' Church was both the 'community of the faithful', and (since faith was given by God's election) the 'body of the elect'.[1] Accordingly Luther redefined the 'Communion of Saints' (*communio sanctorum*) referred to in the creeds, simply as those people, living or dead, who belonged to the elect. Since sinners were only 'holy' in the sense that an 'alien' righteousness was draped over them, the 'saints' were simply the community of true believers.[2] This definition of the Church as the 'Community of the Faithful' was shared by such other reformers as Melanchthon, Zwingli, Bucer, Bullinger, and Calvin.[3] It was a cliché; Luther remarked in 1537 that a 'child of seven' knew that this was how one defined the Church.[4] Nor was it original to protestantism. The Church had been defined as the community of the 'elect' or 'predestined' in the Augustinian tradition throughout the Middle Ages. The doctrine that the essential, true Church was a 'mystical body', transcending the faults of some who seemed to belong to it, had originally been used to refute those who claimed the value of the sacraments depended on the worthiness of priests (who might be notorious sinners). Wyclif and Hus had used the definition to reject the Roman Church's claims to authority.[5]

If the elect were known only to God, some of the living might appear to be damned, yet in fact be predestined to be saved, and vice versa; society was full of 'hypocrites'. So, the community of *true* believers was unknowable, invisible, and an object of faith. If this 'invisible Church' were all there was, of course, there would be no basis for an organized Christian community. Yet leading reforming theologians were passionately concerned with the reform of religion in the *whole* community. They therefore spent more and more time describing the 'visible' as well as the 'invisible' aspects of the Church: the Church as known, experienced, and lived within, as well as the Church as 'believed'. Luther spoke of the Church having a purity and holiness 'hidden' under the veil of human failings and errors. On the other hand, the 'spiritual' Church was also visible, just as the preached Word was audible. Wherever the heritage of Word and sacrament was truly conserved *some* members of the true Church would be found (and this could even include medieval catholicism). However, the true Church could not exist in the total absence of faith.[6]

In the hands of most other reformers the relationship between 'visible' and 'invisible' Church was less dynamic, but clearer and more organized. Zwingli, for instance, wrote that there was 'one ... universal Church, and that this Church is either visible or invisible'; the visible Church was the body of all those who for the time being publicly professed faith in Christ, including hypocrites. A third sense of the Church was the local or regional church, which made up a part of the universal.[7] Bucer discussed the 'visible' Church very fully. For him it was the 'usual' means by which the Spirit governed and guided the Christian community.[8] Calvin added to Bucer's ideas a characteristic argument that, since human nature was inadequate without help to grow in faith, God had 'accommodated' himself to believers' needs by offering a visible structure in which they could grow in 'sanctification'. The believer could not know which of the members of the visible Church were indeed saved, but should charitably assume that those who joined in the life of the community were of the elect.[9]

The reformers' view of the Church rejected the idea that the 'visible Church' could be indissolubly linked to one institution with a fallible human being at its head and a corruptible hierarchy as its leadership. The 'universal', 'visible' Church was the aggregate of the regional churches, the 'essential' body within which Christ was preached. How, then, could one *know* which were true and authentic examples of such churches? The answer emerged that the true church could be seen wherever certain 'marks' or 'signs' were present in its conduct and principles. Luther suggested in 1520 that Christian baptism and the preaching of the Gospel were visible signs that some Christians would be present in such a church. These criteria proved that *some* believers were present; they did not validate the Church as a whole. Roman Catholicism could therefore be said to have 'marks of the Church' in this sense. Elsewhere he defined such signs as 'baptism, the bread [the Eucharist], and most important of all the Gospel'. In the Augsburg Confession Melanchthon similarly insisted that the Church was present wherever 'the Gospel is rightly preached and the sacraments are rightly administered'. Later, in 1539, Luther added to the list of 'signs': besides the Word and sacraments there were the office of the keys [discipline], the presence of ministers and offices in the Church, prayer, the public praise of God and the 'cross' of temptation and persecution.[10]

Luther gradually moved from regarding the 'signs' as indications of the presence of *some* Christians, to taking them as a sign that a given church *as a whole* was basically sound. He may have been influenced in this by Melanchthon and perhaps even by Bucer, with their greater concern for the education and discipline of a Christian population. Bucer wrote in the early 1520s that a church was present where the Gospel was preached and heard, and where people were subject to Christ. In the tract *On the True Care of Souls* of 1538 he seems to have added discipline (moral supervision) to these essential 'marks': he defined the Church as a 'community where there reigns the Word and the sacraments, love and discipline'. Discipline remained a primary concern of Bucer's, though by 1550 he restricted the vital marks to the hearing of the voice of Christ, the ministry of teaching, suitable ministers, lawful dispensation of the sacraments, and righteousness and holiness of life.[11] For Calvin the two basic 'marks' were the pure preaching of the Word and the scriptural administration of the sacraments. The presence of these defined their possessor as a genuine church, deserving due obedience and respect. One should not therefore separate from a church on the pretence either that it taught some minor and insignificant heresy, or that it included some scandalous members.[12]

The protestant doctrine of the Church, then, campaigned on two fronts: against sectarian exclusivism and hierarchical catholicism. As the reformers grew more sure that the 'marks' of the Church were valid criteria by which to judge a whole community, so they hardened their attitude towards the status of Rome. Luther, perhaps surprisingly, was slow to reject Rome outright. He departed from the traditional liturgies and rituals of the Church slowly and hesitantly. At first he distinguished between sound and corrupt aspects of catholicism; even between the (partly redeemable) traditional church and the (corrupt) papacy.[13] As protestantism grew into an entire, self-sufficient church, it identified surviving catholicism completely with the papacy. Calvin turned the notion of 'marks of the Church', which for Luther were a reason to continue to respect *some* catholics, into a reason for consigning the Roman Church bag and baggage to perdition:

Instead of the ministry of the Word, a perverse government compounded of lies rules there, which partly extinguishes the pure light, partly chokes it. The foulest sacrilege has been introduced in place of the Lord's Supper. The worship of God has been deformed by a diverse and unbearable mass of superstitions. Doctrine (apart from which Christianity cannot stand) has been entirely buried and driven out ... In withdrawing from deadly participation in so many misdeeds, there is accordingly no danger that we may be snatched away from the church of Christ.[14]

This change in attitudes reflected the progressive hardening of outlook on all sides under political pressure. As the protestant churches were forced to frame their own structures and ideas entirely without reference to the Church of Rome, so they denounced it more absolutely.

2. *Sacrificing Priests to Preaching Ministers*

In the Middle Ages the priesthood was set apart from and above other Christians, by the 'indelible character' of sacramental ordination, its legal privileges, ritual celibacy, clerical dress and tonsure, and above all by the sacrificial and miraculous ritual of the mass.[15] The assumption underlying all these, that God consistently transmitted holiness and power through predictable channels, was quite alien to the reformers' principles. For them, God did not invest certain institutions or certain kinds of people with palpable 'holiness' to do with as they wished: he gave grace inscrutably to whom he chose. No artificially separate class of people could presume to a higher degree of God's favour. As early as 1520 Luther denied that priestly orders made someone a superior kind of Christian:

Baptism, gospel, and faith alone make us spiritual and a Christian people ... the Pope ... can never make a man into a Christian or into a spiritual man by [the rituals of ordination] ... He might well make a man into a hypocrite or a humbug and blockhead, but never a Christian or spiritual man ... we are all consecrated priests through baptism ... whoever comes out of the water of baptism can boast that he is already a consecrated priest, bishop, and pope.[16]

The polemical flourish with which Luther enunciated this 'Priesthood of all believers' can easily mislead. Luther was writing to secular powers who felt (legally) impotent to redress well-known faults in the Church, because the clergy claimed that they, as the 'spiritual estate', were set apart from and above the rest, that only they could judge themselves, only they could reform themselves.[17] However, if any one Christian was as much a 'priest' as another, every Christian was equally entitled and equally competent to take the Church's welfare in hand. However, such 'priesthood' was to be held by believers not individually but in common with their neighbours. Repeatedly Luther emphasized that the 'priesthood' of all Christians did not give anyone and everyone the right to dash out without further ado and start preaching the Word or administering the sacraments. Such actions would usurp the *common* rights of the community, which must be administered by consent; such usurpation would lead to chaos. To exercise priestly authority someone needed proper installation; once installed, he held his position only so long as he discharged its function, and could be removed if he ceased to do so.[18]

A 'priest', for the reformers, was an equal member of a community who happened to be entrusted with the special task of preaching the word of God and seeing to the needs of the Church. He was a functionary, not the holder of a title or a piece of property. Therefore Luther, and subsequent protestants, called the office of preaching a 'ministry', a word connoting the work of a *servant*. These arguments—that the ministry was only a function, to be performed by a specialist—were echoed by Zwingli and became definitive.[19] What *were* those proper functions? Very broadly, one could divide them into preaching, dispensing the sacraments, and pastoral work. In Luther's writings these aspects were often implicit rather than clearly laid out. When defining marks of the Church in 1539, Luther listed 'offices of the Church' after the Word, sacraments, and discipline, implying that these three duties were the scope of the Church's officers. Such officers derived their authority both from their communities (since they carried the delegated responsibility of the common 'priesthood') and also from God, since officers of the Church had been prescribed in the New Testament.[20]

About the same time, Martin Bucer articulated a detailed vision of the different offices in the Church. In his biblical commentaries of 1536 he suggested that the Church needed, besides ministers to preach the Word and offer the sacraments, doctors to teach, deacons to see to the relief of the poor, and 'elders' able to maintain spiritual order and discipline within the community. In the *True Care of Souls* of 1538 he claimed that the order of pastors, elders, and deacons was necessary by divine right.[21] Calvin (based at Strasbourg during 1538–41) developed from Bucer's example the 'orders of the ministry' later identified with Calvinism. Some ministries of the New Testament were temporary and now lost, like those of apostles and evangelists; two however, 'doctors' charged with preserving pure belief, and 'pastors' charged with a whole community, were permanent. For the latter the titles of 'bishop', 'presbyter', 'pastor', or 'minister', were interchangeable. In addition to these ministers of the Word, each community needed a 'senate' of elders to correct moral faults within it; and a body of 'deacons' to oversee the gathering of alms and the care of the poor.[22]

From where did such ministers and officers derive their authority? Traditionally, authority came from the laying-on of hands in episcopal ordination, which conferred the Holy Spirit and linked the ordinand with a 'succession' reaching back to the Apostles.[23] This doctrine, like all the others which linked grace consistently to an organic institution, was discarded. In its place came the reformers' doctrine of the 'true call' or 'vocation' to the ministry. Luther wrote of two calls, an 'inner' one to the conscience, and an 'outward' one, expressed through the community and carried out in orderly fashion. In the early 1520s Luther seems actually to have envisaged congregations electing their own pastor; later on he reverted to more traditional views on patronage. Calvin echoed the distinction between the two calls, and likewise Luther's preference for 'due order'. He proposed that pastors should be chosen with the consent of the people (meaning the congregation) and with the oversight of other pastors. This plan corresponded, on the theoretical level, to the way in which local consistories, colloquies, and synods, and ultimately the Genevan Company of Pastors supervised the conduct of ministers in the French-speaking Calvinist churches.[24]

Sweeping practical consequences flowed from the reformers' changes to the priesthood. First, hierarchy and order went into the melting-pot. If the 'Church' was simply the aggregate of local churches decently observing the 'marks' of the Church, then the paraphernalia of prelates, international law-making, and of course the papacy itself, could be entirely discarded.

The local church could become bounded and defined by the local political unit: a city-state, a province of a federation, a great noble's estate, or a kingdom. Hence Church and State relations were put in question.[25] Secondly, the ritual separateness of priests was done away with, along with compulsory celibacy for priests, and of all forms of monasticism. Asceticism was not just morally dubious or superstitious: the vow itself rested partly on the notion of 'merit' and partly on the belief that God was pleased with a form of service which he had neither instituted nor approved. The 'religious life' was therefore to be taken out of the cloister and into the life of the everyday, married, householding, pious individual, regardless of whether that individual was a minister or an ordinary lay person.[26] Thirdly, the new ministers' tasks were both simpler and more difficult than the old priests'. All forms of religious activity besides congregational ministry were at best unnecessary. Bishops ruling great tracts of land, and monks or chantry priests saying prayers with no one but themselves to hear, were alike redundant. The old Church's peripheral tasks in social, legal, or educational affairs ceased to be 'religious' as they had been.[27] On the other hand, the minister *was* now expected to minister; he had to be present, functioning, and above all *qualified* according to much more demanding standards. To preach and discipline effectively required much more train- ing, more books, and more character than simply to recite the mass and the Hours to an inattentive or indeed empty church, relying on the mysterious power of the sacrament. By stripping away the accumulation of priests without parish duties, the reformers realized the dream of 'reformers' like Geiler: they put the talented graduate back into the parish. Whether the talented graduate would succeed in preaching and the moral supervision of people used to the more lax rule of their mass priest was quite another matter.

3. *Church and State*

The medieval papacy sought political prestige and influence to protect the western Church. The reformers rejected the popes' claims to a 'primacy' unknown to the early Church, to worldly sovereignty over lands and even rulers, to be (as Luther put it) vicars of Christ triumphant in heaven, who needed no substitute, instead of vicars of Christ the suffering servant of men on earth.[28] Instead of making spiritual activities autonomous, the papacy had made their own caste of people a race apart, repudiating their role as subjects and citizens, using physical punishments to domineer over others.[29] However, the reformers also opposed the view of sixteenth-century anabaptists (and of some medieval heretics) that the true believer and the world of sinful men could and should have nothing whatever to do with each other. They condemned such perfectionist sectarianism—justly or unjustly—with the simple argument that no one knew for certain who the elect were, and no one within this life was wholly 'pure' and 'spiritual' anyway: so the idea that those who were 'saved' and 'spiritual' could form a community apart was absurd.[30]

Because the Church was neither a consecrated élite of clergy, nor a huddle of self-proclaimed 'godly', the European reformers had to rework the relationship between the local, regional, or national 'Church', and the secular power which already laid down the rules in everything except religion. As soon as the Reformation became in any way organized, it appealed to lawful worldly authority to protect and foster it.[31] In 1520 Luther reassured noblemen that religious renewal was indeed their business, and suggested an agenda. Leading reformers throughout the sixteenth century dedicated their tracts to secular rulers who might (they hoped) implement their proposals.[32] In return much protestant political theory stressed how Christians ought to obey such rulers.[33] On the other hand, the Reformation was not to be left to the mercy of worldly politicians. The realm of the spirit concerned spiritual things and was distinct and autonomous from politics. Concepts such as the 'headship of Christ in his Church', and 'the law of God' were invoked to restrain politicians from tampering at will with the reformed Church. In practice protestant ministers claimed to decide the (technical) question of what the Church ought to be like, and expected the politicians to do as they advised. Worldly power was given to rulers 'to build up the Church, not to tear it down'.

The reformers recognized no separation of persons in Church–State relations, only a separation of functions to be observed within the unitary community. Luther's ideas on Church and State can only be understood in the light of a body of ideas known as the 'Doctrine of the Two Kingdoms and the Two Governments', stated at its clearest in 1523. The (much debated) meaning of this doctrine seems to be as follows. God had instituted two orders of being, with two regimes or forms of government on earth. One, the 'realm of the spirit', dealt only with the relationship between Christ and the believer's soul. This (spiritual) realm operated through the Word, not through any institution. The second, the 'realm of the World', was the order of secular society, operating by visible structures, published rules, and coercive force. This second 'regime' applied to all men irrespective of their belief or unbelief. Confusingly, Luther also wrote of

'God's kingdom' being opposed and at war against the 'kingdom of the devil' in the world: *both* the forms of government were means by which God restrained men from sin. Luther insisted that the Christian, the believer, the member of the elect, should be subordinate to both worldly *and* spiritual government, partly as an act of charity and 'Christian freedom'; but also because, as 'at once a sinner and justified', he always contained in himself those sinful elements which needed worldly government to restrain and suppress them. Conversely, everyone needed the 'spiritual regime', because the Word and the promises had to be preached to all.[34]

Luther at first thought that the Word would achieve reform by itself, and did not define what kind of real, visible authority was competent to introduce religious change. His theory had the defect that for secular authority (the prince) to interfere in religious matters amounted to a 'confusion of the two realms', one of the things Luther most deplored. Yet, if the spiritual realm (the Church) could not and must not coerce, how could it introduce new laws? When in 1527 the elector of Saxony had to authorize a visitation of the Saxon churches, Luther justified the step as an 'emergency' use of the universal priesthood: the elector was here acting as a christian 'emergency bishop', not as a secular ruler. However, Melanchthon became progressively more positive about the prince's right and duty, as the 'chief member of the Church', to authorize reform. Luther's complex and sometimes foggy theory lagged far behind practical reality: ultimately, the Lutheran churches became very largely departments of state in their respective territories, according to the principle later known as 'Erastianism'.[35]

Luther was exceptional in that he saw 'the Word' as an experience above all for the individual soul. Almost all other leading reformers emphasized the communal character of the Church, and the need to define its position *vis-à-vis* the secular state. This difference of emphasis (though seen in later Lutherans) appeared from the first in the so-called 'reformed' tradition of Zwingli, Oecolampadius, and Bucer. All three worked in cities where secular authority (in this case the council) had a long tradition of claiming to supervise religious affairs. Zwingli regarded both Church and council as servants of God's rule over the community. The council was bound to pass secular laws consistent with Scripture, to heed the advice of the Word (as interpreted) in religious matters, and to back up the Church by seeing that the Word was duly preached. Through the 1520s, under pressure from anabaptist separatists, Zwingli emphasized more and more the power and duty of the council to act in religious matters. However, this interconnection of the two spheres did not confuse them: the preacher (or 'prophet') handled the subject-matter of religion, while the community, as perhaps expressed in the council, legislated in outward, formal matters. Once again, theory lagged behind practice: Zwingli needed the council's assistance.[36] After his death in 1531 his successor Bullinger relied on the magistrates to discipline the Church.[37]

Joannes Oecolampadius set out the classic 'reformed' attitude to Church–State relations at Basle in 1529. From the establishment of a reformed Church there, he proposed that the structures of Church and State should be clearly separated. The religious congregation was to discipline its members, using only exhortation and spiritual sanctions. Respected laymen, some representing the congregation and some the magistracy, were to carry out the disciplinary functions of the Church. He failed to convince the Basle authorities; but gave an example to other reformers.[38] After working with Oecolampadius to introduce the Reformation at Ulm in 1531, Bucer concluded that a secular magistrate must have different priorities from the moral ones proper to a pastor: so the Church needed its own independent structures to carry out discipline. In the early 1530s Bucer attempted unsuccessfully to turn Strasbourg's *Kirchenpfleger* (officers appointed by the council to keep the churchmen in line) into lay ruling elders of the Church. In his *True Care of Souls* in 1538 he committed himself to instituting a separate disciplining eldership, in the face of relentless opposition both from the council and from some of his brother clergymen.[39]

Calvin drew momentous lessons from his contacts with Bucer during 1538–41. In a crucial chapter inserted in the *Institutes* in 1543, he passed over in silence any question of the secular power contributing its say or its authority in Church offices: the Church was to act independently in its own sphere.[40] Two years before, Calvin had begun to translate this principle into practice in the celebrated *Ecclesiastical Ordinances of the Church of Geneva*. In these ordinances the fourfold offices of the Church (pastors, doctors, elders, deacons) were again set out; provision was made for elders and pastors to meet on a regular basis at local levels, and more occasionally in a synod of all the Genevan clergy.[41] In practice the Genevan church's autonomy was severely restricted by the typical determination of local magistrates to keep a firm hold over something as vital to the order and morale of a city as its Church.[42] In theory, however, clerics and laymen would co-operate in ruling the church, but solely within 'Church' structures: elders ruled the church because they were elders, not because they might also happen to be local magistrates. Thereafter many local Calvinist churches organized themselves in a hierarchy of synods (local 'consistory' or 'session', then district 'presbytery', 'colloquy', or 'classis', then provincial or even national synods) without (in the classic phrase) 'tarrying for the magistrate [to approve]'. In The Netherlands, France, Scotland, and for a brief period England, the parallel structures of State and Church envisaged in the reformers' theory came close enough to reality to arouse the jealousy and mistrust of monarchs and politicians. It also allowed a people to put pressure on their rulers to introduce the Reformation; until such a vision of State–Church relations existed, this kind of pressure had been restricted to the compact society of corporate towns.[43]

I I

The Reformers' Message
Sacraments

The sacraments were the most solemn of the rituals whereby the medieval Church claimed to mediate divine grace reliably and predictably to the believer. They were also alleged to be based on Scripture; two, baptism and the Eucharist, seemed to have a clear origin or 'institution' in the New Testament. These two aspects posed a serious problem for the consistency of the entire Reformation movement. The reformers insisted that salvation came as an unmerited free gift direct from God, apprehended through the preaching of the Word; therefore *any* rituals which claimed to 'confer grace', let alone to 'win merit', should have been drastically curtailed or entirely abolished. However, because they also insisted on the supreme authority of Scripture, they were obliged to find a role for ceremonies and symbols which had a precedent and warrant in the New Testament. In short, the reformers were saddled with the sacraments; the inner logic of their basic theme, which gave the rest of their teaching such tight logical coherence, on this topic gave them conflicting messages.

Thus the divergent preferences of Luther and Zwingli came into play. Luther's instinct was to preserve as much of the old order as was not clearly opposed to his vision of the truth, at least in the first instance. Zwingli's instinct was only to retain what was clearly necessary to conform to his vision of God's plan.[1] In the very beginning, in the 1520s, these differences in instinct and preference—whatever their rationale on the level of theology—kept the various Reformation movements separate.[2] For the rest of the sixteenth century, however, there were not simply two distinct 'schools' of thought, one Lutheran and the other Zwinglian, on the sacraments. Rather there were 'ultra' Lutherans at one extreme, and rather fewer dedicated followers of Zwingli at the other; and a huge mass of more moderate Lutheran and 'reformed' theologians in between, some trying to find mutually acceptable middle positions, others deliberately fanning the flames of theological controversy.

This chapter will sketch out four areas of Reformation thought: first, it will set out what the reformers claimed that a 'sacrament' really was, and what it did; then it will examine in turn the two 'biblical' sacraments which the reformers retained; and finally consider the five traditional sacraments which they rejected.

1. *Defining 'Sacraments'*

On this issue like others, the reformers began by rewriting the medieval theologians' glossary. Most agreed on two basic components in a true 'sacrament': a promise of God, to which a sign was added. Thus Luther wrote 'to every promise of his, God usually adds some sign as a memorial'; Melanchthon: 'Christ instituted [sacraments] as signs to signify his promise'; Calvin: a sacrament is 'an outward sign by which the Lord seals on our consciences the promise of his good will'.[3] This definition defied traditional teaching along classic Reformation lines. For late medieval thinkers a sacrament consisted of a 'matter', the material element or action, combined with a 'form', the correct verbal blessing, which if added to the appropriate 'intention' on the part of the participants, conferred 'grace' on those who received, so long as they did not impose an 'obstacle' of intent to sin.[4] For Luther and the rest, therefore, this interpretation wrongly derived grace and merit from a work performed apart from faith. In the Reformation, the sacraments depended for effect not upon rituals or intentions, but upon (given) faith.[5] Since they worked through faith, sacraments had to be publicly proclaimed: they were, in effect, simply a different way of setting forth the Word. Therefore the late medieval custom, by which the consecration of the Eucharist was thought to contain words so holy that they should be whispered by the priest into the elements on the altar without laymen even hearing, was repugnant. Every reformed sacrament had to be accompanied by public, explicit preaching of its purpose in the vernacular.[6]

However, what the sacrament *did* remained unclear: did the recipient of a sacrament derive a specific benefit from it? And if so, was this human ritual not in some sense presuming to 'manipulate' God's promises? Luther seems to have been clear that since 'where there is a divine promise, there faith is required',[7] the sacraments should be offered (by Christ's institution) in the Church, and they would 'work' through the faith given by God to the individual believer. 'The sacraments were instituted to nourish faith'.[8] Indeed, faith was so powerful that it could operate outside the sacraments as well. Always, of course, the sacrament was a sign of God giving something to man: it was not the Church giving something to its members to make them acceptable to God.[9]

The problem with this line of reasoning was that, if the Word and faith could operate without the sacraments, then why have sacraments at all? Zwingli resolved this worry thus: 'Christ abolished external things, so that we are not to hope in them or to look to them for justification ... Yet to us ... he has bequeathed two ceremonies, two external signs ... undoubtedly he has done this as a concession to our frailty.'[10] Calvin (who modified Zwingli on much else) took over this vision of the sacraments partly as God 'tempering himself to our capacity ... condescending to lead us to himself even by these earthly elements'.[11] Zwingli went far further than most in opposing the traditional catholic dogma that sacraments correctly performed automatically, even magically, conferred benefits. Sacraments were 'signs' of holy things, not those holy things themselves. Taking up baptism or the communion was a public statement of intent, like wearing the badge of a member of the Swiss confederation. To expect benefits from the sacraments was to make them into Gods.[12] At the very most, Zwingli later allowed that they 'represented' holy things by analogy, and as such were aids to the contemplation of faith.[13] The early Bucer likewise denied that sacraments achieved anything *of themselves* to aid salvation, calling them 'protestations' and 'memorials' of God's blessing. Calvin later struck a balance. One could say that sacraments 'confirmed and increased' faith in the sense that they were one of three means—the teaching of the Word, the confirmation of the sacraments, and the direct illumination of the Spirit—by which God enlightened believers. Sacraments could be a channel for the work of the Holy Spirit.[14]

These debates set the scene for decades of mutual misunderstanding and recrimination among reformers. On one hand they strove against a 'magical' belief that sacraments invariably, predictably, mechanically conferred grace. On the other their logic threatened completely to obliterate a biblical ministry. Luther's conservative view of the sacraments as 'nourishing' faith could be misunderstood as giving intrinsic, quasi-magical powers to the rituals themselves. Zwingli's destructive rationalistic critiques threatened to cut faith completely adrift from worship. The debates over baptism and the Eucharist illustrate these issues at work.

2. *Baptism: An Uncertain Role*

Applying their agreed criterion of a true 'sacrament', a divine promise with a sign attached, the reformers reduced the sacraments to two, baptism and the Eucharist, the only ones which were demonstrably instituted by Christ. Baptism raised the problems associated with an outward sign of a spiritual process: what did it actually 'achieve'? It also became the major issue between the mainstream or 'magisterial' reformers, who continued the traditional practice of baptizing infants, and most of the sectarian extremists known as 'anabaptists', who reserved baptism to adult believers and 'rebaptized' their followers, holding infant baptism to be meaningless. The variety of arguments with which the reformers defended their positions continuously from the mid-1520s testifies to their difficulties.

The reformers criticized the catholic view of baptism on two counts: it claimed too little for the sacrament in one way, and too much in another. Traditionally, baptism set the believer free from inherited 'original' sin; but after he sinned again in later life, he had to turn to further means of forgiveness, essentially the sacrament of penance. In St Jerome's phrase baptism was the 'first plank [clung to] after shipwreck', and penance the 'second plank' to which one turned after sin submerged the benefits of baptism.[15] For Luther and Melanchthon, the effects of baptism were permanent, of value throughout life. It promised salvation to those who believed and were baptized; it gave the sign of 'death and resurrection, that is, full and complete justification'.[16] Calvin likewise rejected the 'second plank' argument. Baptism was not so wiped out by sin that it should not be 'recalled to the memory of the sinner whenever he thinks of forgiveness of sins, so that from it he may gather himself together, take courage, and confirm his faith that he will obtain the forgiveness of sins, which has been promised to him in baptism'.[17] The importance of baptism, then, increased as the 'sacrament' of penance was abolished. Baptism *was* the 'sacrament of penance'; penance was 'nothing but a return to baptism'; baptism was 'a sufficient substitute for all the sacraments which we might need as long as we live'.[18]

However, baptism was not the magical, physical 'elimination' of one little parcel of sin, so much as the sign of its being no longer 'imputed'. This distinction was not always clear in Luther, who called 'the washing away of sins' 'too mild and weak ... to bring out the full significance of baptism'. Baptism signified *total* renewal of the soul, which (as seen earlier) was achieved by imputed righteousness and gradual regeneration.[19] As Calvin put it, 'baptism indeed promises to us the ... mortification of our sin, but not so that it no longer gives us trouble, but only that it may not overcome us ... if we faithfully hold fast to the promise given us ... in baptism, [traces of sin] shall not dominate'.[20] Zwingli went further to eliminate the idea that baptism 'removed' sin in some mechanical way. The sacrament, the water and the word, was for him still an 'external' thing which could not remit sin; forgiving sins was God's work alone. When the Bible spoke of 'living water' cleansing and saving the soul, it was really Christ, not baptism, which was meant. Zwingli persistently emphasized that the sacrament could not *give* faith or grace. He went further still, arguing against baptism washing away original sin by denying that such 'sin' conferred guilt in the first place. Guilt could not attach to the innate corruption of human nature: baptism could not 'cleanse children from a sin which they never had'.[21] Zwingli saw baptism as so 'external' a thing that he repeatedly called it 'an initiatory sign or pledge initiating us to a lifelong mortification of the flesh and engaging or pledging us like the soldier at his enlistment'.[22] Those who were baptized grew in 'sanctification' afterwards, like novices learning the rules of a monastic order as they wore its cowl.[23]

The reformers had some difficulty in describing the role which 'faith' played in baptism. In 1520 Luther agreed with tradition that the infant 'believed' through the faith of those who brought it for baptism, or indeed the faith of the Church as a whole. By 1525 he seems to have said that infants really had their own, individual faith: since faith was inspired, it could come to infants as well as adults.[24] Baptism (as nearly everyone, except Zwingli, agreed) in some way confirmed, increased, and stimulated faith, not of itself, but because of the promises appended to it and the action of the Spirit.[25] This argument, that children could acquire 'passive' belief, in the same sense that adults did, became crucial to the case against the anabaptists who reserved baptism to fully believing adults. Calvin insisted that while faith *usually* came through hearing and understanding, God could give faith however he chose, including giving justifying faith to children who died in infancy. Those who grew up would grow into an understanding of the baptism which they had received.[26]

The mainstream reformers used a host of other arguments to condemn the anabaptist practice of baptizing only professing adult members of their sect, and to justify continuing the traditional practice of routinely baptizing newborn infants into the Church community. Not all of these need detailed study. The reformers could not, of course, consistently argue from the traditions of the Church, and they admitted that there was no *specific* proof of the baptism of infants being prescribed in the New Testament. That point, as several insisted, proved nothing, since (for instance) the Bible did not specifically portray women as receiving the Eucharist either.[27] The most important reasons were first, that as baptism continued and simplified the Old Testament rite of circumcision, baptism likewise should be administered to infants.[28] Much more fundamentally, since the sacraments were about promises of God's goodness to man, rather than the other way around, those promises applied to children no less than to adults.[29] Finally, Zwingli's favourite argument was that the anabaptists insisted that those who were baptized should not only have full faith, but actually be able to live after baptism without sin. Such an attitude was not only 'works righteous' in a way repugnant to the reformers; it also contradicted the fundamental protestant insight that even the saved continued to sin throughout their lives. To exclude infants because they did not have the discretion to make such an undertaking was therefore absurd.[30]

However, it is reasonable to suppose that the reformers rejected believers' baptism not *because* of the sometimes rather specious analogies or arguments which they used, but for the much more fundamental reason that they were not about to found a sect rather than a community church. They insisted that the promises of the Gospel be preached and applied to everyone; they founded *churches*, not sects or heresies. Their traditional view of baptism mirrored their universal vision of reform itself.

3. *The Communion: A Bone of Contention*

The Lord's Supper, Eucharist, or communion is chiefly famous as the issue which produced the sharpest and most bitter disagreements between reformers who on many other topics were basically at one. It is sometimes said that it 'divided' the Reformation, though this is misleading: rather, disagreements over the communion brought differences of temperament and presuppositions into the open, and prevented an already diffuse movement from becoming united. Ironically, the reformers were overwhelmingly agreed in what they did *not* want: the catholic mass, with all its implications and appendages. Abolishing the old mass, and transforming it into a communion rite, was a major milestone wherever a reformed order was established.[31] Like baptism, the communion ritual was impeccably biblical, and a natural focus for worship. However, the essential reformed message did not help in positively defining what it was, how it worked, or what kind of 'reality' it represented. For that the reformers were thrust back on their diverse intellectual instincts and training: they produced, not two tidily opposed schools of thought, but decades of confusion, disagreement, and searches for acceptable compromise.

The features of the catholic mass which the reformers condemned are clear enough. Above all they rejected its claims to be a 'sacrifice', a 'good work' beneficial to the living and the dead.[32] For the reformers the idea that man could 'offer' anything to God to atone for human sin was an offence against Christ's unique, sole sacrifice on the Cross. From 1519 onwards Luther wrote vehemently against the idea of the mass as a 'good work' and a sacrifice conferring merit.[33] Zwingli was just as clear: Christ 'was offered up but once, wiped out all the sins of all men ... this faith is not offered up, but is an enlightenment from God'.[34] Melanchthon and Calvin distinguished between the 'sacrifices' of animal blood in the Old Testament which ended with Christ, and the 'sacrifices of thanks' which acknowledged God's benefits but did not *give* him anything.[35] Evidently, this rejection of the 'sacrificial' quality of the mass followed logically from the reformers' teachings on salvation.

However, other things were equally unacceptable. The adoration of the Eucharistic elements was (typically) not condemned at once by Luther, but steadily fell from favour as idolatrous.[36] Secondly, the reformers condemned the withholding of the wine from lay people (by which the sanctity of both the mass and the priesthood itself had been emphasized); it was a 'tyranny' and 'robbery' against the laity without warrant in Scripture or the early Church.[37] Much idolatry and superstition had grown up around the mass through misunderstandings of the dogma that the 'substance' of bread and wine was miraculously transformed into that of the body and blood of Christ, while the outward 'species' or 'accidents' remained unaltered: hence the crude cults of bleeding or indestructible hosts which proliferated before the Reformation.[38] Although the reformers disagreed over the sense (if any) in which Christ's body *was* present in the Eucharist, they agreed that it was *not* present according to the 'scholastic subtleties' of transubstantiation.[39]

What positive features were emphasized about the Eucharist? The reformers taught that the Eucharist most effectively portrayed and recalled Christ's sacrifice. It was, said Luther,

as if [Christ] were saying, 'I promise you ... the forgiveness of all your sins and life everlasting. And that you may be absolutely certain of this irrevocable promise of mine, I shall give my body and pour out my blood, confirming this promise by my very death, and leaving you my body and blood as a sign and memorial of this same promise'.[40]

Melanchthon wrote: 'With this bread and wine [Christ] attests that he accepts us, makes us his members, grants us forgiveness of sins.'[41] For Calvin, Christ in the Eucharist 'attests himself to be the life-giving bread upon which our souls feed unto ... immortality'.[42] Even Zwingli (finally) agreed in 1531: 'you come to the Lord's Supper to feed spiritually upon Christ, and when ... you share with your brethren in the bread and wine which arc now the *symbolic* body of Christ, then truly you eat him *sacramentally*, ... your soul being strengthened by the faith which you attest in the tokens.'[43] The reformers had different views of how often the Eucharist should be celebrated. Luther envisaged a regular weekly celebration, as of old, though whether all the congregation were to take communion so often is doubtful. Zwingli expected the evangelical communion to be offered perhaps three or four times a year. Calvin saw a weekly communion as ideal, though it was hard to enforce this in practice. *All* deplored the catholic custom of receiving only once a year, at Easter, and simply hearing mass the rest of the time.[44]

Finally, there was the question of just what it meant to say that Christ's body and blood were 'present' in the elements of bread and wine in the Eucharistic rite. This issue involved more mutual misunderstandings, clashes of character, and forced exegesis of Scripture, than almost any other issue of the Reformation. Luther described in 1520 his own anxieties on the issue; he had resolved them by concluding that 'real bread and real wine' remained on the altar, 'in which Christ's real flesh and real blood are present ... no less than the others assert them to be'. *Two* realities, then, were present simultaneously. The idea that the 'substances' of bread and wine were annihilated when the words of consecration were spoken was (he said) a novelty hatched out of scholastic philosophy, unknown to earlier Church Fathers. The two things, bread and body, could be present together just as fire and iron existed together in a red-hot iron, or the natures of man and God coexisted in Jesus. Beyond that he preferred not to speculate: 'let us not dabble in too much philosophy ... [Christ] desired to keep us in a simple faith, sufficient to believe that his blood was in the cup.'[45] Although Luther described the details variously, he clung to this essential insistence, that the *body* of Christ was physically, materially present in the Eucharist, ever afterwards. Controversy only led him to insist more strongly on the *bodily* presence which he believed the text required.[46]

It is impossible to separate the strife of ideas over the Eucharist from the context and the personalities which produced it.[47] From 1524 Luther's estranged and exiled Wittenberg colleague Andreas Karlstadt published tracts where he claimed that the words 'this is my body' in the Last Supper were used by Christ of his own body, not the bread. In general he separated Christ's sacrifice and the memorial ritual very sharply. Luther, already disgusted with Karlstadt because of his precipitate moves in altering worship at Wittenberg[48] and his tactlessness, despised him yet more on this issue. When Luther heard that Karlstadt's ideas were gaining adherents in Switzerland he was at once predisposed to listen no further.[49]

Karlstadt probably played no real part in shaping the ideas of Zwingli and Oecolampadius, though he did a great deal to prejudice Luther against them. After discovering, through a meeting with Hinne Rode (the ex-rector of the Hieronymus Gymnasium at Utrecht) in early 1524, a tract by Corneliszoon Hendrixzoon Hoen (d.1524) on the Eucharist,[50] Zwingli developed a distinctively new view of the Eucharistic presence, first clearly stated in a letter to Matthäus Alber of Reutlingen in November 1524.[51] From this point Zwingli drew a very sharp distinction between flesh and spirit, body and soul, Christ as divine and Christ as human: this distinction dominated and shaped the rest of his thought on the issue. On one hand, he insisted that the words 'this is my body', like many other such statements in the Bible, were a metonymy, a figure of speech which described a symbol as 'being' what it 'represented'. On the other hand, and in keeping with his general views on the sacraments, he regarded 'faith [as] the only true feeding on Christ'; the 'spiritual presence of Christ ... is not to be in any way identified with the element [the bread and wine] itself'. He reinforced this by repeated references to John 6: 63, 'it is the spirit that gives life; the flesh profiteth nothing'.[52] The twofold argument, on figures of speech, and the essentially *spiritual* presence of Christ, were essential to Zwingli.

In the mid-1520s the issue aroused a violent pamphlet dispute between Zwingli and Luther and their respective partisans. Zwingli's *Commentary on True and False Religion* (March 1525), *An Addition or Summary on the Eucharist* (August 1525), and *The Lord's Supper* (February 1526)[53] made his position widely known. Lutheran clergy meeting at Schwäbisch-Hall in October 1525 adopted a formula devised by Johannes Brenz (1499–1570), published as the *Swabian Syngramma* in 1526. Bucer replied with his *Apology* (1526), where he tried pacifically to recommend the cause of Zwingli and Oecolampadius to Brenz, while insisting that what he called 'the carnal presence of Christ in the bread and wine' produced no benefit at all to the Christian mind.[54] In February 1527 Zwingli wrote his *Friendly Exegesis* to Luther, which immediately sparked off a series of increasingly bitter personal exchanges between the two reformers. In March 1528 Luther stated his position on this (and the rest) of his theology in his

Confession on Christ's Supper, soon answered by both Zwingli and his ally Oecolampadius.[55]

This dispute threatened the survival of the Reformation, in the face of the Emperor's hostility; it also dissipated the reformers' energies in contests for the allegiance of several southern German towns. Early in 1529 Philipp of Hesse, a vigorous supporter of the Reformation, inveigled both Zwingli and then Luther into accepting invitations to a dispute in his state capital of Marburg. The discussions (involving most of the leading lights of the movement) took place between 1 and 4 October 1529. Luther from the very start refused to give way or even to admit that logical argument *could* sway him on what he regarded as a mystery. Zwingli insisted on his favourite texts with similar obstinacy. However, each side undertook to be more charitable to the other (an ill-kept promise) and they subscribed a common (if perhaps ambiguous) statement of beliefs on fourteen out of fifteen articles of faith, and on several points on the Eucharist *apart* from the nature of Christ's presence in the sacrament. None the less, the aim of a political union of all reformed communities failed; the movement was split into a spectrum of allegiances ranged between Wittenberg and Zürich. Whether such a union of Swiss and German reformed churches would have brought real benefits anyway, in view of the political problems, may be doubted.[56]

The unresolved debate between Zwingli and Luther was *not* the end of the story. The German (as opposed to Swiss) reformed cities could not indefinitely remain estranged from the Lutheran churches. As early as the 'Four Cities' Confession' (*Confessio Tetrapolitana*) produced by the 'Zwinglian' cities of Strasbourg, Constance, Lindau, and Memmingen at the Augsburg *Reichstag* in 1530, it was affirmed that 'true body and true blood' were 'truly eaten and drunk', not mere bread and wine. Between March and May 1536 Bucer (for the south Germans) and Luther, Melanchthon, and Bugenhagen negotiated the 'Wittenberg accord'. Amongst other issues, this accord stated that body and blood were 'truly and substantially' present and received in the Eucharist. It allowed the full political (and later doctrinal) unity between north and south Germany which had been so elusive seven years before.[57] Switzerland, too, saw shifts in Eucharistic teaching. In Calvin's hands Luther's and Zwingli's *positive* emphases, without their destructive elements, were reconciled into a complete system. On one hand Calvin taught that Christ's 'fleshly' presence was a reassurance of his closeness; his 'flesh and blood' fed the soul as food and drink fed the body; Christ penetrated into the believer's 'bones and marrow'.[58] On the other he agreed with Zwingli that 'this is my body' was figurative, a metonymy: Christ's body was not 'physically' present in a gross sense. Believers were lifted up spiritually to Christ; he was not dragged down 'bodily' to them.[59] On this basis, Calvin's allies Théodore de Bèze and Guillaume Farel (who had earlier taught an even more extreme rejection of the physical presence of Christ than Zwingli)[60] could claim that their beliefs on the Eucharist were essentially those of the Lutherans.[61]

Fast as some theologians sought for harmony, others insisted on stressing divisions. Some of the heirs of Luther, notably the Württemberg theologian Johannes Brenz, and the Hamburg churchman Joachim Westphal, developed into a prime principle of Christ's presence in the communion the notion that Christ's resurrected body could be present everywhere in creation. This doctrine of Christ's so-called 'ubiquity' was pressed vehemently not only against Calvin, who complained that it reduced Christ's body to a 'phantasm', but also against Melanchthon, who was accused of not being dogmatically 'Lutheran' enough in insisting on the bodily presence of Christ.[62]

Theologians sometimes analyse the sources of these different visions of the real presence in subtle and highly complex ways. The historian may doubt how far the reformers themselves actually derived their positions from subtle theory, or how far they took up a position on instinct and then devised reasons to defend it. Certainly the communion caused the greatest problems of all the issues in the Reformation. However, those issues were not always clear-cut and sharply defined. One should not argue from these differences that there were two categorically divided and easily defined 'types' of Reformation movement. Conflicts over ideas will only make sense within the context, limited in time and space, where they occurred.

4. *Rejecting the Rest*

The criterion of a true sacrament—a word with a promise—led the reformers to deny the name of 'sacrament' to the remaining five rites, for reasons which need no long discussion. The notion of seven sacraments had been made current by Peter Lombard in the twelfth century, though only enunciated as an official doctrine in 1439.[63] Once accepted, this implied that penance, confirmation, marriage, extreme unction, and holy orders conferred grace in basically the same way as baptism and the communion.

Luther, Melanchthon, and Calvin spent most time over penance. Their objections to the practice of confessing every individual sin, and to regarding penance as a 'second plank' replacing baptism, were discussed earlier.[64]

Because penance was essentially a 'return' to baptism, it could not be regarded as a separate sacrament in its own right.[65] Other sacraments were downgraded to mere rites of the Church, because they had no precedent in Scripture, and attested to no specific divine 'promise'. Such were confirmation, ordination, and extreme unction. Extreme unction had the added fault that in place of the New Testament rite of praying for and anointing the sick, it had been turned, effectively, into a practice reserved for the dying.[66] Calvin made fun of the sacrament of holy orders actually comprising seven different rituals for the different levels of priesthood, which (if all were separate sacraments) would raise the real number of sacraments to the extremely inauspicious total of thirteen.[67]

Marriage was traditionally seen as a sacrament on the grounds that it was an analogy of the relationship between Christ and the Church. The reformers denied that this was sufficient reason to turn it into a 'sacrament' as such. Calvin mischievously remarked that on those grounds burglary would be a sacrament, since 'the day of the Lord comes like a thief in the night'.[68] So might anything else to which the message of the Gospel was compared, like a star, a mustard seed, yeast, or a shepherd.[69] Finally, Luther, Calvin, and the others denounced details in the 'rites' which they saw as 'human' regulations, especially those which claimed to bind consciences like the impediments to marriage or the reserved sins which only bishops or even popes could absolve.[70]

There was more to the drastic reduction in the number and the roles of the sacraments than doctrinaire adherence to a principle or to the letter of Scripture. The Reformation dispensed with the elaborate sequence of little rituals which had disciplined and consoled earlier generations. It inaugurated a religious life based on prayer, simplified worship, and *learning*. That such an austere creed was adopted by popular demand presents an interesting puzzle.

12

The Conversions of the Reformers

By the early 1520s the Reformation was a public movement with political implications; it entailed a deliberate, drastic, public breach with the basic beliefs, rituals, and rules into which everyone in Europe had been brought up. To become a reformer, one had to be so convinced of the value and truth of the basic message that one dared to renounce an entire system of belief, law, and culture; and to face the (possibly fatal) consequences. Yet the movement only achieved its phenomenal spread because literally dozens of talented, intelligent, often successful priests and scholars *were* so convinced within a few years of each other. Those preachers spread the message too fast and too widely for the remnants of 'catholic' authority to suppress it. Never before had so many of the learned clergy defected from orthodoxy; that fact marked the Reformation off absolutely from any previous heresy since antiquity, and challenges any historian trying to explain its success.

1. *Martin Luther: Development and Influences*

Unlike every other Reformation theologian, Martin Luther had no other figure's example to imitate when he became a reformer. He developed his ideas in the course of a normal academic career; they were forced into relief by accusations and rebuttals; he responded by sharpening his teachings into defensible form and giving them a controversial 'edge'. Luther's development into such a figurehead is therefore a subject by itself, different in kind from the rest. The subject is far, far more complex than appears at first; and has been made even more so by the prodigious literature devoted to it. His early life offers few clues. For his first twenty-two years (1483–1505) Luther followed the conventional career of a scholar of limited means, at school in Magdeburg and then Eisenach, then studying arts at the University of Erfurt from 1501. In 1505 he abruptly and unexpectedly decided to enter the house of observant Augustinian Eremites at Erfurt, after an ill-defined mental crisis. Whatever his motives, Luther was successful enough to become a full member of his order (1506) and to be ordained priest (1507). He then began to study Theology and quickly obtained the minor degrees (1509). He moved permanently to the University of Wittenberg in 1511 and received his doctorate in Theology soon after. At that point he began the twice weekly lectures on the Bible which lasted the rest of his life.[1]

In his crucially formative period Luther was, quite simply, one of the Theology professors in a new, undistinguished, small north German university. His fascination rests not in his life but in the subtle shifts in his *teaching* (above all his teaching on man's justification before God) which ultimately brought him to the stage represented by his controversial pieces of 1520 1. His ideas survive in the notes either taken by his students or prepared for publication by himself; they take the form of a running exposition of selected books of the Bible, namely *Psalms* (1513 15), *Romans* (1515–16), *Galatians* (1516–17), *Hebrews* (1517–18), and *Psalms* again (1519–21). His thought evolved steadily, with repeated overlaps in language between one stage and the next; so no agreement on just when he moved from his first position to his last, and by what stages, has ever been reached.[2] To pretend to offer a definitive solution would be futile. The clearest course (at the risk of over-simplification) is to discuss possible answers to several separate questions:

(1) At what point did Luther break out from the 'Occamist' scholastic tradition in which he was trained at Erfurt?

(2) What was Luther's teaching on man's salvation just after he broke with the Occamist opinion?

(3) When did Luther develop a recognizably and exclusively 'Reformation' doctrine of justification?

(4) What was the so-called 'Tower-experience' which Luther later claimed that he had undergone, and how did it contribute to his teaching on justification?

(5) At what point did Luther's teaching transgress the bounds of 'catholic' orthodoxy?

The answers to these questions are by no means necessarily the same, nor is the connection between them a simple one.

1. At what point did Luther break out from the 'Occamist' scholastic tradition in which he was trained at Erfurt? Luther's teachers, like Bartholomäus Arnoldi, were faithful though subtle followers of the traditions of Occam and Gabriel Biel.[3] Luther later called Occam 'his master'.[4] It is usually assumed that Luther began at Wittenberg teaching this school's theology, as his appointment required him to do. It has been proposed, in

contrast, that Luther might have been influenced in a more specifically 'Augustinian' direction in his first Wittenberg years, since the works of followers of Gregory of Rimini like Simone Fidati, Hugolino of Orvieto, and Jacobus Perez were available in his workplace and current in his order.[5] However, this rests on circumstantial evidence and is disputed.[6] The most persuasive evidence for a first shift away from the broadly Occamist consensus on salvation is found in the course of Luther's first series of lectures on the Psalms (1513–15). In those lectures Luther still used the framework of Occamist ideas, such as the principle that God graciously sets up a system within which the believer prepares himself for grace, and the notion that God responds to those who 'do what is in them'. However, at points Luther's thoughts seem to have sat uncomfortably within that framework. *His* 'doing what is in one' seems to have been an act of prayer, an act of self-accusation, an act of humility, rather than the pure 'love of God above all else' which Biel had envisaged. The emphasis on man's faith and God's mercy was there, though not yet the crucial dynamic element.[7]

2. What was Luther's teaching on man's salvation just after he broke with the Occamist opinion? The departures (if they really existed) from the usual Occamist views in the Psalms commentaries were a long way from generating even an academic dispute, let alone a Reformation. Much more significant changes appear from the beginning of the lectures on Romans in 1515. From the first he stressed how 'the summary of this epistle is to destroy and overturn ... all the wisdom and righteousness of the flesh'. Many of the most familiar slogans and themes of Luther's mature ideas made their first appearance at this point, as for instance:

Inasmuch as the saints are always aware of their sin and seek righteousness from God in accord with his mercy, for this very reason they are always also regarded as righteous by God ... they are actually sinners, but they are righteous by the imputation of a merciful God ... Christ, our Samaritan, has brought this half-dead man into the inn to be cared for, and he has begun to heal him, having promised him the most complete cure into eternal life, and does not impute his sins, that is, his wicked desires, unto death, but in the meantime in the hope of the promised recovery he prohibits him from doing or omitting things by which his cure might be impeded ... Now, is he completely righteous? No, for he is at the same time both a sinner and a righteous man; a sinner in fact, but a righteous man by the sure imputation and promise of God that he will continue to deliver him from sin until he has completely cured him.[8]

It seems reasonable to claim that these passages offered a more radical critique than that of Augustine or Staupitz, in particular by a specially emphatic insistence that man's righteousness came not from within him, but from without, by the sovereign action of God.[9] Moreover, the polemical anger against 'good works' and those who trust to be saved by them came through clearly.[10] This angry, aggressive rejection of Biel and his followers was made sharper and more intense in the *Disputation against Scholastic Theology* of September 1517.[11]

However, there were important differences between the teaching on salvation in the lectures on Romans, dramatic as its rejection of Occam's followers seems to be, and the thought of the 'mature' Luther of the polemics of 1519–21. Although Luther spoke about 'imputation' and 'extrinsic' or 'alien' righteousness as early as 1515–16, he seems to have meant the righteousness which does not belong to man, but which God gives to man to 'cure' his desires. While God was 'curing' him (purifying him internally) man remained forgiven. This medical analogy linked the external position (being forgiven by God) with the internal state (becoming more holy because of Christ's indwelling righteousness). Now the logical distinction between these two states, 'justification' and 'sanctification', was the crucial prerequisite of the critique of medieval piety which led the reformers to do away with ritual penance and all the rest. For this reason, by 1521 Luther abandoned such medical analogies which compared sins to ulcers or fevers which needed to be 'cured'.[12] If that logical separation was not sharply defined and clear-cut, as it is not in the Romans lectures, to that extent Luther's thought in 1515–16 was not 'Reformation' thought.

3. When did Luther develop a recognizably and exclusively 'Reformation' doctrine of justification? For these (and various other) reasons several historians have become steadily more convinced that Luther did not reach his 'mature' reforming stance until about 1518–19, or after the debate on indulgences had been afoot for some months. It is in fact very reasonable to suppose that the heat of controversy led Luther to reformulate his ideas in a sharper, more destructive form than they had assumed in his years of soul-searching.[13] The mature, sharpened form of his teaching is found, for instance, in the sermon 'On twofold righteousness' of 1519.[14] From this point 'justification' was the *wholly* external decision of God not to regard the sins of the sinner when choosing to save him by free grace: typically, this form entailed that the justified man remained 'essentially' a sinner.[15]

4. What was the so-called 'Tower-experience' which Luther later claimed that he had undergone, and how did it contribute to his teaching on justification? Study of Luther's development has been bedevilled by his own decidedly confusing accounts of it. From the 1530s onwards Luther

several times described over long afternoon meals in the former Augustinian monastery how the phrase 'the righteousness [or 'justice'] of God' terrified him in his early years, because he took righteousness to mean God's just punishment of sinners; however, when meditating 'in the tower' of the monastery on the words of Romans 1: 17 'the righteous (or just) shall live by faith', he realized that God's 'righteousness' here meant the *vindication* offered to men by faith, and was consoled by that discovery.[16] In a famous preface to his works written a year before he died, he recounted this so-called 'Tower-experience', and gave far more details, dating the event specifically to his second lectures on the Psalms of 1518–19.[17]

Many scholars have accepted that Luther's insight must have come as a sudden flash of inspiration amid the gloom of spiritual temptation. They have generally taken the account to mean that Luther's theology was formed, crucially, by this turning-point. One has even extended Luther's spiritual experience and generalized it to explain why so many lay people found the Reformation attractive.[18] Yet *when* did this flash of insight occur? The evidence of the lectures shows that Luther moved gradually from one position to another, shedding the assumptions and the vocabulary of his earlier periods slowly and piecemeal. So the 'Tower-experience' has been variously dated by scholars to 1508–9, 1511, 1512, 1513, 1514, 1515, or 1518–19.[19] The problem is that Luther described the experience as liberating him from anxiety about sin and works righteousness, but dated it himself to 1518–19: the date which he supplied was far too late for the substance of the revelation he described. So either the topic, or the date, of his 'experience' as described cannot be exact. It seems, in fact, that far too much of a meal has been made of the 'Tower-experience'. There was a literary tradition of this kind of spiritual autobiography, and Luther was concerned with the spiritual message, not the precise autobiographical details.[20] The search for 'breakthroughs' and 'turning-points' does not necessarily enlighten.[21]

5. At what point did Luther's teaching transgress the bounds of 'catholic' orthodoxy? This question, which fascinated some older scholars, rests on an assumption unacceptable to most modern historians: namely, that there exists an eternal standard of 'catholic' truth independent of time and place against which Luther can be judged.[22] In fact, the confusion between 1517 and 1521 over whether Luther was or was not a 'heretic' required just the opposite to be true: there was much uncertainty about whether his reading of Paul and Augustine was a valid one. As late as the mid-sixteenth century there were those, even within the papal curia, who believed that a core of catholic truth could be extracted from Luther's message.[23] To lay

down a frontier, and then try to point to where Luther crosses it, is an artificial exercise.

It is reasonable to conclude, then, that Luther's beliefs about man's justification evolved, gradually and in stages, from a position broadly (if uncomfortably) within the Occamist school when he began lecturing, to a point where he vigorously and publicly rejected Occamist and Scotist teachings, at the very latest by the time of the *Disputation against Scholastic Theology* in September 1517. His ideas then developed a further 'edge', to the point where they inherently threatened the whole fabric of medieval piety (by 1518–19). Meanwhile, of course, Luther had done far more than ponder justification. By late 1516 he had become an academic reformer, overturning the entire medieval syllabus and study techniques in the name of the Bible and the Fathers. This attack on 'Aristotle' deserves perhaps more attention than the 'Tower-experience'; for it was this purely scholarly revolt which won Luther his first allies and defenders, and helped him to win the admiration of the humanists that was so important in the early months after the indulgence quarrel.[24]

However, when one has charted Luther's development from nominalist professor to reformer, one has not explained *why* it happened, or what influences most shaped his mind. At various stages in his career Luther was exposed, or exposed himself, to all the main currents of thought in vogue at the time: nominalism, in its various senses; the 'Augustinian' movement of educated piety represented by Johannes von Staupitz; German mystical theology of the fourteenth century; and finally humanism, especially biblical and scholarly humanism. All these movements of thought to some extent provided Luther with techniques, skills, or assumptions. From philosophical and theological 'nominalism' Luther may have inherited an appreciation for precise logic, an awareness of the importance of context when using terms, and even a taste for paradox.[25] It is claimed that Staupitz on one hand, or the 'nominalist' Augustinian theology of the followers of Gregory of Rimini on the other, may have helped to shift or 'correct' Luther's thought at crucial stages in the devising of the first lectures on the Psalms. However, the evidence on these issues is too scanty, and the judgements of specialists too contradictory, to allow a safe conclusion.[26] From the mystics, including the author of the *German Theology* which he republished, Luther drew an intense sense of God's direct action in the believer; at a particular stage of his development, during the preparation of his Heidelberg theses in 1518, he developed the 'Theology of the Cross', a series of stark paradoxes between the 'Theologian of Glory' who exaggerated human ability, and the 'Theologian of the Cross' who recognized the meaning of Christ's sacrifice. However, the mystical elements and language occasionally used by Luther were always servants to his dogmatic message.[27]

No less problematical is Luther's debt to humanism. Luther used and needed the texts of the Bible and the Fathers which textual scholarship provided. He echoed (in his own way) humanist suspicions about sterile philosophizing at one end of the social scale, and vulgar superstition at the other. He and his allies both admired and exploited rhetorical techniques polished by the humanists. Finally, the superficial resemblance between Luther's protests and the humanists' campaign against scholasticism and dogmatic bigotry won him many early allies. However, Luther was always a theologian exploiting humanist techniques, rather than endorsing humanist value-systems for their own sake. The more that emerges about how much humanism was current in the Wittenberg milieu up to 1517, the more limited Luther's use of it appears.[28]

Neither meticulous reconstruction of his theological odyssey, nor listing and debating the component influences in his thought, actually *explain* Luther. His native pugnacity, combined with the ham-fisted response of the papal authorities to his 'case', had much to do with the 1517–21 crisis. However, in two other ways Luther was unusual. His instinct, from as early as 1517, was to pre-digest his message into a pungent form for a wide public. His *Seven Penitential Psalms* of 1517 were, he said, 'not for the Nurembergers [Staupitz's allies], for highly sensitive and sharp-nosed souls ... but for rude Saxons, for whom Christian erudition can never be chewed fine enough'.[29] Never before had academics been so keen to take their disputes to the 'rude Saxons' in such pungent prose. Secondly, Luther so readily saw his mission in terms of a conflict of God and the devil, that he could cast caution and political prudence to the winds when it suited him.[30] No more, of course, does 'explaining' Luther of itself 'explain' the Reformation. The paradox remains, that the religious, social, and intellectual ferment was brought to a boil, quite unconsciously, by a collision of ideas, temperaments, and insights so unpredictable that Luther could justly claim that 'the Word' (the message) had done its work without him.[31]

2. *The Non-Humanist Reformers*

The vast majority of the first-generation reformers were deeply influenced by the northern Renaissance humanist movement *before* they turned to supporting ecclesiastical reform in the name of the free gift of divine grace. They thus progressed from holding traditional piety in supercilious contempt, to denouncing it for more substantial theological reasons. This spiritual odyssey, through which so many different reformers passed, raises special problems of its own.[32] However, a handful of early reformers were *not* humanists first: loyal churchmen of a largely traditional type, they abruptly and often tempestuously turned to preaching vehemently against the institution in which they had been brought up. Three examples from very different milieux illustrate this kind of reformer: Andreas Bodenstein von Karlstadt (*c.*1480–1541), Mathis or Matthäus Zell of Kaysersberg (1477–1548), and the first major French-speaking reformer, Guillaume Farel (1489–1565).[33]

All three were somewhat older than the leading reformers within their circle: Karlstadt older than Luther, Zell older than Bucer or Capito, Farel older than Calvin or Pierre Viret (1511–71). All had passed (slowly and rather late) through the traditional university curriculum and become secular priests. Karlstadt studied at Erfurt from 1499, then under the followers of the Thomist or 'ancient' school at Cologne, before moving to Wittenberg in 1505. Zell also studied at Erfurt, then (after a break) at Freiburg-im-Breisgau, where he took up Theology and became rector of the university in 1517. In 1518 he was made pastor of the church of S. Lorenz at Strasbourg and penitentiary to the bishop.[34] Guillaume Farel grew up among a family of notaries, lawyers, and ecclesiastics from the bourgeoisie and petty nobility of the Dauphiné, then studied arts and philosophy at Paris from 1509, obtaining a post at the Collège du Cardinal Lemoine in 1517. Most striking of all the parallels, each of these reformers grew up under the moral and spiritual influence of great figures of the fifteenth-century 'reform' of religious life: Karlstadt under Staupitz, Zell under Geiler von Kaysersberg, and Farel under Jacques Lefèvre d'Étaples.[35]

It is not clear just why these three figures were so little touched by Renaissance humanism. Zell's Freiburg was quite remote from the academic mainstream, but the same cannot be said of Karlstadt's Wittenberg, where the Nuremberger Christoph Scheurl taught from 1507,[36] still less of Paris around 1500, one of the great European centres of classical scholarship. Quite simply, the humanist desire for good literary style never captivated these men; indeed their writings were always pungent, laborious, and inelegant. Karlstadt dabbled in poetry and classical languages, but seems to have lacked the necessary talent.[37] The absence of Renaissance leaven in Farel's mind (despite his admiration for Lefèvre) left him conventionally devoted to the cults of the Holy Cross.[38]

The reasons why reformers were converted are always elusive; even the process, and the date, are often obscure. In Karlstadt's case the presence, personality, and intellect of Luther, the 'modern' theologian in the faculty to Karlstadt's 'ancient', was critical. Luther shocked Karlstadt by the unorthodox views he proposed at the disputation for Bartholomäus Bernhardi's promotion in September 1516.[39] Karlstadt was moved to buy a copy of Augustine's works, read both that and possibly Staupitz's *On Eternal Predestination*, and by April 1517 was writing fervently Augustinian, anti-scholastic theses of his own.[40] Karlstadt was, of course, just one of those converted to Luther's drastic reform of the theological curriculum. Nikolaus von Amsdorf, who taught Scotist philosophy at Wittenberg, was similarly converted by a gift of Augustine's works from Luther.[41] As Luther developed and refined his theology still further Karlstadt was drawn along after him; he, rather than Luther, provoked the debate with Eck of Ingolstadt which ended in the Leipzig debate of 1519. Karlstadt reverted, after his estrangement from Luther and departure from Wittenberg, to something like his earlier neo-Augustinian position.[42]

Zell's conversion was a literary rather than personal experience. His early studies were in the teachings and sermons of Geiler von Kaysersberg, who normally preached an Occamist theology of salvation.[43] In 1521 he abruptly announced to his hearers in Strasbourg that he would preach the 'pure Gospel', beginning with the Epistle to the Romans, and defended Luther from his pulpit. In December 1522 he was hauled before the bishop's officials, and during the struggle manipulated popular feeling on his behalf, as well as defending himself in print with his *Christian Defence* in 1523.[44] Farel's transition to reformer is perhaps the most obscure. He himself gave all the credit to Lefèvre, who he claimed 'drew me away from the false opinion of [human] merit, and taught me that everything came by grace only through the mercy of God'.[45] By the time Farel knew him (perhaps as early as 1515) Lefèvre was working in semi-retirement at Saint-Germain-des-Prés; he remained loyal to traditional worship.[46] The harassment of Lefèvre and his circle by the scholastics of the Sorbonne probably alienated Farel from academic religious orthodoxy; but only between 1521 and 1523 did he translate his sympathies for Augustinian-

style theology and purified worship into public pressure for religious change, first at Meaux, then at Paris, then at Basle.[47]

Once converted, reformers of this type made a particular contribution to the Reformation movements for which they worked. All became fervent, aggressive, unquestioning enthusiasts for the reform of worship and an end to those 'corrupt' or 'diabolical' religious practices which they had just renounced. Karlstadt at Wittenberg, Zell in Strasbourg, or Farel in Switzerland were alike urgent, furious, and unrestrained. Consequently, they counterbalanced the caution and moderation of others. Karlstadt helped to devise the first reformed 'church order' at Wittenberg during 1521-2.[48] Zell shamed Wolfgang Capito into becoming an overt protestant, just as Farel later shamed Calvin into staying in Geneva as a working churchman rather than a scholar.[49] A vital role in converting others, and in turning reforming theology into the Reformation, was undoubtedly played by the unsubtle enthusiasm of these essentially second-rate intellects.

3. *Humanist Reformers: Origins and Backgrounds*

The term 'humanist' could embrace an enormous variety of temperaments, ideals, and levels of learning. It is not easy to generalize when one is dealing with men as diverse as Melanchthon and Zwingli, or Calvin and Conrad Grebel. Moreover, the issue has been complicated by those historians who have sought to identify a particular 'humanist' type of reformation thought, or spoken of a 'humanist Reformation' in opposition to the Lutheran— usually meaning the Reformation of Zwingli, Oecolampadius, Bucer, and their allies.[50] In fact, humanists and non-humanists worked in uneasy concert in all sorts of Reformation milieux. The non-humanists discussed in the last section belonged to three different regions of the movement; while from Scotland to Transylvania men trained in the learning of the Renaissance played a vital part in determining how far the Reformation spread. Furthermore, the progress from humanist to reformer might be an easy and apparently natural evolution, where the boundary-lines are hard to draw and the throw-backs to earlier patterns of thought are obvious; or it might involve soul-searching and a fundamental lifetime change of principles and values.

The humanist reformers came from diverse backgrounds, but a few broadly common features attract notice. Most were born in towns or cities: Zwingli, born in the village of Wildhaus in the remote Swiss territory of Toggenburg, was an exception. Most were born to fathers of at least the

rank of artisan, like Bucer, the son of a shoemaker at Sélestat, or Capito, son of a smith at Hagenau. The fathers of several were prominent in their municipalities: Johannes Brenz came from a patrician family of Weil der Stadt; Joachim Vadian's father sat in the inner council of St Gallen; Justus Jonas's father was *Ratsmeister* of Nordhausen. For others, like Lazarus Spengler, literary competence ran in the family.[51] The obvious reason why most came from such relatively well-to-do backgrounds was that a fair amount of money was needed to support long periods of study at those universities where the humanist cadres of Germany and Switzerland were formed.[52] Particular urban and university centres attracted their own cliques of young humanists. One such was Heidelberg, where at various times during the 1510s Oecolampadius, Brenz, and Melanchthon studied Greek together, and Oecolampadius first met Capito. Bucer apparently escaped from the uncongenially scholastic atmosphere of the Heidelberg Dominican cloister to study classical literature with this group. A slightly more unlikely centre of future reformers was the University of Vienna, whose students included Joachim Vadian, the Strasbourgeois Nikolaus Gerbel and Jakob Bedrot, Simon Grynaeus (later prominent at Basle), and Johannes Honter, reformer of the German towns of Transylvania. More predictably, Erfurt and nearby Gotha, where the humanist scholar Mutianus Rufus presided, nurtured students such as Johannes Lang, Georg Burckhard 'Spalatinus', later secretary to the elector of Saxony, and Justus Jonas. Finally, Nuremberg and Augsburg, though not university towns, provided important foyers for future reformers: Spengler and Wenceslaus Linck at Nuremberg, Oecolampadius at Augsburg.[53]

By far the majority of the humanist reformers were ordained clergy and theologians. The principal exceptions were Joachim Vadian, who studied Medicine at Vienna before turning to protestant theology (though he put his medicine to use later), and Lazarus Spengler, who studied Law at Leipzig before taking up the family profession of civic secretary at Nuremberg on his father's death. A fair proportion were members of regular religious orders. Some of these spent short and not very happy periods in the cloister while still seeking a vocation. Bucer joined the Dominicans when he found it impossible to support his education any other way, and soon regretted doing so. Oecolampadius spent a few unhappy months as an adviser with the Bridgettine order at Altomünster in 1521. Others, however, seem to have been both sincere and successful in their monastic calling. Wenceslaus Linck had been prior of the reformed Augustinian house at Wittenberg for several years before he took up Staupitz's mantle as spiritual leader of the Nuremberg élite. Ambrosius Blarer rose to be

prior of the Benedictine house at Alpirsbach shortly before he left it abruptly in 1522.[54]

There were numerous other such cases: Konrad Pellicanus, who followed humanist studies at Heidelberg in the 1490s, became a Franciscan, only to leave the order in 1525 to teach at Basle. Besides Luther himself, the Augustinian order produced Wenceslaus Linck, Johannes Lang, and Heinrich of Zutphen, who preached at Bremen; the Franciscans included besides Pellicanus Eberlin von Günzburg, preacher at Ulm, Friedrich Myconius, pastor at Gotha, and Johann Briessmann, who worked in northern Germany; while Urbanus Rhegius of Augsburg was a former Carmelite, and Johannes Bugenhagen, Luther's emissary to the Baltic cities, a former Premonstratensian canon.[55]

A final characteristic stands out: the humanist reformers were almost without exception as young or younger than Luther, some (like Melanchthon, only 20 in 1517) very young indeed.[56] This set of academic, religiously minded humanists was far more than an aggregate of individuals sharing roughly similar backgrounds and training. The humanists formed a self-conscious and interconnected series of brotherhoods sharing not only ideas, but also partisan loyalties against common foes (such as the Cologne scholastics who persecuted Reuchlin). As it turned out, the bonds which bound this generation of young scholars together were stronger than those which linked them to their humanist elders. Once one group converted, many others followed, and brought their cohesiveness and drive to a new movement.

4. *Humanist Reformers: Conversions*

Those humanist scholars who admired and clustered round Luther crossed to the Reformation decisively, but fairly painlessly. Several of them participated in his programme of turning from 'Aristotle' to the Bible and the early Fathers, which looked superficially very like the long-desired humanist reform of theology. They made a conscious, but fairly straightforward transition, from cultivating scholarship with an ethical twist, to applying their learning to interpreting the Bible and the Fathers along what they took to be Luther's terms.

Perhaps the most important, and certainly the most academically precocious, was Philipp Melanchthon. Classically educated almost from infancy, he studied at Heidelberg (1509–12) and Tübingen (1512–18), graduating MA and beginning to teach the classics in 1514, aged 17. He went as a classicist to Wittenberg in 1518 on Reuchlin's recommendation, already intending to lecture on Homer *and* the Bible. He attended the Leipzig disputation, and graduated in Divinity on 3 October 1519 with theses extensively influenced by Luther. From 1519 to 1521 he wrote down Luther's sermons on Genesis, transforming them into a commentary by 1523. By the time that he published the first edition of his *Common Places* in 1521, he was actually a more concise and systematic exponent of Luther's ideas than Luther himself—as the latter readily acknowledged.[57] On the negative side, Melanchthon broke decisively with his humanist elders. When Reuchlin joined Eck at Ingolstadt in 1519, Melanchthon refused to accompany him, and contacts between the relatives ceased in 1521. He broke with Erasmus, like so many younger humanists, over the 'Freedom of the Will' in 1524–5.[58]

Other reformers likewise changed careers under Luther's personal influence. The Pomeranian Johannes Bugenhagen (1485–1558) had progressed from studying the humanities (1502–4) to Erasmian religious humanism (from 1504) and to ordination (1509). Having already become involved with Saxony via a project for histories of both Saxony and Pomerania, he read Luther's *Babylonian Captivity*, wrote to Luther for moral advice, and received a reply enclosing *On Christian Freedom*. In April 1521 he informally joined the Wittenberg theologians.[59] Justus Jonas (1493–1555) was by his early training a lawyer and initiate of the Erfurt–Gotha circle of Eobanus Hessus, Mutianus, Urbanus Rhegius, and Spalatin. He studied Law at Wittenberg during 1511–14, becoming in due course a professor at Erfurt. All the while he was drawn to Erasmian ideas, and actually carried letters between Erasmus and Luther during 1518–19. After he returned to Wittenberg in 1521 he soon moved from teaching Law to Theology.[60] Erasmus and Cochlaeus were left ineffectually to bemoan the loss of the scholar who had so suddenly slipped sideways into a different career and ideology.[61] Close personal contact with Luther was not essential. The Nuremberg humanist coterie which had been dominated by pre-reform figures like Willibald Pirckheimer and Johannes von Staupitz experienced a crucial change of leadership in the late 1510s. From 1517 Wenceslaus Linck (1483–1547), Augustinian Eremite and Wittenberg-trained theologian, replaced Staupitz as its spiritual adviser, preaching to humanists like Hieronymus Ebner, Caspar Nützel, and above all Lazarus Spengler. Linck circulated Luther's *Ninety-Five Theses*, and even expounded them from the pulpit. Gradually the Nurembergers became deeply alienated from Luther's adversary Johannes Eck, who included Spengler and Pirckheimer with those condemned in the 1520 bull. Their literary enmities, no less than their friendships, drove the younger Nurembergers into partisan support for Luther.[62]

With those reformers who were *not* closely connected with Luther by academic or literary ties, there is much more difficulty in tracing their passage towards the Reformation. Not surprisingly, they denied that they were introducing anything 'new' in the Church, rather than restoring the teaching of the Scriptures and the early Fathers. While Luther was a banned heretic with an uncertain future, to acknowledge him publicly as Zell did would have been imprudent. Moreover, the non-Lutheran reformers were genuinely independent minds, well able to 'rediscover' the basic Reformation message on their own terms and with their own emphases.

Huldrych Zwingli became a reformer of worship and doctrine *through* being a preaching humanist. During 1522–3 he abruptly emerged as a supporter of fast-breaking and clerical marriage, then an exponent of justification by free grace, predestination, the unique sacrifice of Christ, and so forth. Moreover, the defining of Zwingli's own position went hand in hand with the development of the Zürich Reformation itself.[63] It is important that Zwingli preached in humanist style, abandoning the medieval formulas, as soon as he arrived in Zürich in 1519. However, he does not seem to have challenged existing practices until Lent 1522. He experienced some kind of turning-point about 1516, when he became a preaching humanist, looking to the unadorned Scripture for guidance; but then developed into a dogmatic and practical reformer until he emerged as such in 1522.[64] It is not enough to say simply that Zwingli was a reforming humanist: he was a reformer who found Erasmian humanism an insufficient vehicle for his beliefs and message. He so described his own development in his *Architeles* addressed to the bishop of Constance in August 1522. He like everyone had been worried about his salvation, and found the available answers insufficient. Recent writers (late scholastics) 'displayed more folly than wisdom'; the 'ancients' beloved of the humanists often differed from Scripture. Every teaching was to be tested against Christ himself. This led him to defy human traditions, and human commands, which conflicted with Scripture.[65]

Inevitably, since Zwingli emerged as a public opponent of Church law and tradition only in 1522, one has to ask how far he was affected by the message and reputation, or indeed the teaching, of Luther. Two extreme positions have been suggested: (*a*) that he preached his own Reformation message as early as *c.*1516–19, quite independently of and anterior to Luther; or (*b*) that he remained a humanist until 1521–2, when Luther's fame and teaching turned him into a reformer.[66] Luther himself wrote contemptuously in 1527 of 'those friends of ours, who without us and before us were nothing, did not dare to open their mouths, and now inflated by our victory turn their attacks on us ...'[67] The truth probably lies somewhere in between. Zwingli was quite enough of a theologian to devise his own system with only passing reference to a cursory reading of Luther's works. Luther could function as an example rather than a strict guide.[68] On the other hand, he apparently copied some phrases verbally from Luther.[69] If Zwingli really did develop the distinctively 'Reformation' message of salvation by free forgiveness, apprehended through faith, simultaneously but *entirely* independently of Luther, it was the most breath-taking coincidence of the sixteenth century.[70] Zwingli deliberately emphasized in his own writings that he read little of Luther, took little notice of him, and derived his teachings from his earlier teachers like the Swiss Thomas Wyttenbach. It is, however, striking that he always emphasized the independence of his ideas, or their humanist origins, *either* when the Zürich movement was still in flux, and when identification with a condemned heretic would have been dangerous, *or* after the Eucharistic dispute had given him other, more potent reasons to deny that he was a 'follower' of, or in any sense subordinate to, the Saxon reformer. He came to see Luther, with his (by Zwingli's standards) exaggerated faith in the sacraments, as perpetuating some of the 'idolatry' of the old Church.[71]

Because of the understandable (if regrettable) antagonism between German historians anxious to prove that Zwingli's thought was derivative, and Swiss scholars wishing to prove the opposite, Zwingli's transition from preaching humanist to reformer has perhaps been over-interpreted. With most other ex-humanist reformers, including the vast bulk of those who preached to the southern German cities, there is much less of a problem. No one is surprised to see that men like Bucer, Capito, or Ambrosius Blarer were first estranged from the scholastic opponents of Luther; that they sided with Luther only partially understanding his teaching; but as they grew to understand it, they became practical, preaching reformers. In most cases the psychological 'moment of truth' is hard to find, if it exists at all.

In 1516 Martin Bucer moved to the observant Dominican house at Heidelberg. He knew Wimpfeling's humanist circle at Sélestat as well as those at Heidelberg, and watched Luther's performance at the Heidelberg Augustinian chapter in 1518. He showed contempt for the role played by the respected Dominican Hochstraten in the Reuchlin affair, and fled from the monastery some time in 1520. He took temporary refuge first with von Hutten, then with von Sickingen at the Ebernburg. In 1522 he married a runaway nun and preached for the local pastor at Wissembourg. Excommunicated by the bishop of Speyer, he fled to Strasbourg in May 1523 and was installed by popular demand at the parish church of St Aurelia. Repeatedly he broke the rules for a priest, burning his bridges behind him: by associating with the priest-hating knights, provoking open disputes with the Wissembourg Carthusians, and eventually defying an official ban on preaching in German at Strasbourg.[72]

Bucer's older ally Capito went through a quite different process. In the 1500s Capito kept in with both the humanists around Wimpfeling and the popular Tubingen Scotist Conrad Summenhart, one of whose works he published in 1502.[73] He read scholastic Theology at Freiburg about 1510, then Hebrew alongside Oecolampadius at Heidelberg during 1513–15. From 1515 he was a professor in Old Testament studies at Basle. While serving as secretary to Archbishop Albrecht of Mainz from 1520, he tried to assist fellow humanists. In that spirit he obtained Bucer his dispensation from his monastic vows, and mediated in the exchange of letters between Luther and Albrecht over indulgences: to such effect that the 1520 papal bull against Luther was not published in the province of Mainz. What impressed Capito about Luther was not so much his fortitude as his orderly moderation in suppressing the 1522 Wittenberg disorders. In 1523 he left Albrecht for a rich post at Strasbourg; but his encounter with the irrepressible Zell turned him into a reformer as Luther had failed to do. When the hierarchy took steps against married priests Capito climbed down off the fence, being installed as a congregational preacher in May 1524. In 1526 he finally resigned his benefice.[74]

Capito was not alone in his conscious effort to delay his transition to outright opposition to the old order. Ambrosius Blarer wrote in July 1522 to his brother that he had remained as long as he could at Alpirsbach monastery, trying to reconcile his respect for the Scripture with the monks' mockery of his 'Lutheran' ideas:

By now Luther's name was exposed to their execration, which I could have put up with, so long as they respected the scriptures. But they got hold of the idea that, whatever I had carefully gleaned from the Gospel and from Paul, they should decry as drawn from Luther and therefore impious and heretical, and should no longer listen to any account of my faith; that injustice, inflicted not on me but on God, was something I neither could nor should tolerate.[75]

When the monks tried to turn him away from reading the Bible, he left.

These cases suggest that the transition from humanist to reformer took many forms. It is widely accepted that a 'constructive misunderstanding' occurred between Luther and the humanists of southern Germany, whereby they took up Luther's cause because they entirely mistook him for another humanist scholar passionate for the 'pure Scripture' oppressed by pedantic and legalistic churchmen. There is abundant evidence that the *content* of Luther's early thought was not understood; hardly surprisingly, since the Heidelberg theses (for instance) were paradoxical, epigrammatic, and highly idiosyncratic even by Luther's own standards. Bucer in 1518 described Luther's performance at Heidelberg in a way that shows quite clearly that he mistook him for a more explicit Erasmus. Oecolampadius, on the other hand, soon realized the 'Augustinian' implications of his thought.[76] However, such a 'misunderstanding' was clearly insufficient to turn scholars into reformers; one could perfectly well be a preaching humanist, or oppose indulgences, without also rejecting the apparatus of Church worship and authority. In their wholehearted shift of loyalties the humanist reformers gave up more than their religious loyalties. They abandoned (with many misgivings for its future)[77] scholarship for its own sake; they gave up the fashionable, snobbish distance which they had previously maintained from the 'barbarous' common people. They became, in large numbers, popular parish preachers: heirs of Geiler rather than Wimpfeling or Mutianus.[78] In many cases the change was forced on them by circumstances and opposition: the Erasmian middle ground simply split and collapsed under them.

Calvin's conversion, a decade or so later than those already discussed, shows a sudden and dramatic change; but it was obscure, and so entangled with the uncertain fate of French humanism that it remains controversial. In 1523 the 14-year-old Calvin went from his native Noyon to study Arts and Philosophy amidst the humanists at Paris. In 1528 he moved from Philosophy to reading Law at Orléans and Bourges, then back to Paris in 1531. In 1532 he published an edition of Seneca's *On Clemency* which showed no *clear* indication of religious heterodoxy. In November 1533 he was chased from Paris after one of his humanist friends, Nicholas Cop, preached a rectorial sermon in the university which adulterated Erasmian humanism with much Lutheran theology, and drew the fire of the dogmatically orthodox theology faculty. He then wandered through France, returning to his native town to renounce his benefices in May 1534. Also in 1534 he wrote a polemical tract against the anabaptists' belief in the 'sleep of souls' from death to the last judgement. Finally settling in Basle, he began early in 1535 to draft the first, short edition of his *Institutes of the Christian Religion*, which was completed by August and published early the following year.[79]

Debates have raged over the exact meaning and date of Calvin's 'conversion'. Clearly (like all the others) it involved a protracted series of changes: his movement from classical scholarship towards 'Lutheran' ideas; his decision to renounce an income from Church benefices; his conscious espousal of 'Reformation' ideas, and consequent rejection of what he called 'papal superstitions'; finally, his self-dedication to writing theology at Basle, and indeed later still, to practical churchmanship under Farel's influence at Geneva in 1536. When he described his spiritual conversion as late as 1557, he spoke of God's intervening by a 'sudden conversion' which released him from respect for the old Church's rituals and dedicated him to (reformed) theology.[80] Clearly Calvin knew exactly what the issues were: 'misunderstanding' was not at issue. However, he probably hoped, out of stubborn respect for the old Church, to remain a reforming humanist as long as possible. Only when allegiances became polarized after Cop's sermon and the 'Placards' scandal in France in 1534,[81] and Calvin's humanist allies were exiled or burned, was this position impossible. Then, no doubt, his decision to come down firmly on the protestant side did feel like a 'sudden' providential change.[82]

The personal motives for the reformers' conversions are ultimately inexplicable. However, this overlooks the fundamental point: they were personal motives. One did not become a first-generation reformer by habit, compulsion, or default. Where any evidence exists, it suggests that the reformers reached their positions only after serious and earnest heart-searching. They were some of the most conscientious revolutionaries ever to rebel against authority.

13

Rejections of Reform

1. The Older Generation

The Reformation protest was generally rejected by those who had taught the future reformers, or led the spiritual cliques in which they matured and formed their friendships. The theory of a 'generation gap' may partly explain this. Nearly all the Wittenberg academics who were older than Luther resisted the innovations, either delaying their own changes as long as possible or turning them down outright and migrating to more orthodox havens.[1] Similarly, nearly all the older generation of German humanists, like Staupitz, Wimpfeling, Reuchlin, Peutinger, or Pirckheimer, turned against the Reformation when its implications for belief and practice became apparent.[2] With the exceptions of Eck and Emser, most of the early anti-Lutheran polemicists, such as Cochlaeus, Wimpina, Hochstraten, and above all Erasmus, were significantly older than Luther, himself one of the oldest reformers.[3] Commonsense psychology suggests that the more years a churchman had devoted to the old ways, the less ready he would be to abandon those ways as wrong—all the more so if the call to do so came from someone younger.

The reactionaries were, however, persuaded with reasons which many, though by no means all, of the younger generation set aside. The reasons given for rejecting the Reformation are therefore instructive. Perhaps the most universal objection was to the reformers' broadcasting debates about rarified, technical theological questions to a wide public. On the very eve of the Reformation the Tübingen theologian Konrad Summenhart published a tract showing how Church tithes were *not* owed on pain of mortal sin, as canon lawyers claimed. However, he insisted that this subversive conclusion should be used either as an academic theory or to console troubled consciences, not broadcast from the pulpit to stimulate popular discontent: the whole truth need not be proclaimed to the people.[4] After the Leipzig debate Karlstadt complained that Johannes Eck had made important concessions to the Wittenbergers' positions, which he had then contradicted from the pulpit: Eck had protested that the uneducated

public should be taught a simple, uncomplicated message, while the subtleties and doubts should be left to the academics.[5] Élitist intellectual
snobbery, and a real fear that to know about academic debates would lead
the masses to disobey, linked scholastics like Summenhart with humanists
like Mutianus or Konrad Peutinger.[6] Many likewise felt that a 'quarrelsome
theology' contributed nothing to making better Christians: this argument,
older than the Reformation, was later used against it.[7]

However, the Reformation was rejected for better reasons than just
academic snobbery. In as much as the reformers rejected *all* the classic
definitions of sin, the law, faith, good works, the Church, sacraments, and
so forth, they drew fire from those older writers who found their redefin
itions either repugnant or quite simply incomprehensible. It is therefore
hard to single out any one theme to which the older theologians objected.
Hochstraten, to take one example, was scandalized by Luther's claim that
the souls of the elect were saved in spite of their continuing state of sin:
'as if Christ takes to himself the most foul bride and is unconcerned about
her cleanliness'. The idea that God's forgiveness might after all *not* be
conditional on the sacramental purifications of the Church was deeply
shocking.[8] Equally perplexing was the reformers' cavalier defiance of tradition and authority: the older generation had interpreted Scripture
through a tradition, rather than contradicting tradition *and* the Church in
the name of Scripture.[9]

One famous and glaring exception to the hieratic, snobbish authoritarianism of most late medieval writers seems to contradict much of
what has just been said. Erasmus had seemed the natural patron and
foreshadower of the reformers. Like them, he regarded the Bible as the
preserve of every layman, and decried the notion that 'Christ taught such
intricate doctrines that they could scarcely be understood by very few
theologians, or [that] the strength of the Christian religion consisted in
men's ignorance of it'.[10] Like the reformers (though for different reasons)
he poured scorn on the excesses of popular 'superstitious' spirituality on
one hand, and the 'Aristotelian' theology on the other.[11] However, these
superficial similarities were more than counterbalanced by a series of more
fundamental differences. First, Erasmus was only willing to spread abroad
the 'truths of the Bible' because he held a very restricted view of what
'truths' were useful or edifying for *any* Christian. He objected to abstruse
and non-instructive scholastic speculation: so, the only kind of dogmas
which lay people *or* theologians were supposed to bother with were ethical
principles—how to 'live well' as a Christian. As Sebastian Brant had put
it:

> But certainly all our beliefe and creede,
> The which is able to save us from hell payne,
> To us is given in wordes clere and playne,
> In our lawe are found no wordes disceyvable,
> No false abusion nor obscure hardnes ...[12]

Consequently, Erasmus rejected Luther's speculations on free will as 'irreverent inquisitiveness' into 'things which are hidden, not to say super-fluous', urging instead that one concentrate on agreed ethical principles.[13] Indeed, he could not see that the essence of Christianity rested in such speculations, whether those of the scholastics or what he called the 'para-doxes of Luther'.[14] Secondly, Erasmus could not endorse broadcasting subversive truths—even if they *were* truths—in such a way as to stir up mass discontent and disorder. As he wrote to Justus Jonas in 1521:

Although it would be prudent to dole out the truth according to circumstances, to urge just enough of it, and what is suitable to each person, [Luther] in so many hurried writings is pouring it all out at once, making even cobblers aware of things which used to be discussed only amongst the learned, as mysteries and forbidden knowledge; and often, as far as I am concerned, his unrestrained enthusiasm carries him beyond what is right ... Above all I would urge that one avoid disorder, which can do nothing but harm. Thus, with a kind of holy guile one should wait for the proper time, so that the treasure of Gospel truth, by which men's minds may be purified, may not be betrayed.[15]

However, Erasmus also objected to what he saw as the substance of Luther's message: that an 'enslaved will' was unable to respond positively to the offer of divine grace: that 'free will [was] an empty title ... God works in us evil as well as good effects, and all things which happen are of mere necessity'.[16] Over this issue, of Erasmus's own choosing, broke out the pamphlet controversy between Erasmus's *'Diatribe' on Free Will* (September 1524), Luther's riposte *On the Enslaved Will* (December 1525), and Erasmus's two-part rejoinder *Hyperaspistes* ('The shield-bearer', 1526–7).[17] Did this, then, mean that his theology of salvation emphasized the free response of man in his 'natural condition', as Occam, Biel, Scotus, and their followers had done?[18]

The issue is deeply controversial, mainly because Erasmus, committed as he was to the unity and consensus of the whole Church, was not willing to advance a single position of his own as the one certain truth. He 'collated' and compared texts and authorities on a contested question, producing a 'sufficiently probable' opinion rather than a defined dogma.[19] However, the 'probable opinion' which he favoured in the 'Diatribe' was that which he drew from Augustine, that God initiated human salvation by a gift of first 'free grace', but man then 'co-operated' by responding to the offer.[20] Likewise, in disputes with Noël Bédier and other Parisian theologians during 1524–6 he approved of 'Luther when he calls us away from frail confidence in ourselves to the most safe harbour of trust in evangelical grace ... Our hope is in the mercy of God and the merits of Christ'.[21] However, he was far from consistent, sometimes entertaining the notion of man acquiring 'congruent' or 'semi-merit', above all in several passages in the *Hyperaspistes* where he regarded it as a possible opinion which *might* be approved.[22] His persistent concern was to deny that man was totally passive before God's grace: a physician's ministrations were not made useless, nor a friend's advice less valuable, just because one was 'free' to accept such aids. As long as he stressed *that* message, the precise dogmatic formula was clearly of secondary interest to him.

Erasmus's tragedy was that his humane middle ground, opposed alike to scholastic obscurities, vulgar superstitions, protestant dogmatics, and popular disorder, was steadily deserted by both sides. Most of the older generation drifted irresistibly towards defending the old religious ways which, whatever their humanistic mockery, they had never truly renounced. Many of the younger scholars found Erasmus's position a half-measure lacking the full-blooded appeal of the protestant 'Gospel'. Consistently loyal to an untenable position, he was left as an awkward anomaly, moving between catholic Freiburg and protestant Basle, really belonging to neither, until his death in 1536.[23]

2. *Some Italian 'Evangelicals'*

The Reformers' message was well known and understood south of the Alps by the early 1520s. In Italy as in Germany, Christian humanist thinkers took an interest in Lutheran and similar ideas, when they seemed to echo their own biblical or patristic preferences. Reformed ideas gained a hearing—or at least a readership—amongst specific kinds of religious orders which had grown up in Renaissance Italy, especially the Oratories of Divine Love and the Theatine Order of 'regular priests', the reformed Franciscans known as 'Capuchins', the reformed Benedictines of the congregation of Monte Cassino ('Cassinese'), and the reformed Augustinians of St John Lateran or 'Lateran canons'.[24] Theologies of salvation either parallel to or actually derived from the reformers were current in Venice during the 1520s, in the circles of the nobleman Gasparo Contarini (1483–

1542), an associate of the Oratorians, and of the Cassinese Gregorio Cortese at San Giorgio Maggiore; and at Padua around the Lateran canon Piermartire Vermigli (1500–62) and the Englishman Reginald Pole (1500–58). Such ideas merged with the theological traditions of their host orders without, at this stage, causing scandal.[25] There was at first no question of 'turning' protestant, since, in the confused climate, none of these figures thought they were departing from Christian orthodoxy anyway.

After the accession of Pope Paul III in 1534 the so-called 'Italian evangelicals' gained a foothold in the papal court with the elevation as cardinals of Contarini, Pole, and Cortese. Moreover, in 1531 Juan de Valdés (*c*.1500–41), brother of Charles V's secretary Alfonso, moved to Italy as a papal chamberlain. After he settled at Naples in 1535 as the religious confidant of the noblewomen Giulia Gonzaga and Vittoria Colonna, Valdés presided over a circle of churchmen, including the Capuchin vicar-general, Bernardino Ochino (1487–1564), the Lateran abbot Vermigli, and the Oratorian Marc'Antonio Flaminio (d.1550). These not only discussed theology in the Gonzaga household but also preached in public. Valdés's writings, ostensibly independent of protestantism, have been shown to borrow verbatim from Luther in places. The Neapolitan group was only dispersed on Valdés's death in July 1541.[26] Meanwhile members of the Cassinese order, which cultivated a theology based on the Greek Fathers, stressing salvation by free grace but in a process of inner renewal, strenuously urged catholics and protestants to overcome their differences, in such works as Isidoro Chiari's *Exhortation to Concord* of 1537 and Luciano degli Ottoni's *Commentary of St John Chrysostom on Romans* of 1538.[27]

However, the ambiguities could not remain for ever. A series of revelations alarmed the entrenched conservatives and threw the Italian 'spirituals' or 'evangelicals' into a crisis where hard decisions had to be made. In 1541 Cardinal Contarini gained papal approval to meet representatives of the protestant churches at the religious colloquy at Regensburg, where he and Melanchthon came to a politically dangerous semi-accord.[28] In 1542–3 a little religious treatise, generally known as the *Beneficio di Cristo*, appeared in Venice. This pamphlet, initially composed by a Cassinese monk, Benedetto di Mantova, had been reworked by Marc'Antonio Flaminio with substantial (unacknowledged) extracts from the 1539 edition of Calvin's *Institutes* inserted into the text. Though the source of the quotations was not recognized, the aggressively protestant tone of parts of the work revealed how far its authors had gone.[29]

The public preaching of some of the 'spirituals' in towns like Lucca,[30] the sweeping concessions offered to protestants at Regensburg, and the

Beneficio provoked a storm from the rival grouping at the Curia dominated by Gian Pietro Caraffa, the future Paul IV and the enduring enemy of the 'evangelicals'. Contarini died in August 1542; as he was dying, Ochino and Vermigli abruptly and sensationally fled north to Switzerland to emerge as fully-fledged protestants.[31] Caraffa obtained from Pope Paul III the bull *Licet ab initio* of 21 July 1542 establishing The Roman Inquisition; he contributed to its buildings and was named as one of the first inquisitors-general. On the other hand, Reginald Pole regrouped his allies at his residence as governor of the papal states at Viterbo, where he and Flaminio reconciled themselves to absolute papal obedience. They resisted in vain the explicitly anti-protestant (though subtle) formula on justification adopted at the Council of Trent, believing that in spite of their friends' defection, their own theological position was authentically catholic.[32] The Cassinese monks remained true to their native traditions, contriving to be accused simultaneously of protestant and Pelagian heresies.[33] After Pole failed to be elected pope in the 1549–50 conclave, and even more after Caraffa's elevation as Paul IV in 1555, most of Ochino's and Vermigli's former associates exiled themselves to Switzerland and beyond. Of those who remained, Cardinal Morone was subjected to a humiliating trial (1557–60), while a minor figure, Pietro Carnesecchi, was executed for heresy in 1567.[34]

The older generation of men like Contarini or even Juan de Valdés probably felt that they followed Luther only in so far as they were themselves convinced of his catholic orthodoxy: and therefore never regarded themselves as 'protestants'. Contarini's complicated theology of salvation clearly lacked the dynamic implications of the authentic Reformation.[35] It was the younger figures who found the pressure to take sides irresistible. Broadly speaking, those who were temperamentally publicists and men of action (like Vermigli and Ochino) sooner or later defected to protestantism; those who were essentially contemplatives and disliked public theological wrangling, like Pole, stood by their basic loyalty to the papal Church and, with gritted teeth, put their beliefs in justification by free grace into a more minor key.

4. *Conclusion: A Novel and Destructive Challenge*

The reformers presented the institutional Church with a challenge of an unforeseen kind from an unexpected quarter. There had been, in the pre-Reformation era, plenty of criticism of a bloated and flawed Church organization, and likewise plenty of vigorous theological debate about the saving of souls: but before 1517–21, the two had not really coalesced; nor had one kind of challenge propped up or validated the other. The Reformation actually combined the two kinds of challenge: it redefined the process of saving souls, so that (*a*) the positive role of the old Church, in purveying the means of grace, became redundant; and (*b*) its faults and blemishes (though less obnoxious than its 'idolatry') need no longer be tolerated for the sake of its ministry.

It is important to grasp the essential novelty and destructive power of the reformers' beliefs about human salvation. 'Saving' a human soul was no longer first and foremost a question of moral or ritual purity, dealt out by the priests in doses according to need. It was a 'cloak', a garment of righteousness draped directly by God over the forgiven believer's sins.[36] Therefore, the nursing of the soul and the conscience through life with sacramental and penitential help was redundant; and so was the institution which purveyed such help. A church which *proclaimed*, rather than channelled, the grace of God needed no supranational organization or a vast bureaucracy; on earth it could be as compact as the local community.

Because recent historians have so subtly and ably shown how the reformers remained men of their time and their scholastic or humanist training, much has been said of how they continued to argue within medieval frameworks and with medieval tools. However, their much more obvious and blatant rejections of old and agreed terms of reference need to be noticed as well. Sin, the law, grace, faith, good works, Scripture and tradition, the Church, the sacraments—all these basic building-blocks of theology were redefined, quite fiercely in Melanchthon's case, so as to exclude the old rituals and ways of thinking.[37] The reformers' message on salvation dictated how other issues were defined, instead of being shaped and balanced by them. The tone of Reformation teaching became, and remained, vehemently antagonistic to the papal, Roman Church which condemned it.

However, the reformers' anti-catholicism was a subtle attitude, based on a rarified intellectual system. It was born in the lecture halls and debating chambers, and only with some difficulty taken into the public arena. If humanist scholars were mistaken about Luther's message at first, what hope was there for those with no academic training at all?[38] Therefore, one cannot just say of the doctrine of salvation, 'this is the essence of the Reformation', and then ask why it had such impact or appeal in society at large. The argument here is *only* that the Reformation teaching on salvation was the intellectual reason—the 'core' idea—behind the reformers' reconstruction of Church and society; that this conditioned the leading figures' revolt against the Church, and distinguished them from superficially similar 'forerunners', whether humanist or 'Augustinian'.

There are two other levels on which the Reformation has to be explained. First, what political consideration led communities and governments to become 'reformed' or 'protestant'? Why was it expedient, or necessary, to turn a matter of conscience into an act of state? Secondly, what was the psychological attraction of the reformed programme for individuals? Ordinary lay people may sometimes have understood and approved of the new message of human justification, but many certainly did not. How were non-theologians drawn to the Reformation, and what feature about it so enthralled them? It is perfectly possible, even likely, that the Reformation appealed on either of these levels for reasons which had very little to do with its 'ideal' essence. Those other levels of interpretation are discussed next.

PART III

Establishing the Reformed Churches

The European Reformation did not remain simply a set of opinions or ideas. It coalesced with the political and social aspirations of classes, societies, and governments to inaugurate unprecedentedly sudden and sweeping changes to the Christian dispensation in those societies which adopted it. The coalition between theologians' theories and lay politicians' animosities gave *both* far greater power than before. In the past, politicians—whether the burghers of Strasbourg or the Emperor Maximilian—had always stopped just short of irrevocably breaching Christian unity in their exasperation with pope and priests. From decisions on genuinely spiritual issues of doctrine or worship, they had been almost entirely excluded. Now lay politicians across Europe heard reputable, sincere churchmen tell them to crush priestly power utterly, in the name of the 'community'; and to inaugurate and protect a restructuring of worship and redefinition of belief which had previously been a 'spiritual' monopoly. Civil authorities took ultimate, or even immediate, responsibility for human souls; 'anticlerical' self-assertion, so far from being potentially irreligious or unlawful, became a Christian ruler's duty. The reforming preachers and theologians, for their part, were called on to become constructive legislators, to turn their theses and pamphlets into codes and systems of belief and worship.

This 'establishing' of the Reformation in the states of Europe marked a transitional period in European cultural history. In the medieval West one had no choice but to be born into the (essentially unique and indivisible) Church. Church affairs had political implications, but within a narrow range of options. At the opposite extreme, after the mid-eighteenth century, post-revolutionary France or the United States of America gave no one creed legal or political privileges over another. To caricature this state of affairs: in the Middle Ages the Church's affairs were matters of State, but only for the élite who made the decisions; in contrast, in the modern West choice of faiths is open to everyone, but is no longer a political issue in the same way. However, during the critical few decades in the sixteenth century when the Reformation movement struggled for the right to exist, religion was *both* a political issue, *and* one which involved every rank in society. The Reformation, then, was a curious threshold between the Middle Ages and the modern world. At its height the local, or national, community still insisted that its Christianity *ought* to be a matter of common policy; indeed, it was sincerely believed that wrong faith, or corrupt religion, would certainly bring divine punishment in the form of famine, plague, or other visitations on the *whole* people. Nevertheless, Europe as a whole, and sometimes even small federations within it, had to accept that variety and choice was inescapable; and that overall religious uniformity, even at the theoretical level, was gone for good.

14

Unsuccessful 'Affiliations' to the Reformed Cause

Amongst both English and German speaking historians, the 'social history of the Reformation' has grown enormously in the past thirty years or so. The movement can be explained, and even narrated, largely in terms of the classes, corporations, or political pressure groups which adopted it; their struggles with the established orders—in Church, State, or both—to influence or overturn them; and the motives, ambitions, and animosities which provoked them to take the stances they did. The social–historical approach changes one's perspective: the guildsman and town mayor replace the theologian and the preacher as the primary actors in the drama, while the petition of grievances and the popular pamphlet overtake the theological tract and the liturgy as documents. More regrettably, however, the two main kinds of Reformation history—theological and socio-political—have mostly been written in separate compartments.[1] Most monographs emphasize *either* dogma *or* social conditions, rather than combining them. This *can* give the impression that theological historians believe ideas had a life of their own and that the context in which they were studied hardly matters;[2] or that social historians regard the establishment of the Reformation as 'really' a matter of power politics and class struggle, to which beliefs were marginal.[3] Probably neither of these crude opinions is really held by scholars; but integrating ideas and society remains difficult. One needs not just a 'social history of the Reformation', but a 'social history of reformed belief', in which all levels of religious experience, from the refined and literate to the oral and non-logical, are studied in their settings: as they were talked over, argued about, used as slogans, and adopted as aims.

To become established, the Reformation had to 'affiliate' itself to some social unit. That affiliation needs to be examined on several levels. One can study the various processes, ideological and political, destructive and constructive, which took place between a state first having the ideas of the reformers discussed within its borders, and its acquiring a fully developed reformed church structure. Secondly, the political pressures within states which led (or did not lead) to a total or partial establishment can be analysed: whose wishes carried the day, and how? Thirdly, did establishing the reforms help or hinder the political self-interest of the ruling groups who eventually authorized it? Finally, since laymen, whether as pressure groups, politicians, or rulers, chose to press for the changes, what features about the reformed programme attracted lay people to it?

As will be seen later, Reformation ideas were readily exploited by city fathers or princes to justify, or even sanctify, their ever tighter grip on Church power, patronage, and property.[4] However, all kinds of social groups and classes, winners and losers, harboured grievances and ambitions against the Church. In the early 1520s two such groups broke out into violence against established authority, spurred on to an uncertain and indefinable degree by the Reformation crisis. These two movements, by the imperial 'knights' and the rural proletariat, failed to create a stable or secure political framework within which the reformers' programme could serve their political aims.

1. *The Petty Nobility of Germany*

The free 'knights' of the Empire (the *Reichsritter*) were casualties of economic and political developments within late medieval Germany. Like the princes, they derived their status and authority immediately from the Emperor; but were so vastly inferior to the greater territorial lords in wealth and lands that they shared in none of the political and legal advances made by the latter. They were most numerous in the middle Rhine, Franconia, and Swabia, where no great principalities had been formed. However, they went largely unrepresented in the *Reichstag*; their own associations (like the *Ritterschaft* of Franconia) were subject to interference and obstruction by the princes. The Swabian League, reconstituted in 1488 by Maximilian I as a structure for the cities and lesser nobility of southern Germany, had from 1500 been infiltrated by the princes, until by 1525 the lesser nobles were overawed within it. Those who could not survive off their estates had to find employment either as mercenaries, as courtier-servants of princes, as literary freelancers like von Hutten, or simply as bandits: hence their collective nickname of *Raubritter* ('robber-knights').[5]

The knights therefore developed a life-style and culture both archaic and embattled. Some at least saw their ideal as a form of chivalry: the knights were the protectors of the oppressed poor, offering to support their pleas for justice with their overlords, or to resist the oppressor by force.

They identified themselves with the Emperor on the one hand, and on the other with the common people of town and countryside, and against the princes and the city merchant oligarchies, with their Roman law, their wealth, and their immunity from most forms of punishment. Equally, the knights' precarious situation prevented them from living up to their ideal. In October 1518 von Hutten graphically described the life of the knights: they lived off impoverished estates, received unreliable protection from princes, were forced always to travel armed, and housed in cramped, noisy, uncomfortable castles open to all manner of unsavoury visitors. To the accusation that they were no more than robbers von Hutten replied in 1521 that his class was less greedy and rapacious than the merchants, lawyers, or higher clergy.[6]

The knightly class articulated its 'grievances' from the 1490s onwards, objecting in detail to how the imperial polity was developing. From the Mainz *Reichstag* of 1495 (which forbad the knights' traditional recourse to the feud, or private war), repeated complaints were made about abusive taxes and elaborate, costly, and corrupt justice. The knights also objected to Maximilian I's attempt to regulate their customs by law in 1517.[7] Following the proclamation of internal peace in the Empire at the Worms *Reichstag* of 1521 the knights of Franconia met in Mergentheim, Mainz, and Schweinfurt, and those of Swabia met at Constance, to discuss the presentation of their grievances. The Franconian grievances, presented early in 1523, protested against exactions made by princely lords from knightly tenants; slow, tortuous, expensive, and intrusive justice, whether from princes or the *Reichskammergericht*; the unruly conduct of the Swabian League; and the rapacity of merchants and higher clergy alike.[8]

Ironically, a private quarrel brought these discontents to a head. Franz von Sickingen (exceptionally for a knight) had money to lend, and had invested large sums in loans to Charles V for the costs of his coronation. In the summer of 1522 he was rewarded with a commission to lead an imperial army against French troops in the Low Countries. The campaign went very badly, his loans were not repaid, and von Sickingen was left with huge debts. In this predicament he revived a personal quarrel with the archbishop-elector of Trier, Richard von Greiffenklau, possibly hoping to plunder one of the rich prelates (a class hated by the knights), who was also a suspected enemy of Charles V, and one of the order despised by the reformers. On 29 August 1522 von Sickingen laid siege to Trier. The archbishop, through the dealings of one of von Hutten's relatives, received no help from nearby Mainz. However, he defended his city so well on his own that von Sickingen's equally ill-supported campaign collapsed after a few weeks, and the knights had to retreat to their strongholds. Von Sickingen's ally, Ulrich von Hutten, had meanwhile dissipated his energies (already weakened by disease) in minor raids. Before the former's defeat he had escaped to Sélestat, Basle, and Mulhouse, to die in August 1523 near Zürich.[9] This outbreak of violence gave the princes in the Swabian League the excuse to suppress the whole knightly order. The archbishop of Trier, the Elector Palatine, and Philipp of Hesse besieged and bombarded von Sickingen's castle at Landstuhl, where he died of wounds on 7 May 1523. They then moved against the knights in Franconia, especially the notoriously unruly Thomas von Absberg. They may have destroyed as many as twenty-three noble castles, and thus ended hopes of redressing knightly grievances, in the cause of the Reformation or anything else.[10]

It is too easy to dismiss the knights and their 'Knights' War' as an irrelevant escapade by decadent members of a doomed feudal class, with little bearing on the Reformation proper. However, misguidedly or not, some members of the knightly class were the first to warm to Luther and his cause, just as many had aspired to some familiarity with the ideas of the Renaissance. Franz von Sickingen was an early patron of Bucer, Oecolampadius, and Melanchthon.[11] Hutten was portrayed in the early 1520s in several pamphlet portraits as a fellow struggler for German liberty alongside Luther, whom he supported rather obliquely with his verse satires.[12] The knight Hartmuth von Kronberg wrote some of the earliest pamphlets in support of the Reformation, combining his own vision of society with Lutheran ideals.[13] The imperial knights have suffered the double stigma, for modern historians, of being both aristocrats and failures. They might, in other circumstances, have deformed the reformers' ideals no worse than the princes or merchants who dispossessed them; or the petty nobility of France, Poland, England, Scotland, or The Netherlands who became 'natural' patrons of a later phase of the Reformation.

2. *Communal Movements in Rural Germany*

Late medieval Germany saw sporadic outbursts of violent rebellion by the rural population. Such outbursts were unevenly distributed across the Empire: they broke out particularly readily in the upper Rhineland, including Württemberg and Baden; in Alsace and Swabia, and the adjoining Swiss confederation; and to the east, in Austria proper, as well as in the Austrian dependencies of Steiermark (Styria), Kärnten (Carinthia), and Krain (Carniola). These revolts grew more frequent in the years up to

1525. Only seven have been identified in the first half of the fifteenth century; six during 1450–74, eight in 1475–99, but no less than eighteen in 1500–24. They arose basically from economic and legal grievances. However, they were unevenly spread; so it is unlikely that harsher economic conditions (common everywhere) alone produced them. They occurred most readily where the peasantry were used to organizing themselves into communities (*Gemeinde*), based on a village, a jurisdiction, or a state. The peasantry, already used to regulating some of their economic, legal, and police needs, felt bound to their lords only in so far as those lords were willing and able to protect them; and argued that the lords' power ought to be limited, conditional, and used responsibly.[14]

Faced with a shortage of tenants and a decline in revenues, late medieval landlords had ruthlessly exploited their remaining privileges, reimposing servile status on unfree tenants, and withdrawing previously conceded rights to commons, woods, and rivers. In smaller principalities and lordships where revolts broke out, the principal grievance seems to have been precisely such revivals of feudal burdens by lords whom the peasants no longer felt morally bound to respect as feudal patrons. The peasants called for a return to the state of things before the new duties: a return to the so-called 'old law' of custom and mutual obligation. In larger principalities (Württemberg or Austria, for instance) taxes, and the activities of a sophisticated princely bureaucracy, were usually the objects of peasant protest.[15] Though these revolts broke out in all kinds of jurisdictions, Church lordships suffered extensively. In 1462 the peasants of the archbishopric of Salzburg rose in protest against an increase in taxes, also citing grievances about landlords' dues and court procedures; further risings occurred there in 1478 and 1504. In other ecclesiastical and monastic estates, there were revolts at Salem (1468), Kempten (1491–2), Ochsenhausen (1496–1502), St Peter (c.1500), and Berchtesgaden (1506). These revolts by no means always ended badly for the peasantry. In most cases where grievances were formally presented, new obligations were henceforth confined to a stipulated, lower level. In Ochsenhausen in 1502 these dues and rights were confirmed by the intervention and arbitration of the powerful Swabian League.[16]

A complex set of pressures widened and deepened the sense of discontent of the rural and urban masses until, between the autumn of 1524 and the spring of 1526, lands as far apart as Swabia and Samland, or the Rhineland and the Tyrol, were convulsed by rebellions of unprecedented breadth and scale; in central and southern Germany only Bavaria escaped. These interlinked revolts are often collectively called the 'Peasants' War'

(*Bauernkrieg*), by analogy with the 'Cities' War' of 1449–53, the 'Knights' War' of 1522–3, and the 'Princes' War' of 1552. In fact, like the abortive *Bundschuh* conspiracies,[17] these involved much more than just the peasantry; but unlike the pre-1521 revolts, more spiritual idealism, and more elaborate and sweeping plans for social reform, were urged than in most of the earlier risings. There were five major areas and complexes of popular rebellion: (*a*) the first risings in the district of Stühlingen just north-west of Schaffhausen, which spread down the Klettgau to Waldshut and across to the Breisgau; (*b*) the revolts in upper Swabia, in the triangle of land between Lake Constance and the valleys of the Iller and the Danube; (*c*) the rebellion in Franconia, around the cities of Heilbronn and Würzburg; (*d*) that in Thuringia, centred around the large town of Mühlhausen; and (*e*) the rebellions in the Austrian provinces, the family lands of the Habsburgs. For the sake of clarity each of the major revolts will be discussed in turn.[18]

2.1. *Stühlingen and the Breisgau*

In June 1524 several hundred tenants of Count Siegmund von Lupfen at Stühlingen rebelled against the detailed and obnoxious exactions imposed by their lord. They chose a leader, a former mercenary called Hans Müller of Bulgenbach, and in August allied with the town of Waldshut, where a popular preacher named Balthasar Hubmaier (1481–1528) had roused the population against its Austrian rulers.[19] When this group allied itself with Zürich, the Habsburgs' representatives were forced to play for time. The peasants of Stühlingen presented their grievances to the *Reichkammergericht* in the following April.[20] In May 1525 Müller of Bulgenbach captured Freiburg-im-Breisgau.[21] This revolt was initially inspired by strictly agrarian and legal issues. Religious enthusiasm became involved only when, during November and December 1524, the preacher Thomas Müntzer (*c.*1489–1525) travelled around Stühlingen and Waldshut looking for support for his own more drastic ideas of revolution.[22] The local Austrian officials had problems nearer home, so they engaged in insincere talks with the rebels at Stockach, and left the revolt to burn itself out.

2.2. *Swabia*

In October and November 1524 the unrest spread eastwards into Swabia, producing risings round Lake Constance in the Allgäu, the Hegau, and the Thurgau. In February 1525 these were joined by the tenants of the abbey of Kempten. In February–March 1525 six armies of rebels gradually coalesced: the Allgäu army, based on Kempten; the Lake army from the northern side of Lake Constance; the Baltringen army, based on Biberach and drawing its support from the Donauried; an army based on the Hegau district on the south-eastern edge of the Black Forest; and armies from the lower Allgäu and the Leipheim district. On 6–7 March 1525 the Allgäu, Lake, and Baltringen armies met at Memmingen in the so-called 'Peasants' Parliament'. There they adopted the 'Twelve Articles', a distillation of dozens of broadly similar lists prepared by the Swabian communities, probably prepared by the Memmingen furrier Sebastian Lotzer with the help of the preacher Christoph Schappeler, and reflecting especially the concerns of the Baltringen army, the largest Swabian band. These articles were then printed and went through twenty-five editions and perhaps as many thousands of copies, circulated throughout the Empire.[23]

Only the Swabian League had the force and authority to tackle such widespread unrest. However, early in 1525 the League's general Georg Truchsess von Waldburg was busy coping with the exiled Duke Ulrich of Württemberg; the latter, dispossessed by the Habsburgs in 1519, briefly besieged Stuttgart in March; his troops then deserted and he fled. The Swabian League negotiated with the leaders of the peasant bands at Ulm until talks were broken off on 25 March. Truchsess and his army then tackled the peasant bands piecemeal. The Leipheim army gave in without a struggle. On 13 April Truchsess defeated the Baltringers, who had been besieging his own castle of the Waldburg, near Wurzach. During 15–17 April, outnumbered by the large Lake army at Gaisbeuren, he negotiated the treaty of Weingarten, which yielded to some demands on condition that the rebels disbanded. Remaining resistance in Swabia was suppressed in July.[24]

2.3. *Franconia*

The rebellion in Franconia, from March and April 1525, was more revolutionary than the Swabian risings. As in the south several separate revolts combined. One of the first broke out at Rothenburg ob der Tauber on 21 March, when the peasants of the village of Ohrenbach delivered a protest to the patricians of Rothenburg and were promptly joined by the town's artisans under a knight, Stephan von Menzingen. In mid-April the town underwent a vehement, iconoclastic Reformation under the hesitant and unlikely leadership of Andreas Karlstadt; on 14 May it joined the towns of Heilbronn, Wimpfen, and Dinkelsbühl in the 'brotherly covenant' of the Franconian peasants to attack the prince-bishop of Würzburg. On 26 March the peasants of the Odenwald had formed an army under the serf

Jäcklein Rohrbach. This army was also joined by minor nobles, like the knights Florian Geyer and Götz von Berlichingen and the lawyer Wendel Hipler. Four other rebel bands were also formed. The Franconian rebels captured the castle of the Weinsberg on 16 April; Rohrbach's group then massacred its noble custodian and seventeen knights the following day. The rebels then took the neighbouring city of Heilbronn, where the lawyers among them soon formed a peasants' assembly like that at Memmingen. After capturing Würzburg they settled down to the siege of the prince-bishop's fortress. Rohrbach's band, disowned by other Franconian rebels after the Weinsberg massacre, terrorized most of the local knights into collaborating with the insurgents. Truchsess then turned from the Swabians to subdue the Franconians. He defeated a peasant army at Böblingen in Württemberg on 12 May, and the news of this, and of the peasant defeat at Zabern (Saverne) in Alsace five days later, forced the delegates at Heilbronn to disperse. The Weinsberg was then recaptured; Rohrbach, as the leader of those who had massacred the nobles there, was burned to death over a slow fire. After a further brief rebel assembly at Schweinfurt on 1–2 June, a detachment of the rebels who had left Würzburg was defeated at Königshofen on 2 June. Florian Geyer's group was then defeated at Ingolstadt, and Würzburg reoccupied after talks during 5–8 June.[25]

2.4. *Thuringia*

The Thuringian revolt was centred in the free city of Mühlhausen, where from early 1523 the preacher Heinrich Pfeiffer had been pushing forward a populist urban reformation. In the autumn of 1524 he had been joined by the fiery preacher Thomas Müntzer, who had just escaped from Allstedt; first expelled, they had returned by February 1525. By mid-March they had replaced the city council (which had originally expelled them) with an 'eternal council' of their party. In late April and early May, as the Twelve Articles circulated in the region, the revolt spread to the rural districts of Allstedt, Sangershausen, and Mansfeld, and to towns such as Fulda, Erfurt, Zwickau, Merseburg, Nordhausen, and Goslar. In May Müntzer, with Mühlhausen and Frankenhausen as his strongholds, threatened the counts of Mansfeld. However, this revolt which the local princes had seemed powerless to combat was abruptly and suddenly suppressed by the forces of Philipp of Hesse and Duke Georg of Saxony. On 15 May they confronted the peasants outside Frankenhausen and routed them. Müntzer was captured shortly afterwards hiding in an attic, and on 27 May he and Pfeiffer with fifty-two others were executed.[26]

2.5. *The Austrian lands*

In February 1525 the Swabian rebels contacted the people of the Tyrol, already wavering in their obedience to Archduke Ferdinand of Austria. In May rebellion broke out in the southern part of the province in the Adige and Isarco valleys. At a gathering at Brixen (Bressanone) on 13 May the rebels chose Michael Gaismair from the region of Sterzing (Vipiteno) as leader. The archduke pacified matters by negotiation in June, but Gaismair fled to Switzerland, to return to besiege Rastadt in May–July 1526. Meanwhile the peasants and miners subject to the archbishop of Salzburg rebelled in June 1525; in Styria rebels under Michael Gruber captured Siegmund von Dietrichstein, the regional governor sent to suppress them, at Schladming on 3 June.[27]

There were numerous other outbreaks of unrest, whether in the west, on the Main around Mainz or Frankfurt, the Rhine Palatinate, Alsace (where rebellion was only suppressed by the active armed intervention of Duke Antoine of Lorraine), Montbéliard, or parts of Burgundy; to the south, in the lands of Schaffhausen and Solothurn; to the north-east in Samland; or to the east, amongst the mining communities of eastern Saxony or Austria. The rural revolts also triggered urban uprisings like those which acted as midwives to the urban Reformations of northern Germany.[28]

The relationship between the Peasants' War and the Reformation has been explained in many different ways.[29] However, it has been assumed rather too readily that one can simply test the demands and behaviour of the peasants against the prescriptions of the reformers, and then judge whether the peasants 'really' belonged to the Reformation. A first way— but an inadequate one—to 'test' the peasants' movement is to examine Luther's own response to it. His response was shaped by the violence and lack of talks peculiar to the Thuringian outbreak, and by its connections with the 'fanatic' Müntzer. Luther's first *Admonition to Peace* was written about 19–20 April 1525, when the Twelve Articles had circulated, but the worst violence had not yet erupted. It laid equal blame on the rulers for oppressing the peasants and the peasants for acting as judges in their own cause. He called for negotiations, and applauded the Treaty of Weingarten when news of it reached him. From 21 April to 4 May he travelled round Saxony preaching to the peasantry and experienced their excited mood at first hand—and at some risk to himself. By 10 May the uproar had spread far and wide, and the princes seemed to have neither the men nor the will to resist the revolt. In some desperation he republished his tract with a notorious addition, *Against the Robbing and Murdering Hordes of Other*

Peasants. The rulers, he wrote, were to do their spiritual duty by praying, offering terms to the rebels, and punishing them with swift and brutal force if they refused. So sudden was the Thuringian rebels' collapse, however, that Luther's addition seemed (and was taken to be) an encouragement to the senseless murder of already defeated rebels, both innocent and guilty, which accompanied the suppression of the revolt; then and later, in fact, he condemned both peasants' and rulers' outrages.[30]

However, was Luther typical? His violent and bloodthirsty language was regretted and resented by temperamental moderates like Melanchthon. His celebration of his marriage during the punitive massacres in mid-June 1525 was seen to be in bad taste.[31] Yet amongst the Lutheran reformers at least, the *substance* of his objection to the revolts, that the use of unlawful means to establish reforms would plunge society into confusion, seems to have been much more widely shared. Many other theologians, including such major figures as Urbanus Rhegius, Johannes Brenz, or Nikolaus von Amsdorf, adopted similarly conservative attitudes.[32] Johann Rurer preached against the peasants' 'misunderstanding' of the Lutheran message in Kitzingen at the height of the unrest.[33] Outside the Saxon context responses were much more equivocal, especially where churchmen could see the more constructive and moderate face of peasant unrest. Even if religious leaders like Müntzer or Balthasar Hubmaier can be set aside for the moment,[34] several preachers in southern and central Germany gave more than a sympathetic ear to the peasants. Karlstadt at Rothenburg, Christoph Schappeler at Memmingen, and probably Sebastian Hofmeister and Sebastian Meyer at Schaffhausen, all became involved in shaping the religious content and expression of the 1525 rebels' demands.[35]

However, this whole approach—examining the reactions of the reformers to the events of 1525—can distort the question. Even if individual reformers disowned the rebels, the whole movement may still fairly be seen as another (unsuccessful) attempt to integrate themes of the Reformation programme into the aspirations of the majority of the German and Swiss proletariat. Recent historians have seen correspondences between elements of the social vision of the early Reformation, especially as represented by Zwingli and the south Germans, and the reforming vision of the peasant manifestoes. Essentially, both reformers *and* peasant leaders urged that the 'community' be reformed by the free preaching of 'the Gospel', the diversion of misused Church funds to the common good, the communal election of a preaching minister to be sustained from reallocated funds, and the replacement of 'human' (defective) ordinances with 'godly' laws. To this extent it is plausible to claim that the (abortive) peasant 'Reformation' and the urban communal Reformations sought many of the same broad ideals.[36] Although the suggestion remains controversial, some recent research on the peasantry of Alsace partly supports the basic thesis: the peasants 'interpreted' the Reformation message just as any other order of early sixteenth-century society interpreted it. The call to instal reformed preaching went hand in hand with political demands; in some cases it was the same 'lord' (the bishop) of whom the demands were made.[37]

Even if one can rehabilitate the more high minded of the peasants' aims, and accept them as a valid modification of the social message of the Reformation for the 'community', their 'communal' Reformation was none the less a short lived failure. The introduction of 'the Gospel' and 'godly law' into the rural community at the grass-roots level, in isolation from or defiance of the territorial sovereign, never progressed—perhaps never *could* have progressed in any normal context—beyond pamphlets and paper projects.[38] With the towns it was very different.

15
Self-Governing Towns and Cities

In most regions of Europe no more than one in ten, and more commonly one in twenty, of the people lived enclosed within the walls of a corporate town. Nevertheless, the overwhelming majority of recent social analyses of the Reformation have studied corporate towns, and mostly large ones at that. A. G. Dickens's memorable remark that the Reformation was an 'urban event' has been endlessly quoted.[1] The point, however, is not that cities were the only, the most important, or even always the first places to become reformed: rather that they above all else possessed the concentration of people, the literary awareness, and the political sophistication to propel the ideas of preachers and pamphleteers to the forefront of the political agenda in the early 1520s. It was much easier for city tradesmen to learn about the Reformation, become enthusiasts for it, and then press reform measures upon the city fathers living a few streets away, than for farmers or villagers even to hear a reforming preacher, let alone to lobby a distant prince or king on that preacher's behalf. The seductive attraction of the urban Reformation lies in the great variety of people whom it allowed to contribute at all levels—from that of a council debate to an image-breaking mob—to the Reformation process.[2]

The distinctive cultural, social, and indeed religious priorities of the towns and cities left them especially well placed, in the aftermath of the Worms *Reichstag*, to translate their approval for Luther's stand into the language of urban politics. The 'coalition' between the Reformation message and the aspirations of the cities was possibly the most successful and complete of all. This was natural, in that many of Luther's prescriptions for moral and social reform in *To the Christian Nobility* were (despite the book's title) most appropriate to a corporate town.[3] Most of the other influential reformers worked in cities larger, more sophisticated, and more autonomous than Wittenberg; so the 'urban component' in their thought coloured their vision of the Christian community even more deeply than Luther's.[4] The urban Reformation coalesced so successfully with civic aspirations that it sometimes took many years before differences in priorities between reforming churchmen and urban reforming politicians emerged as a serious problem.[5]

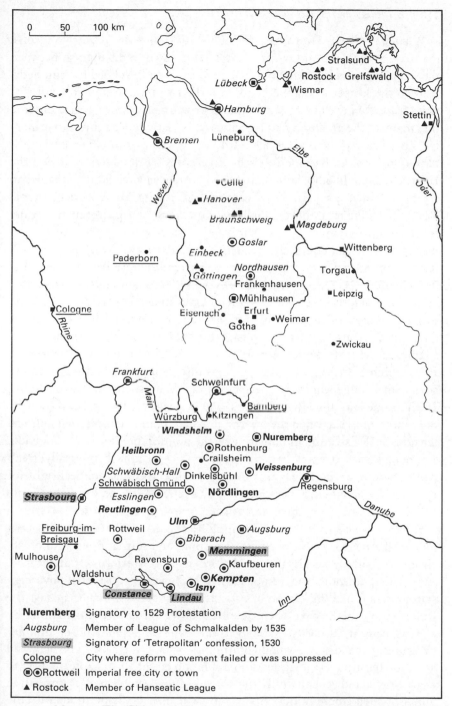

0   50   100 km

Stralsund
Rostock Greifswald
Lübeck ●
Wismar
Stettin
Hamburg
Lüneburg
Bremen
Elbe
Weser
Oder
Celle
Hanover
Braunschweig
Magdeburg
Goslar
Wittenberg
Einbeck
Paderborn
Nordhausen
Torgau
Göttingen
Frankenhausen
Leipzig
Mühlhausen
Cologne
Erfurt
Eisenach
Weimar
Rhine
Gotha
Zwickau
Frankfurt
Schweinfurt
Main
Bamberg
Würzburg Kitzingen
Windsheim
Nuremberg
Heilbronn
Rothenburg
Crailsheim
Schwäbisch-Hall
Weissenburg
Schwäbisch Gmünd Dinkelsbühl
Strasbourg
Esslingen
Nördlingen
Regensburg
Reutlingen
Danube
Freiburg-im-
Breisgau
Ulm
Augsburg
Rottweil
Biberach
Mulhouse
Memmingen
Ravensburg
Kaufbeuren
Waldshut
Kempten
Constance
Isny
Lindau
Inn

Nuremberg Signatory to 1529 Protestation
Augsburg Member of League of Schmalkalden by 1535
Strasbourg Signatory of 'Tetrapolitan' confession, 1530
Cologne City where reform movement failed or was suppressed
◉◉Rottweil Imperial free city or town
▲ Rostock Member of Hanseatic League

MAP 1. The Cities and Towns of the Empire and the Reformation

What was a 'self-governing city'? This question is far harder to resolve than at first appears. In German history it is usual to distinguish between the sixty-five or so 'free imperial cities' (*Reichsstädte*), subordinate immediately to the Emperor, on one hand, and the two thousand or so territorial cities (*Landstädte*) ruled by some kind of prince on the other; and to observe that many of the greater territorial cities (especially those subject to prince-bishops) had by the end of the Middle Ages cut down their overlord's power so far as to become in effect 'free cities' (*Freistädte*).[6] Outside the Empire one could add to the number of clearly sovereign cities the urban capitals of such northern Swiss cantons and territories as Zürich, Berne, Basle, Schaffhausen, or St Gallen. However, 'self-government' really involved more complex issues than whether an emperor, prince, or prince-bishop was ultimately in charge. Inasmuch as every 'town' or 'city' was (by definition) a community somehow chartered or privileged to conduct its own affairs, *every* town was 'self-governing' until and unless its ultimate ruler chose to intervene. Many 'subject' cities in fact experienced the same social pressures for the Reformation, and adopted it as enthusiastically, as their 'free' rivals. Erfurt was ultimately subject to the archbishop of Mainz, Zwickau to the elector of Saxony, Kitzingen to the *Markgraf* of Brandenburg-Ansbach; yet they yield as interesting social lessons, or more so, as small but technically 'free' cities like Windsheim or Dinkelsbühl.[7] In the same way the cities of Lausanne or Geneva, though governed by the canton of Berne when they were reformed, underwent internal political tensions as decisive and illuminating as the political pressures from outside. At the opposite extreme, *every* city-state, no matter how theoretically 'free', had to beware of threats from powerful neighbours. The political rights of the 'free' imperial cities were drastically curtailed by the Emperor in the 1550s, while one, Constance, was turned into a territorial town.[8]

A city was effectively 'self-governing' to the extent that it made its own policy whether to establish the Reformation, and how and when to do so, as opposed simply to carrying out the orders of its overlords. It might have gained that freedom and responsibility by being a substantial sovereign state in itself, like the canton of Zürich; or the decision for or against the Reformation might have been devolved downwards to the commune by a weak central authority. Whatever the external diplomatic or military pressures, such self-governing communities made their own alliances and stood or fell by their own decisions. The object of this chapter is first to chart briefly and schematically the spread of the 'established' Reformation amongst such communities; an attempt will then be made to identify the various processes, ideological and political, destructive and constructive, which took place between a state first having the reformers' teachings discussed openly within its borders, and its acquiring a fully developed reformed Church liturgy, structure, and confession of belief.

1. *The Urban Reformation in Germany*

The urban Reformation movements consisted of a whole series of collective decisions by individual communities against a shifting set of external and internal pressures. Such complexity absolutely precludes a continuous narrative from being both clear and readable. The only course—at the expense of any lingering claims to elegance—is to present short, summary discussions of the various areas in which the different types of urban Reformation took place, and then resort to tables and lists.

1.1. *Wittenberg*

During Luther's absence at the Wartburg other reform-minded clergy turned words into deeds at Wittenberg. Karlstadt and Luther's fellow Augustinian Gabriel Zwilling (*c.*1487–1558) pressed for changes in worship in line with the ideas Luther had taught. They urged the giving of the wine (traditionally reserved to the clergy) to all in the communion, and from Michaelmas 1521 did so; they wished to abolish all 'sacrificial' private masses said without a congregation. That same autumn Augustinian Eremites began to abandon their vows, rules and cloister. At Christmas 1521 Karlstadt celebrated a drastically revised and simplified mass, repeated twice early in 1522 before large congregations. On 19 January 1522 Karlstadt married publicly. Meanwhile the reform of the Wittenberg Augustinians degenerated into rioting and the destruction of altars. Matters were further heated by the arrival in Wittenberg of three 'prophets' from Zwickau, a student (Marcus Thomae or Stübner) and two weavers, Nikolaus Storch and Thomas Drechsel, preaching strange notions about dreams and the coming millennium.[9]

On 25 January 1522 Wittenberg's town council adopted a new Church order. This provided for a common fund to support the needy, banned begging (religious or otherwise) and prostitution, and laid down rules for church worship. The plan was Karlstadt's, though the ideas were from Luther's works, especially *To the Christian Nobility*.[10] The cautious Elector Friedrich, however, disowned the order and disapproved of the changes;

his intervention caused confusion and insecurity. In this atmosphere Luther returned to Wittenberg on 6 March 1522. From 9 March he preached a series of eight sermons, with a message which ended the disorders: the timing, not the essence of the changes had been wrong; more teaching was needed, and when it was absorbed reform of worship could follow.[11] He dismissed the 'prophets' with contempt (unfortunately forming his own view of more enthusiastic reformers from their example). Most of the changes in worship were postponed.

Thereafter Wittenberg was reformed gradually, according to Luther's method. In 1522–3 he published works on marriage, political questions, and the rights of congregations to elect pastors. Meanwhile lay people were offered the wine in communion at Wittenberg (late 1522), and in 1523 Luther published a first (Latin) *Formula of the Mass*. Late in 1524 the old mass ceased to be said anywhere in the town's churches. That same year Luther published some of his soon to be famous German hymns. By October 1525, Luther's hesitancy had led to a host of divergent services being established by others; he therefore devised the *German Mass*, which was published, along with a purified Latin rite, in 1526.[12] In these rituals Luther retained as much of the old as he could: the communion host continued to be 'elevated' before the people at Wittenberg until 1542. In the late 1520s Luther began to preach sermons on the 'catechism', the question-and-answer formulary used for basic religious instruction. In April 1529 he published his (long) *German Catechism*, an advanced manual for instructing pastors, teachers, and parents in his understanding of the Gospel; it was supplemented by the simpler *Small Catechism* in May.[13]

1.2. *Saxony*

The combination of fervent preaching and the involvement of the town council, which had led to such upheavals in Wittenberg, was meanwhile repeated in other parts of Germany subject to Luther's influence. Up to and beyond Elector Friedrich's death in 1525 the towns of Saxony were given little guidance from their overlord, and partly left to find their own way towards Reformation. Table 15.1 gives some indication of the process of change.[14] After 1528–9 events in the towns of electoral Saxony were overtaken by Elector Johann's own measures to organize the territorial church through visitations.[15] Meanwhile Lutheran influence also reached towns theoretically subject to princes of the Church. At Erfurt Johannes Lang and Johannes Culsamer preached to such effect that the laity were given the communion cup in 1523, Church property was seized in 1524, and a new Church order was instituted in 1525, ultimately secured by the

TABLE 15.1

Town	Preacher	New orders	Dates
Allstedt	T. Müntzer	Service orders	1523–4
Altenburg	W. Linck	Common chest	1522
Coburg		Service order	1524
Colditz	W. Fues		
Eilenburg	G. Zwilling	Cup to laity	1523
Eisenach	J. Strauss		
Gotha	F. Myconius		
Leisnig		Common chest	1523
Schweinitz		German mass	1524
Torgau		Church orders	pre-1529
Zwickau	N. Hausmann	German liturgy	1524–5

Treaty of Hammelburg with the archbishop of Mainz in 1530. Meanwhile the episcopal town of Naumburg adopted a new Church order in 1527.[16]

1.3 *Lutheranism in Franconia and central Germany*

Having received and protected so many Lutheran preachers, Nuremberg was able, up to 1524, to equivocate by instructing its preachers to maintain order and leave the old rites intact.[17] Notwithstanding, matters moved gradually towards a crisis in March 1525, after which the adoption of fully reformed orders followed, as shown in Table 15.2.[18]

TABLE 15.2

Date	Measures
1522	Mandates on preaching
	Order for poor relief
1524	German baptism order
	Prior Volprecht's reformed mass
	Provosts' articles
1525	Disputation
	Suppression of monasteries and expulsion of some monks
	New German mass orders
1528	Nuremberg articles on doctrine
	Nuremberg–Brandenburg–Ansbach Church order
1533	Nuremberg–Brandenburg–Ansbach Church order
	Catechism

TABLE 15.3

Town	Preacher	New orders	Dates
Crailsheim	Adam Weiss	Church order	1526
Heilbronn		Reformation	1525–32
Kitzingen		Order for the poor	1523
		Edict on preaching	1524
		Baptism order	1526
		Church orders	1528[a]
Reutlingen	M. Alber	German liturgy	1523–4
Schwäbisch-Hall	J. Brenz	Church order	1526
Weissenburg		Service order	1528
Windsheim		Common chest	1524
Rothenburg		Church order	1559
Schweinfurt		Church order	1543

[a] Through intervention of the local prince.

During the 1520s the Lutheran movement found its geographical limits in central and southern Germany, with the introduction of reforming measures in the towns shown in Table 15.3.[19]

1.4. *Lutheranism in north Germany and the Baltic coast*

The politics of introducing the Reformation in the north German towns listed in Table 15.4 tended to follow a pattern. Lutheran sermons crystallized urban unrest amongst those excluded from power by the increasingly exclusive urban oligarchies. The Reformation was introduced in the wake of constitutional upheavals and the replacement or inhibition of the city patriciates by so-called 'citizen committees' (*Bürgerausschusse*) in the late 1520s. However, the introduction of the Reformation Church order itself (usually through the intervention of Luther's ally Johannes Bugenhagen) was peaceful and orderly, and managed to survive when the oligarchies reasserted themselves in the mid-1530s. Similar movements brought the Reformation into Germanic cities within Poland, such as Danzig, Thorn, and Braunsberg.[20]

1.5. *Strasbourg and the cities of the 'tetrapolitan' confession*

Strasbourg was by 1523 even better endowed with eloquent reforming clergy than Nuremberg; its preachers, above all Zell, Bucer, Capito, and Hedio, looked more and more readily towards Zürich for guidance, less towards Wittenberg with its preference for gradual change. Somewhat like

TABLE 15.4

Town	Dates of major change
Bremen	to 1528
Braunschweig	1528
Celle	1526
Einbeck	1529–32
Göttingen	1529–31
Greifswald	1531–2
Goslar	1528
Hamburg	1528
Hanover	1533 4
Lübeck	1531
Lüneburg	1531
Magdeburg	1524
Northeim	1539
Rostock	1531
Stettin	1535
Stralsund	from 1525
Wismar	1535

Nuremberg, the city council there tried to have its preachers 'confine themselves to preaching from Scripture' and avoid irrevocable breaches with the old Church as long as possible. However, the crucial transition came early in 1524, and the measures shown in Table 15.5 ensued.[21]

Reformed Strasbourg most readily found allies amongst some towns in Swabia which had turned earliest to the Reformation. A discernible 'south

TABLE 15.5

Date	Measure
1.12.1523	Edict on 'scriptural' preaching
16.2.1524	Eucharistic cup given to laity
19.4.1524	First German mass and baptism
1524	Bucer publishes his *Grund und Ursache aus göttlicher Schrift*
11.1524–4.1525	Most celebrations of the mass forbidden piecemeal
1527	Capito's *Catechism* issued
1529	Mass forbidden altogether
	Monasteries closed
	City signs *Protestation* against edict of Speyer *Reichstag*
1530	Submits 'tetrapolitan' confession
1531–4	Church orders introduced

TABLE 15.6

Town	Preachers	Preaching mandate	Mass banned	Church orders
CONSTANCE	A. Blarer	9.2.1524	1528	1531–4
	J. Zwick			
MEMMINGEN				
(i)	C. Schappeler	1523–4		Cup to laity
				End to priestly privileges
				(measures revoked 1525ᵃ)
(ii)	S. Schenck		1528	1528 Church orders
				1529 Liturgy
				1532 Discipline
				1531–3 *Städtetag* orders
LINDAU	T. Gassner			1525 Reformed mass
				1527 German psalter
				1533 discipline, poor relief

ᵃ The temporary reversal of the Memmingen Reformation was a direct result of its involvement with the Swabian 'peasant bands' during 1525.

German' civic pattern emerged, quite different from that in the north: preaching, followed in several cases by a 'preaching mandate' urging restraint, then pressure from the trade guilds, culminating (usually) not in a constitutional coup but a tactical change of heart by the town council, sometimes backed up by a census of opinions within the city's guildsmen or householders. Matters developed more or less as shown in Table 15.6.[22]

1.6. *Other south German cities*

In free cities apart from the above the Reformation gained a foothold rather more slowly. In several cases a change (albeit a peaceful one) in the magistracy was necessary to break the deadlock and introduce the reforms.[23] Of the cities listed in Table 15.7, Augsburg (by far the richest and most populous) deserves special mention. Contests between Lutheran and Zwinglian preachers during the 1520s led the council to make no official changes, and to preserve catholic worship, and accept the anti-reforming Speyer edict in 1529. Charles V ordered all the evangelical preachers to be dismissed when the *Reichstag* met there in 1530; the city declared it could not comply. Augsburg was thus neutral and isolated: the lead was then taken up by the city's physician Gereon Sailer (d.1562), who drew the city closer to Strasbourg, and by the newly arrived preachers Wolfgang Müslin ('Musculus', 1497–1563), and Bonifatius Wolfhart (d.1543). In January 1533 the city's preachers petitioned the city council to do something against the hitherto tolerated catholic worship. The council was faced with

TABLE 15.7

Town	Preachers	Mass banned	Church orders	Alliances
Augsburg	W. Musculus	1537	7/1534 Mandate	1536 Schmal
			1537 Church order	
			Catechism	
			Sacraments	
Biberach	B. Millius	1531	1531	
Esslingen	J. Otther	1532	1533–4	
Frankfurt[a]	D. Melander	1532		1532 Schmal
Isny	P. Fagius		1531–4	1531 Schmal
Kempten		1532–4	Details settled c.1540	
Mulhouse[b]		1528–9	1523 Worship reformed	
			1528–9 Church order	
Ulm	K. Sam		1528 School orders	
			1529 Hymnbook and Psalter	1531 Schmal
	M. Frecht	6/1531	8/1531 Liturgy and discipline	

[a] Frankfurt-am-Main is far to the north of Swabia, but adopted a Swabian-type Reformation under the influence of Dionysius Melander from Ulm.
[b] Mulhouse (Mühlhausen in Alsace) was reformed under direct influence from neighbouring Swiss churches.
[Dinkelsbühl, Nördlingen, Ravensburg, and Regensburg hesitated even longer, and finally introduced the Reformation in the 1540s.]

conflicting advice: its most respected personality, civic secretary Konrad Peutinger (with others), advised doing nothing against the laws of the Empire; in spite of this, the need to respond to popular pressure and the spiritual concerns of some leading citizens forced the council to decide on principle for reform in April 1533, and to carry it through in the summer of 1534, with elaborate safeguards for the power of the council.[24]

2. *The Reformation of the Urban Cantons of Switzerland*

2.1. *Zürich*

Zwingli had regarded his performance in the January 1523 disputation as a victory; the council probably still thought themselves safe in imposing their criterion of 'conformity to Scripture' on the preachers.[25] However, worship in Zürich began to change irrevocably in mid-1523. Zwingli's ally Leo Keller, known as Leo Jud (1482–1542), devised a German baptism order, first used on 10 August; he and Zwingli began to raise objections to images (including crucifixes) in the churches, and to the form of the mass. On 26–8 October 1523 a second disputation was held. Zwingli was barely opposed in this debate, although the council deferred further changes in

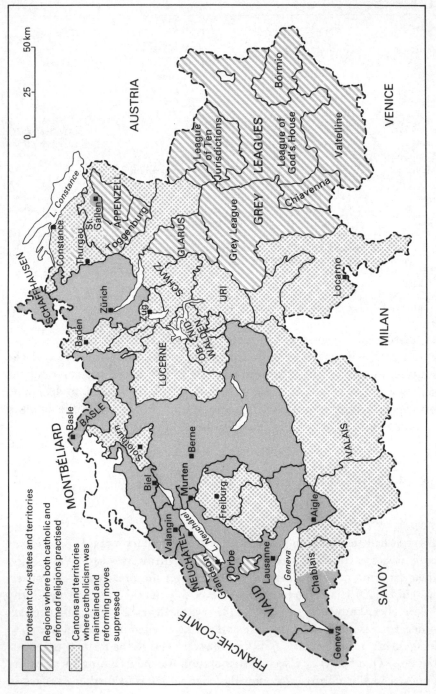

MAP 2. The Swiss Confederation, *c.*1540

worship. A third disputation (13–14 January 1524) broke the opposition, and on 15 June the council approved a disciplined removal of images. In April 1525 Zwingli prepared and printed a German mass; on 12 April the council ordered that the old mass should cease. Meanwhile monasticism was also taken in hand. Most monks and friars were won over, and on 3 December 1524 the remainder were amalgamated at the Franciscan house and the other houses confiscated. Within two years Zürich had destroyed the old religious order as thoroughly as any imperial city.[26]

2.2. *Berne, Basle, St Gallen, Schaffhausen*

Zürich's neighbours in northern Switzerland moved rather more gradually. By the early 1520s several churchmen in Berne, a small city with its large rural hinterland, were sympathizers of Luther and Zwingli, most notably Berchtold Haller (*c*.1492–1536). Berne's Reformation, however, took the course shown in Table 15.8.[27]

TABLE 15.8

Date	Measure
15.6.1523	Edict on scriptural preaching (repeated 22.11.1524, 21.5.1526, and 17.5.1527)
Easter 1527	City council has reforming majority; priests marry openly; corporate masses abandoned
6.1.1528	Berne disputation, attended by leading Swiss and south German reformers
26.1.1528	City bans the mass, provides for removal of altars and images, and for new service order, formally allows priests to marry, and confiscates Church property
9–14.1.1532	Berne synod establishes church structures

A similar slow Reformation occurred further north at Basle. The city council ordained 'scriptural' preaching in May 1523; but, as at Berne, no visible change resulted, and catholic preachers were if anything stronger and more stubborn in their resistance. During 1527 and early 1528 the council tried to suppress the hostilities by assigning places of worship to the reformers; sporadic image-breaking, and the city's active printing presses, aggravated tension. A guildsmen's meeting in December petitioned for the abolition of the mass; in January 1529 the council went half-way, and then, on 9 February, amid image-burning by the populace, decided for reform. The reforming ordinance of 1 April 1529 laid down rules for worship, church reorganization, social discipline, and education.[28]

Two other major towns in northern, German-speaking Swiss territories followed suit. In February 1524 St Gallen's council issued a typical decree that all preaching be 'according to the Gospel', a decree monitored by Vadianus[29] and others. In 1525 the council was faced by fervent bible-teaching from Zürich-trained visitors and by emergent and violent ana-baptism; this led on 5 June 1525 to a moderating decree favouring the Zwinglians. Late in 1525 Vadianus was made *Bürgermeister*; late in 1526 images were removed, and a new communion was instituted in time for Easter 1527. The mass was abolished in 1528 and monasteries within the city were secularized. Despite attempts from 1529 onwards, however, the town of St Gallen ultimately failed to win lasting control of the great abbey.[30] At Schaffhausen, rather like Memmingen, the militant first effort of the Reformation under Hofmeister and Meyer had failed when the two preachers were expelled in August 1525, possibly in the wake of the Peasants' War. They were succeeded by Benedikt Burgauer (1494–1576) and Erasmus Ritter (d.1546). The crunch came late in 1529 when Schaff-hausen joined forces politically with Zürich; late in 1529 a commission began to prepare an order for worship, issued in 1530. Acceptance of Leo Jud's catechism followed in 1536.[31]

2.3. *The Swiss civic Reformation finds its limits*

Unlike the urban Reformations in Germany, those of northern Switzerland reached their political limits by the early 1530s. In rural territories like Appenzell and Glarus, neither creed gained ascendancy and arrangements were made for both confessions to be practised. Similarly in the *Graubunden*, or Grey Leagues, reformed teachings made inroads, but the 'Ilanz articles' of April 1524 and June 1526 only granted a form of toleration and the right for the reformers to convert communities piecemeal (ultimately to include Rhaeto-Romanic-speaking Switzerland).[32] In fact, the catholics fought back. At first they staged a not wholly successful propaganda disputation at Baden on 19 May–9 August 1526, where heavyweight catholics like Eck and Johann Fabri outgunned Oecolampadius, the only major reformer to attend.[33] Then matters turned to alliance-building and outright hostility. In 1527 Zürich negotiated an alliance with Constance; after Berne's conversion further alliances matured into what from early 1529 became known as the *Christliche Burgrecht* or 'Christian Civic Union'. The inner conservative cantons (Lucerne, Fribourg, Uri, Schwyz, Unterwalden, and Zug) then negotiated the 'Christian Union' at Waldshut (22 April 1529), by which the Emperor's brother Ferdinand of Austria promised to help their defensive alliance.[34]

The clash came over a number of issues, especially the attempts made by Zwinglian preachers to spread their movement into certain rural territories administered by the whole confederation. The conservatives feared that a Zwinglian take-over in these areas would extinguish their political influence as well as their creed. Late in May 1529 Zwingli suggested to the Zürich government a short, preventative war against the central cantons. In spite of the caution of Berne, war was declared on 8 June 1529, and the bloodless invasion of the central territories was ended by negotiations at Kappel on 24 June. The 'First Peace of Kappel' lasted until the middle of 1531; by then Zwingli believed that further war was necessary to defend the reform. Again notwithstanding Berne's hesitation, in May a blockade of grain, wine, iron, and salt was imposed on the central cantons. By late September the catholics were desperate and resolved on fighting. Inexplicably, the Zürichers ignored rumours of their preparations. When Zürich was threatened early in October, only an inadequate force was available to defend it. When the small Zürich army met the catholics at Kappel on 11 October, it was routed almost at once; Zwingli was killed fighting, along with at least nine other clergy. On 24 October a further force of the reformed cities was cut to pieces at Gubel. Peace was made in November; the expansion of the Reformation by political means in the Swiss territories was stopped.[35]

2.4. *The French-speaking dependencies of Berne*

The spread of the Reformation in the Swiss cantons tempted every reformed state to convert its neighbours and dependencies, simply for reasons of self-protection. Even before its own civic Reformation was complete, Berne chose to encourage reforming sermons in its French-speaking territories. Not least of its worries was the neighbouring catholic canton of Fribourg (Freiburg-im-Uechtland), with which Berne jointly ruled Orbe, Grandson, and Morat (Murten) in the Pays de Vaud around the Lake of Neuchâtel. The Bernese recruited a French-speaking reformer in Guillaume Farel (1489–1565),[36] who had learned reforming dogmas from Oecolampadius at Basle. Farel gathered around him a group of pastors and scholars who provided the first generation of Francophone reformers: Pierre Viret (1511–71), Pierre Robert (alias Louis Olivier, or Olivetanus, *d.*1538), who would publish the first French protestant Bible in 1535, and Antoine Saunier. Under Bernese protection he began to preach reform in the small towns of the canton in 1526. By the spring of 1528 he had established the reform in the Bernese dependencies of Aigle and Bex; during 1529–30 Neuchâtel and Morat accepted Farel's message, while

Grandson reacted with civil strife and rioting. Catholic Fribourg agreed with Berne on 30 January 1532 that both reformed and traditional religions were to be tolerated at Grandson and Orbe.[37]

By 1530 *the* political issue in western Switzerland was the fate of the episcopal city of Geneva. The city was poised between the authority of its nominal overlord, the bishop of Geneva, and the dukes of Savoy, theoretically the bishop's subordinates within Geneva itself but actually dominating the bishops (five of whom came from the ducal family between 1451 and 1522) and the city alike. During the duke's absence in 1526–9 a party of urban 'patriots' allied with Berne and Fribourg, who thwarted the duke's siege of the city in 1530, extorting control of the Pays de Vaud as security. In 1534 Fribourg withdrew from the alliance with Geneva, allied with Savoy, and attacked the city. However, François I's attack on Duke Carlo III of Savoy in the winter of 1535–6 (part of François's greater designs on Italy) distracted the duke; during his absence the Bernese occupied Geneva and annexed the Pays de Vaud in February 1536. As a direct consequence the Bernese imposed a reformed order on the city of Lausanne; a disputation was stage-managed, 'papal' rites forbidden, and a protestant minister appointed late in 1536; the reformed Church structure was set up in May 1537.[38] Meanwhile, by a treaty of 7 August 1536 Geneva had become a Bernese protectorate while retaining its nominal independence.[39]

The introduction of the Reformation in Geneva was visibly interwoven

TABLE 15.9

Date	Measure
10.1532	City blocks a visit by Farel
1.1533	Antoine Fromment, Dauphinois schoolmaster, preaches reform; Berne tries to protect him versus the council
5.1533	Rioting: Canon Pierre Werly of Fribourg murdered
7.1533	Bishop of Geneva fails to regain control of city
11.1533	City imprisons Dominican Friar Furbiti for denouncing the Bernese
27.1–3.2.1534	First disputation
1.3.1534	Reformers given use of a church
4.1535	Farel and Viret settle in Franciscan friary
6.1535	Second disputation
8.1535	Council provisionally abolishes mass and secularizes religious houses; most monks and friars leave city
21.5.1536	General Assembly of city vows to live by 'the holy law of the Gospel'

with these events, as shown in Table 15.9.[40] Yet one cannot regard the Reformation in Geneva as purely the outcome of external political pressure and Bernese aggression: external circumstances and the internal dynamics of urban preaching and social tensions were closely interwoven. Moreover, the Bernese annexation and the vow and treaty of 1536 did not establish a 'reformed order' in Geneva as such; matters remained chaotic. On 8 August 1536 Farel met Jean Calvin (1509–64) at Geneva and fervently pressed him to stay in the city as a preacher and teacher.[41] Farel and Calvin tried to establish a comprehensive pastoral system of discipline in a city which had initially adopted the Reformation in a flush of politically motivated enthusiasm.

Thereafter the Genevan Reformation became the plaything of internal Genevan politics as shown in Table 15.10.[42] Calvin returned to Geneva in September 1541 on the understanding that he would be allowed to establish the kind of Church polity which he had pressed for during 1536–8 and further articulated in principle while at Strasbourg. Between 16 September and 20 November 1541, however, the proposals ultimately published as the *Ecclesiastical Ordinances of the Church of Geneva* were repeatedly

TABLE 15.10

Date	Measure
1536–7	Farel and Calvin draft Church orders, revised by city councils
2.1536	Reform-minded city magistrates ('syndics') elected
1537–8	Small council tries to impose Calvin's *Confession of Faith* and give clergy power to excommunicate; larger councils reject this proposal
2.1538	New syndics (tactically) insist that Farel and Calvin accept rites of Church of Berne, on pain of expulsion
23.4.1538	Farel and Calvin ordered out of Geneva; Calvin settles at Strasbourg
1539	Berne commissions Calvin to write reply to catholic tract by Giacomo Sadoleto, bishop of Carpentras; Geneva endorses and publishes Calvin's reply; pro-Bernese faction at Geneva now in disgrace for surrendering freedoms agreed in August 1536
2.1540	Syndics elected from Farel's supporters
6.1540	Leaders of pro-Bernese faction ('Artichauds') executed
10.1540	Calvin invited back to Geneva
13.9.1541	Calvin, under protest, returns to Geneva

adjusted by the councils to preserve their own control. During 1542 he published his second *Catechism* and *Form of Church Prayers*, and the 'consistory' or Church court of Geneva began to operate.[43] However, Geneva remained riven by discord. The surviving 'Artichauds' returned to power and ratified the agreement with Berne on 19 February 1544. Between 1544 and 1549 Calvin repeatedly conflicted with prominent residents of the city over issues of moral discipline; while beneath these individual cases the crucial question—whether the consistory was to be allowed to excommunicate citizens on its own authority—was unresolved. The Genevan political pendulum swung two more times, until a riot by Calvin's enemies on 16 May 1555 gave the reformers' party the excuse to expel or execute their rivals. Only then was Geneva sufficiently in Calvin's grasp to become the centre for spreading his kind of Reformation to French-speaking Europe.[44]

Within fifteen years of Luther's appearance at Worms no other kinds of political units had committed themselves to the Reformation in such numbers as had the cities of Germany and Switzerland. Such a large number of near-independent units only chose to establish the Reformation after a complex series of social, political, and cultural factors had come into play. Some of those components in the process of urban Reformation will now be analysed.

3. *Introducing the New Ideas in the Cities*

Within any sovereign city, enough people had to *want* the Reformation (for whatever reason), if it was to be established. So the first stage in the political 'process' of establishing the Reformation happened when some people—even if only a small clique—took an interest in the new ideas, and gave them local support. *Why* they took such an interest initially is a problem.[45] They may well have been influenced by long-standing animosities quite independent of the Reformation message: nationalist antagonism to an 'Italian' papacy; a fiscal, economic, or political grievance against the local bishop or great abbey; an aversion to the excesses of cultic piety as practised in the local pilgrimage centres; even some internal problem in the old Church, such as rivalry between orders of mendicant friars.[46] However, to account for interest in the Reformation *entirely* in such terms makes the general explain the particular. These feelings had existed for centuries before the 1520s, even where protestantism arose late or not at all.[47] In any case, the people of the cities *did* read and hear about the new ideas; they bought pamphlets, heard sermons, and supported their preachers with sometimes violent partisanship.

Luther's *Ninety-Five Theses* were published by his correspondents, in separate editions in at least four cities within a few months. This first spectacular example of rapid opinion-forming set the tone for later years. Up to 1530 Germany was flooded with perhaps 4,000 titles of small, short-run pamphlets for mass distribution in a rapid turnover of editions, based in printing centres in northern Germany (Wittenberg, Erfurt, Zwickau), central and southern Germany (Nuremberg, Strasbourg, Augsburg), and Basle in Switzerland.[48] However, *printing* a pamphlet was only part of the communication process. Grandiose trading arrangements like the Frankfurt book fairs would have been too elaborate for circulating the small-format pamphlet (most often of eight or sixteen pages) or the single-leaf illustrated picture of most reformed propaganda. Such pieces were carried from town to town by pedlars and small traders in whom the sixteenth century abounded.[49]

Pamphlet- and tract-reading must not be envisaged in too narrowly modern a way. Even in the most sophisticated of towns 'literacy' may not have exceeded 30 per cent, while between 5 and 10 per cent may have been nearer the norm. Most, therefore, would neither have read pamphlets from start to finish, nor indeed bought their own copies. To have a mass effect they were almost certainly read aloud in inns, workshops, or market-places, or even posted up on walls in public places. The *fact* of a Reformation tract being handed around might have had much more impact than its actual *content*; and that content might easily have been misunderstood, so that it would only generate a general 'awareness' of the Reformation issues.[50] In the Lutheran movement especially, much use was made of pictorial pamphlets and flysheets, which served to remind readers of the message they had heard from the pulpit, rather than to convert and instruct believers by themselves.[51]

The vast majority of pamphlets were written by the leading reformers themselves. Like Luther, they took their message to 'the rude Saxons' (or Swabians, or Swiss) in pungent vernacular, breaking all the previous rules of how theology was to be discussed.[52] They produced short, simple manuals of their teaching, like Farel's *Summary and Brief Declaration*, Bucer's *Summary of his Sermons*, and the *Union of Dissenting Passages in Scripture*, sometimes also attributed to Bucer.[53] Works of popular contro-versy or self-defence also appeared, like Zell's *Christian Reply*, Sebastian Meyer of Schaffhausen's reply to the bishop of Constance, or the tract *On the Old and the New God*, once attributed to Joachim Vadian. Vadian was also credited with the dialogue *Karsthans* satirizing the anti-Lutheran pamphleteer Thomas Murner, while Bucer published the *New Karsthans* soon after.[54] The ex-Franciscan Eberlin von Günzburg produced a whole sheaf of such pamphlets under the title *Fifteen Confederates*.[55] Such tracts formed only a part of the reformers' much wider literary output, including systematic, controversial, and didactic theology for educated, mostly clerical readers.

In contrast to the ecclesiastics, fairly few laymen wrote or published pamphlets. They divide approximately into two categories: prominent lay authors who wrote pamphlets because they knew and worked alongside reforming churchmen; and those who wrote only one or two pieces as a wholly exceptional response to the stimulus of the early 1520s. Of the first type, Lazarus Spengler, city secretary to Nuremberg, published two tracts in defence of Luther in 1519 and 1522, the second in association with Nikolaus von Amsdorf.[56] Willibald Pirckheimer published anonymously a notorious satire on Johann Eck, and wrote on the Lutheran concept of the Eucharist before eventually reaffirming his support for the old Church.[57] Still at Nuremberg, the prolific poet Hans Sachs turned his talents to versifying protestant dogma, most famously in his *Die wittenbergisch Nachtigall* ('The Wittenberg Nightingale') of 1523.[58] Jörg Vögeli, civic secretary at Constance, wrote in defence of one of his town's reforming preachers. In Berne Niklaus Manuel produced devastating satirical plays in the early 1520s, including *The Devourers of the Dead*, *The Indulgence-Seller*, and *The Pope and his Entourage*, which did much to popularize reforming ideas at a critical period.[59]

The minor lay pamphleteers were, in comparison, something of a motley crew, the interest of those writings lies rather in showing how their authors absorbed the ideas of the Reformation, than in what they contributed to influencing it. They included minor nobles like the Alsatians Matthias Wurm von Geydertheym and Eckhard zum Treubel; students like Lux Gemigger von Heinfelt; artisans like the painter Hans Greiffenberger, the furrier Sebastian Lotzer or the weaver Utz Rysschner; and a handful of women, including the noblewoman Argula von Stauffen, Ursula Weyda, a tax-collector's wife, and Catherine Schütz, wife of the Strasbourg preacher Matthäus Zell.[60] Lay people made the Reformation possible by *responding* to it; they did comparatively little to *create* its ideas. After the shock of the 1525 rebellions made the 'common man' seem more threatening than the mythically poor but upright peasant 'Kartshans', lay Reformation pamphlets ceased almost completely.[61]

With such a vast variety of genres and types of author, any generalizations about the manner and approach of the pamphlets must be very tentative. However, it seems that this form of literature emphasized what one might call the 'secondary' messages of the Reformation which were deduced by the reformers from their primary insights, and made them themes in themselves. The negative aspects, in particular the assaults on traditional practices, were thus stressed. The insufficiency of human 'works' and rites; the false claims made by the priesthood and papacy; the exaggerated powers attributed to masses or indulgences; the superfluous detail demanded in auricular confession; pamphlets addressed all these kinds of topics. Only occasionally did they need to refer back to the doctrine of 'imputed' or 'alien' righteousness. It was enough to put across the practical reforms which that dogma implied—assuming that the pamphleteer had grasped it, as only some did.[62] Even where the fundamental insight *was* present, the pamphlet would not stress a logical deduction from premisses to conclusions. It would communicate memorable slogans and arouse partisan feeling. These qualities of pamphlet propaganda emerged even more clearly in the pictorial images produced on behalf of the Lutheran Reformation. In such broadsheets, the (approximate) lessons included: personal admiration for the person, or more properly the image, of Luther; exploitation of the slogans and emblems of popular insult and parody to denounce the old Church; the drawing of sharp antitheses between 'true' and 'false' religion, to the extent of representing the papacy as the antichrist of the apocalypse; and only later the somewhat laborious portrayal of dogma through diagram and allegory.[63]

In most cases propaganda did not operate on its own; it complemented the preaching, persuasion, and encouragement of the urban reforming clergy. The process by which reformers reached their hearers was just as important as that by which pamphlets reached their readers. Some reformers were already established preachers in their community, and gravitated to the Reformation as they carried out their duties, through their own reading or contacts. Besides Luther himself, this occurred with Zwingli, Matthäus Zell, Wolfgang Capito, Berchtold Haller, Brenz of Schwäbisch-Hall, Schappeler of Memmingen, and doubtless many others.[64] Such preachers could carry their hearers with them on the basis of their existing reputation. Others travelled as students to a reformed centre, say, Wittenberg, Zürich, Strasbourg, or Geneva, and returned to their birthplace to spread the message among those they knew. Wittenberg siphoned an astonishing number of visiting students through its schools, several of whom became prominent as reformers of their native districts. The Scandinavians Hans Tausen and Olav Pedersson studied there before returning to spread the message in Denmark and Sweden respectively.[65] Leonhard Stöckel spent time there before reforming the Saxon cities of northern Hungary.[66] Johannes Kessler's spell at Wittenberg assisted the reforming of his native St Gallen. While, rather later, Geneva turned religious exiles into missionaries to their homes almost as a matter of routine, not least because of Calvin's distaste for clandestine or 'Nicodemite' protestantism and his wish to see 'settled' churches.[67]

Thirdly, a preacher might simply launch himself unprepared on a community, in hopes of a favourable reception. Guillaume Farel exemplifies this approach: expelled from Montbéliard, he was accepted by Aigle and Bex, rejected by Lausanne and Geneva (at first), but then successful at Neuchâtel. Often such evangelizers had to rely upon the protection of a powerful, if distant, authority against a hostile local community, as Farel relied upon the Bernese government.[68] Such distant patronage was, of course, denied to all the preachers of extreme or sectarian tendencies, as is shown by Müntzer's attempts to establish himself at Allstedt, Mühlhausen, and even Prague; or by the careers or men like Balthasar Hubmaier or Melchior Hoffmann.[69] On the other hand, a reforming preacher might actually be invited by a community already receptive (perhaps through the influence of a group of committed laymen) *before* that community made any formal steps towards reform. Luther preached around several towns in Saxony during the spring of 1522, and prompted civic requests for preachers. Bucer was installed as a preacher in Strasbourg following pressure from the gardeners' guild. A less talented reformer might summon a more powerful personality in the midst of the struggle, as Farel detained Calvin at Geneva. In a quite different way, preachers might be summoned to organize a local reformation *after* the decision in principle had been made. Such a summons is distinct from 'opinion-forming' and belongs to the later, constructive period; instances are Bugenhagen's work in Braunschweig, Lübeck, or Hamburg; Ambrosius Blarer's at Augsburg, Esslingen, Isny, Lindau, Memmingen, and Ulm, and the second phase of Calvin's work at Geneva.[70]

A preacher might have hoped to count on the support of particularly receptive groups in the urban population. It could be assumed that humanist coteries would be receptive; many of this type became reformers themselves. The Nuremberg group of Luther's correspondents is perhaps the most famous example; others would be Vadianus's allies at St Gallen, or Johannes Adelphi's at Schaffhausen.[71] However, humanists were not always so sympathetic. Much depended upon age.[72] Strasbourg's older humanists do not seem to have emulated those of Nuremberg,[73] while leading Augsburgers like Konrad Peutinger resisted the establishment of reform. Humanism produced eloquent opponents of protestantism like Thomas More in England, Josse Clichtove in the Low Countries, Thomas Murner at Strasbourg, or Paul Helgesen at Copenhagen.[74] University students might help, as happened at Wittenburg, Erfurt, and Zwickau; even some young theology masters at the otherwise catholic University of Leipzig proved sympathetic. However, a university could just as well turn out to be predominantly hostile, as in Rostock, Cologne, or Louvain.[75] Finally, those burghers who were sufficiently articulate and prosperous to be concerned with more than bare survival, but not so wealthy and well connected as to have a vested interest in the old order, might listen and respond. As organized in the lesser guilds of the free cities, such people figured enormously in the urban Reformation.[76]

Any reasonably eloquent and plausible reformer soon found an enthusiastic and sometimes raucous following which rapidly drew the attention of both the ecclesiastical and civil authorities. Preaching usually, but not invariably, was the starting-point for vigorous popular involvement. Such mass popular enthusiasm was neither rare nor surprising: fifteenth-century preachers often had a similar cult following. At Strasbourg in the autumn of 1522 Matthäus Zell found that his sermons on Romans drew crowds far too large for his pulpit in the St Lorenz chapel, and when refused permission to use Geiler von Kaysersberg's pulpit in the nave, he preached from a portable wooden one constructed by local carpenters. In the following year several of the city parishes installed reforming preachers in defiance of the rights of the patrons.[77] In Leipzig, not a free city but the territorial capital of the fiercely catholic Duke Georg of Albertine Saxony, suspected Lutheran sympathizers were found to be preaching in the autumn of 1522. The council refused to discipline one of them; the churchwardens of a hospital then petitioned the duke for a permanent reforming preacher, and invited one, Sebastian Fröschel, to preach in their hospital. Locked out of the church, he preached to a large and militant crowd in the churchyard.[78] When the clergy of St Mary's church in Memmingen attempted to prevent a reforming sermon at vespers on Christmas day 1524 the service degenerated into a riot.[79]

The defenders of the old order took to the pulpit rather reluctantly and not always very effectively. However, rival sermons by preachers of different dogmas or creeds could set a community by the ears: like those between the traditionalist Bartholomäus Arnoldi von Usingen and the reformer Johann Culsamer at Erfurt, or those at Zwickau between the firebrand Thomas Müntzer and Johannes Sylvius Egranus, not a reactionary but an

Erasmian reformer opposed to religious schism. Müntzer's partisans posted up twenty-four articles against Egranus; the latter's supporters may have thrown a libellous note through Müntzer's window; after further scandals and mutual insults, both preachers left. Meanwhile, a hostile catholic priest who had attended one of Müntzer's sermons had been pelted with stones and injured by the listeners.[80] Similarly at Geneva, the preaching of Farel and Fromment caused riots in late March and early May 1533, culminating in the murder of Canon Pierre Werly; later that same year the Dominican Guy Furbiti stirred up yet more trouble from the catholic side. Early in 1534 a protestant gang forced their way into the Franciscan friary and installed Farel in the pulpit.[81] Just as much tension was generated by simultaneous preaching by enthusiasts of different protestant creeds. In the cities of southern Germany the later 1520s saw intense rivalries between 'Lutheran' and 'Zwinglian' preachers contending for audiences, respectively Urbanus Rhegius versus Michael Keller at Augsburg, or Johannes Rotach and Johannes Seeger versus Jakob Haystung at Kempten. Usually it was the Zwinglians who had the better of it.[82] Equally, the presence of extremist or anabaptist preachers could pose a problem, as was discovered not only during the brief period of Müntzer and the 'prophets' at Zwickau, but in St Gallen during 1525 and even in Augsburg, not to mention Strasbourg.[83]

Sermons soon led to the call, as at the cities' assembly at Ulm on 6 December 1524, for 'not only evangelical teaching, but also evangelical deeds and actions'.[84] The popular challenge to traditional worship could completely by-pass the preacher. It might express itself in attempts to prevent catholic worship and ceremonial; in deliberate insult, mocking, or parody of such ceremonial; or in abuse and profanation of cultic objects venerated by the traditionalists. From 5 October 1521 Wittenberg students deliberately and systematically disrupted the hermits of the order of St Antony as they begged and consecrated holy water. Services were interrupted on All Saints' day. Early in December priests were stopped from saying mass and singing the hours in the parish church by having service-books torn from their hands or being pelted with stones. At Christmas the first 'reformed' services were held, while in the parish and castle churches candles were snuffed and chanting drowned out with singing of secular songs and howling. At Memmingen on Christmas afternoon 1524 a noisy crowd blocked a religious procession in the nave of St Mary's church (a procession which had been deliberately arranged to prevent a reforming sermon). The highly theatrical religious 'plays' held in some cities attracted particular attention. Pirna, in Saxony, saw Easter processions and the ritual raising of the crucifix from the sepulchre disrupted; some ten years later, in 1533 at Augsburg, the catholic patron and protestant churchwarden of St Moritz's church engaged in extraordinary subterfuges, on the one hand to maintain, and on the other to sabotage, the representations of the Resurrection and Ascension.[85]

Satirical plays and carnival processions were designed to make holy objects ridiculous, rather than (as happened somewhat later in the process) to destroy them altogether as diabolical. Several times in Germany and Switzerland between *c*.1520–*c*.1540 during the carnival or *Fastnacht*, 'carnival popes', bishops, priests, monks, or nuns were either represented in satirical plays, or chased through city streets in derision; notably, it was citizens dressed as clergy, not the clerics themselves, who were actually subjected to this mockery. In June 1524 the Saxon mining village of Buchholz staged an elaborate and apparently hilarious parody of the ritual disinterment of the relics of St Benno of Meissen which had just taken place across the border in Albertine Saxony. Crucifixes, which had been paraded round the streets in traditional Easter processions, were subjected to mock processions, in Nuremberg in 1525, Basle in 1529, and Hildesheim in 1543.[86]

Sacred objects were deliberately profaned in various grotesque ways, from the smearing of images with cow's blood, to the dismemberment of images, or the beating or pouring of beer over them, or finally to spitting, urinating, or defecating into sacred utensils (such as fonts or holy water vessels) or images. In August 1524 at Magdeburg flowers and herbs just consecrated to the Virgin Mary were scattered on the ground and danced on. Letters of indulgence, finally, were used for every purpose from carnival costume material to lavatory paper.[87] These episodes were anything but trivial; inasmuch as such a great part of the religion of the later Middle Ages consisted of ritual acts centred upon cultic objects, the systematic desecration of those same objects would have made an enormous impression on the popular mind: it demonstrated the 'powerlessness' of hitherto holy rites and objects as dramatically as any sermon could possibly have done.

The atmosphere of heady enthusiasm generated by this first phase of the urban Reformation confronted civic authorities with a serious problem. They had to show that they could keep order, yet not forfeit the basic popular assent without which an early modern city was ungovernable. They had to harness the 'social movement'[88] of the early Reformation so as to exploit its possibilities for an anticlerical coup, while deflecting its anti-authoritarian implications away from themselves. Finally, they had to satisfy their own consciences (presumably no more and no less active than those of the populace) that they were acting in a 'Christian' fashion. These considerations help to explain the sometimes tortuous course of events which followed.

4. *The City Councils become Arbiters*

The spontaneous enthusiasm shown towards so many of the urban reforming preachers presented civic governments with an entirely new dimension to an old problem. In the past they had intervened in the legal or fiscal privileges of the clergy, in the choice of candidates for city preachers, in disputes with the bishops' officers—in virtually everything except the theological content of their preachers' sermons. City fathers were disqualified, whether by training or simply by being one small component of a larger Church, from judging Christian rites or dogma, as the bishop of Constance's delegates pointed out at the Zürich disputation in January 1523.[89] However, just as they had previously intervened in the 'spiritual' realm out of concern for the city's tax base or its defences, so now further intervention was demanded to preserve order and cope with dangerously illegal acts by the populace. One need not assume that city fathers willingly embraced the opportunity to intervene; though, of course, that opportunity may have been welcomed, for political *or* ideological reasons.

Many cities which received reforming preachers lay under the jurisdiction of a non-resident alien bishop: Erfurt under the archbishop of Mainz, Zürich within the see of Constance, Nuremberg in that of Bamberg, and Memmingen in that of Augsburg. In each case, and also in those cities which had a bishop of their own such as Strasbourg or Geneva, at some stage or other the council had to decide to defy episcopal discipline of its preachers. Thus Zell was protected against the bishop of Strasbourg (ironically, he also benefited from rivalry between the bishop and the chapter); Schappeler was protected by Memmingen against the bishop of Augsburg; Bartholomäus Metzler was shielded by the town of Constance against the local bishop; Nuremberg (later) ignored the bishop of Bamberg's excommunication of Osiander.[90] Besides protecting established preachers, cities were called on to instal new (reforming) ones as well. In the justly famous case of Strasbourg the city council was faced with a virtual *fait accompli* when parishioners installed their own pastors and the council had to give belated approval. At Ulm popular pressure brought about the installation of Konrad Sam in 1524; something similar might have happened at Leipzig but for Duke Georg.[91]

However, perhaps the most interesting, and certainly the most ambiguous, interventions by secular authority in the early stages of a popular reformation movement were the so-called 'preaching mandates' or 'Scripture mandates'. On the face of it, in these cases the state intervened in the pulpit battles which accompanied the debates over reformed ideas with a directive that, by their decree, all the preachers within the state's jurisdiction should preach 'only according to Scripture', or 'confine themselves to Scripture' or preach 'only what was consistent with Scripture'. Zürich issued a series of such mandates in the early 1520s: the first may have been as early as 1520 or 1521, and subsequent ones were issued on 21 July 1522, 1 December 1522, 3 January 1523, and 29 January 1523.[92] Zürich's example was widely followed as the list of these 'Scripture mandates' in Table 15.11 shows.[93]

Just what did these 'Scripture mandates' imply about the attitudes of the cities or assemblies which issued them? They have been described as arbitrating between rival beliefs, committed to neither; as calculatedly ambiguous; and also as forming the first decisive step towards full reformed establishment.[94] Most states which issued such mandates did eventually adopt protestantism, if not always as the sole official creed.[95] Nevertheless, it does not follow that, when such a mandate was issued, the ruling group which authorized it had actually decided in favour of reform. In fact, there were several different explanations for their behaviour. One reason might have been to prevent mutual acrimony between reforming and conservative preachers, carrying as it did the risk of public disorder. In 1522 the traditionalist theologian Bartholomäus Arnoldi von Usingen engaged in a furious preaching battle with the Lutheran preacher Johann Culsamer in Erfurt; the Erfurt councillors summoned both clerics and told them to preach 'only what could be proved from Scripture'; their successors repeated the command in 1529 to the feuding priest and preacher at nearby Sömmerda, and meanwhile continuously protected lawful incumbents from riotous interference. In November 1522 the Strasbourg council likewise commanded Matthäus Zell and Peter Wickram, the city preacher, to stop attacking each other from the pulpit and stick to the New Testament.[96]

Alternatively, such edicts might have dissuaded over-zealous preachers from showing too much sympathy for Luther (after 1521 a banned heretic) in a way which might embarrass the government. The first Berne edict of 15 June 1523 commanded all preachers to avoid disturbances and uproar, preach 'only the holy Gospel', and avoid 'all teachings contrary to Scripture from Luther or other doctors'. Zwingli and his allies (who had not been specifically condemned) were not mentioned.[97] Such often-repeated

TABLE 15.11

City	Dates issued
Basle	5–6.1523
Berne	15.6.1523 (the so-called 'Viti und Modesti' edict)
	22.11.1524
	7.4.1525
	21.5.1526
	27.5.1527
Constance	before 12.12.1523
	9.2.1524
Erfurt	1522
Esslingen	8.1531
Frankfurt-am-Main	before 5.4.1524
Kaufbeuren	early 1525
Mühlhausen (Thuringia)	?1523
Mulhouse	29.3.1523
Nuremberg	14.2.1522
	7.3.1523
Reutlingen	?1524
St Gallen	5.4.1524
Stolberg	4.5.1525
Strasbourg	2.8.1522
	17.11.1522
	14.3.1523
	23.3.1523
	18.11.1523
	1.12.1523
Ulm	21.3.1522
	9.12.1523
	6.1524
Worms	10.3.1523

phrasing may well have drawn inspiration from the reply of the *Reichstag* to Legate Chieregati on 5 February, that the princes should see that preachers 'should not spread ideas by which the people might be moved to tumult or to error ... but preach only the true, pure, entire holy Gospel, ... according to the teaching and exposition approved and received by the Christian Church'.[98] Such a posture, in no way intended to favour Lutheranism, had been adopted in the official edicts of the Nuremberg *Reichstag* on 9 February and 6 March 1523.[99]

The 'preaching mandates' even echoed old-fashioned bourgeois impatience with the extravagances of preaching friars: in 1513 the guildsmen of Cologne had petitioned the council to insist the clergy should preach 'Scripture, and not the fables invented by men'. In this case they objected to the patronizing legends of saints handed down to popularize (and finance!) their cults.[100] Nevertheless, with a subtle alteration of phrasing, such mandates could be taken to embody the most evocative of reforming slogans, with their emphasis on 'the Gospel' and 'the Word of God'. The Zürich council's declaration in 1523 that all pastors and preachers in its jurisdiction were only to preach 'what they can prove according to the holy Gospel and true divine Scripture', echoed Zwingli's own catch-phrases; in the following year they were able to claim that this had been their policy 'since before they had heard of Luther'. Bucer had already urged that Scripture was the basis of reformed teaching before the Strasbourg magistrates passed their mandate in December 1523.[101]

The very ambiguity of such mandates was their chief value. Since they could seem to conform simultaneously to the Bible, the *Reichstag*, and the reformers, it was hard for anyone involved in the complex politics of the period to take exception to them. They created a framework of 'fictitious agreement', within which the city fathers could discover what they really thought about the issues. As the situation changed subtly—as for instance in Berne or Basle during the 1520s—the undertones of 'Scripture alone' changed with them.[102] By a series of minute and (taken by themselves) innocuous steps secular authorities discovered, perhaps to their own surprise, that they had inaugurated a religious revolution. As at Zürich, 'only with time would the Council find out what they had decided upon'.[103]

Having decreed 'Scripture alone' as their criterion, city councils were trapped by their own logic into policing the 'Scripture mandates', and thus into assuming responsibility for what was or was not 'according to Scripture'. This arbitration over the meaning of 'the Gospel' produced the 'disputations' characteristic of the early urban Reformation. Traditionally, disputations were held in Latin, in an academic institution, before an audience of experts, under the adjudication of a senior expert whose teachings would form the basis of what was discussed.[104] However, academics or clergy could no longer arbitrate in the 1520s controversies: the Church was divided, churchmen were partisans. So, the *reformed* disputation had to be in the vernacular, before laymen, and under the presidency either of a persuadable lay judge, or of a reformed clergyman. Zwingli passionately urged the Zürich council to regard itself as a Christian assembly, just as fully authorized to resolve issues in the Holy Spirit as any General Council of the Church; only hesitantly did the council begin to oblige him.[105]

For practical as well as theological reasons city councils were unwilling to be drawn into the unpredictability, passion, and uproar of an open disputation. Only occasionally did they happen before a council had made up its own mind. During the Christmas 1524 riots at Memmingen the merchants' guildmaster announced a debate, sponsored by the city council, for which Christoph Schappeler submitted seven articles. It began on 2 January and lasted five days with no conclusion reached; soon after the city became embroiled with the rebellious Swabian peasants.[106] Farel and Viret, in the early stages of the movement in Geneva, were summoned to dispute with Guy Furbiti over three days from 27 January 1534 in the presence of the council and the Bernese ambassadors. The council later judged Furbiti to have broken the rules.[107] Such open-ended debates were more common in the countryside.[108]

Most—*not* all—reformed disputations served as propaganda for a movement which had already won a significant proportion of the hearts and minds which mattered. These were not real contests in which the decision was in doubt and the adjudicators really did not know where to turn; they were occasions stage-managed by governments—or significant factions within them—so as to give public vindication for the decision to reform, by demonstrating (according to the previously agreed criteria) that the reformers' ideas were indeed 'provable by Scripture'. Not *all* disputations were 'rigged' in this way, as has sometimes been suggested; but a sufficient number were, from both sides.[109] The city council of Nuremberg called a religious colloquy, which opened on 3 March 1525 and where Andreas Osiander debated against those of the catholic clergy who still remained. Not only did the council adjudicate; it appointed Christoph Scheurl, a prominent city lawyer and equally prominent reforming enthusiast, as chairman. Though held in the city hall, the people could hear the proceedings (and react!) through open windows. At the last session the monks left Osiander to make his peroration uninterrupted.[110] For the Zürich disputation of 26–8 October 1523, Bürgermeister Röist appointed Joachim Vadian, Sebastian Hofmeister, and Christoph Schappeler to preside; shortly afterwards the larger council of the city took charge of policing the 'Scripture mandate'.[111] While not perhaps totally one-sided, the great Berne disputation of 6–26 January 1528 was undoubtedly stage-managed to be a reformed triumph; Haller was abetted by Zwingli (with sixty-nine others from Zürich!), Oecolampadius, Vadian, Benedikt Burgauer, Ambrosius Blarer, Bucer, and Capito, against a much more lightweight, though adept, catholic deputation. The reformed 'theses' were adopted by 235 votes to 46, and Berne's Reformation mandate followed on 7 February. By the time of the Lausanne disputation of 1–9 October 1536 the Bernese had already dominated the territory since the previous April; they named the presidents, and Farel based his theses on those of Zwingli.[112]

It was not only protestants who would try to arrange 'rigged', or perhaps more fairly 'weighted', disputations. The catholics tried to arrange a debate at Solothurn in October 1522, while they succeeded—though not perhaps as well as they should have—in stage-managing the Baden disputation of 1526 as a set piece for orthodoxy.[113] Rigged, weighted, or just decisive, the reformed disputations propelled the city authorities into the next stage: demolishing the old order in the community church with which they had had such ambivalent relations in the past.

5. *The Political Pressures:* Coup d'état, *Consensus, or Compulsion?*

Matters had to reach a crisis before secular governments, which were rarely captivated *purely* by religious enthusiasm, would take drastic steps to abolish the old order. This crisis might simply have meant, as in some cities, that popular enthusiasm was so out of hand that a regime which failed to keep in step would forfeit its credibility as the old Church had done. In Germany, it was often entangled either with the 1524–5 rebellions, or with the political struggles in the *Reichstag* during 1529–30. A legal or jurisdictional issue was sometimes involved: for instance, the Strasbourg magistrates 'fudged' the issue of their protection of the reforming preachers for as long as they could, until a public act—the marriage of several leading clergy—brought relations between the city and the bishop of Strasbourg to a crunch.[114] Who gave the crucial 'push' which made a city respond to the crisis by (finally) taking decisive and unambiguous steps towards the Reformation? Any 'established' reformed settlement required the participation, even if only a reluctant, passive, or late participation, of the official governing body of the community. In this sense, *every* Reformation was a councillors' Reformation.[115] However, some movements are regarded as 'people's and some as 'rulers' reformations'; not necessarily because the formal processes were so different, but because the political realities—who gave the decisive 'push'—were diverse. The problem boils down to two basic questions:

(1) From what position in the social and political structure did those who promoted the Reformation come?

(2) How far did circumstances allow the reforming agitators to press their programme on the ruling group?

The following were some of the possible answers:

(1) If the reforming agitators were largely or wholly *excluded* from the governing élite, they would either fail, or succeed only by overwhelming and evicting the old government.

(2) If the agitators came mostly from a class, a layer of society of broadly similar status and wealth, and had some political rights, then they might effect a Reformation by putting pressure on their 'betters' or increasing their own share of political influence.

(3) A reforming party might comprise members of many different classes, a faction dividing society at all levels, *including* the ruling élite. Here the move towards the Reformation would be less of a 'class war' and more of a sectional, partisan conflict.

(4) The effective agents of the Reformation might have come predominantly, or even exclusively, from members of the élite itself. Popular support, whether strong or weak, would be irrelevant to its *initial* political success.

One comes nearest to the first of the above options—a *coup d'état* against an unsympathetic regime by agitators excluded from real power—in some of the towns and cities of northern Germany and the Baltic coast: trading ports of the Hanseatic League like Rostock, Wismar, Stralsund, Greifswald, and most importantly Lübeck; or inland territorial Hanseatic cities which maintained some solidarity in the face of their princes, such as Braunschweig, Lüneburg, Göttingen, Hanover, or Lemgo. The Hanseatic city Reformations were marked by a sharp distinction between popular campaigns for religious and social change and resistance from a closed patrician class. Unlike the guildsmen of some south German cities, the middling bourgeoisie in the Hanseatic towns were excluded from the town councils, although competent and experienced in organizing themselves in other subordinate bodies. As a rule neither the city patricians nor the local princes showed any sympathy for the Reformation in the crucial period in the late 1520s and early 1530s; they identified themselves with the old Church hierarchy and accordingly shared its unpopularity. Popular agitation on a broad social base led to the formation of a 'burgher committee' (*Bürgerausschuss*), usually under the leadership of the merchants and craftsmen who were socially just below the level of the patriciate. They pressed for a more open constitution, and (with increasing unity as Lutheran propaganda spread) also for religious reform.

Either wholesale or piecemeal, the old oligarchies which had obstructed change were removed or replaced. A particularly dramatic form of this change occurred at Lübeck, where after five years of negotiations the burghers seized control of the council in February 1533 and elected their leader, a Hamburg merchant named Jürgen Wullenwever, as *Bürgermeister*. Wullenwever embroiled Lübeck unsuccessfully in the Counts' War in Denmark, and the oligarchs regained control of the city during his absence in August 1535. Generally speaking, the anti-patrician ferment in the north did not last more than a few years. If the noisiest of the agitators were integrated into the élite, they helped to suppress the rest. In some cases the burghers' oath was restored and the alienation of the city's subjects lessened. After these agitations had passed their peak the citizen committees, having gained their objectives, died away. The residuary legatee, whatever the constitutional implications, was the Lutheran Church settlement: the resurgent oligarchs and the new masters alike found that the Reformation (usually in the high organized form marketed by Bugenhagen) offered the best way to quieten popular demands.[116]

Elsewhere popular pressure against the magistracy also verged on an attempted coup. The effect which the Peasants' War had on the city Reformations is debatable, and varied greatly from place to place even within the heartlands of the revolt. In several cases it can be shown to have produced abortive city reformations, or at least 'false starts', which were followed by a period of restructuring on more conventional political lines, as in the Hansa. At Erfurt, where tentative measures against the old order had already been allowed by the council, the Thuringian peasants stirred up a revival of civic unrest in April 1525. The peasants, encamped in the city, joined with the urban populace to force the appointment of a 'new' council and a new civic seal, the abolition of obnoxious taxes, and a complete reordering of the structure of the Church. When the revolt collapsed the political changes were revoked; the Lutheran settlement was subsequently moderated.[117] At Kitzingen, south-east of Würzburg in Franconia, a similar revolt broke out also in April 1525, apparently directed by the populace against a plutocratic council. It led (temporarily) to an opening of the political structure and to the town joining the peasantry. That June Markgraf Kasimir of Brandenburg-Ansbach invaded the town, punished the rebels, and imposed his own kind of Reformation.[118] The 1525 rebellions produced several other false starts to a civic Reformation: Memmingen (where Schappeler ministered), Rothenburg (exposed to

Karlstadt's preaching), Heilbronn or Würzburg (like Rothenburg epi-centres of the Franconian peasants' revolt), or Schaffhausen (whose pastors changed abruptly in 1525).[119] After an unsuccessful uprising by the weavers' guild in 1525, the impatience of the citizenry of Basle between Christmas 1528 and February 1529 nearly caused a rebellion. Pressure for the total abolition of catholic worship led to the formation of a guilds' committee, with calls for civic restructuring as well as religious change.[120]

Versions of the second and third 'options' mentioned above—Re-formations resulting either from class agitation, or from sectional, partisan pressure transcending class boundaries—are found, in varying permu-tations, in most of the civic Reformation movements for which central and southern Germany and northern Switzerland have become famous. Because cases of such negotiation between rulers and ruled were specially common in (largely self-governing) imperial free cities, they are sometimes described in terms of a stereotype of 'imperial city Reformation'. According to this 'pattern', preaching and discussion of the new ideas spread from small groups of enthusiasts to the populace at large; where it aroused support, the councils usually put the brakes on; first they allowed reforming preach-ing, then made modest concessions in other areas; finally, under pressure from the community and in agreement (voluntary or forced) with the agitators, the patriciate consented to complete the abolition of the old order and instituted a strict, comprehensive Church ordinance to satisfy popular demands while preserving their own authority.[121]

Various problems have been identified with this pattern in the immense amount of detailed local research which has been conducted since it was formulated. It tends to take insufficient account of external pressures from other cities, prelates, princes, or indeed the Emperor, whose impact varied from place to place. The constitutional and social structures within the free cities differed, in particular the relative strength or weakness of craft guilds again producing variety.[122] Moreover, 'the Reformation' presented itself in numerous confessional guises (Lutheran, Zwinglian, extremist, sectarian), whose social appeal could be different. Finally, the pattern of imperial city Reformation should not be applied too narrowly to the fifty or so (mostly small) partly or wholly reformed cities out of the sixty-five directly dependent on the Holy Roman Empire.[123] Other kinds of semi-autonomous civic state experienced vibrant, argumentative episodes in their early Reformations: cities subject to a remote bishop, whose power had already been restricted; cities under a prince who was as yet uncommitted in religion, as in parts of the Saxonies; and, of course, the city-dominated cantons of northern Switzerland. No short sketch can do justice either to the communities or their historians, but an outline of a few examples must be attempted.

In several Swabian free cities the movement was ushered in by a period of constitutional struggle between different levels of socio-economic privilege, where the oligarchy was pushed into co-operating with the agitators, rather than overthrown by them as in the Hansa. At Ulm and Esslingen in the late 1520s the city councils were clearly torn between popular support of the preachers and the external threat posed by the imperial administration. Pressure for religious innovations combined with protests against the wealthy, if anything making the oligarchs less willing to endanger their links with the Emperor. Neither city adopted either of the protestant confessions in 1530. The decree which closed the Augsburg *Reichstag* convinced Ulm's representative there, Bürgermeister Bernhard Besserer, that a decision could no longer be put off. The issue of accepting or rejecting the decree was put to a vote of the guilds, fraternities, and master craftsmen early in November 1530; 87 per cent of those asked voted against the imperial edict. Esslingen was influenced by Ulm's example. In September 1531, when the council had just refused to accept a new parish priest at the hands of the Speyer chapter, the city secretary Johann Machtolf discussed entry to the Schmalkaldic League with the protestant guildmaster Bernhard Motzbeck. On 25 September the council approved membership. In November the council held a vote on the abolition of the mass and images, and the introduction of 'apostolic' orders of service, which were approved overwhelmingly. During this period of change the council's membership shifted, with many old catholic, imperialist members leaving their posts; those who remained could feel that joining a protestant league made heresy less of a risk.[124]

In the much larger and politically significant city of Augsburg somewhat similar forces were at work. The decree of the *Reichstag* just held there was unacceptable to the guildsmen and to the greater (broader) of the city's councils, where the guilds predominated; the decree was challenged on 25 October 1530. By 1533 (after the deaths of Zwingli and Oecolampadius had made the Reformation seem less 'Swiss') the patricians Rehlinger and Seitz, sympathetic to a Bucerian type of reform, replaced the Lutherans Imhof and Vetter as *Bürgermeisters*; the larger council decided formally for the Reformation in July 1534. Elsewhere shifts at the top of the city councils were also important: the election of the reforming agitator Christoph Gräter as *Bürgermeister* of Biberach in 1528, or that of the carpenters' guildmaster Bartholomäus Hensler at Ravensburg in 1544, were turning-points in each case.[125] While the power struggles between guilds and councils threatened to divide the community, the referenda carried out, especially over such unpopular decrees as those of the *Reichstag* meetings at Speyer in 1529 and at Augsburg in 1530, tended to reintegrate the citizenry to face the consequences. Besides Ulm and Esslingen, such polls were taken (either by individual enquiries or mass meetings) at Biberach, Constance, Memmingen, and Reutlingen in the south, and at Goslar, Heilbronn, and Weissenburg further north.[126]

So far these case-studies support the paradigm: the movement was supported by those classes who were literate and influential enough to express their concern about the salvation of their city, but far enough from actual decision-making not to think so much about princes and Emperor. The councils, caught between the upper millstone of the Empire and the nether of their own bourgeoisie, had to compromise and survive, or abdicate.[127] However, there is something suspiciously self-serving about the councillors' protests—which began, after all, in the *Reichstag* in the early 1520s—that, try as they might, the 'common man' would not allow them to enforce the edicts against heresy.[128] By locating the pressures on them outside their own number, they could paper over any divisions which might exist *within* the élite themselves. Such divisions undoubtedly existed; alongside, and sometimes in place of, a simple 'up-and-down' set of class pressures for the establishment of the reform, there occurred factional, 'sideways' pressure from a party, or parties, pressing for the Reformation from all levels of society *including* the élite. Strasbourg offers an interesting example. Between 1522 and 1524 there occurred typical guildsmen's agitation for the installation of reforming preachers and attacks on the privileges of the old Church. Strasbourg's regime was a fairly open one in which the guilds had much say, although predictably the wealthier members tended to dominate an apparently balanced system.[129] The oligarchy was 'badly split' by 1523: into an 'old guard' of elderly, rich, entrenched catholics, who mostly resigned between 1524 and 1530, a party of Zwinglian 'enthusiasts' (both patricians and guildsmen) led by Claus Kniebis, and soon after a politically prudent group of protestant councillors led by the patrician Jakob Sturm, who towered over protestant diplomacy during the 1530s. In such circumstances guild pressure would have (conveniently) abetted reformed agitation within the oligarchy itself.[130]

In Nuremberg, Luther's earliest adherents were within the circles of power from the very start: most importantly Lazarus Spengler, the civic secretary, and Christoph Scheurl, one of the city's permanent legal advisers. Their contacts with Luther derived from their literary and religious interests: their civic positions were coincidental. During the disputes with the

Empire, papal legate, and local bishop, Scheurl adroitly disabled the Church's disciplinary structure within Nuremberg, allowed the reforming clergy to go ahead without interference, and finally (as president of the March 1525 disputation) oversaw the transfer of civic 'legitimacy' to the reformers.[131] Nevertheless, the Nuremberg council was not united in the calls for the religious changes—older 'humanists' such as Willibald Pirckheimer distanced themselves from them—nor was it immune to popular pressure. A peasants' revolt in the countryside around nearby Forchheim in 1524 influenced some of the less privileged citizens to riot and disturbance in support of extremists of the Müntzer type. In this case the council was led to a much harder, strict Lutheran line (against both catholic reaction and extremist reformism) to preserve unity, order, and its own control.[132]

Such tension between authoritarian Lutheran patricians and proletarian followers of more extreme reformers characterized Zwickau in the early 1520s. To popular indifference, the council's favoured preacher Nikolaus Hausmann instituted a Lutheran settlement with much emphasis on obedience and order; such popular enthusiasm as existed was diverted to the followers of Müntzer and the 'prophets', Storch, Drechsler, and Stübner. The councillors steered between the extremists and the remaining catholics to set up their own type of church establishment.[133] What held for Zwickau's radicals also held for some of the Swabian cities, though here it was not so much sectarianism (though it had adherents), as Zwinglian beliefs and rituals which aroused most enthusiasm; support for Zwinglian preachers tended to be associated with the more unruly elements in the guilds, and civic authoritarianism with more cautious Lutheran reform, for instance at Augsburg or Kempten.[134]

At Zürich itself council, city, and reformers seem to have acted in the most surprising harmony. One interpretation sees the city councillors of Zürich committed fairly early, between 1520 and 1522, to supporting Zwingli and his criteria for reform, and sees tensions and opposition chiefly in terms of the bishop of Constance on the one hand and the extremists, alienated from the council, such as Grebel and Mantz on the other. An alternative analysis explains the delay (for instance in abolishing the mass at Zürich) in terms of conflict between 'a new and energetic group of oligarchs, mostly young, grown prosperous in crafts and trade', favouring Zwingli, and a faction of old patricians combined with traditional traders holding out against him; the displacement of the latter between 1524 and 1528 becomes crucial.[135] It is unlikely, to say the least, that Zürich politics were entirely calm in the Reformation era: *after* the abolition of the mass, Zwingli still had to wage a campaign against political opposition, concentrated in the headquarters of the *Konstaffel*, a corporation of city aristocrats, disgruntled with the ending of mercenary service and pensions from foreign powers.[136]

The final political 'option', namely that the *effective* agitation for reform might come more or less exclusively from within the élite itself, does not exclude the possibility that the cause of the Reformation might gain support among the unprivileged; it simply means that the wishes of the unprivileged played a limited political role, or none at all, in bringing the reformed establishment into being. Just as most of the 'community' Reformations were found in the geographically smallest political units, so the most authoritarian Reformations occurred within territorial monarchies, where sheer distance as well as constitutional custom prevented mass participation. However, there were authoritarian reformations even in the cities: at Zwickau in the 1520s, as seen earlier, the councillors foisted Hausmann's gospel of civic obedience on to an unenthusiastic populace; further south the small Council of Dinkelsbühl likewise used a strict Lutheran settlement to validate its control on the town in the 1530s; in Colmar, in Alsace, a change in the opinions of the city's political élite was the crucial factor in the very late Reformation which occurred there in 1575.[137]

6. *Demolishing the Old Order*

Finally, then, city governments went beyond mere 'baiting' of the old Church hierarchy and flouting of its orders to acts of abolition and destruction in spheres where, in the past, they had had no agreed competence whatever. Once the decision to end the old order was taken, it was attacked on at least three broad fronts: (*a*) the jurisdiction, status, and privileges of the catholic priesthood and hierarchy were challenged; (*b*) the ceremonial and worship of the old Church (above all the mass itself) was abolished, in varying degrees and at varying speeds; (*c*) the material wealth and property of the churches was confiscated or destroyed. These areas also overlapped each other: destruction of images, shrines, and altars ended the cult of saints, relics, and the host, but also entailed confiscation of church plate; monasticism was abolished and monastic property re-used at least partly because a life spent in secluded prayer, private worship, and self-mortification was no longer valued.

6.1. *Abolition of priestly power and privilege*

The rejection of the authority and jurisdiction of pope, bishops, and clergy was more often implicit than explicit; as was seen in the case of episcopal protests against heretic preachers, it usually suited governments simply to disobey without stating reasons. Later in the process, some cities actually forced their bishops to leave: Bishop Hugo von Hohenlandenberg of Constance and his chapter left Constance for Meersburg in 1526–7; Bishop Christoph von Utenheim of Basle resigned and left in 1527; Bishop Paul Ziegler of Chur lived from 1526 in exile, as did Sebastian de Montfaucon of Lausanne after 1536. Many late medieval bishops had already long since been forced to reside outside their sees, as at Strasbourg or Geneva.[138] When diocesan authority lapsed the clergy lost the power to control their own membership, tax themselves, and to make and enforce their own rules and regulations both upon themselves, and on laymen in matters like marriages, wills, and the church's upkeep through taxes and fees. However, the priesthood lost not only power, but also privilege.[139] Priests were made subject to criminal and civil law in ordinary courts. They were obliged to swear loyalty to their city, prince, or king, and to pay their governors the usual taxes. By joining the ranks of married fathers of families they were integrated into lay society.

This process began very early in the German and Swiss cities. The magistrates in Erfurt took advantage of an anticlerical riot in 1521 to remove priestly privileges.[140] Zwickau and Nuremberg gradually removed clerical tax exemptions, the former from 1523, the latter after 1525.[141] The Strasbourg city council, which had long experience of trying to integrate its clergy into civic life, in April 1523 abruptly increased the demands it made of the clergy in return for civic protection and privileges: citizens' oaths were to be taken, citizens' taxes paid. After eighteen months of deadlock with the conservative chapters the council issued an ultimatum in 15 November 1524; the canons reacted on 6 December by leaving the city; full civic duties were enforced on the rest on 16 January 1525. This 'domestication' of the civic clergy was a feature of other south German cities such as Constance, Memmingen, Biberach, and Augsburg, as well as Swiss cities such as Zürich and Schaffhausen.[142] Protestant clerics completed their integration with the citizenry by marriage, usually contracted long before they were 'allowed' to. Karlstadt announced his marriage at the height of the 1521–2 movement; Zwingli married early and in secret; Bucer was an embarrassment to the Strasbourg council by being already married when he arrived in the city. Their marriages were retrospectively recognized.

6.2. *Abolition of traditional worship*

It can be—and is—disputed just how new the campaign against clerical power and privilege was. The wholesale abolition of the rites and ceremonies at the heart of medieval catholicism was indubitably a radical and unheard-of departure. The traditional sacrificial mass had been the focus of the liturgical rhythm: performed daily by the priesthood, watched by the laity, deemed to have a quantitative and qualitative value for the good of the soul.[143] Luther stamped upon those communities which respected his views a consistent preference for gradual, partial change rather than sudden, dramatic gestures.[144] After suspending the new order tumultuously introduced by Karlstadt and Zwilling on his return to Wittenberg in March 1522, Luther introduced changes very slowly: the chalice was given to the laity late in 1522; on 11 March 1523 he gave up daily mass, leaving only the weekly communion; the old mass was abandoned in Wittenberg late in 1524.[145] Nicolaus Hausmann at Zwickau followed Luther's example: in July 1523 the Eucharistic Host ceased to be carried round the churches in procession; the following March the mass was said in German and the laity were given the cup; the whole liturgy was said in German from April 1525. Particular kinds of masses were often abandoned *before* the central, congregational rite, as when private masses for the souls of benefactors were abolished early in Nuremberg. Numerous details of the old rite were changed at the same time, before uniform new orders were instituted: detailed individual confession before communion was abandoned, at Nuremberg or Reutlingen for instance, in 1524; the 'hours' of prayer, and certain fasts and feast-days, were simplified at the same time.[146]

There was a vital difference between suspending or abolishing the old mass in *some* of the churches within a given jurisdiction, and banning it *everywhere*. Reformers were often able to discard parts of the old rite (and, of course, employ their own new forms) long before the mass was banned altogether. However, in the Swiss and southern Germanic Reformations the finishing of 'the mass' meant far more for the popular imagination and reformed propaganda than in northern Europe. Luther remarked caustically of the 1528 Berne disputation: 'they have done nothing, except that the mass is abrogated, and the children sing in the streets that they have been freed from the baked God'.[147] Notwithstanding, even in the south abolishing the mass was sometimes a long-drawn-out process. At Zürich the mass was almost the last feature of the old Church to be abolished. Some of Zwingli's most trenchant writings, the *Epicheiresis* of August 1523 and the *Isagoge* of November, as well as most of the October

1523 disputation, were devoted to it.[148] However, the Zürich council remained cautious. In Lent 1524 most of the rites surrounding holy week were discarded by the people, including displays of images and a procession to Einsiedeln. By June 1524 many of the priests discarded the 'canon' of the mass; by the following April Zwingli and his allies prepared a new liturgy and confronted the council with a demand for the end of the old mass; the council gave in on 12 April 1525, and the liturgy changed abruptly midway through holy week.[149]

In cities which followed the Zürich tradition the banning of the mass was thereafter the principal event marking the final end of the old ways. After the Berne disputation in 1528, the mass was forbidden at both Berne and St Gallen; at Basle daily celebrations had already been confined to three churches when it was abandoned following the riots of February 1529. At Strasbourg particular celebratory masses were steadily abandoned; the old mass was confined to the chapter churches after Easter 1525, but only forbidden altogether in 1529.[150] Similar edicts followed at Mulhouse (1528–9), Constance (1528), Memmingen (1528), Ulm and Biberach (1531), and Esslingen (1532).[151]

6.3. 'Iconoclasm'

Reformed worship required a building large enough for the congregation, but no larger than one unaided preacher's voice could fill. It needed a table and utensils for communion and baptism; pulpits, equipped with bibles; and little, if anything, else. Nearly all the ornaments of late medieval churches, and many of the churches themselves, were superfluous. The question was how much should be removed; how far the apparatus should be stripped to bare essentials. 'Iconoclasm', meaning strictly the 'breaking of images', is a term often used of the events of some parts of the Reformation. It is slightly inadequate to describe what happened; for not only 'images'—pictures and statues—were destroyed in the ritual 'cleansing' of churches from 'idolatry'. Altars themselves, their ornaments and hangings, rich communion vessels and monstrances, relics and their bejewelled housings, even organs, were destroyed. Reformation 'iconoclasm' was not a campaign against 'graven images' as such, but a campaign against the veneration of all that detracted from the free and sufficient grace of Christ—so relics or mass vestments, not 'images' as such, might none the less be denounced and destroyed as 'idols'.

The first portentous 'iconoclastic' episode accompanied the riotous movement at Wittenberg during 1521–2. On 4 December 1521 an altar in the Franciscan friary was destroyed. On 10 January 1522 Gabriel Zwilling persuaded the Wittenberg Augustinians to burn all their images and mutilate the stone statues. Threats were made to 'cleanse' altars. The town council tried to take matters into its hands, issuing a 'Church ordinance' on 24 January 1522 promising to abolish all images, and all altars save three, in the churches, 'to avoid idolatry'. In February Zwilling led bands of unofficial image-breakers around the town.[152] Luther restrained and partly reversed this programme on his return in March. He bequeathed to the 'Lutheran' churches the attitude that images should not be made the object of rules and regulations; he came to regard the fetish of abolishing them as just as 'legalistic' and wrong as the fetish of worshipping them.[153] At least partly through his influence, the Lutheran communities of northern Germany left the physical appearance of their churches very largely unchanged. Johannes Bugenhagen's ordinances for the northern cities declared images to be a matter of free choice, and discouraged disorderly image-breaking.[154] Nuremberg saw no programme of image-breaking. Nikolaus Hausmann simply removed one altar and a choir-screen from St Katherine's church at Zwickau in March 1524.[155]

In contrast, the thorough removal of images and their associated paraphernalia became a recognizable feature of the Reformation movements of Switzerland and southern Germany (later copied in The Netherlands, England, and Scotland, and in the 'second Reformation' in parts of the Empire itself).[156] However, image-smashing was not always carried out in the same spirit. Broadly speaking, there are perhaps four different patterns seen in the movement across Europe:[157]

(1) Orderly image removal by civic officials, with popular approval.
(2) Riotous popular image-breaking at a time of official religious changes, but outside official control.
(3) Riotous popular image-breaking *against* official religious policy.
(4) Orderly image removal by government officials *against* popular wishes.

The first pattern occurred in Zürich after the October 1523 disputation. There was much preaching against 'idols' and some small-scale removal of pieces by their donors, but the council's temporizing orders prevented widespread destruction until an edict on 15 June 1524 promised an orderly removal. The city architect and three clerics supervised teams of craftsmen as over two weeks from 20 June they removed all images, altars, and ornaments, and whitewashed the walls. A similar commission removed images in Augsburg after the decision to reform in 1534, and similar episodes occurred in Constance (1528–9), Ulm and Biberach (1531), and Ravensburg (1545). At Strasbourg the magistracy countenanced the removal of images in slow instalments from October 1524, punctuated by some spontaneous outbursts of destruction.[158]

Slightly different versions of the second pattern occurred at Berne, St Gallen, and Basle. After the end of the Berne disputation the city council ordered the removal of all images and altars within eight days; in only two days, 27–8 January 1528, the destruction was completed by a mob. Zwingli preached to the rioters on the second day, and the wealth recovered by the destruction was given wholesale to the poor. The movement spread through the canton. Just under a month later, Vadianus led the people of St Gallen to destroy not only images and altars, but also the shrines of two local saints (whose 'relics' turned out to be a skull, a large tooth, and a snail-shell). At Basle the council's attempt to go gently backfired. Two churches were illegally stripped of images in April 1528; a crowd petitioned for the abolition of the mass and images on 8 February, and the following morning the cathedral and remaining catholic churches were cleansed (one by its own, catholic, parishioners). The attempt to distribute the wood for firewood broke down in disorder.[159]

The third and fourth patterns—where the citizenry and government were completely out of step with each other—were much rarer in free cities than in territorial states. Unofficial image-breaking occurred in The Netherlands in 1566,[160] while unpopular official demolition of shrines occurred several times in England from 1538 onwards, and in the Palatinate under Friedrich III after 1560, even though the old (Lutheran) order may have enjoyed much popular affection.[161] Equally uncommon in the central European city Reformations was the demolition or conversion of superfluous churches which featured in Scandinavia and Scotland.[162]

6.4. *Abolition of the monastic order*

The houses of monastic orders, whether of monks, nuns, friars, or whatever, all disappeared, sooner or later, wherever the Reformation was established. Although the theological reason for abolition—that vows, repeated masses, celibacy, and self-mortification were not 'good works' and had no value for the soul of the monk or anyone else—was the same everywhere, the actual politics and sentiments behind the process varied. Friars were particularly disliked, as the source of most resistance to the Reformation within the towns; their houses were sometimes destroyed by mob action. Some urban orders, like the Wittenberg Augustinians, spontaneously dissolved themselves, leaving Luther's family to rattle around in the rambling cloister.[163] Rural monasteries were usually less odious, except where they presented a threat, commercial or political, to the nearby town; in such cases they could be attacked by a reformed city nearby, as St Gallen monastery was by the town, Weingarten by Ravensburg in Swabia, or Grunhain by Zwickau in Saxony.[164] In the bulk of the city Reformations the monasteries were surrendered at the same time as the mass was abolished, with their members given the choice of conformity to the new order or exile.[165] A particularly resilient order might last longer, as for example the Franciscanesses (Poor Clares) at Nuremberg, whose formidable patrician abbess Caritas Pirck-heimer secured temporary survival, without new admissions, for her community; or at Biberach, where they lasted till 1536, five years longer than the rest.[166]

The destructive processes of the Reformation marked a decisive change in the experience of the people of great areas of Europe. A system of law and a factor in diplomacy was eliminated. A ritually separate class of people lost their separateness and their 'holiness'. A whole range of sacramental services to confer 'grace' was abolished. In many areas the sights and sounds of worship were drastically purged, while everywhere the learned language retreated to the seats of learning. Yet the destruction of the old religious order went hand in hand with, and was justified by, the attempt to build up the new; however, it sometimes proved easier to pull down than to build up.

7. *Constructing the New Order*

Although the 'breakthrough' which ended the restraints of clerical power upon secular government or lay consciences is sometimes portrayed as the end of the interesting part of the story, no one at the time regarded a purely negative, destructive act of Reformation as adequate or complete. The reformed churches had to prove themselves as decorous, disciplined, and 'orderly' as the catholicism which they replaced, or preferably more so. Long-standing complaints about ill-trained priests and superstitious laity had to be addressed. The constructive aspects of the Reformation, there-fore, were as interesting and as fruitful in political controversy as the years before the breakthrough. A reformed church settlement may be divided into at least three aspects:

(1) The adoption of a distinctively protestant 'confession', or common statement of belief.
(2) The introduction and use of a reformed standard of worship, for the communion rite and all other remaining church services.

(3) Thirdly, the institution of a church structure, comprising not only a replacement for the old priesthood, but also bodies to continue the moral and social oversight which the old Church had exercised.

However, the process by which these changes took place in any given city was complex, protracted, and sometimes haphazard.

7.1. *Belief*

Consciously partisan statements of belief made by individual communities were a novelty in sixteenth-century western Europe. The old Church had inherited and used the Apostles', Nicene, and Athanasian creeds; but up to and including the Fifth Lateran Council on the very eve of the Reformation, only specific issues of faith had regularly been resolved in the medieval western councils. Reformed 'confessions' were offered either to show communal solidarity when threatened, or to reassure a higher power that the protestants were really peaceful and respectable Christians. The prime instance of this kind of confession was Melanchthon's Augsburg Confession of 1530. In twenty-two articles of doctrine it stated the Lutheran message, but asserted its 'catholic' orthodoxy, and counterpointed its affirmations with denials and denunciations of old heresies (for instance on the Trinity) and new 'anabaptist' ones (such as the rejection of baptism or civil authority). In its second part, the Augsburg Confession claimed that the Lutherans only 'omitted a few abuses' of the catholic Church; denying the wine to the laity, priestly celibacy, detailed confession, food regulations, monastic vows, prelatical power.[167] At similarly 'threatened' stages other protestant Churches adopted confessions. The Augsburg *Reichstag* also produced the *Tetrapolitana* of Strasbourg and three reformed cities in Swabia, as well as Zwingli's *Fidei Ratio*.[168] The threat of a Church council in 1537 inspired the first 'Helvetic' confession agreed at Basle in the early months of 1536.[169]

Once the Augsburg and Four Cities' confessions were available, new entrants to the protestant fold within Germany tended to adopt them retrospectively. Before then, however, a few reformed states produced their own standards of belief in the form of statements requiring their clergy to teach the people in such and such a way. One of the first of these was the 'Notice' (*Anzeigen*) issued by Markgrafen Kasimir and Georg of Brandenburg-Ansbach in August 1525 for their clergy: this ordered them to teach that faith alone—but a living faith active in good works—was enough for salvation, and (predictably in the year of popular revolts) that secular powers were to be obeyed. Nearby Nuremberg issued a particularly succinct and complete set of 'doctrinal articles' (*Lehrartikel*) for examination of its clergy in 1528.[170] Thereafter Lutheran Church ordinances usually contained sections on doctrine: in the *Instructions to the Visitors* of 1528, which laid down standards for the towns of Electoral Saxony, articles on 'teaching the whole Gospel', Christ's satisfaction for sin, free will, and Christian freedom, alternated with prescriptions on ritual and morality. The great Church ordinance devised by Brenz and Osiander for Nuremberg and Brandenburg-Ansbach and ratified in 1533 likewise contained a large doctrinal element; this ordinance profoundly influenced others in central and northern Germany.[171] Closely related to ordinances for preaching were the formal catechisms, question-and-answer formulae used in the instruction of the young. Usually these were employed to consolidate rather than introduce reformed ideas, as in the case of Luther's catechisms of 1529.[172] However, the adoption of a catechism to bring up the new generation could equally be a landmark in installing the Reformation itself: instances are the publications of Osiander's elaborate *Kinderpredigten* for Nuremberg in 1533, the adoption of Leo Jud's catechism at Schaffhausen in 1536, or Calvin's production of an 'Instruction and Confession of Faith' (later entitled 'Catechism') for Geneva in November 1537.[173]

7.2. *Worship*

At first individual drafts for particular services were produced, above all for the two remaining protestant sacraments, baptism and the communion. New vernacular baptisms were amongst the first reformed rites: Luther's (1523 and 1526), Leo Jud's (10 August 1523), Matthäus Zell's at Strasbourg (27 January 1524), or Osiander's at Nuremberg (also 1524).[174] However, the centre of the new worship was the vernacular Eucharist. Luther's conservatism and caution contrasted not only with the Swiss reformers, but also with his own Saxon colleagues. After March 1522 he suspended the immensely popular public Eucharists which Karlstadt and Zwilling had introduced, and gradually introduced his own. He produced some recommendations for the Saxon town of Leisnig in January 1523. In November, at the request of pastor Nikolaus Hausmann of Zwickau, he produced a Latin *Formula of the Mass*. His detailed German mass was first used at Wittenberg on 29 October 1525 and published the following year.[175] Meanwhile many other German towns had already produced their own reformed communions. One of the first may have been that used by Caspar Kantz at Nördlingen in 1522.[176] Thomas Müntzer made some poetic (and quite influential) contributions to liturgy during his time at Allstedt during 1523–4. Nuremberg saw experiments with a variety of both German and

Latin masses. Even within Saxony towns like Erfurt or Coburg devised their own rituals. In the basically Lutheran rites only the most obnoxious elements of the old mass, those which suggested that it was a repetition of Christ's sacrifice, were deleted; and Latin, for instance at Nuremberg, was only gradually and partially supplanted.[177]

Even in non-Lutheran Strasbourg the changes were gradual, from the first German masses celebrated by Anton Firn and Theobald Schwartz in February 1524 to the much more thoroughly reformed orders (omitting all unscriptural additions) introduced in 1525-6.[178] In these later orders the Strasbourg pastors consciously drew themselves closer to Zürich. There Zwingli (as seen earlier) had pushed and pushed for the wholesale abolition of the old mass. He had his own *Action oder Bruch des Nachtmals* ready to replace it right in the middle of holy week 1525. In this ritual, and those which drew upon it, German was used for all the major elements and only unexceptionally evangelical elements of the old mass were retained.[179]

Gradually these experimental orders of service matured into complete schemes for the entire range of church services. By the late 1520s or early 1530s directions on the conduct of services formed part and parcel of the state ordinances which also regulated the structure of the new churches. Johannes Bugenhagen's parallel ordinances for several north German cities, for instance Hamburg in 1529 or Lübeck in 1531, made detailed recommendations for worship in the midst of educational and social provisions.[180] Further south worship was settled for Weissenburg, near Nuremberg, in its ordinance of November 1528; in 1545 Luther's amanuensis Veit Dietrich drew all the Nuremberg orders together in his massive *Agendbüchlein* of 1545.[181] Strasbourg settled its liturgical forms during 1533-5.[182]

Converting a liturgy from Latin into a vernacular *could* have drawn clergy and laity closer together, and ended the self-imposed isolation of spiritual and secular worlds which the *hearing* of an incomprehensible rite had tended to create. That would have depended, however, on finding a *truly* accessible vernacular (not always easy in sixteenth-century Europe, with its babel of provincial dialects), and on adjusting the arrangements of the Church so as to make the new liturgy audible and immediate. One of the most dramatic ways in which the Reformation involved the congregation more closely in the weekly rite was the much greater role which it gave to hymn and psalm-singing. These had been anything but unknown in the late Middle Ages; indeed, Luther at first relied on German medieval hymns before devising his own. However, the 'spiritual songs' of the Lutheran and reformed traditions grew into metrical and musical emblems, slogans, and indeed war-cries, for the protestant confessions to a previously unheard of extent.

In his *Formula of the Mass* of 1523 Luther proposed that the 'canticles' accompanying the mass should be sung by the whole congregation as in antiquity, not by the choir alone; he recommended a few of the medieval hymns (suitably amended) and called for poets to come forward and produce new ones.[183] Luther did literally write around Saxony asking for poets to write verse translations of the Psalms; but he soon burst into verse himself. He wrote a long poem on the first Lutheran heretics burnt at Antwerp in 1523, and early in 1524 published at Nuremberg, with Paul Speratus, a first book of eight German hymns. Within two years Luther had written some twenty-four hymns; his most famous, many times translated, remain easily his best-known writings.[184] His devotion to church music even moved him to write in October 1530 to a court musician in catholic Bavaria for a tune.[185] In this as in other respects Luther's arch-enemy Thomas Müntzer had made some pioneering and, to appearances at least, comparatively conservative contributions. In the *German Church Service* which he composed for Allstedt *c*.1523–4 Müntzer built in antiphons, metrical hymns, and some free renderings of parts of the Psalter.[186]

In Bucer's Strasbourg from the early 1530s complete Psalters in German were prepared for the use of the congregation. Possibly the most internationally significant impact of this move was its effect on Calvin, who had already called for the revival of congregational psalm-singing at Geneva as early as 1537. Shortly after his arrival in Strasbourg, Calvin issued in 1539 a small volume entitled *Aulcuns Psaumes et Cantiques mis en Chant*. This included translations by Calvin himself of five Psalms, the Song of Simeon (the *Nunc dimittis*), and the Ten Commandments; but, even more importantly, it introduced eight Psalm translations by the French former court poet and *valet de chambre* of François I, Clément Marot. Fifty of Marot's Psalms were published at Geneva in 1543; in 1562 Théodore de Bèze issued a yet further enlarged edition. Marot's translations were soon enthusiastically set to music or adapted by writers and composers such as Loys Bourgeois, Claude Goudimel, Philibert Jambe-de-fer, and Claude le Jeune.[187] The Marot Psalter, perhaps above all else, became the standard vehicle for the devotional life of French-speaking protestantism; while metrical versions of the Psalms in English (if one excepts the ponderous efforts of James VI), acquired similar status in Scotland.

7.3. *Structure*

Luther, it is sometimes said, regarded the institutional Church as less important than the community of the truly faithful scattered in society. Be that as it may, communities which adopted the Reformation had very quickly to fill the gaps left by the abolition of the papal hierarchy and the monastic orders: to pay pastors' stipends, relieve poverty, educate children, regulate marriages and wills, and supervise public morals. Here also piece-meal instructions were produced, then consolidated into great 'ordinances'.

The Church ordinances of the early Reformation made frequent references to the organization of elementary schools. Unlike that concerning doctrine and the bulk of the liturgy, the task here was not to tear down and rebuild from the foundations; it was to attempt to bring some sort of harmony and uniformity into a bewildering and complex array of institutions. By the early sixteenth century European schools included some entirely secular institutions run by municipalities; village schools associated with the pastor and taught either by him or by a minor clerk; schools annexed to friaries or other religious foundations; and entirely independent bodies run by private trusts which might or might not have a religious dimension.[188] The reformers wanted sound doctrine taught from the first; secular authorities wanted control and uniformity; both wanted more of the right kinds of schools. In 1523 Luther contributed to the small town of Leisnig a detailed 'common chest order', which provided for all the revenues of the 'community church' to be concentrated in the chest and disbursed by the community's officers for the upkeep of the pastorate, education, and poor relief. This included requiring a pious schoolmaster to be hired, and a respectable widow to teach the young girls.[189] In the latter part of the 1520s reformers such as Melanchthon, Agricola, Aepinus, Brenz, and Bucer made similar recommendations for towns under their influence.[190] In Bugenhagen's reforming Church ordinances for cities like Hamburg (1529) and Lübeck (1531), the first section of all was dedicated to setting out the grade, syllabus, personnel, and salaries of the cities' schools and their teachers.[191] Besides the inevitable catechism classes for religious instruction, the curricular regime for the Latin schools (which occupied far more of the reformers' attention than the German schools) remained a largely conventional one, with the medieval grammatical stand-bys of 'Donat' and Dionysius Cato leading on first to Aesop's Fables, then to Terence and Plautus, then Virgil, Ovid, and Cicero.[192]

Such urban regulations established patterns which were followed in the school ordinances issued by the princes in the mid-century, of which perhaps the most influential was that issued by Duke Christoph of Würt-temberg in 1559.[193] The results of such efforts were incomplete: money was short, teachers scarce, and parents often recalcitrant when it came to supporting school discipline or even sending their children to school at all. Nevertheless, in the most closely managed reformed states a degree of harmony, and an overall increase in the numbers of schools, was achieved.

In 'social control', the regulation of the poor, needy, and marginal elements of society, civic authorities leapt into the breach with predictable enthusiasm to bring yet another aspect of community life under their sway. They introduced orders for combining all the old funds for poor relief into a so-called 'common chest'. One of the first of these was introduced—long before any other reforming changes apart from preaching—in the Nuremberg alms order of 1522. This inspired imitations at Kitzingen in 1523 and Windsheim in 1524.[194] Meanwhile Luther's detailed common chest order for Leisnig banned begging and made detailed plans for requiring the able-bodied poor to work and for giving alms to sustain the young, old, and sick. Magdeburg copied this move in 1524. The Zwickau common chest acquired an unfortunate reputation when the city fathers were suspected of using its funds to provide themselves with loans at favourable terms of interest.[195] In Bugenhagen's ordinances, for example for Braunschweig (1528), Hamburg, and Lübeck, the common chest was a major component, its revenues to be administered by 'deacons'.[196] In Calvin's *Institutes*, the office of 'deacon', the lay supervisor of poor relief and social welfare, became one of the four offices of the Church; in Genevan practice this meant taking two pre-existing civic officers (the 'hospitallers' and the 'procurators') and giving them a New Testament title and a place in the *Ecclesiastical Ordinances*.[197] Important by-products of these arrangements in protestant states were: the discouragement or banning of irregular begging; the confiscation and amalgamation of endowments made for the poor as pious offerings for the good of the donor's soul; the prohibition of religious begging, practised as a mortification by certain religious orders, above all friars; and, less predictably, the closing of municipal brothels.

However, it is not quite clear just how distinctively 'protestant' or indeed religious these initiatives were, apart from the banning of begging friars and (possibly) of prostitutes. Elsewhere in the early sixteenth century, cities in heavily urbanized regions of Europe, whether Venice in northern Italy or Ypres, Mons, or Lille in the Low Countries, found traditional indiscriminate and random private charity, usually in the form of pious bequests or foundations, unsuitable for the numbers and types of poor within their walls. A structured programme of poor relief was gradually developed, comprising enclosure and care of the young and the disabled, enclosure and compulsory work for the able-bodied but un- or underemployed, and severe repression of public begging and vagrancy.[198] This programme reflected (at least in part) Renaissance humanists' praise of the ideal of the busy, wealthy, lay husband and father against that of the monastic, contemplative, celibate, idle mendicant.[199] The civic and humanist trends coalesced in the tract *De Subventione Pauperum* (*On the Support of the Poor*) published by Juan-Luis Vives at Bruges in March 1526: it denounced the idleness of the rich and the deceitfulness of the picaresque poor alike, and called for existing charitable foundations to be so regulated as to supervise all categories of poor and make random charity redundant.[200] This model was later copied in the reform of poor relief at Lyons.[201]

Separating the humanist and protestant input into the social control legislation of the early Reformation is a difficult and probably quite artificial task. In the case of England, it can be shown that the ideas of Vives and The Netherlands towns were circulated in England in the 1530s and practically realized in the post-Reformation legislation of the Elizabethan period.[202] Here humanist and protestant impulses coincided and are indeed barely distinguishable. However, in central Germany perhaps the most influential text on this issue was not Vives's tract, but rather the second part of Luther's *To the Christian Nobility*, whose 'prescription' of social remedies included: reducing feast-days to prevent idleness (no. 18); the abolition of all begging, with the imposition of systematic, prudent relief of the poor within each city (no. 21); restraints on luxuries and usury, and a ban on municipal brothels (no. 27).[203] Humanist influences are less obvious; indeed, several of the German common chest orders were instituted well before either the Ypres scheme or the publication of Vives's *De Subventione*.

More importantly, however, historians of the Reformation city tend to attribute the haste with which many cities created common chests to very practical motives. Simply, such chests were used as a means to confiscate and bring under the city fathers' control the great confused mass of medieval charitable endowments—not to mention houses of mendicant friars—which formed substantial enclaves of clerical power and fiscal immunity.[204] Signs of lay impatience with the disorderly and sometimes erratic nature of religious charities were already visible in the late Middle Ages, when the Augsburg city fathers campaigned against begging, or secular and Church authorities vied for control of charitable endowments around Avignon.[205] The issue may be not whether protestantism or humanism was the ideological motor force behind systematic poor relief; but rather why Luther, Vives, and the rest independently found ideological reasons to support developments upon which the late medieval bourgeoisie insisted (once the fear of treading upon clerical toes was removed) for economic and political reasons.

It was only too easy to persuade civic authorities to institute common chests, to take away the powers of the old priesthood. It was much harder to erect a Church discipline as such, which might give new power to the new clerics over laymen. Some replacement of the old bishops' or archdeacons' courts was indispensable: to regulate marriages, for example. However, reformed clergy saw more to their role than regulating the proprieties of bourgeois legality. Blasphemy, irreverence, inattendance at church, or bad neighbourliness were moral evils to be cured, no less than obvious civil crimes; they were also, one might note, offences which the rich and powerful committed as readily as the poor and unfranchised. One of the earliest reformed Church disciplines emerged in Zürich under Zwingli. A marriage court was set up in May 1525, combining clerics and lay councillors; by 1526 the city council was responsible for excommunicating those found guilty of adultery by the marriage court. From 1528 a 'synod' of the Zürich clergy organized its regulatory pronouncements: these culminated in an important moral ordinance (*Sittenordnung*) passed by synod and council in March 1530.[206] Zürich was exceptional in the mutual co-operation shown by city council and pastorate towards each other. Much more normal was a protracted period of wheedling between the civil and religious powers. An important example of this tension showed itself at Strasbourg. The magistracy did nothing to fill the void left by the rejection of the bishop's authority until 1531; that October they created the office of *Kirchenpfleger*, 'church curators', essentially to supervise the conduct of the pastors (not their flocks!). In the Strasbourg synod of 1533 and the *Ecclesiastical Ordinance* and *Disciplinary Ordinance* which followed in 1534 and 1535 respectively, the clergy attempted to harness the 'curators', with so little success that Bucer discarded them as religious officers by 1538. When the clergy attempted to set up a voluntary discipline on their own in the late 1540s prolonged and bitter rows with the council ensued.[207]

Even in Geneva, which is still apt to be regarded as a reformed Utopia, the establishment of a Church discipline entailed a prolonged and determined struggle on the part of Calvin and his allies. The 'consistory', or Church 'court', as set up in the 1541 ordinances, was composed of the company of pastors and a dozen lay 'elders' chosen from the members of the city councils. However, the consistory did not have the clear power to excommunicate (exclude from the sacraments) and absolve until 1555; by acquiring even that power the Genevan consistory was more successful than its counterparts elsewhere. In Augsburg, for instance, council control over the clergy in the mid-1530s settlement was almost obsessively vigilant.[208] Consistories appeared in Lutheran north Germany as well, but more slowly and with less furore than in the southern civic Reformations. The first forms of moral discipline were envisaged as part of the preparation for receiving communion. Luther discussed such a (voluntary) discipline in his edition of the mass in 1526, but declined to enforce it in practice. In the Brandenburg–Nuremberg ordinance of 1533, Brenz and Osiander directed the pastors to urge their communicants to seek absolution for their sins first: not (as they insisted) by way of restoring the popish enumeration of *all* sins, but as a means of moral instruction. The Hamburg ordinance of 1535 likewise urged the retention of private confession and absolution. Wittenberg's own 'consistory' was established by a comprehensive edict of Elector Johann Friedrich in 1542. This body was to oversee all kinds of moral issues—especially within marriages—backed up by the force of excommunication.[209]

8. *Unsuccessful Civic Reformation Movements*

In some cities where a favourable climate of opinion did *not* lead to a successful urban Reformation, one finds a valuable 'control sample' to compare with the political analyses of those states and communities which became protestant.

The small imperial free town of Schwäbisch Gmünd incurred a heavy debt to the Swabian League during the revolts of 1525; in the suppression of these revolts the first wave of reforming preachers, Althamer, Gundelfinger, and Sigwyn, were driven out. Nevertheless, strong pressure from the guildmasters to open up the oligarchic council structures was combined in July 1531 with a petition for evangelical preaching and a revision of the traditional calendar of feast- and fast-days. The council reacted by instituting a rigorous supervision of the clergy, especially the regular orders, and curtailing some of their commercial privileges; but throughout the 1530s and thereafter, in keeping with its pro-Habsburg policy, it interpreted such measures in terms of the old faith, and gave no scope to *protestantism* as such.[210] At Leipzig, despite Duke Georg of Saxony's own entrenched catholicism, the burghers treated Luther's opponents with derision in

1518–22; during 1523–4 they heard reforming preachers (Dominikus Schleupner and Andreas Bodenschatz) with enthusiasm and petitioned for them to be appointed to permanent places in the town churches. When the duke refused, a proportion of the citizens took to hearing Lutheran sermons across the Ernestine border, and to passive avoidance of catholic confession. In the early 1530s the duke felt strong enough to act against these (mostly quite wealthy) closet Lutherans: some seventy or so were expelled in mid-1533, and official changes waited until Georg died in 1539.[211]

A series of 'failed' Reformations occurred in urban sees of prince-bishops, such as Paderborn in the north, Cologne in western Germany, or Würzburg or Bamberg in Franconia. These cities were by no means under their bishops' heels: they had considerable privileges and exemptions from their authority, though the fear of losing such privilege was persistent. In Cologne, capital of the electoral archbishopric, the city council acted quickly and decisively against the merest discussion of Lutheran ideas from the first. In 1522 they allowed the burning of Luther's books, partly to earn the papal legate Aleander's help against the new archbishop's pretensions. The city oligarchs endowed, appointed, and even in part staffed Cologne University's resolutely conservative theology faculty; in 1522–4 the theologians acted quickly to purge Lutheran ideas from the Augustinian Eremites' house, and throughout maintained a reasonably effective censorship of the press and a very efficient stranglehold on the city's pulpits.[212] In several episcopal sees the vital ingredient of a broadly based popular movement was forestalled by the events of 1525. In Würzburg a civic revolt in April 1525 prompted the city council to consider a 'common chest' order like Kitzingen's; in Bamberg the height of popular pressure for reform was reached in the same year; in Cologne some of the guilds pressed for curtailment of Church privileges and sermons based on the 'right word of God' during a disturbance in 1525; thereafter the city fathers used the tight guild structure to prevent any further such agitation. Three years later a riot at Paderborn in May 1528 led the bishop to fine the city heavily. In each of these episcopal cities popular agitation, associated with a widespread failed revolt, proved unable to ally with whatever enthusiasm there might have been for reform among humanist clergy and élite reformers. The fear of disorder, on the contrary, justified harsh repression by bishops or councils.[213]

A major ingredient in 'failed' civic Reformation movements in Germany, heavy-handed intervention or pressure from an external authority like a duke or an archbishop, was absent in those cantons of Switzerland which rejected the reform. At Lucerne, Zug, and Fribourg (Freiburg-im-Uechtland) modest humanist circles entertained reforming ideas and tried to attract preachers, reaching a peak in their activities in 1522–4; they failed, however, to win over either the city oligarchies or any significant interest group among the populace. In the face of official disapproval the (rather minor) reformers of these places left for greener pastures; Hofmeister, Myconius, Xilotectus, and Kilchmeyer had left Lucerne by 1524, while Werner Steiner left Zug in 1529. At Zug the citizens themselves declared a wish to stay with the old Church in 1526.[214] Only at Solothurn did the authorities temporarily adopt a neutral, rather than uniformly hostile attitude. A minority group of agitators, centred on the boatmen's guild, were given a brief period of limited rights of worship from 1530 to about 1533.[215]

It would be rash to generalize from these case-studies, or to suggest that their experience was shared more widely elsewhere in Europe. However, in these instances, several points stand out. First, civic authorities, princes, bishops, or theologians reacted quickly, decisively, and (except at Solothurn) conclusively to resist the Reformation. Regardless of *why* they did so, their resolution contrasts with the benign, uncommitted inactivity which was clearly so vital in shortly-to-be-reformed cities. Secondly, the chief effect of this resolute policy was to prevent widespread reformed preaching, and thereby to discourage the coalition between humanist ideas and guildsmen's grievances which was found elsewhere. Finally, the very fact that some cities elsewhere were *already* reformed had a doubly discouraging effect. First, cities which distrusted their neighbours would also resist their neighbours' religion: Bamberg versus Nuremberg, Zug versus Zürich, Solothurn versus Basle. Secondly, unsuccessful reformers could hardly be blamed for taking themselves off to more congenial environments; protestant Switzerland could not help draining surrounding regions of protestant talent, from as far away as northern Italy.[216] The success of the reforms in one place might of itself dictate its failure somewhere nearby.

The Reformation in the cities demands attention not because of the mere numbers involved, nor because the urban reforms represented a particularly 'pure' form of the protestant Gospel. Simply, the cities offered the earliest and fullest opportunity for the citizen's response to the religious, social, and political challenges of the Reformation movement to translate itself into practical acts. If one considers bare numbers, the city Reformations represented a minor proportion of sixteenth-century protestants.[217] If one looks rather at how many people participated in the political process of choosing the Reformation, the contribution of the cities probably does deserve the extraordinary attention which historians have lavished on it.

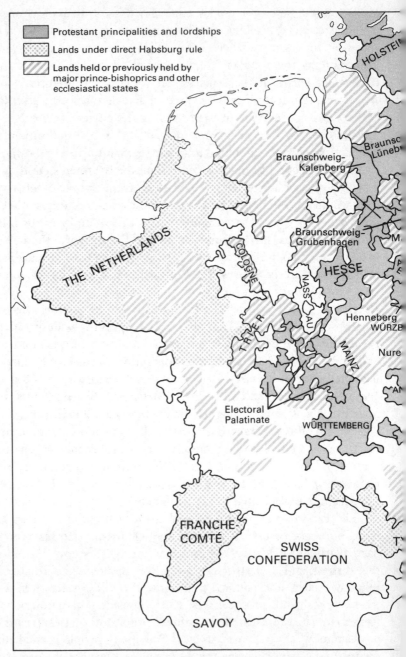

MAP 3. The German Principalities on the Eve of the Schmalkaldic War, *c.*

POMMERN-WOLGAST

POMMERN-STETTIN

EAST PRUSSIA

ENBURG

G

ELECTORAL
BRANDENBURG

chweig-
büttel

POLAND

ERNESTINE

Liegnitz

O N Y

ALBERTINE

BOHEMIA

ER
TINATE

MORAVIA

euburg

VARIA

AUSTRIA

HABSBURG HUNGARY

STYRIA

CARINTHIA

CARNIOLA

0   50   100   150 km

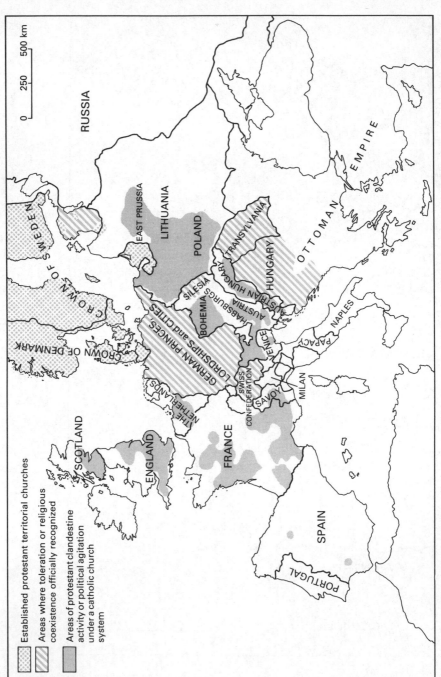

MAP 4. The Religious Complexion of Europe in the Period c.1555–8

Established protestant territorial churches

Areas where toleration or religious coexistence officially recognized

Areas of protestant clandestine activity or political agitation under a catholic church system

RUSSIA

CROWN OF SWEDEN

CROWN OF DENMARK

SCOTLAND

ENGLAND

THE NETHERLANDS

FRANCE

SPAIN

PORTUGAL

GERMAN PRINCES AND CITIES
LORDSHIPS and CITIES

EAST PRUSSIA

LITHUANIA

POLAND

SILESIA

BOHEMIA

AUSTRIAN HUNGARY

HABSBURGS

TRANSYLVANIA

HUNGARY

OTTOMAN EMPIRE

SWISS CONFEDERATION

SAVOY

MILAN

VENICE

PAPACY

NAPLES

0   250   500 km

16
Principalities and Kingdoms

It is much harder to analyse how the Reformation merged with the purposes of territorial sovereigns than with cities. The crucial decisions were made in smaller, less public circles. Monarchs could afford to be less responsive to their subjects' feelings; political, diplomatic, and military calculations blended with very variable degrees of real interest in religion.

1. *The German Princes*

The 'princes' were the substantial territorial sovereigns of northern, central, and south-eastern Germany. Great dynasties like the Wettin in the Saxonies, the Hohenzollern in the Brandenburg lands, the Wittelsbach in Bavaria and the Upper and Lower Palatinates, contained in one of their branches the dignity of an elector (*Kurfürst*) of the Holy Roman Empire. Along with lesser houses, they varied in their titles of 'princes' (*Fürsten*), 'dukes' (*Herzöge*), or 'counts' (*Grafen*, the latter often prefixed by *Mark* or *Land*); and in their degree of superiority over the lesser nobles. The greatest possessed rich courts, sophisticated chanceries, substantial urban capitals, and other trappings of power and wealth. The Habsburgs in the Austrias were only the greatest of this class. They represented the future of the *Reich*; their states fared best in the century of intermittent local and national warfare to which the Reformation led.

1.1. *Saxony*

As was seen earlier, the spread of Lutheran ideas in the towns of Saxony was diffuse, partly because Luther had no wish and made no effort to lead and organize a movement, because not all preachers followed his lead, and finally because Elector Friedrich never explicitly supported or authorized, but only tolerated and refused to suppress, such moves. When Elector Johann 'the Constant' (1525–32) succeeded Friedrich, he became a much more active protector of the new churches, partly at least under Luther's promptings that he should do something to replace the rapidly crumbling old Church structure.[1] He commanded the saying of mass in German on Christmas day, 1525. Between December 1526 and February 1527, after further urgings from Luther, he appointed a small committee of electoral councillors and university theologians to prepare a church visitation of his lands. Their instructions were issued on 16 June.[2] Between August 1527 and March 1528 Melanchthon and others worked up a full set of instructions for the visitors, translating Lutheran ideals into princely decrees for the first time. Luther wrote the preface.[3] The Saxon reformed Church organization was developed through the 1530s. The office of 'superintendent', the Lutheran replacement for the episcopacy, grew in importance with the appointment of Johannes Bugenhagen as *Obersuperattendent* for the north German churches in 1533. Church discipline stabilized when the proposal made in 1537 for 'consistory' (Church) courts for Electoral Saxony matured into the Wittenberg consistory ordinance in 1542.[4]

1.2. *Other principalities*

With the important exceptions of the elector of Saxony at Wittenberg and the archbishop of Mainz at Erfurt, the princes were less exposed to the destabilizing pressure from the lower bourgeoisie which forced otherwise cautious or reactionary city oligarchies, like those of Nuremberg, Lübeck, or Augsburg, to institute or allow a Reformation. Where such pressure arose and was either successfully resisted or defeated, as in the capitals of the archbishop of Cologne in the 1520s or the prince-bishop of Münster in 1531–5, the backlash may even have favoured princely authority. Conversions amongst the princes were therefore steady and gradual, in contrast to the somewhat explosive suddenness of the urban Reformation in the 1520s.[5]

Some of the changes shown in Table 16.1 were unusual in various ways. The East Prussian lands were created out of the estates of the Order of Teutonic Knights, converted into a duchy of the kingdom of Poland by Albrecht von Hohenzollern, the former Grand Master of the Order.[6] Two states were reformed through military intervention: Württemberg when Duke Ulrich, exiled by the Habsburgs since 1519, was restored to his lands by Hessian troops and Saxon mediation at the Peace of Kaaden (June 1534);[7] while Heinrich of Braunschweig-Wolfenbüttel, who had been harassing protestant towns near his lands, was overrun by Hessian and Saxon troops in July–August 1542 and his lands (temporarily) reformed under a commission of protestant princes.[8]

More studies of the 'Princes' Reformations' are needed before one can safely generalize about the political pressures behind the adoption of the Reformation. Some features stand out. The princes were generally more

TABLE 16.1

Territory	Changes	Prince
East Prussia	1523–5	Albrecht of Hohenzollern
Brandenburg-Ansbach	1524–8	Kasimir (d.1527), Georg (d.1543)
Hesse	1526–8	Philipp (1518–67)
Braunschweig-Lüneburg	1526–7	Ernst (d.1546), Otto (d.1549), Franz (d.1549)
Mecklenburg-Schwerin	1526 (i)	Heinrich (reversed 1528)
	1533 5 (ii)	Magnus (1516–50)
Anhalt-Köthen	1526–	Wolfgang
Mansfeld	1525–6	Gebhard (d.1558), Albrecht (d.1560)
Liegnitz	1527	Friedrich II
Anhalt-Dessau	1532–4	Johann (d.1551), Georg (d.1553), Joachim (d.1561)
Pomerania	1534–5	Philipp (1531–60), Barnim (1532–73)
Württemberg	1534	Ulrich (d.1550) (with L. of Schmalkalden)
Brandenburg Neumark	1536 8	Johann von Küstrin (1513–71)
Braunschweig-Grubenhagen	1538	Philipp (1494 1551)
Electoral Brandenburg	1539–40	Joachim II (1535–71)
Albertine Saxony	1539 (i)	Heinrich (1539–41)
	1541 (ii)	Moritz (1541–53)
Braunschweig-Kalenberg	1540–	Erik II (1540–84)
Holstein	1542	
Braunschweig-Wolfenbüttel	1542–3	(Saxon and Hessian occupation)
Neuburg	1543	Ottheinrich
Henneberg	1545	Wilhelm, Georg Ernst
Electoral Palatinate	1546	Friedrich II (1544–56)

remote from their populations than the city councillors, and relatively closer (legally and politically) to the Emperor; so they tended to fear imperial retribution more than their own subjects (except in 1525!) and delayed introducing reform accordingly. Hence, for example, Electoral Saxony, Hesse, and Brandenburg-Ansbach were only beginning to reorganize their churches in the late 1520s, while major cities like Zürich, Nuremberg, or Strasbourg had already taken major steps by the end of 1525.[9] Insecurity had another consequence: like the Swiss cantons, catholic and protestant princes alike tended to form defensive leagues from the mid-1520s onwards. Following the inconclusive *Reichstag* at Nuremberg in 1523–4 two catholic leagues were formed: the League of Regensburg (June–July 1524), comprising the Emperor's brother Archduke Ferdinand, the dukes of Bavaria, and a dozen south German prelates; and the League of Dessau (July 1525), formed by Duke Georg of Saxony, Archbishop Albrecht of Mainz, the elector of Brandenburg, and the dukes of Braunschweig-Kalenberg and Braunschweig-Wolfenbüttel, with the approval of Charles V.[10]

In response Elector Johann of Saxony and Landgraf Philipp of Hesse met at Gotha on 27 February 1526 to form what on 2 May became called the League of Torgau, and which was enlarged to include more members on 12 June.[11] A fictitious alliance, the Breslau League, supposedly formed in May 1527 between Ferdinand, Electoral Brandenburg, Mainz, Bavaria, and the southern bishops (actually invented by Otto von Pack, a former vice-chancellor of the duke of Saxony), stirred Philipp of Hesse to further aggression in 1528.[12] In the face of a hostile *Reichstag* on 22 April 1529, Electoral Saxony, Hesse, Strasbourg, Ulm, and Nuremberg came to a secret understanding to defend each other if attacked. Although Philipp of Hesse failed to persuade the Saxon and Swiss theologians to reconcile themselves at Marburg,[13] he did orchestrate the 'Protestation' against the decrees of the 1529 Speyer *Reichstag* jointly subscribed by southern German cities (hitherto aligned with Zürich) and Lutheran princes, which first earned them the name of 'Protestants'.[14]

In answer to the decrees of the Augsburg *Reichstag* of 1530[15] Elector Johann of Saxony and other princes gathered at Schmalkalden at Christmas 1530, where they protested against the proposed coronation of Ferdinand as 'King of the Romans' (effectively heir apparent to the Empire).[16] At a second meeting on 27 February they formed the League of Schmalkalden. The League's constitution was to be settled at a meeting at Frankfurt in December, and its regular organization at Schweinfurt in April 1532. This League was far more structured and formal than the alliances of the 1520s; it replaced the *Reichstag* or the Swabian League as the natural forum for the protestants in the Empire; it enabled them to renounce allegiance to imperial institutions which they distrusted. Its membership was different from the subscribers of the 'Protestation': some cities (like Nuremberg) stayed out for reasons of security, while some of the Baltic cities joined.[17] The League members, with cities in square brackets, are shown in Table 16.2.

The intermarriage and partition of inheritances between different noble

TABLE 16.2

League	Members
Torgau, 1526	Electoral Saxony, Hesse, Braunschweig-Lüneburg, Braunschweig-Grubenhagen, Mecklenburg-Schwerin, Mansfeld, Anhalt-Köthen, [Magdeburg]
Speyer, 1529	Electoral Saxony, Hesse, Brandenburg-Ansbach, Braunschweig-Lüneburg, Anhalt-Köthen,
('Protesters')	[Nuremberg, Nördlingen, Heilbronn, Reutlingen, Weissenburg, Windsheim, Strasbourg, Ulm, Constance, Lindau, Memmingen, Kempten, Isny, St Gallen]
Schmalkalden, 1530–1	Electoral Saxony, Hesse, Braunschweig-Lüneburg, Anhalt, Mansfeld,
	[Strasbourg, Ulm, Constance, Reutlingen, Memmingen, Lindau, Biberach, Isny, Lübeck, Magdeburg, Bremen]
1532	Brandenburg-Ansbach,
	[Esslingen, Heilbronn, Schwäbisch-Hall, Kempten, Weissenburg, Windsheim, Braunschweig, Goslar, Einbeck, Göttingen, Nordhausen, Hamburg]
1535	Pomerania, Württemberg, Anhalt-Dessau,
	[Augsburg, Frankfurt, Hanover]

families helped dynastic rivalries to express themselves in religious divisions. All three of the electoral dynasties (Wettin, Hohenzollern, Wittelsbach), at some stage included a catholic duke opposed to a protestant elector, or vice versa; such rivalries led to the transfer of the electoral dignity of Saxony from the Ernestine to the Albertine branch (though by this stage both were protestant) in 1547, and to the catholic Bavarian absorption of lands and titles from the protestant Palatinate in the seventeenth century.[18] Lesser dynasties like Braunschweig, Mecklenburg, or Anhalt were just as readily fragmented. No doubt matrimonial problems played a role, as when Elizabeth, the Lutheran wife of the elector of Brandenburg, fled in March 1528 to join her relative Johann of Saxony.[19] Generation gaps may also have been involved: only the death of zealously anti-protestant princes like Duke Georg of Saxony or Elector Joachim I of Brandenburg allowed religious changes to take place in those lands.

The princes' turning 'protestant' left the religious politics of the Empire very delicately balanced. Of six participating electors in the *Reichstag*, the three lay members were now protestants, naturally suspicious of all imperial authority. Of the three ecclesiastical electors, Cologne only barely escaped falling into reformed hands both in the 1540s and in the 1580s. A swathe of protestant territories now stretched from the Baltic coast down to the Black Forest and the borders of Switzerland. Of major catholic powers, only Bavaria and Austria itself were left alongside the numerous remaining prince-bishoprics and great abbey estates. Catholic security was dangerously identified with Habsburg power; while the bishoprics aroused both cupidity and insecurity in their neighbours.[20]

2. *Kings, Nobles, and Bishops: The Scandinavian Kingdoms*

The monarchies of Scandinavia were the first 'kingdoms' to part company decisively with the old religious institutions and traditions. Since 1397 the lands occupied by the present-day countries of Denmark, Norway, Iceland, Sweden, and Finland (with, from 1460, the addition of the north German provinces of Schleswig-Holstein) had been held in a fragile confederation known as the Union of Kalmar. Christian II of Denmark (1513–23) precipitated the final break-up of this union in the face of a movement for Swedish autonomy led by the 'administrator' Sten Sture and the bishop of Linköping. After successfully invading Sweden in 1519–20 and being crowned in Stockholm on 8 November 1520, Christian judicially massacred around ninety opposition leaders in the 'Stockholm bloodbath'. Within a few years Gustav I Eriksson 'Vasa' (1496–1560) secured recognition in all save the extreme south of Sweden. For the destiny of the Reformation in both Danish and Swedish lands the survival of the monarchy was entangled with the prestige—or lack of it—of the bishops, who played crucial roles in the civil wars. Control over the Church was a vital political prize, and the dogmas of the reformers too convenient a temptation to be ignored.

2.1. *Denmark*[21]

Christian II took an interest in the Reformation without really having time to become clear about its implications. He listened to some reformed sermons, and issued on 6 January 1522 a comprehensive but probably ineffectual law code for the clergy, the so-called *Byretten*, which claimed to restrict the clergy's recourse to Rome and the scope of their jurisdiction, as well as their accumulation of landed property. His despotic handling of the higher clergy led some bishops and the Danish nobility to renounce their loyalty to Christian and on 14 April 1523 to elect his 53-year-old uncle as Fredrik I (1523–33). Fredrik inherited a deadlock with the papacy over the appointment to the archbishopric of Lund, and on 19 August 1526 confirmed Christian's original candidate, Aage Sparre, in defiance of the pope, and thereafter filled Danish sees with his nominees as 'bishops-elect'. The king secured approval for his measures against prelates' authority at a noble assembly (*Herredag*) at Odense in December; apparently by bartering noble power over the Church in return for their consent. Some clergy resisted the tide of secularism, particularly the Copenhagen Carmelite and humanist Paul Eliasen or Helgesen (*c.*1485–1534) and the Cologne Franciscan Nikolaus von Herborn (*c.*1480–1535). However, as elsewhere, politically motivated secularism was harder to denounce effectively than outright heresy. A *Herredag* at Odense in August 1527 restored the payment of tithes (which had recently been unofficially refused to the bishops) but did nothing about the bishops' complaints of clerics marrying and preaching heresy.

From the early 1520s Lutheran ideas were preached at Husum, in Schleswig, in the far south, by Hermann Tast (1490–1551), and at the opposite end of the country, at Malmø in Skåne by Klaus Mortensen (1500–?), who also reformed the local liturgy and hymns. From 1525 Viborg, in Jutland, fell under the influence of Hans Tausen (1494–1561), a member of the order of St John who had studied at Rostock, Copenhagen, and finally Wittenberg, and who had been sent to Viborg to be cured of his Lutheran errors. He began to preach Lutheranism publicly, was from 1526 placed under royal protection to evade the bishop's jurisdiction, and in 1528 set up a Lutheran press like that set up by Olof Ulriksen at Malmø. In 1529 Fredrik allowed the demolition of twelve churches in Viborg, leaving only the cathedral and two civic churches, former friaries; Lutheran canons introduced a Danish service in the cathedral; Tausen and his associate Jørgen Sadolin were made preachers to each of the remaining parish churches. A Danish mass-book was printed at Malmø in the same year. About this period many religious houses, especially those of orders of friars, were quietly suppressed on local initiatives. At the Copenhagen *Herredag* on 2 July 1530, the conservative clergy denounced the heretics, and Tausen and his followers presented their answer to the Augsburg Confession, the *Confessio Hafnica* in forty-three articles. The assembly concluded an equivocation worthy of a south German city, by decreeing 'each one who has the grace may clearly proclaim [the Gospel] ... whosoever shall preach or teach anything other than what he can prove is agreeable with Scripture shall be brought to justice'. A proposed disputation was abandoned when neither the language nor the adjudicators could be agreed upon. Later that year an attempt to combine old and new rites at Copenhagen led to such serious rioting that the church was closed for eleven months and the catholics then restored.

Fredrik I's death on 10 April 1533 left a balance of power between the bishops and traditionalist nobility on one hand, and Fredrik's Lutheran son Duke Christian of Schleswig-Holstein on the other. Duke Christian had fostered Lutheranism in his duchy and founded a school for reformed clergy at Haderslev. By 1534 the tension led to the Counts' War between Count Christoph of Oldenburg, on behalf of the deposed Christian II, and Duke Christian; by the summer of 1536 the latter entered Copenhagen as Christian III (1534–59). The bishops had wholeheartedly sided with the losing faction, and Christian needed money: so, on 11–12 August 1536, Christian arrested the bishops of Roskilde, Lund, and Ribe, and by consent of the council or *Rigsraad* abolished the episcopal office. A national assembly (*Rigsdag*) at Copenhagen on 15–30 October 1536 confirmed the abolition and reorganized ecclesiastical property. Johannes Bugenhagen arrived on loan in Copenhagen in July 1537, crowned the king and queen, ordained seven 'superintendents', published a Church ordinance (on 2 September 1537), and reformed the syllabus of the University of Copenhagen. In 1538 Christian joined the League of Schmalkalden and adopted the Augsburg Confession as authoritative. On 10 June 1539 a *Herredag* at Odense confirmed the Church ordinance. During the 1540s and 1550s details of ritual and order were gradually resolved, especially by the indefatigable Church visitor, Peder Palladius, bishop of Sjaelland and author of the definitive Danish service-book in 1556. Denmark's Lutheranism, unlike that of Sweden, was to prove largely uncontroversial and even intellectually arid once established.

2.2. *Sweden*[22]

Sweden's religious history shows the perils for the reformers of a 'royal Reformation' almost as well as that of England. Following the Stockholm bloodbath Gustav Eriksson 'Vasa' gradually took possession of Sweden; he was named as administrator of the kingdom in August 1522 and elected king at Strängnäs on 7 June 1523. His secretary and chancellor Lars Andersson (d.1552), archdeacon of Strängnäs and later of Uppsala, seems to have helped introduce Gustav to Lutheran ideas. As in Denmark, the civil strife had left most episcopal sees vacant or held by bishops-elect awaiting papal confirmation. The pope would only confirm Peder Mansson (d.1534), brother of the papal legate and archbishop-elect of Uppsala, as bishop of Västerås. Gustav, having unsuccessfully petitioned his clergy for grants of money to pay military costs, protested at the Estates (*Riksdag*) at Västerås on 24 June 1527 that unless the clergy surrendered some of their property he would himself abdicate. The *Riksdag* accepted the formulae known as the 'Västerås Ordinances', by which Church property, and the jurisdiction of clergy over laymen, were drastically curtailed and subjected to royal oversight. Much Church land was to be returned to nobles and crown, and the 'Pure Word of God' to be preached. Secularization, as elsewhere, had preceded Reformation. Three bishops-elect were consecrated by royal command and duly crowned the king. Meanwhile the chancellor and others set about quietly plundering Church lands.

Meanwhile cells of Lutheranism had developed, much as in Denmark. German in training and influences, they depended on royal patronage and protection. Olav Pedersson (also known by his Latinized name as 'Olaus Petri', 1493–1552), had studied at Rostock, Leipzig, and finally Wittenberg before entering the service of the bishop of Strängnäs, where he probably converted Archdeacon Andersson, the future chancellor. When his sermons raised protests he was placed under royal protection and in 1524 given a preachership in the main church in Stockholm. He wrote pastoral works such as *A Useful Instruction* of 1526, works on the sacraments and marriage in 1528, his *Swedish* (liturgical) *Handbook* of 1529 and *Swedish Mass* of 1537. Olav's brother Lars Pedersson ('Laurentius Petri', 1499–1573) helped to translate the New Testament into Swedish in 1526 and on his return to Sweden from study in 1531 was made archbishop of Uppsala.

From 1527 Gustav moved slowly and hesitantly to 'reform' his national church. Lars Andersson's Swedish Church council held at Örebro on 7 February 1529 directed study of the Bible, curtailed the penitential system and Church festivals, and reinterpreted ceremonies. By 1530 the old mass was fully banned at Stockholm. During the 1530s the bench of bishops was gradually filled with protestants; in October 1536 a Church council at Uppsala prescribed that all cathedrals should use the Swedish mass, that clergy living with women should marry them, and that Pedersson's *Handbook* was to be used in baptisms and marriages. In 1538 a German knight named Bernhard (or Berend) von Melen, an estranged former ally of Gustav, intrigued to have Sweden excluded from membership of the League of Schmalkalden. At the same time, and somewhat paradoxically, Gustav grew to distrust the Pederssons as wishing to set up a too autonomous ecclesiastical institution and turned to German immigrants whom he hoped would be more amenable to a thoroughgoing royal supremacy over the Church. A theologian named Georg Norman (d.1553) and an Augsburg lawyer named Konrad von Pyhy were summoned to Stockholm. In August 1539 Pyhy, as royal secretary, presided over a Church council at Uppsala which witnessed a sharp clash of views between himself and Olav Pedersson, the two having already conflicted over personal questions. Late in 1539 Norman was made 'superintendent' of the Church as a royal vicar. In December a noble council or *Herredag* at Örebro charged Lars Andersson and Olav Pedersson with treason. They were condemned, reprieved, and fined heavily. Norman produced a draft reformed Church order in 1540, and Gustav took the title of 'Supreme defender of the Church'.

Olav Pedersson was rehabilitated in 1543 and made pastor of the main church in Stockholm for life. A full translation of the Bible, edited by his brother, had meanwhile been published in 1541. In 1543 von Pyhy was dismissed. At a *Riksdag* at Västerås in 1544 the acts of Reformation (such as they were) were confirmed. For the rest of Gustav's reign superintendents were introduced into the dioceses, somewhat undercutting the bishops, and the clergy were gradually made more Lutheran in character; but otherwise no national confession of faith was adopted, nor were any Church ordinances on discipline or education introduced. Matters were left to local or provincial initiatives. Monasteries were allowed to decay gently, or abolished by local landowners. Only after royal flirtations with crypto-Calvinism (in the 1560s) and crypto-catholicism (in the late 1570s), was the Augsburg Confession finally adopted in 1593.

2.3. *Dependencies*

In the Danish dependencies of Norway and Iceland, and the Swedish dependency of Finland, the introduction of Lutheranism followed its political success in the capitals. Despite the bitter conflicts which ensued in Norway and Iceland, these lands did ultimately breed their own indigenous reforming enthusiasts, such as Geble Pederssøn, bishop of Bergen and friend of Peder Palladius, in Norway, Gissur Einarsson (1515–48), bishop of Skálholt, in Iceland, and the Wittenberg-trained churchman Mikael Agricola (1508–57), bishop of Åbo (Turku) in Finland from 1544.

3. *Fragmented Kingdoms: Eastern Europe*

In Scandinavia kings allied with their lay nobles, or a faction of them, to humiliate the bishops and higher clergy; the 'protestant' programme was then introduced in the wake of political adjustments. On the eastern boundaries of Latin Christendom, in Poland and Hungary, almost the reverse occurred. Lutheran and later Calvinist ideas found a hearing amongst noble cliques, who rejected the disciplinary authority of the bishops and then demanded from their kings, as a price of continued support, control over religion within their own jurisdictions.

3.1. *Poland*[23]

Sixteenth-century Poland was fragmented geographically into Little Poland (around Cracow), Great Poland, (including Poznań), to the north, and the Grand Duchy of Lithuania to the east. It was also politically fissile, with an elective monarchy, a Senate of 139 magnates, and a Chamber of Deputies of 200 of the numerous and powerful lesser aristocracy, or *szlachta*. The meetings of the Estates, or *Sejm*, became an important forum for religious debate. Though its church was on the margins of the Roman obedience, Poland was a full part of the European cultural milieu, not least through the marriage of Sigismund I in 1519 with the Italian Bona Sforza, who became famous both for her patronage of scholars and her simony in Church appointments.[24]

Lutheran ideas made precocious progress among towns, nobles, and even some bishops along the Baltic coastline of Poland in the early 1520s, as was seen in East Prussia or the town of Danzig. However, these gains were made chiefly among the Germanic population, and did not naturally spread to the Poles themselves. However, Lutheranism was preached at Kościan in 1524, and Poznań (until the local bishop took a hand and expelled the preachers in 1535) was a reformed centre. Cracow itself heard Lutheran sermons in the late 1520s.[25] The clergy responded with energetic but probably ineffectual orders that bishops maintain inquisitors and preachers (1527); restrictions on book imports (1530 and 1532); bans on study at heretical universities (1534 and 1540); and exclusion of (suspect) Germans from holding Polish abbeys (1538). In 1539 the wife of a Cracow councillor, a woman called Wiegel, Weiglowa, or Zalaszowska, was executed for heresy, though whether of a protestant kind is unclear.[26]

About 1540, reformed ideas, those of Calvin in particular, gained a hearing among the Polish nobility and priesthood. Calvin dedicated his *Commentary on the Mass* to Crown Prince Sigismund Augustus in 1539, and corresponded with the *Hetman* Tarnowski about 1540. Within a few years the future reformers of Poland were converted: in 1541 the Dominican Andrzej Samuel, in 1542 Jan Łaski (1499–1560), nephew of the primate of Poland (based at Emden at that stage), in 1543 the Dominican Jan Seklucjan (1500–70), and in 1546 Felix Krzyżak or Cruciger. The Dominican Francesco Lismanini (1504–66), previously confessor to Queen Bona and Polish provincial of his order, circulated Calvinist books and ideas both among the Cracow nobility and at the royal court itself. These conversions did not at once stir up a reforming movement within Poland, as most Polish reformers worked until the 1550s at the new university founded at Königsberg (now Kaliningrad) in Albrecht von Hohenzollern's lands of East Prussia in 1544. They produced a formidable protestant literature, of catechisms, liturgies, and a New Testament from the Königsberg presses.

From the mid-1540s Calvinist cells or conventicles grew up under noble protection at Cracow, Poznań, Radziejów, Pińczów, Chęciny, and Koźminek. Such voluntary noble-sponsored churches resembled those later found in France or Scotland. The first Calvinist synod in Little Poland met at Pińczów in 1550. Felix Cruciger became superintendent in 1555. From the accession of the tolerant Sigismund II Augustus (1548–72), the noble patrons of these reformed cells, anxious to protect their legal position, pressed in the *Sejm* for the right to practise the faith of their choice. At first Sigismund withstood the pressures and upheld the rights of the bishops. However, in 1552 the Calvinist Raphael Leszczyński was made president of the Chamber of Deputies (one of a series of protestants to hold the office until 1565); along with Tarnowski in the Senate, he denounced the senior clergy for their prosecutions in absence of protestant nobles and their attacks on married clergy, and forced all Church jurisdiction in the matter to be suspended for a year. The suspension was continued through the meetings of the *Sejm* in 1555 and 1556. In 1558–9 the attack was broadened to a call for all ecclesiastical justice to cease and the clergy to bear the burden of military taxes. In 1562–3 the heresy laws were effectively annulled as far as the *szlachta* were concerned; by 1565 they could no longer be summoned for non-payment of tithes. By 1569 the lay senators were, by a small majority, predominantly protestant; and after Sigismund's death in 1572 the 'Pact of Confederation' on 28 January 1573 embodied an undertaking that no future king would be elected without first promising to guarantee religious freedoms.[27] Protestantism was therefore 'established' in Poland only in the negative sense that its persecution would not be tolerated by the nobility. The nobles, once won for one 'heresy', could either be reconverted to catholicism or persuaded into something more exotic still. In due course both these problems afflicted the Polish Reformation.

3.2. *Hungary*[28]

Hungary was fragmented ethnically, into Székely or Szeklers (the original Hunnish inhabitants), Magyars (tenth-century settlers), Saxon peoples settled since the twelfth century, and in some areas Vlachs or Romanians, who were thirteenth-century arrivals. To ethnic and religious divisions (for the Vlachs were Eastern Orthodox) were added after 1526 political confusion. The catastrophic defeat of the Hungarian armies by the Turks at Mohács on 29 August 1526 saw the deaths of King Lajos (Louis) II along with two archbishops and five bishops. Thereafter Archduke Ferdinand of Austria ruled the northern and western areas, with a substantial no man's land in the plain around Buda, contested during the late 1520s and early 1540s; the east and south was directly administered by the Turks; to the north-east the province of Transylvania, with its own Estates, was semi-autonomous under János I Zápolya (1526–40), a vassal of the Turks, then Bishop György Utjesenovich 'Martinuzzi' (d.1551), of Nagyvárad, as regent for Sigismund János Zápolya II (1540–71). In this context rigorous orthodoxy could not be sustained. Even before 1526 the royal court had been open to Lutheran influence; after the division of the kingdom neither aspirant to the allegiance of the Hungarians could afford the political liability of religious persecution. Besides all these divisions the Ottomans, splendidly indifferent to which type of infidels they governed, allowed religious toleration in their own sector.

The initial gains for the Reformation were ethnically conditioned. Saxon inhabitants took up Lutheranism. In northern Hungary from 1539 Wittenberg-trained Leonhard Stöckel (1510–60) spread Lutheran ideas from the school at Bartfeld. In 1549 he persuaded the five 'free cities' of Bartfeld, Eperies, Kaschau, Klein-Zeben, and Leutschau to adopt his *Confessio Pentapolitana*, subsequently accepted elsewhere in Hungary. In the 'seven cities' (*Siebenbürgen*) of the Transylvanian Saxons, the humanist scholar Johannes Honter (1498–1549) performed a task similar to Stöckel's, establishing a school and press at Kronstadt in 1533. In the early 1540s he won over the governor and the clergy; in 1542 he reformed the liturgy, and in 1543 produced a draft Church ordinance at the Estates of Transylvania at Weissenburg. The Augsburg Confession was accepted in 1544; and the Transylvanian Saxon Church order, based on Honter's, in 1547–50. However, Lutheranism also found adherents among the Magyar and Szekler populations. Johannes Sylvester (c.1504–52) established a school and printing-house at Ujsziget near Sárvár in the north-west of the country in the late 1530s, issuing a grammar and New Testament in Hungarian. In the 1540s influential Magyar protestant leaders emerged: the preacher and pamphleteer Mátyás Dévai Bíró (c.1500–45); the theologian and pedagogue István Szegedi Kis ('Stephanus Szegedinus', 1502–75); the preacher and hymn-writer Mihály Sztarai (c.1500–75). Two Hungarian-speaking Transylvanians of German descent, Kaspar Heltai and Ferenc Dávid (c.1510–79), converted the Magyar population there to Lutheranism.

However, Magyar Lutheranism was soon adulterated. Even the Saxons favoured Melanchthon's eclectic moderation; by the late 1540s and early 1550s a number of 'Lutheran' Magyar churchmen drifted from 'Philippism' to positions on, for example, the interpretation of the communion which were Swiss inspired, and much closer to Calvinism than Lutheranism. At a meeting of the Estates of Transylvania at Torda on 1–14 June 1557 Saxon Lutherans, ambivalent Magyars under Ferenc Dávid, and explicitly Calvinist Magyars under their leader Martin Santa Kálmáncsehi were all alike given provisional toleration. In March 1558 the Calvinists suffered a temporary reverse and their leadership was taken over by Péter Méliusz Juhasz. Méliusz was behind the 'Eucharistic Confession of Maros-vásárhely', issued in 1559; and progressively other Magyars such as Szege-dinus aligned with his positions. Méliusz's base at Debrecen, on the frontiers of Turkish and eastern Habsburg Hungary, became the centre of Magyar Calvinism. The synod at Nagyenyed in 1564 marked a final parting of the ways between Lutherans and Calvinists. Already the Transylvanian Estates had resolved that the 'confessions of Hermannstadt' (Lutheranism) and 'of Kolozsvár' (Calvinism) should enjoy equal freedoms. In 1567 the Calvinist synod at Debrecen formally adopted the second Helvetic (Swiss) Confession, devised the year before.

The protestantism of Hungary was by about 1560–70 undoubtedly more firmly and articulately established than that of Poland; the dependence on noble patronage was less crippling, and the Church structures more developed. However, in exactly the same way as in Poland, religious leaders were to find the drift into unusual and heretical religious beliefs hard to resist. In each case the Reformation's survival depended on the weakness of the old Church hierarchy and the forbearance of contending sovereigns. These factors might only prove temporary.

4. *Partial Reformation: England before 1559*[29]

Europe's offshore islands enjoyed continuous diplomatic, commercial, and cultural contact with all parts of Europe, and were as readily exposed to the ideas of the Reformation as anywhere on the Continent. As a fairly unitary state (at least compared with the Empire, Switzerland, or Poland) England might have undergone a territorial Reformation similar to that in Scandinavia. However, England was too closely involved with France and central Europe to escape entanglement with both Swiss protestantism and the plots of the kings of France and Spain.

Early in the 1520s clerics and students began to study the reformers' teachings through books and pamphlets. The most famous such group was at Cambridge, where the priest Thomas Bilney (*c*.1495–1531) introduced others to some (selected) reformed ideas. The prior of the Cambridge Augustinians, Robert Barnes (d.1540), led discussions in Cambridge and later at London; William Tyndale (*c*.1494–1536) also presided over a group which included future protestants such as Hugh Latimer (*c*.1485–1555), Thomas Cranmer (1489–1556), and Nicholas Shaxton (*c*.1485–1556). By the mid-1520s the movement had spread to Oxford and had attracted the attention of Church dignitaries. As a result most of the 'Lutheran' sympathizers were forced either to recant or exile themselves; Tyndale's New Testament was printed at Cologne and Worms in 1525–6, and easily shipped into England. England in the 1520s was perhaps most remarkable for its efficient persecution of early forms of protestant thought: not least because the most effective anti-Lutheran persecutor and polemic was a leading lay lawyer and politician, Thomas More (d.1535).[30]

Two important features of the English religious picture changed about 1529. First, King Henry VIII's long-standing alliance with the Habsburg Emperor and king of Spain had lost much of its rationale, and become a positive embarrassment. Charles V had effectively broken the alliance in 1525 by abandoning his plan to marry Henry's daughter Mary. Henry's Queen, Catherine of Aragon, Charles V's aunt, was not only a tediously pious middle-aged lady with no son; she also represented a redundant foreign alliance. Since June 1527 Henry had been suing explicitly for the annulment of his marriage, and in 1529 Catherine had appealed to Rome. Secondly, the cardinal-legate of England, Thomas Wolsey (d.1530), whom the king had largely supported despite his high handedness and unpopularity, ceased to be useful. His chief virtue (apart from unflagging dedication to the king's interest) had been his papal connections. However, after Charles V's troops had run amok in Rome in 1527 Pope Clement VII had been effectively in the Emperor's power, and could hardly solve Henry's matrimonial problems by allowing him to discard Charles's relative.[31]

In this atmosphere Henry VIII embarked on a programme of humiliation of the higher clergy reminiscent of Gustav Vasa. Wolsey was himself stripped of office in October 1529; he was then pardoned, and died in November 1530. On 3 November 1529 Henry opened a Parliament which promptly proposed a series of measures to regulate absentee and pluralist clerics, and to restrict the powers and fees of some Church courts. Some of these proposals, to the apparent fury of the Lords, became acts and led to some 200 lawsuits, mostly unresolved. Meanwhile the Crown indicted seven bishops and eight lesser clergy on a wholly preposterous charge that by abetting the cardinal-legate they had offended against the statutes of Praemunire, fourteenth-century devices to restrict clerical intervention in the legal sphere. In the spring of 1531 the clergy were 'pardoned' on payment of a combined fine for the two Church provinces of £118,840. In the spring of 1532 the payment of the clerical tax known as 'Annates' to Rome was provisionally suspended, and the clergy were required (on 15 May 1532) to refer all their canons to the king for authorization.[32]

May 1532 seems, in fact, to have marked the crisis in a struggle around the monarch over policy. Conservatives, discreetly led by Lord Chancellor More, had tried to dissuade the king from his marriage plans, and to continue the heresy-hunting; more radical intellectuals such as Edward Foxe, Thomas Cranmer, and the rising political star Thomas Cromwell (d.1540) urged that the marriage problem be solved by the king's clergy within England; if that meant schism and using the talents of religious heretics, so be it. By the time the lord chancellor resigned in May 1532 the king seems to have been committed to the 'go-it-alone' option. In the first months of 1533 Thomas Cranmer was nominated archbishop of Canterbury; a session of Parliament between 4 February and 7 April enacted that appeals in cases of wills, marriages, and certain kinds of grants to the Church could only be decided within England; in May a special court annulled the king's marriage; and on 7 September the new queen, the former courtier Anne Boleyn, gave birth to Elizabeth Tudor.[33]

Between its spring and autumn sessions in 1534 the English Parliament tidied up some of the legal implications of this royal supremacy in Church affairs. The king's marriage was recorded and protected by penal provisions. Royal justice filled the gaps left by papal instruments and licences; the royal fisc more than made up for the ending of papal taxes. A statute 'corroborated and confirmed' the king's title as supreme head of the Church. Between 1535 and 1540 these changes in jurisdiction and procedure were backed up by a formidable propaganda exercise varying from philosophical treatises on obedience by the otherwise conservative Stephen Gardiner (c.1490–1555) to satirical plays by the protestant John Bale (1495–1563). They were protected by an equally formidable testing of loyalty on oath, and prosecution of the suspect or refractory: this led to some 400 prosecutions and claimed sixty-five victims, most spectacularly Thomas More and Bishop John Fisher of Rochester, as well as the unbending members of strict religious orders, executed by a variety of barbarous means.[34]

Again like other European monarchs, the king of England set about stripping the Church of its property before the reasons for such action were clear. The smaller monasteries, friaries, and convents (worth less than

£200 per annum) were dissolved on the presumption that small houses were usually ill-disciplined ones. The question, as with Gustav Vasa, was how much protestant teaching Henry would now accept. In the mid-1530s the king's secretary of state, Thomas Cromwell, displayed a number of decidedly Lutheran characteristics, though how far the king recognized or approved of them as such is doubtful. Cromwell was appointed 'vicegerent in spirituals' to visit and value the English Church, like the chancellor of a Lutheran state. He inspired the 'Ten Articles' (1536), embodying Melanchthon's language and beliefs on justification, and reinterpreting traditional rites in somewhat Erasmian fashion; issued the *Injunctions* (1536 and 1538) enforcing the articles, requiring the clergy to instruct in the Bible, and attacking relics and pilgrimage centres; and presided over the issuing of the so-called *Bishops' Book*, a bewilderingly ambiguous amalgam of reformed ideas about the Church and modest recommendations on worship. Finally, Cromwell courted the League of Schmalkalden in a somewhat desultory way, hampered by rivals at court; this finally bore fruit in the king's disastrous marriage to Anne of Cleves in 1540.[35]

In fact the king's secretary headed a clique at court which almost certainly contained some committed protestants. However, their protestantism was a hostage to fortune in the sanguinary context of the court battles of the late 1530s. Cromwell and his allies adeptly survived the challenge of the complex of revolts in the autumn of 1536 and early 1537 (the 'Pilgrimage of Grace'), when rebel leaders called explicitly for their removal as heretics.[36] In 1538–40, however, their rivals at court, the duke of Norfolk and the bishop of Winchester, discredited the secretary. They aroused alarm about 'sacramentaries' (a label uniquely calculated to frighten monarchs, Henry VIII and François I alike), promoted several conservative religious measures (the 1538 proclamation, the June 1539 'Six Articles', and a persecution of 'heretics'); and by June 1540 had Cromwell executed on a wholly spurious charge of treason.[37]

Thereafter the regime's religious policy wavered in the breeze of royal favour. A king who had refounded some monasteries at the same time as dissolving others,[38] and decreed that vows of chastity be strictly kept while destroying the institutions which protected such vows, found no problem in ambiguity. In 1543 there was a heresy hunt and a statute restricting who was allowed to read the Bible; meanwhile Cranmer continued to struggle with liturgical reform, producing a litany in 1544 and a *Prymer* in 1545. Nevertheless, Henry VIII died on 28 January 1547 with no comprehensive statement on doctrine, the diocesan and parish structure of the English Church unchanged save at the top, and regular worship still essentially in the medieval forms, with only a few festivals omitted and centres of pilgrimage abolished.[39]

The faction which had come uppermost in the king's last months of life, that of Edward Seymour, earl of Hertford (soon made duke of Somerset and Lord Protector for the boy King Edward VI), began to locate the English Church decisively in the protestant camp. Matters were, however, tackled step by step, with an eye to the parlous state of European protestantism in the late 1540s, as well as the divided state of opinions within England. In 1547 the Eucharistic wine was ordered to be given to the laity, some of Henry's anti-protestant legislation was repealed, and the following Easter some prayers in English were inserted in the mass. The confiscation of endowments for prayers for the dead ('chantries'), begun under Henry, was completed. The marriage of priests was formally condoned. Cranmer's first English Prayer Book was authorized in January 1549 and imposed from Whit Sunday: this was so cautious and eclectic (keeping such catholic features as vestments, saints' masses, and chanting) that it was deemed acceptable by the imprisoned conservative Bishop Gardiner and denounced by Cranmer's protestant allies on the bench of bishops.[40]

Protector Somerset was blamed for a wave of agrarian revolts in the summer of 1549 and ousted from power by John Dudley, soon made duke of Northumberland. Religious opinions in England became more polarized; the bench of bishops was purged, and Bishops Hooper of Gloucester and Ridley of London imposed local liturgical change. Cranmer imported numerous distinguished refugees from the troubles in Germany, who arrived during 1549; the inevitable effect was to confirm the minority of English protestants in their orientation towards south German and Swiss models. This bore fruit especially in the appointments of the protestants Piermartire Vermigli (1500–62) and Martin Bucer as Regius Professors of Divinity at Oxford and Cambridge respectively, and in the second Prayer Book, devised by Cranmer with Bucer's advice during 1551 and approved in April 1552. With this formula the liturgy was decisively and visibly altered across the country for perhaps the first time: vestments and ornaments were drastically simplified, leavened bread was given in place of communion wafers into the laity's hands, and tables in the body of the church replaced altars in the chancel.[41]

Cranmer seems to have intended the complete reformation of religion in England which Henry VIII had denied him: besides changes in public worship, the rites and rules of ordination were changed (1550), a decidedly Swiss or south German statement of beliefs, the *Forty-two Articles*, was issued (1553), and when the young Edward VI succumbed to tuberculosis on 6 July 1553 a programme for revising Church law was in progress, never to be completed. Moreover, the secular power intervened in religious affairs as absolutely as under Henry, appointing bishops during the royal pleasure (for the only period in the century) and inserting into the 1552 liturgy a warning to the laity not to worship the Eucharistic bread when they knelt to receive it.[42]

Whether this importation of state-sponsored protestantism would have established itself had the king lived longer is debatable. However, the political classes in England refused to accept Northumberland's cobbled plot to divert the succession to creatures of his own family; Mary, Catherine of Aragon's daughter, swept to power in perhaps the only wholly successful rebellion of the Tudor era. She treated the 'heretical' religious statutes as void at once, but found that the legal niceties protracted themselves none the less. Edward VI's religious laws were repealed in the late autumn of 1553; but the restoration of papal supremacy was delayed by the curious combination of Charles V, who wished to make the papal restoration seem a result of Mary's impending marriage to his son Philip, and of the (traditionalist) English gentry, whose loyalty to the old religion did not stretch to surrendering *gratis* their rights to Church lands for which they had paid good money. The pope was readmitted, in the shape of Cardinal-Legate Reginald Pole, in November 1554. The cardinal, soon made archbishop of Canterbury, began a conscientious renewal of the Church's infrastructure, which was cut short in April 1557 when he fell victim to the new Pope Paul IV's deep distrust of Pole's orthodoxy and his master Philip's loyalty, and was stripped of his legatine powers.[43]

Early in 1555 Mary's regime began to try protestants as heretics. The 300 or so victims between 1555 and 1558, overwhelmingly from southeastern England and (despite five bishops, seventeen other clerics, and ten gentry) predominantly artisans or labourers, were balanced by the 800 or so gentlemen, clerics, and students who evacuated safely to the Continent. The two aspects of the 'suffering' English protestant Church complemented each other to turn a largely foreign-inspired minority clique into a national legend. The martyrs' records were collected and ultimately published by the exiles. The exiles became a voluntary society consciously loyal to the 'English Church' of the reign of Edward VI, and were to form the core of the protestant missionary effort in the English countryside after 1559. This exiled church might (like the churches of Italian protestants in Switzerland somewhat later) have led a shrivelled, fugitive existence, had not Mary and Pole died disillusioned on the same day, 17 November 1558, leaving Anne Boleyn's daughter Elizabeth as heir.[44]

England might, with a less irresolute series of monarchs or a less factionalized aristocracy, have settled down to a Lutheran Church settlement based on the decrees of ruler and estates. In the event it postponed the revision of liturgy, doctrine, and Church structure (the last of these for ever) until they fell victim to the varied allegiances of the various Tudors. By the time that the definitely protestant Elizabeth I acceded in 1558, a nationalistic settlement with moderately reformed belief and a vaguely recognizable old-style liturgy, which might have satisfied most agitators fifteen or even ten years earlier, could find hardly any senior protestant clerics ready to operate it.

5. Reformations Delayed: France and Scotland before 1559

5.1. France

In France the Church's haste to denounce Luther and his allies may actually have given them additional publicity. The Sorbonne Faculty of Theology's condemnation of Luther on 15 April 1521 in no way prevented the growth of religious free thought elsewhere in the university. An early casualty of its rather frantic orthodoxy was Guillaume Briçonnet's programme of clerical improvement, liturgical simplification, and public exposition of the Bible at Meaux. Neither Briçonnet nor his vicar-general Jacques Lefèvre d'Étaples (c.1455–1536), adopted the Reformation, though several of their subordinates, like Pierre Caroli and above all Guillaume Farel, later did so. But for Luther the Meaux experiment might have enjoyed élitist celebrity like the pious societies of the Rhineland or Nuremberg. François I (king of France, 1515–47) had no wish to preserve orthodoxy at the price of stifling all literate intellectual discourse; his sister Marguerite d'Angoulême patronized and protected the Meaux group. Only during the king's absence from France after his capture at the military disaster of Pavia (25 February 1525) did the academics get their way, investigating the diocese of Meaux and driving several of Briçonnet's group into refuge at Marguerite's court at Nérac, or at Strasbourg.[45]

François I's religious policy seems superficially as tortuous as his English counterpart's, though a plausible case can be made for its consistency.[46] Returning to Paris in March 1526 the king rescued some of those threatened with the penalties of heresy, and disgraced the leader of the Sorbonne theologians, Noël Bédier or Beda. However, since his diplomacy required good relations with the pope, prosecution of a handful of 'heretics', like the Parisian Louis de Berquin in 1529, was allowed to proceed. *Parlementaires* and senior clergy combined to define the ground rules for persecution of notorious heretics, like those who smashed images in 1528. Nevertheless, at this stage François hoped to reconcile moderate reformers—so long as they respected the mass—rather than burn them. The du Bellay brothers, Jean, bishop of Paris, and Guillaume, seigneur de Langeay and royal diplomat, dangled before François the possibility of coaxing some of the protestants back to catholicism and thereby scoring a major coup against Charles V. To this end François negotiated indirectly with Jakob Sturm of Strasbourg and even with Melanchthon in late 1533.[47]

In spite of François's order to the Paris *Parlement* in December 1533 to investigate Lutheranism in the university there (inspired by the ill-advised Lutheran sermon preached by the rector Nicholas Cop in November), some protestants expected the king of France to be amenable to persuasion. However, the posting of the Placards against the mass in Paris and Amboise during the night of 17–18 October 1534 was a disastrous miscalculation. These crudely abusive denunciations of the priests as 'damnable deceivers, apostates, wolves, ... idolaters ... execrable liars and blasphemers' who had 'plunged the whole world into public idolatry', by Antoine Marcourt, one of the Neuchâtel pastors, had the doubly unfortunate effect of alienating many protestants and of clarifying François's opposition to heresy. A series of burnings of protestants followed during 1534 and early 1535; printing was placed under rigid controls; and several literary figures, such as the court poet Clément Marot, thought it best to flee the country.[48]

France's foreign affairs now intervened once again. In the spring of 1535 negotiations with the German reformers were reopened, although the elector of Saxony refused to co-operate. To clear the decks for the forthcoming invasion of Italy, François issued on 16 July 1535 the edict of Coucy, suspending heresy prosecutions for six months to allow heretics time to recant. A clause excluding 'sacramentarians' from the amnesty was generally ignored, and the edict stayed in place into 1537 while the French armies dispossessed Duke Carlo III of Savoy and overran Piedmont. French Savoy was, initially at least, tolerant of heresy, since the king's lieutenant in Piedmont, Guillaume du Bellay, employed as subordinates the Lutheran German mercenary Wilhelm von Furstenberg, and Guillaume Farel's brother Gauchier.[49]

Once the war was over persecution resumed within France. Two royal edicts (June 1539 and 1540) turned heresy jurisdiction over to secular courts, provincial *parlements*, and bishops acting jointly. Since 1531 at the latest the archbishop of Aix-en-Provence had been investigating the allegedly 'Lutheran' Waldensian immigrants from the Dauphiné and Piedmont settled in the villages east of his capital. The *Parlement* of Aix, alarmed by reports that the heretics intended to rebel and 'turn Swiss', by a sweeping decree of 18 November 1540 condemned all the villagers to death and ordered their dwellings to be razed. The decree was suspended while François I commissioned a report on the intended victims from Guillaume du Bellay; then, after the villagers had taken up arms in 1543, the persecutors' lobbyists at court obtained royal letters patent enforcing the decree on 1 February 1545. In mid-April one of the first of the devastating religious massacres to disfigure sixteenth-century French history occurred in Provence, prompting an international outcry and, in 1549–51, a painfully protracted trial of the persecutors themselves in the *Parlement* of Paris. Despite the carnage this area became a centre of French rural Calvinism.[50]

The 1540s saw other persecutions besides the Waldensian massacres. In March 1544 the Sorbonne issued a list of prohibited books. On 8 October 1546 Pierre Leclerc and thirteen members of the informal church at Meaux were executed. After François I's death his successor Henri II put the persecutions on a more established footing. A special tribunal of the Paris *Parlement*, to be known as the *Chambre ardente*, was instituted late in 1547, issued a stream of edicts against heresy, and indicted over 300 individuals in the three years or so of its existence. Provincial *parlements* and ecclesiastical judges alike participated in the repression. The edict of Châteaubriant of 27 June 1551, an astonishingly comprehensive manual for State persecution, deprived those accused of heresy of all municipal or judicial office. Indeed, possibly the only restraint on Henri II's campaign against heresy was his own continual preoccupation with war against the Habsburgs up to the Peace of Cateau-Cambrésis, signed 3 April 1559. Once peace was signed, the king of France (like the king of Spain and the duke of Savoy) was expected to set about a vigorous purging of heresy in his lands, and might have done so had he not died from a jousting accident shortly after the peace. The regency which he left behind was ill-equipped to respond decisively to the new forms which protestantism had suddenly assumed.[51]

For meanwhile small 'conventicles' of protestant sympathizers had grown up at random, drawing inspiration and support from the French emigré community at Strasbourg, where Calvin himself (to 1541), Pierre Brully (d.1545), and Valérand Poullain ministered during the 1540s. Such conventicles existed in Sainte-Foy, Aubigny, Meaux, Tours, and Pau, and included all ranks of society, with perhaps an overrepresentation of the literate bourgeoisie.[52] From the mid-1540s Calvin, in a series of letters, objected to the easy-going way in which such covert protestants participated in catholic services and did not form coherent churches. By the early 1550s he was advising them to elect their pastors and to set up a consistory; in 1552 he sent one of the first settled ministers, Philibert Hamelin; and in 1555 the first organized church congregation was established in Paris under the pastor Jean Le Maçon de Launay.[53] The years 1555 to 1559 saw something of an explosion in the establishment of settled churches all over France, with centres in Touraine and Anjou, south-west of Paris, in Normandy, in the west around La Rochelle, at Lyons, and in the traditional peripheral regions of religious dissent, Dauphiné, Provence, and Languedoc. Willing or not, Calvin's company of pastors at Geneva was obliged to supply an insatiable demand for barely trained pastors to such communities, beginning with the sending of Jacques Langlois to Poitiers in 1555.[54]

5.2. *Scotland*

France's ally Scotland saw no official endorsement or imposition of any form of the Reformation before about 1560 which could compare with that tried in England. However, new ideas were decidedly in the air; open-mindedness in some of the clergy and vacillation on the part of the government laid some of the foundations for the sudden and largely bloodless transition to protestantism thereafter. In the 1520s Scottish intellectuals dabbled in Lutheranism, much like Bilney and Barnes in England at the same time. The import of Lutheran pamphlets was specifically forbidden by law in 1525. Patrick Hamilton (d.1528), abbot of Fearn, studied at the Hessian capital of Marburg, and published a short Lutheran treatise, traditionally known as *Patrick's Places*, at Antwerp. Hamilton was tried and burnt as a heretic at St Andrews in 1528; but the university there, and particularly St Leonard's College, acquired a reputation for heresy. Other tracts (John Johnsone's *An Confortable Exhortation*, John Gow or Gau's *Richt Vay to the Kingdom of Hevine*, and the *Gude and Godly Ballatis*, attributed to James, John, and Robert Wedderburn) were published abroad and imported. As Thomas Cromwell dabbled in Lutheranism in 1530s England, several Scots reformers settled there, among them the Augustinians Alexander Alesius and Robert Richardson, John MacAlpine or Maccabeus, John Willock, and George Wishart; some treated England as a stopping-off point on the way to the Continent. Others, like the friars William Arith and Alexander Seton, preached a non-specific 'reform' in Scotland as best they could.[55]

James V (1513–42) was fairly uniformly hostile to heresy, though equally (and hypocritically) hostile to some of the Church's administrative abuses. A series of acts of parliament attempted to shore up the Church's authority against contempt and disobedience, upholding excommunication in 1535, and the honour of the sacraments, Virgin, and saints, and the authority of the pope in 1541. Ordinary people, sometimes merely guilty of conspicuous irreligion rather than protestantism, were executed, for instance in 1539 and 1544. Meanwhile, an extraordinary change came over the lands of the Church. At the first breath of serious royal criticism, the Church's leaders leased away as 'feus' the greater part of their estates, largely to the benefit of the more powerful and wealthy lay landholders. Plunder of lands preceded religious reform.[56] The king's death in 1542 left the infant Mary as queen and politics, religious and otherwise, in flux. The regent, James Hamilton, earl of Arran, abruptly passed an act permitting the reading of the Bible in English (in the English versions), and there was a short-lived explosion of interest in Lutheran ideas, also (ironically) associated with Henry VIII's project of obtaining a marriage alliance between Edward and Princess Mary, which ended in a bloody war fought intermittently from 1544 to 1550. Some noblemen and towns dabbled in protestantism, including the earl of Glencairn and John Erskine of Dun, and circles in Aberdeen, St Andrews, Perth, and Dundee. However, the friar George Wishart, who had been preaching around southern Scotland, was burnt at St Andrews on 3 March 1546; this in turn provoked, less than three months later, the savage murder of Archbishop David Betoun and the capture of the archbishop's castle, eventually ended by a French raid in July 1547.[57]

In the late 1540s and early 1550s Scots religious affairs were dominated by the efforts of Mary of Guise-Lorraine, the queen mother, to keep Scotland allied with France. In the face of English invasion Mary was betrothed to the French Dauphin (the future François II) in 1548; Mary of Lorraine mitigated her predictable anti-protestant stance as the price of noble support. This move allied the queen mother's party with the Hamilton family. The earl of Arran reconciled himself to catholicism and passed the regency to Mary. Arran's half-brother, Archbishop John Hamilton of St Andrews, held a series of reforming councils between 1549 and 1559 with the apparent aim of redressing old faults in the clergy, adopting what was best in the compromise documents circulating on the Continent, and generally stealing whatever of the protestants' clothes seemed wearable. The councils called for moral and intellectual improvement in the priesthood, introduced a moderate catholic *Catechism*, and probably drew upon the reform programmes (*Canons* and *Consultation*) proposed for the diocese of Cologne in the early 1540s by its archbishop with the help of Bucer and

Melanchthon. Finally they even suggested liturgical revision. By 1559, however, it was too late to avoid the thoroughgoing and explicitly anti-papal protestantism into which so many even of the archbishop's household, let alone of the other clergy and nobility, suddenly and unexpectedly lapsed.[58]

In France and Scotland rulers were squeezed between their traditional political loyalty to a Church order which (at that stage) did so little to make itself attractive to its followers, and new waves of ideas which were hard to pin down. Petty-bourgeois urban Lutheranism would have been easy enough to recognize; but literate 'reformism' which infected the upper bourgeoisie and parts of the aristocracy was much harder to identify as 'heretical', and almost impossible to prosecute effectively until too late. While these kingdoms avoided the political disintegration suffered by Poland, their monarchs were caught out by new movements which simply bypassed the larger state community as Lutheranism had not done.

This brief survey of the territorial Reformations suggests that the social 'profile' and the probable motives of the protestant agitators were as complex and variable as those seen in the cities. Some sort of 'coalition' was formed between the ideals of the reformers and the new aspirations of the politicians, though *which* politicians—monarchs, princes, or lesser aristocrats—evidently varied enormously. Such variety reflects what the effective political unit within a given society actually was: it says something about the state and its society rather than about the Reformation. Charles V could not restrain the princes or the cities; the Swiss cantons were always stronger than the Federation; the Polish *szlachta* could dictate to their king. Before about 1555 the territorial Reformation had to establish itself in an effective political community, which would then reform its 'community church' along the new lines. That community could be a town, a canton, a principality, or a kingdom; but for the preservation of peace, it had to be an acknowledged, stable, self-sufficient unit. In contrast, real instability developed when the effective monarch was temporarily weakened (as in France after 1559, or Scotland after 1542) and prey to conflicting political pressures; or when a monarch had conflicting priorities, like François I or Henry VIII. The aftermath of such conflict or weakness produced the *late* sixteenth-century Reformation pattern, where it was no longer the effective community which was reformed wholesale, but aggressive emergent voluntary groups within it.

17

Motives for Establishing the Reformation?

It becomes obvious that the Reformation was only established because somebody, somewhere in the political process, very much wanted it to be. Analysing the pressures or infighting which led to the crucial corporate decision only serves to identify individuals or groups of people: it does not, of itself, explain *why* they wanted the Reformation so much. As seen earlier,[1] the crucial *push* for the new order came from many different sections of society: guildsmen, civic oligarchs, or landed nobles. The *motives* of such diverse people as the agitators for the Reformation are therefore a complex topic in themselves. No single explanation of the Reformation's appeal should be expected to fit even most—let alone all—instances. The many and varied explanations devised by scholars to explain why the Reformation attracted lay support resolve themselves into three basic groups:

    1. Political and material explanations. These suggest that the Reformation was adopted because it justified lay people in seizing greater wealth, or more power, from the riches, status, and privileges of the old Church.

    2. Explanations based on the Reformation's alleged appropriateness to a class, order, or constitution. These claim that the reformers' message, as perceived by the laity, seemed to 'coincide' with the world-view of classes or estates which adopted it; or that a particular form of the Reformation was specially well suited to the political experience and thinking of certain types of communities.

    3. Psychological and Spiritual Explanations. These look at the essential, spiritual message of the Reformers, and account for laymen's response to it in terms of psychological needs which may be supposed to exist in everyone, rather than in specialized interest groups. These offer the most far-reaching kind of argument, but also the hardest to prove; and are therefore better left until the possibilities of the others have been exhausted.

It *should* seem almost ludicrous to assert that one of these classes of motive was the 'correct' one, and that all the others were mistaken. Most people do not leave evidence of their motives; even the few who do are hard to introspect. Reforming agitators might well have justified their actions in one way to their political superiors, and in other ways to their allies or equals, or to themselves. This chapter will first consider whether an argument which accounts for the Reformation purely on the basis of its political and material usefulness really is sufficient or persuasive, and if so in which cases. The other types of explanation will then be examined, with the reasons for and against explored.

1. *Wealth and Power?*

Hypothesis: rulers adopted the Reformation in order to seize and exploit the Church's excessive wealth.

Territorial sovereigns undoubtedly gained great new wealth—and new responsibilities as well—through establishing the Reformation. In one sense, *every* protestant state became the proprietor of the entire Church establishment within its borders. However, material gains would only help to explain the decision to reform if rulers made a significant *net* gain: that is, if they were able to pocket a substantial balance after they had paid for the clergy, poor relief, education, and whatever other services the state took over from the old Church.

The imperial cities do not seem to have gained very much in this way: pressure from the south German reformers on one hand and neighbouring states on the other forced them to devote most Church property to something like its old religious and social uses.[2] Indeed, the city oligarchs may have missed the old Church foundations. Monastic churches, their art, and their memorial masses had celebrated patrician families' previous munificence; monasteries had given their younger sons and daughters an easy and respectable living; the old benefice system had given prestige and patronage to families of the urban nobility.[3] The personal benefits from founding a school or a hospital were less obvious.

Territorial monarchs, on the other hand, took amounts varying from the significant to the enormous. Duke Ulrich of Württemberg, restored to his duchy by protestant armies in 1534, was perhaps the most blatant princely plunderer of the Church: in two years he confiscated all monastery lands, which provided twice his own original income; ultimately he seized three-quarters of *all* Church property, and even had gold paint scraped off the altar-paintings.[4] Other princes were equally successful but less brazen. The

Landgraf of Hesse raised 75,000 Gulden from monasteries in 1527–40 alone; with the parish clergy paid out of parish funds, monastery lands grew in value to provide something like one-seventh of ordinary income by 1565. Electoral Saxony spent more Church money on paying off the elector's debts than on all 'pious' purposes put together. The electors of Brandenburg used Church property to increase their (modest) share of land in regions where landownership was otherwise dominated by the lesser nobles.[5]

The German princes' acquisitiveness was eclipsed by the massive plundering carried out under Henry VIII, Edward VI, and Elizabeth I of England. The clergy were first fined and taxed to the tune of over £400,000 between 1535 and 1540; between 1536 and 1540 the entire property of the religious orders was confiscated. Sales of such land (mostly to lesser gentry) before 1547 raised nearly £800,000, and plate and jewels nearly £80,000. Rents raised from lands before they were sold brought the total profit to the Crown in twelve years to some £1.3 million.[6] Thereafter fresh lucre was sought in the endowed wealth of memorial masses or 'perpetual chantries', confiscated after about 1545, and the landed estates or 'temporalities' of the bishops, which were 'exchanged' for theoretically equivalent (but actually less profitable) 'spiritual' incomes based on parish tithes, during the reigns of Edward and Elizabeth.[7] Similar, if smaller, gains were made by the kings of Denmark and Sweden at the same stages.

Given the repeated complaints in the late Middle Ages about the money ill-gotten and worse spent by rich prelates, fat monks, or lazy mass priests, it would have been astonishing if the new reformed Church establishment had *not* been cheaper to run than the old one. It is therefore no argument against the 'profit motive' to point out that churches, schools, and almshouses had to be supported out of the confiscated revenues. Where this happened, it left a surplus for the ruler, as in the case of Haina monastery in Hesse, refounded as a hospital.[8] Even land spent on 'pious' purposes like education might indirectly serve the state's needs, by preserving peace and order, and providing educated civil servants for the prince.[9] Finally, rulers could delay founding schools or hospitals and make a healthy, if temporary, profit from the endowment.[10]

However, did the profit motive lead rulers to establish the Reformation? It is not enough simply to show that material gains were made. The following possible objections have to be considered:

(1) Did the 'hidden' costs of the Reformation entail expenses to counterbalance the short-term profits?

(2) Was the seizing of Church property the one crucial turning-point which led to the Reformation being established?

(3) Could rulers seize control of Church property without turning protestant at all?

First, neither the princes of Germany nor the kings of England became massively rich through the Reformation. They gained huge sums of money; but then spent as much, or more, in the search for security and political stability. Hesse and Electoral Saxony embarked on military mobilization and frantic diplomatic activity to defend their confessional position, which swallowed up the increased income which they received from the Church, and quite possibly more.[11] While some German princes had to spend the added *income* on increased security, the kings and queens of England actually squandered the *capital* within a few decades. Two-thirds of monastic lands were sold by 1547, three-quarters by 1558, and almost everything by the early 1600s.[12] Henry VIII's wars against France and Scotland in the 1540s did not, of course, derive simply from the need to defend 'heretical' England against catholic powers. However, by the 1580s and 1620s some of the English nobility, at least, assumed that their protestant homeland would fight for less fortunate co-religionaries abroad. By this stage the significant gains made from the Church were long gone, and the Crown was (after due allowance made for inflation) in a worse financial state than before.[13]

Secondly, there was no clear causal link between confiscating lands and turning protestant. In several instances the 'plunder' was successfully extracted from the Church many years before the ruler's religious position was defined. In Sweden and England the Crown confiscated Church property on grounds of expediency or legal precedent which made little or no reference to the Reformation, and antedated the adoption of reformed belief or worship by many years. In Denmark Church property was handed over to the nobles as early as the 1520s.[14] In Scotland the nobility secured favourable 'feus' on Church property in the decades before the Reformation, as the old Church sought to protect itself with a massive heap of vested interests.[15] Finally, some rulers of catholic lands were just as effective as the protestants in squeezing extra income out of their churches: in the sixteenth century the dukes of Bavaria actually used the threat of making concessions to the protestants to extract more money from the estates of the catholic Church—but remained catholic themselves.[16]

Hypothesis: rulers adopted the Reformation to justify abolishing priestly privileges and consolidate their rule.

Added *power* won by rulers who turned protestant is even harder to quantify than additional money. However, it has been very strongly urged that *political* gains offered a spectacular blandishment to secular rulers to adopt the Reformation. In both the cities and the territorial monarchies—the argument goes—secular rulers had long resented the rights and privileges held by the Church, which restricted their freedom for manœuvre. Such antagonism had already led them to enact 'anticlerical' legislation of various kinds and with varying degrees of success.[17] The Reformation gave them the excuse to carry such initiatives to their logical conclusion, by overruling *all* clerical privilege and subsuming all Church activities within the state. The proponents of this argument can cite the apparently close continuity between the moves to turn 'priests into citizens' in the late Middle Ages and similar moves in the Reformation.[18] Such motives varied from the worries of the Strasbourg council about shrinking taxable land in the city to the Zwickau fathers' resentment of monks infringing their monopoly on brewing beer.[19] One can also cite, no less impressively, the deliberately medieval language in which so much of the early legislation of the English Reformation was couched; or Henry VIII's 'discovery' that his clergy were only 'half our subjects'.[20]

The basic difficulty with this argument is that it only explains why *rulers* might have wished to impose the Reformation from above. In most territorial states this is fair enough. However, historians have claimed plausibly 'the Reformation was never the work of a city council';[21] at least in the sense that city councils were normally 'the brakes rather than the motor of reform'.[22] Explaining the *urban* Reformation in terms of the city councillors' motives is accounting, in most cases at least, for the attitudes of the wrong people. Therefore, a *political* explanation for the establishment of the Reformation has to explain the motives of agitators just outside the ruling class; and account for tensions between rulers and ruled. Hence one finds a variant of the previous hypothesis:

Hypothesis: rulers endorsed their subjects' demands for the abolition of priestly privileges, so as to deflect any challenges to their own power on to the clergy.

Most self-governing cities in the late Middle Ages experienced struggles between increasingly authoritarian and closed oligarchies on one hand, and aggressive pressure groups within trade and craft guilds on the other.[23] Since these 'socially and intellectually mobile' groups were probably some of the most receptive to protestant preaching, *their* pressure for the Reformation can be represented as an extension of their social ambitions:

thrusting the new doctrines on to the city fathers became a new way to challenge those same city fathers for the moral headship of the community. This argument works especially well where the introduction of the Reformation was accompanied by pressure from the guilds and changes, whether temporary or permanent, in the city constitution.[24] It suggests that those patriciates which adopted, or endorsed, the Reformation deflected criticism of their *own* privileges by allowing the lower orders to vent their antagonism on the clergy. Hence T. A. Brady commented:

in 1524–5 Strasbourg's well-integrated ruling class staved off a conjuncture of social revolt with the reform movement by sacrificing the old ecclesiastical order, a maneuver which, performed rapidly and without major losses or severe factionalism, is an index of this class's internal solidarity and strong political will.[25]

H. Schilling remarked of the northern German cities:

the Reformation should be seen as a continuation of the civic conflicts of the middle ages . . . Lutheranism had to establish itself from below, from social groups which had no such inhibitions [i.e. about loyalty to the old ecclesiastical structures]. Thus the Reformation could be linked to communal movements concerned with the civic constitution and social order.[26]

Needless to say, something of the same pattern can be found in the constitutional struggles of the southern German cities discussed earlier.[27]

Such reasoning has obvious affinities with Marxist principles that class conflict is omnipresent and that economic motives are always the underlying mainsprings of popular political action. In different ways Marxist historians (chiefly, but not solely those within the historical tradition associated with the former regime in eastern Germany) have portrayed the Reformation as an 'early bourgeois revolution' conforming to the Marxist typology of social development.[28] The 'deflection' of popular attacks on an urban oligarchy on to the Aunt Sally of the privileged clergy affords an interesting instance of a 'false consciousness' being generated in a discontented, politically aggressive bourgeoisie. The ruling classes thus seem to be coping with a class-based attack on themselves by allowing the people to persuade themselves that the priests are their 'real' enemies. Nevertheless, such arguments transcend crude political dogmas and appeal to scholars of all backgrounds; they must be taken very seriously in their own right. The coincidence between guild struggles, political 'anticlericalism', and the Reformation cannot now be belittled or ignored by any serious historian.

However, both these 'political' arguments raise several problems. They work better in some contexts than in others. In some cases where 'anticlerical' social tensions existed they either did not lead at once to a Reformation (as at Colmar) or could be appeased without reference to protestantism (as in Schwäbisch Gmünd).[29] Even in strictly political terms the Reformation was not necessarily the most natural vehicle for politicians' ambitions. It was and remained a movement of clerics,[30] which soon created an even more high-minded and obnoxious 'clericalism' than the ethos which it replaced.[31] Whereas late medieval politicians had made threatening noises and passed only partially effective laws against their clergy's privileges, reforming politicians paid their ministers' stipends and told them what to preach. This transition was *not* an automatic, gradual, steady progression. *Something* quite dramatic broke down the late medieval equilibrium between 'anticlerical' distaste for the Church's flaws and 'conventionally pious' belief in its rituals. The political–material explanation, with its insistence on continuity, inherently cannot explain what that 'something' was.[32]

In *all* political–material explanations there is an imbalance between the political or material gains which were in prospect, and the enthusiasm displayed, the risks taken, and the sacrifices made for the Reformation's sake. 'Few people embrace martyrdom or even exile merely in the expectation that a new creed may lighten their taxes or give some of their friends seats on a city council.'[33] Political self-interest is not a uniformly satisfying explanation for the establishment of the Reformation. Several princes were ready to run immense political *risks* for their creed, like Georg of Brandenburg-Ansbach or Philipp of Hesse.[34] Several rulers who had *already* weathered the political crisis of abolishing the old Church ultimately 'reformed' worship or doctrine as well, for instance in ducal Saxony, England, or Sweden. In those lands where the pressure to reform came from subjects rather than rulers, it is arguable, to say the least, that a sovereign could thwart the establishment of the Reformation if really determined to do so, like Duke Georg of Saxony, Elector Joachim I of Brandenburg, or cities like Würzburg, Bamberg, or Cologne.[35] Neither the search for political advantage nor the need for political survival, then, adequately explain the changes, however subtle and stimulating the arguments which show beyond doubt that they played a part.

2. *Appeal to Classes or Social Structures?*

Explanations based on political or material advantage suggest why there was a crisis in Church and State in the first half of the sixteenth century. They do not explain why the Reformation, a programme of changes in belief, worship, and Church politics, rather than any other movement or slogan, apparently offered such a widely acceptable solution to people's problems. One must try to explain what made the reformers' message *appear* to apply particularly closely to those social groups or communities who took the critical decisions.

> *Hypothesis: the Reformation message confirmed the ruling élites' view of man as essentially sinful and in need of discipline, and thereby justified their paternalistic restrictionism.*

This argument seeks to explain the attraction which the Lutheran message apparently held for the ruling classes of central and northern Germany. Originally developed by Gerald Strauss for the particular case of Nuremberg, it suggests that Lutheran teachings, by dwelling so insistently on the topic of human sin and inadequacy,[36] struck a chord in the minds of the city magistrates. Their statecraft apparently rested on chronic distrust of their subjects: every aspect of city life was subject to minute, paternalistic, oppressive scrutiny and supervision. The pessimistic Lutheran anthropology seemed to echo their view of man more persuasively than catholic hopes that believers might be partially purified by penitential exercise: therefore they found Lutheranism congenial.[37]

It is easy to make fun of this argument, the suggestion (according to Steven E. Ozment) 'that the Reformation succeeded, as it were, by insult'.[38] However, there are perhaps even better reasons than Strauss suggested why Lutheranism was an appropriate creed for paternalist governments. Luther's doctrine of the 'Two Kingdoms', correctly understood, emphasized that *all* people, as 'both sinners and righteous', needed to have the sinful side to their nature bridled and restrained by worldly discipline and secular government.[39] It cannot be coincidence, for example, that strict Lutheran preachers were usually those chosen by rulers most anxious to secure obedience and restraint, whether Nikolaus Hausmann in mid-1520s Zwickau, or the preachers approved of by the rulers of Brandenburg-Ansbach, Augsburg, or after 1548 by the regimes installed in cities like Ulm or Strasbourg.[40] Even in Hesse, where more religious diversity was allowed, Lutheran ideas seem to have contributed to the development of a paternalist, even 'mercantilist', attitude towards trade and industry, combined with the characteristically Lutheran reform of poor relief.[41]

No doubt princes and city fathers warmed to Lutheranism (rather than Zwinglianism or some sectarian creed) when *some* form of Reformation was either materially attractive or necessary to keep control. However, this was at best a negative reason to choose the least socially subversive and politically risky heresy; it only partly explains the enthusiastic adherence shown from the very first to the Lutheran protests by Nuremberg citizens like Lazarus Spengler.[42] Even less does it explain why the *people* clamoured for the Reformation, and then forced reluctant rulers to shop around for the reforming creed which entailed the least risks and the best chance of obtaining moral and religious reinforcement for the state. Ironically, after the 1550s princely absolutism became associated, not with Lutheranism, but with the German version of 'Calvinism', which actually derived not so much from Geneva as from the reformed schools of Heidelberg in the Palatinate. The new creed could only be introduced (in the face of popular apathy or, in some cases, active resistance) by autocratic, despotic imposition: hence princely absolutism and 'Calvinism', in contrast to the situation elsewhere in Europe, went hand in hand.[43]

Hypothesis: the Reformation message echoed the preferences of the progressive urban bourgeoisie for a simpler, purer more practical everyday creed.

It has been long and persistently suggested (possibly because of the different ways in which catholics and protestants behaved in nineteenth-century France and Germany) that protestantism was inherently more suited to an economically aggressive, upwardly mobile bourgeois class. The key to the argument seems to be that reformed worship, simple, cerebral, austere, and (in comparison to the saint- and festival-filled calendar of the Middle Ages) not too time-consuming, was the ideal way for early modern, proto-industrial, proto-capitalist man to address his God. It offered a means for society to organize and discipline its way out of the Middle Ages.[44] Historians of the Reformation in France, for instance, have found that the 'merchant manufacturers, craftsmen, and artisans' were the first class of people to reject catholicism in favour of the new beliefs. Henry Heller has recently urged in very circumstantial detail that the revolt of the Calvinist urban artisanate was a protest against a creed dominated by the aristocracy, which was both extravagant and grasping of money without regard to the welfare of a community threatened by the economic crisis of the century.[45]

The 'bourgeoisie' thesis, however, rests on more than just economics. In the classic form advanced as long ago as 1904 by Max Weber, an 'ethos', a sociological 'ideal-type', was alleged to represent the 'essence' of a reformed mentality which suited, and indeed helped to produce, the characteristic attitudes of bourgeois capitalist production. Those attitudes included thrift, diligence, sobriety, careful use of time, and high moral standards.[46] The Weberian approach has been criticized, reformulated, and argued over endlessly. For present purposes the main dispute between Marxists and Weberians—whether religion *reflected* the modes of economic development, or actually helped to *create* them—are less important than the broad consensus that there was something definitely 'bourgeois' about the protestant outlook.[47]

That consensus has been weakened by the recognition that, for whatever reasons, many noblemen were also attracted, at least for a few generations after about 1540, to the supposedly 'bourgeois' protestant creed.[48] One suspects that urban artisans and guildsmen were specially numerous in the early Reformation for simple, circumstantial reasons rather than as 'ideal-types': city-dwellers were the first to hear preachers and read (or indeed print) reforming pamphlets; those just below the social level of the oligarchies (i.e. the middling bourgeoisie) would be on one hand aware enough of new ideas, and self-assertive enough to challenge the Church, but on the other not rich enough to have a vested interest in the old Church fabric and structures.[49] Secondly, the austere, protestant work ethic cannot easily explain the popular appeal of the *early* Reformation. The primitive Reformation experience entailed riot, disorder, carnival enthusiasms, and satirical lampoons: hardly the stuff of which the Weberian 'proto-capitalist' was made.[50] Weber's 'ideal-type' explains the end of the process better than the start.

> *Hypothesis: the Reformation message with its anticlerical and anti-authoritarian overtones appealed to those who felt oppressed by their political or economic masters.*

Almost any subversive dogma can be expected to appeal, if only in a rather temporary and superficial way, to those with a sense of grievance against their immediate social superiors. This kind of interpretation assumes a rather simpler, two-tier system of class antagonism than the Weberian preoccupation with the middling bourgeoisie: a 'them and us' struggle between rulers and ruled.[51] Thomas A. Brady's study of the political structures of Strasbourg claims to discover great potential for social subversion behind the pressures for the Reformation on the part of the citizens:

The forms and institutions of property did not much differ between ecclesiastical and lay owners. When, therefore, the rulers yielded to the argument that ecclesiastical property should be administered for the public good regardless of historic rights and the intentions of donors, not far beyond this idea lay the position that all property should be so administered ... This is why the regime's invasions of ecclesiastical property rights was truly dangerous: there was no fundamental reason why all property should not be socialized as ecclesiastical property was ... What the aristocrats sacrificed in 1523–5 suggests what the Reformation might have become. What was saved in 1523–5 suggests how that potential was thwarted.[52]

These remarks partly justify Steven E. Ozment's testy observations that this reduces the Reformation to 'a modest class war', and that 'we would find it laughable to interpret the price revolution of early modern history solely in terms of religious belief, yet seem willing to take seriously the explanation of a religious revolution in the near exclusive terms of economic self interest'.[53] The kind of protestant allegiance which was based on social tensions was, however, fickle and even reversible. This was shown by Natalie Z. Davis's classic survey of the printers' journeymen of Lyons, who espoused protestantism at a time of bitter strife with their masters only to turn round and revert to catholicism when the masters themselves became protestants.[54]

In fact, *all* kinds of social strata—rulers, middling producers, under-dogs—have been found at some stage to have a class-based socio-economic reason for finding the Reformation attractive. Allegiances between particular socio-economic groups and particular religious ideologies were, like the 'coalition' of Reformation and political units itself, temporary marriages of convenience rather than permanent bonds forged into the essential natures of people and ideas.[55]

> *Hypothesis: particular forms of the Reformation corresponded to the assumptions of particular city types, nation-states, or ethnic groups.*

Many historians, whether temperamentally or for ideological reasons, prefer to take communities and their structures as a whole, rather than fractured 'classes' or interest groups. The classic instance of this approach is Bernd Moeller's comparison of the cultural, constitutional, and religious differences between the cities of northern Germany and southern Germany. Put very simply, Moeller's argument was that on one hand, the more personal outlook of Lutheran teaching was appropriate to the *northern* German cities in which authority and culture were the preserves of a fairly closed élite. On the other the 'reformed' tradition of Zwingli and Bucer emphasized the 'community' as the primary unit of religious life rather than the individual soul; it therefore suited the social experience of the *southern* cities of Swabia and Switzerland, in which participation in the political and cultural life of the city was spread much more widely across the population: 'The victory of the 'Reformed' Reformation in the Upper German [i.e. south German] imperial cities is finally explained by the encounter of the peculiarly 'urban' theology of Zwingli and Bucer with the particularly vital communal spirit in Upper Germany.'[56]

This thesis began a vigorous discussion which carried all the participants beyond their original positions. Both sets of distinctions, between the social dimensions of Lutheran versus 'reformed' theology, and between the communal spirit in northern and southern cities, have been questioned.[57] Perhaps, also, the social context in which the south German reformers worked actually *shaped* their ethical outlook; this explanation may be just as likely as Moeller's suggestion that those reformers' social context simply *decided* whether their (predetermined) theology was accepted or not. However, the search for parallels between ideas and types of community has continued. Guy Swanson's *Religion and Regime* developed a complex and highly controversial classification of types of government; he then suggested that the adoption of one or other type of protestantism, or the retention of catholicism, each corresponded 'naturally' to a particular type of regime: hence the *ultimate* religious profile of a state could be explained in terms of its type of constitution.[58] Mary Fulbrook's recent comparison of seventeenth-century regimes in Germany and England in terms of their attitude to voluntary protestant ideas stands in this same tradition.[59]

All these explanations do at least attach themselves to some distinctive feature of protestant thought or teaching, rather than considering the purely external and coincident implications of a more drastic assault on the old Church. However, in many cases that distinctive feature, whether of protestant thought in general, or of a particular religious confession, is isolated in a rather impressionistic and approximate way. Perhaps it cannot be otherwise, given the uncertainty about just what *was* understood to be the basic protestant message within lay society. The arguments so far discussed cannot *fully* satisfy. One still must address the basic question: what impact did the 'preached message' of the Reformation have on the people who heard it, and how did it affect their political support for the movement?

3. *Answering a Spiritual Need?*

Since social and economic explanations have held the centre of the stage in much recent religious history, it would be easy to be either apologetic or militantly defensive in broaching the *spiritual* appeal of the Reformation. In fact, though, recent experience across the world suggests that people will do things to their society for the sake of an ideology—and especially for the sake of what they call 'God'—with far less prudence, forethought, or moderation than they would ever do for the sake of material profit. That religion is far, far more than a tool for imposing social harmony on the simple-minded is as obvious now as it was in the crisis years of the mid-1520s and 1530s.

However, the 'core' message of the Reformation was really very *inappropriate* to what seem to have been the commonest spiritual needs of the masses.[60] Late medieval people chose to support the cultic, ritualistic, often entertaining features of their religion. They worried about bodily survival and well-being;[61] and used the available rites to care for their souls in the hereafter.[62] Reformation teaching knocked away the psychological 'props' of reassurance offered in both these departments, for technical academic reasons which were (in their entirety at least) hard for the untrained mind to grasp. The problem, therefore, is to decide just what the Reformation message *meant* for its hearers and partisans; and then to account for its evident popularity in a plausible way.

Hypothesis: the Reformation offered a release from the spiritual 'oppression' imposed by the penitential cycle and the intolerable material and psychological demands which it made on the believer.

This thesis claims that the so-called 'Burden of Late Medieval Religion' is the key to the Reformation's appeal. The origins of the argument lie in the work of the nineteenth-century German historian Johannes Geffcken; but its major present-day exponent is Steven E. Ozment. Since Professor Ozment's work is more widely read than many other works cited here, it requires fairly full discussion.[63] The argument is that the penitential mechanisms of late medieval Christianity, and above all the process of privately confessing each individual sin, imposed a 'burden' of scrupulous self-examination and moral rigour on the lay penitent. It is claimed that (*a*) this 'burden' was becoming more inquisitive and obnoxious as the Middle Ages ended; (*b*) it did not offer a suitable set of moral principles for the layman, expecting him to live by a toned-down version of monastic morality; (*c*) it actually *failed* to reassure consciences troubled by the awareness of their sins. Therefore, when the reformers offered a form of spiritual advice and comfort which was less inquisitive and censorious, more sympathetic to laymen's values, and cheaper, lay people grasped at it eagerly and adopted the Reformation as a means of spiritual reassurance. This 'conversion' experience corresponded to the moral soul-searching which the older Luther described having gone through himself in his youth.[64] As Professor Ozment sums it up:

What the Reformation did have in common with late medieval reform movements was the conviction that traditional church authority and piety no longer served the religious needs of large numbers of people and had become psychologically and financially oppressive. Luther's inability to satisfy his own religious anguish by becoming a self-described 'monk's monk' was an experience many laity also knew in their own way, for they too had sought in vain consolation from a piety based on the penitential practices of monks ... Many laity derived no more consolation from the sacrament of confession than Luther from monastic exercises. This shared religious experience formed the basic bond between Luther and the multitude who became protestant.[65]

This argument has not gained widespread acceptance (despite being restated several times by its author)[66] and is not endorsed here. However, it has the major virtue of recognizing that the fundamental change brought into religion by the Reformation was the abolition of the 'penitential cycle'—the rhythmic progress through sin, confession, absolution, penance, grace, and further sin—which was at the heart of late medieval pastoral theory.[67] The spiritual 'core' of the Reformation was the change from a justification through a great sequence of little atonements, to a justification 'draped' over the believer in a single, once-for-all act of redemption.

However, Ozment's argument raises at least four questions before it can be accepted as a really comprehensive explanation of the Reformation's appeal:

(1) Is its assessment of late medieval pastoral theory (let alone practice), as fussy, inquisitive, tormenting, and 'psychologically burdensome' fair and balanced?
(2) Was the 'torment' of the confessional really the key to Luther's spiritual development?
(3) Did the reformers denounce as the old Church's primary failing that it 'tormented' lay people with the discipline of the confessional?
(4) Is there evidence to warrant attributing Luther's conversion experience

(as he described it) to the entire 'multitude [of laymen] who became protestant'?

1. Ozment's thesis rests on a selection of the most extreme of the popular manuals for confessors, as he himself admitted at one point.[68] Thomas N. Tentler's comprehensive survey of the theory found that confessional theologians required a balance to be struck between arousing a sense of sin and comforting a troubled or 'scrupulous' conscience.[69] When one turns to examine the *practice* of confession and absolution, the image conjured up by Ozment is so distorted as to resemble a caricature.[70] Laymen had a wide choice of confessors and could pick the most lenient and reassuring if they wished for their (annual) spiritual 'cleansing'. By the eve of the Reformation the sellers of 'full confessional letters' fell over themselves to lighten the burden. The point was not to 'torment' laymen, but to bind them (morally and financially) to the Church's services.[71] It is possible to overrate the moral power of the confessional if one equates it with its twentieth-century counterpart, administered every few weeks by priests striving to hold on to hearts and minds in a secular world.[72]

2. Luther undoubtedly did speak of his struggle to overcome his fear of God's judgement through monastic discipline.[73] However, as was shown earlier, his remarks at table or in the 1545 'autobiography' were not precise historical accounts, but rather a spiritualized over-simplification which does *not* correspond neatly to the evidence of his lecture notes and letters at the time.[74] To treat the soul-searching remarks of an observant eremite and theologian not only as accurate autobiography, but also as typical of the spirituality of the mass of lay people in pre-Reformation Europe is therefore, to say the least, imprudent.

3. It is at best a half-truth to say that the reformers condemned the medieval confessional because they thought it 'oppressive' and 'burdensome' to consciences. 'What seems to have scandalized so many Protestants earlier in this century was their conviction ... that it was *shockingly easy* for Catholics to cleanse themselves of their sins in the confessional on Saturday so that they could, with sanguine conscience, receive the Body and Blood of Christ on the next day.'[75] This observation holds good for Luther, Melanchthon, Zwingli, and Calvin as well. To imagine that anyone *could* simply list, and then atone for, all their sins in some fixed brief period of time was bad enough; to think that a yearly flushing-out of one's moral plumbing dealt with the gravity of man's offences against God was far worse.[76] The confessional, they said, encouraged complacency by lifting artificial or imaginary burdens instead of revealing real sins.

4. It is very difficult to look beneath the surface of popular attitudes. However, the abolition of the confessional (as opposed, say, to the abolition of the mass or the removal of images) does not seem to have been a very high priority in the popular Reformation. The reformers blew hot and cold over it, intending still to retain some sort of private confession of sins before communion as a means of reassurance.[77] The chief example whom Ozment cites of a reformer militantly opposed to the confessional above. all else, Jakob Strauss of Eisenach, is a fairly minor and in other ways somewhat eccentric figure who seems to have influenced few others.[78] In the pamphlets written by ordinary laymen, a doubtful but exceptional source for lay attitudes, the confessional did not figure as the one supremely important grievance against the old Church; it was only ever (at most) one issue among many.[79]

Hypothesis: the message preached by the reformers seemed both more plausible and more biblical than the one purveyed by its opponents.

Finally one may consider the simplest, most face-value explanation of all: that people listened to, and believed, the reformers quite simply because their ideas seemed to make sense; indeed, because they seemed to enshrine some very important principles.[80] Such a theory involves the problem that, first of all, the basic Reformation message led to the abolition and rejection of many of the aids, comforts, entertainments, and reassurances of medieval religion, which clearly were popular in town as well as countryside.[81] Secondly, that message *was* a complex, difficult thing, as the rather halting attempts made by some artists to represent it in diagrams and pictures prove very well.[82] Religious historians justly resist any doctrinaire insistence that economic or political objectives are somehow more 'real' than religious ones; they reject the view that attributing disinterested religious motivation to people of varying social class can only be 'romantic idealism'.[83] Nevertheless, there remains a credibility gap between the austere intellectual qualities of the idea, and the down-to-earth antagonisms of everyday politics: a gap arising out of any teacher's common-sense experience, not from dogmatic assumptions about human motivation.

In this light several questions arise:

(1) What message actually *reached* the ears and eyes of the inhabitants of a city or state on the way towards Reformation?
(2) How did people *apprehend* the message which was delivered to them?
(3) Did that message, as apprehended, answer their spiritual concerns so appropriately as to arouse vigorous partisanship?

1. Opinions vary as to just how the core Reformation message was transmitted to the people. Of course Luther himself, with his idiosyncratic preference for very slow changes in ritual, his retention of old-style worship and even of images, and his aggressive insistence on a *bodily* presence of Christ in the Eucharist, was in no way normative for the rest of the movement. To regard the primitive hero-figure as the bench-mark by which other reformers or Reformation movements were judged is plainly absurd.[84] However, it is equally extreme to assert that Reformation ideas spread in a totally random fashion. Franz Lau spoke of a 'disorderly growth' (*Wildwuchs*) of the Reformation in the early 1520s, in which he assumed that all kinds of ideas, sharing nothing with Luther's theology save common enemies, were current in the towns and cities.[85] An even more reductionist position claims that the real unity in early Reformation preaching lay in the unbridled hostility which it encouraged and fomented against the old priesthood.[86]

Against this assumption Bernd Moeller recently studied a collection of thirty-two summaries of sermons issued by twenty-six reformers, addressed to twenty-seven cities in a total of fifty-six editions between 1522 and 1529. The survey covered all kinds of preachers representing all the main German-speaking areas in which the urban Reformation developed.[87] In spite of the diversity of peoples and places, a consensus emerged. The preachers presented the basic common denominator of the early Reformation message in a series of fundamental primary themes. The primacy of the Bible, the supreme importance of belief in Christ for the forgiveness of sins, the Church as the communion of all who believe, the sufferings of the Church in the context of the last days, were all expounded in broadly similar fashion. The coherence of the *early* Reformation message rested in a polyphony of many individual minds spreading broadly the same message in their own words.[88]

2. However, what preachers preached and what people heard may have been very different things. A. G. Dickens concluded:

One could not substantiate any claim that the German public rapidly obtained an accurate grasp of Luther's doctrine of justification, let alone of his still more difficult doctrine of the Eucharist. One could indeed cite a few passages in other men's pamphlets where the former is reasonably grasped and summarized, but it remains hard to avoid the impression that the years of pamphleteering must have left some blurred and simplified impressions of Luther's central doctrine.[89]

What seems to us to be the intellectual core of his message may not be the core of his political or psychological appeal. Some pamphlets indeed presented, not so much 'blurred and simplified impressions', as rhapsodic variations with only tenuous connections to the major themes. Paul Russell has recently studied the 'economies of salvation' presented by the lay pamphleteers Sebastian Lotzer, Haug Marschalck, Hans Greiffenberger, and Argula von Grumbach. In these 'justification by faith' was much less prominent than the call to turn works of 'piety', 'good works' to harness the old Church to the good of one's soul, into works of 'charity', that is, moral and social goodwill towards one's neighbour and the community.[90] This message was of course a practical consequence, rather than a primary part, of reformed teaching. C. M. N. Eire has found a similar stress on the consequences of protestant preaching, in this case the rejection of old-style catholic piety, in early pamphlets by minor figures, priests and laymen alike.[91]

Nevertheless, there is also evidence that a basic grasp of the implications of the reformed teaching on justification *did* reach beyond the preaching élite. In March 1525 a committee of Strasbourg citizens petitioned against the mass, saying that whereas the priests claimed it was a work to earn salvation, 'Christ has done everything once and for all believers'.[92] Indeed, it is hard to imagine that the mass, object of such devotion and investment, could have been energetically denounced and abolished by popular demand if the people had *not* been given a good reason why.[93] If some of the lay pamphleteers were erratic in their theology, the prolific Nuremberg poet Hans Sachs presented (at least in his early works) a uniformly faithful versification of Luther's basic message.[94]

3. However, even if the basic spiritual message *did* filter through to some of the laymen who mattered, *why* was this so? It is unsatisfactory to resort to mass psychology, to claim that there was some special 'anguish' about life in the early sixteenth century which only the reformers knew how to appease:

[Humanism] was not enough for the masses who had a specifically acute sense of sin and nonetheless felt unable to escape from it ... If Renaissance people were capable of the greatest heroism in action, nothing was more alien to them than the patient overcoming of one's own self. So theology had to come to their aid—the sacraments of the Roman Church, or the justification by faith of the Lutheran Reformation ... In the Bible, many humanists sought and discovered above all an ethic. But the anguished Christians of the start of the sixteenth century needed first of all a faith ... [95]

Nor is it enough to say simply 'they read the Bible and found that the reformers' teaching derived from it'.[96] Even if Bible-reading was more common than some historians suggest,[97] one suspects that people read the Bible because they already found the ideas of the Reformation congenial— not the other way around. Even at the purely spiritual level it is difficult to find a convincing reason *why* the reformers were heard and supported with such enthusiasm. Historians may have been much too subtle.

4. Conclusion: The 'Flattery' of Reformed Preaching

A much simpler explanation can now be considered:

Hypothesis: The Reformation 'flattered' its hearers by treating them as fit to hear and to judge the most arcane doctrines of the religious élite, and by portraying the layman as the true custodian of biblical truth.

Envisage the alternatives presented to that minority of Europe's ordinary people who were able to choose whether to espouse the Reformation or not. On the one hand was the old Church. It was suddenly deserted by many of its most talented members, sometimes in the most humiliating circumstances, as when one after another of the catholic preachers called to Strasbourg announced their conversions.[98] It proved pathetically slow to spring to its own defence in really popular propaganda.[99] When offered the chance to tout its wares before a lay audience, its 'champions' retreated into the old attitude of refusing even to discuss the mysteries of religion before laymen in their own language.[100] When they *did* defend themselves, traditional theologians like Eck, Cochlaeus, or Mazzolini often had to appeal to the authority of a papal supremacy which was (politically) unpopular among clerics, let alone laymen.[101] They were handicapped by defending an institution into which so many 'abuses', or rather 'misuses' of money, people, and legal systems had become deep rooted.[102] The spiritual prestige of the old rituals had preserved the Church from the consequences of its many failings as long as that prestige was unchallenged. Now everything was open to question, the 'power of the keys' could no longer carry that weight.[103]

On the other hand there were the reformers. They resided and preached; they wrote; they worked hard, took risks, and actually expected to have a more professional, smaller, and above all *cheaper* establishment to support their work. Hero-worship is outdated; but it is surely a major fact of history that their leaders at least were seen to be figures of transparent integrity. After decades of 'anticlerical' satire, nothing worse could be said against them than that they disagreed with the Romanists, that they were married (a technical offence but arguably further proof of their rejection of hypo-crisy), and that they were single-minded, often politically naïve enthusiasts. They satisfied laymen's moral criteria.[104] They also appealed, directly and openly, to the 'Christian community' of laymen to judge in issues from which they had been excluded. Lay people saw some of the best talents in the Church turn towards them for approval and support.[105] Nothing could have been more surprising or more intoxicating. This was the astonishing way in which the Reformation flattered lay susceptibilities. From being hesitant trespassers on the margins of the spiritual domain, laymen were actually *invited* to judge issues at the very heart of their dealings with the Almighty, and by clerics at that! When one views the choice open to laymen—rulers or people—in the early days of the Reformation's spread, it is not the fact that people adopted the movement which is puzzling; it is that there were anywhere in Europe people loyal enough to the old catholicism to nip the new movement in the bud before it was too late.[106]

In other ways too the reformers 'flattered' laymen's spiritual self-esteem in the crucial early years of the Reformation. In the late Middle Ages an established literary cliché contrasted the simple, straightforwardly pious layman with the devious and hypocritical priest.[107] Before this romantic and unrealistic image of the ordinary layman—the peasant especially—was revealed as a delusion by the events of 1524–5, it gave a heaven-sent opportunity to reforming pamphleteers. In numerous dialogues, notably the *Karsthans* (probably by Joachim Vadian) and the *Neu-Karsthans* by Martin Bucer, the honest peasant was portrayed either as the champion of the new biblical faith or the honest open-minded soul converted to it.[108] One preacher even went so far as to live out the myth: Diepold Peringer, known as the 'Peasant of Wöhrd', preached around Franconia during 1523–4, representing himself (despite a proven knowledge of patristic and scholastic theology) as an inspired layman preaching to other laymen. His claims were taken seriously at the time (and by some historians since); but he seems actually to have been a runaway ex-priest in disguise.[109] Romantic myths aside, the reformers could 'flatter' the lay estate in other ways, as for instance by comparing the useful, sociable piety of the working layman with the 'useless' religious idleness of the monks, nuns, and friars.[110]

To explain the alliance or 'coalition' of reformers and politicians in these terms has several advantages: (*a*) it takes the spiritual priorities of all kinds of people seriously, and so is not bound to particular classes or contexts, as so many of the social-historical arguments are; (*b*) it does not exclude any of the other arguments so far advanced, which no doubt function well enough in their particular contexts; (*c*) it is not tied rigidly to any detail of a theological scheme, with the need to prove that laymen either understood or were attracted by any such scheme. Thus it can accommodate the 'misunderstandings' of the message by imperial knights, peasants, or humanists. The argument rests only on the obvious fact that no one in the sixteenth century liked being patronized by those priests in whose expertise they had suddenly ceased to be confident.

The reformers' flattery of lay people was politically naïve rather than insincere or consciously manipulative.[111] The early reformers had really believed their lay followers would be the pious paragons portrayed in their own propaganda.[112] In practice laymen's enthusiasm for diligent Reformation of religion and society proved fickle as clerical and lay interests began to diverge.

The context for the history of both city and Reformation was formed by a symbiosis between their specific interests, but that symbiosis was an interim, a *temporary* coalition ... Each defined the basis of the common weal in a different manner: in the 'obedience of faith' on the one hand and a 'sense of civic virtue' on the other.[113]

Despite the 'coalition' of clerical and lay interests which was apparently created when the reformed order was established, reformers and secular politicians had really only been allied at arm's length. Very few lay politicians indeed could realistically have forfeited everything—including their authority in their own communities—for the sake of a set of principles as the reforming preachers did. Very soon after the inception of the 'established' Reformation the cracks in the alliance began to show through, in the sectaries' disenchantment with the 'alliance', the manipulations of princes, and the internecine quarrels of protestant clerics. Such cracks in the surface of the alliance mark the final phase of the sixteenth-century Reformation movement as well as of this book: this theme, too, is better explained by an alliance born of flattery than one based on closely matched political interests or widely shared spiritual anguish.

PART IV

The Coalition of Reformers and People Breaks Down

The coalition between the leaders of the movement and their patrons and allies among the laity was thus based on a partial sharing of interests and a degree of mutual respect and convenience. It inherently required compromise. Some reformers, like Martin Bucer or Philip Melanchthon, were habitual, almost obsessive compromisers, and would have compromised with the papacy itself if their more stiff-necked colleagues had allowed them to. However, the task of simultaneously upholding principles and preserving political stability was bound sooner or later to frustrate one side of the coalition or the other. In various sixteenth-century developments this 'breakdown' of the Reformation coalition can be observed.

Very early indeed some figures from within the broad current of reforming thought turned away in disgust from the slow, piecemeal negotiation towards Reformation of an entire state; they thus condemned themselves to becoming, in fact and soon on principle, exclusive sectarians at odds with secular society (Chapter 18). At the other extreme, lay politicians grew impatient with the reformers' impractical attitude towards their political survival: gradually the political thinking of the mainstream Reformation was dragged to a position where it reflected the need to defend a Church against attack at all costs (Chapter 19). Reformation thinking on the proper way to form a Church crystallized, so that instead of a whole society reforming itself with reference to local conditions, a series of 'patterns' of reformed religion, above all 'Lutheran' and 'Calvinist', were thrust on to rulers who had to take them or leave them. In Germany above all, the strife of different 'confessions' scarred the reformed churches very deeply in the later sixteenth century (Chapter 20). Finally, churchmen and politicians in Germany, France, the Low Countries, or the British Isles alike tussled over just how much power the Church should have to instruct and direct its people in the principles which they had (supposedly) endorsed by setting up the Church order (Chapter 21).

18

The Sects Reject the 'Coalition'

The sectarian tendencies and movements in the Reformation period are hard to classify. On the one hand, their leaders, mostly literate ex-clergy, came from the same milieux, appealed to the same kind of support, and used some of the same anti-Roman or anticlerical arguments as did the preachers of the early civic Reformations.[1] Many led conventional protestant careers before, or even in some cases after, their time as sectaries. Some claimed merely to draw out to their conclusions arguments which the orthodox reformers had initiated. For this reason they are sometimes called 'radical' reformers, in contrast to the mainstream or 'magisterial' reformers.[2] Unlike the mainstream reformers, however, they had no time for the compromises necessary to establish on a legal footing a reformed church embracing and serving the whole community. They desired instant information; failing which, a reformation of the 'godly'. Among most this aspect was in due course to be symbolized by the rite of believers' (adult) baptism, which for most at that period meant rebaptism: hence Zwingli, and later historians, called them 'anabaptists'. Since they disdained a settled relationship with secular society, secular society could not long tolerate them, and they were invariably persecuted.

The sectaries did not subscribe to the classic protestant view of man as a sinner even when he has been saved; nor did they accept that the saved were known only to God. Therefore some of them could envisage a church of 'visible saints'; they were thus estranged from the fundamental beliefs of the leading reformers. They disagreed with each other and split their sects so readily that even these generalities barely apply to them all; many also denied the most basic tenets of the early Church on which protestants and catholics agreed. Persecution made their leaders mobile, elusive, and very short lived. As they were voluntary groups, the sects tended to flare up, gain adherents, and quickly shrivel to a tiny core. They were a tiny proportion of Europe's population; the literature on them is vast, mainly because they flourished in a more *laissez-faire* atmosphere across the Atlantic in later centuries.[3]

1. *Sectarian Developments to 1535*

1.1. *Thomas Müntzer*

Thomas Müntzer (*c*.1490–1525), complex, enigmatic, and flawed, exerted an uncertain influence on the sectarian trends of the Reformation. A university-trained priest, he worked as a conventional 'Lutheranizing' pastor at Jüterbogk (1519) and then from 1520 at Zwickau. There his fervour and militancy emerged in his quarrels with the humanist preacher Sylvius Egranus, and his espousal of the Zwickau 'prophets' Storch, Drechsel, and Stübner.[4] In April 1521 he was driven from Zwickau after a civic disturbance, and moved to Prague, where he demonstrated the apocalyptic and partisan character of his ideas in his 'Manifesto'.[5] He failed to gain supporters, and returned to Germany, distancing himself all the while from the Lutherans. By the summer of 1523 he was at Allstedt, where he produced a pioneering—and very poetic—German service order for the town.[6] Meanwhile he antagonized the local aristocracy and the Lutherans alike. In July 1524 two Ernestine princes visited Allstedt and heard Müntzer preach a full-blooded version of his belief in revelation through dreams and visions, the direct communication of the Holy Spirit with the elect, and the call for the elect to turn on the 'ungodly' with violence. Meanwhile he had organized 'covenanted leagues' of his supporters in the region. Under their princes' scrutiny the Allstedters distanced themselves from the preacher, and Müntzer fled from the town in August.[7] He moved to Mühlhausen, which was in the midst of a riotous urban Reformation movement led by Heinrich Pfeiffer. Mühlhausen saw coups and counter-coups which led the city into the epicentre of the Thuringian Peasants' War, with the fatal results already described.[8]

Müntzer's chief claim to be a founding sectarian rests on his apparent assumption that the 'godly' were to be found amongst the masses of the small-town poor, and that religion could be reformed for their benefit, in preparation for the second coming, by overwhelming their religious and class enemies. However, Müntzer was a theologian obsessed with the mystical movement of the soul to God through tribulation, not essentially a social or political writer. His peculiarities—violent anticlericalism and emphasis on direct inspiration—did not appear consistently, but became more prevalent under the pressure of repeated failures and betrayals. Such influence as he exerted on the sectaries came through followers like Hans Römer, Hans Hut, or Melchior Rinck.[9]

1.2. The 'Swiss Brethren'

As at Wittenberg, so at Zürich, enthusiasts impatient of Zwingli's habitual waiting for the magistrates spread their ideas in private discussion groups. Their earliest leaders included two local parish clergy, Simon Stumpf and Wilhelm Röubli or Reublin (c.1484–1559); two scholar-priests, Felix Mantz (c.1500–27), and Ludwig Hätzer (c.1500–29); and Konrad Grebel (1497–1526), son of a Zürich patrician, a gifted if rather florid humanist and brother-in-law of Vadianus of St Gallen. On the fringes of this group was the theologian Balthasar Hubmaier ('Pacimontanus', c.1481–1528), formerly preacher at Waldshut. By the October 1523 disputation the enthusiasts were publicly dissatisfied with the slow pace of Zwingli's reforms; and beginning to question the appropriateness of infant baptism. In 1524 they were joined by Georg Cajakob ('Blaurock', c.1492–1529), and Johannes Brötli (d.1529), who was made a preacher at Zollikon. By August 1524 Röubli seems to have persuaded several farmers in his parishes of Wytikon and Zollikon to withhold their infants from customary baptism. These protests were accompanied by the refusal of tithes from four villages during 1523–4, by objections raised to rents and mortgages and other 'usurious' payments exacted from farmers, and the disruption of sermons by the city's ordinary clergy.[10]

Baptism, rather than tithe, became the sticking-point, since the Zürich council readily insisted on its being observed (11 August). After a public dispute between Grebel and his allies and Zwingli on 17 January 1525, the city councillors sided with Zwingli and renewed their orders on baptism. On 21 January they ordered Grebel and Mantz to keep silence and expelled several others. That same day Grebel defiantly rebaptized Blaurock and fifteen others in Felix Mantz's house. The group moved out to Zollikon and in the following weeks rebaptized dozens of converts. The Zürich magistrates responded quite patiently. At the end of January Blaurock and Mantz were arrested, briefly imprisoned, re-arrested, and expelled from the city. By November 1525 most of them were back in Zürich where they were imprisoned. Mantz, Grebel, and Blaurock confronted Zwingli, Jud, Vadianus, and others in debate in the *Grossmünster* on 6–8 November, and were released the following March. Hubmaier, also imprisoned, was twice forced to recant his heresy and then expelled. During 1526 the Zürich council made rebaptizing and attending 'anabaptist' meetings punishable by drowning: on 5 January 1527 Felix Mantz, who had sworn to leave Zürich and cease rebaptizing and broken both promises, was drowned by the Zürich executioners in the river Limmat. Blaurock was flogged and expelled in the same month, to be ultimately captured and burnt by the Austrian government in September 1529. Grebel had meanwhile died of disease in 1526.[11]

Röubli and his ally Michael Sattler visited Strasbourg and then made new converts in the Neckar valley in Württemberg (where Röubli had once been a priest). In February 1527 they gathered at Schleitheim, where they debated and adopted the 'brotherly union', also known as the 'Schleitheim Confession'; this creed set out the principles and organization of a pacifist sectarian creed which was to avoid civil oaths, public office, and participation in bloodshed. The Schleitheim Confession seems to have been intended to distinguish Sattler's group of anabaptists from other more erratic enthusiasts who had meanwhile sprung up. While Sattler was at Schleitheim his groups at Horb and Rottenburg were discovered; Sattler was arrested, tried, tortured, and burnt at Rottenburg on 21 May 1527. Röubli was to appear in Moravia.[12]

1.3. *The south German urban sectaries*

Another group of sectaries, largely independent of the 'Swiss Brethren', grew up at more or less the same time in the cities of southern Germany. It owed its origins at least in part to Johannes (Hans) Denck (*c*.1500–27), a Bavarian scholar who via proof-reading at Basle had come to Nuremberg, where he associated with some of the city's heterodox painters. He became influenced by the writings of Müntzer and the later Karlstadt; expelled from Nuremberg, he moved to Augsburg, where in April 1526 he met Balthasar Hubmaier, just driven from Zürich. Hubmaier rebaptized Denck; on 26 May 1526 Denck rebaptized Hans Hut (d.1527), a bookbinder and book-pedlar, and refugee from the defeat of Müntzer's followers in Thuringia. Hut renounced for the time Müntzer's and the peasants' violence, but still earnestly believed that the second coming was imminent. He preached briefly round Franconia; then in 1527 went on to Nicolsburg (Mikulov) in Moravia, where he engaged Hubmaier (based there since the previous July) in debate. Hut was imprisoned, then escaped bringing with him the ex-Lutheran pastor of Nicolsburg Oswald Glait. In due course Hut left Glait at Vienna as pastor to the Austrian anabaptists, whose widespread but ephemeral sectarianism was ruthlessly stamped out by the Habsburg authorities.[13]

In 1526 Denck meanwhile engaged in a pamphlet controversy with Urbanus Rhegius, the chief Lutheran pastor at Augsburg. When a public disputation was proposed Denck abruptly left the city. He moved on to Strasbourg and mingled there with various exotic heretics, but after a public debate with Martin Bucer in December 1526 the city council asked him to leave. Early in 1527 he was at Worms, together with Ludwig Hätzer and Melchior Rinck (d.*c*.1544), a scholar who had passed from Lutheranism to supporting Müntzer. The three converted the local Lutheran preacher Jakob Kautz, but their public opposition to baptism and the hostility of other Lutherans led to their being driven out on 1 July. In August 1527 some sixty anabaptists gathered at Augsburg in the so-called 'martyrs' synod'; Rhegius and his party managed to convince the magistrates that this large gathering was a conspiracy threatening civic peace. In mid-September the protectors and leaders of the group, including Hut, were arrested; Hut was to die mysteriously in prison in December. Denck left Augsburg and made his way to Basle where he was apparently reconciled to Oecolampadius and to more orthodox views shortly before his death the same year. Hätzer was later to be tried and executed in Constance in February 1529 for an adultery allegedly committed at Augsburg.[14]

1.4. *Moravia and the 'Hutterites'*

The margraviate of Moravia ultimately became the nearest thing to an anabaptist refuge. However, their first communities fared badly. In July 1526 Balthasar Hubmaier converted to his views the pastor of the recently formed Lutheran church at Nicolsburg, Oswald Glait. Hubmaier was willing to allow the 'godly' normal dealings with the rest of society; an extremist group, however, wished for absolute separation from society and total community of goods, and actively prepared for the second coming. In 1527 Hans Hut arrived and took the extremists' side against Hubmaier in the ensuing disputation. Soon afterwards the extremists moved to Austerlitz, where they gathered refugees from the Austrian persecutions. Hubmaier, meanwhile, was taken to Vienna and executed in March 1528 for his part in the 1524–5 rebellion at Waldshut. The Moravians were gathered together by the Tyrolean Jakob Hutter (d.1536), who had replaced Blaurock as pastor in the Tyrolean communities when Blaurock was burnt in September 1529. Hutter organized a drift of refugees from Austria to Moravia; and during his own visits to Moravia (the longest in 1533–5) laid the foundations of the highly structured, rigorous, communal life-style of the Moravian 'Hutterite' anabaptists. The communities were temporarily evicted from their refuges in the spring of 1535; Hutter was captured and executed in February 1536.[15]

1.5. *The Strasbourg sectaries*

Strasbourg, like Augsburg, offered a temporary foyer for sectarian dissent. From mid-1524 the gardeners' guildsman Clement Ziegler pressed for immediate reforms in much the same way as others elsewhere. Likewise, in 1526, Röubli, Hätzer, Denck, Sattler, and others arrived, were soon imprisoned, and forced to leave in 1527. Röubli and Kautz (the ex-Lutheran from Worms) ministered to those who remained. In 1528 a further hundred refugees, followers of Hut, arrived from Augsburg. In September 1528 the Tyrolean Pilgram Marpeck (*c*.1495–1556) arrived and joined Röubli's group. He organized a strict, sober, heterodox community; wrote and disputed against Bucer; and was obliged to leave early in 1532.[16]

More striking than 'ordinary' anabaptists, so to speak, were the more free-thinking figures who also gathered in Strasbourg. In May 1529 there appeared Caspar Schwenckfeld (1489–1561), an exiled nobleman from Silesia. He stayed in Strasbourg until 1533, for part of that time as Capito's house guest, and aloof from the other sectaries. He has been called a 'spiritualist'; he disdained to build up a reformed church himself, but by his formidable intellect and contacts made life very difficult for those who were trying to do so. Very different was Melchior Hoffmann (d.1543), a Swabian furrier and lay preacher who came to Strasbourg in June 1529 after preaching the Reformation in Livonia, Stockholm, Schleswig-Holstein, and East Frisia. He gathered a group of loyal followers (the 'Strasbourg prophets'). After several attempts to capture him, the city council finally imprisoned him from 1533 until his death. He contributed a fervent apocalyptic expectation to the movement, which transmitted itself to his followers in The Netherlands and Münster.[17] Despite Capito's partial sympathy, from November 1532 to the 'Strasbourg synod' of June 1533 Bucer and the other clergy brought matters to a head. Leading sectaries were examined; the city clarified its stance on contested issues; in April 1534 irreconcilable anabaptists were ordered to leave. The clergy won the council to their views, but failed to secure disciplinary power for themselves.[18]

1.6. *Melchiorite anabaptists in the Low Countries and Münster*

Between visits to Strasbourg Melchior Hoffmann, based at Emden in East Frisia, had rebaptized many of the dissenters who had emerged in the Low Countries in the mid-1520s. From 1530 to 1531 his followers made conversions in Amsterdam, but the sudden betrayal and execution of several of them late in 1531 made him hesitate. The example of these

Dutch sectaries converted two future leaders, Obbe Philips of Leeuwarden and Jan Matthijs of Haarlem. These two were to lead divergent strains of dissent. Matthijs's followers became ever more vehement and public in their protests, culminating in an armed procession through Amsterdam in March 1534 which led to the execution of many. Philips's group responded to the violence by becoming ever more quietist and undemonstrative.[19]

After the débâcle of the armed demonstration of March 1534 many 'Melchiorite' followers of Matthijs migrated to Münster in nearby West-phalia, where the preacher Bernard Rothmann (c.1495 ?1535) had led the city towards a typical popular civic Reformation, enacted between August 1532 and March 1533. From May 1533 Rothmann had begun to question infant baptism. He weathered the ensuing crisis with popular support and bypassed the city council in the winter of 1533-4. Meanwhile the followers of Matthijs had learned of what was happening the previous autumn. Early in 1534 Rothmann was rebaptized by two followers of Matthijs, and soon afterwards the anabaptists arrived in large numbers. In February 1534 Rothmann's patron Bernard Knipperdolling was made *Bürgermeister*; soon afterwards all those who would not join the anabaptists in their new apocalyptic community were warned to leave.

The prince-bishop of Münster laid siege to the city in late February 1534. In a raid by the citizen army outside the walls Matthijs was killed on 4 April. He was succeeded by Jan Beukelsz of Leiden, who had been the first to bring news of Rothmann's reforms to the Dutch Melchiorites. Beukelsz was responsible for most of the brutal and eccentric behaviour which made the Münster episode notorious. In May he dissolved the city council, appointed twelve 'elders' of his choosing, and imposed a harsh moral code with compulsory polygamy. He executed the leaders of a failed coup against himself late in July (and also executed one of his own wives); early in September he had himself anointed as a universal 'king of righteousness'. By January 1535 the total encirclement of the city made conditions harder and harder; no practical help came from any other anabaptists, and on 25 June the city was taken by storm after the keepers of one of the gates betrayed it. Knipperdolling and Beukelsz were exhibited around northern Germany for some months, then tortured and hanged in irons in January 1536.[20]

2. *Restructuring and Survival, 1535–c.1600*

The violent end of the Melchiorite extremists at Münster was a watershed for all anabaptism, even though Münster itself only involved a tiny minority. Beukelsz's reputation turned states against all anabaptists. Protestantism settled into the civic and political fabric, and established its distinctness from the 'radical' vision. As the sectarians realized that the second coming was *not* imminent, they faced three options: they could compromise with the world like protestant churches, and aspire to 'respectability'; stay separate in remote and tolerant places; or sit tight and worship in secret. As voluntary 'elect' communities they faced two threats (apart from persecution): discontent leading to schism, or apathy leading to extinction. The pacifist Melchiorites, as the 'Mennonites' of north-western Europe, became settled and legal; the 'Hutterites' of Moravia survived in remote regions as long as possible; the remainder, especially those in south Germany, were progressively extinguished.

2.1. *From Melchiorites to Mennonites in the Low Countries*

Even after the capture of Münster, a group of fanatics under Jan van Batenburg (1495–1538) known as 'swordsmen' or 'Batenburgers' indulged in sporadic terrorism in The Netherlands for nearly a decade after 1535. However, after a meeting between moderates from both the non-violent and the militant wings of Melchioritism at Bocholt in Westphalia in the summer of 1536, the pacifists began gradually to take over Netherlands anabaptism. They were led briefly by Obbe Philips (1500–?), the West Frisian barber-surgeon who had led opposition to Matthijs. However, he disappeared from the movement altogether about 1540, to be followed by David Joris (c.1501–56), a glass painter from Delft, who drew many former Batenburgers into a more passive sectarianism. In 1539 thirty-one of Joris's followers were executed at Delft. In 1542 he issued a volume of his writings known as the 'Book of Wonders' (*'t-Wonderboek*); and the following year settled at Basle with his family and some followers, under the assumed name of Jan van Brugge. Nicolas Meyndertsz van Blesdijk corresponded with Joris and sustained his Dutch followers before himself moving to Basle in 1546 and rapidly becoming disillusioned with his leader. After Joris's death in 1556, Blesdijk, interrogated, revealed Joris's identify and his scandalous life; Joris's remains were burnt and his followers submitted to orthodox protestantism in Basle.[21]

The most credible 're-founder' of Dutch anabaptism was, however, Menno Simons (1496–1561), a parish priest from Witmarsum in West

Frisia. Through doubts about the Eucharist and a Lutheran belief in Scripture he came to doubt infant baptism; the repercussions of the Münster episode seem to have shocked him into abandoning his parish early in 1536; he then worked as an anabaptist elder and preacher to about 1540. In that year he issued his 'Foundation Book' (*Fundamentboek*) outlining his communitarian, suffering creed. He taught in Holland during 1541–3, thereafter exclusively in East Frisia (around Emden) and in northern Germany. An encounter during 1544 with Jan Łaski, leader of the hybrid Lutheran Church at Emden, led Łaski to coin the phrase 'Mennonites' (*Mennisten*) to describe quietist, non-Münsterite anabaptists whom he thought should be spared harsh persecution.[22]

From mid-century the pressing issue for the Mennonites was how strict or lenient their discipline should be: whether those excluded from the community should be totally 'shunned' by the 'brethren'. An associate of Menno's, Leenaert Bouwens (1515–?), an elder in West Frisia, by his excessive severity split both the Emden and the Franeker congregations during 1556–7 into rigorists and laxists; the latter became known as 'Waterlanders', who diluted their rejection of civic life, even holding some public office. Discipline, along with theological issues, also split the central and south German anabaptists from Menno and Bouwens in 1557; mutual excommunications followed. After Menno died in 1561 the strict Mennonites were led by Dirk Philips (1504–68), brother of Obbe, an ex-Franciscan who had defended the movement in debate in 1537 and 1546 but remained under Menno's shadow in his lifetime. Under his leadership another schism occurred, this time between the native West Frisian congregations and the 'Flemings' who settled *en masse* at Franeker after Alva's repression forced them into exile. In a row over the choice of a preacher during 1566–7 Philips found himself on the side of the 'Flemings' and Bouwens on that of the 'Frisians' based at Harlingen. There were thus by the outbreak of the northern Dutch revolt in 1572 three distinct anabaptist groups: Waterlanders, from 1575 led by Jan de Ries (1553–1638), 'Flemish' Mennonites, and Frisian Mennonites. During 1577–8 the minority Calvinist church lacked sufficient authority to force a general persecution; William of Orange and the rebel Estates-General adopted a policy of toleration to the various groups, who thus acquired a degree of legal security.[23]

2.2. *The 'golden age' of the Hutterites and its end*

The Hutterites in Moravia enjoyed the best fortunes of all anabaptists up to—but not long after—the 1590s.The earlier, already fragmented, movement having been dispersed during 1535–6, it was reconstructed in the later 1530s by the Bavarian weaver Jakob Amon (d.1542), Ulrich Stadler (d.1540), and the writer and missionary Peter Riedemann (1506–56). Riedemann was one of a number of Hutterite missionaries sent from Moravia into central Germany to draw recruits, the vast majority of whom were executed. Riedemann himself was captured in Hesse in February 1540; Landgraf Philipp kept him in easy confinement in Wolkersdorf castle, where Riedemann wrote his 'Account of our Religion, Teaching, and Belief' (*Rechenschaft*) before finally breaking his 'parole' and returning to Moravia in 1542. After the deaths of Stadler and Amon the Hutterites accepted Leonard Lanzenstiel (d.1565) as their 'overseer'; with Riedemann, he led the communities through a difficult period in which Ferdinand I tried to force the Moravian nobility to revoke their tolerance of the anabaptists. The problems of persecution, dispersal, and a flood of refugees from elsewhere were partially eased when Maximilian II succeeded in 1564. Riedemann's authority as principal theologian of the movement passed on his death in 1556 to Peter Walpot (1521–78), a Tyrolese. He drew up a response to a Lutheran literary attack on the Hutterites in 1557 and succeeded Lanzenstiel as overseer in 1565. At this time the Hutterites enjoyed their 'golden years'; the authorities tolerated them; their structured communism worked; they numbered perhaps as many as 30,000.[24]

The Austro-Turkish war of 1593–1606 concentrated the Habsburgs' attention on Moravia. The Emperor Rudolf II (1576–1612) and the Cardinal Franz von Dietrichstein (1570–1636) levied taxes on the Hutterites for the war effort and introduced militant catholicism at Mikulov and Olomouc. Hutterite numbers, already depleted by the war, were shattered by the decree of expulsion issued on 28 September 1622, which drove them to Slovakia or parts of Germany. Even the most introverted of anabaptist movements was seemingly too much to take.[25]

2.3. *The 'Swiss Brethren' become extinct*

Anabaptist ideas had spread from Switzerland and from the south German cities into the Rhineland and the Low Countries; the remnants of this expansion lingered precariously into the middle of the century. Generally known as 'Swiss Brethren' to distinguish them from the Mennonites on one hand or the Moravian Hutterites on the other, they maintained tiny, mostly rural, communities in the Palatinate, Alsace, Baden, Württemberg, Swabia, and Bavaria. They rarely surfaced; exceptionally, Elector Palatine Friedrich III called some to a disputation at Frankenthal on 28 May– 19 June 1571 and thereafter was fairly tolerant of them, unlike his successors.[26]

Pilgram Marpeck (d.1556), exiled from Strasbourg in January 1532, travelled round Germany and Moravia until in 1541 he settled in southern Germany and gathered a fellowship of followers, including the noblewomen Magdalena and Walpurga Marschalk von Pappenheim. Marpeck also involved himself in a heated debate with Caspar Schwenckfeld (and Schwenckfeld's patroness) during 1542. From about 1544 to his death in 1556 Marpeck worked as a hydraulic engineer to the Augsburg city council. His usefulness and powerful patrons ensured that he was periodically dressed down for holding conventicles, but was not seriously persecuted. Two of his collaborators collected Marpeck's writings in a manuscript known as the *Kunstbuch*.[27] By letters and personal contracts, Marpeck spread his influence as far as Alsace, the Grisons in Switzerland, and Moravia, but very thinly; there were perhaps as few as fifteen 'Pilgramite' communities, mostly rural cells of ten to twenty members. In Augsburg itself no more Pilgramites were punished for holding meetings or evading infant baptism after 1573.[28]

Even in the very seed-bed of the 'Swiss Brethren' in the villages of Zürich canton, they collapsed in the late sixteenth century. Under Bullinger's headship Church and State united to threaten anabaptists with imprisonment, confiscation, or exile, while denying them martyrdom. Cells survived in the villages on both sides of the lake of Zürich. In April 1589 one group passed a 'supplication', composed by Andreas Gut of Zwillikon, to the cantonal authorities. In that year sixteen anabaptists were arrested at Horgen, on the south side of the lake. In 1608 more steps were taken against them in Horgen and its neighbours, Wädenswil and Hirzel. Under the pastor J. J. Breitinger, Zürich effectively exterminated its anabaptists during 1613–14.[29]

3. *New 'Heresies' in Eastern Europe*

In Poland and Transylvania the broadly 'Calvinist' camp, established since the 1540s and 1550s, split during the 1560s and 1570s into orthodox reformed, who wished to adhere to the usual beliefs of the Swiss, Dutch, and Rhineland churches, and more free-thinking, extreme groups. The latter usually rejected the traditional understanding of the Trinity, especially the relationship between Christ and God the Father, so as to go beyond the pale for catholic and orthodox protestant alike. Some also held 'heretical' opinions about baptism and participating in public office, which brought them close to anabaptism. By the end of the century such groups acquired a formal identity as 'Unitarian' or 'Socinian' churches, with synodal structures, noble patronage, and legal recognition.

3.1. *From antitrinitarianism to Socinianism in Poland*

Protestantism was only established in Poland in the negative sense that no one could punish it; so the nobility were free to choose more unorthodox creeds. Piotr Giezek of Goniądz ('Gonesius', *c*.1530–*c*.1571), a product of the Paduan school of philosophy, returned to Poland in 1555 and first presented his eccentric views on the Trinity at the 1556 synod at Secemin. He was denounced and excluded at the reformed synod of Pińczów in 1556 and condemned as an anabaptist at Wodzisław in 1558. However, at a synod in Brest in Lithuania Gonesius impressed Anna Kiszka, sister to Prince Mikolaj Radziwiłł; she installed him as preacher on the family estates at Węgrów. In the late 1550s the Radziwiłłs took up two other future sectarian leaders, Marcin Czechowić (1532–1613), and Szymon Budny (1538–?).[30] Protestant 'heresy' in Poland was further encouraged by Italian émigrés, the more eccentric of whom had been forced to move on by mainstream protestants elsewhere in Europe. One, Francesco Stancaro (d.*c*.1574), ironically encouraged ideas which *limited* Christ's participation in the Godhead, by teaching the exact opposite too energetically. During a visit to Poland in 1559–60 he denounced as 'Arians' (heretics who denied or minimized Christ's divinity) mainstream reformers like Melanchthon, Łaski, and Lismanini. The row was aired at a series of synods during 1560.[31] In response to Stancaro the Piedmontese Giorgio Biandrata (*c*.1515–88) suggested abandoning the description of the Trinity found in the creed of Nicea, in favour of simpler, biblical—but also 'Arian'—language.[32]

Biandrata's suggestion bore fruit in the early 1560s in the hands of Grzegorz Pawel (1526–91), the real founder of Polish 'Unitarianism'. At synods at Książ and Pińczów in March 1562 Biandrata persuaded Lismanini to abandon the Nicene creed. Pińczów itself became a centre for both Italians and antitrinitarian ideas. Pawel published his *Table of the Trinity* in November 1562, and his group won support from the judge Jan Niemojewski and Czechowić's Lithuanian followers.[33] An 'orthodox' Calvinist backlash, led by Stanislas Sarnicki and Christoph Tretius, caused King Sigismund Augustus to issue an edict expelling the Italian 'apostates' on 7 August 1564; the reformed church in Poland was finally split by the debate at Piotrków in March 1565.[34] The radical, antitrinitarian group under Pawel and his allies with the nobles Niemojewski, Lutomirski, Filipowski, and Siennicki confronted Sarnicki and Tretius, who eventually withdrew after heated debates. The antitrinitarians, eventually to be known as the 'minor Church', met as a group for the first time at Brzeziny in June 1565 and again at Węgrów in December, to discover how widely they disagreed among themselves over baptism (at what age, and whether total immersion or 'sprinkling'), pacifism, and office-holding.[35]

In 1569 Grzegorz Pawel founded a sectarian community of anti-trinitarians on woodlands belonging to the noble Jan Sieninski at Raków near Sandomierz. The community took up weaving, pottery, and paper-making, and attracted all sorts of antitrinitarians. Contacts with the Moravian Hutterites, superficially similar to the Racovians, proved abortive; instead Raków reorganized itself from 1572 under the Cracow apothecary Simon Ronemberg. One tension, however, remained: between the militant, socially conservative Lithuanian followers of Szymon Budny, who were taking the denial of Christ's divinity to the extreme of ceasing to pray to him; and the more conventional, but pacifist and communistic, Racovians under Ronemberg.[36] Yet another Italian found a way out of the impasse, this time Fausto Sozzini of Sienna ('Faustus Socinus', 1539–1604), who came to Poland in 1579 and joined the Racovians in 1580. He sided with them against Budny, and brought his own distinctive theology to Polish Unitarianism, especially over the Trinity and the atonement. He tried, and ultimately failed, to have baptism omitted altogether; total immersion became the rule. Nevertheless, the Raków *Catechism* of 1605, produced under his influence, became definitive for the 'Socinian' churches, and was to outlast the suppression of Raków (1638) and the exile of the Socinians from Poland (1658).[37]

3.2. *Unitarianism is established in Hungary and Transylvania*

In Transylvania many of the same forces were at work; here 'Unitarian' ideas won over even more leading protestant clergy. Stancaro visited Transylvania in 1554 and became court physician to the *voivode*; for spreading his peculiar ideas Stancaro was attacked in print during 1555, and defeated in debate by Ferenc Dávid and other Kolozsvár clergy in 1557. Stancaro's challenge, and Biandrata's response, probably had the same effect here as in Poland. The Magyar-speaking reformers Kaspar Heltai and Ferenc Dávid played a similar role to Grzegorz Pawel. Just when the Magyar 'Lutherans' under Ferenc Dávid had formally lapsed into 'Calvinism' at the synod of Nagyenyed in 1564, Giorgio Biandrata appeared as physician (and part-time diplomat) at Sigismund Janos Zápolya's court. Up to 1565 Dávid, court preacher to Sigismund Janos at Gyulafehérvár, was steadily won over to Biandrata's ideas. In 1566 the issue came to a head in a sequence of synods, culminating in a confrontation in April at Gyulafehérvár, where Biandrata and Dávid engaged Méliusz in debate.[38] Thereafter the Transylvanian reformed Church moved steadily towards formal Unitarianism. In 1567 Biandrata and Dávid replaced the (Calvinist) Heidelberg catechism with an explicitly Arian one at Torda; whereat Méliusz summoned an orthodox Calvinist synod of his own at Debrecen. On 28 January 1568 a royal edict extended formal religious toleration to Unitarians as well as catholics, Lutherans, and Calvinists. From about 1569 Unitarianism became the most powerful protestant creed in Transylvania; Kolozsvár became its spiritual focus, with a prolific press managed by Dávid's associate Kaspar Heltai.[39]

After the death of Sigismund Janos II on 15 March 1571 the post of *voivode* (regional governor under the Sultan) of Transylvania passed in rapid succession to the catholic Stefan Báthory and, when he became king of Poland in 1574, to his elder brother Christoph. Unitarianism became dangerously linked with the failed rebellion of the Székely population under Kaspar Békés in 1575. Moreover, some elements in Transylvanian Unitarianism drifted from denying Christ's place in the Godhead to ceasing to worship him altogether. By the synod of Torda in 1578 Fausto Sozzini and (ironically) Biandrata were desperately trying to restrain Biandrata's pupil Dávid from suspending both the sacraments and Christ worship. Biandrata ultimately had the *voivode* and the Kolozsvár council arrest Dávid, who died in prison in November 1579. A splinter group of Dávid's followers under Andras Eössi nevertheless turned to 'Judaizing', restoring the mosaic ceremonial code, worshipping on the Jewish sabbath, and abandoning the Christian sacraments altogether. It was among these followers of Dávid, who seem to have influenced the Lithuanian followers of Szymon Budny in their practices, that the rejection of medieval Christian worship was taken to its most eccentric extreme.[40]

The eastern European Unitarians differed, of course, from the central and northern European anabaptists (except perhaps the Hutterites) by enjoying and cultivating the support and protection of the powerful. They were also more formidable in intellectual strength and numbers. However, all these movements breached the boundaries, whether of social cohesion or of loyalty to the basic agreed standards of belief and practice, which the mainstream protestants observed. They followed the logic of their beliefs without much compromise or moderation. They are exceptions which help to define the rules by which the main Reformation worked.

4. *Religious and Social Teachings*

The greatest single difficulty to be found in setting out the teachings of the sectarian movements is their variety.[41] No rigid scheme or pattern can fit even a majority; while any attempt to do justice to their diversity in a short section can only confuse. However, one can examine just a few features of the thought of some of the most prominent or influential of the sectaries, simply for the contrasting light which it sheds on the distinctive features of the mainstream, or as it is sometimes called, the 'magisterial' Reformation. For this purpose most use will be made of elements of the mature teaching of the 'Swiss Brethren' and the later Dutch Melchiorites, especially under Menno Simons. These were the least eccentric and flamboyant of the various anabaptist groups, and the closest in their training and attitudes to the mainstream reformers. The ways in which they differed from the latter, therefore, are especially revealing.[42]

4.1. *Justification and regeneration*

Many of the sectarian writers echoed the language of the Reformation on justification by faith.[43] At the very least, they echoed its *negative* emphases, condemning the medieval Church's penitential system, the belief that 'grace' could be predictably bestowed by an earthly institution, that 'pious' acts done within the context of Church ritual could acquire a kind of 'merit', and so forth. However, it is less certain that they understood or endorsed the *positive* determining principle of Reformation theology on this issue. The reformers' classic dogma that man was saved by an 'alien' righteousness 'draped' over his continuing sin ensured that 'the saved' would still, in themselves, be real sinners who could in no sense deserve God's favour, and might appear no different from the 'hypocritically righteous' who were not so saved. 'Sanctification', the visible evidence of the growing work of grace within men, would always be incomplete and impossible to judge by external standards.[44] This subtlety seems to have been lost on the earliest anabaptist leaders. Konrad Grebel taught that a sinner was converted by the preaching of the Word, and thus brought to a point where he would abandon his sins and turn to a 'new life'. This new life would be the fruit of a real faith; if the believer persisted in this way and avoided sin, he could be sure of salvation.[45] Menno Simons developed this into a theory of the soul's progress from a state of servile fear which led to repentance; the soul was then given the 'gift of faith' in which the divine nature lost at the fall was restored; the knowledge of the Gospel then led to love of God and its outpouring in 'fruits of the Spirit'.[46] Denck and Hut, possibly following Müntzer, elaborated the so-called 'Gospel of all Creatures': the 'creaturely' state of man would be affected by the 'redeeming word that suffering is the way of all', leading to an 'interior baptism' or conversion.[47] Some anabaptists, therefore, rehabilitated man's 'free will' to do good.[48]

This vision of human salvation conflated and combined the processes of 'justification' and 'sanctification', which the main reformers had kept *logically* separate.[49] In pastoral terms, it combined protestant and—surprisingly—catholic features. The Reformation made justification a once-for-all act of God in forgiving sins, rather than a piecemeal, cyclical process; it also detached the state of 'being saved' from the apparent moral condition of the soul at any given moment. Catholicism linked the 'state of grace' to the actual moral state of the soul, but then insisted that souls were saved by the bit-by-bit process of sacramental purification. The anabaptists took from the reformers the once-for-all nature of salvation, but then harnessed salvation to the visible state of the believer's soul as the catholics did. So, anabaptist believers were expected to experience a sudden transformation in their lives, and not to lapse back again to their old ways. This composite attitude made stricter—and perhaps more unrealistic—moral demands than either of the faiths which it opposed.

Did this mean that the anabaptists thought that after regeneration they could actually live without sin, and that they could be 'perfect'? It seems that while some enthusiasts like David Joris did, the more sober majority did not. There was not to be a 'perfect' or 'sinless' church.[50] Menno Simons and his follower Dirk Philips were aware of the charge of 'perfectionism' and refuted it. However, the inner logic of their arguments required them to strain after sinlessness, to strive to be as perfect as possible, and to regard moral lapses in a very serious light. Melchior Hoffmann apparently taught that someone who tasted the Christian life and abandoned it was irretrievably damned.[51]

4.2. *Baptism*

The pastoral practice even of the moderate anabaptists in two crucial areas—baptism and excommunication—reflected precisely this seeking after a degree of personal and corporate purity in a way utterly alien to the Reformation mainstream. The baptism of adult believers was the most public and, to majority sixteenth-century opinion, the most shocking, anabaptist deviation. It was the act by which the first 'Swiss Brethren' marked themselves off, and was taken up by several sectaries like Hubmaier or Hoffmann who had not stressed it at first.[52] Since for *converts* it actually meant a second baptism, it implied contempt or profanation of the first (catholic) baptism. All anabaptists agreed that the baptism of infant children who could not understand the preached word or enter into any 'covenant' to lead a Christian life was of no value or effect. Despite this there was much disagreement as to what the rite did achieve in adults: whether its effects were inherent, or whether it simply testified to a transformation which had already happened.[53]

Nevertheless, the ritual marked a psychological turning-point. Zwingli remarked how anabaptist converts claimed that in baptism they felt a sudden great release of tension at the moment of baptism;[54] he also remarked that this same sudden (artificial) reassurance used to be produced by sacramental penance. Denck and Hut saw the exterior baptism as the second part of a three-stage process, consisting of the interior conversion, the external 'covenant' (baptism), and finally the personal testimony in blood (martyrdom). Hoffmann described baptism in highly emotional terms as a 'nuptial union'.[55] At the very least baptism was a 'sign of a change in the inner man, a new birth, a washing away of sin, and accordingly a pledge of obedience to Christ and of the purpose to "walk according to Christ"'.[56] Menno denied that God's grace could be bound into a physical element, but saw the transformation of the soul, achieved through preaching and understanding, as a prerequisite before baptism could be given.[57]

4.3. *The Church and 'separation'*

Those who were baptized were initiated into a community which had set itself apart from the rest of society. Whether they regarded themselves as 'perfect' or 'sinless' in a theological sense is less important than that anabaptists by their *actions* represented themselves as a spiritual élite, more godly than the rest, for whom neither contamination nor backsliding was acceptable. From Grebel's thought onwards the Church was seen as a voluntary society of those who confessed their faith, forsook sin, and gave evidence of a new and holy life.[58] The visible Church was to strive to resemble the invisible society of true believers, the elect: members should recognize the 'divine nature' in each other.[59] Hence the 'marks' of the Church recognized by Menno Simons or Dirk Philips were much more subjective and more exclusive than among the reformers: they included 'unfeigned, brotherly love', 'discipleship', 'evangelical separation', and 'oppression and tribulation'.[60]

Negatively, the believers' Church was defined by 'separation': separation of the Church from the rest of the sinful world, and separation of its own unworthy members from the fellowship. Instead of the community reforming itself wholesale (as in the Reformation), the Church was to remove itself from the world: 'believers were to separate themselves from the unbelieving mass and to unite in the fellowship of believers.'[61] Such unity between believers, and separation of believers from the mass, was emphasized in articles 3 and 4 of the Schleitheim confession.[62] Among the Mennonites this principle of 'non-conformity to the world' became enshrined visibly, and controversially, in the principle of marrying only those within the sect.[63] It also prohibited believers from participating in the secular state. Taken to extremes it produced the exiled, self-sufficient, communistic Hutterite colonies.[64] The profound social implications of this attitude are discussed below.

Since the Church was separate from the world, and contained the baptized minority who had turned from sin, it followed that it had to exercise discipline by excluding, banning, or 'shunning' those members who fell short of or rejected its standards. In the unstable state of affairs where former followers of Müntzer, violent Münsterites, or other enthusiasts were being confused with those 'Swiss Brethren' or pacifist Melchiorites who sought the high moral ground, it was inevitable that rival groups should mutually anathematize each other.[65] However, once such communities were established the object of discipline was more to punish moral failings than (as in the medieval Church) to punish errors of belief or offences against the hierarchy. The normal punishment for grave sins committed by a baptized believer was not simply exclusion from communion (the most to which the disciplinarian protestant reformers aspired) but total separation from the anabaptist community.[66] Among the sixteenth-century Mennonites discipline became progressively ever more severe, producing several schisms between extremists and moderates. One congregation banned the wife of an excommunicate because she refused to 'shun' her husband altogether. It may be that, as the psychological pressure of maintaining a high moral standard became more oppressive, anabaptists felt the need to punish lapses more harshly so as to confirm the remaining members in their loyalty to the code.[67]

4.4. *Church and State*

Almost from the very beginnings at Zürich, the moderate anabaptists saw themselves as alienated from the secular State, as they were from secular society. Grebel held that Church and State operated on different and exclusive levels. The Church had no right to try to use the mechanisms of the State to endorse its regulations.[68] (The contrast with mainstream Reformation teaching and practice is obvious.) The idea that a magistracy might arise which would consist of 'Christians' (i.e. anabaptists) was allowed as a possibility, but non-Christian magistracies were to be kept at arm's length.[69] In a kind of exaggerated version of Luther's 'Two Kingdoms' theory, some anabaptists acknowledged that the State used violence legitimately—but not Christianly—to punish evil-doers.[70] Most important of all, however, believers separated themselves from the State, as well as vice versa. The vast majority of anabaptists could not envisage taking part in any form of worldly magistracy in which they would be required to consent to or order judicial execution. They for the most part refused to swear the judicial oath, including the oaths required of the citizens of self-governing cities. They would not engage in any military activity or obligations.[71]

In some of the earliest phases of the sectarian movement this estrangement from ordinary society can be explained by a practical expectation of sudden change, either the imminent end of the world and the second coming, or the duty of Christians to make war on ungodly society and reform it to their standards.[72] However, the degree of real anticipation of the end of the world varied. Alienation from the State, in the case of the 'Swiss Brethren', may rather have resulted from disillusionment with the compromises on which the world (in which case the Zürich council) insisted before reforming religion.[73] Moreover, estrangement from the state became more, not less marked after the catastrophes of the 1524–5 rebellions and the 'kingdom' of Münster. Its prime manifestation was in the Hutterite communities, who asked for nothing more from secular society than land on which to settle and to be left in peace.[74]

The morphology of the sects is a fascinating topic in itself worthy of the vast literature it has generated. For this survey, however, the point is that, whatever their primitive intent, the sectaries very rapidly opted out of the essential social and religious process which was the Reformation. First, they rejected the crucial principle that believers' 'sanctification' was always incomplete: that even the saved were, in reality, as much sinners before God as the damned. So they believed that the elect could be known, and therefore that the elect, not the community, could constitute the limits to the Christian Church. For them, the Reformation 'coalition' moved from being distasteful to become wrong on principle. Of the other non-anabaptist sectaries, 'Spiritualists' like Schwenckfeld rejected all visible forms in worship, and 'Rationalists' (Unitarians) rejected the otherwise agreed

Christian position on the Trinity.[75] Though interesting, these also can fairly be regarded as marginal to the major themes surveyed here.

However, the Reformation of whole political units or 'communities' could break down even without conscious sectarianism. In due course 'conventicles' of Calvinist worshippers (in particular) in France and the Low Countries would find themselves in practice, though not in principle, forming 'gathered churches' of the persuaded (though not, as they would have insisted, of the elect). The difference between anabaptist and 'confessional' groups might at times have seemed to be one of attitudes and goals rather than of visible behaviour.

19

Crisis, Survival, and Compromise in Politics

In Germany or France the lay patrons of the Reformation, while responding to popular pressure for religious change, had also to look carefully over their shoulders at their political overlord. It never proved possible, despite some hopeful attempts, to persuade any German Emperor or French king formally to adopt the Reformation on the same basis as Roman Catholicism. So, for most of the sixteenth century establishing the Reformation in Germany or France entailed at some stage defying the sovereign's will. During much of the crisis of 1517–22 Luther probably expected to face trial and execution. To preserve his spiritual and moral integrity was his chief aim; bodily survival, let alone self-defence, mattered less. Lay rulers, however, who took the political risk of adopting the Reformation had thereafter to use all their political skills to preserve their lives, estates, and power. The Reformation, for cities and princes alike, became the focus of purely political allegiances and manœuvres, the morality of which was governed by much the same rules as any other political decision. That change entailed much heart-searching and conflicts of principle between clerics and laymen.

1. *German Politics to 1555*

The Reformation became *the* issue in the *Reichstag* for over thirty years from 1521 onwards. It determined the German princes' attitudes to the Emperor, the popes, and each other. In an older school of Reformation history, deriving from the work of Leopold von Ranke in the early nineteenth century, the movement's entire history was written around these political stresses.[1] Although this kind of narrative political history has lost favour recently, it is still clear that calculations of political risk played a major role in the story; and that various secular governments followed different religious policies because of such calculations.[2]

1.1. *The Nuremberg* Reichstag, *1522–3 and 1524*

The papal bull of 3 January 1521 and the edict of Worms of 26 May should, in principle, have deterred not only the Saxon Elector but all supporters of Luther from further action. In the event, the 'establishment' of various types of Reformation provoked repeated interventions by the Emperor Charles V, his brother Ferdinand of Austria, and the popes in the religious question in Germany. On 21 August 1521 Charles V and François I went to war; on 1 December Pope Leo X died. The papal vacancy and the short reign of Adrian of Utrecht (Adrian VI) distracted Empire and papacy alike from the Luther affair. On 17 November 1522 the *Reichstag* reassembled at Nuremberg, where the new pope sent his legate Francesco Chieregati, bishop of Teramo (1522–39). During December and January the legate offered to reform *disciplinary* failings in the Church, but insisted that Luther's utterances against official *doctrine* be suppressed. The Estates of the *Reichstag* would not allow the issues to be thus separated. On 5 February they claimed that harsh repression of Luther would be looked on as a defence of the Church's faults and would lead to popular rebellion; conversely, their price of supporting the Church against Luther was a 'Free Christian Council' in Strasbourg, Mainz, Cologne, or Metz. They then reiterated (7 February) the 'Grievances of the German Nation' in an especially full form. The closing edict or *Recess* of this *Reichstag* of 6 March ordered the Estates themselves to ensure that 'only the Gospel according to the interpretation of Scripture now approved and received by the Church' was taught in their jurisdictions until a future council.[3]

These encounters set the tone for the first part of the 1520s. The new Pope Clement VII (Giulio de' Medici, 1523–34), appointed Lorenzo Campeggio (1474–1539) as cardinal and papal legate for German affairs. Campeggio arrived at the Nuremberg *Reichstag* (resumed January 1524) in mid-March and tried to cajole the Estates into enforcing the Worms edict. In the ensuing *Recess* of 18 April the Estates promised only to observe the edict 'in so far as they recognize themselves as bound to it', and 'as far as it was possible to obey and implement it'; and suggested that a German national council at Speyer should discuss religion pending a general council.[4]

1.2. *Speyer, 1526, and the Turks*

The insecurity caused by this failure to resolve matters showed itself in the informal leagues formed among both catholic and reforming princes in the 1524–6 period.[5] The *Reichstag* convened at Speyer under Archduke Ferdinand's presidency on 25 June 1526 in this heated atmosphere. The archduke's opening speech called for immediate implementation of the Worms edict. The Estates prevaricated until Ferdinand cut short the debates by reading on 1 August Charles's letters (written on 23 March) forbidding further innovations. Three days later the imperial cities declared themselves unable to comply with the edict; the *Recess* of 27 August resolved that each of the Estates would govern their own affairs 'as [they] hope and trust to answer to God and his Imperial Majesty'. This meant that the eventual solution—to leave control over religion to individual sovereign bodies within the Empire—was already adopted as a temporary expedient for want of any practical alternative.[6]

Even without the princes' leagues, the Habsburgs could not have enforced their edict for military reasons. On 22 May 1526 François I of France, the pope, the duke of Milan, and the doge of Venice had concluded the League of Cognac, wiping out some of Charles's gains by his victory at Pavia in 1525, threatening his position in Italy, and moderating his pro-papal enthusiasm. From April 1526 the Ottoman Sultan Suleiman I (1520–66) led one of his most successful invasions of south-eastern Europe, defeating a Hungarian army at Mohács on 29 August, wiping out the last Jagiellon king, Lajos (Louis) II, and a substantial number of the Hungarian nobility. From then until 1527 Ferdinand was thoroughly occupied striving for the thrones of what was left of Hungary and of Bohemia.[7]

1.3. *Speyer, 1529*

Meanwhile the political temperature was raised by Philipp of Hesse's belief in Otto von Pack's forgeries and his aggressive response to them.[8] For this and other reasons (such a new accord between Emperor and pope), the *Reichstag* which met again at Speyer on 21 February 1529 was much less sympathetic to the Lutherans than that of 1526. Ferdinand's opening address on 15 March expressed horror at the widespread religious changes, forbad further 'violence ... against ancient usages and customs', and declared that the terms of the first Speyer *Recess* were no longer to be 'expounded at every man's pleasure'. On 6–7 April the majority in the *Reichstag* resolved that religious changes should be halted, and that 'sacramentarian' errors (meaning reformed ideas which denied a physical presence of Christ in the communion) should not be tolerated.[9] The minority who had adopted the reforms, however, had already prepared their objections to the expected resolution. On 19 April they submitted a *Protest* against the abrogation of the 1526 *Recess*. When they were refused permission to have their protest registered among the official acts of the session, they published on 25 April the *Instrument of Appeal*, stating their resolve to abide by the decisions of 1526. On 22 April Electoral Saxony, Hesse, Strasbourg, Ulm, and Nuremberg came to a secret understanding to defend each other if attacked. The very same day Philipp issued his invitation to Zwingli to what became the Marburg colloquy. Theological rifts thwarted unity with the Swiss; but in spite of that, southern German cities (hitherto aligned with Zürich) and Lutheran princes jointly subscribed to the 'Protest' and so earned the name of 'Protestants'.[10]

1.4. *Augsburg, 1530*

After the Treaty of Barcelona with the papacy (29 June 1529), the Treaty of Cambrai with François I (3 August 1529), and his imperial coronation at Bologna (24 February 1530), Charles V finally found himself free to devote all his energies to tackling the 'Protestant' threat, as he saw it. He summoned the *Reichstag* for 8 April; it eventually opened on 20 June at Augsburg. From mid-March the Saxon elector canvassed his theologians for opinions as to how to respond to the summons. By May Melanchthon had formulated a *Confession* and *Apology* defending the Lutherans from the charges of extreme heresy and defining their position as closely as possible within the Church's tradition. The confession was compiled from the *Schwabach Articles* (drafted by Luther in the summer of 1529 and published just after the Marburg talks) and fresh statements on Church rites and rules drafted at Torgau in March; it was formally approved by Luther, signed by the Lutheran princes and the cities of Nuremberg and Reutlingen, and submitted at the third session of the Augsburg *Reichstag* on 25 June. Strasbourg, Constance, Lindau, and Memmingen submitted their own 'Four Cities' Confession' or *Tetrapolitana* on 11 July.[11] The catholic majority regarded the Augsburg Confession as a heretical document to be examined and judged. In private, Melanchthon offered vast concessions in the search for an accord with the Emperor's humanist secretary Alfonso Valdés and Campeggio. However, the catholic response (orchestrated by Johann Eck) was to produce a *Confutation* of the confession, not wholly reactionary, but in no way helpful to unity. On 26 August Luther wrote to advise Melanchthon to abandon the search for compromise. On 22 September Charles proposed in the *Recess* that the

Worms edict be suspended until the following April and that meanwhile the protestants should prevent further changes and muzzle their printing presses. The princes and cities renewed their protests and left the *Reichstag*. The final decree of 19 November left the Worms edict in force and threatened both armed and legal measures against the protestants after 15 April 1531.[12]

1.5. *The League of Schmalkalden and continuing tensions*

As seen earlier,[13] the princes' direct response to the Emperor's threatening moves was to form the League of Schmalkalden as a regular, permanent forum for the defence of those protestant states who joined it. Thereafter the question was not whether the protestants could be brought back into the fold, but for how long war between catholic and protestant states could be averted. Sultan Suleiman's invasion in mid-1532 led to the Peace of Nuremberg on 23 July 1532. Its signatories had their prosecutions in the imperial court or *Reichskammergericht* suspended. However, the catholic League of Halle from 1533 fomented prosecutions of non-signatories to the Nuremberg peace, such that the imperial court was repudiated by all protestants in January 1534.[14] The protestant princes flexed their political and military muscles by restoring Ulrich of Württemberg in 1534 and protestantizing Braunschweig-Wolfenbüttel in 1542. In the 'Wittenberg Accord' of May 1536, Bucer and his allies with the help of Melanchthon and Bugenhagen arrived at a formula on the Eucharist which obscured the question of the Eucharistic presence and glossed over remaining theological differences. The Wittenberg Accord resulted partly from experience gained in arranging for Lutheran and south German reformed clergy to co-operate in Württemberg and Augsburg. It was, no doubt, a spurious piece of semantic juggling; its political importance lay in that the Lutherans sought and agreed a *doctrinal* accord with their south German allies: the League of Schmalkalden no longer represented two rival and potentially hostile creeds.[15]

The position began to threaten once more when the pope summoned a General Council to Mantau, and the protestant rulers had to decide whether to ignore it or not. Differences between the clergy and the politicians were thrashed out at Schmalkalden in February 1537 and the summons was defied.[16] In August 1538 the League concluded a defensive alliance with the king of Denmark. The imperial vice-chancellor, Held, cajoled catholic princes into the League of Nuremberg in June 1538; but before it could act the Turks and the French went to war again, the council was prorogued (eventually to meet at Trent in 1545), and negotiations restarted. Ferdinand

and the Elector Joachim II of Brandenburg, a conservative with reforming sympathies, suggested a purely *political* accord between the parties in Germany to allow for joint action against the Turks. Long and delicate talks at Frankfurt, held under the constant threat of war, led on 19 April to the 'standstill' agreement, which gave a short period of truce and an end to legal harassment of protestants, but also blocked any extension of the League of Schmalkalden and the further conversion of Church lands to secular uses.[17]

Several factors had delayed a decisive resolution of the religious division of Germany during the 1530s. Besides the obvious external threats from Suleiman and François I, the catholics would not negotiate realistically, the papacy seemed incapable of initiating a General Council of the Church, and the protestant princes were united. During the 1540s the foreign threats remained, but the catholics became more conciliatory, the council was summoned, and the protestants started to quarrel amongst themselves.

1.6. *Catholic moderates*

By the late 1530s a group of moderate theologians emerged as the leaders of catholic thought. They combined an earnest wish to reconcile the protestants to the catholic Church, with a theology of salvation close enough to that of moderate protestants to make agreement with them seem possible. Prominent among them were Julius Pflug (1499–1564), Dean of Meissen, and the lapsed protestant Georg Witzel (1501–73); also Johann Gropper (1503–59) of Cologne, and his mentor the Netherlander Albert Pighius (1490–1542). This group engaged in talks with conciliatory protestants, notably Bucer and Melanchthon. Bucer and Witzel tried at Leipzig in 1539 to produce a hybrid reform programme for the duke of Saxony.[18] After an unsuccessful attempt at Hagenau in 1540, delegates assembled at Worms in November 1540. Discussions took place publicly between Melanchthon and Eck from 14 January 1541, and privately between Bucer and Gropper much earlier. Bucer and Gropper produced a draft compromise agreement on a host of major issues, including original sin, justification, and the authority of Scripture.[19]

The Worms draft was discussed during the meeting of the *Reichstag* at Regensburg from April to July 1541. With the catholics represented by Pflug and Gropper as well as Eck, the pope by Gasparo Contarini, and the protestants by Melanchthon, Bucer, and the Hessian Johannes Pistorius, a more conciliatory group could hardly have been found. Over late April and early May an agreement was reached, to the participants' own astonishment, on justification. However, accord soon proved impossible on the

Eucharist, penance and absolution, and the pope and the Church. Worse still, both Luther and the Roman Curia rejected such draft compromises as had been reached. By the end of the *Reichstag* on 29 July 1541 the religious issues had to be referred again to the proposed General Council, and the 'standstill' agreement was renewed for a further eighteen months. Fatal damage had been done to the plan of resolving the religious split by negotiation; and fatal discredit brought (as noted earlier) upon the conciliatory group at the papal court.[20] Finally, the plan which had been concocted between Bucer and Gropper to introduce moderate 'catholic reform' in the electoral archbishopric of Cologne under its Archbishop Hermann von Wied (1515–47) collapsed when Bucer and Gropper quarrelled in 1543 and, after appeals to pope and Emperor, the archbishop was publicly deposed on 3 July 1546.[21]

1.7. *Rifts and scandals among the protestant princes*

At sessions of the *Reichstag* at Speyer (February–April 1542) and Nuremberg (July–August 1542 and January–April 1543) the protestants repeatedly quibbled over giving help and money to fight the Turks and the French unless their protests (above all about the behaviour of the *Reichskammergericht*) were discussed.[22] Yet the protestant princes' position had been seriously weakened by a series of scandals and disputes. During 1539–40 Philipp of Hesse had cajoled Bucer, Luther, and Melanchthon into authorizing his secret second marriage to a lady-in-waiting at his court, and the secret soon leaked out. As a result Philipp, notoriously guilty of the capital crime of bigamy, found no help from other members of the League of Schmalkalden against the Emperor or the *Reichskammergericht*; while Charles V blackmailed him into agreeing on 13 June 1541 to cease some of his diplomatic activity and stop new accessions to the League of Schmalkalden.[23] Thus, when Duke Wilhelm of Jülich-Cleves petitioned to join the League of Schmalkalden in 1542–3, Philipp blocked his admission; this allowed Charles V to force the duke to submit, surrender Guelders and Zutphen, enter a marriage alliance with the Habsburgs, and renounce the Reformation. Moreover, Philipp, unlike the cities and lesser princes, raised no objection to Charles's demands for money at the *Reichstag* at Speyer during February–June 1544.[24]

The invasion of the lands of Duke Heinrich of Braunschweig-Wolfenbüttel by Philipp of Hesse and Johann Friedrich, elector of Saxony, in 1542[25] could be justified as defence of the protestant towns of Goslar and Braunschweig; however, the feud between the belligerents was older than the Reformation, and the *coup d'état* was unpopular with many princes. A worse rift opened up in the early 1540s between the two branches of the ruling house of Saxony over ecclesiastical lands. In 1541 the elector of Saxony intruded the Lutheran theologian Nikolaus von Amsdorf as protestant bishop of the see of Naumburg, in spite of the regular election of the catholic Pflug by the chapter, and his endorsement by the *Reichstag* in 1545. This issue, and a dispute over Wurzen, an estate of the bishops of Meissen, estranged Duke Moritz of Albertine Saxony, a recent Lutheran convert, from the Ernestine Saxon-Hessian axis of protestant power.[26]

1.8. *The Council of Trent and the Schmalkaldic War*

Charles V had accepted the temporary religious truces on the strict understanding that they were provisional arrangements until a General Council of the Church was called. On 30 November 1544 a papal bull formally summoned a council to Trent, in the Adige valley on the frontiers of Italy and the Tyrol, for 15 March 1545; it was actually to open on 13 December. Charles mistakenly expected that it would act entirely as an agent of his German policy, and both he and the council fathers rapidly lost patience with each other. However, it deprived the protestants of one of their oldest excuses for not co-operating with the Emperor.[27]

Although the *Reichstag* at Worms (March–August 1545) prepared for another pointless religious conference (held at Regensburg, January–March 1546), by this stage it was clear that the Emperor was resolved on using force to end the schism.[28] He secured large grants of men and money from Rome and from the Spanish Church. At the Regensburg *Reichstag* (June–July 1546) he formally rejected the protestants' demands on the council and the *Reichskammergericht*. He meanwhile made treaties with the pope, the dukes of Bavaria, duke Moritz of Saxony, and two Hohenzollerns, Hans von Küstrin and Albrecht Alcibiades of Brandenburg-Kulmbach. By these treaties Charles doomed the actual restoration of Roman Catholicism before he began, since he knew that the papacy could not endorse the promises which he had made to his (Lutheran) Saxon and Brandenburger allies. His main objective, however, was to destroy the political and military power of the *Landgraf* of Hesse and the elector of Saxony. Charles justified his attack as a punishment of these two for the Braunschweig-Wolfenbüttel affair, concealing the religious character of the war as best he could.[29]

After the Schmalkaldeners' general Sebastian Schärtlin von Burtenbach's swift march down into the Tirol in July, matters settled down into a bloodless campaign of strategic marches by the two matched armies around the Danube valley. By November the protestants had run out of money and Johann Friedrich of Saxony was forced north to repel an invasion of his lands by Duke Moritz. The south Germans were left to their fate: in December Schwäbisch-Hall, Ulm, and later Strasbourg surrendered, while the Elector Palatine and duke of Württemberg were glad to make favourable terms with Charles. In the spring of 1547 Charles joined up with Moritz of Saxony's army in Saxony. By 24 April the imperial and League armies confronted each other across the river Elbe at Mühlberg, between Dresden and Torgau. The imperial army outflanked its opponents and routed them; Elector Johann Friedrich was taken prisoner shortly afterwards, and his capture ensured the capitulation of Wittenberg (19 May) and Gotha (30 May). Duke Moritz was instantly given his promised reward of Johann Friedrich's electorate, and Philipp of Hesse was induced to surrender to Charles on 19 June.[30]

1.9. *The Augsburg* Reichstag *and the* Interim

Charles V had broken up the protestant leagues, but only by exploiting existing jealousies, humiliating only his most dangerous opponents, and in effect giving up a complete restoration of catholicism.[31] When the 'violent' or 'iron-clad' *Reichstag* met at Augsburg on 1 September 1547, the pope had moved the council to Bologna in the papal states and conducted its business in disregard of Charles's diplomatic needs. Charles had to try to impose a provisional or 'interim' settlement, essentially a moderate catholic reformation, on the *Reich*; he used a reform sketch based on the work of Gropper and Pflug, and took advice on it himself when the *Reichstag* would not help. His victory thus turned into administrative and political chaos. When the bulk of the protestant princes rejected a first form and it was amended, the catholic princes then refused to adopt the revision. In the end Charles had to publish the 'Imperial Clarification of Religion' (the *Interim*) on 15 May 1548 as a creed and law for the protestants only, with a separate reform edict for the catholics.[32]

Enforcing it was a nightmare. The south German cities took oaths from their clergy to obey it and expelled the recalcitrant (Osiander from Nuremberg, Musculus from Augsburg, Brenz from Schwäbisch-Hall, Bucer from Strasbourg, and Blarer from Constance); Constance was actually absorbed by Austria in October 1548 and re-catholicized. In Württemberg only force brought obedience; there proved to be insufficient clergy to operate the new system. In Albertine Saxony Moritz and the Wittenbergers rejected the *Interim* and laboriously negotiated their own version, the Leipzig *Interim*, in November–December 1548, the only practical result of which was the wearing of surplices by the clergy; in Ernestine Saxony and northern Germany resistance was nearly total.

Charles had to be content with the spiteful and pointless exercise of emasculating the constitutions of the Swabian cities. Augsburg and Ulm were thus dealt with during 1548; in 1551 Charles's official Heinrich Has toured the remaining cities suspending their charters and installing new corporations (catholic where possible) submissive to the Emperor. With grim humour the new councils were known as *Hasenräte* ('rabbit councils') in a pun on the official's name.[33]

1.10. *The Princes' War*

By late 1551 Charles's fragile alliance was, predictably, itself breaking up. Elector Moritz of Saxony, disillusioned with Charles's treatment of him and in fear for his own security, negotiated with Hans von Küstrin, Albrecht of Prussia, and Johann Albrecht of Mecklenburg, who had allied at Königsberg to defend protestantism. He then treated with Henri II of France, who by the Lochau heath agreement of October 1551 and the treaty of Chambord of 15 January 1552 agreed to subsidize a protestant revolt against Charles V in return for the chance to take Cambrai, Metz, Toul, and Verdun unresisted. In the event, the 'Princes' War' (*Fürstenkrieg*) was a private affair between Moritz, Wilhelm of Hesse, and the brigandly Albrecht Alcibiades of Brandenburg-Kulmbach on the one hand and the Habsburgs on the other. The Ernestine Saxons, Württembergers, and most Hohenzollerns stayed aloof. In March 1552 Moritz drove Charles from Innsbruck to refuge at Villach in Carinthia; but then allowed himself to become involved in long talks with King Ferdinand at Passau. Their peace treaty of 10 August 1552 postponed the religious issue to the next *Reichstag*. Albrecht Alcibiades then changed sides to fight for the Emperor in Alsace, returning to Saxony only to be defeated by Moritz at Sievershausen (9 July 1553); Moritz himself died of wounds two days later.[34]

1.11. *The Augsburg* Reichstag *of 1555*

Thoroughly disenchanted with the nightmare of imperial politics, in June 1554 Charles left the forthcoming *Reichstag* entirely to his brother. When it opened at Augsburg on 5 February 1555 Ferdinand, astonishingly, still wanted a religious reunification of the *Reich*; but the electors swung the assembly round to the plan of a detailed religious peace. The next few months were spent sorting out the detailed legal consequences—especially for Church property—of the peace. The death of Pope Julius III on 23 March and Charles's refusal to be involved on 8 April doubtless cleared the air. The terms were settled by 25 September, and provided, in essence, for sovereign princes and lords to choose to follow either the Augsburg

Confession or catholicism, and thereby to determine the faith of their subjects, who could emigrate if dissatisfied. Free cities were allowed to adopt Lutheranism only on condition of accepting some residual or restored catholic worship within their walls.[35] However, several elements of the peace, above all a provision forbidding further protestantizing of prince-bishoprics, were not accepted by all. Even the exclusion of non-Lutheran protestantism was soon diluted by the advent of Calvinism. The *Interim* died quietly, and affairs returned to a more fixed version of the state in which they had been after 1526.[36]

2. *Political Theory: From Non-Resistance to Godly Rebellion*

The reformers, it was remarked earlier, were painfully conscientious revolutionaries, whose grasp of principles was usually sounder than their understanding of political realities. Their response to the foregoing political challenges shows this clearly. Individual clerics and preachers sought to keep their consciences unsullied by declaring that they would never resist lawful authority by force; but territorial rulers, responsible for large populations, could not establish the Reformation in their states and then, at the theologians' bidding, make no efforts to defend their states from the political consequences. The history of sixteenth-century protestant political theory is one of the progressive erosion of the principle that the Gospel should not be propagated or defended by violence. In this erosion pressure of circumstances played a part; but so did the politicians' determination not to have their security undermined by the hesitations of their ideologues.

The reformers' primary imperative was to return to what they saw as New Testament principles, including Romans 13: 1–5:

Let every soul be subject unto the higher powers. For there is no power but of God: the powers that be are ordained of God. Whosoever therefore resisteth the power, resisteth the ordinance of God: and they that resist shall receive unto themselves damnation. For rulers are not a terror to good works, but to evil ... He is the minister of God, a revenger to execute wrath upon him that doeth evil. Wherefore ye must needs be subject, not only for wrath, but also for conscience sake.

Luther's doctrine that political obedience to the ruler was a Christian obligation was first clearly formulated in the early 1520s, in his *Of Good Works* (1520) and above all his *Secular Authority: To What Extent it should be Obeyed* (1523).[37] He regarded the authority of rulers over their subjects as akin to the authority of fathers over their children. Although good rulers should indeed be 'fathers to their people', failure to live up to that standard did not deprive them of divine sanction. Luther knew perfectly well that most princes in his day were inept, unqualified, and immoral.[38] By insisting that secular authority ruled by the ordinance of God, Luther incorporated government securely into his theology. Even regenerate believers, according to Luther, remained prone to the same sins as the rest of mankind; to that extent they, like other people, needed to be restrained by secular discipline. This discipline fitted into the theory of the 'two regiments' or ways in which society and Christian life was regulated.[39]

In Germany life was not quite so simple. All kinds of powers could claim to be 'sovereign'; the argument as to whether the Emperor alone, or both the Emperor and the territorial princes, could command the highest authority in law-making, and war and peace, was a long-standing debate among imperial lawyers.[40] By that token Luther—protected as he was by the elector of Saxony—might from the start have suggested that princes were also 'powers that be' as envisaged in Romans 13. He did not. On 5 March 1522, warning Elector Friedrich that he was about to disobey his instructions and return to Wittenberg, Luther urged his patron not to resist the Emperor's officials if they came to arrest Luther once he had emerged from hiding.[41] Much later, when in 1529–30 Luther was presented with arguments from Philipp of Hesse's lawyers to the effect that territorial princes were 'sovereigns' of equal standing with the Emperor, he explicitly repudiated them, convenient though they were.[42]

This high-minded but impractical stance was nevertheless the basic starting-point for almost all the other reformers who worked in Germany or France. Melanchthon in his *Common Places*, and early English Lutherans like Barnes and Tyndale, wrote in a similar vein about the duties of subjects to obey their rulers, however imperfect those rulers might be.[43] Calvin himself insisted for successive editions of the *Institutes* that all rulers, good and bad, were appointed by God.[44] Even Zwingli, exceptional in so many ways, spoke of the need for government to regulate man's lower nature, and of the duty of obedience set out in Romans 13. As a citizen of a city-republic he was well aware of the risk of tyranny and abuse of power within monarchies: he taught that an unworthy ruler should be censured by the pastors, but still obeyed by the people 'until the Lord removes him from the seat of authority or a way is found whereby those whose duty it is may deprive him of his functions and restore order'.[45]

However, from the twentieth-century perspective 'obedience' and 'subjection' to rulers can easily be misunderstood. The reformers did *not* teach 'unlimited and unqualified obedience to established powers'.[46] 'Obedience', as commended by Luther and the other reformers, meant not defying the will of the ruler with violence. It did *not* extend to willing co-operation with 'ungodly' commands. Rulers, Luther said, were the 'masks of God', bound by obligations; if they commanded something directly contrary to God's will, they must never be obeyed. Hence in that same letter of 5 March 1522 just quoted, Luther excused his disobeying the Elector, claiming that the call to take charge of matters at Wittenberg was a case where 'God should be obeyed rather than man'.[47] In due course a ruler who insisted on upholding the Roman Catholic faith would be seen as making precisely such an 'ungodly' demand. However, Luther was even ready to recommend that where a ruler commanded something which was manifestly unjust in the secular sphere, or declared an unrighteous war, he should be denied the co-operation of Christian subjects.[48] All this was very far from the insistence of twentieth-century totalitarians that their subjects owe allegiance heart and soul to every decree of the State whatever.

The options left open to those bound in conscience not to co-operate with 'ungodliness' were limited. Only passive disobedience was countenanced: believers should act true to their beliefs and face the consequences. Calvin agreed that the only choices open were to flee the country or endure punishment with fortitude.[49] The basic primordial doctrine of the reformers on political duty, then, was one of discriminating co-operation, and if need be passive disobedience to the ruler's will.[50] It was a teaching appropriate to private individuals, especially to those élite souls willing to face martyrdom. After the establishment of the Reformation within certain states of Germany, however, it could only embarrass cities and princes in a complex political quandary in the mid-1520s. The doctrine had to go; and it soon did.

A diverse medieval heritage of arguments could be called upon to justify active resistance to a properly constituted regime. The most sophisticated anti-monarchial ideas of all had been propounded by theologians and canon lawyers in the period of the Great Schism and the councils.[51] Theologians like Gerson held that authority in the Church on earth ultimately derived from a General Council, and that in appointing its head the body of the community (the Church in this case) transmitted authority to the ruler in trust on its behalf. Since the Church and secular government ought both to reflect the paradigm of a 'perfect' society, Gerson was able to suggest that in *all* political societies power was held by the ruler not absolutely, but in trust for the people.[52] The Italian legal tradition, represented in the sixteenth century by Renaissance scholars like Andrea Alciati and Mario Salamonio, held the same basic principle, that power was held by rulers in trust for the people, and must be wielded by their consent.[53]

A second legal tradition claimed that the Holy Roman Empire was more complex than a 'mere' monarchy. Late in the twelfth century a celebrated dispute had arisen over whether the 'inferior magistrates' in the Empire could wield some of the same kind of authority as the Emperor.[54] The imperial 'Golden Bull' of 1356 gave great importance to the electoral princes, and furthered a drift towards an almost 'federal' concept of Empire.[55] Such ideas were propounded in the early sixteenth century by another humanist lawyer, Ulrich Zasius of Freiburg. In this tradition the Emperor could be seen as much less powerful in the Empire than a king in his kingdom, limited by a host of privileges and previous decisions.[56] Finally, a third legal tradition extended the Roman private law right of self-defence to the judicial context. According to the fifteenth-century canon law commentator Niccolò de' Tudeschi ('Panormitanus'), a judge who proceeded outside his own jurisdiction or with 'notorious injustice' might lawfully be resisted by his victim with violence. This theory tended to develop into a general principle that 'force might lawfully be resisted with force'.[57]

There was nothing particularly scriptural, or even theological, about these arguments. The reformers hesitated to meddle with them, and only yielded to them under political pressure. Having once made the vital concession, protestant writers, including Luther, adapted and extended their arguments and gave them a more specifically religious flavour. However, the adoption of a more sensitive theory of political obedience was a major departure from original principles, quite different in kind from the 'coalition' which created the reformed churches in the first place.The steps towards this change coincided with each of the short-term crises and threats to the reformed faith described in the previous section.[58]

During the league-forming between rival groups of princes in the mid-1520s Luther would only make the modest concession that if the Lutheran princes were attacked by a league of catholic princes acting *without* the Emperor's permission, then the Lutherans might defend themselves.[59] The real crux came with the Speyer *Reichstag* of 1529, the 'Protestation', and the Augsburg *Reichstag* of the following year. In 1529 Johannes Bugenhagen broke ranks by writing to Elector Johann of Saxony that if the Emperor meddled with religious affairs outside his own sphere, the princes could not only disobey but resist with force.[60] In December 1529 Philipp of Hesse tried to persuade the elector of Saxony and Georg of Brandenburg-

Ansbach to his jurists' opinion that the 'powers that be' included princes as well as the Emperor, who were bound by reciprocal obligations. Luther refused to be convinced by this argument.[61]

After the Augsburg *Reichstag* the elector of Saxony obtained from his chancellor, Gregor Brück, by October 1530, a series of lawyers' opinions justifying the formation of the league of protestant princes on the private law argument that if the Emperor were to attack the Lutherans before the Church council had met he would be using 'unjust force' and might be resisted within the terms of imperial law.[62] Elector Johann summoned Luther and his colleagues to Torgau during 25–8 October 1530 to put the lawyers' arguments to them. At the end of the meeting the theologians announced their conversion to an at least grudging acceptance that the lawyers' position might be valid. They announced that they would no longer invoke the New Testament in direct opposition to the case being put forward by the lawyers.[63] What their 'conversion' really meant is disputed. Two contradictory points have emerged. First, the reformers did not positively or warmly embrace theories of lawful resistance at Torgau; they only conceded that they *might* after all be valid in the legal sphere. They showed their hesitancy by making the alternative recommendation that princes should simply refuse to co-operate with the Worms edict, so that without their aid a restoration of catholicism would soon collapse. Secondly, having once opened the door to violent resistance, the reformers did not try to backtrack once the crises were past, but actually developed and amplified the arguments. Their *initial* hesitancy, then, gradually matured into a willing, considered defence of resistance.[64]

In 1536, 1539, and 1550 Lutheran writers showed how they were moving ever further away from passive disobedience. In 1536 Melanchthon and his colleagues submitted pieces of advice (*Gutachten*) which endorsed the view that hostile actions by the Emperor would amount to 'notorious injustice'; and claimed that German princes had a *duty* to protect and defend their Christian subjects from unjust violence, even when it came from the Emperor.[65] It was natural for Melanchthon, who had already been more keen to see princes as the 'chief members' of the new churches, to portray them as those churches' protectors as well.[66] In 1539 Luther endorsed most of the existing arguments, but more strikingly added others of his own. The propagandists of the Schmalkaldic League had already devised the notion that if the Emperor were to act against the Lutherans not in his own right, but simply as the 'pope's hireling', his actions could be resisted. Luther embellished this by pointing out that in a truly Christian commonwealth the pope with his hybrid form of authority had no place:

he was a monstrous deformity like the *Beerwolf* (a German folk-tale monster), whose ravages on Christian people had to be resisted at all costs and without hesitation.[67]

Meanwhile outside Saxony other writers had similarly changed their tune.[68] A second wave of theorizing was generated when Duke Moritz of Saxony laid siege to Magdeburg in the last stages of Charles V's war. In April 1550 the city pastors led by Luther's former colleague von Amsdorf published a famous *Confession* in which they justified their resistance to the Emperor's forces. By this stage the arguments for lawful resistance were basically twofold: first, the 'constitutional' principle that 'lesser magistrates' had a right or a duty to restrain monarchs from unjust acts against true religion; and secondly the 'private law' theory of lawful resistance against a judge's unjust violence.[69] The intellectual arguments to justify and defend acts of violent resistance to a tyrannous ruler were articulated by Lutheran writers in the 1530s and 1540s, such that several scholars agree that there was little distinctively 'Calvinist' content in the resistance theories produced by the writers of the 'Calvinist' movement after 1550 at all: the Lutherans had prepared the ground for them.[70] This view is disputed by those who see a greater preoccupation with changing ungodly worship, and suppressing idolatry, among Calvinists than Lutherans; but that issue concerns the motivation *behind* the resistance rather than the moral reasoning used to justify it.[71]

Perhaps more important is that the contexts for Lutheran and 'Calvinist' resistance theories were very different, and the ideologies which they produced therefore had distinct nuances. Early 'Calvinist' movements either relied on noble support and a weak monarchy (as in eastern Europe) or on keeping quiet and lying fairly low while the ruler was hostile, as in France.[72] In France, the Low Countries, or the British Isles the peculiar German situation of well-established territorial princes contending with the Emperor did not obtain in the same way. The rulers of these countries, Henri II, Charles IX, Philip II, or Mary Tudor, could send officials to persecute individuals and whole communities if they chose—as Charles V could not, say, in Saxony. The question posed of French or English theologians was not, as in Germany, 'may some prince lawfully put an army into the field to defend his subjects against his (nominal) sovereign?'; it was, 'how does a ruler forfeit the right to be regarded as a ruler?' or 'how minor an official may count as a "lesser magistrate" and lead opposition to the king?' Religious rebellion, rather than religious warfare, had to be justified.[73]

Calvin's own response to these problems was hesitant and his writings on the subject fragmentary. From the very first edition of the *Institutes* in 1536 he admitted that there *might* be, in certain states, officials who, like the 'ephors' of Sparta, were responsible to the people for 'restraining the wilfulness of kings': in such instances their religious duty was to perform their constitutional obligations.[74] However, he was vague about how this principle might be applied in practice. Secondly, Calvin offered tantalizing suggestions that princes who claimed that 'God was not to be served and honoured' were 'no longer worthy to be counted as princes'.[75] His most subversive comments along these lines, however, appeared in biblical commentaries published after his death; works accessible to fellow theologians and clergy, but hardly political manifestoes. Calvin's strongest card was a wholly traditional insistence that rulers who made ungodly demands were to be disobeyed, and God obeyed rather than man. The same attitude was taken, equally firmly, by Pierre Viret.[76]

Hard-line Calvinist defenders of revolution were those pamphleteers who wrote under the pressure of some spectacular persecution: John Knox, Christopher Goodman, and John Ponet in the time of Mary Tudor's burnings in England, or François Hotman, Théodore de Bèze, and Philippe Duplessis-Mornay in the France of the religious wars. This wave of propaganda sharpened the analysis of what kind of rulers could really be regarded as 'ordained of God'. Knox, Goodman, and Ponet in different ways laid aside the idea that a thoroughly bad ruler must still be 'ordained': if he was ungodly, the people had been mistaken in allowing him to rule in the first place. In the view of Duplessis-Mornay's *Defence against Tyrants* a ruler who turned to 'ungodliness' had forfeited the right to his kingdom, and could expect to forfeit control as well.[77] Secondly, the idea of 'lesser magistrates', which had been at first a face-saver to allow for constitutions where the ruler was not absolute, became a guiding principle. François Hotman's *Francogallia* actively sought out such magistrates in the French constitution, while de Bèze's *Right of Magistrates* combined arguments from actual law with those drawn from more basic principles of what *any* state should be like.[78]

It is hard to avoid the conclusion that the political theory of 'godly' resistance or rebellion was shaped and conditioned by political circumstances. Obvious as this may seem, for circumstances to shape beliefs reverses the pattern found in the rest of the Reformation. The theological principles of the Reformation both transcended and pre-dated the events within which they became practical realities. The new political theories, on the other hand, only arose after the context had made armed resistance by the princes inevitable; and the major outpourings of ideas occurred at particular flash-points in the story. England after 1560 had a protestant queen, so its political theory (with Goodman and Knox shut out of the kingdom) was strictly monarchist; when a protestant prince became heir to the French crown in 1584 it was catholic thought which suddenly became republican and protestant attitudes loyalist.[79]

However, the theologians' responses to the political dilemma *were* of interest to others besides just theologians. It was important that the Reformation should be *seen* to be defended in accordance with law and morality, and not just by crude force. Some (only some) of the writings discussed here did much to justify the reformed cause: the Magdeburg Confession and the works of the Huguenot pamphleteers above all. The anti-monarchist writings in English became an embarrassment to their authors' supporters only because of the unexpected death of Mary Tudor and the sudden collapse of the Guise regime in Scotland. Such public writings helped to reconcile the protestant public to the changes which had befallen the original principle that the Reformation should restore 'religion within the community'. Other, more academic treatments of the theme in *Gutachten* or biblical commentaries must be presumed to have reached few people beyond the clergy itself. Yet the most persuasive defence of resistance was far simpler than all these.

3. *Teaching by Example: Martyrs and Warriors of the Gospel*

To the popular mind, involved arguments drawn from Roman or canon law, history, or political theory to justify resistance to persecution probably made much less impact than teaching by *example*. Throughout the later sixteenth century protestant writers depicted the edifying way for a Christian to practise principled disobedience to his superiors. Although both passive and active disobedience were portrayed, the former was usually depicted as more dignified and more heroic: the reformers' original preference for non-violent resistance to ungodliness still remained their highest ideal. Most major protestant churches produced their 'martyrology', a literary memorial to those who took their passive disobedience of catholic rulers and judges to the bitter end. These collections grew in number and bulk to become a part of the corporate heritage of their movement, no less than confessions of faith or catechisms.

Martyrologies needed individual victims to celebrate. The first Lutheran martyrs, members of the Augustinian house at Antwerp, were executed at Brussels as early as July 1523, and the Habsburgs' Netherlands probably witnessed the largest number of executions for religion before 1555— though most of the victims were anabaptists.[80] Elsewhere, the Reformation was set up community by community (in Germany, Scandinavia, Switzerland, and eastern Europe), where the risk to individuals was slight; or else it was cultivated by furtive, conformist, 'Nicodemite' dissent as in France, which was hard to detect. Therefore *comparatively* few people within the orthodox Reformation fell foul of the law before the mid-1540s; the bulk of the martyrs, and the wave of martyrologies, began with the activities of Henri II's *Chambre ardente* from 1547, with Mary Tudor's persecutions in England from 1555 to 1558, and with the sudden emergence of active, public, Calvinist communities in France, the Low Countries, and the duchy of Savoy in the late 1550s and early 1560s.[81]

This literature was partly stimulated by one major exception to the pattern, the massacre of the Waldensian or 'Vaudois' communities of the Luberon in Provence, which erupted in 1545 after five years of legal wrangles.[82] The Vaudois' *social* pattern of completely voluntary, unofficial, and semi-public heretical activity, most unusual for the early Reformation, almost certainly owed more to their medieval heretical traditions than to protestantism.[83] Without effective patrons among the aristocracy, they were thus exposed to armed attack like few other protestants of the time. The massacre itself followed a pattern set by the pogrom carried out in the Dauphiné in 1487–8, although there were many more victims in 1545.[84] The killings in Provence caused an enormous scandal, and abundant details became known when the perpetrators were put on trial at Paris in 1550–1. In 1554 Jean Crespin (*c.*1520–72) published the first edition of his *History of the Martyrs*, containing what became the definitive account of these massacres.[85] This account of the first major religious massacre was copied and reissued by numerous others for the following hundred years.[86]

Most of the martyrs celebrated in Crespin's martyrology were, however, private individuals caught out by François I's and Henri II's tribunals carrying protestant books, reading Bibles in the vernacular, or discussing religion with indiscreet neighbours. Once caught, such people behaved quite differently from their heretic predecessors in the Middle Ages. In the past those accused of heresy used to deny before their judges— sometimes quite honestly—that they had ever heard of the 'criminal' opinion or belief which they were supposed to have held. Most heresy trials ended with an 'abjuration'—a formal renunciation of wrong belief by the victim and promise to live and believe like a good catholic thereafter.[87]

Protestant martyrs, however, took a quite different line. A trial was regarded as an opportunity to confess one's beliefs boldly and defy the judges to their face in the name of the Gospel. Hence there were far more executions than in the past, as obstinate (technically, 'pertinacious') heresy carried the death penalty; under the *Chambre ardente* and Mary Tudor death became the normal punishment for protestant 'heresy'.[88] The declarations made by quite ordinary protestants in the face of burning made the most potent propaganda texts. Perhaps in recognition of this threat, the French authorities in mid-century reputedly burned the record of the trial with the victim.[89]

Crespin's work was copied and imitated in all the major protestant communities of Europe. Between 1554 and 1557 Ludwig Rabus (1524–92), a native of Memmingen educated at Strasbourg, Tübingen, and Wittenberg, published from his final workplace at Ulm a massive martyrology in German, incorporating some of Crespin's material.[90] Matthias Flacius Illyricus (1520–75), an ultra-Lutheran controversialist otherwise chiefly known for his work on the *Magdeburg Centuries* of Church history in the mid-century, published in 1556 his *Catalogue of Witnesses to the Truth*: though most of this was designed to show that the Lutherans had respectable and heroic medieval forebears, elements from the martyrologies were built in as well.[91] In 1563 Heinrich Pantaleon (1522–95), whose religious allegiances wavered during his life, issued a Latin martyrology based partly on Crespin; exceptionally, he used the sufferings of the martyrs to show not the heroism of the one true way, but the evils of religious intolerance and persecution.[92] In 1559 there appeared the chief martyrology of the mainstream protestants of the Low Countries, the *History and Death of the Pious Martyrs* of Adriaen van Haemstede (*c*.1525–62), while the first anabaptist equivalent appeared in 1562.[93] Perhaps the largest and most celebrated of these works, John Foxe's *Actes and Monuments*, appeared in its first full-length English edition, after partial Latin sketches of 1554 and 1559, in 1563. This combined the aims of Crespin and Flacius Illyricus. On one hand Foxe celebrated in epic fashion the martyrs of the 'true Church' down the ages who had resisted the tyranny of Rome, culminating in copious and generally accurate accounts of the trials of Mary Tudor's victims; on the other he used the evidence of such resistance to the papacy since the eleventh century or so to show that the protestant Church was not the 'novelty' which some of its opponents claimed.[94]

However, protestant propaganda writers did not just narrate the heroic endurance of defenceless victims of persecution (as they saw it). They also commemorated armed rebellion. Here again the former 'Waldensian' heretics were important. In February 1560 the duke of Savoy, newly restored to his duchy following peace between the French and the Habsburgs, began to take action against his heretic subjects. The latter were already well supplied with ministers sent from Geneva, and had begun to establish formal churches in the valleys leading up from Piedmont to some of the Alpine passes. When persuasion and threats failed, the duke resorted to sending in troops. In a series of skirmishes the 'Waldensian' protestants of Savoy defended themselves so energetically that the duke was forced to call a halt, pardon his subjects for their rebellion, and grant them, by a treaty of June 1561, limited rights of protestant worship within their enclave.[95] For reformed propaganda this military victory was immensely important. Detailed narratives were issued as separate books in 1561 and 1562; they were then incorporated into the martyrological literature and general histories of the period, even those written by moderate catholics.[96]

Accounts of the Waldensian rebellion in Piedmont of 1560–1 showed 'godly rebellion' actually at work in the countryside. Following Calvin's instructions, their ministers told the villagers to escape to the mountains with their belongings when the soldiers approached. The people, however, knew that this way they would soon be starved out. So:

Certain other ministers ... wrote to them [those who advised flight] ... that in such an extremity and necessity, it was lawful for them [to defend themselves]; especially, the quarrel being so just, that is, for the defence of true religion, and for the preservation of their own lives, and the lives of their wives and children; knowing that it was the Pope and his ministers which were the cause of all these troubles and cruel wars, and not the Duke.[97]

The duke as the pope's misguided assistant could, then, reasonably be resisted.[98] The same account went on to relate how the clergy accompanied the mountaineers to lead them in prayer before battle and keep them in order, such that they terrified their enemies simply by the sound of their group prayers.[99] Yet the lesson was clear: the clergy acquiesced in armed resistance with reluctance, and insisted that it must be 'holy' warfare, conscientious and restrained.

In comparison the even-handed accounts of the Schmalkaldic War written by Johannes Sleidan (1506–66) in his *Commentaries* on events in the reign of Charles V were mild stuff.[100] The prevailing impression, whether from theory or from propaganda, was that the Reformation was defended by political and military means only when no other course was feasible. How much better, if possible, to restrain the persecutor by force of persuasion alone. In the 1540s and 1550s major reformers devoted much time to writing to monarchs like François I or Henri II, sometimes with the backing of German princes or Swiss cities, to try to make those kings desist from shedding their own subjects' blood.[101]

Alternatively, protestants could escape to a friendly country. Exile communities of protestants sprang up all over Europe at times of persecution: French reformed churches in 1540s Strasbourg, and later of course at Geneva;[102] Dutch and French churches in England under Edward VI and Elizabeth;[103] English churches in Frankfurt, Strasbourg, Zürich, Geneva, and elsewhere in the reign of Mary;[104] Italian communities in Geneva and Zürich, or even in the very south-eastern corners of Switzerland close to Milan.[105] Such diplomatic efforts and displacements of people were almost always politically embarrassing; but once again, they conformed to the reformers' original ideals. The priorities of politicians and devotees were very different.

20

Reformers at Odds
The 'Confessional' Reformation

Since the early Reformation devised a new religious order for each effective political unit, and the movement comprised diverse and independent minds, it was natural—and not in itself alarming—that different churches and allegiances should grow up. If each of these 'churches' had confined itself to its native territory, and disagreements between them had avoided acrimony, no political harm need have been done: the damage caused *within* Germany by the strife between Zwingli and Luther, serious as it was in 1529, was at least partly repaired by 1536. However, as the century progressed the various ideal patterns of a true 'Reformation' tended to become ideologically fixed and—what was worse—politically self-sufficient. Loyalty came to be owed, not to a community whose church was reformed in this or that way, but rather to the manner of Reformation itself, to the 'creed' or 'confession' which embodied that particular vision of protestantism. In short, while the early Reformation movements often consolidated political loyalties within a state, the 'confessional' movements set up an external standard of a 'perfect' church, and so tended to strain or even divide those loyalties.

1. *Lutheran Controversies, c.1540–c.1580*

Nowhere were the results of 'confessional' antagonisms more obvious than in Germany. However, the spread of 'Calvinism' there can only be understood against a background of Lutheranism weakened by ideological and personal infighting among its second-generation leaders. Luther's death in 1546 and the defeat of the leading protestant princes in the Schmalkaldic War precipitated unprecedented internal strife within the Lutheran Churches. Quarrels had already begun between Lutheran theologians before 1546; without a living arbiter or referee, no one could judge between two parties of roughly equal standing who both claimed to represent Luther's legacy.

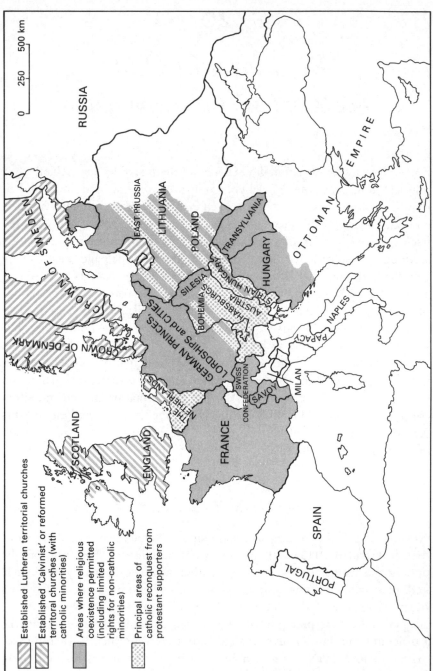

MAP 5. The Religious Complexion of Europe, c.1600

Established Lutheran territorial churches

Established 'Calvinist' or reformed territoral churches (with catholic minorities)

Areas where religious coexistence permitted (including limited rights for non-catholic minorities)

Principal areas of catholic reconquest from protestant supporters

RUSSIA

CROWN OF SWEDEN

CROWN OF DENMARK

EAST PRUSSIA

LITHUANIA

POLAND

TRANSYLVANIA

SILESIA

BOHEMIA

HABSBURGS

AUSTRIA

S'THAN HUNGARY

HUNGARY

GERMAN PRINCES, LORDSHIPS and CITIES

THE NETHERLANDS

SWISS CONFEDERATION

SAVOY

MILAN

FRANCE

SCOTLAND

ENGLAND

SPAIN

PORTUGAL

OTTOMAN EMPIRE

NAPLES

PAPACY

0   250   500 km

1.1. *Two Saxonies, two Lutheranisms*

After the defeat of Johann Friedrich, the new Elector Moritz and his successor August (1553–86) received not only the electorate from the Ernestines, but also the lands, city, and university of Wittenberg.[1] The Ernestines therefore established their own university at Jena (chartered in 1558 but active earlier); the two universities thereafter tended to reflect the different policies of the two branches of the Wettin house. Because Moritz initially made terms with Charles V, his Wittenberg under Melanchthon's guidance became eclectic, moderate, and revisionist in theology; the defiance of the Ernestines was symbolized by the so-called 'Gnesiolutherans' or 'ultra-Lutherans' at Jena, who emphasized the distinctively *Lutheran*, as opposed to just protestant, character of their creed. The alignment of parties was of course more complex than that; but political rifts, personal jealousy, and ideological strife clearly fed on each-other.

1.2. *The 'Adiaphorist' controversy*

The first quarrel arose directly out of the post-war conditions of 1548. Moritz, as noted earlier, negotiated in late 1548 the Leipzig *Interim*, by which numerous peripheral details of traditional worship were (in theory) supposed to be restored. Melanchthon, who had after all been ready to make similar concessions before in 1530 and 1541, acquiesced in the proposal, on the grounds that such details were 'matters indifferent' (*adiaphora* in Greek). He expected (correctly) that neither the *Interim* nor the Emperor would last much longer. In contrast Nikolaus von Amsdorf (1483–1565), Matthias Flacius Illyricus (1520–75), and Nikolaus Gallus (1516–70) set up a rival school of Lutheranism in Magdeburg, which sustained an epic resistance to both Moritz and the *Interim* until the city surrendered on favourable terms in November 1551. After the *Interim* was buried the 'Gnesiolutherans', Amsdorf, Flacius, and their allies, still persecuted Melanchthon and the so-called 'Philippists' over their acquiescence in 'popish' ceremonial.[2]

1.3. *The 'Majorist' and 'synergistic' controversies*

The hostilities continued on a broader front, however, because Amsdorf and Flacius alleged that the terms of the *Interim* had diluted not only the peripherals of the Reformation, but its essence: the rejection of the idea that 'good works' began the process of saving souls; the primary insight which had entailed Luther's rejection of the special status of the Roman

Church. The 'Gnesiolutherans' in effect accused the moderates of selling out to the Emperor and the catholics. Melanchthon's allies, on the other hand, believed that an 'ultra-Lutheran' approach to this question threatened the foundation of ethics, the reason for doing *any* 'good works'. The Philippist Georg Major (1502–74) of Wittenberg, with Johann Bugenhagen, attacked the Magdeburg school in 1551 over their charges, to be met by furious rejoinders from Amsdorf. The 'Majorist' controversy spiralled in the 1550s, with Amsdorf making his notorious claim that 'good works' could actually harm man's salvation.[3]

The controversy flared up again in 1555 when the Philippist Johann Pfeffinger (1493–1573) of Leipzig discussed man's 'co-operation' (or, technically, *synergia*) in the process of being converted by grace. Melanchthon and his followers at this period were trying to analyse the way in which conversion *worked*; their enquiry inevitably tended to introduce confusing subtleties and distinctions into the issue of human 'free will', and the question whether a Christian in being converted could contribute his efforts (guided by divine grace) towards the process. In 1558 Amsdorf and Flacius bitterly attacked Pfeffinger's position, too, as crypto-catholic. Ironically, this 'synergistic' controversy split not just the Saxonies from each other but the Jena theological faculty within itself. When in 1557 Duke Johann Friedrich (known at the time as 'the middle one') commissioned a statement on the controversies, Viktorin Strigel, a protégé of Melanchthon's working at Jena, prepared a draft only to find it revised into something much more vitriolic by Flacius Illyricus. When he refused to accept this revised 'Weimar Confutation Book' he was imprisoned, then set against Flacius in a protracted disputation in August 1560. Strigel eventually moved to Leipzig in 1562, while Flacius soon fell from the favour of the Ernestine dukes and became a more marginal figure.[4]

1.4. *The Eucharistic controversy*

In the debates over 'good works' and 'co-operation', the Philippist 'revisionists' had been accused of crypto-catholicism. In another set of controversies over the meaning of the Eucharist, the reverse happened: the Philippists appeared too extremely protestant—too close, in fact, to the Swiss and Calvin in particular—while the Gnesiolutherans preserved the more nearly 'catholic' feature of Luther's legacy. This dispute was sparked off by a treatise written against Calvin's doctrine of the communion by Joachim Westphal (1510–74), a Lutheran preacher at Hamburg, apparently worried by the arrival of Calvinist ideas in Germany. Calvin himself responded with a series of tracts up to 1557 and with passages in the final *Institutes* in 1559. However, Elector Palatine Friedrich III asked Melanchthon for an opinion on a debate about this issue between the academic Tilemann Hesshusen (1527–88), a staunch Lutheran, and the Calvinistically inclined deacon Wilhelm Klebitz, both churchmen at Heidelberg. Melanchthon's opinion was deemed insufficiently 'Lutheran' by the Gnesiolutheran Nikolaus Gallus, and another intra-Lutheran feud ensued. When the theologians of Tübingen University, followers of the south German Lutheran Johannes Brenz, put forward at the Maulbronn colloquy of April 1564 Brenz's own doctrine of the Eucharist, a new rift opened between the Tübingen and Wittenberg theology faculties.[5]

1.5. *The Osiander controversy*

However furious the debates between these different wings of Saxon Lutheranism were, they were largely united in a further storm which blew up around the head of Andreas Osiander, who had fled from Nuremberg and settled at Königsberg in East Prussia after the *Interim*. Two disputations staged by Osiander on 5 April 1549 and 24 October 1550 announced his highly personal theology of salvation, much more revisionist than Melanchthon's. Osiander stressed how Christ's divine nature was somehow 'infused' into the saved believer: he became 'essentially' righteous, not just by imputation. Osiander thus committed what for the senior protestant theologians was the cardinal sin: he muddled and confused the doctrines of justification and sanctification, and obscured the idea of 'imputation'. Melanchthon, Flacius, Amsdorf, and Calvin all wrote against him, the first leading a formal condemnation at the Naumburg assembly on 23 May 1554.[6]

1.6. *The beginnings of reconciliation*

It took some thirty years from the 'iron-clad' Augsburg *Reichstag* before these rifts were partly healed. The two sides favoured different approaches to reconciliation: the Philippists wanted a mild, non-controversial formula to which everyone should subscribe, after which the theologians would bury their hatchets. The Gnesiolutherans wanted absolute victory, with the formal condemnation and public humiliation of their opponents. In the end the princes of Württemberg, Braunschweig-Wolfenbüttel, Hesse-Kassel, and the elector of Saxony made the breakthrough. A decade or so of talks and attempts at compromise, held at Worms (August 1557), Frankfurt (1558), Naumburg (1561), and Altenburg (October 1568), only led to bitter recriminations. In 1568–9 Jakob Andreae (1528–90), chancellor

HOLST

Bremen

Brauns
Lüne

Braunschweig-
Kalenberg
Lippe

CLEVES

BERG

JÜLICH

THE NETHERLANDS

LOWER
HESSE
(HESSE-KASS

NASSAU

Wetterau

Hesse-
Darmstac

Electoral
Palatinate

WÜRTTEMBERG

Baden-
Durlach

FRANCHE-
COMTÉ

SWISS
CONFEDERATION

SAVOY

MAP 6. The Spread of the 'Calvi

of the University of Tübingen in Württemberg, entered the story. After being sent by his prince to organize the Church in Braunschweig-Wolfenbüttel, he tried to gain support in northern Germany for a peace-making confession of his own in 1569. This initiative led to the well-attended synod at Zerbst in May 1570, which was unfortunately wrecked over disagreements between Andreae and the Wittenbergers.[7]

In the early 1570s the situation changed in several ways, some quite extraneous to theology. Andreae became a credible mediator after his *Six Sermons* dedicated to the duke of Braunschweig-Wolfenbüttel in February 1573 distanced him from Wittenberg, reconciled himself to some Gnesio-lutherans, and generally improved his theological stature. Secondly, the Wittenberg Philippists suffered a humiliation when in 1574 Elector August found how Calvinist Eucharistic ideas had been spread around at Wittenberg in the hands of the physician Kaspar Peucer (1525–1602) and the theologians Christoph Pezel (1539–1604) and Joachim Curaeus (1532–73). August imprisoned or exiled members of the group, purged the Wittenberg theological faculty, and issued the 'Torgau Eucharistic Confession'. Finally, in 1573, on the death of Duke Johann Wilhelm, the administration of the Ernestine lands passed to August. The elector was no longer Wittenberg's patron against Jena, since he governed both.[8]

1.7. *The Formula of Concord*

From late 1573 moves to Lutheran unity proceeded rapidly. A series of drafts prepared: the 'Swabian Concord' (November 1573); the 'Swabian–Saxon Concord' and 'Maulbronn Formula' (1575); the 'Torgau Book' of 1576 amalgamated these. In March 1577 Andreae and two of his principal allies from Braunschweig, Martin Chemnitz and Nikolaus Selnecker, edited the definitive form of a new confession at the monastery of Bergen near Magdeburg, which was presented to August on 28 May 1577. This 'Book of Bergen', also called the 'Solid Declaration', or simply the 'Formula of Concord', was ceremonially presented on the fiftieth anniversary of the Augsburg Confession on 25 June 1580. The Formula of Concord was endorsed by the three secular electors of the Empire, twenty dukes and princes, twenty-four counts, four barons, thirty-five imperial cities, and their theologians, comprising perhaps two-thirds of all the German Lutheran territories. The text was moderate and balanced enough for historians still to disagree over precisely how it aligned itself on some of the issues.[9]

2. *Germany's 'Confessional' Movement, c.1560–1600*

While Lutheranism was distracted by its internal divisions, the Swiss reformed tradition, as exported by followers of Bullinger and Calvin, made inroads in formerly Lutheran states. The term 'Calvinism' as applied to this movement is convenient but misleading. It did not bow to Calvin's personal authority (in any case, Calvin died in 1564, when the German movement was only in its early years); its leaders were mostly Germans who drew inspiration from Zürich as much as from Geneva, and set their own standards. For some it was merely the next step on the road from 'Philippism' to a comprehensive restructuring of worship and discipline. It is therefore sometimes called the 'second Reformation'.[10] It purged ritual and ceremonial more thoroughly than the Lutherans had done; saints' days, religious pictures, altars, fonts, organs, and hymn-singing were mostly rejected. Above all, it implied a more 'sacramentarian' denial of the *bodily* presence of Christ in the Eucharistic bread, symbolized by breaking every-day bread, instead of wafers, for the laity to eat.[11]

2.1. *The Lower Rhine towns*

The movement first arose through congregational pressure on city-states in the Lower Rhine. In the 1540s refugees from The Netherlands instituted separate services from those of the local Lutherans, for instance in the town of Wesel. The militantly Lutheran Tilemann Hesshusen stirred up a Eucharistic dispute at Wesel in the 1550s, which led in 1557 to the expulsion of the refugees, and shortly afterwards to a reaction against Hesshusen. After Alba's repression from 1567,[12] immigrants arrived in such numbers that they swamped the native Lutherans. An assembly of pastors and lay representatives ('elders') met at Wesel on 3 November 1568 and organized the local churches into 'classes' (district synods) in precocious imitation of similar arrangements in France; the Emden synod of 4–14 October 1571 endorsed these orders. 'Classes' spread into the Rhine-land provinces, appearing in Jülich in 1570, in Cleves in 1572, and Berg in 1589. The Wesel 'classis' met regularly between 1573 and 1609, after which a general synodal union of the Rhineland principalities was resolved at Duisburg. The movement thereafter depended on the dynastic struggles over the local princedom.[13]

2.2. *The Palatinate*[14]

In the Lower Rhineland the new order grew 'from beneath' at community level. Yet even here noble support was given by houses such as Mörs-Neuenahr, Dhaun-Falkenstein, Quadt, and Hardenberg.[15] In the rest of the 'Second Reformation' unrestrained princely autocracy brought the changes about. The first and most important state to become involved in this development was the Rhine Palatinate. Under Electors Friedrich II (1544–56) and Otto-Heinrich (1556–9) the Palatinate had initially adopted Lutheranism. When Friedrich III (1525–76) succeeded to the electorate in February 1559 he had already been converted to Lutheranism by his Hohenzollern wife Maria, and Tilemann Hesshusen had been made superintendent at his capital of Heidelberg after leaving Wesel. Between 1559 and 1562, however, Friedrich III drifted through Philippism to Swiss ideas, influenced by Melanchthon's advice about the Eucharist question,[16] and by a disputation at Heidelberg University in June 1560 where Pierre Boquin (d.1582) tried to reconcile Calvinist ideas with the Confession of Augsburg.[17]

Friedrich III then forced his ideas on his state. He made binding the Eucharistic formula devised in 1541 by Melanchthon in the so-called 'Varied Augsburg Confession' (the *Augustana Variata*); he replaced Hesshusen and on 12 August 1560 ordered that those clergy who would not accept the *Variata* must leave, thereby purging his church of ultra-Lutherans. On his own initiative he drastically simplified the Church's calendar and ornaments, and introduced everyday white bread in the communion late in 1561. Most importantly, he attracted talented theologians of Swiss orientation to Heidelberg, above all Zacharias Beer ('Ursinus', 1534–83), made director of the theological school, and Kaspar von Olewig ('Olevianus', 1536–87), professor and pastor.[18] The most influential product of this movement was the Heidelberg catechism, probably drafted by Ursinus and Olevianus, corrected by the elector, and approved by a territorial synod in December 1562. A composite and moderate document, it drew on various authors, especially Bullinger; its final version issued in November 1563 became one of the basic standards for 'Calvinist' churches all over Europe and beyond. It was supplemented with a new order for the Church council (the *Kirchenrat*, a branch of the electoral bureaucracy administering religion) in 1564, and one relating to religious discipline in 1570.[19]

On Friedrich III's death in 1576 his successor Ludwig VI (1576–83) employed the same authoritarian methods to restore strict Lutheranism.

Between five and six hundred pastors and teachers loyal to the new order were expelled; Olevianus moved to Nassau-Dillenburg, while Ursinus took refuge in the miniature court of the elector's still 'Calvinist' relative Johann Kasimir (d.1592), whose capital at Neustadt-an-der-Hardt preserved this religious tradition until Ludwig VI's death in 1583. During the minority of Elector Friedrich IV (1583–1610) Johann Kasimir, as leader of a group of regents of mixed confessions, re-established the 'Calvinist' settlement once more. In the hands of Friedrich IV and even more Friedrich V the Palatinate became the primary centre of militant, internationalist protestantism in early seventeenth-century Germany.[20]

2.3. *Nassau-Dillenburg and its allies*

Dynastic, diplomatic, and some genuine spiritual pressures introduced the movement elsewhere. Count Johann VI of Nassau-Dillenburg (1559–1606), brother to William of Orange-Nassau who led the Dutch revolts, called Gerhard Eobanus Geldenauer from Philippist Hesse to be his Church superintendent in 1572. In 1577 he welcomed some of those expelled from the Palatinate by Ludwig VI. The synod of Dillenburg on 8–9 July 1578 adopted a confession of faith composed by Christoph Pezel, the former Philippist expelled from Wittenberg by Elector August. A 'presbytery' was set up in the same year, and a General Assembly of the county in 1581 adopted the Palatine Church order and the Heidelberg catechism. Specially significant for the European scene was the foundation in 1584 of the Johannea University at Herborn, a theological 'high school' whose first leading teachers were Olevianus and Johannes Piscator.[21]

Johann VI sought to expand the influence of his confession. He converted the five counts of the Wetterau, whose lands were included in the Herborn synodal organization of 1586.[22] They in turn helped convert Count Simon VI of Lippe (1554–1613), who had been trained in Philippism and had gradually replaced Lutheran worship with 'Calvinist' forms about 1600.[23] After 1592 Landgraf Moritz 'the Learned' of Lower Hesse (1592–1627) was also drawn into the system.[24] Prince Joachim Ernst of Anhalt (1546–86) refused to accept the Formula of Concord despite being sandwiched between Brandenburg and Saxony; from 1578 he encouraged Wolfgang Amling, the superintendent, and others at Zerbst to produce their own religious standards; in the 1590s and 1600s his successors simplified worship and adopted the *Variata* and the Palatinate liturgy and catechism.[25]

In several instances the 'confessional' movement caused serious political fractures between princes and their towns, or princes and their estates. Lemgo, the major town in the county of Lippe, refused to change from

Lutheranism; the counts gave up the struggle in 1617.[26] Some princely estates, who had accepted Lutheranism without a murmur, now stuck to it resolutely in spite of their ruler. In contrast to his father August, Christian I of Saxony (1586–91) actively encouraged 'Calvinist' ideas under the influence of his Philippist adviser Dr Nikolaus Krell, and suspended allegiance to the Formula of Concord. The estates and officials of the electorate protested vigorously, and after Christian's death the regents for his successor had Krell tried (1594) and executed (1601).[27] Less dramatically, Elector Johann Sigmund of Brandenburg, who had been taught at Strasbourg and Heidelberg, turned to Calvinism in 1613 and tried in vain to persuade his staunchly Lutheran estates and people to follow him.[28] Markgraf Ernst Friedrich of Baden-Durlach, similarly unsuccessful in trying to convert his people, even wrote his own Calvinist confession of faith in 1599.[29]

Not only was such 'Calvinism' sometimes damaging to political unity *within* states; it made a mockery of the Augsburg religious peace of 1555. At Naumburg in 1561 Philipp of Hesse and Friedrich III tried to have their adherence to Melanchthon's *Variata* form of the Augsburg Confession accepted as falling within the terms of the 1555 peace; but it was anathema to the 'Gnesiolutherans'.[30] The rift wrecked the Lutheran princes' hopes of achieving an alliance with the new Emperor Maximilian II (1564–76), the nearest of all the Habsburgs to showing protestant sympathies. At the *Reichstag* at Augsburg from 23 March 1566 Maximilian II, together with the princes of Württemberg, Zweibrücken, Mecklenburg, and Brandenburg, called on Friedrich III to abandon his 'Calvinism'; August of Saxony, and most of the estates, accepted Friedrich's protests of loyalty to the Augsburg Confession except for his Eucharistic ideas. Although the consequences only surfaced in the next century, the legal ambiguity of the 'Second Reformation' lay like a land-mine under imperial politics.[31]

3. *Religion and Revolt: France and the Low Countries*

In France and The Netherlands 'Calvinist' protestant churches grew up as voluntary assemblies of zealots, created not by the cohesive reform of a whole region, but by piecemeal conversions *within* a given district. Private gatherings at first, these gatherings of believers were soon thrust into public view. The rights of a minority of voluntary enthusiasts became the major issue for the kings of France and the regents of The Netherlands under Philip II of Spain. In each case the result was a more destructive and prolonged conflict than anything which the Lutherans in Germany had so far generated. Rather than reinforcing the cohesion of the municipality or the state, this form of protestantism caused splits at all levels. In France the result was some forty years of intermittent strife, the so-called 'Wars of Religion'; in the Low Countries a revolt which permanently divided southern from northern provinces and transformed the society and economy of both. In each case, of course, the conflict arose from much more than just religious division; but the 'confessional' divide provided many of the slogans and made the strife more bitter and merciless.

3.1. *France*[32]

As was noted earlier, 'settled' protestant churches emerged almost explosively between 1555 and 1559 in the west and south of France. They required stable, qualified pastors as ministers, and some eighty-eight pastors are known to have been sent from the Company of Pastors at Geneva between 1555 and 1562: a dozen or so in each of the years 1557, 1560, 1561, and 1562, with twenty-two in 1558 and thirty-two in 1559. Perhaps one-third were already protestant ministers elsewhere; the rest included ex-students, former schoolmasters, and converted catholic clergy. This 'Calvinist' church began to organize itself because of a local emergency at Poitiers. In the winter of 1557–8 the protestant clergy there met to discuss with Antoine de la Roche-Chandieu from Paris a dispute with a heterodox minister called La Vau: the outcome was an agreement to federate congregations and organize discipline at regional level. This example was subsequently copied elsewhere.[33] Thereafter the consistories and synods gave the French churches their particular social and religious character. Rarely after about 1560 were they to expand at such a rate.[34]

In the second half of the 1550s the leaders of two princely families had converted (with varying degrees of sincerity or staying power) to protestantism: from Bourbon-Vendôme, Antoine de Bourbon (d.1562) and his wife Jeanne d'Albret, queen of Navarre and daughter of Marguerite d'Angoulême; also Louis, prince de Condé (d.1569) and his first wife Eléonore de Roye; and from the Montmorency-Châtillon family the brothers Gaspard II de Coligny, admiral of France (converted 1555), François Dandelot, colonel-general (converted 1556), and Odet de Châtillon, cardinal-bishop of Beauvais (converted 1561). Under such patronage, the Paris protestants engaged in a series of provocative demonstrations. They met in hundreds in September 1557 and armed themselves for defence. Over three days in May 1558 several thousands held public psalm-singing in the Pré-aux-Clercs district of Paris. Finally, during 26–9 May 1559 the 'first national synod', actually a gathering effectively involving eleven churches from west and north-western France, was held at Paris. Calvin, initially very angry at the proposal because of its rash timing, eventually sent delegates with a draft confession of faith; this was heavily amended by the synod and adopted, along with a disciplinary code based on the Poitiers draft and addressed to local conditions.[35]

The Crown responded inconsistently to the sudden wave of public protestant activity. Henri II had little time to initiate the threatened persecution before he died following a bizarre jousting accident on 10 July. The regency for the young François II was dominated by the militantly catholic Guise family, which included the mother of François's queen, Mary Stuart. The prince de Condé, the pastor La Roche-Chandieu, and the sieur de La Renaudie hatched a plot to seize the court from Guise control. This 'tumult of Amboise' misfired badly: news leaked out, and an assault by a few plotters on the court at Amboise on 17 March 1560 failed. Anti-protestant reprisals were forestalled when François II himself died on 5 December, leaving the throne to his younger brother Charles IX. The queen mother, Cathérine de Medici, ended persecution and seemed ready to make concessions to protestantism. At a meeting of the French clergy at Poissy from 9 September 1561, arranged to coincide with the Estates-General at Pontoise, she probably envisaged a 'religious conference' like those attempted in Germany in the 1540s. The diplomatic Théodore de Bèze represented Geneva. However, a predictable row arose over the Eucharist; the Jesuit delegate would not discuss doctrines pending at Trent. Though the colloquy of Poissy failed to reconcile the factions, it did lead Queen Cathérine to issue the liberal first edict of Saint-Germain-des-Prés on 17 January 1562, which granted limited rights of assembly and worship to the 'Huguenot' protestants. This led to an immediate, sometimes violent, expansion of the movement and to greater militancy on the part of the catholic nobles.[36]

On 1 March 1562 the duc de Guise sent a force of troops against a congregation of some 1,200 protestants attending a sermon near Vassy: seventy-four were killed. The massacre inaugurated the first of the 'Wars of Religion'. It lasted until the edict of Amboise (19 March 1563) and saw the deaths of Antoine de Bourbon and François, duc de Guise, as well as the capture of Condé. From this point up to about 1576 the essential purpose of the wars, from the protestant point of view, was to avenge the victims of, and to defend the churches against, violent persecution; and to obtain acceptable guarantees of safety and toleration from the Crown. Further fighting broke out between 1567 and March 1568; from September

1568 to August 1570; from August 1572 to July 1573; and from June 1574 to May 1576. The peace negotiated on 6 May 1576 by François duc d'Anjou, known as the 'Peace of Monsieur', or as the edict of Beaulieu, marked the high point of privilege granted to a militant Huguenot faction. It offered complete freedom of worship except at Paris and royal towns, free assembly, and access to office, as well as military and legal protection. Thereafter the catholic reaction became more hardened and embittered.[37]

This phase of the fighting saw the most notorious inter-confessional bloodshed. In the summer of 1572 Gaspard de Coligny, effectively the Huguenot leader at this point, was well received at court and aroused catholic fears about his influence over the king. The Guise faction plotted his assassination; a first attempt on 22 August wounded him. On the night of 23–4 August (the eve of the feast of St Bartholomew) Coligny and numerous other leading Huguenots in Paris were massacred; the killing was taken up by the people and became a widespread slaughter. A few days later numerous provincial cities began similar massacres of protestants, believing (rightly or wrongly) that they were acting on royal orders. A non-partisan account estimated that 30,000 were killed in the massacres. The young prince de Condé and Antoine de Bourbon's son Henri de Navarre were forcibly returned to catholicism.[38]

Following the St Bartholomew episode, 'republicanism' developed amongst the Huguenots, both in theory and practice. Theories which justified resisting or repudiating rulers who committed outrages such as the massacres were expounded in learned fashion in François Hotman's *Francogallia*, published in French in 1574 and again in 1576, Beza's related *Right of Magistrates*, printed in 1574, and the *Defence of Liberty against Tyrants*, published anonymously in 1579 but usually attributed to Philippe Duplessis-Mornay. They received more popular expression in the *Reveille matin des françois*, 'The Frenchmen's Alarm Bell', probably issued in 1575.[39] In practice, a sequence of meetings from December 1573 to July 1575, held mostly at Millau-en-Rouergue in southern France, articulated a federated 'Huguenot state', with regular assemblies, later placed under the protection of Henri, king of Navarre.[40]

Before 1572 the French protestants were troubled by a prolonged internal quarrel over the constitution of their churches. In 1562 Jean Morély, sire de Villiers, published a *Treatise of Christian Discipline and Polity*, dedicated to Pierre Viret, then pastor at Lyons, criticizing the 'aristocratic' Genevan method by which pastors co-opted other pastors into parishes, and recommending a more open, 'congregational' arrangement, less under the clergy's control. The Genevans, and their allies in France, condemned the book repeatedly. However, other French protestants, championed from 1567 by the academic philosopher Pierre de la Ramée ('Ramus', 1515–72), proved more sympathetic to Morély. The row, into which Beza and Bullinger were drawn, was still alive at the time of the 1572 massacres, in which most of Morély's party, including Ramus, were killed; thereafter the French protestant Church became definitely oligarchic in character.[41]

After 1576 the French protestants were but one faction among many in an ever more confused and anarchic struggle; peace or war in the regions came to have little connection with events at court. Catholic extremists, distrustful of the Valois, in 1577 and again after 1584 formed their own 'league' to defend the catholic cause, if need be against the king of France and with the aid of the king of Spain (given by the Treaty of Joinville, 31 December 1584). They drew support from Guise clients among the nobility and from the populace in Paris.[42] The death of François d'Anjou on 10 June 1584 made Henri de Navarre, by now a distinguished soldier as well as the Huguenot leader, heir presumptive; the murder of Henri III, the childless last Valois king, on 1 August 1589 made Navarre the royal candidate of all the non-league factions. 'Henri IV' timed his accession to power carefully, reconverting to catholicism on 25 July 1593 at the crucial moment to secure the surrender of Paris. Meanwhile the Huguenot assemblies, in regular session during the 1590s, negotiated with Henri IV for religious rights, which culminated in the edict of Nantes of 13 April 1598. This gave a fresh version of the privileges offered in 1576: freedom of conscience, right of assembly where it already existed, access to education and high office for protestants, and judicial and military safeguards against attack. This settlement was, like that in the Empire in 1555, a recognition that no other pacification or reunification was practicable. Its armed truce depended on the protection of a sympathetic Crown and zealous nobility, and was not to survive the disappearance of both.[43]

3.2. *The Low Countries*

The Reformation in the Low Countries has many apparent similarities to that in France: at first, a widespread but quite thinly supported voluntary movement, which did not put sufficient pressure on a hostile regime to establish itself in the first generation; then the appearance of Genevan-inspired reforming ideas in the 1540s or 1550s among select members of the nobility and the bourgeoisie; then a period of political turmoil beginning in the 1560s out of which some sort of partial reformed settlement emerged. However, the geographical, social, economic, and political diversity of the region made the whole story much more complex. Seventeen distinct provinces, from Artois in the south-west to Groningen in the north-east, had passed during 1477–82 from the Valois dukes of Burgundy to the Habsburgs, in the shape of Maximilian I; and by the Augsburg arrangement of 1548 were definitively hived off from the Empire to be ruled by the future King Philip II of Spain, who received them from his father Charles V in 1555.[44] The south and south-west spoke a dialect of French ('Walloon'), and was rural, feudal, and aristocratic; the southern central regions of Flanders and Brabant were urban, commercial, politically and culturally sophisticated, and Flemish-speaking; the north-western provinces of Holland and Zeeland were maritime, bourgeois, with an impoverished noble class, and spoke Dutch; the north-eastern provinces were mostly rural, speaking a form of Frisian known to the Dutch as 'Oosters'. Finally, late medieval religion in these areas had been sophisticated and multiform; elaborate ritual, preaching, and, especially in the Rhineland, Gelderland, and Overijssel, the heartland of the Brethren of the Common Life and their devotional style.[45]

Unlike most northern European rulers, the Habsburgs in the Low Countries reacted to the Reformation with immediate harshness. Between 1523 and 1555 some 1,700 were burnt for heresy in the southern provinces, and another 240 in the north. It has been estimated that the majority (two-thirds, more or less) of the victims in each case were anabaptists. Charles V's persecuting edicts were codified on 14 October 1529 as the 'Placards', revived in 1535 and 1538, unpopular with the magistrates, and erratically enforced.[46] Notwithstanding, a range of reformed ideas found a readership. Ninety-four editions of works by Luther were published in The Netherlands by 1541. Editions, complete or partial, of Bullinger's sermons (the *Decades*) sold well in the 1550s. Calvin, by contrast, fared badly: only four Dutch editions of his works appeared in his lifetime. Moreover, local protestant authors developed their eclectic ideas, especially Jan Gerritz ('Anastasius Veluanus') in his 'Laymen's Guide' (*Leken Wechwyser*) of 1554. Netherlands protestantism became distinct from strict Lutheranism under the influence of Jan Laski, who, expelled from England in 1553, revised the liturgy of Emden in East Friesland in the direction of Strasbourg and set an example for Dutch exiles who settled there (as they had done in London and Frankfurt-am-Main).[47]

Calvin exerted only literary influence upon Flemings or Dutch before the 1560s; few of the preachers before 1566 had any ties with Geneva. In the French-speaking areas, however, he tried to persuade the protestants to set up public churches (as he did in France) with his treatises against the 'Nicodemites' in 1543 and 1544, and sent a pastor, Pierre Brully, to

Tournai and Valenciennes, who was burnt on 19 February 1545. It was in these French-speaking areas that settled Calvinist churches emerged around 1560. Crucial to this development was Guy de Brès (1522–67), a native of Mons in Hainault who had worked in London and in Switzerland; he settled at Tournai in 1560 and fostered the growth of churches in Lille, Valenciennes, and around Cambrai. In 1561 he collaborated with three other pastors to edit the 'Belgian confession', a revision in Walloon of the 1559 French confession of faith, translated into Dutch in 1562 and made binding on the Dutch protestants by the Emden synod of 1571.[48] At about the same time the movement crossed the linguistic divide into Flanders: a congregation was set up in Antwerp under Hermann van Strijker (known as Moded) and Pieter Daten (Dathenus), and others in Ghent, Bruges, Hondschoote, and Breda somewhat later.[49]

Religious persecution became a political issue in the mid-1560s when the king, the regent, his half-sister Margaret, duchess of Parma, and her chief minister Antoine Perrenot de Granvelle, faced hostility from the Flemish nobility over their plans to establish a more elaborate—and controllable—catholic church hierarchy in the region. In mid-1565 the leading nobles of The Netherlands, under the prince of Egmont, petitioned for moderation of the edicts against heresy. Philip's response was to insist on full enforcement of the Placards; a panic developed over the threat of an 'inquisition' being introduced. Early in 1566 a document known as the 'Compromise', probably drafted by one of the fairly few genuinely Calvinist nobles at this period, Philippe Marnix, seigneur of Ste-Aldegonde in Hainault, called for leniency to heretics and rejected the idea of an inquisition. It was passed around secretly for signature among the nobility by Marnix de Ste-Aldegonde in alliance with Louis of Nassau. This protest therefore continued the policy by which an aristocracy afraid of being by-passed obstructed the Madrid government.[50]

What fragile unity there was in such protests was then broken, in the summer of 1566, by the activities of the protestants in the towns of Flanders and Brabant. Following a catholic religious procession at Antwerp on 18 August, a series of riots culminated in a hundred or so townspeople entering the cathedral in the night of 20–1 August and destroying all the images and ceremonial ornaments. The destruction spread to the rest of the city and province, and to Malines (Mechelen), Tournai, and Valenciennes in succeeding weeks. The violence was apparently reserved to objects, not people: in places there was an orderly 'cleansing' of churches to suit them for reformed worship. Nevertheless, the fright administered to the nobility destroyed the Compromise; some aristocratic leaders like

Egmont returned to Philip's allegiance; William, prince of Orange-Nassau (d.1584), the future leader of the revolt, fled to safety in his lands of Nassau-Dillenburg in the Empire. From August 1567 the hardline Spanish government of the duke of Alva conducted a thorough purge of rebels, although acquiescence in his regime, brutal in its punishments and voracious in its tax demands, was at best partial.[51]

From the early 1570s the momentum both of the revolt and also (to some extent) of Dutch protestantism moved to the north, especially to the provinces of Holland and Zeeland. William of Orange licensed a squadron of rebels as privateers, who based themselves in England until they were evicted by Elizabeth in April 1572; soon afterwards they captured Den Briel on the Maas, then Vlissingen on Walcheren in Zeeland, allowing them both to blockade Antwerp and to extend their power over Holland and Zeeland as a whole. *Coups d'état* in the principal towns, and the adoption of William of Orange as provincial governor by the Holland Estates in July 1572, consolidated rebel power. Protestant universities were set up to rival catholic Louvain: Leiden in 1575, and Franeker, near Leeuwarden in Friesland, in 1576. However, establishing a protestant settlement in rebel towns, which sometimes involved purging the magistracy (as at Amsterdam in 1578) was a slow and painful process: by the 1620s Calvinists even in quite major towns of Holland were only between 5 and 20 per cent of the population.[52]

For a brief period in the mid-1570s the Dutch revolt almost recovered its character as a political strike by the whole seventeen provinces against Spanish occupation; but once again urban Flemish protestantism divided the rebels against each other. When Philip II stopped paying his creditors (1 September 1575), his governor-general, de Requesens, died (5 March 1576), and his unpaid troops first mutinied and then ransacked Antwerp (4 November 1576), the catholic noble faction under the duke of Aerschot forced through the 'Pacification of Ghent' of 8 November 1576, uniting to rid The Netherlands of foreign troops and religious persecution. However, in August 1577 the towns of Flanders erupted in revolutions combining Calvinist fervour with guildsmen's constitutional assertiveness. Only in the southern cities did this recognizable Reformation 'coalition' occur. The most famous of these revolts occurred in Ghent under the petty nobles Hembyze and Rijhove, abetted by the preacher Pieter Dathenus; the environs of Ghent, Brussels, Antwerp, and 's Hertogenbosch in Brabant also rebelled. The association of Calvinists with these urban rebels, jealousy between the duke of Aerschot and the prince of Orange, and rebel defeats, caused the resistance movement to break into separate northern and southern confederacies in 1579. The northern rebels assembled their own States-General and renounced allegiance to Philip II in 1581. They flirted disastrously with François, duc d'Anjou, and scarcely more happily with Elizabeth I as sovereigns; then finally accepted their unique status as distinct, 'united provinces' under the loose headship of the house of Orange, but without a formal monarch. Philip's new general, Margaret of Parma's son Alessandro, duke of Parma, meanwhile stabilized the Crown's relations with the Aerschot faction and crushed the southern cities' revolts between 1583 and 1585.[53]

The Reformation in the rebel provinces of the north therefore rested on the military coups of the early 1570s, the personal prestige of the Orangists, and the exodus of artisans from the southern towns to the north following the failure of the revolts of 1577–85. Protestantism remained a minority creed in the 'United Provinces' of the northern Netherlands well into the seventeenth century; while commitment to 'Calvinist' consistorial discipline, excommunication, and a hierarchy of Church synods, was rarer still. So catholic worship was slow to be abolished even in the heartlands of the Dutch revolt; heterodox forms of protestantism—apart from anabaptism— emerged, as in the case of Dirk Coornhert's spiritualism in the 1560s, or when Caspar Coolhaes and Cornelis Pieterszoon Hooft argued (in the 1580s and 1600s respectively) that Church discipline was unnecessary after the civil powers had been converted. The most notorious of all heretics against Calvinist orthodoxy, Jakob Hermandszoon ('Jacobus Arminius', 1560– 1609), professor at the University of Leiden from 1603, developed a doctrine which rejected the strict predestinarian views of most Calvinists of his age: the ensuing debate raged in The Netherlands from 1603 until long after Arminius's death, and had repercussions throughout protestant Europe.[54]

In both these cases the impact of the 'confessional' form of the Reformation has to be seen as fundamentally divisive. No doubt, after the first wave of enthusiasm was passed by about 1550, the voluntary, piecemeal process of conversion was the only practicable way to establish protestantism where the ruler was hostile. However, the formation of militant creeds, informal consistorial structures, and the defiance of weak rulers only gave *just* enough strength to the protestant movement in these countries to cause chaos and fragmentation. Not only did it lead to fighting in the short term; it left a legacy of social tensions, shown in the struggles between strict and tolerant protestants in Holland throughout the seventeenth century, and in the waning of protestant support—especially among a nobility grown impatient of Church discipline—in France up to Louis XIV's expulsions in 1685.

4. *England and Scotland, 1559–1603*

England and Scotland were the most important, if not the only, kingdoms to adopt the south German or Swiss pattern of Reformation as their sole official faith. However, in both these countries the reformed settlement led to decades of controversy: not whether to allow protestantism or not (as in France), nor yet what 'confession' to choose (as in the Palatinate), nor even (at first) how to keep doctrine pure (as in the intra-Lutheran feuds). The disputes were over how *thoroughly* 'reformed' the kingdoms were to be; how far the new creed could be enforced; and how the zealots' desire for thoroughness could be reconciled with a monarch's concern to keep the movement under rigid control. In both kingdoms the monarchy faced energetic voluntary protestants striving to promote the 'confession' at the expense of the monarch's authority.

4.1. *England*

At their deaths on 17 November 1558 Mary I and Reginald Pole left a church of zealous catholic bishops and technically celibate clergy, but still poor and humbled after decades of plunder. Elizabeth I (1558–1603) wasted no time in offending catholic sensitivities when on Christmas day 1558 and 15 January 1559 she pointedly left mass when the officiating bishop insisted on elevating the Host. The Parliament which opened on 25 January heard a sermon from Richard Cox (*c*.1500–81), a protestant academic just back from exile in Frankfurt. By 29 April 1559 that same Parliament had passed the Acts of Supremacy and Uniformity which re-established the monarch's control over the Church (as 'Supreme Governor' rather than 'Supreme Head', a distinction whose real significance is debatable), and restored the second Prayer Book of Edward VI's reign (dating from 1552), purged of some of its more violent anti-catholic rhetoric.[55]

This drastic and definitive settlement, which the queen afterwards refused to alter, reflected several pressures: a touchy diplomatic position; the strength of conservative opposition among bishops and some peers; the determined but politically astute protestantism of royal advisers like Anthony Cooke, Francis Knollys, and William Cecil, and perhaps that of the queen herself; and the scruples of the talented clergy who had been in exile in Frankfurt, Worms, Strasbourg, Aarau, and Zürich, without whose co-operation the queen would have had no bishops to whom to turn. It had a tortuous passage through Parliament, for uncertain reasons.[56] It was accompanied by a final scramble for Church land, the plunder this time being the considerable landed estates of the bishops. Worship was settled by the 1559 statutes; the structure of the Church remained traditional except for the royal supremacy; belief and doctrine waited a further four years until the convocation of 1563 adopted the 'Thirty-nine Articles' of faith, a statement based on the explicitly and militantly protestant Forty-two Articles of 1553. Proposals dating from Cranmer's time to reform Church law were revived but abandoned once again.[57]

Elizabeth nurtured and defended this settlement, at times single-handed, for the rest of her reign. Her own religious views are as unclear as her father's. She was no catholic, and there is no evidence that the amended 1552 liturgy dissatisfied her. Herself celibate, she resented priests marrying but could do nothing to stop them; she kept altars and crosses in her chapels, but allowed them to be removed elsewhere; she feared the social risks of protestant preaching much more than she hoped for any political benefit from it. Aware that she was the only hope of the protestant loyalists, she made more superficial concessions to potential rebels among the old catholics than to zealous protestant disciplinarians among her own supporters. Elizabethan religious politics were thus in tension between positive protestants trying to realize the potential of the settlement, and the queen—and a few of her bishops—trying to stop them.[58]

The choices made of archbishops of Canterbury were crucial. During 1559–60 most vacant sees were filled with protestants returned from exile; but Canterbury was given to Matthew Parker (1504–75), who had lain low in England after deprivation for marriage under Mary. He consistently but moderately enforced the queen's demands for basic conformity to the settlement from protestants during the quarrel over clerical 'vestments' in 1564–7 and over the prayer book in 1571–2. His successor, Edmund Grindal (?1519–1583), a former exile, regarded the clergy as 'experts' in the subject of God's will, to whose advice mere monarchs should submit. For refusing during 1577 to suppress preaching 'exercises'—effectively, retraining courses for protestant clergy—he was suspended from office until his death. His suspension did not stop the 'exercises' or 'prophesyings', which continued in some dioceses with positive encouragement from local bishops. Only in 1583 did Elizabeth find a primate entirely to her taste in John Whitgift (c.1530–1604), who instituted a series of judicial purges of insubordinately protestant clergy. His 'inquisitions' shocked some royal counsellors; but Whitgift relied on the queen's approval, and passed his see on his death to his former chaplain Richard Bancroft (1544–1610).[59]

A wide range of steps, public and private, national and local, statutory and voluntary, moderate and extreme, were taken to make the English Church more positively protestant during Elizabeth's reign. With gross over-simplification one may identify three trends:

(1) Attempts to alter the liturgy and ornamentation of Church services to a distinctly reformed type.
(2) Proposals to incorporate into the largely unaltered medieval structure of the English Church the system of local, provincial, and ultimately national synods or 'classes', in deliberate imitation of European Churches.
(3) Initiatives to further the twin aims of doctrinal instruction and moral discipline at parish level.

1. The new bishops themselves raised the first objections to Elizabeth's tastes in worship: early in the reign Bishops Cox of Ely, Edwin Sandys (c.1516–88) of Worcester, and John Jewel (1522–71) of Salisbury made such complaints about the queen's traditional crucifix and candles in her chapel that they feared deposition from their sees. When this issue blew over, attention shifted to the 'vestments' of officiating clergy. The 1559 book appeared to insist on the whole traditional paraphernalia of surplice, alb, cope, and chasuble; protestants clearly expected this to change. In the 1563 convocation a proposal to drop all 'mass-vestments' except the surplice failed in the lower house by only one vote. During the spring of 1565 Parker and four other prelates drew up the so-called 'Advertisements'; these directions on enforcing at least *some* of the vestments were published in March 1566 without the queen (who was their real instigator) giving any public support. Parker only really tried to enforce them in Oxford and Cambridge Universities, where they met vigorous resistance, and in the London diocese, where a compromise was struck. With Mary Stuart's defeat in Scotland in June–July 1567 the diplomatic pressure eased; strict laws once again were laxly enforced.[60] The Prayer Book itself, with its (to protestants) obnoxious and trivial concessions to tradition, also came under attack. Four attempts were made in Parliament either to replace it or to make it only voluntary for protestants, in April 1571 ('Strickland's Bill'), the spring of 1572, 1584 ('Turner's Bill and Book'), and 1586–7 ('Cope's Bill and Book'). These met with opposition from queen and council, even from those councillors who like Francis Knollys had strong protestant tastes, and failed.[61]

2. A potentially serious challenge to the hybrid English Church structure came from the movement to introduce reformed-style 'presbyteries' or 'classes'. The ideologue of this campaign was Thomas Cartwright (1535–1603), briefly Lady Margaret Professor of Divinity at Cambridge during 1569–70, whose lectures on Church government during the spring of 1570 caused a furore and led to Cartwright's departure to Geneva. His ideas were taken up by John Field (1545–88), who issued during 1572 a series of manifestoes for Church government by presbyteries, beginning with the first *Admonition to Parliament* in June which was answered at ever greater length by John Whitgift, the future archbishop. A scandal in October 1573, when a protestant fanatic attempted to murder someone whom he thought was the queen's favourite and Whitgift's patron, Christopher Hatton, discredited and damaged the campaign.[62]

In the early 1580s the idea was revived at local level with the informal and unofficial establishment of voluntary 'conferences' of enthusiastic protestant clergy, including one in London under Field and his allies Thomas Wilcox and Walter Travers, and a particularly famous one at Dedham in Essex. In the mid-1580s Field even tried to organize an informal 'General Assembly' of delegates from the rural conferences at the time of parliamentary sessions. This project was never more than a means to co-ordinate mutual encouragement and communication between protestant pastors who often felt embattled in their parishes. It did not incorporate (lay) 'ruling elders' in its hierarchy in the same way as the continental or Scottish examples. Its discipline lacked 'teeth'. It was overtaken by events: Field died in 1588, the anonymous publication of the first of the outrageous (if entertaining) *Marprelate Tracts* against Whitgift and his ally Bishop John Aylmer of London alienated moderate protestants; and Whitgift subjected Cartwright and his allies to a long unsuccessful prosecution during 1590–2. More importantly, the 'Anglican' hybrid of high reformed doctrine, mixed liturgy, and traditional structure won devoted supporters. The *Laws of Ecclesiastical Polity* published in 1594–7 by Richard Hooker (c.1554–1600) was the most famous and thorough defence of the hybrid; but works were written in the same cause by Richard Bancroft, the Flemish exile Adrian Saravia (1531–1613), and others.[63]

3. Meanwhile, all through the reign, measures were proposed in Parliament and elsewhere to further the protestant cause directly, rather than by attacking the 1559 settlement. These aimed to create a cadre of zealous, resident, preaching protestant ministers, to require attendance and obedience to them, and to harry the remaining catholics. Elizabeth repeatedly attempted to stop the introduction of religious bills by private members,

but seems to have been only half-heartedly supported in this by some of her own councillors. In 1566 she rejected a handful of bills, including one to enforce the Thirty-nine Articles; in 1571 she accepted modified versions of some of these but rejected others; by 1584, when similar bills appeared, Whitgift was in place to resist them.[64]

In the country at large patrons and ordinary laymen alike strove for the same goals. They endowed 'lectureships', stipends usually held by already settled clergy to preach to parishes or corporations.[65] They adapted the medieval patronage system to support preaching ministers.[66] People travelled from one parish to another to hear a specially popular preacher; and churchwardens constituted themselves as a *de facto* parish 'presbytery'.[67] Whitgift's and Bancroft's campaigns against such initiatives were cut short by the end of the 1600s, when Archbishops George Abbott of Canterbury (1611–33) and Tobie Mathew of York (1607–28) reverted to an attitude similar to Grindal's. With such a broad Church establishment, actual sectarianism in England remained extremely rare, instances being dealt with by the bishops in the late 1560s and early 1590s.[68]

4.2. *Scotland*

Unlike that in England, the protestant settlement in Scotland resulted, at a first glance, from a *coup d'état* against the monarchy and the French, supported by a vigorous movement of voluntary protestant churches in the towns. In a deeper sense, however, both countries' reformations depended on the allegiance of a highly motivated minority of the nobility to the cause, and on the careful exploitation of the twists and turns of international affairs. As in France, so in Scotland local churches were set up, and important noblemen converted, in the later 1550s. The so-called 'privy kirks' were (deliberately) obscure at first, but seem to have met for worship with increasing regularity in Edinburgh, St Andrews, Dundee, Perth, Ayr, and elsewhere, worshipping with elements drawn from the 1552 English liturgy. By the middle or later months of 1559 these churches, at least in St Andrews, Dundee, and Ayr, were semi-official bodies, the object of civic regulations and keepers of their own records. Meanwhile, on 3 December 1557 the duke of Argyll and his sons, the earls of Morton and Glencairn, and John Erskine of Dun signed the 'First Band' of the 'Lords of the Congregation', a document of confederacy adapted from Scots civil practice to unite the protestant magnates.[69]

The Lords of the Congregation temporized with the regent, queen Mother Mary of Lorraine, until the accession of Elizabeth in November 1558 suddenly made England, rather than potentially Huguenot France, their natural ally. In May 1559 civil disturbances began: John Knox (*c*.1513–72), who had led some disgruntled English exiles from Frankfurt to Geneva and been excluded from England by Elizabeth, returned to Scotland and preached in Perth; the ensuing iconoclastic riot led to the devastation of the friaries and charterhouse there. On 22 May the Lords of the Congregation warned the regent that they would take up arms; later in 1559, after 'suspending' the regency in October, they several times occupied Edinburgh and then had to withdraw. In March 1560 Elizabeth intervened and sent troops to besiege the French in Leith; in April the Lords took over Edinburgh; in June Mary of Lorraine died; by July the Treaty of Edinburgh provided for the withdrawal of the English and French troops, and ensured the Lords' hold on power. Meanwhile, elsewhere in Scotland, numerous leading churchmen abruptly and seemingly without difficulty deserted to the protestant cause; in some towns catholic priests and protestant preachers even worked in parallel for some years. For all its dramatic results, the coup involved little bloodshed and few martyrs.[70]

After the Scottish 'Reformation Parliament' met in August 1560, the political insurrection and ecclesiastical reform movements in Scotland coalesced in a programme. Papal authority was abolished, the mass prohibited, and the Scottish confession of faith adopted, though subscription to it could in no way be enforced. Some catholic bishops retired into obscurity, others actively aided the reformers. In an attempt to solve the muddled Church structure, the *First Book of Discipline*, compiled during 1560 by a committee combining fervent protestants like Knox with the moderate Augustinian ex-subprior of St Andrews, John Wynram, proposed a coherent protestant system to reallocate the Church's wealth and appoint 'superintendents' to oversee the clergy. It was adopted by a General Assembly and by the 'Secret Council' of the nobility, but its provisions for Church land asked too much of the laymen who had in recent decades secured favourable leases of those lands. During the winter of 1561–2 a compromise allocated one-third of the income from benefices (endowed posts in the old Church) to the Crown for the new Church, and the rest to its 'old possessors'. In 1562 an English service-book of Genevan inspiration was printed and prescribed by General Assemblies in 1562 and 1564.[71]

By the early 1560s Scotland had a catholic monarch, Mary Stuart, ruling over a protestant church allowed to worship but poorly funded, and a catholic establishment forbidden to worship but well endowed. The rebellion against Mary after her intricate matrimonial scandals, her defeat at Carberry Hill (15 June 1567), imprisonment, and abdication (24 July), left the protestant Lord James Stewart, earl of Moray, as the first of a series of ill-fated regents to hold sway to the early 1580s. Gradually the lands of the old Church passed piecemeal to the new. However, the Scottish Church establishment, which is sometimes supposed to have been uniformly 'Calvinist' and 'presbyterian', remained in flux. In January 1572 an extraordinary General Assembly at Leith consented to the filling of the old bishoprics and archbishoprics by protestant clerics as government nominees.[72]

By the mid-to-late 1570s two points of the Scottish Church structure caused heated ideological controversy, rather than undogmatic compromise. The first issue was that of 'parity' among clerics (the idea that ministers should all be of the same rank); the second, of the Church's autonomy and right to manage its affairs distinct from the civil power. Coincidentally, since the bishops, whose offices had never really lapsed, were the natural figures to implement State control over the Church, the survival of their office became an issue as well. The figure traditionally associated with the call for an autonomous, presbyterian Church polity in Scotland is the academic Andrew Melville (1545–1622), who was recruited from Geneva to become principal of Glasgow University in 1574. Rightly or wrongly, Melville is usually regarded as the leader of that faction in the Church from 1574 to his imprisonment in London in 1607. In fact, the struggle between a would-be-Erastian civil government seeking to establish firm secular control over the nascent structure of the reformed Church, and the divines of that Church trying to preserve their autonomy and purity, dated from the origins of the Scottish Reformation itself, not just from the 1570s.[73]

The fate of the presbyterian system hung largely on the tortuous politics of the time. The *Second Book of Discipline*, adopted by a General Assembly in 1578, enunciated the principle of Church autonomy and some aspects of a presbyterian polity, but was blocked by the Scottish Parliament under first Regent Morton and then James VI's favourite, the earl of Lennox. None the less new presbyteries were set up (and a violently anti-catholic confession of faith adopted) in 1581; after the earls of Gowrie and Mar seized James from Lennox's hands in the 'Ruthven Raid' of 1582, more advances were made by presbyteries in some areas. However, in August 1583 James escaped from the tutelage of this faction and a reaction ensued. The 'Black Acts' of May 1584, passed under the earl of Arran's influence, denounced the regional 'presbyteries' (the most contentious topic), reaffirmed episcopal powers, and most importantly asserted royal and parliamentary supremacy, exercised through the bishops, over the Church.

Both the defeated conspirators and the Melvillian ministers went into temporary exile in England. In 1585 Arran fell from grace and the presbyteries made advances again, reaching an accommodation with the bishops in 1586 and fully eclipsing them in 1592. After 1600 the situation reverted once again: James VI, naturally enough, wished to use the episcopate as a means to oversee an otherwise unruly body. The issue of Church–State relations, which in so many protestant Churches either was of purely abstract interest or was resolved on a day-to-day basis, in Scotland became a spectre which haunted the nation for most of the seventeenth century.[74]

The 'confessional' period marked a distinct change from the primitive, even naïve enthusiasm of newly reformed states in the early sixteenth century towards a more hard-headed attitude on the part of both reforming clerics and secular politicians. Above all there was a much greater understanding that the reformed Church might *not* be a convenient tool of the emerging state: that religious zealots had priorities and enthusiasms of their own which were hard to harness or contain. This chapter has shown how the movement, in very different ways, acquired and used *sectional* political support to set itself up as a potent and disruptive minority force in several countries. The next chapter will show how clerics and laymen had divergent ideas as to what 'godliness' implied *within* an established church: how the ambitions of churchmen to educate, chasten, and control could exasperate their former patrons.

21

Reformers and Laymen
A Conflict of Priorities

The Reformation did not just redefine the means of human salvation and radically alter the Church's relationship to secular society. It tried to instil a comprehensive new vision of the Christian life. A Christian under the new dispensation was required to abandon nearly all the traditional cultic psychological props and comforts against the insecurity of life: including those rites and entertainments which gave medieval life its rhythm and colour. The Church itself, now simply a vast brotherhood of other learning, praying lay people, no longer had special virtue available to be 'transferred' to one's spiritual account. Laymen, therefore, acquired a daunting new range of religious duties. They had to *learn* about their belief; to pray on their own behalf; and to exhibit their 'sanctification' in moral goodness towards their neighbour, rather than in candles lit or masses paid for. Fathers of families especially found their duties extended: in the first (naïve) vision of the reformers they were virtually to become ministers to their households; to instruct, to lead in prayer, and to discipline their families in 'godliness'. For none of this was any spiritual or material 'reward' promised whatever.

All this was inherent in the basic logic of the reformers' teaching. However, these implications were not self-evident from the first spate of pamphlets, sermons, and disputations. The Reformation whipped up enthusiasm for abolishing the old rituals, promising 'freedom' from the expensive and corrupt business of saving souls through the ministry of a human institution. The other side of the coin, that believers had now to find in faith the reassurance which before they had found in rituals, only emerged as the new order settled down after the upheavals of 'establishing' a reformed church. Some politicians had already foreseen the dangers of unrestrained 'clericalism', when for instance they haggled over or simply obstructed the demands of the new clergy for the authority to bar sinners from the Eucharist.[1] As time passed it became progressively clearer that not even the most potentially 'godly' lay people—let alone the majority— necessarily shared the reformers' vision of a purified, godly community.

This was the final way in which the 'coalition' between reforming preachers and their lay supporters dissolved: into varying degrees of alienation between the 'magisterial' clergy, who soon acquired a caste mentality not so very different from that of their priestly forebears, and the lay people whom they tried to shape into their mould.

1. *Protestant Ministers become a 'Profession'*

In many parts of Europe there was in the first instance little change either in the personnel of the priesthood or in its behaviour, because the old incumbents simply remained in their posts and conformed, with good or ill grace, to the new demands made of them. In Zürich, many German principalities, England, and Scandinavia, most of the parish clergy obeyed their rulers' instructions to adopt the reformed order.[2] Where the introduction of the Reformation was most politically divisive (as in Geneva, or even more so in France or the Low Countries), or where catholic priests were allowed to keep parts of their old revenues (as for instance in Scotland), many more old priests kept to their old ways.[3] Where the old clergy remained, the problem of shaping the new pastorate was simply deferred for a generation; and so, in all probability, was the real impact of the Reformation itself.

However, after a generation or so many of the clergy serving the new reformed churches were quite different socially, intellectually, and economically from their medieval predecessors. The medieval clergy, a vast many-faceted society with immense diversity of incomes, social origins, and roles, had mirrored the variety of the secular world which produced and supported it.[4] The basic principles of the Reformation, however, inherently homogenized both what kinds of clergymen there were and what tasks they performed, by stripping away the peripherals and reducing the Church's work to teaching, preaching, giving the sacraments, and pastoral work. They also injected a large intellectual element, requiring knowledge and understanding of both pastors and people.[5] To the extent that these changes were realized in practice, they set a distance between the pastors and their flocks. The clergy developed an intense self-consciousness as a profession, and subscribed to a particular collective set of values. Lay people might reasonably have felt that their ministers were actually *less* familiar and recognizable than their priests had been.[6]

Just which types and classes of people were drawn into the new pastorate was determined both by circumstances and by the vision of its leaders. The drastically simplified new Church lost its social extremes, its aristocracy and its proletariat. The prince-bishoprics and great abbeys in Germany and Switzerland were either retained by catholics or became secular lordships. The office of 'superintendent' in Lutheran lands carried much less prestige, and certainly less money. Even the bishops of Elizabethan England, inheriting what had been some of the richest sees in Christendom, found their revenues cut and their costs increased.[7] At the other end, the minor orders of doorkeepers, exorcists, and acolytes disappeared, and even the deacons changed their function. The mass of poorly paid chaplains who had satisfied the demand for memorial masses became redundant. Correspondingly, therefore, very few noblemen or peasants would have wished to become reformed ministers: for the former the prospects were too poor, for the latter the educational demands too expensive.[8]

At the core of the new ministry was the parish clergyman, expected to be literate, resident, and attentive. Naturally, this model was shaped by the kind of people who served the urban Reformation movements in the first generation. A survey of 176 urban preachers active in the early German Reformation revealed some of their social characteristics. The vast majority were either secular priests or monks or friars when they started preaching; some who were not were schoolteachers, on the fringes of the clergy.[9] Much more strikingly, no fewer than three-quarters had studied at universities; over half of these had studied for higher degrees; and the majority of those had studied theology. Both in the depth of their education, and in their orientation towards theology rather than law, these were an élite of society *and* a special interest group among the career clergy of the time.[10] Finally, of those whose social origins are known a quarter were sons of town councillors or patricians, the majority of the remainder being modest bourgeois. The middle and upper classes were overrepresented, while 90 per cent came from towns, exactly reversing the contemporary norm for the population as a whole.[11]

Although generalizations are dangerous, those who were ordained afresh to the new ministry in its early decades do seem, like the pioneering preachers, to have been an unrepresentative sample of society, unlike the multifarious old priesthood. Those ordained at Wittenberg before 1550 were first and foremost the graduates of its university; their social origins were almost certainly 'the non-noble, non-wealthy, non-peasant strata ... that is, the mostly urban lower middle class'.[12] In the rush to provide sufficient numbers of pastors for the burgeoning new churches other people were temporarily drawn in from other professions: former teachers and scribes, as well as former sextons and choirmasters, took orders. Around

1540 Wittenberg ordained a minority of former craftsmen, printers, clothiers, and so forth, but only as an emergency measure.[13] The reformed pastorate, whether in southern Germany or Switzerland, remained the preserve above all of middle-class townspeople just below the levels of the rich and privileged. The really wealthy, if they put their sons into a profession, made them lawyers.[14] Sooner or later the pastorate began to propagate itself. In the Middle Ages the clergy had been set apart by not marrying (although illegitimate sons of priests were often legitimized and accepted into the clergy); this formal 'separateness' was supposedly set aside when reformed ministers married like other laymen. Like other laymen, however, they tended to promote their sons into their calling, and marry their daughters to others of their kind; and so the 'separateness' was perpetuated in another way. In Switzerland, Württemberg, the Rhineland, or Brandenburg the sons of ministers were a large proportion, sometimes an outright majority, of candidates for the ministry.[15] In England there were dynasties of parsons, and even of bishops.[16]

Just as the new clergy were set apart socially from most of their flocks (above all in the countryside), so their wealth and life-style slowly rose above the average. Since the new pastors were expected to raise and feed families, and to devote time to reading and preparing sermons, they could no longer be expected to eke out a living from tithes and part-time farming their parish lands or 'glebe'. Here the changes were probably slowest of all to take effect, and distinguished the towns (where preaching beneficed clergy had always been an élite) sharply from the countryside.[17] Nevertheless, as the missionary fervour of the first generation abated, lay rulers and patrons realized that properly qualified people simply could not be found for the old pittances. Inflation ate away at those parts of clerics' incomes paid in money rather than kind, forcing further improvements. One reason why 'common chests' were set up in the very first place was to reallocate Church income to pay the new style of pastor better.[18] In the Saxon districts of Weida and Gotha, the electors were forced to supplement the gradually rising incomes of many parishes with new endowments from the lands of dissolved monasteries.[19] Even in country districts where protestantism was not the sole creed, as in the Valtelline, the pressure on rulers to set a minimum income for preachers became irresistible by the 1550s.[20] In England town and country vicarages alike were poorly paid at first, but an élite of more wealthy parishes gradually emerged to support the more highly born clerics and retired academics; while the old vices of absence and plurality persisted to the nineteenth century.[21]

However, the major factor which turned the reformed ministry into a distinct self-conscious 'profession' was the increasing level of higher education which its members received.[22] Luther's 'priesthood of all believers' from the first implied that the *common* priesthood should be exercised by the duly qualified and appointed specialist.[23] Possession of suitable learning set the minister apart—in reality, rather than in a nominal, ceremonial way—from the rest of humanity, and made him the representation of urban, academic, bourgeois ways of thought in town and countryside alike. In the first generation, of course, there was a basic problem that old priests could not easily be taught new doctrines, let alone new tricks, very quickly. The main effect of the electoral visitations held in Saxony from 1528, ostensibly to 'improve' the clergy, was simply to reveal the huge scale of 'gruesome blindness, lack of understanding, ignorance, and animosity towards the light' among the resident priests. Such recognition of the problem in turn prompted the writing of manuals and catechisms, and the tentative beginnings of permanent supervision.[24] At Zürich, Zwingli and his colleagues began in June 1525 to hold meetings, known as the *Prophezei*, five times a week at which the more learned of the city clergy expounded the Scriptures, read in their original languages, to their less talented colleagues.[25] In the first decades of the Elizabethan settlement some of the more enthusiastic protestant clergy in England began similarly to gather regularly for the comparing of notes and for the moral and intellectual strengthening of the weak. Such entirely voluntary initiatives, known variously as 'lectures by combination', 'exercises', and 'prophesyings', received little support, and in England positive hostility, from the ruler.[26]

Some of the parish clergy responded well to such initiatives, like the parish priest in backwoods Essex who supplied his church with a lectern and books, and aroused a keen appetite for sermons among his hearers.[27] However, obedience to such exercises could not be enforced. Many parishes had to wait for a new incumbent before protestant zeal reached them. In the first instance the universities provided the bulk of the new clergy. Above all, from about 1520 to about 1560 a stream of graduate trainees issued from Wittenberg to many corners of Lutheran Europe.[28] Erfurt and (after the conversion of Albertine Saxony) Leipzig, trained many. In southwestern Germany Tübingen and Heidelberg were prominent, especially after the latter became a centre of 'Calvinist' teaching. In the north Bremen and Rostock produced their quota of ministers.[29] Other universities were created at least partly to supply the demand which the Reformation created. Basle's university was refounded in 1532. Philipp of Hesse founded the Philipps-Universität in Marburg in 1527, while the princes of Orange helped establish the university at Franeker in Frisia in 1576. The university set up at Leiden in the mid-1570s began to train large numbers of protestant ministers after 1592. In Scotland medieval universities were refounded with faculties to train for the ministry, while Cambridge saw new colleges, Sidney Sussex and Emmanuel above all, founded explicitly as protestant seminaries. Oxford issued the largest number of degrees of Bachelor of Divinity in its history during 1610–39, at the peak of the improvements.[30]

However, in the rush to train pastors new kinds of theological training colleges were set up, many of which can be traced to the direct or indirect influence of Strasbourg. In March 1538 a *gymnasium* was inaugurated there under the influence of the humanist educator Johann Sturm (1507–89), a former pupil of the Brethren of the Common Life at Liège and probably an acquaintance of the French pedagogue Mathurin Cordier (*c*.1480–1564).[31] Just two years after Sturm's arrival in the city he was called on by the magistrates to organize and lead the college. His primary contribution was a rigidly disciplined hierarchy of study, comprising nine years of 'secondary' and five years of 'further' education, beginning with a sound grounding in pure classical Latin, grammar, rhetoric, and dialectic. Tests had to be passed before a student could be 'promoted' to a higher level of study; the mere passage of time was not enough, as it sometimes seems to have been in the past. Sturm's college (favoured with the title of 'academy' in 1566) was not exclusively devoted to theology: it comprised nine faculties in all, including the full range of contemporary educational ideas.[32] Sturm's reforms to the arts curriculum belonged to a wave of educational improvement in the mid-century, which also saw foundations at Bordeaux and Nîmes.[33]

Sturm's plan was adapted by others to the more specialized purpose of training protestant clergymen in large numbers. The Bernese government set up a college and academy at Lausanne in the Vaud in 1537, but its statutes were only defined in 1547 through the work of Simon Sulzer of Berne (1508–85), probably under the influence of Pierre Viret and Mathurin Cordier. It contained fewer levels of study than Strasbourg, and was initially limited to a theological faculty, but otherwise followed Sturm's methods.[34] However, tensions developed between the Berne regime at Lausanne and Viret's followers at the academy, especially over the typically Genevan issues of Church discipline and debates on predestination. From May 1558 onwards the disagreements reached the point where the Bernese government expelled forty of the 'Calvinist' pastors and professors from Lausanne. To make up for this loss the academy of Geneva was soon established. It was inaugurated on 5 June 1559 with Théodore de Bèze as its first rector, and based on the principles of both Sturm and Sulzer. It began with only 162 students but by 1564 had 1,500; thereafter numbers wavered, reaching a peak after the massacres in France in 1572 but declining under pressure from the duke of Savoy in the 1580s.[35] Unlike full universities, the two Swiss academies did not award degrees, but gave commendations for good character, often after only a few months' study as candidates for missionary pastorates in France were rushed through the basic training.

France and the neighbouring regions soon followed the lead of Lausanne and Geneva. Academies for teaching protestant theology, with their secondary 'colleges', were set up by the town of Nîmes in 1561; by the queen of Navarre at Orthez, in Béarn, in 1566; by the de la Marcks at Sedan, in the Ardennes, between 1579 and 1602; and by the protestant communities of Montpellier (1596), Montauban (1598), Saumur (c.1601), and Die (1604).[36] In the house of Orange Nassau Dillenburg, a theological college was added to an existing foundation at Orange in 1573, while Johann of Nassau-Dillenburg created the Johannea at Herborn to train his clergy in 1584.[37] Political emergencies in Germany's 'confessional' period could lead to new foundations: Johann Casimir of the Palatinate founded the 'Casimirianum' at Neustadt-ad-der-Hardt to keep up the 'Calvinist' tradition during the electorship of the Lutheran Ludwig VI of the Palatinate.[38]

These specialist academies tended to be found where the Reformation was intruded piecemeal, where a previously catholic, or previously Lutheran, clergy could not be relied on to teach the new 'Calvinist' precepts. They took long to be established, and were not found everywhere they were needed. Rural territories with no academy of their own often could only support prospective ordinands for two or three years at a foreign university, while some Rhineland students had to find their own costs. Once there, students chose literary and linguistic study of the Bible, often in preference to the rigid dogmatics with which they had been trained in childhood.[39] Before these institutions appeared the reformers regularly bewailed the shortage of suitable trainees. In 1541 Luther wrote to his elector that supplying pastors for newly converted areas had stripped Wittenberg of trained men and left only boys.[40] Twenty years later Calvin described even more graphically how the frantic search for pastors for the new French churches had exhausted his resources, and 'we are reduced to searching everywhere, *even in the artisan's workshop*, to find men with some smattering of doctrine and piety as candidates for the ministry'.[41]

Their predominantly bourgeois origins, slightly raised incomes, and better education made of the new minister an intrusion of the cultivated élite world into the everyday community. Ministers were told to rise above the level of their neighbours; the Saxon visitors expected clerics to desist from the violent and crude ways of the peasantry, and to refrain from drinking with them in taverns. In identical tones 'puritan' sentiment in Jacobean England denounced 'tippling ' and the 'vice of good fellowship' amongst clergymen.[42] As with all historical 'transformations', the turning of ministers into a 'profession' must not be simplified or exaggerated.[43] Nevertheless, all these changes, however partial, can hardly have failed to establish a 'separateness' between pastors and people; a barrier which threatened those very improvements which the reformers wished to work in their society.

2. *Instilling Correct Doctrine*

The title of this section ought to cause surprise. Luther observed with astonishment in 1522 how his message, 'the Word', spread through Germany by its own power.[44] Did not the people of northern Europe flock to hear the new teachings preached? If so, what need was there for formal, pedantic instruction? In fact, there had always been something of a gulf between preachers and hearers. The reformers' sermons had been heard with enthusiasm mostly by town-dwellers, and by those country people willing to trek into the towns to hear them; whereas the 'established' Reformation provided for the rural majority in city-states' hinterlands and monarchies alike. Secondly, hearing a few sermons, or reading a pamphlet, did not necessarily produce the complete, coherent religious awareness demanded by the new concept of 'faith'.[45] Finally, if the 'flattery' of teaching a subversive message attracted hearers to the reformers' preaching against the Romanists, it might just as well attract hearers to a sectarian preaching against the reformers' 'new orthodoxy'.[46]

If the reformers ever had any doubts that a formal, structured, course of education was called for, they were dispelled by the first waves of visitations in electoral Saxony from 1528 onwards. As Luther wrote in the preface to his *Shorter Catechism* in 1529, describing his experiences as a visitor:

Dear God, help us! What misery I have seen [as a visitor]! The common man, especially in the villages, knows absolutely nothing about Christian doctrine, and unfortunately, many pastors are practically unfit and incompetent to teach. Nevertheless, they are all called Christians, have been baptized, and enjoy the holy sacraments even though they can recite neither the Lord's Prayer, the Apostle's Creed, nor the Ten Commandments. They live just like animals and unreasoning sows ... [47]

This experience was repeated wherever the Reformation spread: initial, feverish enthusiasm amongst townspeople, not always shared by those in the country; then a cooling-off period in which interest might be diverted to other more exotic creeds, and which certainly did not prepare people for a lifelong, universal course of dogmatic religious instruction. Reformed theologians and writers soon became impatient and despairing of adult listeners, especially the 'fickle rabble', on whose tastes, ironically, the whole movement had in its early days depended.[48]

In this context the teachings of the Reformation had to be passed on in a quite different fashion from the first wave of preaching and pamphleteering, which had emphasized dramatic and often negative slogans.[49] What was needed later on was a structured, balanced presentation of the beliefs shared with the continuous history of the Church, integrated with those new and distinctive to the Reformation. Such a presentation was made through a distinctive literary form: the Reformation catechism.[50] Most major reformers produced at least one of these basic manuals of religious instruction: Luther wrote his *Greater* and *Shorter Catechism* in the spring of 1529 after the shock of the visitations the previous winter.[51] Brenz and Capito also issued catechisms in 1529;[52] while Osiander wrote a somewhat extreme Lutheran *Catechism, or Childrens' Sermon* for Nuremberg and Brandenburg-Ansbach in 1533.[53] Martin Bucer produced his in 1534. In 1537 Calvin, probably in collaboration with Farel, produced the first catechism for Geneva;[54] on his return to Geneva in 1541 he hurriedly compiled a second, fuller text based on the form of Bucer's, probably issued in 1542 and certainly printed in 1545.[55] However, the major figures were not the first to write catechisms, nor were their versions the only ones available. In 1530s Germany at least, local pastors were positively encouraged to try drafting their own versions to suit local conditions and dialects, even if they wrote nothing else. In consequence, eleven or twelve different catechisms circulated in sixteenth-century Nuremberg, thirty to forty in Saxony, and some fifty in Hamburg.[56] Only gradually did those of Luther gain ascendancy in German states anxious for uniformity, while Calvinist churches generated a family of catechisms, perhaps the most famous being the Heidelberg catechism written by Olevianus and Piscator in 1563, which became in effect the rallying-point of German 'Calvinism'.[57]

The backbone of a catechism consisted of the basic formulas and practices of the reformed churches. Four major pieces of the liturgy, the Ten Commandments, Lord's Prayer, Apostles' Creed, and the two sacraments of baptism and the Eucharist, were in turn and in varying orders, recited and then expounded, usually in an exchange of questions and answers. In the longer, fuller treatments such as Luther's *Greater Catechism* or Osiander's *Children's Sermon*, the text consisted in effect of a series of sermons handling each major point of doctrine as they arose in the Commandments, Creed, and Prayer: thus specimen sermons were provided for pastors unwilling or unable to strike out on their own. The *order* in which these elements were presented may have been significant. Luther and his followers grouped the texts thus: (*a*) the Ten Commandments (i.e. the law, and how impossible it is to fulfil it); (*b*) the Creed (where help against the law's 'curse' is to be found); (*c*) the Lord's Prayer (how to approach the source of that help); (*d*) the sacraments (external symbols by which that help is attested). However, in the catechisms themselves this was not always made explicit.[58] In the Calvinist tradition the order of Creed, then sacraments, then Commandments, then Prayer was followed, suggesting that everything, including obedience to the law, flowed from right faith. This order *may* have been chosen to suit the mid-century tendency to revalue 'the law' as part of 'sanctification'.[59]

These texts could not all be used in the same way; nor was their purpose identical from around 1530, when many ordinary parish clergymen in reformed areas had little idea of what the Reformation meant, to the end of the century. They were handled differently for adults and children, and depending on whether the vernacular or Latin versions were used. The comparatively short texts could in principle be memorized, a part at a time, until all was known. To make this easier churchmen from Luther onwards stressed that the text had to be read in *exactly* the same words time after time.[60] The first basis of instruction, therefore, was repetition of a formula of words, time after time, until it was thoroughly learned. The longer texts formed the base for detailed exposition; only the most talented could be expected fully to absorb and remember catechisms which sometimes ran to many thousands of words.[61]

Catechisms were dinned into lay people in a variety of contexts. First of all they could be expounded from the pulpit. A large part of many Sunday sermons probably consisted of no more than catechetical exercises; or similar repetition of the 'Postills', 'model' sermons published by the reformers.[62] Secondly, pastors might hold separate meetings, perhaps several times a week, at which the catechism was studied and examined. In theory, all those who were insufficiently instructed were supposed to attend these. Johann Langepeter, Lutheran pastor of Kapellendorf near Weimar about 1570, faithfully preached his catechism on Sundays and examined the 'young and simple' during the week. Scipione Lentolo, Calvinist pastor to a 'Waldensian' congregation at Prali in the mountains of Piedmont, preached repetitively on the Creed, created his own mini-catechism which he rehearsed at the end of his sermon, and then examined his hearers on it during the week.[63] In protestant states, however, school and household (theoretically) also took a hand. Those children whose parents obeyed instructions to send them to school were drilled in the catechism as they learned to read; while the rubrics of Luther's *Shorter Catechism* assumed that parents would rehearse it to their children at home.[64] In visitations Lutheran states tried to discover whether these basic requirements were being attained.[65]

Such methods assumed that the congregation were at least prepared to listen (if only out of obedience rather than zeal). In some cases protestant clerics grew so impatient of the indifference or resistance of the mass of the people that, consciously or otherwise, they allowed religious instruction to slip sideways into voluntary, sectional gatherings. The most public and controversial of these gatherings occurred during and just after Martin Bucer's last years in Strasbourg in the late 1540s. After frustrating years of trying to gain civic authority for comprehensive spiritual discipline and pastoral care, Bucer and a group of his allies among the Strasbourg clergy collected names of those willing to participate in a *voluntary* programme of religious instruction and spiritual discipline. Initiates were to meet regularly in private gatherings under the supervision of the parish minister. This experiment, so easily confused with sectarian activities, split both the laity *and* the clergy of Strasbourg; the 'communities' (*Gemeinschaften*) only met for a few years between 1547 and 1551.[66]

However, informal arrangements of the same type grew up out of private and household devotions among zealous 'puritan' protestants in England. 'Voluntary religion' resulted when crusading zeal among preaching ministers met with zealous, but patchy support under a basically indifferent regime. Enthusiasts for 'godly' instruction would travel long distances to hear a favoured preacher; they would attend 'exercises' in addition to normal church services, to listen to the clergy edifying each other; several families (as Archbishop Whitgift complained) would gather together for 'repetition' or rehearsal of the contents of a lately heard sermon. 'Conferences' between zealous families, held every few weeks, might contain catechism classes for the young, sermons, 'repetition', prayer, and psalm-singing.[67] Although moral discipline and exhortation was no doubt part of such gatherings, their overwhelming purpose seems to have been mutual comfort through the shared business of hearing doctrine preached.

This obsession with learning as the primary protestant religious activity raises the question of how far Reformation doctrine *could* be represented accurately for mass consumption.[68] One problem was that the reformers strove to persuade their flocks to be religious, while also teaching that 'good works' of piety were worthless to earn salvation. Though consistent in an abstract intellectual way, these claims were psychologically inconsistent; the problem was only partly solved by saying that one 'ought' to be zealous for religion in order to show that one's faith was real and not counterfeit.[69] A second difficulty was how to balance instilling fear about sin with inspiring hope of God's mercy and favour—especially when such mercy could not be 'earned'. This was just the problem felt by the pastoral theologians of the late Middle Ages when dealing with confession; despite the early talk of 'evangelical freedom' and 'lightening burdens', it was no easier to tackle in the Reformation.[70] A third contradiction arose out of the educational aims themselves. The catechisms drove relentlessly for *reasoned* understanding: 'why do you say this?', 'what does it mean to say so-and-so?', 'how does this happen?'. Luther emphasized from the first that rote-learning had to be followed by *understanding* based on logical exposition.[71] However, the method followed was calculated so to dull the senses by endless repetition as to *suppress* curiosity in all but the most dedicated.[72] Indeed, as far as most people in rural Europe were concerned, the thought patterns of school logic, where one proposition led to another by formal rules, were themselves foreign and inappropriate.[73] This aspect of the Reformation was a form of intellectual imperialism, the 'acculturation' of popular thought to alien, academic standards.[74]

3. *Imposing New 'Piety' and 'Godliness'*

That the Reformation entailed new, or at least different, belief was obvious. It was less evident that different ethics were implied as well. The old and the new orders shared the pristine New Testament message of love of God and one's neighbour. Yet when the reformers abolished the 'reliable' value of a ritual performed in the face of a sacrificing Church to aid human salvation, they set aside a whole class of 'good works' and gave fair warning that the meaning of being a 'good Christian' was to change.[75] Their message, however, faced the more serious accusation of undermining the very reason to do 'good' in the first place. If the moral law was impossible to fulfil, and if good works done by 'natural' mankind were worthless to earn grace, how could people be induced to try to obey the moral law at all?[76] Lutheran writers from Melanchthon onwards addressed the pastoral implications of this issue:

The people should be diligently warned, that this faith cannot exist without earnest and sincere repentance and fear of God ... and it should be made known, that only in faith can they experience true repentance and sorrow for their sins ... where there is no repentance, it is a counterfeit faith. ... These two are the first points of the Christian life, penitence, or repentance and sorrow, and faith, through which we obtain forgiveness of sins, and become righteous before God ... the third part of Christian life is *to do good works*, such as to be chaste, to love and help one's neighbour, not to deceive, not to steal, not to murder, not to be vindictive, not to trust to one's own strength etc. Therefore, once again, the Ten Commandments must be energetically preached, wherein all good works are set out.[77]

Good works proved that the faithful were really faithful. Even for those who might not have faith, however, some social value attached to good works done simply to remain on good terms with one's neighbours and one's rulers. As the Lutheran Ambrosius Moibanus pointed out in his 1535 catechism, such 'counterfeit piety' consisted of avoiding outward sins such as theft, adultery, or blasphemy; though it could not save souls, it enabled human society to function. Men might be sinners, but they could restrain themselves from being public sinners.[78]

So what was the Reformation standard of 'piety' and 'godliness'? Gerald Strauss painted a picture of Reformation ethics both sombre and fundamentally boring:

Civility, good manners, tidy dress, and neat personal habits were the outward signs of the disciplined youngster. A modest demeanour in keeping with his age and station marked his carriage; humility and deference guided his deportment towards his fellowmen. At a deeper level, his behaviour exemplified his epoch's ingrained principles of sub- and coordination. He was a sturdy, responsible, but otherwise unremarkable member of his society, a docile subject, a good citizen. His foremost attachment, after his allegiance to God, was to his social and political order, his major task to uphold it.[79]

In fairness, the object of this portrayal was to show how ill-suited Lutheran ethics were, either to the prospering bourgeoisie (individualists for whom the talk of upholding the status quo and staying in one's station in life was ill-suited) or to the proletariat (who probably resented being patronized by the clergy anyway).[80] However, the issue is surely not how Reformation ethics compared with modern liberal individualism, but whether they changed any existing assumptions about which ways of life were better than others. From this point of view the reformers were almost as revolutionary in their ethics as they were in their doctrine.

3.1. *Rejecting marriage, parenthood, and daily work ceases to be the height of holiness*

The late medieval clergy's attitude (at least in the confessional advice books) had been that, since marriage and child-rearing involved the constant risk of committing sins of varying gravity, it was far preferable, if possible, to avoid them altogether and remain celibate.[81] Two Reformation arguments demolished this: first, the distinction between types of sin was removed, so 'venial sins' could no longer be guarded against;[82] secondly, no 'good work' was regarded as good unless it was specifically commanded by God, which religious chastity was not.[83] As Bucer pointed out, the dangers in a hypocritical celibacy were much worse than those in marriage; marriage entailed a kind of chastity pleasing to God.[84] Likewise, the 'idleness' of monks who did nothing but cultivate 'holiness' by performing rites not demanded in Scripture was deemed to be much less worthy and Christian than discharging one's duty usefully to society. The Lutheran Christoph Vischer encouraged readers of his catechism to feel that doing even the humblest useful work made them 'holier than the Carthusian who killed himself by fasting to death'. To have a 'sincere desire and a good will to give honest, useful service to human society', for Melanchthon, made one a truly disciplined Christian.[85]

No doubt it was flattering to servants and labourers to hear their lifestyles and daily work described as holier than an ascetic's devotions. However, it also removed a psychological prop: the ordinary lay person could no longer feel supported by the spiritual endeavours of an élite. The community's moral welfare depended upon all its members pulling their weight. In an age where public sins were expected to bring punishment on the whole community which failed to suppress them, the end of the monastic ideal might actually *increase* the sense of burden on the remainder.

3.2. *The position of women*

All mainstream protestants, and the vast majority of the sectaries, agreed with their age in excluding women from the ministries of the Church and from civic office. Princesses and queens, of course, transcended the normal limits assigned to women; but the power acquired over the conduct of

English religious affairs by an Elizabeth I (for example) did nothing for the status of women as a whole. Neither as ministers nor as burghers could women participate *publicly* in the Reformation process. Though undoubtedly involved intimately in the movement at all levels, women's distinctive participation was usually masked by that of a male partner. How far, then, did the evolving Reformation widen, narrow, or simply adjust the opportunities and roles offered to women?[86]

Quite soon after the establishment of the Reformation, nunneries and convents of female religious went the way of their male counterparts. On the face of it, this development restricted women's independent access to a spiritual life. The role models for spiritually minded women in the Middle Ages had nearly always presupposed celibacy and life in the cloister. Such women saints were more abundant between about 1350 and about 1500 than at any other time in the Middle Ages. In a late medieval nunnery some women practised an intense, often materialistic contemplative devotion: saints' lives related nuns' visions of bathing, and even suckling, the infant Christ; such women could gather 'spiritual families' of followers. Those who tried to combine spirituality with marriage and life in the world were often suspected of heresy.[87] In such a context religion formed an alternative, not an enhancement, to family life for all but a tiny minority like Sts Margaret of Scotland, Elizabeth of Hungary, or Brigid of Sweden. Several historians consider that women in cloisters achieved greater independence and responsibility, even something closer to a 'career', than they would ever attain during the Reformation.[88]

However, in the heat of the early Reformation the late medieval nunneries were roundly condemned in the pamphlet literature, and their reputation has never quite recovered. It was claimed that in nunneries women were subjected to stricter enclosure and a harsher regime than monks, and that their spiritual independence was curtailed by the intrusive supervision of male monastic overseers. Pamphleteers alleged that a nun received less respect than a married woman in her own household.[89] In the early years reformers sponsored 'raids' to 'rescue' women from convents and protected the runaways. In several cases, including that of Luther's own wife Katharina von Bora, the ex-nuns were married off to reform-minded clergy.[90] The problem is that while some nuns were clearly relieved to have escaped the cloister, and reported the fact in print, others (like the Poor Clares of Nuremberg or Biberach) strove hard to be allowed to stay.[91] One cannot generalize about nunneries any more than monasteries; nor can one tell whether women loathed or cherished the cloistered regime because they had protestant or catholic sympathies, rather than the other way around.

Austerity might be embraced as a means to holiness, then detested when its sanctifying value seemed to be in doubt.

Convents and nunneries would only have been missed if women had had no other outlet for their religious ambitions, and if the position of a protestant housewife had been one of unrelieved domestic subordination and inferiority. In practice, domesticity did not always preclude the religious life for women, any more than for the now married ministers. A handful of women actually published religious pamphlets in the early 1520s, of whom the most important was probably Catherine Schütz, wife of Matthäus Zell of Strasbourg. Catherine Zell entered into the vigorous debate surrounding the marriage of priests, which offered for one class of women at least—priests' mistresses—the prospect of new-found public recognition and respectability.[92] She was also one of the few lay people, male or female, who continued writing pamphlets after 1525. While women soon ceased to involve themselves in public religious controversy, devotional activity, including devotional writing and even publishing, remained a privileged area for protestant women. Women's influence as patrons and protectors of reforming ideas was often crucial: as when French noblewomen embraced Calvinism ahead of their husbands;[93] when Italian aristocrats like Vittoria Colonna and Giulia Gonzaga encouraged the early stirrings of similar ideas in Italy;[94] when south German ladies like Helen Streicher and Magdalena von Pappenheim protected and encouraged sectaries like Marpeck and Schwenckfield;[95] or, finally, when noble ladies like Lady Margaret Hoby or the countesses of Warwick or Bridgwater presided over ponderously devout 'puritan' households in late sixteenth- and seventeenth-century England.[96]

Protestant teaching, by emphasizing the *personal* obligation of all lay people to hear and understand religious teachings, coincidentally extended women's spheres as it extended those of other lay people. Since girls no less than boys needed to undergo the programme of catechetical instruction, reforming clerics envisaged schools being founded where older women should instruct young girls in religion. Women might not speak in church, but they might certainly teach 'godliness' elsewhere.[97] One catechist reminded husbands that their wives were 'no dish-clouts, ... nor no drudges, but fellow-heirs with them of everlasting life, and so dear to God as the men'.[98] Indeed, women's spiritual standing placed them and their children in the same political relationship to their husbands as subjects towards rulers: namely that their subjection extended only to 'godly' commands, and that ungodly orders could and must be disobeyed.[99] Some of this stress on women's moral and spiritual potential may well have been very largely drawn from pre-Reformation sources, above all from certain Christian humanists, Erasmus in particular; however, the spiritual fervour and constant religious emphasis which suffused protestant ethics was distinctive to the post-Reformation era.[100]

The inherent message of the Reformation thus offered women some limited alternative role models to the old female monasticism, or to the resuscitated social crusading found in counter-Reformation catholicism. However, its message cannot be separated from its actual political impact on women's status. The net effect of abolishing the old independent ecclesiastical jurisdiction in most protestant states was to bring the regulation of marriage and the family within the purview of secular systems and values.[101] Protestant law codes tended to enshrine civic concepts of social obligation (drawn from the burgher protectors of the movement) in a sometimes awkward fusion with the personal morality of the reforming clergy (drawn, as seen above, from the humanists). In effect, the early reformed cities tended to reinforce paternal, patriarchal authority in various ways. Marriage was confined and delayed until the age of financial independence, subject to more stringent parental controls, and turned decisively into a public, official, civic ritual. Clandestine marriages (valid, even though punishable, in the old canon law) were more harshly punished by the new marriage courts. In some cases women's rights to manage property and to make legal transactions as individuals distinct from their husbands were whittled away.[102] Yet it was not only young women whose lives were regulated: as the age of marriage was forced up, so prostitution was also banned, prescribing long periods of sexual abstinence to both sexes in early adulthood.

Inferring decisive social changes from *either* ethical principles *or* legal structures is, however, very dangerous. The Reformation simplified the structures of society, for men and women, by making domesticity the religious as well as the secular norm. Whether women experienced more or less religious fulfilment in the re-spiritualized home surely depended on their family context, their own personalities, and those of their families. Spiritualizing, or sanctifying, women's household role was simply the natural counterpart of sanctifying ordinary people and daily work of all kinds.

3.3. *Work, and making a living, becomes a spiritually respectable and worthy activity*

The Reformation, by spiritualizing everyday work, encouraged the concept of the 'calling', the idea that ordinary secular tasks were a moral and religious duty, and that diligence and success in one's work need arouse no scruple of conscience. There had been, in the Italian Renaissance above all, abundant encouragement to lay people to work hard, prosper, and raise their families diligently and carefully.[103] However, in the protestant north of Europe this ideal no longer had to *compete* with the vision of religious poverty which attracted orthodox and heretic alike in the Middle Ages.[104] From Luther onwards the concept of 'calling' or 'vocation' (*Beruf*) was applied to all forms of useful work. This concept can be misunderstood. If it had meant that people were 'called' into the occupation and condition in which they were born, they would have had a religious duty to persevere as servants, artisans, merchants, or whatever, and not to try to 'better' their status. However, Luther does not seem to have envisaged 'calling' in this narrowly restrictive way. What mattered was the 'life of service' and 'consideration for the needs of society', rather than maintaining the status quo. In practice Lutheran universities became potent instruments for the social betterment of boys and students from humble families.[105]

For those whose 'callings' were inherently upwardly mobile, there was the contrary risk that protestant ethics would encourage or at least condone unlimited acquisitiveness. Importantly, *Lutheran*, and not just 'puritan' or 'Calvinist' writers gave conditional approval to acquiring wealth by trade, and even by modest money-lending within secular laws. Osiander was exceptional in taking a bite out of the hand which fed him by condemning profiteering merchants for 'concealed theft'.[106] This argument must not be pressed or distorted. Protestant moralists were not alone in finding means to condone mercantile activity, and protestants were not even the most distinguished of the great merchant classes in sixteenth-century Germany.[107] The ethics of the Reformation endorsed the priorities of the bourgeoisie because they could not realistically have done otherwise. The Reformation accommodated itself ethically to the standards of the people who ran the towns, just as it accommodated itself to them politically in the 'establishment' of the new religious order. Within that context there was room for some reformers (like Christoph Schappeler at Memmingen) to appeal to the lesser burghers and craftsmen, and for others (say, Nikolaus Hausmann at Zwickau) to build good relationships with the patricians.[108]

3.4. *'Orderliness', rather than 'purity' in morals becomes the ideal: rectitude rather than penance*

A range of moral offences had been denounced, dissuaded, and punished in laymen and clerics alike by the ecclesiastical courts of medieval Europe. Disrespect to religion and to the clergy, disorderly conduct falling short of actual criminal violence, and sexual lapses of various kinds, were investigated and punished. While this area of life was only part of the work of ecclesiastical courts,[109] it aroused much controversy in the Reformation. No one seriously doubted that scolding, adultery, incest, or irreverence were sins. Austere protestant moralists objected rather to the apparently feeble sanctions provided by the old style of Church discipline: atoning penitential exercises, assessed by the confessor according to circumstances.[110] Afterwards, offences against the moral code laid just as much stigma on the community, but could not be ritually 'wiped away' so easily. Purification was insufficient; for the protestant zealot, the sin itself had to cease. The moralist would find the idea of a modest public humiliation and reconciliation totally inadequate, and question whether it actually *deterred* the guilty party from sinning again in the same way.[111] In England the problem was exacerbated by the repeated failure of attempts to reform the medieval Church jurisdiction, the sometimes comical efforts of some parliamentarians to replace the old Church procedures with a more 'puritan' approach, and the way in which moral discipline tended to fall to a 'godly' clique in some areas.[112]

A most austere, controlling attitude to moral behaviour is traditionally associated with Calvin's Geneva, and the Churches which grew up under its example. This is only partly misleading. In Saxony the 1528 *Visitation Articles* already recognized that 'Christian Freedom' was being misinterpreted as licence, but could only recommend pastors to the princely chancery for advice. By 1542 the Wittenberg consistory was directed to investigate adultery, 'whoredom', incest, disorder, idolatry, and so forth.[113] Zürich had established its 'marriage court' much earlier.[114] Where Geneva may have been different was neither in the aims nor even in the institutions it created, but in the level of *enforcement* and the deterrent quality of the punishments employed.[115] Perhaps because the foundation of the consistory entailed such a political struggle for the pastors, they embarked after their decisive victory in 1555 on a somewhat frantic pursuit of immoral offenders: such cases reached a peak in 1557–8. It is estimated that during the 1560s the consistory excommunicated on average five people each week; a much larger number of offenders were reported to it, but then reconciled to the Church. One delegation to the council alleged that if the consistory insisted on such austere standards of purity all their wives might be tied in weighted sacks and thrown into the river (the severest punishment in adultery cases).[116] However, the narrowly ecclesiastical nature of Genevan discipline must not be exaggerated. It relied upon the legislation of the city councils, who passed a whole series of strict moral laws between 1536 and 1541, and their power to punish, for its 'teeth'. Often it operated by reconciling quarrels rather than inflicting punishments. Civic consensus was vital to the best years of the Genevan consistory; the respect shown towards it by magistrates and citizens alike declined rapidly in the 1570s, and the pastors found they could do little to restore it.[117]

3.5. *'Popular culture' is denounced*

Most of these themes of protestant ethics, the moral worth of marriage, the family, and secular work, and the need for punishment of public immorality, would have been acceptable in principle (if not always in execution) to most of the respectable bourgeois who, irrespective of political structures, probably formed the majority of enthusiastic protestant lay people. There would even have been enthusiastic support for a moralistic campaign against the sexual irregularities which led to unprovided infants depending on communal charity.[118] It may have been a quite different story with the protestant campaign to suppress all forms of 'superstition', 'idolatry', and 'frivolous entertainments'—in short, the whole texture of magic, rituals, popular rites, and festivities, which had been grafted on to medieval religion, and only partly domesticated or regulated by the old Church. These almost certainly represented for the majority their most authentic dealings with the supernatural universe.[119] The Reformation tried to sweep them away, with varying thoroughness and success.

The reformers' attacks on such practices were far more thoroughgoing than medieval moralists', because their new vision of worship allowed them to take a much simpler and more hostile attitude to 'superstition'. For the protestant, the conditions and circumstances of life were governed by divine providence. Prayer, perhaps accompanied by a sign of humiliation such as fasting, was the acceptable way to address God's judgement.[120] No 'manipulation' of the cosmos by acts of worship or charming, and certainly none involving the mechanical application of prayers or religious formulae, could achieve anything good by itself. The reformers had attacked the element of 'charming' and mechanical manipulation implicit in catholic rituals: so, by transference, in attacking popular religious rites they were attacking *both* 'superstition' *and* 'popery'.[121] Therefore, in sermons and visitations, manifestations of the popular view of the supernatural were sought out and denounced. In 1569 the Lutheran Caspar Huberinus condemned popular cults as 'unchristian, pagan, idolatrous, frivolous, . . . seductive, ungodly, devilish'. Visitors of reformed churches in various parts of Germany complained about casting of spells using Christian prayers, ringing of church bells against storms, and protestants visiting catholic territories to obtain blessings and consecrations. In Nassau-Wiesbaden in

1594 a visitor remarked that 'the use of spells is so widespread among the people here that no man or woman begins, undertakes, does, or refrains from doing, desires or hopes for anything without using some special charm, spell, incantation, or other such heathenish medium'.[122] Charming and invoking old saints were being observed and complained of in England well into the industrial era.[123]

Not only conjurations and blessings, but also festivals and entertainments associated with the old rite, drew the reforming preachers' fire. Much of the protestant distaste for processions, holidays, and even the theatre might be explained by the prominent role these played in the old catholic order and the 'superstitious' view of the universe which it implied; and also by the associated sociability and drinking, thought likely to produce idleness, drunkenness, disorder, and sexual licence.[124] Nor was this hostility entirely a rural phenomenon. In stolidly Lutheran Nuremberg the *Schembartlauf*, a traditional masked carnival procession with a float called the 'Hell', was discontinued between 1524 and 1538. Presumably by popular demand, it was reinstated in 1539, when the 'Hell' float contained a representation of the preacher Osiander surrounded by fools and devils: the old ritual was thus used as a means of protest against the new religious austerity.[125] Similarly the Calvinist Scipione Lentolo complained about young men in his Piedmontese Waldensian congregation dressing as women and rolling other villagers in the snow.[126]

Taken to its extreme, the campaign to impose 'godliness' demanded that Sunday be kept entirely within the terms of the new pieties: the day of rest was to be occupied in hearing sermons, reciting catechisms, and private household devotions. This was the object of so-called 'sabbatarianism', the drive by some protestant clerics, and their lay supporters, to give the new religion pre-eminence in people's leisure time, and thus, negatively, to suppress sports and entertainments which competed with it.[127] It was neither universal nor practical everywhere in reformed Europe; just persuading people to come to church once in the day was, in many a rural parish, quite enough.[128] However, from Bucer's days in Strasbourg the clergy strove to persuade the burghers to desist from going for walks in the environs outside the city for all of Sunday afternoons.[129] In England the complaints of sabbath-breaking, and campaigns to suppress drinking, sports, and dancing on Sundays engaged and divided all social classes, and became a major political issue in the early seventeenth century.[130]

How is one to sum up these elements of the 'godliness' demanded by so many representatives of the Reformation, above all after the middle of the sixteenth century? It would be easy, neat, and tempting, to sum it all up as bourgeois: to say that Reformation standards of behaviour, formed among the middle classes of the corporate towns, exported modern, proto-capitalist attitudes into the European countryside at large. However, many of the most eloquent and powerful *opponents* of protestant morality and standards (say the Perrins at Geneva or the Fuggers at Augsburg) were just as 'bourgeois' as those (admittedly more numerous) counterparts who embraced protestantism.[131] Rich burghers might actually find it easier to defy a cleric to his face than simple country people, provided they avoided political minefields like 1550s Geneva. Certainly many, if not most, active early protestants were bourgeois in their origins and attitudes; that did not *infallibly* make them adopt every priority of the reformers. In some cases, for instance over marriages or usury, their wishes conflicted with those of the reforming clergy.

Rather than searching for ideal-types based on social class, one can partly explain Reformation ethics as a new kind of response to the pressures of life. Medieval (and primitive) cultures assumed a complex series of semi-physical, semi-spiritual 'levers' by which one's fate in this world could be controlled. Appeal to the spiritual goodness of a holy man or a holy order, penitential purifications to wipe out the stains of one's shortcomings, homespun charms and festivities both to mark out and to influence the rhythm of seasons and circumstances: these were ways to respond to an inexplicable predicament which had nothing to do with being 'good' in a narrow, moral sense. They were ceremonial comforts, depending essentially on the correct performance of a rite. This entire outlook on life was discarded by the reformers as fifteenth-century moralists like Gerson had never *quite* resolved to do. After the Reformation, the human response to divine providence was to be both rational and moral: rational, because the false logic of attributing virtue and potency to symbols themselves, rather than to God, was rejected; moral, because 'piety', the 'good works flowing from true faith', consisted *entirely* of obeying ethical rules, rather than purification through ritual.[132] Even learning a catechism or hearing a sermon was only provisional, persuasive evidence that one was one of the elect being 'sanctified'—not a certain 'goodness' of itself. It would be grossly anachronistic to suppose that any one social or economic class of people had a prerogative on this sort of world-view in the sixteenth century. It was through this outlook that the European mind tenuously groped its way out of essentially primitive world-views; and did so, paradoxically, in the cause of ever greater religious zeal.

4. *The Layman's Response: Resistance, the 'Inner Ring', and 'Erastianism'*

Finally, one reaches perhaps the most basic question of all: how did the people of protestant Europe respond to the torrent of instruction and exhortation which the reformed clergy thrust upon them? The Reformation, for whatever reasons, became an officially established programme of change in belief, worship, Church structures, and discipline. It set up standards of religious duty and ethics significantly different from those of the Middle Ages. Therefore, one wishes to know how far it actually achieved the aims which its architects devised for it. The degree of 'popularity'—or lack of it—which the Reformation enjoyed once it was established can indicate how far those who agitated for its introduction really understood what they were letting themselves in for; or whether the Reformation only revealed its true colours as time passed. That in turn might suggest how its initial political success depended upon all sorts of misunderstandings or partial self-deception on the part of its supporters.

Obviously any sweeping generalization about what people 'really' thought about the new churches would be very dangerous. However, one can compare different pieces of evidence left by different witnesses. Unfortunately, energetic reformed pastors often recorded very different impressions from those received by other more dispassionate observers. After riding an exhilarating wave of popular enthusiasm in the early days, perhaps they were bound to be somewhat disillusioned. In any case, reformers and pastors from all over protestant Europe complained of their flocks' conduct. People hardly seemed grateful to the ministers who had 'liberated' them from the papacy. Luther himself wrote in 1530 to a beleaguered Zwickau pastor: 'For our ministry to be thus scorned, regarded with hate and malediction, and then extinguished by hunger is a hidden and most noxious sort of persecution.'[133] In 1553 Johann Marbach, chief pastor in Strasbourg, wrote of the 'shocking scorn and little regard for the ministry of the Church' among the people of his city.[134] In 1592 Théodore de Bèze was still complaining that the ministry was 'the vocation most despised of all nowadays, though more necessary than the very air we breathe'.[135]

Partly, this 'scorn' of the ministry concerned the commonplace business of money: people paid for sermons preached less willingly than they had for masses said; in 'voluntary' churches in remote areas this problem was especially dire.[136] However, from all sorts of protestant churches ministers complained that their ministry itself, and not just its incidental expenses, was rejected. Gerald Strauss has assembled evidence from a formidable range of territories, including Saxony, Thuringia, Coburg, Magdeburg, Braunschweig, Hesse-Nassau, Neuburg, and a string of cities both princely and self-governing. The results were mixed: in occasional, scattered instances groups of people were found to be learned and pious, and devoted to the Gospel. However, in the overwhelming majority of cases pastors complained bitterly that their efforts to introduce doctrine and discipline were alike treated with contempt and neglect. At Borna, in Saxony, in 1578 it was 'the chief complaint of nearly all pastors that when they announce the catechism examination, no one will come to church'. In 1572 visitors in Braunschweig-Wolfenbüttel related 'the greatest and most widespread complaint of all pastors hereabouts that people are too lazy to go to church ... on weekdays, when the catechism is preached, only the least part of the parishioners come, so that the pastor preaches to an empty church'.[137]

Lutheran pastors were in no way unique. Elizabethan England was full of what has been called the 'literature of complaint', in which enthusiasts, principally but not exclusively ministers, fulminated against the neglect of religion by most of the people. What they meant was, *not* that people failed to attend church; but that they did not show enough *extra* devotion in wishing to learn the new religious pattern and conform to it. Simple attendance at church on Sunday morning was regarded as no better than popery or 'atheism'. In Kent one writer observed 'most doe glorifie God no more than their brute beast'; another commented:

Let the preacher speake never so plaine, although they sit and looke him in the face, yet if ye enquire of them so soone as they be out at the church dores, ye shall easily perceive that ... it went in at the one ear, and out at the other ... but aske, what doctrine did [the minister] handle? Then are they at a pause, and set at a dead lift.[138]

Extraordinary as it may seem, exactly the same complaints, of contempt and resistance both to theological instruction and to moral censure, were made by the pastor of a Piedmontese Waldensian congregation. By practising their 'heresy' in a catholic state, the duchy of Savoy, these people were putting their very lives at some risk. They would *be* protestants— that was their identity—but that did not extend to being bored stiff or humiliated by an alien preacher wished upon them by the Company of Pastors at Geneva.[139]

The 'literature of complaint' is only one side to the story. If the observer applied a different set of criteria, different results emerged. In some cases even pastors could be more realistic. Johann Marbach of Strasbourg was after 1552 in an unusual position. Forbidden to hold visitations within the city itself, a highly talented corps of clerics conducted *annual* visitations (something almost unheard-of in a principality) until 1581 in a small string of Alsatian villages ruled by the Strasbourg council. After 1563 Marbach gave up general overviews of 'piety' and concentrated on particular problems: warning children not to give up attending catechism when they reached adolescence; chivvying people to turn up to sermons on time, and not to become too drunk at weddings and baptism celebrations. When a remarkably talented body of men oversaw a small area, some measure of success, by modest criteria, could be achieved.[140] By standards as modest as these many other parts of Europe would probably have fared quite well. In the late sixteenth-century Rhine Palatinate, a modicum of observance was the norm; nearly everyone turned up to weekly worship; catechism classes were attended by younger children, but hardly at all by adolescents or adults; weekday services were only attended by the 'respectable' classes, especially the elderly and female.[141] None of this would surprise any country pastor in any age.

In other words, the standpoint from which one judges 'success' or 'failure' is crucial. This is illustrated by the otherwise puzzling fact that administrators and judges, even within Church institutions, seem to have been comparatively unworried by the neglect of catechism duties or resistance to moral instruction. If one relies primarily upon such official records, societies can appear as largely quiescent under the new religious regime: in Elizabethan and Jacobean Wiltshire there were only occasional instances of outrageous blasphemy, hardly any of witchcraft or sorcery, minimal cases of sabbath-breaking or wilful absenteeism from sermon or communion, and a tendency on the part of the authorities to leave well alone where commonplace peccadilloes like tippling and traditional sports, games, and festivals were concerned. 'Typical of the village, and apparently as true of the poorer householders as of the wealthier inhabitants, was a stolid conformity which stopped well short of enthusiasm ... most people ... professing some degree of unspectacular orthodoxy'.[142]

One should not, then, insist that there was *either* gross, flagrant, universal resistance to protestant pastoral efforts, *or* that there was a rapid, effective adoption of the essentials of the Reformation at all levels of society.[143] The polarity is rather between:

(1) those communities where clergy, whether as parish pastors or as ecclesiastical visitors and judges, made realistic demands of the people and

were content with a steady, uniform, unspectacular mediocrity; and
(2) those where the clergy insisted on trying to impose the new code of
religious behaviour with little regard either to the wishes or the capabilities of their congregations.

In the former case the resulting impression would be of widespread
'indifference' to religion, or of reasonable success, depending on the observer's standards. In the latter (assuming the pastor was not so thoroughly
obnoxious as to be driven out altogether), most likely only a minority
would be willing to adopt 'godliness' as their central obsession. Again
depending on circumstances, a potentially dangerous split could develop
between the majority of the people and the 'inner ring' of zealous
supporters, often transcending class barriers, which gathered around the
pastor.

The reformers were from the very first aware of the possibility that a
circle of specially devout believers might develop within the context of a
universal parish ministry. Luther even sketched out possible ways in which
such a society of true believers might operate in 1526, though he refused
to try to put it into practice.[144] However, few reformers in continental
Europe went so far as to address the idea as Martin Bucer. Out of his
frustrations with the constant refusal of the Strasbourg magistrates to
enforce discipline was born the idea of a society of specially enthusiastic
believers, meeting together, disciplining each other, educating each other
under the pastor.[145] Unfortunately, this enterprise not only split the laity,
but also split the Strasbourg clergy as well, into those who co-operated
with these pastoral initiatives and those who felt that the parish was the
only unit of pastoral work. None the less, the offer of extra pastoral attention
was briefly taken up by many Strasbourg artisans, suggesting that not all
shared the city fathers' views. Some even ventured to lecture their pastors
on keeping the promises of extra teaching which they had made.[146]

Strasbourg around 1550 was exceptional in continental Europe.
However, the problem of a socially divisive protestant campaign surfaced
in post-1559 England. Although the evidence is geographically somewhat
patchy and debatable, there is abundant evidence that 'puritanism' was
primarily the formation of *de facto* 'inner rings' of those who espoused a
controversial and demanding pastor against the sentiments of the rest of
society:

The meaning of puritanism is not only doctrine ... but a social situation: the
partly self-inflicted isolation of the godly, which contributed to a significant change
in the pattern of cultural and social relations. ... Perhaps it was inevitable that a

century of protestant endeavour should have led not to the new Jerusalem ... but to communities scandalously divided between those who embraced the godly way of life or had it thrust upon them and those who resisted it.[147]

There is no clear evidence that such communities split along lines determined by social, educational, or any other factors besides the simple fact of finding 'godliness' either compelling or repulsive.[148] The numbers and scale of such adherence, and the degree of division resulting, varied from place to place.[149] At worst, the rift could produce litigation and complaints to higher authority, prosecutions for disorder on one hand and non-conformity on the other, and an embattled 'puritan' mentality quite unre-lated to social class or national politics.[150]

Lay authority could respond to such 'godliness' in one way: by reas-serting the control of the 'community' (meaning ordered, hierarchical lay society) over the conduct of religious affairs. By the late sixteenth century this principle, that religious discipline and authority should depend ulti-mately on laymen, became known as 'Erastianism', a term which is often, and imprecisely, applied to the movement for lay control of the clergy at any period and place. The name derived from Thomas Liebler ('Erastus', 1524–83), court physician to the Electors Palatine and a Heidelberg aca-demic. At a crucial stage in the 1560s Erastus issued theses against the Calvinist principle that an independent Church consistory should have the power to excommunicate defaulters; instead he ascribed such authority to the civil power. This involved him in bitter exchanges with the English exile George Withers, Kaspar Olevianus, and other 'Disciplinists', and eventually in exile.[151] From that point the term 'Erastian' has been used of a very common instinct, and one which played no small part in the beginnings of the Reformation itself: an instinctive distrust of the poten-tially divisive and authoritarian ambitions of some clergy, and the need to contain the Church within the bounds of lay authority and lay consensus.

To judge the Reformation by its 'success' or 'failure' in imposing new standards of behaviour on the people slightly misses the point. The ambition to enforce a basic outward conformity to a programme of education, discipline, and moral regulation, in the hope of allowing as many as possible to be confronted with the challenge of the Reformation message, was inherently paradoxical. It tried to impose on everyone what, by common consent and even by definition, could only elicit a suitable response from a few. In so far as some protestant ministers embraced this ideal, they were attempting a gross transformation of normal human nature. The pastors' ambition utterly to revise the basic principles behind sixteenth-century people's dealings with their God, their cosmos, and their predicament was a piece of intellectual imperialism of colossal proportions. Even in the first age of relatively cheap paper, the printed book, and bureaucratic record-keeping, it was far beyond the realistic capabilities of sixteenth-century opinion-forming techniques. It is astonishing that the reforming clergy were so swept up with their mission that they even tried; even more remarkable that they were given the qualified encouragement and support of so many of the powerful; and more surprising still that, in varying degrees across Europe, they had at least some superficial measure of success. Whatever they were doing, however, they were *not* fostering a 'popular movement' based on that slightly muddle-headed coalition of inconsistent slogans, resentments, and ambitions which had made the whole exercise politically practical in the first place.

22

Conclusion

The course of the Reformation was full of paradoxes. It began with an attack on the 'oppression' of elaborate codes of ritual piety: it ended by erecting a more severe, rational, and demanding code of conduct than had ever been expected of all Christian people in the Middle Ages. It began by tearing down the separate, exalted status of the priesthood; it ended by creating a more evenly professional, highly qualified, and dedicated body of religious and cultural missionaries than had ever been seen within Europe. It began by attacking an elaborate, technical, recondite theology in the name of 'the simple Gospel' and 'return to the sources'; yet by 1600 protestant theology was a complex body of academic teachings, far more widely distributed than ever was medieval scholasticism, and sustained with much more doctrinaire determination. Yet these paradoxes appeared only because the real impact of the Reformation's true message took several decades to show itself. Despite its internal feuds and inconsistencies, and the infinitely diverse social and political contexts in which it was adopted, there was an essential, underlying coherence to the Reformation process.

The Reformation was not a foreseeable explosion from a discontented lay society which had long since outgrown the religious forms which the Church purveyed. On the contrary, by 1500 Europe's people had learned how to choose, select, invest in, and indeed develop the forms of religious piety and reassurance which suited them best. The 'monopoly' held by the catholic Church was mitigated by the competition for laymen's offerings between different religious orders and different local cults. Undoubtedly, the priesthood was suspected and mistrusted for its extravagance, misuse of resources, and its strivings for political autonomy and influence. However, its sternest critics were its own members, whose high ideals and reforming zeal counterpointed the Church's inherent failings, and offered the eventual prospect of modest improvements to learning, pastoral care, and administrative efficiency. The flaws and blemishes on the visible institution could be partly excused by the contact which it promised to the reliable, trustworthy divine economy of human salvation by dispensing grace in the sacraments.

The reformers' teaching differed from most previous 'anticlerical' attacks on the old Church: instead of criticizing an acknowledged weakness— extravagance, pomp, political aggression, or whatever—in the Church, it called into question what was always presumed to be the Church's principal strength and justification. Indeed, Martin Luther's primordial insight into the relationship between God and the human soul was not at first meant to have social or political implications. He envisaged—somewhat foggily at first—souls being saved by the direct intervention of a sovereign God considering only his own inclination to mercy, rather than the sinner's disposition. Yet the remorselessly coherent logic of the basic protestant message about human salvation entailed and demanded that one abandon the search for quantitative 'grace' through acts of ritual, ceremonial piety done in the face of Mother Church. If souls were not saved by acquiring through religious exercises the 'grace' to atone for one's sins, then the entire mechanism which channelled, measured out, and dispensed such 'grace' was redundant. The arguments from Scripture and tradition with which it buttressed that mechanism had to be spurious; the claims which the Church made to administer and adjudicate both 'grace' and 'scriptural truth' had to be erroneous and arrogant. Thus, doctrines of the authority of Scripture, and of the relationship between the ideal and the actual Church, were devised to uphold and coincide with the reformers' teaching on salvation, and to defend it against arguments from the 'authority' of the established human institution, the Roman Catholic Church.

This vision of the relationship between the believing community, or the believing soul, and its God should not be dismissed as 'mere' theology, as though it were somehow less 'real' than the nitty-gritty business of class antagonism, economic self-advancement, or political ambition. The ulti- mate effect of Reformation teaching was an overall cultural shift of funda- mental importance for the emergence of the modern world. It abolished ritual purification through expiatory rituals, the natural source of spiritual comfort for any basically primitive society. In its place it erected a system by which the moral faults and failings, whether of the individual or the community, were first sheltered under the promise of divine grace, and then gradually rectified through instruction and moral discipline. Religious worship served to inculcate correct behaviour, not to make up for its absence. It does not matter that the shift of emphasis from ritual to ethical 'goodness' had been anticipated by small cliques of northern Renaissance humanists and their readers. It took the Reformation to turn the rarified scruples of literate intellectuals into a complete pattern of new belief, worship, and Church polity. It required a full, comprehensive, theological system to persuade people (not least the priests themselves) that memorial masses, indulgences, fasts, relic-worship, or the sacrament of penance were not just vulgar practices for the ignorant and simple-minded, but actually idolatrous and diabolical.

Despite acrimonious debates between or within individual reformed churches over issues like the meaning and role of the sacraments, the interlocking body of basic Reformation beliefs attracted progressively wider support from the clerical and intellectual élite of the sixteenth century. Where medieval heresies—except for Hussitism—had degenerated into popular movements shunned by most of the clergy within a generation or two, the Reformation seduced more and more of the best qualified and most committed of the younger generation of churchmen and scholars. Roman Catholicism was in places left reeling from the shock: only after several decades could it muster an effective counter-attack, or inspire its priests with the same combative and proselytizing fervour. That counter-attack, moreover, was only brought to bear at the cost of suppressing the most sensitive, moderate, and thoughtful trends in sixteenth-century Italian religious thought.

It still remains puzzling—if one looks purely at its religious core—that the Reformation message *also* attracted immediate and widespread support from peasants and princes, from knights and bourgeois, across Germany and Switzerland, then into Scandinavia and the rest of central and northern Europe. Some previous historians have tried to explain the successful political 'establishment' of the Reformation in terms of a real harmony between the religious values of the reforming churchmen and the socio-political ambitions of so many different constitutions, classes, ranks, orders, or ethnic groups within European society. This book suggests, on the contrary, that the essential Reformation message was rather badly suited to the cultural needs and ambitions of most of the lay people who espoused it. So far from offering additional spiritual comfort, or emancipation from clerical dominion, it reduced the scope of available religious comfort and reassurance, while raising both the professional standards of the clergy and the moral or intellectual demands which they made of the laity.

Therefore, the ready adherence by all kinds of political interest groups to the various campaigns for protestant reform can be better explained in terms of a short-term coalition, born partly of misunderstanding and confusion of ideas, but also out of the reformers' outrageous, if innocent, flattery of lay susceptibilities.

1. The misunderstandings were natural, in that many of the demands which flowed as consequences from the Reformation programme resembled

other campaigners' slogans and ambitions in previous decades. The rhetoric against greedy popes and Italian curialists echoed the 'grievances' of the *Reichstag*, or the complaints of monarchs in dispute with the papacy. Luther's denial of a special spiritual 'status' to the priestly caste corresponded to the ambitions of city burghers to turn their priests into 'good citizens'. The denunciation of hypocritical monasticism or of superstitious saint and relic cults precisely matched Erasmus's more sarcastic utterances. The offer to preach the 'pure Scripture' rather than 'fables' struck a chord not only with humanists, but also with the urban laymen who had endowed and supported the better class of late medieval preachers. The advocacy of a personal, inner piety, finally, should have appealed to those who had already cultivated the 'modern devotion' style of spirituality.

Yet none of these correspondences 'explains' the unique character or course of the Reformation. When the Reformation appeared as anti-papal, bourgeois, humanist, scriptural, or devout, it showed only one of its facets, and not its most original or distinctive features. If people supported it because of those appearances, they were misled: for its implications went far deeper. To explain the Reformation as a continuity with these older trends is to cut out the very thing which made it different. For all these late medieval movements in religious politics or piety had stopped short of questioning fundamentally the received economy of salvation, of altering the basic role of the Church, or of breaching Christian unity. The Reformation did all of those things, and only coincidentally echoed traditional criticisms and dissent.

2. When the reformers appealed to the (supposedly) straight-thinking, honest, pious layman to hear, read, adjudicate, and implement an elaborate programme of religious change, they gave him on a plate something which the patronizing ways of the old Church had always denied him. City fathers were presumably both bewildered (since they took so long actually to make firm decisions on religion) and flattered to be called upon to extend their competence in this way. Where the old priests had retreated into their privileges and cloisters, the reformers went into the squares and council chambers and asked for lay support. Instead of burying dogma in a technical jargon, they translated it and insisted that any layman learn its tenets. While, with experience, lay people might eventually decide that they did not actually *want* to have the Bible, the catechism, or issues of Church polity and discipline thrust upon them at every turn, at first the effect must have been of a cornucopia of forbidden fruit suddenly poured out before their eyes.

It is essential to show how the 'coalition' between reformers and lay people was only *temporary*, because otherwise one cannot make sense of its ultimate paradoxes: that the Reformation was, according to period and context, both anticlerical and theocratic, liberating and disciplinarian, vulgarizing and élitist, and, in short, popular and unpopular. When it stirred up enthusiasm and uproar, and demolished the old order, it showed its populist side; when it rebuilt its own vision of the 'godly community', and claimed the right to educate, discipline, and erect its own institutions, its clericalist colours emerged. Hence the delays in producing the Christian community on earth led some more impatient reformers to peel off into sectarianism or spiritualism, despairing of the wiles of worldly politicians. Unease at the dubious morality of imperial and international politics eventually forced theologians to forsake some of their principles in the sphere of political theory, and retreat into the cult of the protestant martyr. In the 'confessional' age after about 1560, the Reformation was presented as a pre-packaged set of dogmas and practices, from which secular rulers tried to pick and choose at their peril. The campaign to educate the community into godly learning and godly conduct entailed potential conflict both at the personal and the political level, as only a minority of the people could ever be persuaded to make 'godliness' their central preoccupation and, so to speak, their hobby.

Social historians commonly point out that the protestant Reformation and the catholic Counter-Reformation sought, at the level of the village community, to 'Christianize' popular culture and behaviour in roughly similar ways. The ultimate social impact of protestant and catholic religious movements was in many ways similar: the clergy were educated, and consciously set apart from the mass of their people; religious dogma was instilled by didactic formulae, including catechisms and the formal rhetoric of the sermon; cults of saints, and external ritual purification in general, were replaced by exhortations to examine the conscience and cultivate moral virtue. 'Superstitious' cults which sought to manipulate the universe through magical charms and incantations, and above all by the mechanical application of Christian prayers or cult objects, were denounced in the parishes, not just in the lecture halls. If the ultimate result was the same, did it matter what precise theological rationale lay behind the suppression of indulgence-selling by itinerant friars?

Much of the common ground between protestant and catholic 'Christianizing' can, almost certainly, be traced to their common ancestry in the values of Renaissance humanism. That such common ground existed is doubtless significant. However, it does not obliterate the vast differences between the routes by which the two movements reached their goals. The catholic process essentially reaffirmed the hieratic, authoritarian quality of the Church; it simply transmuted its 'separateness' from that of a ritual caste into that of a qualified profession. The Reformation moved from clericalism to clericalism within two generations. In the midst of that process, though, it appealed directly to lay society for support and endorsement: it laid aside its privileges and status and descended into not one, but a whole series of political arenas. The difference between catholic and protestant reformations was that between evolutionary and revolutionary change. The unique quality of the protestant Reformation consists in that it took a single core idea; it presented that idea to everyone, and encouraged public discussion; it then deduced the rest of the changes to teaching and worship from that idea; and, finally, it tore down the entire fabric of the institutional Church and built again from scratch, including only what was consistent with, and required by, the basic religious message. That is to say:

(1) doctrine was subjected to public debate;
(2) the test of the value and 'rightness' of any religious act (whether 'popular' or 'élite') was its conformity to one fundamental dogma;
(3) religion was simplified by a complete rebuilding of the structures of western Christianity.

How far, then, was the Reformation a 'necessary' or fundamental event in shaping western European culture and society? The experience of catholic countries shows that one could leave the Middle Ages and the popular pre-industrial world by several routes, of which the Reformation was only one. However, those people who had taken the route of public debate and mass involvement would learn by the experience. The Reformation gave large groups of people across Europe their first lessons in political commitment to a universal ideology. In the sixteenth century, religion became mass politics. Other ideologies, ultimately more secular in tone, would take its place. The Reformation was the first.

Abbreviations Used in the Notes

Althaus, *Luther*	P. Althaus, *The Theology of Martin Luther*, trans. R. C. Schultz (Philadelphia, 1966)
AHR	*American Historical Review*
ARG	*Archiv für Reformationsgeschichte* (also *Archive for Reformation History*)
BSLK	*Die Bekenntnisschriften der evangelisch-lutherischen Kirche, herausgegeben im Gedenkjahr der Augsburgischen Konfession 1930* (repr. Göttingen, 1976)
Bornkamm, *Mid-Career*	H. Bornkamm, *Luther in Mid-Career 1521–1530*, ed. K. Bornkamm and trans. E. T. Bachmann (London, 1983)
CO	*Joannis Calvini Opera Quae Supersunt Omnia*, ed. G. Baum, E. Cunitz, and E. Reuss, *CR* 29–87 (Braunschweig and Berlin, 1853–1900)
COD	*Conciliorum Oecumenicorum Decreta*, ed. J. Alberigo *et al.* (3rd edn. Bologna, 1973)
CR	*Corpus Reformatorum*
DDC	*Dictionnaire de droit canonique*, ed. R. Naz *et al.* (Paris, 1935–65)
Dickens, *German Nation*	A. G. Dickens, *The German Nation and Martin Luther* (London, 1974)
DThC	*Dictionnaire de théologie catholique*, ed. A. Vacant *et al.* (Paris 1903–72)
EE	*Erasmi Epistolae*, ed. P. S. and H. M. Allen, 12 vols. (Oxford, 1906–58)
EHR	*English Historical Review*
Eire, *Idols*	C. M. N. Eire, *War Against the Idols: The Reformation of Worship from Erasmus to Calvin* (Cambridge, 1986)
F and M	*Histoire de l'église depuis les origines jusqu'à nos jours*, ed. A. Fliche, V. Martin, and E. Jarry, 21 vols. (Paris, 1946–52)

von Greyerz, *Rel. and Soc.*	K. von Greyerz (ed.), *Religion and Society in Early Modern Europe 1500–1800* (London, 1984)
Hay, *Church in Italy*	D. Hay, *The Church in Italy in the Fifteenth Century: The Birkbeck Lectures, 1971* (Cambridge, 1977)
Hefele-Leclercq	C. J. Hefele, rev. and trans. H. Leclercq, *Histoire des conciles,* 11 vols. (Paris, 1907–52)
HThR	*Harvard Theological Review*
HZ	*Historische Zeitschrift*
IGJ	E. Iserloh, J. Glazik, and H. Jedin, *Reformation and Counter Reformation,* trans. A. Biggs and P. W. Becker, vol. v of *History of the Church,* ed. H. Jedin and J. Dolan (London, 1980)
Inst.	J. Calvin, *Christianae Religionis Institutio/Institution de la religion chrestienne* (1559–60). References are to the chapter headings of the definitive Latin edn. of 1559; see the edn. by J.-D. Benoît, *Jean Calvin: Institution de la religion chrestienne,* 5 vols. (Paris, 1957–63), and that ed. J. T. McNeill and trans. F. L. Battles, *LCC* 20–21 (Philadelphia, 1960)
JEH	*Journal of Ecclesiastical History*
Kidd, *Documents*	B. J. Kidd (ed.), *Documents Illustrative of the Continental Reformation* (Oxford, 1911)
L and B	F. Lau and E. Bizer, *A History of the Reformation in Germany to 1555,* trans. B. A. Hardy (London, 1969)
Léonard, *Protestantism*	E. G. Léonard, *A History of Protestantism,* ed. H. H. Rowley and trans. J. M. H. Reid and R. M. Bethell, 2 vols. (London, 1965–7)
LCC	*Library of Christian Classics,* ed. J. Baillie, J. T. McNeill, and H. P. van Dusen, SCM Press
Locher, *ZR*	G. W. Locher, *Die zwinglische Reformation im Rahmen der europäischen Kirchengeschichte* (Göttingen and Zürich, 1979)
LW	*Luther's Works,* American edition, ed. J. Pelikan and H. T. Lehmann, 55 vols. (Philadelphia and St Louis, 1955–)

Melanchthon, ed. Manschreck	*Melanchthon on Christian Doctrine: Loci Communes 1555*, ed. and trans. C. L. Manschreck (New York, 1965)
Moeller, *Imperial Cities*	B. Moeller, *Imperial Cities and the Reformation: Three Essays*, ed. and trans. H. C. E. Midelfort and M. U. Edwards (Philadelphia, 1972)
MWA	*Melanchthons Werke in Auswahl*, ed. R. Stupperich (Gütersloh, 1951–)
NDL	*Neudrucke Deutsche Literaturwerke (16.–17. Jahrhunderts)*
Oakley, *Western Church*	F. Oakley, *The Western Church in the Later Middle Ages* (Ithaca and London, 1979)
Oberman, *Forerunners*	H. A. Oberman, *Forerunners of the Reformation: The Shape of Late Medieval Thought Illustrated by Key Documents* (2nd edn., Philadelphia, 1981)
Oberman, *Harvest*	H. A. Oberman, *The Harvest of Medieval Theology: Gabriel Biel and Late Medieval Nominalism* (Cambridge, Mass., 1963)
Oberman, *Masters*	H. A. Oberman, *Masters of the Reformation: The Emergence of a New Intellectual Climate in Europe*, trans. D. Martin (Cambridge, 1981)
ODCC	*The Oxford Dictionary of the Christian Church*, 2nd edn., ed. F. L. Cross and E. Livingstone (Oxford, 1974)
Ozment, *Cities*	S. E. Ozment, *The Reformation in the Cities: The Appeal of Protestantism to Sixteenth-Century Germany and Switzerland* (New Haven, Conn. and London, 1975)
Ozment, *Guide*	S. E. Ozment (ed.), *Reformation Europe: A Guide to Research* (St Louis, Mo., 1982)
Ozment, *Perspective*	S. E. Ozment (ed.), *The Reformation in Medieval Perspective* (Chicago, 1971)
Ozment, *Reform*	S. E. Ozment, *The Age of Reform 1250–1550: An Intellectual and Religious History of Late Medieval and Reformation Europe* (New Haven, Conn. and London, 1980)
P and P	*Past and Present*
Pelikan, *Dogma*	J. J. Pelikan, *Reformation of Church and Dogma (1300–1700)*, vol. iv of *The Christian Tradition* (Chicago, 1984)

PL, ed. Migne	*Patrologia Latina*, ed. J. P. Migne, 221 vols. (Paris, 1844–90)
Prestwich, *Int. Calv.*	M. Prestwich (ed.), *International Calvinism 1541–1715* (Oxford, 1985)
Rapp, *Église*	F. Rapp, *L'Église et la vie religieuse en occident à la fin du moyen âge* (Paris, 1971)
Rapp, *Réformes*	F. Rapp, *Réformes et réformation à Strasbourg: église et société dans le diocèse de Strasbourg (1450–1525)* (Paris, 1974)
Rupp, *Patterns*	G. Rupp, *Patterns of Reformation* (London, 1969)
S and S	*Huldreich Zwinglis Werke*, ed. M. Schuler and J. Schulthess, 8 vols. (Zürich, 1828–42)
SCH	*Studies in Church History* [papers presented at the meetings of the Ecclesiastical History Society]
Scheel, *Dokumente*	O. Scheel (ed.), *Dokumente zu Luthers Entwicklung (bis 1519)* (2nd edn., Tübingen, 1929)
Scribner, *PC and PM*	R. W. Scribner, *Popular Culture and Popular Movements in Reformation Germany* (London, 1987)
Sehling	E. Sehling (ed.), *Die evangelischen Kirchenordnungen des XVI. Jahrhunderts*, i–v, (Leipzig, 1902–13); vi–viii, xi–xiii (Tübingen, 1955–)
Skinner, *Foundations*	Q. Skinner, *The Foundations of Modern Political Thought*, 2 vols. (Cambridge, 1978)
SMRT	*Studies in Medieval and Reformation Thought*
Southern, *W. Soc. and Church*	R. W. Southern, *Western Society and the Church in the Middle Ages* (Harmondsworth, 1970)
Stadtbürgertum und Adel	W. J. Mommsen, P. Alter, and R. W. Scribner (eds.), *Stadtbürgertum und Adel in der Reformation: Studien zur Sozialgeschichte der Reformation in England und Deutschland* (Stuttgart, 1979)
Städtische Gesellschaft	I. Bátori (ed.), *Städtische Gesellschaft und Reformation* (Stuttgart, 1980)
Stephens, *Bucer*	W. P. Stephens, *The Holy Spirit in the Theology of Martin Bucer* (Cambridge, 1970)
Stephens, *Zwingli*	W. P. Stephens, *The Theology of Huldrych Zwingli* (Oxford, 1986)

Strauss, *Pre-Ref. Germany*   G. Strauss (ed.), *Pre-Reformation Germany* (London, 1972)

Strauss, *Manifestations*   G. Strauss (ed.), *Manifestations of Discontent in Germany on the Eve of the Reformation* (Bloomington, Ind., 1972)

Strohl, *Pensée*   H. Strohl, *La Pensée de la réforme* (Neuchâtel and Paris, 1951)

T and O *Holiness*   C. Trinkaus and H. A. Oberman (eds.), *The Pursuit of Holiness in Late Medieval and Renaissance Religion*, *SMRT* 10, (Leiden, 1974)

Thomson, *Popes*   J. A. F. Thomson, *Popes and Princes 1417–1517: Politics and Piety in the Late Medieval Church* (London, 1980)

WA   M. Luther, *Werke: Kritische Gesamtausgabe*, 58 vols. (Weimar, 1883–1948)

WA.B   D. Martin Luthers Werke. Briefwechsel, 12 vols. (Weimar, 1930–67)

Williams   G. H. Williams, *The Radical Reformation* (London, 1962)

Z   *Huldreich Zwinglis sämtliche Werke*, ed. E. Egli *et al.*, *CR*, 88 et seq. (Berlin, Leipzig, and Zürich, 1905–)

ZKG   *Zeitschrift für Kirchengeschichte*

Notes

Introduction: The Reformation and Europe

1. As remarked by Erasmus, in *EE* iv. 1155 n.; see R. H. Bainton, *Erasmus of Christendom* (London, 1972), 204 and n.

2. Rare exceptions included the books of Reformation instruction printed in glagolitic script for use in Croatia by Johannes Ungnad von Sonneck at Urach in Württemberg: see IGJ 325 and n.; H.-M. Maurer and K. Ulshöfer, *Johannes Brenz und die Reformation in Württemberg* (Stuttgart, 1973), 187. Among the Romanian people in Hungary, previously of orthodox faith, protestantism was the first form of western Christianity to be taught there: L. Makkai, *Histoire de Transylvanie* (Paris, 1946), 168 ff.

3. Estimates from K. H. Helleiner, 'The Population of Europe from the Black Death to the Eve of the Vital Revolution', in M. M. Postan and H. J. Habakkuk (eds.), *The Cambridge Economic History of Europe*, iv (Cambridge, 1967), 1–95; R. Mols, 'Population in Europe 1500–1700', in C. Cipolla (ed.), *The Fontana Economic History of Europe*, ii.: *The Sixteenth and Seventeenth Centuries* (London, 1974), 38–9; H. Miskimin, *The Economy of Early Renaissance Europe, 1300–1460* (Cambridge, 1975), 28; J. R. Hale, *Renaissance Europe 1480–1520* (London, 1971), 33 ff.; T. H. Hollingsworth, *Historical Demography* (London, 1969), 375 ff.; H. A. F. Kamen, *European Society 1500–1700* (London, 1984), 31 ff., 45 ff.

4. M. W. Flinn, *The European Demographic System, 1500–1820* (Brighton, 1981), 13 ff.; Kamen, *European Society*, 28 ff.

5. Mols, 'Population in Europe', 39–44; see also id., *Introduction à la démographie historique des villes d'Europe du xive au xviiie siècle*, 3 vols. (Gembloux and Louvain, 1954–6).

6. Flinn, *European Demographic System*, 22 ff.

7. Dickens, *German Nation*, 179–80, remarks that even in the most urbanized parts of Germany town-dwellers were a minority.

8. J. Heers, *L'Occident aux xive et xve siècles: aspects économiques et sociaux* (4th edn., Paris, 1973), 78 ff., 139 ff.; Miskimin, *Economy of Early Renaissance Europe*, 32–72; see also G. Duby, *Rural Economy and Country Life in the Medieval West*, trans. C. Postan (London, 1968), 293 ff., 520 ff.

9. On price movements see A. de Maddalena, 'Rural Europe 1500–1750', in Cipolla (ed.), *Fontana Economic History*, esp. ii. 304 ff.; F. Mauro, *Le xvie Siècle européen: aspects économiques* (Paris, 1966), 209 ff.; on Baltic grain see P. Burke (ed.), *Economy and Society in Early Modern Europe: Essays from Annales* (London, 1972), 93.

10. See for instance R. W. Scribner and G. Benecke (eds.), *The German Peasant War of 1525: New Viewpoints* (London, 1979), 19 ff., 63 ff.; T. Scott, 'The Peasants' War: A Historiographical Review', *Historical Journal*, 22 (1979), 695 ff., and nn.; see also Ch. 14. 2.

11. W. Minchinton, 'Patterns and Structure of Demand 1500–1750', in Cipolla (ed.), *Fontana Economic History*, esp. ii. 151 ff.; B. H. Slicher van Bath, *The Agrarian History of Western Europe, A. D. 500–1850*, trans. O. Ordish (London, 1963), 195 ff.; Kamen,

European Society, 52 ff.; Burke (ed.), *Economy and Society in Early Modern Europe*, 72 ff., 92 ff.

12. On so-called 'proto-industrialization' see T. Scott, 'Economic Conflict and Co-operation on the Upper Rhine, 1450–1600', in E. I. Kouri and T. Scott (eds.), *Politics and Society in Reformation Europe: Essays for Sir Geoffrey Elton on his Sixty-Fifth Birthday* (London, 1987), 213 ff.; see also P. Kriedte, H. Medick, and J. Schlumbohm (eds.), *Industrialization before Industrialization: Rural Industry in the Genesis of Capitalism* (Cambridge, 1981); Kamen, *European Society*, 79 ff.

13. T. A. Brady, *Turning Swiss: Cities and Empire, 1450–1550* (Cambridge, 1985), 9 ff.; Moeller, *Imperial Cities*, 44 and n.; see also R. A. Rotz, '"Social Struggles" or the Price of Power? German Urban Uprisings in the Late Middle Ages', *ARG* 76 (1985), 64–95, for a more political and less economic explanation.

14. On European aristocracies in general see the brilliant analysis in Kamen, *European Society*, 93–119; on the German *Ritter* see Ch. 14. 1, and V. Press, *Karl V, König Ferdinand und die Entstehung der Reichsritterschaft* (Wiesbaden, 1976), 8 ff.

15. See the somewhat overstated case made by C. Lis and H. Soly, *Poverty and Capitalism in Pre-Industrial Europe* (Brighton, 1982), *passim*.

16. See Ch. 4. 5, and C. Trinkaus, *The Scope of Renaissance Humanism* (Ann Arbor, Mich., 1983).

17. H. Holborn, *A History of Modern Germany*, 3 vols. (New York, 1959–69), i. 106; F and M xiv. 459 ff.; M. Aston, *The Fifteenth Century: The Prospect of Europe* (London, 1968), 37–9; H. Rashdall, *The Universities of Europe in the Middle Ages*, ed. F. M. Powicke and A. B. Emden, 3 vols. (Oxford, 1936), ii. 211–80; A. B. Cobban, *The Medieval Universities: Their Development and Organization* (London, 1975), 116–21.

18. See Ch. 15. 3.

19. As is to some extent implied by E. L. Eisenstein, *The Printing Press as an Agent of Change*, 2 vols. (Cambridge, 1979), i. 303–450; id., 'L'Avènement de l'imprimerie et la réforme', *Annales: économies, sociétés, civilisations*, 26 (1971), 1355–82.

20. B. Moeller, 'Religious Life in Germany on the Eve of the Reformation', in Strauss, *Pre-Ref. Germany*, 21–3 (this article is also translated as 'Piety in Germany around 1500', in Ozment, *Perspective*, 50–75); Aston, *Fifteenth Century*, 74; L. Febvre and H.-J. Martin, *The Coming of the Book: The Impact of Printing 1450–1800*, trans. D. Gerard (London, 1976), 249 ff., 278; R. Hirsch, *Printing, Selling and Reading 1450–1550* (Wiesbaden, 1967), esp. 128 ff.

21. See the remarks of A. Hudson, *The Premature Reformation: Wycliffite Texts and Lollard History* (Oxford, 1988), 510 ff., on the relationship between Wycliffism and the presence or absence of print. For a critique of 'Justification by Print Alone', see A. G. Dickens, 'Intellectual and Social Forces in the German Reformation', in *Stadtbürgertum und Adel*, 22; also Febvre and Martin, *Coming of the Book*, 288.

1. *The Religion of the People of Europe*

1. This persistent but crude simplification dates back to such works as J. A. Babington, *The Reformation: A Religious and Historical Sketch* (London, 1901); against which compare e.g. F. Clark, *Eucharistic Sacrifice and the Reformation* (Chulmleigh, 1981), 72.

2. See the debate in von Greyerz, *Rel. and Soc.* between R. Muchembled (56–65) and

J. Wirth (66–78); also N. Z. Davis, 'Some Tasks and Themes in the Study of Popular Religion', in T and O *Holiness*, 307–36.

3. As described in J. Delumeau, *Catholicism between Luther and Voltaire: A New View of the Counter-Reformation* (London, 1977), 175ff.; K. Thomas, *Religion and the Decline of Magic* (London, 1971), *passim*, but esp. 58–89.

4. Such texts included Henricus de Gorinchem, *Tractatus de supersticiosis quibusdam casibus* ... (Esslingen, 1473 and 1475; Cologne, 1488, etc.); Martinus de Arles y Andosilla, *Tractatus insignis et exquisitissimus de superstitionibus contra maleficia seu sortilegia* ... (Paris, 1517), here cited in the edition in *Tractatus Universi Juris*, xi, pt. 2 (Lyons, 1584), fos. 402ᵛ–8ʳ; M. Plantsch, *Opusculum de sagis maleficis* (1507), as discussed in Oberman, *Masters*, 162–72; a later ex. is J.-B. Thiers, *Traité des superstitions* (Paris, 1679); see N. Z. Davis, *Society and Culture in Early Modern France* (London, 1975), 229, 336. On the definition of 'superstition' see also M. O'Neil, 'Magical Healing, Love Magic and the Inquisition in Late Sixteenth-Century Modena', in S. Haliczer (ed.), *Inquisition and Society in Early Modern Europe* (London, 1987), 88–9.

5. The phrase used by Thomas, *Religion and the Decline of Magic*, 800; cf. R. Muchembled, *Popular Culture and Élite Culture in France 1400–1750*, trans. L. Cochrane (Baton Rouge, La., 1985), esp. 71ff., 92ff., 101ff. On the application of popular magic to healing and love-magic see O'Neil, 'Magical Healing', 92ff., 98ff.

6. Thiers, *Superstitions*, 316; C. Ginzburg, *The Night Battles: Witchcraft and Agrarian Cults in the Sixteenth and Seventeenth Centuries*, trans. J. and A. Tedeschi (London, 1983); Thomas, *Religion and the Decline of Magic*, 222.

7. Thomas, *Religion and the Decline of Magic*, 237 f.; Thiers, *Superstitions*, 422ff.

8. *Tractatus Universi Juris*, xi, pt. 2, fos. 404ᵛ–5ʳ; J. Toussaert, *Le Sentiment religieux en Flandre à la fin du moyen-âge* (Paris, 1963), 364ff.; Thomas, *Religion and the Decline of Magic*, 214.

9. *Tractatus Universi Juris*, xi, pt. 2, fo. 403ʳ. On the parasitic relationship between popular magic and the liturgy see also O'Neil, 'Magical Healing', 91.

10. Delumeau, *Catholicism between Luther and Voltaire*, 177ff.; Thiers, *Superstitions*, 316.

11. R. W. Scribner, 'Cosmic Order and Daily Life: Sacred and Secular in Pre-Industrial German Society', in von Greyerz, *Rel. and Soc.*, 19; id., 'Ritual and Popular Religion in Catholic Germany at the Time of the Reformation', in Scribner, *PC and PM* 31ff.

12. *Tractatus Universi Juris*, xi, pt. 2, fos. 403ʳ, 404ᵛ, 406ʳ⁻ᵛ.

13. Oakley, *Western Church*, 117ff.; Thomas, *Religion and the Decline of Magic*, 28–31; A. N. Galpern, *The Religions of the People in Sixteenth-Century Champagne* (Cambridge, Mass., 1976), 53–5.

14. *Tractatus Universi Juris*, xi, pt. 2, fo. 404ᵛ.

15. Scribner, 'Cosmic Order', in von Greyerz, *Rel. and Soc.*, 21–3.

16. *Tractatus Universi Juris*, xi, pt. 2, fo. 403ʳ.

17. Bornkamm, *Mid-Career*, 291.

18. F and M xiv. 728–9; Bibliothèque Nationale, Paris, MS Latin 3375. ii, fos. 17ᵛ–37ʳ; it was stipulated by the decree *Omnis Utriusque Sexus* of the Fourth Lateran Council in 1215 that all lay people should confess their sins and receive communion at least once a year: see Hefele-Leclercq, v, pt. 2, 1349–51; cf. Ozment, *Cities*, 29 f.

19. Oakley, *Western Church*, 126; T. N. Tentler, *Sin and Confession on the Eve of the Reformation* (Princeton, NJ, 1977), 16ff., 82ff.

20. T. N. Tentler, 'The Summa for Confessors as an Instrument of Social Control', in

T and O *Holiness*, 103–26; on the infrequency of laymen's confessions see Toussaert, *Sentiment religieux*, 122.

21. E. J. D. Douglass, *Justification in Late Medieval Preaching: A Study of John Geiler of Kaisersberg*, SMRT 1 (Leiden, 1966), 154–5.

22. Oakley, *Western Church*, 122–3.

23. For full details on this topic see Ch. 6 nn. 12–13.

24. Oakley, *Western Church*, 120–2.

25. E. W. Monter, *Ritual, Myth and Magic in Early Modern Europe* (Brighton, 1983), 14–15; J. Chiffoleau, *La Comptabilité de l'au-delà: les hommes, la mort et la religion dans la région avignonnaise à la fin du moyen âge (1320–1480)* (Rome, 1980), 323–56; B. Moeller, 'Religious Life', in Strauss, *Pre-Ref. Germany*, 15–16; Rapp, *Église*, 154–5; H. Heller, *The Conquest of Poverty: The Calvinist Revolt in Sixteenth-Century France* (Leiden, 1985), 49–50 and refs.; on the contrast between pious bequests from catholics and heretics in Provence see G. Audisio, *Les Vaudois du Luberon: une minorité en Provence (1460–1560)* (Mérindol, 1984), 208ff. For English instances see P. Heath, 'Urban Piety in the Later Middle Ages: The Evidence of Hull Wills', in R. B. Dobson (ed.), *Church, Politics, and Patronage in the Fifteenth Century* (Gloucester, 1984), 209ff. and esp. 213ff.; C. Burgess, '"For the Increase of Divine Service"; Chantries in the Parish in Late Medieval Bristol', *JEH* 36 (1985), 46–65; N. P. Tanner, 'The Reformation and Regionalism: Further Reflections on the Church in Late Medieval Norwich', in J. A. F. Thomson (ed.), *Towns and Townspeople in the Fifteenth Century* (Gloucester, 1988), 129–47, esp. 133ff., 138ff. On the English chantry see A. Krieder, *English Chantries: The Road to Dissolution* (Harvard, 1979).

26. Oberman, *Forerunners*, 247–51.

27. Oakley, *Western Church*, 232.

28. Southern, *W. Soc. and Church*, 30–1.

29. *WA* vi. 447 f.; *LW* xliv, 185 f. and nn.; see I. Rothkrug, 'Popular Religion and Holy Shrines: Their Influence on the Origins of the German Reformation and Their Role in German Cultural Development', in J. Obelkevich (ed.), *Religion and the People, 800–1700* (Chapel Hill, NC, 1979), 20–86.

30. Ozment, *Cities*, 139.

31. Monter, *Ritual, Myth and Magic*, 15.

32. See Ch. 6. 1.

33. Rapp, *Église*, 143–5. Some extremists demanded that communion be administered to them much more often: see Moeller, 'Religious Life', in Strauss, *Pre-Ref. Germany*, 15 and n. 8.

34. Scribner, 'Cosmic Order', 19–21, also his *The German Reformation* (London, 1986), 11–12; also id., 'Ritual and Popular Religion', in Scribner, *PC and PM*, 36–41.

35. On the social value of the mass see J. Bossy, 'The Mass as a Social Institution', in *P and P* 100 (1983), 29–61; M. E. James, 'Ritual, Drama, and Social Body in the Late Medieval English Town', *P and P* 98 (1983), 3–29; on confraternities, K. Schlemmer, *Gottesdienst und Frömmigkeit in der Reichsstadt Nürnberg am Vorabend der Reformation* (Würzburg, 1980), 341ff.; Monter, *Ritual, Myth and Magic*, 15–16; Moeller, 'Religious Life', in Strauss, *Pre-Ref. Germany*, 16, notes the existence of 99 confraternities in 16th-cent. Hamburg; further details are found in C. F. Black, *Italian Confraternities in the Sixteenth Century* (Cambridge, 1989), *passim*; Hay, *Church in Italy*, 66 f;

J. Heers, *L'Occident aux xive et xve siècles: aspects économiques et sociaux* (4th edn., Paris, 1973), 322–31.

36. Galpern, *Religions of the People*, 52–68.
37. J.-P. Gutton, 'Confraternities, *Curés* and Communities in Rural Areas in the Diocese of Lyons under the Ancien Régime', in von Greyerz, *Rel. and Soc.*, 202–12; F and M xiv. 666 ff.
38. Galpern, *Religions of the People*, 78–85; see also F and M xiv. 605 ff.
39. On such *Functiones sacrae* see R. W. Scribner, 'Ritual and Popular Religion', in Scribner, *PC and PM*, 23–9; id., 'Ritual and Reformation', in Scribner, *PC and PM*, 110–11.
40. Scribner, 'Ritual and Reformation', 108–9.
41. F and M xiv. 760–1; xv. 343 and nn.; Schlemmer, *Gottesdienst*, 260 ff.
42. On this theme in general R. C. Finucane, *Miracles and Pilgrims: Popular Beliefs in Medieval England* (London, 1977); J. Sumption, *Pilgrimage: An Image of Medieval Religion* (London, 1975); specific to this period are for instance M. Hellmann, 'Eine Pilgerreise ins heilige Land im Jahre 1480', in K. Schulz (ed.), *Beiträge zur Wirtschafts- und Sozialgeschichte des Mittelalters: Festschrift für Herbert Helbig* (Cologne and Vienna, 1976), 261–72; Schlemmer, *Gottesdienst*, 331 ff.; and Rothkrug, 'Popular Religion', as cited above, n. 29.
43. Monter, *Ritual, Myth and Magic*, 9–11, based on L. Rothkrug, *Religious Practices and Collective Perceptions: Hidden Homologies in the Renaissance and Reformation* (Waterloo, Ont., 1984).
44. F and M xv. 342–3; Monter, *Ritual, Myth and Magic*, 11; Hay, *Church in Italy*, 69.
45. F and M xiv. 783–4; xv. 339–41; Rapp, *Eglise*, 149–51; Oberman, *Harvest*, 283–5; Pelikan, *Dogma*, 45–50.
46. F and M xv. 343; Moeller, 'Religious Life', in Strauss, *Pre-Ref. Germany*, 16.
47. Moeller, *Imperial Cities*, 47 and n. 21; Moeller, 'Religious Life', in Strauss, *Pre-Ref. Germany*, 25; Ozment, *Cities*, 38–42; Schlemmer, *Gottesdienst*, 254 ff.; Rupp, *Patterns*, 6 n. 2; P. A. Russell, *Lay Theology in the Reformation: Popular Pamphleteers in Southwest Germany 1521–1525* (Cambridge, 1986), 30.
48. A. Renaudet, *Préréforme et humanisme à Paris pendant les premières guerres d'Italie (1494–1517)* (2nd edn., Paris, 1953), 163–70; H. R. Guggisberg, *Basel in the Sixteenth Century* (St Louis, 1982), 12–13; F and M xiv. 636 ff.; xv. 266–74; Rapp, *Église*, 130–6; Douglass, *Justification, passim*.
49. COD 610 ff.; *Praise of Folly/Moriae Encomium*, ed. B. Radice, in *Collected Works of Erasmus*, xxvii, ed. A. H. T. Levi (Toronto, 1986), 132 ff.; see also his *De Ratione Concionandi*.
50. For some moralizing views on such 'aberrant' forms of thought see Toussaert, *Sentiment religieux*, 361 ff., 371; also I. Schairer, *Das religiöse Volksleben am Ausgang des Mittelalters nach Augsburger Quellen* (Leipzig, 1914), 104 ff.; cf. F and M xiv. 821 ff.; Rapp, *Église*, 159–62.
51. On such a world-view see e.g. C. Webster, *From Paracelsus to Newton: Magic and the Making of Modern Science* (Cambridge, 1982); D. P. Walker, *Spiritual and Demonic Magic from Ficino to Campanella* (London, 1958); R. W. Scribner, *For the Sake of Simple Folk: Popular Propaganda for the German Reformation* (Cambridge, 1981), 123 ff.; id., 'Demons, Defecation and Monsters: Luther's "Depiction of the Papacy" (1545)', in Scribner, *PC and PM* 277 ff.; L. W. Spitz, *The Religious Renaissance of the*

German Humanists (Cambridge, Mass., 1963), 93–5, 162; P. Baumgart, 'Formen der Volksfrömmigkeit: Krise der alten Kirche und reformatorische Bewegung', in P. Blickle (ed.), *Revolte und Revolution in Europa: Referate und Protokolle des internationalen Symposiums zur Erinnerung an den Bauernkrieg 1525 (Memmingen, 24.–27. März 1975)*, Historische Zeitschrift Neue Folge Beiheft 4 (1975), 196ff.; on Melanchthon, see F. Hildebrandt, *Melanchthon: Alien or Ally?* (Cambridge, 1946), p. xviii; and in more detail D. Bellucci, 'Mélanchthon et la défense de l'astrologie', *Bibliothèque d'humanisme et renaissance*, 50 (1988), 587–622.

52. Oakley, *Western Church*, 116–17; Rapp, *Église*, 152–3; F and M xiv. 763ff.; Moeller, 'Religious Life', in Strauss, *Pre-Ref. Germany*, 23–4; Monter, *Ritual, Myth and Magic*, 13–14 and n. 14; Russell, *Lay Theology*, 45; Baumgart, 'Formen der Volksfrömmigkeit', 195 f.

53. See Ozment, *Cities*, 15–22 and nn.

54. As portrayed above all by J. Huizinga, *The Waning of the Middle Ages: A Study of the Forms of Life, Thought and Art in France and the Netherlands in the Fourteenth and Fifteenth Centuries*, trans. F. Hopman (London, 1924), *passim*.

55. Scribner, *German Reformation*, 7–10. Those who most deplored such popular religious practices themselves attest their popularity.

56. See J. R. Lander, *Government and Community: England 1450–1509* (London, 1980), 109.

57. Chiffoleau, *Comptabilité*, 211ff.

58. Ibid. 229ff., 240ff., 248ff.

59. See esp. Ch. 21.

2. The Vulnerability of the Church

1. On the use of the term 'corruption' in political theory see *Aristotle's Politics and the Athenian Constitution*, ed. J. Warrington (London, 1959), 133ff.; *Machiavelli: The Discourses*, ed. B. Crick (Harmondsworth, 1970), 106ff., 157–64.

2. See e.g. Southern, *W. Soc. and Church*, 34–44.

3. See *DDC*, 'Curé', iv, cols. 889ff.

4. A. E. McGrath, *Luther's Theology of the Cross: Martin Luther's Theological Breakthrough* (Oxford, 1985), 27.

5. On the late medieval universities see H. Rashdall, *The Universities of Europe in the Middle Ages*, ed. F. M. Powicke and A. B. Emden, 3 vols. (Oxford, 1936), ii. 211–80; J. Verger, 'Géographie universitaire et mobilité étudiante au moyen âge: quelques remarques', in A. Paravicini Bagliani (ed.), *Écoles et vie intellectuelle à Lausanne au moyen âge* (Lausanne, 1987), 11ff. and nn.; H. Jewell, 'English Bishops as Educational Benefactors in the Later Fifteenth Century', in R. B. Dobson (ed.), *Church, Politics and Patronage in the Fifteenth Century* (Gloucester, 1984), 146–67; C. Harper-Bill, 'Dean Colet's Convocation Sermon and the Pre-Reformation Church in England', *History*, 73/238 (1988), 200.

6. See e.g. B. Andenmatten, 'Les *Studia* des ordres mendiants à Lausanne (xiiie–xvie siécles)', in Paravicini Bagliani (ed.), *Écoles et vie intellectuelle à Lausanne*, 75ff., with ref. to *Le Scuole degli ordini mendicanti (secoli xiii–xiv)* [proceedings of a conference at Todi, 1976] (Todi, 1978); or N. Orme, 'Education and Learning in a Medieval English Cathedral: Exeter 1380–1548', *JEH* 32 (1981), 265–83.

7. P. Dubuis, 'Les Écoles en Suisse romande à la fin du moyen âge: quelques jalons', in Paravicini Bagliani (ed.), *Écoles et vie intellectuelle à Lausanne*, 103–4, based on L. Binz,

Vie religieuse et réforme ecclésiastique dans le diocèse de Genève pendant le grand schisme et la crise conciliaire (1378–1450), i (Geneva, 1973), 289–90. For chantry priests holding schools see A. Hamilton Thompson, *The English Clergy and their Organization in the Later Middle Ages* (Oxford, 1947), 144 and nn.

8. R. H. Fife, *The Revolt of Martin Luther* (New York, 1957), 20–31; cf. also J. A. H. Moran, *The Growth of English Schooling, 1340–1548* (Princeton, NJ, 1985), 150–84 and esp. 169ff.; N. Orme, 'Schoolmasters, 1307–1509', in C. H. Clough (ed.), *Profession, Vocation and Culture in Later Medieval England* (Liverpool, 1982), 218–21.

9. On lay measures in poor relief see R. Kiessling, *Bürgerliche Gesellschaft und Kirche in Augsburg im Spätmittelalter: Ein Beitrag zur Strukturanalyse der oberdeutschen Reichsstadt* (Augsburg, 1971), 216ff.; on confraternal charity B. Pullan, *Rich and Poor in Renaissance Venice* (Oxford, 1971), *passim*; C. F. Black, *Italian Confraternities in the Sixteenth Century* (Cambridge, 1989), 130–233; J.-P. Gutton, 'Confraternities, *Curés* and Communities in Rural Areas in the Diocese of Lyons under the Ancien Régime', in von Greyerz, *Rel. and Soc.*, 202 f.; see also P. Slack, *Poverty and Policy in Tudor and Stuart England* (London, 1988), 114ff.

10. On monastic charitable obligations see e.g. D. Knowles, *The Religious Orders in England*, 3 vols. (Cambridge, 1948–59), iii. 264ff.

11. See Ch. 1 n. 25 (wills usually combined charitable giving with the request for memorial masses); and also for instance C. Burgess, '"By Quick and by Dead": Wills and Pious Provision in Late Medieval Bristol', *EHR* 102 (1987), 837–58; J. Chiffoleau, *La Comptabilité de l'au-delà* (Rome, 1980), 302ff.; R. N. Swanson, *Church and Society in Late Medieval England* (Oxford, 1989), esp. 299–308.

12. Southern, *W. Soc. and Church*, 37–9.

13. *DDC*, 'Juridiction ecclésiastique', vi, cols. 236ff., 'Official', vi, cols. 1105ff.; A. Lefebvre-Teillard, *Les Officialités à la veille du concile de Trente* (Paris, 1973), esp. 116ff., 145ff.; also P. Fournier, *Les Officialités au moyen âge: étude sur l'organisation, la compétence et la procédure des tribunaux ecclésiastiques ordinaires en France, de 1180 à 1308* (Paris, 1880). On England see R. Houlbrooke, *Church Courts and the People during the English Reformation, 1520–1570* (Oxford, 1979), 21–54; C. Harper-Bill, *The Pre-Reformation Church in England 1400–1530* (London, 1989), 54ff.; Swanson, *Church and Society*, 140ff., and esp. 166ff.; R. M. Wunderli, *London Church Courts and Society on the Eve of the Reformation* (Medieval Academy of America Publications; Cambridge, Mass., 1981), 7–62.

14. On the Inquisition see B. Hamilton, *The Medieval Inquisition* (London, 1981), and sources cited there. The classic work remains H. C. Lea, *A History of the Inquisition in the Middle Ages*, 3 vols. (New York and London, 1888).

15. On the papal monarchy in Italy see P. Prodi, *The Papal Prince: One Body and Two Souls: The Papal Monarchy in Early Modern Europe*, trans. S. Haskins (Cambridge, 1987); P. Partner, *The Lands of St. Peter: The Papal State in the Middle Ages and the Early Renaissance* (London, 1972); Thomson, *Popes*, 114–42.

16. Skinner, *Foundations*, i. 202; D. R. Kelley, *Foundations of Modern Historical Scholarship* (New York, 1970), 34–9; L. Valla, *De Falso credita et ementita Constantini Donatione Declamatio*, ed. W. Seitz (Weimar, 1976).

17. For some effects of the Avignon enclave see R. Moulinas, *Les Juifs du pape en France: les communautés d'Avignon et du Comtat Venaissin aux 17ᵉ et 18ᵉ siècles* (Paris, 1981), 25ff. and refs.

18. On the (partial) laicization of government servants see R. L. Storey, 'Gentleman-Bureaucrats', in C. H. Clough (ed.), *Profession, Vocation and Culture in Later Medieval England* (Liverpool, 1982), 101–9.

19. On crown servants among the higher clergy see Swanson, *Church and Society*, 103–8; Harper-Bill, *Pre-Reformation Church*, 30–6, and id., 'Archbishop John Morton and the Province of Canterbury, 1486–1500', *JEH* 29 (1978), 1–21; on Fox see Oakley, *Western Church*, 285–94 and refs.; on Georges d'Amboise see Y. Labande-Mailfert, *Charles VIII et son milieu, 1470–1498: la jeunesse au pouvoir* (Paris, 1975), 52 f., 65, 150, 238, 421, 435, 517, and 507 for Archbishop Briçonnet; on Matthäus Lang see H. Wiesflecker, *Kaiser Maximilian I: Das Reich, Österreich und Europa an der Wende zur Neuzeit*, 5 vols. (Munich, 1971–86), v. 230–6.

20. Southern, *W. Soc. and Church*, 157–69.

21. Thomson, *Popes*, 145 ff.; see Ch. 4. 2.

22. *DDC*, 'Dîme', iv, cols. 1234 ff., and 'Temporel', vii, cols. 1182 ff.

23. See for instance lay pressure on mortuary fees in England, as in Swanson, *Church and Society*, 216–17; and the protests against such fees in 1529, as in A. G. Dickens and D. Carr (eds.), *The Reformation in England to the Accession of Elizabeth I* (London, 1967), 20.

24. See the attempts to restrict bequests to the Church as in Ch. 4. 3; Thomson, *Popes*, 178 ff.; and English regulations on Mortmain in 1279 and subsequently, as in Swanson, *Church and Society*, 196 ff.

25. Swanson, *Church and Society*, 117.

26. On the diversion of gifts to reformed orders see Chiffoleau, *Comptabilité de l'au-delà*, 229 ff.; on the orders themselves see Ch. 3. 2.

27. A. Hamilton Thompson, *The English Clergy and their Organization in the Later Middle Ages* (Oxford, 1947), 109–16; M. Zell, 'Economic Problems of the Parochial Clergy in the Sixteenth Century', in F. Heal and R. O'Day (eds.), *Princes and Paupers in the English Church* (Leicester, 1981), 19 ff.; see Kidd, *Documents*, 117, for analogous complaints about the diversion of German monastic revenues to Italian churchmen.

28. Hamilton Thompson, *English Clergy*, 137, 182–5.

29. For the workings of the system see e.g. J.-L. Gazzaniga, *L'Église du midi à la fin du règne de Charles VII d'après la jurisprudence du parlement de Toulouse* (Paris, 1976), 83–101.

30. W. E. Lunt, *Papal Revenues in the Middle Ages*, 2 vols. (New York, 1934), i. 63–103; Thomson, *Popes*, 167–80 and refs.

31. Southern, *W. Soc. and Church*, 37–9.

32. *DDC*, 'Clerc', iii, cols. 864–72; W. S. Stafford, *Domesticating the Clergy: The Inception of the Reformation in Strasbourg* (Missoula, Mont., 1976), 109–10, and 264 n. 5, with ref. to K. Hofmann, *Die engere Immunität in deutschen Bischofsstädten im Mittelalter*, Diss., Tübingen (Paderborn, 1914).

33. Thomson, *Popes*, 187 ff.; F and M xv. 143 ff. and refs.

34. See Ch. 16. 4.

35. Thomson, *Popes*, 83–5; Lunt, *Papal Revenues*, i. 60. See also J. Delumeau, *L'Alun de Rome* (Paris, 1962).

36. J. Toussaert, *Le Sentiment religieux en Flandre à la fin du moyen-âge* (Paris, 1963), 435–46; P. Adam, *La Vie paroissiale en France au xive siècle* (Paris, 1964), 179–206; Kidd, *Documents*, 119; Strauss, *Manifestations*, 59, 63; A. G. Dickens, 'The Shape of Anti-

clericalism and the English Reformation', in E. I. Kouri and T. Scott (eds.), *Politics and Society in Reformation Europe: Essays for Sir Geoffrey Elton on his Sixty-Fifth Birthday* (London, 1987), 394 f., 409; S. Brigden, 'Tithe Controversy in Reformation London, *JEH* 32 (1981), 285–301; J. A. F. Thomson, 'Tithe Disputes in Later Medieval London', *EHR* 78 (1963), 1–17; Wunderli, *London Church Courts,* 108–13.

37. S. Fish, *The Supplication of the Beggars* (1529), as quoted in Dickens and Carr (eds.), *Reformation in England,* 16 ff.

38. For protests against benefit of clergy see Strauss, *Manifestations,* 58; Kidd, *Documents,* 118–19; and in England, Swanson, *Church and Society,* 149 ff.

39. See S. C. Karant-Nunn, *Zwickau in Transition 1500–1547: The Reformation as an Agent of Change* (Columbus, Ohio, 1987), ch. 1.; Swanson, *Church and Society,* 228 ff.

40. Papal abuse of 'spiritual' status in political quarrels was a recurrent theme of Marsilius of Padua, *The Defender of Peace,* ed. and trans. A. Gewirth (New York, 1956), esp. Bk. II; see Skinner, *Foundations,* i. 18 ff.; cf. Wessel Gansfort's criticism of Pius II's claims to demand laymen buy papal alum on pain of mortal sin, cited by Thomson, *Popes,* 182.

41. Thomson, *Popes,* 181–200.

42. Ibid., 89–90; Hay, *Church in Italy,* 41–5; F and M xv. 87 f.; further details are found in Lunt, *Papal Revenues,* i. 135–6, and in L. Celier, *Les Dataires du xvᵉ siècle et les origines de la daterie apostolique* (Paris, 1910).

43. *WA* vi. 417–18; *LW* xliv. 142–3; Strauss, *Manifestations,* 43; cf. F and M xv. 88.

44. *WA* vi. 425–7; *LW* xliv. 153–5; cf. Kidd, *Documents,* 113.

45. Thomson, *Popes,* 89 ff., 111–12; Lunt, *Papal Revenues,* i. 129–33; Celier, *Dataires,* 88 ff.; J. A. F. Thomson, '"The Well of Grace": Englishmen and Rome in the Fifteenth Century', in Dobson (ed.), *Church, Politics and Patronage,* 102 ff.

46. The political features of this system are discussed in Ch. 4. 2.

47. Southern, *W. Soc. and Church,* 158.

48. *WA* vi. 419–21; *LW* xliv. 145–8; Thomson, *Popes,* 153 ff.; Strauss, *Manifestations,* 54–7.

49. Kidd, *Documents,* 115–16; Strauss, *Manifestations,* 44.

50. *WA* vi. 423–4; *LW* xliv. 150–3; Kidd, *Documents,* 116–17; Strauss, *Manifestations,* 55.

51. The religious orders are discussed more fully in Ch. 3. 2.

52. Hay, *Church in Italy,* 33–7.

53. L. von Pastor, *History of the Popes from the Close of the Middle Ages,* trans. F. I. Antrobus, R. Kerr, E. Graf, and E. F. Peeler, 40 vols. (London, 1891–1953), vi. 128 ff., 192 ff.

54. Hay, *Church in Italy,* 35–9.

55. F and M xv. 37 ff., 68 ff., 88; Pastor, *History of the Popes,* ii. 165 ff., iii. 299 ff., iv. 67 ff. and 432 ff.

56. F and M xv. 35 ff.

57. Ibid. 194 ff.; Hay, *Church in Italy,* 41, 46–8.

58. Thomson, *Popes,* 134 ff.; Pastor, *History of the Popes,* vi. 103–41, 232–88.

59. Pastor, *History of the Popes,* iii. 311–74.

60. F and M xv. 126 ff.

61. Ibid. 153–5; the anonymous satire *Julius Exclusus,* attributed to Erasmus, is translated with an introduction by M. Heath in *The Collected Works of Erasmus,* xxvii (Toronto, 1986), 155–97.

62. *Loci e libro veritatum*, ed. J. E. T. Rogers (Oxford 1881), 52, as cited by Hamilton Thompson, *English Clergy*, 24.

63. Hamilton Thompson, *English Clergy*, 16–38; on the qualifications and origins of English bishops at this period see also R. G. Davies, 'The Episcopate', in Clough (ed.), *Profession, Vocation and Culture*, 51–89; Swanson, *Church and Society*, 79–82; Harper-Bill, *Pre-Reformation Church*, 24–35.

64. F. R. H. Du Boulay, *Germany in the Later Middle Ages* (London, 1983), 189; F and M xv. 314 f.; Hay, *Church in Italy*, 12–20.

65. Gazzaniga, *L'Église du midi*, 54–62.

66. See Ch. 3. 3.

67. As for instance in Gazzaniga, *L'Église du midi*, 76 ff.

68. Hamilton Thompson, *English Clergy*, 46 ff., 187 ff.; Harper-Bill, 'Colet's Convocation Sermon', 201 and refs.; id., *Pre-Reformation Church*, 30; Lefebvre-Teillard, *Les Officialités*, 25–43.

69. E. J. D. Douglass, *Justification in Late Medieval Preaching* (Leiden, 1966), 98 and n. 7; for real examples of warrior and noble prelates see F and M xv. 314–17.

70. The extremes can be seen in the case of Archdeacon Thomas Magnus, who from some 14 benefices received a combined income of nearly £770 in 1535 (see Hamilton Thompson, *English Clergy*, 122 and n. 2); and in that of chaplains in Italy living on a labourer's wage or less (see P. Burke, *Culture and Society in Renaissance Italy* (London, 1972), 242 f.); the socio-economic condition of the German lower clergy is discussed in D. Kurze, 'Der niedere Klerus in der sozialen Welt des späteren Mittelalters', in K. Schulz (ed.), *Beiträge zur Wirtschafts- und Sozialgeschichte des mittelalters: Festschrift für Herbert Helbig* (Cologne and Vienna, 1976), 273–305.

71. Hay, *Church in Italy*, 51–2; but cf. the more modest requirements of Bishop Wedego of Havelberg, who in 1471 stated that prospective priests should be able to recite the Lord's Prayer and Apostles' Creed, know what the 7 sacraments were, and know enough Latin to read mass, or at any rate know more than their congregations: S. C. Karant-Nunn, 'Luther's Pastors: the Reformation in the Ernestine Countryside', *Transactions of the American Philosophical Society*, 69/8 (1979), 20. Cf. also Swanson, *Church and Society*, 58 ff.; Harper-Bill, *Pre-Reformation Church*, 44–53; P. Heath, *The English Parish Clergy on the Eve of the Reformation* (London, 1969), 15 ff.; M. Bowker, *The Secular Clergy in the Diocese of Lincoln 1495–1520* (Cambridge, 1968), 41 ff.

72. Hay, *Church in Italy*, 53–4.

73. A. Renaudet, *Préréforme et humanisme à Paris pendant les premières guerres d'Italie (1494–1517)* (Paris, 1953), 166–7.

74. Heath, *English Parish Clergy*, 86 ff.; but on ignorance elsewhere see Gazzaniga, *L'Église du midi*, 68–70; also B. Moeller, 'Religious Life', in Strauss, *Pre-Ref. Germany*, 28–9 and n. 102.

75. L. Febvre and H.-J. Martin, *The Coming of the Book* (London, 1976), 251 ff., cite the enormous popularity in the first decades of the printing of such works as the *Epistola de Miseria Curatorum*, the *Manipulus Curatorum* of Guy de Montrocher, the *Confessionale* of S Antonino of Florence, and the *Modus Confitendi* of Andreas de Escobar, which may be presumed to have been sold to clerics above all; other indications of priests' reading are found in Rapp, *Réformes*, 167 ff.; M. U. Chrisman, *Lay Culture, Learned Culture: Books and Social Change in Strasbourg, 1480–1599* (New Haven, Conn., 1982), esp. 60 ff.

76. i e. F and M xv. 331.
77. This was claimed especially of Hugo von Hohenlandenburg, bishop of Constance from 1496 to 1532, whom the reformer Sebastian Meyer alleged to have made a significant part of his income from fines on clergy who had fathered illegitimate children; see Ozment, *Cities*, 59; compare a similar charge made by Catherine Zell in P. A. Russell, *Lay Theology in the Reformation* (Cambridge, 1986), 205.
78. R. W. Scribner, *For the Sake of Simple Folk* (Cambridge, 1981), 38–40; but cf. Strauss, *Manifestations*, 61, 63.
79. E. Cameron, *The Reformation of the Heretics: The Waldenses of the Alps, 1480–1580* (Oxford, 1984), 217, based on M. Venard, 'Jacques Sadolet, évêque de Carpentras, et les Vaudois', in *Bollettino della Società di Studi Valdesi*, 143 (1978), 44.
80. Kidd, *Documents*, 120; Strauss, *Manifestations*, 61; C. Harper-Bill, 'Archbishop John Morton and the Province of Canterbury, 1486–1500', *JEH* 29 (1978), 1–21, and esp. 12.
81. Dickens and Carr, *Reformation in England*, 15–16; Harper-Bill, 'Colet's Convocation Sermon', 192 f.; Dickens, 'Shape of Anti-clericalism', 385.
82. Kiessling, *Bürgerliche Gesellschaft*, 306–7; on clerical poverty see for instance Harper-Bill, 'Colet's Convocation Sermon', 203 and refs.; also id., *Pre-Reformation Church*, 45 ff.

3. *'Reform' from Within and its Limits*

1. R. W. Scribner, *The German Reformation* (London, 1986), 3–5; *COD* 608, 614, 625, etc.
2. Strauss, *Manifestations*, 3–31.
3. *ODCC*, 'Form'; L. B. Pascoe, *Jean Gerson: Principles of Church Reform*, SMRT 7 (Leiden, 1973), 17–48; J. W. O'Malley, *Giles of Viterbo on Church and Reform: A Study of Renaissance Thought*, SMRT 5 (Leiden, 1968), 190–1.
4. See for instance the remarks of Michel Bureau in 1496, in Rapp, *Église*, 208–9.
5. On these see Hefele-Leclercq, vi, pt. 1, 181 ff.; vi, pt. 2, 661 ff.; Oakley, *Western Church*, 219–20.
6. A. Black, *Council and Commune: The Conciliar Movement and the Fifteenth-Century Heritage* (London, 1979), 16 ff., 40 f., 44 ff.
7. F and M xiv. 907–8; A. Hamilton Thompson, *The English Clergy and their Organization in the Later Middle Ages* (Oxford, 1947), 56 ff., 73 ff.
8. See Ch. 4. 1.
9. F and M xiv. 907 and refs.; E. J. D. Douglass, *Justification in Late Medieval Preaching* (Leiden, 1966), 93 and nn.
10. F and M xv. 164–5, 187 ff.; O'Malley, *Giles of Viterbo*, 155 ff., 160 ff.; Oakley, *Western Church*, 229–31; see also the remarks of Jakob Wimpfeling, in J. Knepper, *Jakob Wimpfeling 1450–1528: sein Leben und seine Werke* (Freiburg-im-Breisgau, 1902), 56, as cited by L. W. Spitz, *The Religious Renaissance of the German Humanists* (Cambridge, Mass., 1963), 52.
11. Thomson, *Popes*, 110; H. Jedin, *History of the Council of Trent*, 2 vols. (Edinburgh, 1957), i. 128–30; Hay, *Church in Italy*, 63–4, 84–5.
12. Jedin, *Council of Trent*, i. 423 ff.
13. F and M xv. 107 ff.
14. Thomson, *Popes*, 108–10; Hay, *Church in Italy*, 86–8; Jedin, *Council of Trent*, i. 117–38.

15. Thomson, *Popes*, 111–13.
16. A survey of this movement is provided in Jedin, *Council of Trent*, i. 139–46.
17. Hay, *Church in Italy*, 75–7; Rapp, *Église*, 218–19; A. Renaudet, *Préréforme et humanisme à Paris* (2nd edn., Paris, 1953), 185–9. For monastic reform in England see D. Baker, '"Old Wine in New Bottles": Attitudes to Reform in Fifteenth-Century England', *Renaissance and Renewal in Christian History*, *SCH* 14 (1977), 193–211; R. W. Dunning, 'Revival at Glastonbury, 1530–39', ibid. 213–22.
18. See Ch. 4. 4.
19. Renaudet, *Préréforme et humanisme*, 173ff.; Oberman, *Masters*, 50ff.; Rapp, *Église*, 219–20.
20. O'Malley, *Giles of Viterbo, passim*; Oakley, *Western Church*, 237–8, R. H. Fife, *The Revolt of Martin Luther* (New York, 1957), 162ff.
21. Hay, *Church in Italy*, 77 8; P. McNair, *Peter Martyr in Italy: An Anatomy of Apostasy* (Oxford, 1967), 70–8.
22. Hay, *Church in Italy*, 60; Rapp, *Église*, 222–3; fuller details in J. Moorman, *A History of the Franciscan Order from its Origins to the year 1517* (Oxford, 1968), esp. 441–585; D. Nimmo, *Reform and Division in the Franciscan Order (1226–1538)* (Rome, 1987), 353–642.
23. Renaudet, *Préréforme et humanisme*, 171–3; Nimmo, *Reform and Division*, 643–5.
24. Oakley, *Western Church*, 232; Hamilton Thompson, *English Clergy*, 181–2.
25. Rapp, *Réformes*, 141–50, 213ff., 354ff., 382ff.
26. B. Collett, *Italian Benedictine Scholars and the Reformation: The Congregation of Santa Giustina of Padua* (Oxford, 1985), 77ff.
27. H. O. Evenett, *New Cambridge Modern History*, ii *The New Orders* (Cambridge, 1958), 278ff.
28. Hay, *Church in Italy*, 88–90.
29. See Ch. 2. 5.
30. See M. Vale 'Cardinal Henry Beaufort and the "Albergati" Portrait', *EHR* 105 (1990), 337–54, and esp. 341–3.
31. Hay, *Church in Italy*, 12–13, 54–7, 97–8; Rapp, *Église*, 214; F and M xv. 333 and refs.
32. R. Kiessling, *Bürgerliche Gesellschaft und Kirche in Augsburg im Spätmittelalter* (Augsburg, 1971), 307 and refs.; Locher, *ZR* 449–50; Ozment, *Cities*, 60; Jedin, *Council of Trent*, i. 148–55, cites other examples of reforming bishops in Germany.
33. Rapp, *Réformes*, 171ff., 321ff.
34. F and M xv. 317, 326f. and nn.; Renaudet, *Préréforme et humanisme*, 348–56; M. Bowker, *The Secular Clergy in the Diocese of Lincoln 1495–1520* (Cambridge, 1968), 16ff.; id., *The Henrician Reformation: The Diocese of Lincoln under John Longland 1521–47* (Cambridge, 1981), *passim*; cf. Hamilton Thompson, *English Clergy*, 178 and refs.; on Fisher see B. Bradshaw and E. Duffy (eds.), *Humanism, Reform and the Reformation: The Career of Bishop John Fisher* (Cambridge, 1989); see also C. Harper-Bill, 'Dean Colet's Convocation Sermon', *History*, 73/238 (1988), 199–201; *The Pre-Reformation Church in England 1400–1530* (London, 1989) id., 29ff.
35. Hefele-Leclercq, v, pt. 2, 1334ff.; Rapp, *Réformes*, 158; Hamilton Thompson, *English Clergy*, 45.
36. Rapp, *Église*, 215; for the analysis of visitation records see U. Mazzone and A. Turchini (eds.), *Le Visite pastorali: analisi di una fonte* (Bologna, 1985), *passim*.
37. As remarked by Luther, *WA* vi. 422; *LW* xliv. 149.

38. Rapp, *Réformes*, 213 ff., 237 ff., 281 ff.
39. Pascoe, *Gerson on Church and Reform*, 118–23; D. C. Brown, *Pastor and Laity in the Theology of Jean Gerson* (Cambridge, 1987), 36–78; Renaudet, *Préréforme et humanisme*, 163 ff.
40. Rapp, *Réformes*, 155 ff.
41. Hay, *Church in Italy*, 56; but cf. P. Adam, *La Vie paroissiale en France au xive siècle* (Paris, 1964), 137 ff.; J. Toussaert, *Le Sentiment religieux en Flandre à la fin du moyen-âge*, 557–62, 581 ff. (Paris, 1963).
42. See the sources cited in Ch. 2 n. 71 for the condition of the lower clergy and the presumed effect of diocesan reform initiatives.
43. Hamilton Thompson, *English Clergy*, 123–8.
44. R. N. Swanson, *Church and Society in Late Medieval England* (Oxford, 1989), 5, 45; notwithstanding amalgamations some tiny parishes remained: early modern Oxford had no less than 4 such churches in a line stretching less than a mile from Carfax to St Giles. Demolition or conversion of 'superfluous' churches was particularly common in post-Reformation Scotland, Denmark, and Norway.
45. P. Heath, *The English Parish Clergy on the Eve of the Reformation* (London, 1969), 86 ff.; but cf. P. A. Russell, *Lay Theology in the Reformation* (Cambridge, 1986), 31, for some evidence to the contrary.
46. Hamilton Thompson, *English Clergy*, 180–1 and nn.
47. Harper-Bill, 'Colet's Convocation Sermon', 192–3.
48. F and M vii. 44–5; J. N. D. Kelly, *The Oxford Dictionary of Popes* (Oxford, 1986), 126–7.
49. Rapp, *Église*, 209 ff.; it was only heretics who (allegedly) dated the decline of the Church specifically to the Emperor Constantine's supposed donation of landed wealth and secular authority to Pope Sylvester I in the early 4th cent.: see E. Cameron, *The Reformation of the Heretics* (Oxford, 1984), 77 and n. 7.
50. F and M xiv. 894–5; A. Coville, *Le Traité "De la ruine de l'Église" de Nicolas de Clamanges . . .* (Paris, 1936), 112–14; N. de Clemangiis, *Opera* (Leiden, 1613), 4–6, 22–3; the biblical allusion is to the statue in the dream of Nebuchadnezzar, Daniel 2: 31–5.
51. F and M xiv. 896; Oakley, *Western Church*, 215; Lydius, *Analecta* [at end of edn. of de Clemangiis, *Opera*, as above], 4–5; the saying about wooden priests and golden chalices is attributed to Savonarola (M. Aston, *The Fifteenth Century* (London, 1968), 126) and was cited by Thomas More in *A Dialogue Concerning Heresies*, ed. T. M. C. Lawler, G. Marc'hadour, and R. Marius, in *The Complete Works of St. Thomas More* (New Haven, Conn., 1963–), vi (1981), 40–1.
52. Harper-Bill, 'Colet's Convocation Sermon', 191–3; H. M. Vose, 'A Sixteenth-Century Assessment of the French Church in the Years 1521–4 by Bishop Guillaume Briçonnet of Meaux', *JEH* 39 (1988), 516–17.
53. F and M xiv. 888 ff.
54. Douglass, *Justification*, 92–3; Rapp, *Réformes*, 157–8.
55. See Harper-Bill, 'Colet's Convocation Sermon', 203–5, for evidence to this effect.
56. Vose, 'Sixteenth-Century Assessment', 512–13, 515–16; see also Rapp, *Église*, 210–11; F and M xiv. 890 ff.
57. See F. R. H. Du Boulay, 'The Quarrel between the Carmelite Friars and the Secular Clergy of London, 1464–1468', *JEH* 6 (1955), 156–74.

4. *Challenges from Outside and their Limits*

1. Hefele-Leclercq, v, pt. 2, 1316–98; F and M x. 194–211.
2. Hefele-Leclercq, vii, pt. 1, 209ff., 459ff.; Oakley, *Western Church*, 133; A. Black, *Council and Commune* (London, 1979), 17–18.
3. Hefele-Leclercq, vii, pt. 1, 610ff., and vii, pt. 2, 663–1141; F and M xiv. 222ff., 227–92; Black, *Council and Commune*, 27–48; see also J. Helmrath, *Das Basler Konzil 1431–49: Forschungsstand und Probleme*, Kölner historische Abhandlungen, 32 (Cologne and Vienna, 1987).
4. On this view see above all B. Tierney, *Foundations of the Conciliar Theory* (Cambridge, 1955), esp. 199ff., 241ff.
5. Black, *Council and Commune*, 118ff., 92ff.; Thomson, *Popes*, 6–10.
6. F and M xv. 156–63, 314; Thomson, *Popes*, 16–23; A. Renaudet, *Le Concile gallican de Pise-Milan: documents florentins (1510–1512)* (Paris, 1922), esp. pp. i–iv.
7. Dickens, *German Nation*, 7; on Mair see Strauss, *Manifestations*, 37ff.; Thomson, *Popes*, 16.
8. Skinner, *Foundations*, ii. 117–23; Thomson, *Popes*, 21–4; for further details see F. Oakley, 'Almain and Conciliar Theory on the Eve of the Reformation', *AHR* 70 (1965), 673–90; id., 'Conciliarism at the Fifth Lateran Council', *Church History*, 41 (1972), 452–63; id., 'Conciliarism in the Sixteenth Century: Jacques Almain Again', *ARG* 68 (1977), 111–32.
9. These texts are discussed by Oberman, *Forerunners*, 213–17, 238–9.
10. H. Jedin, *History of the Council of Trent*, 2 vols. (Edinburgh, 1957), i. 106–15.
11. See the examples cited in Thomson, *Popes*, 25–8.
12. Black, *Council and Commune*, 35–8, 47–8 and refs.
13. H. Rashdall, *The Universities of Europe in the Middle Ages*, 3 vols. (Oxford, 1936), i. 574ff.; F. R. H. Du Boulay, 'The Fifteenth Century', in C. H. Lawrence (ed.), *The English Church and the Papacy in the Middle Ages* (London, 1965), 209–12; Thomson, *Popes*, 30; Helmrath, *Basler Konzil*, 47–51.
14. Thomson, *Popes*, 72ff.; W. E. Wilkie, *The Cardinal Protectors of England: Rome and the Tudors before the Reformation* (Cambridge, 1974); D. S. Chambers, *Cardinal Bainbridge at the Court of Rome, 1509 to 1514* (Oxford, 1965), 72–81, 57.
15. F and M vii. *L'Église au pouvoir des laïques (888–1057)*, esp. 231ff., 273ff., 293ff.
16. Southern, *W. Soc. and Church*, 36–41; for extreme denigration of the lay estate see I. S. Robinson, 'Gregory VII and the Soldiers of Christ', *History*, 58 (1973), 169ff.
17. See Henry II's alleged, and possibly apocryphal, message to the chapter of Winchester, as quoted in A. L. Poole, *From Domesday Book to Magna Carta 1087–1216* (2nd edn., Oxford, 1955), 219–20; cf. C. Harper-Bill, *The Pre-Reformation Church in England 1400–1530* (London, 1989), 25.
18. Thomson, *Popes*, 29, 35; E. Cameron, *The Reformation of the Heretics* (Oxford, 1984), 59, based on A.-L. Fabre, *Recherches historiques sur le pèlerinage des rois de France à Notre-Dame d'Embrun* (Grenoble, 1860), 127, 296–8; M. Bloch, *Les Rois thaumaturges* (Paris, 1961), 89ff., 185–215, 309–27.
19. See J. N. Hillgarth, *The Spanish Kingdoms 1250–1516*, 2 vols. (Oxford, 1976–8), ii, 427–8.
20. Though extreme and impractical, the substance of papal claims in the bulls of 1301–2 was not actually new. See J. N. D. Kelly, *The Oxford Dictionary of Popes*

(Oxford, 1986), 'Boniface VIII', 208–10 and refs.; *ODCC*, 'Boniface VIII' and 'Unam Sanctam'.

21. V. Martin, *Les Origines du gallicanisme*, 2 vols. (Paris, 1939); N. Valois, *La France et le grand schisme en occident*, 4 vols. (Paris, 1896–1902); id., *Histoire de la pragmatique sanction de Bourges sous Charles VII* (Paris, 1906); R. J. Knecht, *Francis I* (Cambridge, 1982), 51–65; P. Ourliac, 'The Concordat of 1472: An Essay on the Relations between Louis XI and Sixtus IV', in P. S. Lewis (ed.), *The Recovery of France in the Fifteenth Century*, trans. G. Martin (London, 1971), 102–84; F and M xv., 56, 78, 171–80.

22. Thomson, *Popes*, 151.

23. Du Boulay, 'The Fifteenth Century', in Lawrence (ed.), *English Church*, 192–3, 205 ff.; Hamilton Thompson, *English Clergy*, 15–25; Harper-Bill, *Pre-Reformation Church*, 9–23; R. N. Swanson, *Church and Society in Late Medieval England* (Oxford, 1989), 11–16; Dickens, 'The Shape of Anti-clericalism and the Engish Reformation', in E. I. Kouri and T. Scott (eds.), *Politics and Society in Reformation Europe* (London, 1987), 386.

24. F. R. H. Du Boulay, *Germany in the Later Middle Ages* (London, 1983), 196–7; for the German concordat at Constance see B. Gebhardt, *Die Gravamina der Deutschen Nation gegen den römischen Hof* (2nd edn., Breslau, 1895), 114–25.

25. Du Boulay, *Germany in the Later Middle Ages*, 199–200; Thomson, *Popes*, 38; Ozment, *Reform*, 188–9; the substance of these grievances is discussed in Ch. 2, and its context in Gebhardt, *Gravamina, passim;* L. W. Spitz, *The Religious Renaissance of the German Humanists* (Cambridge, Mass., 1963), 55–7; Strauss, *Manifestations*, 52 ff.

26. D. E. R. Watt, 'The Papacy and Scotland in the Fifteenth Century', in R. B. Dobson (ed.), *Church, Politics, and Patronage in the Fifteenth Century* (Gloucester, 1984), 115–29.

27. Thomson, *Popes*, 156 ff.; Hillgarth, *Spanish Kingdoms*, ii. 395–9.

28. Thomson, *Popes*, 180.

29. At least in some areas: see C. Haigh, 'Anticlericalism and the English Reformation', *History*, 68 (1973), 391–407, and the reply by Dickens, 'Shape of Anti-clericalism'.

30. Du Boulay, *Germany in the Later Middle Ages*, 201, based on Hefele-Leclercq, vii, pt. 2, 690 ff.; Rapp, *Réformes*, 419 and refs.

31. A point made by J. R. Lander, *Government and Community: England 1450–1509* (London, 1980), 148.

32. Rapp, *Réformes*, 397–404.

33. See Ch. 1 n. 29.

34. M. G. Underwood, 'Politics and Piety in the Household of Lady Margaret Beaufort', *JEH* 38 (1987), 39–52; and cf. Lander, *Government and Community*, 111 ff.

35. C. Harper-Bill, 'Dean Colet's Convocation Sermon', *History*, 73/238 (1988), 196–7; A. Hamilton Thompson, *The English Clergy and their Organization in the Later Middle Ages* (Oxford, 1947), 132–60; on the scale of such donations in England see Ch. 1 n. 25.

36. Dickens, 'Shape of Anti-clericalism', 381–3.

37. Ibid. 387–8.

38. Strauss, *Manifestations*, 100–3, 109–15; but for more light-hearted criticism of priests' morals see P. Aretino, *Selected Letters*, ed. G. Bull (Harmondsworth, 1976), 148–9.

39. Strauss, *Manifestations*, 3–31.

40. Above all in the cases of humanists like Sebastian Brant or Erasmus: see below sect. 4. 5.

41. Du Boulay, *Germany in the Later Middle Ages*, 191, 202–4.

42. Rapp, *Réformes*, 404ff.

43. Dickens, 'Shape of Anti-clericalism', 384 and refs.; cf. 396.

44. Quite apart from the revolts led by peasants against their ecclesiastical (and other) landlords: on these see P. Blickle, 'Peasant Revolts in the German Empire in the Late Middle Ages', *Social History*, 4 (1979), 223–39.

45. Rapp, *Réformes*, 406ff.; Strauss, *Manifestations*, 144ff.; A Rosenkranz, *Der Bundschuh*, 2 vols. (Heidelberg, 1927), *passim*; G. Franz, *Der deutsche Bauernkrieg* (11th edn., Darmstadt, 1977), 53–79; id. (ed.), *Quellen zur Geschichte des Bauernkrieges* (Munich, 1963), 59–81. The episodes are discussed in regard to their economic significance by T. Scott, *Freiburg and the Breisgau: Town–Country Relations in the Age of Reformation and Peasants' War* (Oxford, 1986), 165–89.

46. Strauss, *Manifestations*, 221–2; Franz, *Bauernkrieg*, 45–52; N. Cohn, *The Pursuit of the Millennium: Revolutionary Millenarians and Mystical Anarchists of the Middle Ages* (London, 1957), 223–34.

47. Rapp, *Réformes*, 108–14, 413–19; W. S. Stafford, *Domesticating the Clergy* (Missoula, Mont., 1976) 111, 119–20.

48. Hamilton Thompson, *English Clergy*, 109ff.

49. G. Strauss, *Nuremberg in the Sixteenth Century* (New York, 1966), 156; G. Seebass, 'Stadt und Kirche in Nürnberg im Zeitalter der Reformation', in B. Moeller (ed.), *Stadt und Kirche im 16. Jahrhundert* (Gütersloh, 1978), 69ff.; R. Kiessling, *Bürgerliche Gesellschaft und Kirche in Augsburg im Spätmittelalter* (Augsburg, 1971), 99–179.

50. Stafford, *Domesticating*, 116ff.

51. Du Boulay, *Germany in the Later Middle Ages*, 193.

52. Rapp, *Réformes*, 410ff.

53. Strauss, *Manifestations*, 140ff.

54. This whole theme is explored fully by B. Moeller, 'Kleriker als Bürger', in *Festschrift für Hermann Heimpel zu 70. Geburtstag am 19.9.1971*, 2 vols. (Göttingen, 1971–2), ii. 195–210; and after the Reformation on 210–24.

55. Strauss, *Nuremberg*, 156–9; cf. Kiessling, *Bürgerliche Gesellschaft*, 296ff.; for other such cases see Ozment, *Cities*, 179 n. 80; and cf. the hybrid position of the Venetian Inquisition as described in B. Pullan, *The Jews of Europe and the Inquisition of Venice 1550–1670* (Oxford, 1983), 15ff., 26ff.

56. Du Boulay, *Germany in the Later Middle Ages*, 192–5 and refs.; see for instance H. Rankl, *Das vorreformatorische landesherrlichen Kirchenregiment in Bayern (1378–1526)* (Munich, 1971), esp. 153ff., 228ff.; but for the limits to such lay control see H. J. Cohn, 'Church Property in the German Protestant Principalities', in E. I. Kouri and T. Scott (eds.), *Politics and Society in Reformation Europe* (London, 1987), 159–62 and refs.

57. See for instance the remark of the city chronicler Burkard Zink, quoted by Kiessling, *Bürgerliche Gesellschaft*, 179; and the argument of Moeller, *Imperial Cities, passim*.

58. E. F. Jacob, *Essays in the Conciliar Epoch* (Manchester, 1943), 122–3, 125–9, 144–50; R. R. Post, *The Modern Devotion: Confrontation with Reformation and Humanism* (Leiden, 1968), 51–175; F and M xiv. 921–7; Rapp, *Église*, 245.

59. Post, *Modern Devotion*, 293ff.; and see Ch. 3. 2.

60. Jacob, *Essays*, 124–5; Post, *Modern Devotion*, 198–272, 343ff.; F and M xiv. 927ff.

61. Rapp, *Éeglise*, 246ff.

62. Post, *Modern Devotion*, 272–92; F and M xiv. 843, 964 n.

63. Jacob, *Essays*, 134–6 and refs.

64. Rapp, *Église*, 246ff.; Post, *Modern Devotion*, 15–17, 552–631; Post's position is a rebuttal of the works of A Hyma, *The Christian Renaissance* (2nd edn., Hamden, Conn., 1965), *The Brethren of the Common Life* (Grand Rapids, 1950), and *The Youth of Erasmus* (Ann Arbor, Mich., 1930).

65. Jacob, *Essays*, 129–34; Oberman, *Masters*, 45–50; cf. Post, *Modern Devotion*, 442ff., 470ff. Post argues, however (471–3), that Johann Pupper von Goch was *not* a brother.

66. Oberman, *Masters*, 52–5.

67. The text of the *Imitation of Christ*, ed. C. Hirsche (Berlin, 1874), M. J. Pohl (Freiburg-im-Breisgau, 1904), etc.; see also B. Moeller, 'Religious Life in Germany on the Eve of the Reformation', in Strauss, *Pre-Ref. Germany*, 20–1; cf. Oakley, *Western Church*, 99–100, 106–7; Post, *Modern Devotion*, 521–36.

68. F and M xiv. 837–69; L. B. Pascoe, *Jean Gerson: Principles of Church Reform* (Leiden, 1973), 104–9. Cf. Gerson's concern that his mystical theology should not endanger orthodoxy: see D. C. Brown, *Pastor and Laity in the Theology of Jean Gerson* (Cambridge, 1987), 202ff.

69. J. Catto, 'Religious Change under Henry V', in G. L. Harriss (ed.), *Henry V: The Practice of Kingship* (Oxford, 1985), 110ff., partly modifies R. Lovatt, 'The *Imitation of Christ* in Late Medieval England', *Transactions of the Royal Historical Society*, 5th ser., 18 (1968), 100; Rapp, *Église*, 312–14.

70. Jacob, *Essays*, 131; Oakley, *Western Church*, 105; Post, *Modern Devotion*, 309–10, 538–50.

71. Oberman, *Harvest*, 335ff.; Oakley, *Western Church*, 94–5; S. E. Ozment, 'Mysticism, Nominalism, and Dissent', in T and O *Holiness*, 67–92; also id., *Mysticism and Dissent: Religious Ideology and Social Protest in the Sixteenth Century* (New Haven., Conn., 1973).

72. F and M xiv. 912–21; R. E. Lerner, *The Heresy of the Free Spirit* (Berkeley, 1972), esp. 192ff.; Rapp, *Église*, 233–5.

73. Swanson, *Church and Society*, 273–4, 285–6; Rapp, *Église*, 227–40.

74. Oakley, *Western Church*, 91–4.

75. Rapp, *Église*, 242–3 and refs.

76. See J. D. Tracy, 'Humanism and the Reformation', in Ozment, *Guide*, 46; see also C. Trinkaus, *The Scope of Renaissance Humanism* (Ann Arbor, Mich., 1983), *passim*.

77. See P. O. Kristeller, 'Rhetoric in Medieval and Renaissance Culture', in J. J. Murphy (ed.), *Renaissance Eloquence: Studies in the Theory and Practice of Renaissance Rhetoric* (Berkeley, Calif., 1983), 1–19, esp. 2; B. Vickers, *In Defence of Rhetoric* (Oxford, 1988), *passim*; see also R. R. Bolgar, 'Humanism as a Value System, with Reference to Budé and Vives', in A. H. T. Levi (ed.), *Humanism in France at the end of the Middle Ages and in the Early Renaissance* (Manchester, 1970), 199–215.

78. Spitz, *Religious Renaissance*, 203.

79. Ibid. 140.

80. Rapp, *Réformes*, 160. For an edited trans. of *Praise of Folly* see *The Collected Works of Erasmus*, xxvii (Toronto, 1986), 77–153.

81. Rapp, *Réformes*, 163; Spitz, *Religious Renaissance*, 52–4.

82. Spitz, *Religious Renaissance*, 66, 112 f.

83. *The Collected Works of Erasmus*, xxvii. 140.

84. O. Clemen, *Das Leben Johann Puppers von Goch* (Leipzig, 1896), 167–81, 203–8; K. H. Ullmann, *Reformers before the Reformation*, trans. R. Menzies, 2 vols. (Edinburgh, 1855), i. 107–20; see also D. C. Steinmetz, 'Libertas Christiana: Studies in the Theology of John Pupper of Goch (d. 1475)', *HThR* 65 (1972), 191–230, esp. 217ff.; another religious figure opposed to the vow *per se* was Catherine of Genoa: see M. Aston, *The Fifteenth Century* (London, 1968), 155–7.

85. Spitz, *Religious Renaissance*, 54.

86. *The Collected Works of Erasmus*, xxvii. 130ff.

87. See *The Colloquies of Erasmus*, ed. and trans. C. R. Thompson (Chicago, 1965), esp. *The Girl with no Interest in Marriage* (99ff.), *The Repentant Girl* (111ff.), *A Fish Diet* (312ff.), and *The Godly Feast* (46ff.).

88. J. P. Massaut, *Josse Clichtove et la réforme du clergé*, 2 vols. (Paris, 1968), i. 433–45.

89. Spitz, *Religious Renaissance*, 162, 183ff.

90. J. H. Overfield, *Humanism and Scholasticism in Late Medieval Germany* (Princeton, 1984), *passim*, but esp. 329–30; and cf. C. G. Nauert, 'The Clash of Humanists and Scholastics: An Approach to Pre-Reformation Controversies', *Sixteenth Century Journal*, 4 (1973), 1–18; J. H. Overfield, 'Scholastic Opposition to Humanism in Pre-Reformation Germany', *Viator*, 7 (1976), 391–420.

91. As in the case of Willibald Pirckheimer: see Spitz, *Religious Renaissance*, 174–5; cf. N. Holzberg, *Willibald Pirckheimer: Griechischer Humanismus in Deutschland* (Munich, 1981), 179ff.

92. *The Collected Works of Erasmus*, xxvii. 127ff.

93. Spitz, *Religious Renaissance*, 48–9.

94. See Ch 7. 2.

95. Spitz, *Religious Renaissance*, 175–7; those named included Cochlaeus, Eck, Emser, and Murner alongside Erasmus, Linck, Luther, and Oecolampadius.

96. Ibid. 137–9.

97. *The Collected Works of Erasmus*, xxvii. 114–15; see also *The Colloquies of Erasmus: Rash Vows* (4ff.); *The Shipwreck* (138ff.); *A Pilgrimage for Religion's Sake* (285ff.); Eire, *Idols*, 37–44.

98. Spitz, *Religious Renaissance*, 126–7.

99. Ibid. 55–7, 152–4, 172, 205, 226; Eire, *Idols*, 48–50.

100. See G. R. Evans, *The Language and Logic of the Bible*, ii. *The Road to Reformation* (Cambridge, 1985), 69–81; H. Holeczek, *Humanistische Bibelphilologie als Reformproblem bei Erasmus von Rotterdam, Thomas More und William Tyndale, Studies in the History of Christian Thought*, 9 (Leiden, 1975), 62ff., 101ff., 138ff., 186ff.; J. H. Bentley, 'Erasmus' *Annotationes in Novum Testamentum* and the Textual Criticism of the Gospels', *ARG* 67 (1976), 33–53; G. Bedouelle, *Lefèvre d'Étaples et l'intelligence des écritures* (Geneva, 1976), *passim*, but esp. 78ff.

101. See Erasmus's letter to Martin Dorp, in *EE* ii. 90ff.; for 'tradition' see Oberman, *Forerunners*, 51–120.

102. Rapp, *Réformes*, 169.

103. See Ch. 16. 5 for fuller discussion; also Eire, *Idols*, 177–81.

104. Spitz, *Religious Renaissance*, 221; the *Enchiridion* is trans. by C. Fantazzi in *Collected Works*, lxvi, ed. J. W. O'Malley (Toronto, 1988), 1–127; for a summary see R. H. Bainton, *Erasmus of Christendom* (London, 1972), 86–94; the work appeared in English, Czech, German, Dutch, Spanish, and French trans. between 1518 and 1529.

See [F. E. van der Haeghen], *Bibliotheca Erasmiana: répertoire des ouvrages d'Érasme*, i (Ghent 1893), 79–84.

105. Evans, *Language and Logic of the Bible*, ii. 81; for the diffusion of vernacular bibles before 1520 see J. Delumeau, *Naissance et affirmation de la réforme* (3rd edn., Paris, 1973), 71–2; on Erasmus's attitudes to laymen reading scripture, see his *Paraclesis*, as cited e.g. by A. G. Dickens, 'Luther and the Humanists', in P. Mack and M. Jacob (eds.), *Politics and Culture in Early Modern Europe: Essays in Honour of H. G. Koenigsberger* (Cambridge, 1987), 203ff.; and cf. Holeczek, *Humanistische Bibelphilologie*, 188–202.

106. As suggested by Moeller, 'Religious life', in Strauss, *Pre-Ref. Germany*, 29–30; or I. Schairer, *Das Religiöse Volksleben* (Leipzig, 1914), *passim*; but cf. H. Heller, *The Conquest of Poverty* (Leiden, 1985), 48ff.

5. Heresy: An Alternative Church?

1. The so-called 'Dictatus of Avranches', in *PL*, ed. Migne, 16, 946, and as cited in E. Caspar (ed.), *Das Register Gregors VII* (Berlin, 1920), 207 and nn.: 'Qui decretis sedis apostolicae non consenserit haereticus habendus est.'

2. R. I. Moore, *The Origins of European Dissent* (London, 1977), p. ix, based on Gratian.

3. Oberman, *Forerunners*, 76–84.

4. Classics of such manuals were B. Gui, *Manuel de l'inquisiteur*, modern edn. by G. Mollat and G. Drioux, 2 vols. (Paris, 1926–7); N. Eymericus, *Directorium Inquisitorum*, ed. F. Pegna (Rome, 1578); and, from 16th-cent. authors, B. de Lutzenburgo, *Catalogus Hereticorum* (Cologne, 1522), and A. de Castro, *Adversus omnes hereses* (Cologne, 1539). However, local inquisitors habitually amalgamated literary citations and their own discoveries into personal manuals and accounts: see E. Cameron, *The Reformation of the Heretics* (Oxford, 1984), 120–6.

5. Oakley, *Western Church*, 177 f., based on M. D. Lambert, *Medieval Heresy: Popular Movements from Bogomil to Hus* (London, 1977), 106–7, 170–1.

6. H. Kaminsky, *A History of the Hussite Revolution* (Berkeley, Calif., 1967), 7–23; on Hussitism see also F. Smahel, *La Révolution hussite, une anomalie historique* (Paris, 1985).

7. P. de Vooght, *L'Hérésie de Jean Huss* (Louvain, 1960); Oberman, *Forerunners*, 208–12, 218–37; M. Spinka, *John Hus' Doctrine of the Church* (Princeton, NJ, 1966) (and other works); R. R. Betts, *Essays in Czech History* (London, 1969), 29–62, 86–106, 132–59, 176–235; Pelikan, *Dogma*, 93–5.

8. Kaminsky, *History of the Hussite Revolution*, 97–161.

9. Ibid. 161ff., 265ff.

10. Ibid. 339–60.

11. O. Odlozilik, *The Hussite King: Bohemia in European Affairs, 1440–1471* (New Brunswick, NJ, 1965), 4–12.

12. Odlozilik, *Hussite King*, 89–262; see also F. G. Heymann, *George of Bohemia, King of Heretics* (Princeton, NJ, 1965), *passim*.

13. Odlozilik, *Hussite King*, 267–72.

14. P. Brock, *The Political and Social Doctrines of the Czech Brethren* (The Hague, 1957), esp. 103ff.; Williams, 207–18 and refs.

15. The senior authority on Lukas is A. Molnár, whose works include *Bratri a král*

(Zelezny Brod, 1947); *Bratr Lukas bohoslovec Jednoty* (Prague, 1948), and numerous articles in the French-language periodical *Communio Viatorum* of Prague.

16. On their Eucharistic teachings see E. Peschke, *Die Theologie des Böhmischen Brüder in ihrer Frühzeit*, i. *Das Abendmahl* (Stuttgart, 1935), *passim*.

17. See Ch. 6.

18. A philosophical intro. to Wyclif is provided by A. Kenny, *Wyclif* (Oxford, 1985); K. B. McFarlane, *John Wycliffe and the Beginnings of English Nonconformity* (London, 1952), is the standard accessible biography.

19. Kenny, *Wyclif*, 91 ff.; K. B. McFarlane, *Lancastrian Kings and Lollard Knights* (Oxford, 1972), 137 ff.; M. Aston, 'Lollardy and Sedition, 1381–1431', in *P and P* 17 (1960), 1–44; also in id., *Lollards and Reformers* (London, 1984); A. Hudson, *The Premature Reformation: Wycliffite Texts and Lollard History* (Oxford, 1988), 60–119.

20. J. A. F. Thomson, *The Later Lollards 1414–1520* (Oxford, 1965); A. Hudson and P. Gradon (eds.), *English Wycliffite Sermons*, 2 vols. (Oxford, 1983–8), *passim*, but esp. i. 189–201; A. Hudson, *Lollards and their Books* (London, 1985), and *The Premature Reformation*, 120 ff.; N. P. Tanner (ed.), *Norwich Heresy Trials*, Royal Historical Society, Camden 4th ser., 20 (London, 1977).

21. Hudson, *The Premature Reformation*, 278–358. For possible differences between the characters of earlier and later Lollardy see C. Harper-Bill, 'Dean Colet's Convocation Sermon', *History*, 73/238 (1988), 197–8, and nn. 28–35. Hudson, *The Premature Reformation*, tends to minimize all such differences.

22. Thomson, *Later Lollards*, 103, 132 f.; Hudson, *The Premature Reformation*, 446 ff.

23. However, Hudson, *The Premature Reformation*, 205 ff., 455 ff., and Thomson, *Later Lollards*, 244, agree that it is impossible to know precisely *how* the surviving Lollard texts were distributed and used in the later 15th cent., though Hudson provides tantalizing glimpses.

24. M. Aston, *The Fifteenth Century* (London, 1968), 132; Hudson, *The Premature Reformation*, 326, 352; ordinary parish clergy did continue to figure among those accused of heresy; but not, presumably, as part of a continuous 'succession', nor as the leaders of the heretic communities: see ibid. 449, 467.

25. Thomson, *Later Lollards*, 80 ff., 104–15, 187–9, 237 ff.; Hudson, *The Premature Reformation*, 128 ff., 466 ff.; D. Plumb, 'The Social and Economic Spread of Rural Lollardy: A Reappraisal', in W. J. Sheils and D. Wood (eds.), *Voluntary Religion*, SCH 23 (Oxford, 1986), 111–29.

26. Thomson, *Later Lollards*, 68 f., 264 f.; Hudson, *Premature Reformation*, 149 ff.

27. P. Collinson, 'The English Conventicle', in Sheils and Wood (eds.), *Voluntary Religion*, 235 ff.

28. Thomson, *Later Lollards*, 240 ff.

29. See J. Catto, 'Religious Change under Henry V', in G. L. Harriss (ed.), *Henry V: The Practice of Kingship* (Oxford, 1985), 114–15, leading to the possibly extreme statement that 'the history of Lollardy from [1420] until the Reformation is, at best, the history of a felony with no more coherence than a history of murder'.

30. On criteria for the detection of Lollardy, see Hudson, *The Premature Reformation*, 165 ff.; compare S. Fish, *The Supplication of the Beggars*, in A. G. Dickens and D. Carr (eds.), *The Reformation in England* (London, 1967), 17.

31. The principal histories of the medieval Waldenses are J. Gonnet and A. Molnár, *Les Vaudois au moyen âge* (Turin, 1974), and G. Audisio, *Les "Vaudois": Naissance, vie et*

mort d'une dissidence (XIIe–XVIe siècles) (Turin, 1979); the discontinuities in medieval Waldensianism are the theme of G. G. Merlo, *Valdesi e valdismi medievali: itinerari e proposte di ricerca* (Turin, 1984), esp. 27–42.

32. For the Alpine Waldenses see Cameron, *Reformation of the Heretics*; for those of Provence, G. Audisio, *Les Vaudois du Luberon: une minorité en Provence (1460–1560)* (Mérindol, 1984).

33. On the German Waldenses see R. Kieckhefer, *Repression of Heresy in Medieval Germany* (Liverpool, 1979), 13 f., 53–73, and refs.; B. Moeller, 'Religious Life in Germany on the Eve of the Reformation', in Strauss, *Pre-Ref. Germany*, 15, 31, and refs.; see also M. Schneider, *Europäisches Waldensertum im 13. und 14. Jahrhundert* (Berlin, 1981).

34. The late 14th-cent. German inquisitorial treatise *Cum dormirent homines* made extensive use of the Italian Moneta of Cremona; 15th-cent. Alpine inquisitors borrowed from the 13th-cent. German handbook *Tractatus de Inquisitione hereticorum*; Archdeacon Cattaneo of Cremona used Pius II's account of the Hussites to describe the beliefs of the Vaudois of the Dauphiné. On the last 2 see Cameron, *Reformation of the Heretics*, 39, 121–2.

35. See for instance Cameron, *Reformation of the Heretics*, 65–119.

36. On Vaudois literature see Gonnet and Molnár, *Vaudois au moyen âge*, 319–70, 443–50, and a series of edns. by E. Balmas and collaborators.

37. Cameron, *Reformation of the Heretics*, 15–24, 49–61; J. Marx, *L'Inquisition en Dauphiné: étude sur le développement et la répression de l'hérésie et de la sorcellerie du xive siècle au début du règne de François Ier*, Bibliothèque de l'école des hautes études, sciences historiques et philologiques, 206 (Paris, 1914), 179ff.

38. On this the evidence of Audisio, *Vaudois du Luberon*, 202–24, supports that of my *Reformation of the Heretics*, 79, 85–102, 124–6, despite the very different interpretations placed upon it by those 2 works.

39. For instance the custom of the Alpine Vaudois of keeping Lent according to the Ambrosian rite, beginning 5 days later than the local catholics: Cameron, *Reformation of the Heretics*, 99.

40. See for instance the exiguous numbers of Fraticelli described in D. L. Douie, *The Nature and Effect of the Heresy of the Fraticelli* (Manchester, 1932), 243–5, and N. Cohn, *Europe's Inner Demons* (London, 1975), 42–54; or the heretics described in R. Lerner, *The Heresy of the Free Spirit in the Later Middle Ages* (Berkeley, Calif., 1972).

41. As suggested by J. J. Scarisbrick, *The Reformation and the English People* (Oxford, 1984), 46–8.

42. See M. Aston, 'Lollardy and the Reformation: Survival or Revival', *History*, 49 (1964), 149–70; Cameron, *Reformation of the Heretics*, 230ff.

43. See A. G. Dickens, *Lollards and Protestants in the Diocese of York 1509–1558* (London, 1959); J. F. Davis, *Heresy and Reformation in the South East of England 1520–1559* (London, 1983); Cameron, *Reformation of the Heretics*, 135–55, 202–10.

44. See Cameron, *Reformation of the Heretics*, 176–99; Dickens and Carr (eds.), *Reformation in England*, 35–6.

6. The Church and the Christian Soul

1. B. Moeller, 'Religious Life in Germany on the Eve of the Reformation', in Strauss, *Pre-Ref. Germany*, 15.

2. See for instance the views in Thomas More, *Dialogue Concerning Heresies*, in *Complete Works*, vi (1981), 189ff.; or id., *The Confutation of Tyndale's Answer*, in *Complete Works*, viii, pt. 2 (1973), 609ff., 669ff.

3. See Ch. 1. 2.

4. Oakley, *Western Church*, 126ff.; T. N. Tentler, *Sin and Confession on the Eve of the Reformation*, (Princeton, NJ, 1977), 318ff.; J. Bossy, *Christianity in the West 1400–1700* (Oxford, 1985), 45–56. On the rise and acceptance of the doctrine of purgatory see Bossy, *Christianity in the West*, 30ff.; J. Le Goff, *The Birth of Purgatory*, trans. A. Goldhammer (London, 1984), esp. 237ff.; and on its acceptance at the grass roots, J. Chiffoleau, *La Comptabilité de l'au-delà* (Rome, 1980) 389ff.

5. Hefele-Leclercq, v, pt. 2, 1349–51. The details of the system are set out in Tentler, *Sin and Confession*, 82ff.

6. T. N. Tentler, 'The Summa for Confessors as an Instrument of Social Control', in T and O *Holiness*, 103–9.

7. Tentler, *Sin and Confession*, 235–45; Oberman, *Harvest*, 146–60; E. J. D. Douglass, *Justification in Late Medieval Preaching* (Leiden, 1966), 147–60.

8. Tentler, *Sin and Confession*, 263–9; K. H. Ullmann, *Reformers before the Reformation*, trans. R. Menzies, 2 vols. (Edinburgh, 1855), ii. 537–41; Oberman, *Forerunners*, 113–16. Cf. also B. Hamm, *Frömmigkeitstheologie am Anfang des 16. Jahrhunderts: Studien zu Johannes von Paltz und seinem Umkreis* (Tübingen, 1982), 272–84.

9. Tentler, *Sin and Confession*, 270–1; Oberman, *Harvest*, 148–50.

10. Tentler, *Sin and Confession*, 280, and 271–80 on this point in general.

11. Ozment, *Cities*, 16–17, 22–8; Ozment's original assessment was based largely on the work of J. Geffcken, *Der Bildercatechismus des fünfzehnten Jahrhunderts und die catechetischen Haupstücke in dieser Zeit bis auf Luther, i. Die Zehn Gebote* (Leipzig, 1855), before Tentler's more thorough survey of the literature appeared.

12. See for instance D. C. Steinmetz, *Luther and Staupitz: An Essay in the Intellectual Origins of the Protestant Reformation* (Durham, NC, 1980), 31–3; Tentler, *Sin and Confession*, 75–8.

13. Tentler, *Sin and Confession*, 70–6; L. G. Duggan, 'Fear and Confession on the Eve of the Reformation', *ARG* 75 (1984), 159–62.

14. Ozment, *Cities*, 15–22, cites instances of greater reluctance to confess, as does M. Aston, *The Fifteenth Century* (London, 1968), 167, for the otherwise pious Catherine of Genoa; for the Waldenses see E. Cameron, *The Reformation of the Heretics* (Oxford, 1984), 87–8.

15. Duggan, 'Fear and Confession', 163–73.

16. The existence of the treasury of merit was officially declared in the bull *Unigenitus* of Clement VI, 27 Jan. 1343: see Kidd, *Documents*, 1–3.

17. On the theology of indulgences see Southern, *W. Soc. and Church*, 136–42; N. Paulus, *Geschichte des Ablasses in Mittelalter*, 3 vols. (Paderborn, 1922–3); H. C. Lea, *A History of Auricular Confession and Indulgences in the Latin Church*, 3 vols. (Philadelphia, 1896); Oakley, *Western Church*, 118–19; Kidd, *Documents*, 3–10, 12–20; and more recently Hamm, *Frömmigkeitstheologie*, 84ff., 284ff.

18. Ullmann, *Reformers before the Reformation*, i. 234ff.; G. Ritter, 'Romantic and Revolutionary Elements in German Theology on the Eve of the Reformation', in Ozment, *Perspective*, 27; cf. Oberman, *Harvest*, 403ff., and id., *Forerunners*, 93–119; Douglass, *Justification*, 157ff., 201ff.

19. *WA* vi. 543; *LW* xxxvi. 82 and refs. including *WA* xxx/ii. 282, and vii. 420–1; *LW* xxxii. 74–5; cf. Oberman, *Forerunners*, 109 and n. 19.

20. On plurality of schools see Pelikan, *Dogma*, 10–12; J. H. Overfield, *Humanism and Scholasticism in Late Medieval Germany* (Princeton, NJ, 1984), 49 ff.; A. Renaudet, *Préréforme et humanisme à Paris* (Paris, 1953), 53–94; Oakley, *Western Church*, 133–4.

21. Oberman, *Masters*, 8 ff., 23 ff.

22. Douglass, *Justification*, 44, 102; L. B. Pascoe, *Jean Gerson: Principles of Church Reform* (Leiden, 1973), 101 f.; Steinmetz, *Luther and Staupitz*, 28.

23. Douglass, *Justification*, 32–4 and refs.; Oberman, *Masters*, 118–24; Rupp, *Patterns*, 75–6.

24. See Fig. 1.

25. *ODCC*, 'Pelagius'; see also B. R. Rees, *Pelagius, A Reluctant Heretic* (Woodbridge, 1988).

26. For a late medieval technical definition of Pelaganism see Douglass, *Justification*, 116; cf. its use in the work *The Case of God against Pelagius* written *c*.1344 by the English theologian Thomas Bradwardine (*c*.1290–1349): Oberman, *Forerunners*, 135 ff., 151–64; also E. G. Leff, *Bradwardine and the Pelagians: A Study of his 'De Causa Dei' and its Opponents* (Cambridge, 1957).

27. W. J. Courtenay, 'Nominalism and Late Medieval Religion', in T and O *Holiness*, 37–43; S. E. Ozment, 'Mysticism, Nominalism and Dissent', ibid. 80–3; Oberman, *Harvest*, 45; Oakley, *Western Church*, 98–9, 143–6.

28. H. A. Oberman, 'Facientibus Quod in se est Deus non denegat gratiam: Robert Holcot O. P. and the Beginnings of Luther's Theology', in Ozment, *Perspective*, 120–7, and also in H. A. Oberman, *The Dawn of the Reformation* (Edinburgh, 1986), 84–103; Oberman, *Harvest*, 42–7.

29. See M. G. Baylor, *Action and Person: Conscience in Late Scholasticism and the Young Luther*, *SMRT* 20 (Leiden, 1977), 25–9, 77–83, 91–103, 113, 178–9; Oberman, *Harvest*, 65–6; S. E. Ozment, *Homo Spiritualis: A Comparative Study of the Anthropology of Johannes Tauler, Jean Gerson and Martin Luther (1509–16) in the Context of their Theological Thought*, *SMRT* 6 (Leiden, 1969), 20–6, 59, 62–3, 70; Ullmann, *Reformers before the Reformation*, ii. 436 f.

30. Oberman, *Harvest*, 121–9.

31. The earliest form of this cliché appears to occur in the pseudo-Ambrosian *Commentary on Romans*, in *PL*, ed. Migne, 17, cols. 47–192, as cited by Oberman, *Harvest*, 132.

32. Oberman, *Masters*, 107–8; for the views of Scotus see Pelikan, *Dogma*, 28–30.

33. Oberman, *Harvest*, 131–45; 160–74.

34. Ibid. 175–8, 181–4, 426–8; the contrary position, however, is taken up by A. E. McGrath, *Luther's Theology of the Cross* (Oxford, 1985), 61–2.

35. Oberman, *Harvest*, 178–81.

36. Steinmetz, *Luther and Staupitz*, 97–102; Oberman, *Masters*, 93–110.

37. Douglass, *Justification*, 112 ff., 134 ff.

38. Thomas Bradwardine, mentioned above, was a largely solitary figure who founded no school comparable to Gregory's.

39. 'Uncreated grace' described the 'direct' action of God within the believer, in contrast to the 'created habit of grace' devised by the Thomists to explain the good works of the regenerate. See Ozment, *Reform*, 41–2; McGrath, *Luther's Theology of the Cross*, 67 ff.; Oberman, *Masters*, 70 ff.; Pelikan, *Dogma*, 18–19, 30–3; and the sources cited there.

40. A. E. McGrath, *Intellectual Origins of the European Reformation* (Oxford, 1987), 86 ff.; id., *Reformation Thought* (Oxford, 1988), 60–1; H. A. Oberman, 'Headwaters of the Reformation: *Initia Lutheri—Initia Reformationis*', in H. A. Oberman (ed.), *Luther and the Dawn of the Modern Era*, SMRT 8 (Leiden, 1974), 69–81; also in id., *The Dawn of the Reformation*, 65–80; id., *Masters*, 64–110.

41. Steinmetz, *Luther and Staupitz*, 11–23; Pelikan, *Dogma*, 16–17.

42. Steinmetz, *Luther and Staupitz*, 13–27, and as summarized in McGrath, *Intellectual Origins*, 86–93; see also Hamm, *Frömmigkeitstheologie*, 303–33.

43. Ullmann, *Reformers before the Reformation*, ii. 478–9; cf. ibid. ii. 63–81, 431–79; O. Clemen, *Das Leben Johannes Puppers von Goch* (Leipzig, 1896), 94–129; Ritter, 'Romantic and Revolutionary Elements', in Ozment, *Perspective*, 30 ff.; D. C. Steinmetz, 'Libertas Christiana: Studies in the Theology of John Pupper of Goch (d. 1475)', *HThR* 65 (1972), 205 ff. E. W. Miller, *Wessel Gansfort: Life and Writings*, 2 vols. (New York and London, 1917), i. 128 ff. and 149 ff., and ii. 142–7, simply finds somewhat facile resemblances between Gansfort's thought and Luther's.

44. Ozment, *Homo Spiritualis*, 30–1, 44–6.

45. D. C. Steinmetz, *Misericordia Dei: The Theology of Johannes von Staupitz in its Late Medieval Setting*, SMRT 4 (Leiden, 1968), 75–131; id., *Luther and Staupitz*, 71–8, 102–8; cf. Oberman, *Forerunners*, 175–203.

46. This comment applies above all to older scholars such as K. H. Ullmann, E. W. Miller, A. V. Mueller, or H. Denifle, who have been shown to explore the issue of 'predecessors' of Reformation teaching with insufficient subtlety. The theme is discussed in detail by Dickens, *German Nation*, 72–101; and A. E. McGrath, 'Forerunners of the Reformation? A Critical Examination of the Evidence for Precursors of the Reformation Doctrines of Justification', *HThR* 75 (1982), 219–42.

47. A point appreciated by Clemen, *Johann Pupper von Goch*, 182 ff., though other scholars such as Ullmann or even Ritter attributed the differences between 'forerunners' and reformers to issues of tactics and temperament rather than essential teaching.

48. See e.g. sources cited above in n. 2.

49. Pelikan, *Dogma*, 72–81.

50. As claimed by Henry of Kalteisen, cited by Pelikan, *Dogma*, 91–2; cf. Hamm, *Frömmigkeitstheologie*, 266–72.

51. Pelikan, *Dogma*, 92–8; Oberman, *Forerunners*, 205–37; Oakley, *Western Church*, 157 ff., 162 ff.

52. Oberman, *Forerunners*, 245–54; other aspects of Giles's doctrine of the Church are discussed by J. W. O'Malley, *Giles of Viterbo on Church and Reform* (Leiden, 1968), 118–38.

53. See Ch. 7. 1. On other aspects of this topic see Pelikan, *Dogma*, 98–118.

54. Pelikan, *Dogma*, 40–3; Oberman, *Harvest*, 281–322.

55. Pelikan, *Dogma*, 43–50.

56. *PL*, ed. Migne, 42, 176, and as cited by Oberman, *Harvest*, 370.

57. Oberman, *Harvest*, 361–422; id., *Forerunners*, 53–120; McGrath, *Intellectual Origins*, 140–51; Oakley, *Western Church*, 148 ff.; Pelikan, *Dogma*, 118–26; for Paltz see Hamm, *Frömmigkeitstheologie*, 182 ff.

58. For the kinds of issues debated see J.-P. Massaut, *Critique et tradition à la veille de la réforme en France* (Paris, 1974); cf. the treatment of this question in the Reformation as in Ch. 9. 1.

59. Cited by Oberman, *Harvest*, 373–4; but cf. the discussion in McGrath, *Intellectual Origins*, 143.
60. Kidd, *Documents*, 31–2; cf. Pelikan, *Dogma*, 106–110, and McGrath, *Intellectual Origins*, 148.
61. F. Clark, *Eucharistic Sacrifice and the Reformation* (Chulmleigh, 1981), 73–95; Pelikan, *Dogma*, 55–6.
62. Oberman, *Forerunners*, 246–67; and cf. late medieval popular practice discussed in Ch. 1.
63. *COD* 547; see *Inst.*, ed. McNeill and Battles, *LCC* xx–xxi. 1425 n. 50.
64. See for instance the debate between Dr Haigh and Professor Dickens over the nature of late medieval English 'piety' and 'anticlericalism' as discussed in Ch. 4. 3.
65. Moeller, 'Religious Life', in Strauss, *Pre-Ref. Germany*, 29–30, as discussed in Ch. 4 n. 106; but cf. 'lay affective piety' as postulated by P. A. Russell, *Lay Theology in the Reformation* (Cambridge, 1986), 37 ff.
66. This argument is implicit in the logic of T. A. Brady, *Ruling Class, Regime and Reformation at Strasbourg, 1520–1555* (Leiden, 1978), as discussed in detail in Ch. 17.

7. The 'Luther-Affair' and its Context

1. See the ch. by R. W. Scribner, 'Images of Luther', in his *For the Sake of Simple Folk* (Cambridge, 1981), 14–36; id., 'Luther Myth: A Popular Historiography of the Reformer', in Scribner, *PC and PM*, 301 ff.; 'Incombustible Luther: the Image of the Reformer in Early Modern Germany', ibid. 323 ff.
2. For instance Locher, *ZR* 90, so characterizes Luther's impact on Zwingli *c.*1520–2.
3. Luther's early life has provoked innumerable biographies. The classic is that of H. Boehmer, *Martin Luther: Road to Reformation*, trans. J. W. Doberstein and T. G. Tappert (Philadelphia, 1946), while R. H. Fife, *The Revolt of Martin Luther* (New York, 1957), is one of the most detailed. The most authoritative recent work is M. Brecht, *Martin Luther: His Road to Reformation 1483–1521*, trans. J. L. Schaaf (Philadelphia, 1985) (161–476 covers the period from 1517); other substantial recent contributions are H. A. Oberman, *Luther: Mensch zwischen Gott und Teufel* (Berlin, 1982) (199–219 on this period), and M. J. Harran, *Luther on Conversion: The Early Years* (Ithaca, NY, 1983) (151 ff. on this period). To simplify the apparatus these works will not be cited minutely throughout this section. Luther's development before his 'reforming' career is discussed in Ch. 12. 1.
4. The *Seven Penitential Psalms* treatise is edited in *WA* i. 154–220, and *LW* xiv. 137–205; the teachings of Scotus and Occam are discussed in Ch. 6. 2.
5. Text in *WA* i. 221–8; *LW* xxxi. 5–16; a partial trans. is provided in J. Atkinson (ed.), *Luther: Early Theological Works*, *LCC* 16 (London, 1962), 266–73.
6. On indulgences, see the discussion in Ch. 6. 1.
7. Luther's letter is in *WA.B* i. 108–12; *LW* xlviii. 43–9, and the theses in *WA* i. 229–38; *LW* xxxi. 19–33. The texts are also ed. in Kidd, *Documents*, 20–8, and trans. in E. G. Rupp and B. J. Drewery (eds.), *Martin Luther* (London, 1970), 17–25. The general reader should beware that the meaning of some of Luther's lapidary theses is not always certain, and translations vary. Whether the theses were actually affixed to the castle church door (Wittenberg's academic notice-board for such purposes) has been debated at least since E. Iserloh's *The Theses Were Not Posted: Luther between Reform and Reformation*, trans. J. Wicks (London, 1968), 76–97, denied that this ever

occurred; see discussions of this point by E. G. Rupp in Rupp and Drewery (eds.), *Martin Luther*, 12–13, and in *Journal of Theological Studies*, 19/1 (1968), 360ff.; by H. A. Oberman in *Masters*, 148–50 (n. 88); and by Brecht, *Martin Luther*, 192–202.

8. The *Resolutions* are ed. in *WA* i. 522–628; *LW* xxxi. 83 252; the *Sermon on Indulgence and Grace* in *WA* i. 239–46; the Heidelberg disputation in *WA* i. 350–74; *LW* xxxi. 37–70; also trans. in Atkinson (ed.), *Luther: Early Theological Works*, 276–307. This period of Luther's 'Theology of the Cross' has received separate studies, for instance W. von Loewenich, *Luther's Theology of the Cross*, trans. H. J. A. Bouman (Belfast, 1976), and P. S. Watson, *Let God be God* (London, 1947), 102–48, and as cited in Rupp and Drewery (eds.), *Martin Luther*, 27.

9. On this episode see J. Wicks, *Cajetan und die Anfänge der Reformation* (Münster, 1983), esp. 72–112; also *Cajetan Responds: A Reader in Reformation Controversy*, ed. and trans. J. Wicks (Washington, DC, 1978); Kidd, *Documents*, 32–9.

10. Luther's *Asterisks* are ed. in *WA* i. 278–314; documents on the Leipzig debate ed. in *WA* ii. 153–61 and 250–383; *LW* xxxi. 309–25; selections in Kidd, *Documents*, 44–51.

11. *On Good Works* is ed. in *WA* vi. 196–276, and in *LW* xliv. 17–114; *On the Papacy at Rome* in *WA* vi. 277–324, and *LW* xxxix. 51 104; *To the Christian Nobility of the German Nation* in *WA* vi. 404–69, and *LW* xliv. 117–217; *The Babylonian Captivity of the Church* in *WA* vi. 484–573; *LW* xxxvi. 5–126.

12. On this aspect of the story, L. W. Spitz, *The Religious Renaissance of the German Humanists* (Cambridge, Mass., 1963), 177 f.

13. Kidd, *Documents*, 82; cf. also the impressions of the Venetian Gasparo Contarini in ibid., 89.

14. The German text of *On Christian Freedom* is found in *WA* vii. 12–38; the Latin version in *WA* vii. 39–73, and *LW* xxxi. 333–77; see also Luther's *Why the Books were Burned*, in *WA* vii. 161–82; *LW* xxxi. 381–95.

15. The cited passage is found in Kidd, *Documents*, 82–5; *WA* vii. 838, and *LW* xxxii. 112–13; other material relating to the *Reichstag* is in *WA* vii. 814–87; *LW* xxxii. 103–31; and Kidd, *Documents*, 85–9. For the final papal bull condemning Luther see the trans. in Rupp and Drewery (eds.), *Martin Luther*, 63–7.

16. As quoted by R. Bainton, *Erasmus of Christendom* (London, 1972), p. 206 and n. 61.

17. For much of Luther's output during late 1521 see *WA* vii. 237–791; the tract *Against Latomus* is ed. in *WA* viii. 36–128; *LW* xxxii. 135–260; and partial trans. in Atkinson (ed.), *Luther: Early Theological Works*, 311–64.

18. G. Benecke, *Society and Politics in Germany 1500–1750* (London, 1974), 5ff.; id., *Maximilian I (1459–1519): An Analytical Biography* (London, 1982), 138ff.

19. F. Hartung, 'Imperial Reform, 1485–1495: Its Course and Character', in Strauss, *Pre-Ref. Germany*, 73–135; K. S. Bader, 'Approaches to Imperial Reform at the End of the Fifteenth Century', ibid. 136–61; H. Angermeier, *Die Reichsreform 1410–1555: Die Staatsproblematik in Deutschland zwischen Mittelalter und Gegenwart* (Munich, 1984), esp. 164–279; also id., 'Reichsreform und Reformation', *HZ* 235 (1982), 529–604; H. Wiesflecker, *Kaiser Maximilian I*, 5 vols. (Munich, 1971–85), v. 121–50.

20. For the background to these arrangements see Ch. 4. 2.

21. Maximilian would have preferred Wimpfeling to have been more ambitious: see Spitz, *Religious Renaissance*, 55–6.

22. B. Gebhard, *Die Gravamina der deutschen Nation gegen den römischen Hof: Ein Beitrag zur Vorgeschichte der Reformation* (2nd edn., Breslau, 1895), *passim*, and as discussed

by Dickens, *German Nation*, 7–8, 28–9. Versions of the 'Grievances' are found in Kidd, *Documents*, 110–21; Strauss, *Manifestations*, 52–63.

23. J. H. Overfield, *Humanism and Scholasticism in Late Medieval Germany* (Princeton, NJ, 1984), 247–53 and refs.; also id., 'A New Look at the Reuchlin Affair', *Studies in Medieval and Renaissance History*, 8 (1971), 167–207; and Spitz, *Religious Renaissance*, 61–80.

24. The text is available in F. Griffin Stokes (ed.), *Epistolae Obscurorum Virorum: The Latin Text with an English Rendering* (London, 1909); the context in Overfield, *Humanism and Scholasticism*, 253–97. In ch. 7 of François Rabelais's *Pantagruel*, a satirical work written in 1532, the hero visits the library of St Victor in Paris and there discovers, amongst others, such books as *The Art of Breaking Wind Decently in Company*, by Ortuinus Gratius, *The Use of Soups and the Propriety of Hobnobbing*, by Silvestro Mazzolini, *The Calibration of Hypocrisy*, by Jakob van Hochstraten, *Ways of Sweeping Flues*, by Johannes von Eck, and *The Old Wives' Tales* of Cajetan, alongside *The Fulminations of the Cologne Doctors against Reuchlin*.

25. See H. Holborn, *Ulrich von Hutten and the German Reformation*, trans. R. H. Bainton (New Haven, Conn., 1937), 101ff., 117ff., 135ff.

26. Ibid. 124ff., 151ff.; H. Eells, *Martin Bucer* (New Haven, Conn., and London, 1931), 11–12; Rupp, *Patterns*, 18.

27. *LW* li. 71; also Rupp and Drewery (eds.), *Martin Luther*, 102.

28. See Ch. 4. 5.

29. This is the theme of B. Moeller's essay 'The German Humanists and the Beginnings of the Reformation', in *Imperial Cities*, 19–38; when confronted with the accusation that he had 'laid the egg which Luther hatched', Erasmus responded that the egg *he* laid was of a quite different species from Luther's: so the 'cuckoo' image may after all be appropriate! See *EE* v. 609, letter no. 1528 of 16 Dec. 1524.

30. On Luther's early impact on Nuremberg see Fife, *Revolt of Martin Luther*, 239ff.; G. Seebass, 'Stadt und Kirche in Nürnberg', in B. Moeller (ed.), *Stadt und Kirche im 16. Jahrhundert* (Gütersloh, 1978), 71ff. and refs.; G. Strauss, *Nuremberg in the Sixteenth Century* (New York, 1966), 161ff.; H. J. Grimm, *Lazarus Spengler, a Lay Leader of the Reformation* (Columbus, Ohio, 1978), esp. 31ff. See also H. von Schubert, *Lazarus Spengler und die Einführung der Reformation in Nürnberg* (Leipzig, 1934).

31. W. Köhler, *Huldrych Zwingli* (2nd edn., Stuttgart, 1952), 45–85; Locher, *ZR* 83ff., 92ff.; G. R. Potter, *Zwingli* (Cambridge, 1976), 47–78.

32. Köhler, *Huldrych Zwingli*, 85–103; Locher, *ZR* 102–15; Potter, *Zwingli*, 78–125; see disputation in Ch. 15 n. 105.

33. Locher, *ZR* 368ff. and refs.; Rupp, *Patterns*, 18ff.; E. Staehelin, *Das theologische Lebenswerk Johannes Oekolampads* (Leipzig, 1939), 158–69, 189ff., 249–52.

34. W. Näf, *Vadian und seine Stadt St Gallen*, 2 vols. (St Gallen, 1944–57), ii. 128–50; Locher, *ZR* 365 f.

35. Locher, *ZR* 373ff. and refs.

36. M. U. Chrisman, *Strasbourg and the Reform: A Study in the Process of Change* (New Haven, Conn., 1967), 98ff.; Rapp., *Réformes*, 467ff.; L. J. Abray, *The People's Reformation: Magistrates, Clergy and Commons in Strasbourg 1500–1598* (Oxford, 1985), 32ff.

37. Locher, *ZR* 459ff.; H.-C. Rublack, *Die Einführung der Reformation in Konstanz* (Gütersloh, 1971), 16–26.
38. Rupp, *Patterns*, 13–15; Locher, *ZR* 464ff.; in general see for Augsburg F. Roth, *Augsburgs Reformationsgeschichte*, 4 vols. (Munich, 1901–11).
39. The detailed political working out of an interest in reforming preachers is discussed in Ch. 15.

8. *The Reformers' Message: Salvation*

1. See Ch. 6.
2. On which see Ch. 6. 2 nn. 27–37.
3. The usual approach by historians of theology is either to study one theologian at a time and to emphasize the individual and distinctive features of their subject, or to seek out and illustrate often quite technical distinctions (dogmatic, stylistic, or rhetorical) between a handful of figures regardless of whether, historically speaking, they should be regarded as allies; however, see the remarks of Strohl, *Pensée*, 261, and G. W. Locher, *Zwingli's Thought: New Perspectives* (Leiden, 1981), 143, on the basic common features of the leading reformers' doctrines.
4. J. T. McNeill, ed. of *Calvin: Institutes of the Christian Religion*, 2 vols., *LCC* xx–xxi (Philadelphia, 1960), points out numerous parallel treatments of major themes by Melanchthon and Calvin: see nn. to i. 252, 354, 359–60, 362, 365, 373–4, 419, etc.
5. See e.g. the concise summary in Huldrych Zwingli's *The Education of Youth* of 1523, in *Z* ii. 540–1, and S and S iv. 151–2.
6. Althaus, *Luther*, 143, 155; *Melanchthon*, ed. Manschreck, 51–2, 70–2; *Inst.* II. i. 1–3; II. ii. 12, Stephens, *Zwingli*, 139–53; *Z* i. 344ff.
7. M. G. Baylor, *Action and Person*, *SMRT* 20 (Leiden, 1977), 154, 157–208.
8. *MWA* II. i. 17ff., 38 40.
9. See for instance Oberman, *Harvest*, 121ff.; D. C. Steinmetz, *Misericordia Dei* (Leiden, 1968), 64ff.
10. *MWA* II. i. 39–40; *Melanchthon*, ed. Manschreck, 76–7; *Inst.* II. i. 8; M. Bucer, *Metaphrasis et enarratio in epist. D. Pauli apostoli ad Romanos* (Basle, 1562), 295; J. P. Donnelly, *Calvinism and Scholasticism in Vermigli's Doctrine of Man and Grace*, *SMRT* 18 (Leiden, 1976) 106–7.
11. *Inst.* II. ii. 12–17; *Melanchthon*, ed. Manschreck, 52.
12. *Inst.* II. ii. 18–24.
13. Althaus, *Luther*, 144–50.
14. *MWA* II. i. 21–2, 24; *Inst.* II. iii. 3–4; cf. also *Z* iii. 656ff., S and S iv. 61–2.
15. *Inst.* II. ii. 4.
16. Cf. Ch. 6. 2.
17. *WA* xviii. 634–8, 736–40, 757ff.; *LW* xxxiii. 64–70, 215–22, 247ff.
18. See Melanchthon's *Augsburg Confession*, in Kidd, *Documents*, 266–7; *MWA* II. i. 12–16, 42, 236–8; Bucer, *Metaphrasis … in epist. … ad Romanos*, 461ff.
19. The debate was reported by the Piedmontese pastor Girolamo Miolo, in his *Historia breve e vera de gl'affari de i valdesi delle valli*, ed. E. Balmas (Turin, 1971), 99–100.
20. *WA* viii. 82–3, 89; *LW* xxxii. 193ff., 203; *MWA* II. i. 19ff.; *Inst.* III. iii. 10.
21. Stephens, *Zwingli*, 149–53; *Z* i. 350ff.; iii. 708ff.; Bucer, *Metaphrasis … in epist. … ad Romanos*, 295–6.
22. e.g. *Inst.* IV. xv. esp. 10–13.

23. On Christianity as 'Law' see E. Cameron, *Reformation of the Heretics* (Oxford, 1984), 21, and F. Conrad, *Reformation in der bäuerlichen Gesellschaft: Zur Rezeption reformatorischer Theologie in Elsass* (Stuttgart, 1984), 98ff.

24. *MWA* II. i. 40ff., 278ff.; *Melanchthon*, ed. Manschreck, 83–5, 128–9.

25. *Inst.* II. viii., esp. 1–9.

26. *MWA* II. i. 49–52, 326–43; *Melanchthon*, ed. Manschreck, 130ff.; *Inst.* II. viii. 56; on commands and counsels see *DThC*, 'Conseils evangéliques', iii, cols. 1176ff.; *DDC*, 'Précepte', vii, cols. 116ff.; on celibacy, *DThC*, 'Célibat', ii, cols. 2068ff., and 'Continence', iii, col. 1633.

27. *Inst.* II. viii. 58–9; III. iv. 28; Bucer made this stark statement about venial and mortal sins in some advice given to Waldensian pastors in 1530: Cameron, *Reformation of the Heretics*, 204; Trinity College, Dublin, MS 259. 104–5.

28. *WA* viii. 53ff.; *LW* xxxii. 161ff.; cf. *Melanchthon*, ed. Manschreck, 66–9.

29. *Inst.* II. vii. 3–5; Stephens, *Zwingli*, 164; *Z* i. 351–2.

30. *MWA* II. i. 74–82; *Melanchthon*, ed. Manschreck, 122–8; *Inst.* II. vii. 7; *WA* i. 361; *LW* xxxi. 51–2; cf. also Bucer, *Metaphrasis . . . in epist. . . . ad Romanos*, 215–16.

31. But cf. also *Melanchthon*, ed. Manschreck, 141–2.

32. *Inst.* II. vii. 6–9; II. viii. 3, 10; Stephens, *Zwingli*, 164–5.

33. Althaus, *Luther*, 261–6; F. Hildebrandt, *Melanchthon: Alien or Ally?* (Cambridge, 1946), 34–43; *MWA* II. i. 321–6; IGJ 341–4; *Inst.* II. vii. 13.

34. See *DThC*, 'Foi', vi. 55–514, but esp. 467ff.; Thomas Aquinas, *Summa Theologica*, II(2), qq. 1–7 esp.

35. e.g. *MWA* II. i. 98–9; *WA* vii. 58f.; *LW* xxxi. 357; *WA* xviii. 604ff., *LW* xxxiii. 22ff.

36. Bucer, *Metaphrasis . . . in epist. . . . ad Romanos*, 14ff; *Inst.* III. ii. 2–5, 14.

37. *MWA* II. i. 91–2; Stephens, *Zwingli*, 161–3; Bucer, *Metaphrasis . . . in epist. . . . ad Romanos*, 16ff.; *Inst.* III. ii. 8–10.

38. *MWA* II. i. 92, 115–16; cf. *Melanchthon*, ed. Manschreck, 87–8, 158–9.

39. *Inst.* III. ii. 15; cf. Stephens, *Zwingli*, 162; also S and S iv. 60–1.

40. Oberman, *Harvest*, 185, 217ff., 227–30.

41. *MWA* II. i. 119–22; *Melanchthon*, ed. Manschreck, 169–71; Bucer, *Metaphrasis . . . in epist. . . . ad Romanos*, 17–18; *Inst.* III. ii. 38–40.

42. Althaus, *Luther*, 44–5; cf. Scheel, *Dokumente*, 312.

43. Althaus, *Luther*, 60ff.; *Inst.* III. ii. 17, 37.

44. Althaus, *Luther*, 47–9, 232–3; cf. H. Boehmer, *Martin Luther: Road to Reformation* (Philadelphia, 1946), 307–8; *WA* vi. 530; *LW* xxxvi. 62; *Melanchthon*, ed. Manschreck, 159, 164; Stephens, *Zwingli*, 162–3; Locher, *Zwingli's Thought*, 138; Stephens, *Bucer*, 63, 65–8; Bucer, *Metaphrasis . . . in epist. . . . ad Romanos*, 15–16; *Inst.* III. ii. 35.

45. *Inst.* III. ii. 35.

46. Ibid. II. xii–xvii; cf. *MWA* II. i. 82.

47. For the Christology of Chalcedon, see *COD* 83ff.; *DThC*, 'Jésus Christ', vii, cols. 1266ff., 'Chalcédoine', ii, cols. 2194f., and 'Hypostatique', vii, cols. 483f.

48. Althaus, *Luther*, 179–80, 183; W. Niesel, *The Theology of Calvin*, trans. H. Knight (Philadelphia, 1956), 110–18; *Melanchthon*, ed. Manschreck, 31–4; *MWA* II. i. 183–5; Bucer, *Metaphrasis . . . in epist. . . . ad Romanos*, 18; *Inst.* II. xiv. 1–8; III. ii. 38–40; Stephens, *Zwingli*, 113–14; I. D. Kingston Siggins, *Martin Luther's Doctrine of Christ* (New Haven, Conn., 1970), 191–243.

49. Stephens, *Zwingli*, 114–18; Locher, *Zwingli's Thought*, 173ff.; S and S, iv. 48–50; see

also the nn. to G. W. Bromiley (ed.), *Zwingli and Bullinger*, *LCC* 24 (London, 1953), 347.

50. On Anselm's interpretation see *Cur Deus Homo*, in *S. Anselmi Opera Omnia*, ed. F. S. Schmitt, 6 vols. (Edinburgh, 1946–61), ii; and an older edn. as a separate work (Edinburgh, 1909).

51. Siggins, *Luther's Doctrine of Christ*, 108–37; Althaus, *Luther*, 202–8; cf. *Melanchthon*, ed. Manschreck, 33, 82, and S and S iv. 4–6, 47–8; Z iii. 691–701.

52. See G. Aulén, *Christus Victor*, trans. A. G. Herbert (London, 1970), 101ff., and the reservations expressed by Siggins, *Luther's Doctrine of Christ*, 108–9, 129–33, 137–43.

53. *Inst.* ii. xii. 1–6; xvi. 1–4; xvii; for Abelard see *DThC*, 'Abelard', i, col. 47.

54. Strohl, *Pensée*, 139–42.

55. Hugh Latimer's *Sermon on the Plough* of 1548, in *Sermons of Hugh Latimer*, ed. G. E. Corrie, Parker Society (Cambridge, 1844), 75; cf. F. Clark, *Eucharistic Sacrifice and the Reformation* (Chulmleigh, 1981), 99ff., 127ff.

56. Locher, *Zwingli's Thought*, 143.

57. Althaus, *Luther*, 224f.; *Inst.* iii. xi. 1; Niesel, *Theology of Calvin*, 131 and refs.; cf. Melanchthon in *BSLK* 158f., 415; and the peroration to Bucer, *Metaphrasis ... in epist ... ad Romanos*, 424ff.

58. See sect. 8. 4.

59. See *Melanchthon*, ed. Manschreck, 163.

60. The issues are analysed at length in Ch. 12. 1.

61. The sermon *On Twofold Righteousness* is ed. in *WA* ii. 143–52, *LW* xxxi. 295–306; the *Freedom of a Christian* in *WA* vii. 12–38 (German text), 39–73 (Latin text), and *LW* xxxi. 333–77; the Latomus riposte in *WA* viii. 36–128; *LW* xxxii. 135–260. See Ch. 12 n.14.

62. *WA* viii. 92–3; *LW* xxxii. 208.

63. *MWA* ii. i. 107–9.

64. S and S iv. 60; cf. several other similar passages cited by Locher, *Zwingli's Thought*, 182–5 and nn.

65. Bucer, *Metaphrasis ... in epist. ... ad Romanos*, 12–13; and cf. ibid. 50ff.

66. *Inst.* iii. xi. 2.

67. Ibid.; cf. *Melanchthon*, ed. Manschreck, 156, 162; Scheel, *Dokumente*, 192, l. 25.

68. See Ch. 6. 1.

69. This classic phrase of Luther's made its first appearance in his *Lectures on Romans* of 1515–16, but acquired a slightly different meaning later: see Ch. 12. 1.

70. See S. E. Ozment, 'Homo Viator: Luther and Late Medieval Theology', in Ozment, *Perspective*, 148–52; cf. also Bornkamm, *Mid-Career*, 195–7, and S. Ickert, 'Defending the *Ordo salutis*: Jacob van Hoogstraten versus Martin Luther', *ARG* 87 (1987), 81–97 and esp. 91ff.

71. See Ch. 6 n. 39 and refs.; Ozment, *Reform*, 32ff.; *DThC*, 'Grace', vi, cols. 1554–1687, and esp. 1604ff.; cf. *Inst.* iv. xvii. 41.

72. *MWA* ii. i. 85–8; *Melanchthon*, ed. Manschreck, 160.

73. Scheel, *Dokumente*, 192, ll. 25–7; *Inst.* iii. xi. 15.

74. Stephens, *Bucer*, 48–61; Bucer, *Metaphrasis ... in epist. ... ad Romanos*, 119.

75. Stephens, *Zwingli*, 154–9, 164–9.

76. *WA* vii. 53; *LW* xxxi. 349–50.

77. *MWA* II. i. 125–37; Stephens, *Zwingli*, 166; Stephens, *Bucer*, 95–8; *Inst*. II. vii. 14–17; III. xix, *passim*.

78. *MWA* II. i. 125–37, as above; cf. Bucer, *Metaphrasis* ... *in epist* ... *ad Romanos*, 26–7, 216–19.

79. Althaus, *Luther*, 261ff.; *Inst*. II. ix–xi.

80. *Inst*. II. vii. 12–13; III. iii, vi–x; cf. Locher, *Zwingli's Thought*, 122; S and S iv. 62–4; Z iii. 714ff.; Bucer also organized his *Summary seiner Predig* of 1523 in this way: see Strohl, *Pensée*, 109.

81. See Ch. 6 n. 17.

82. *WA* viii. 107; *LW* xxxii. 229; cf. also the 'Resolution' of thesis 58 of the 95 theses, in *WA* i. 605ff., and *LW* xxxi. 212ff.; see Althaus, *Luther*, 299; *MWA* II. i. 136–7, also 108, 265; *Inst*. III. iii. 11; xiv. 9; xv; M. Bucer, *Martin Bucer: résumé sommaire de la doctrine chrétienne*, ed. F. Wendel (Paris, 1951), 42–3.

83. e.g. *Inst*. III. iii. 5.

84. *MWA* II. i. 149; *Inst*. III. iii. 9.

85. Althaus, *Luther*, 234–50.

86. Ibid. 270–1; *WA* vii. 64ff.; *LW* xxxi. 364ff.; *MWA* II. i. 112–13; *Inst* III. vii, viii, x; Stephens, *Bucer*, 92; Bucer, *Résumé sommaire*, 38ff.

87. e.g. *Inst*. III. vii. 4.

88. See Ch. 6 n. 17.

89. *WA* i. 229–38; *WA* xxxi. 19–33; cf. *Inst*. III. v. 6–10.

90. J. Haroutunian and L. Smith (eds.), *Calvin: Commentaries*, LCC 23 (London, 1958), 201; *Inst*. III. ix; Stephens, *Bucer*, 100; also S and S iv. 50.

91. See the discussion in Althaus, *Luther*, 248.

92. This position is suggested by, amongst others, Stephens, *Zwingli* and *Bucer*.

93. See Hildebrandt, *Melanchthon: Alien or Ally?*, xix; cf. also C. E. Maxcey, *Bona Opera: A Study in the Development of the Doctrine in Philip Melanchthon* (Nieuwkoop, 1980), and in the introd. to *Melanchthon*, ed. Manschreck.

94. For these see Ch. 20. 1.

95. *WA* xviii. 614–16; *LW*, xxxiii. 36–9; Locher, *Zwingli's Thought*, 125; Strohl, *Pensée*, 152.

96. *Inst*. III. xxiv. 12.

97. *WA* i. 225; *LW* xxxi. 11; *WA* xviii. 684ff.; *LW* xxxiii. 138ff.; Althaus, *Luther*, 274–86.

98. *MWA* II. i. 10–17.

99. Locher, *Zwingli's Thought*, 128–9, 132–3, 208–9; cf. S and S iv. 61.

100. *Inst*. III. xxi. 5; F. Wendel, *Calvin: The Origins and Development of his Religious Thought*, trans. P. Mairet (London, 1963), 263–8.

101. *Inst*. III. xxiii. 5; Haroutunian and Smith (eds.), *Calvin, Commentaries*, 298.

102. See Ch. 6.2; also Oberman, *Harvest*, 182–215.

103. Ibid.; E. J. D. Douglass, *Justification in Late Medieval Preaching* (Leiden, 1966), 126–8; Steinmetz, *Misericordia Dei*, 79ff.

104. *WA* xviii. 714–19; *LW* xxxiii. 184–90; cf. Wendel, *Calvin*, 271–2.

105. *WA* xviii. 614–16; *LW* xxxiii. 36–9.

106. Bucer, *Metaphrasis* ... *in epist*. ... *ad Romanos*, 409–10; id., *Praelectiones doctiss. in epistolam D. P. ad Ephesios* (Basle, 1562), 21–4.

107. *Inst*. III. xxi. 5; xxii; xxiii. 6; Haroutunian and Smith (eds.), *Calvin, Commentaries*, 294, 305ff.

108. *DThC*, 'Prédestination', xii, esp. cols. 2935–59; and above, n. 102.
109. Althaus, *Luther*, 282–6; *WA* xviii. 709–14; *LW* xxxiii. 175–84.
110. Locher, *Zwingli's Thought*, 132–6, 209; R. T. Kendall, *Calvin and English Calvinism to 1649* (Oxford, 1979), 29–30 n. 3 and refs.; Strohl, *Pensée*, 148–50; for a similar asymmetric position in later Lutheranism see *BSLK* 816ff.
111. Bucer, *Metaphrasis ... in epist. ... ad Romanos*, 410; id., *Praelectiones ... in Epistolam ... ad Ephesios*, 23–4; Stephens, *Bucer*, 23ff.
112. *Inst.* III. xxiii. 1–11, xxiv. 12–17; Haroutunian and Smith (eds.), *Calvin, Commentaries*, 293–4.
113. Strohl, *Pensée*, 148–50.
114. *MWA* II. i. 12; see R. Stupperich, *Melanchthon*, trans. R. Fischer (London, 1966), 67; cf. *Melanchthon*, ed. Manschreck, 187–91, and *MWA* II. i. 229–36.
115. Wendel, *Calvin*, 264 and n. 101; *Inst.* III. xxi. 3.
116. *WA* xviii. 620ff., 630ff.; *LW* xxxiii. 44ff., 58ff.; *Inst.* III. xxi. 4; xxiii. 12–14.
117. Bucer, *Metaphrasis ... in epist. ... ad Romanos*, 411–12; id., *Praelectiones ... in Epistolam ... ad Ephesios*, 20; *Book of Common Prayer*, Art. XVII; Locher, *Zwingli's Thought*, 132; *Inst.* III. xxi. 1–2, and as ed. McNeill and Battles, 992 n. 6; Haroutunian and Smith (eds.), *Calvin, Commentaries*, 303; *WA* xviii. 688ff.; *LW* xxxiii. 144ff.; Althaus, *Luther*, 281.
118. Niesel, *Theology of Calvin*, 169–81; Bucer, *Metaphrasis ... in epist. ... ad Romanos*, 411–12; Stephens, *Bucer*, 30–6; and cf. *Inst.* III. xxiv. 10; Locher, *Zwingli's Thought*, 184–5. There is a major debate over whether and how far predestination played a subtly different role in later Calvinism from that of the mid-16th cent. See B. Hall, 'Calvin against the Calvinists', in G. E. Duffield (ed.), *John Calvin* (Abingdon, 1966), 26ff.; Kendall, *Calvin and English Calvinism*, *passim*; J. S. Bray, *Theodore Beza's Doctrine of Predestination* (Nieuwkoop, 1975), esp. 137ff.; and the recent survey by R. Letham, 'Theodore Beza: A Reassessment', *Scottish Journal of Theology*, 40 (1987), 25–40.
119. For this process see Ch. 6. 1.
120. For general confessions, see T. N. Tentler, *Sin and Confession on the Eve of the Reformation* (Princeton, NJ, 1977), 79–80, 115–16; cf. *Inst.* III. iv. 11.
121. *MWA* II. i. 63–4, 149–55; *WA* vi. 543–9; *LW* xxxvi. 81–91, and refs. on 81 n. 147; *Inst.* III. iv, *passim*; on the varied fate of the confessional in the Reformation see Ozment, *Cities*, 49ff.; *IGJ* 352; Sehling, xi. 186ff.
122. *WA* vi. 548; *LW* xxxvi. 90; *Melanchthon*, ed. Manschreck, 240; *Inst.* III. iv. 2, 16–18; also Eberlin von Günzburg, as cited by Ozment, *Cities*, 96–7; see also Tentler, *Sin and Confession*, 349–62. This aspect of the reformers' attack on confession is the core of the argument of Professor S. E. Ozment discussed in Ch. 17. 3.
123. *WA* vi. 545, 548–9; *LW* xxxvi. 85, 90.
124. *Melanchthon*, ed. Manschreck, 238; *Z* iv. 253.
125. *Inst.* III. iv. 19.
126. *WA* i. 229–38; *LW* xxxi. 19–33; also trans. in E. G. Rupp and B. J. Drewery (eds.), *Martin Luther* (London, 1970), 19ff.; *S and S* iv. 16–17, 50; *Inst.* III. v. *passim*; but Melanchthon simply omitted purgatory altogether from the Augsburg Confession and the *Apology*: see *Inst.*, ed. McNeill and Battles, 676 and nn.
127. Althaus, *Luther*, 297–303; *Inst.* III. xx. 21–7; Strohl, *Pensée*, 58ff.
128. Eire, *Idols*, 54–104, and 195–233 for Calvin's views; *Z* iii. 900ff.; iv. 84–149; Oberman,

Masters, 292f., explains the varying reformed positions towards images in terms of their scholastic training. For their effects see Ch. 15. 6.

129. On the possible extent and limits to lay understanding see Chs. 17. 3 and 21. 2.

9. The Reformers' Message: Scripture

1. See Ch. 6 nn. 53 and 60.
2. e.g. Strohl, *Pensée*, 63.
3. As described in Ch. 7. 1.
4. As for instance in Kidd, *Documents*, 27ff., 82ff.; or *WA* iii. 98–9; *LW* xxxii. 216–17.
5. Althaus, *Luther*, 75 and refs.; *Z* i. 378, and cf. i. 368ff.; M. Bucer, *Metaphrasis ... in epist. ... ad Romanos* (Basle, 1562), 18ff.; id., *Praelectiones ... in Epistolam ... ad Ephesios* (Basle, 1562), 43.
6. *Inst.* I. vii. 3, and cf. Luther's *Von Menschenlehre zu meiden und Antwort auf Spruch, so Man führet, Menschenlehre zu stärken*, in *WA* x/ii. 89ff.; in general see *Inst.* I. vii. 1, and IV. viii. 9–10; Bucer, *Praelectiones ... in Epistolam ... ad Ephesios*, 44–5; id., *Metaphrasis ... in epist. ... ad Romanos*, 20–1.
7. Althaus, *Luther*, 81–6; Kidd, *Documents*, 104–5; E. G. Rupp and B. J. Drewery (eds.), *Martin Luther* (London, 1970), 91–9; cf. Stephens, *Bucer*, 147; W. Niesel, *The Theology of Calvin*, trans. H. Knight (Philadelphia, 1956), ch. 2; J. Haroutunian and L. Smith (eds.), *Calvin, Commentaries*, LCC 23 (London, 1958), 34.
8. Stephens, *Zwingli*, 56–7.
9. But cf. Niesel, *Theology of Calvin*, 22ff., 30ff.; Haroutunian and Smith (eds.), *Calvin, Commentaries*, 33ff.
10. *Z* i. 361–77; Stephens, *Zwingli*, 55ff., 59ff.
11. Bucer, *Praelectiones ... in Epistolam ... ad Ephesios*, 46–7; Stephens, *Bucer*, 134; *Inst.* I. vii. 4–5; cf. *WA* xviii. 606–9; *LW* xxxiii. 25–8.
12. Cf. G. W. Locher, *Zwingli's Thought: New Perspectives* (Leiden, 1981), 254f., on the prayer used at meetings of the Zürich *Prophezei*.
13. Cf. Ambrosius of Speyer, discussed in Ch. 6 n. 59.
14. G. Ebeling, *Luther: An Introduction to his Thought*, trans. R. A. Wilson (London, 1970), 108–9 and refs.; Stephens, *Bucer*, 137 and nn.; *Inst.* I. ix.
15. As set out in Ch. 6. 3.
16. Althaus, *Luther*, 338–41; Stephens, *Zwingli*, 52ff.; *Inst.*, preface, §4, and as ed. McNeill and Battles, 19, and IV. viii. 10–16; ix. 14; x.
17. W. Pauck (ed.), *Melanchthon and Bucer*, LCC 19 (London, 1969), 7, 19; *Inst.*, prefatory material, as ed. McNeill and Battles, 4–8.
18. Oberman, *Forerunners*, 279ff.
19. Ebeling, *Luther*, 98–107; A. E. McGrath, *Intellectual Origins of the European Reformation* (Oxford, 1987), 158–62.
20. Althaus, *Luther*, 92–102; Ebeling, *Luther*, 107–8; McGrath, *Intellectual Origins*, 162–4.
21. Stephens, *Zwingli*, 62ff.; Stephens, *Bucer*, 152–3; H. Bullinger, *The Decades of Henry Bullinger*, trans. 'H.I.' and ed. T. Harding, 4 vols., Parker Society (Cambridge, 1849–52), i. 70–80.
22. Haroutunian and Smith (eds.), *Calvin, Commentaries*, 19, 21; *Inst.* II. x, xi, *passim*.
23. On allegories, see McGrath, *Intellectual Origins*, 152ff.
24. Ebeling, *Luther*, 102–4, and McGrath, *Intellectual Origins*, 152ff., 171; Stephens, *Bucer*, 152–3.

25. Stephens, *Zwingli*, 78–9; McGrath, *Intellectual Origins*, 169–170; *Inst.* II. xi. 1–6; for rejection of allegory, Haroutunian and Smith (eds.), *Calvin, Commentaries*, 27–9.
26. See Ch. 4. 5.
27. For Luther's opinion on Hebrews, Althaus, *Luther*, 84 and refs.
28. See Luther's Open Letter *On Translating*, in *WA* xxx/ii. 632–46; *LW* xxxv. 181–202; excerpt in Rupp and Drewery (eds.), *Martin Luther*, 87–91.
29. See Ch. 15 esp. n. 101.
30. Cf. Strauss, *Manifestations*, 143.
31. McGrath, *Intellectual Origins*, 124–5 and refs.
32. As in Ch. 8. 2 nn. 34–6.
33. Erasmus, *Paraclesis*, as cited in Ch. 4 n. 105.
34. E. G. Rupp and P. S. Watson (eds.), *Luther and Erasmus, LCC* 17 (London, 1959), 37–42, 108 17, 121 39; *WA* xviii. 604–14, 617–39; *LW* xxxiii. 22–37, 41–70 (emphasis added).
35. See Ch. 4 n. 100.
36. See Ch. 10. 2.
37. As described in Ch. 21. 2.
38. See Ch. 15. 1.
39. See Luther's so-called 'Invocavit sermons' in *WA* x/iii. 1–64; *LW* li. 69–100; see also McGrath, *Intellectual Origins*, 138–9 and refs; G. Strauss, 'Lutheranism and Literacy, a reassessment', in von Greyerz, *Rel. and Soc.*, 109–23; R. Gawthrop and G. Strauss, 'Protestantism and Literacy in Early Modern Germany', *P and P* 104 (1984), 31–55.
40. Bullinger, *Decades*, i. 70–5, as above n. 21.
41. For catechisms see Ch. 21.2; Strauss, 'Lutheranism and Literacy', 114; on the effects of this procedure on the training of ministers see also B. Vogler, *Le Clergé protestant rhénan au siècle de la réforme (1555–1619)* (Paris, 1976), 51–5

10. *The Reformers' Message: The Church*

1. See for instance Luther's Resolution XII of the 1519 Leipzig disputation, in *WA* ii. 428–32; H. Boehmer, *Martin Luther* (Philadelphia, 1946), 275.
2. Althaus, *Luther*, 287–8, 294–303.
3. Melanchthon in the *Augsburg Confession*, as in Kidd, *Documents*, 264; Stephens, *Zwingli*, 260–1; *Z* iii. 741 3; S and S iv. 8–9, 58; Stephens, *Bucer*, 159, 164–6; M. Bucer, *Praelectiones ... in Epistolam ... ad Ephesios* (Basle, 1562), 36; H. Bullinger, *The Decades of Henry Bullinger* (Cambridge, 1849–52) i. 161–3; *Inst.* IV. i. 2–3.
4. See Luther's *Schmalkald Articles*, in *BSLK* 459–60, and as cited in Strohl, *Pensée*, 207.
5. See Ch. 5; and cf. *Inst.*, as ed. McNeill and Battles, 1022 n. 14.
6. Althaus, *Luther*, 290–3, 333–4; W. D. J. Cargill Thompson, *The Political Thought of Martin Luther* (London, 1984), 123–4; Strohl, *Pensée*, 177–8; cf. Bucer, *Praelectiones ... in Epistolam ... ad Ephesios*, 37.
7. S and S iv. 9, 58–9; Stephens, *Zwingli*, 262–70.
8. Stephens, *Bucer*, 158–66.
9. *Inst.* IV. i. 1, 7–8.
10. Strohl, *Pensée*, 178–9, 188–9, 207ff.; Althaus, *Luther*, 289–90; Kidd, *Documents*, 264.
11. Strohl, *Pensée*, 197ff.; Stephens, *Bucer*, 156–65; Bucer, *Praelectiones ... in Epistolam ... ad Ephesios*, 37–8; for Bucer's reasons see A. Duke, 'The Ambivalent Face of

Calvinism in the Netherlands, 1561–1618', in Prestwich, *Int. Calv.* 124–5. See also J. Courvoisier, *La Notion d'église chez Bucer dans son développement historique* (Paris, 1933), *passim*, but esp. 97ff.

12. *Inst.* IV. i. 9–29; this was in response to anabaptist extremist views on the Church. Cf. e.g. T. Maruyama, *The Ecclesiology of Theodore Beza: The Reform of the True Church* (Geneva, 1978), 209ff.

13. Althaus, *Luther*, 333ff.; *WA* vi. 434, 453, and cf. 414, 416, 422; *LW* xliv. 165, 193, and cf. 138, 140, 149; cf. Boehmer, *Martin Luther*, 276, 318–19. Luther may also have distinguished between the person of the pope and his office.

14. *Inst.* IV. ii. 2; cf. 9–12.

15. The 'indelible' character of ordination was defined by the bull *Exultate Deo* of Eugenius IV in 1439, as in *COD* 542, 549–50; *DThC*, 'Sacrements', xiv, cols. 594ff., and 'Ordre', xi, cols. 1315ff.

16. *WA* vi. 407–8; *LW* xliv. 127–9; also *WA* vi. 564; *LW* xxxvi. 112–13; see also on this theme, Luther's tracts against Jerome Emser, esp. *Answer to the Hyperchristian, Hyperspiritual, and Hyperlearned book by Goat Emser in Leipzig, including some thoughts regarding his companion, the fool Murner*, in *WA* vii. 614–88; *LW* xxxix. 139–224. For Luther's later attitude to the rituals of ordination, see S. C. Karant-Nunn, 'Luther's Pastors', *Transactions of the American Philosophical Society*, 69/8 (1979), 56ff.

17. As emphasized in Ch. 6. 4.

18. *WA* vi. 408; *LW* xliv. 129–30; *WA* vi. 566–7; *LW* xxxvi. 116; Althaus, *Luther*, 323 and refs.

19. *WA* vi. 541, 567; *LW* xxxvi. 78, 117; Stephens, *Zwingli*, 274–7.

20. Althaus, *Luther*, 323–9.

21. Strohl, *Pensée*, 198–200; E. Cameron, 'The "Godly Community" in the Theory and Practice of the European Reformation', in W. J. Sheils and D. Wood (eds.), *Voluntary Religion, SCH* 23 (Oxford, 1986), 137 nn. 23–4 and refs.

22. *Inst.* IV. iii. 4–9; xi. 6; on the deacons see G. Lewis, 'Calvinism in Geneva in the Time of Calvin and Beza, 1541–1608', in Prestwich, *Int. Calv.* 44. For texts of the *Ordonnances ecclésiastiques* see Ch. 15 n. 43.

23. *DThC*, 'Ordre', xi, esp. cols. 1298ff.; 'Succession apostolique' in the *Tables générales*, cols. 4093f.

24. Althaus, *Luther*, 329–32; *Inst.* IV. iii. 10–16.

25. As in sect. 10. 3.

26. See Luther's *The Judgment of Martin Luther on Monastic vows*, in *WA* viii. 564–669, and *LW* xliv. 245–400; also *WA* vi. 438–43; *LW* xliv. 172–9; *WA* vi. 538ff.; *LW* xxxvi. 74ff.; Bornkamm, *Mid-career*, 29ff.; cf. e.g. *Inst.* IV. x; xii., 22–8, and xiii.

27. Cf. the state of affairs described in Ch. 2. 1.

28. e.g. *WA* vi. 415–16, 433–6, 462–5; *LW* xliv. 140, 164–9, 208–12; *Inst.* IV. v–vii, *passim*.

29. *WA* vi. 407ff.; *LW* xliv. 127ff.; see also Cargill Thompson, *Political Thought*, 55–6, on the papacy as exemplifying a *confusio regnorum*.

30. But cf. anabaptist attitudes as summarized by Duke, 'The Ambivalent Face of Calvinism', in Prestwich, *Int. Calv.* 115.

31. See Part III.

32. e.g. Calvin's 1536 *Institution* and Zwingli's *Exposition* (S and S iv. 44) and *De Vera et Falsa Religione* (*Z* iii. 628) were dedicated to François I; Melanchthon's 1535 *Loci* was dedicated to Henry VIII; Bucer's *De Regno Christi* and Calvin's *Commentary on Isaiah*

were dedicated to Edward VI; on Beza's political dedications see Lewis, 'Calvinism in Geneva', in Prestwich, *Int. Calv.* 67–8.

33. See Chapter 19.2.

34. The principal source for this doctrine is *Temporal Authority: To What Extent it should be obeyed* of 1523, in *WA* xi. 245–80; *LW* xlv. 77–129. Older studies on this subject are cited in Ozment, *Cities*, 216 n.73 (cf. also ibid. 135–8); Cargill Thompson, *Political Thought*, 35–61; id., 'The "Two Kingdoms" and the "Two Regiments": Some problems of Luther's Zwei-Reiche-Lehre', in Cargill Thompson, *Studies in the Reformation: Luther to Hooker*, ed. C. W. Dugmore (London, 1980), 42–59; G. Ebeling, *Luther* (London, 1970), 175–209; and most recently P. Manns and H. A. Oberman in *Luther und die politische Welt*, ed. E. Iserloh and G. Müller (Stuttgart, 1984), 3–34; D. C. Steinmetz, *Luther in Context* (Bloomington, Ind., 1986), 112–25.

35. Cargill Thompson, *Political Thought*, 135–54; Strohl, *Pensée*, 183–8, 239–45.

36. Stephens, *Zwingli*, 286–95; Strohl, *Pensée*, 189–92, 245–6.

37. On this see H. U. Bächtold, *Bullinger vor dem Rat: Zur Gestaltung und Verwaltung des zürcher Staatswesens in dem Jahren 1531 bis 1575* (Berne and Frankfurt, 1982), *passim*, esp. 37ff., 277–8.

38. Strohl, *Pensée*, 192–3; E. Staehelin, *Das theologische Lebenswerk Johannes Oekolampads* (Leipzig, 1939), 500–27; Léonard, *Protestantism*, i. 157–60; Rupp, *Patterns*, 38–40.

39. Cameron, 'Godly Community', 136–7, 142–3; Strohl, *Pensée*, 195–203.

40. *Inst.* IV. iii. 8–16; cf. Strohl, *Pensée*, 216–24.

41. For texts of the *Ordonnances* see Ch. 15 n. 43; see also H. Höpfl, *The Christian Polity of John Calvin* (Cambridge, 1982), 90ff., 128ff.

42. J. T. McNeill, *The History and Character of Calvinism* (New York, 1954), 159–65; G. Lewis, 'Calvinism in Geneva in the Time of Calvin and Beza, 1541–1608', in Prestwich, *Int. Calv.* 43ff.

43. See Ch. 20. 2–4, and compare with Ch. 15.

11. *The Reformers' Message: Sacraments*

1. See Ch. 8, esp. n. 128.

2. The differences in tone and approach between Lutherans and Zwinglians have variously been explained in terms of their respective origins in scholasticism versus humanism (McGrath), the 'modern' versus the 'ancient' scholastic trends of thought (Oberman), or more basic differences in understanding of Christ's nature (Locher).

3. *WA* vi. 517–18; *LW* xxxvi. 43; *MWA* II. i. 140–3; *Melanchthon*, ed. Manschreck, 202f.; *Inst.* IV. xiv. 1; cf. Bucer's description of sacraments as 'visible words': M. Bucer, *Metaphrasis … in epist. … ad Romanos* (Basle, 1562), 155ff.

4. *WA* vi. 531–2; *LW* xxxvi. 64–5; *DThC*, 'Matière et forme dans les sacrements', x, cols. 335–54, and 'Sacrements', xiv, esp. cols. 532ff., 579ff.; see also the refs. in *Inst.*, as ed. McNeill and Battles, 1289 n. 24.

5. *WA* vi. 532ff.; *LW* xxxvi. 65ff.; cf. *Melanchthon*, ed. Manschreck, 203; Bucer, *Metaphrasis … in epist. … ad Romanos*, 153–4; *Inst.* IV. xiv. 14–17.

6. *Inst.* IV. xiv 4; Bucer, *Metaphrasis … in epist. … ad Romanos*, 152ff.; the words of consecration were traditionally described as 'five words which only the priest should hear': for Luther's complaints against this practice see *WA* vi. 516; *LW* xxxvi. 41 and refs.

7. *WA* vi. 533; *LW* xxxvi. 67.

8. *WA* vi. 529; *LW* xxxvi. 61.
9. *Melanchthon*, ed. Manschreck, 223.
10. *Z* iv. 217.
11. *Inst.* IV. xiv. 3.
12. *Z* iv. 217–18; cf. *Inst.* IV. xiv. 13; Stephens, *Zwingli*, 184 ff.
13. S and S iv. 56–8; cf. Stephens, *Zwingli*, 180–93.
14. Bucer in D. F. Wright (ed.), *Common Places of Martin Bucer* (Abingdon, 1972), 319 ff. (and cf. ibid. 347); *Inst.* IV. xiv. 7–9.
15. *PL*, ed. Migne 22, col. 1115; cf. *Inst.*, as ed. McNeill and Battles, 1465 n. 43.
16. *WA* vi. 527–35; *LW* xxxvi. 58–70; *MWA* II. i. 144–9; *Melanchthon*, ed. Manschreck, 206–7.
17. *Inst.* IV. xix. 17.
18. *WA* vi. 572; *LW* xxxvi. 124–5; *Inst.* IV. xix. 17; cf. *MWA* II. i. 155.
19. *WA* vi. 534; *LW* xxxvi. 68; and see Ch. 8.
20. *Inst.* IV. xv. 11.
21. *Z* iv. 248 ff.; cf. *Z* i. 350 ff. (as cited in Ch. 8 n. 21); also S and S iv. 10–11; see Stephens, *Zwingli*, 194–217; cf. ibid. 149–51.
22. *Z* iv. 238–47.
23. Ibid. 231.
24. *WA* vi. 538; *LW* xxxvi. 73; cf. *WA* xvii/ii. 81–3.
25. See for instance *Inst.* IV. xv. 1, 15; Bucer, *Metaphrasis ... in epist. ... ad Romanos*, 320–1, 326; and cf. F. Wendel, *Calvin* (London, 1963), 318–21.
26. *Inst.* IV. xvi. 17–21.
27. Ibid. 8; Zwingli's arguments on infant baptism are found e.g. in *Z* iv. 292 ff.
28. *Melanchthon*, ed. Manschreck, 210–11, 217; *Inst.* IV. xvi. 3–6, 10–16; Wendel, *Calvin*, 325–6; Bucer, *Metaphrasis ... in epist. ... ad Romanos*, 327–8.
29. *Melanchthon*, ed. Manschreck, 211–16; *Inst.* IV. xvi. 7–9; Bucer, *Metaphrasis ... in epist. ... ad Romanos*, 328–31; cf. also Stephens, *Bucer*, 221–37; Trinity College, Dublin, MS 259. 25–46.
30. *Z* iv. 231 ff.; also 292 ff.
31. See Ch. 15. 6.
32. See in general F. Clark, *Eucharistic Sacrifice and the Reformation* (Chulmleigh, 1981), 73 ff., 93 ff.
33. The lectures on *Hebrews*, in *WA* lvii/iii. 102, 207 ff., 222 ff; *LW* xxix. 112, 208 ff., 224 ff; also *WA* vi. 512 ff, 520 ff; *LW* xxxvi. 35 ff., 46 ff.; *De Abroganda Missa Privata* (1521), in *WA* viii. 398–476; *The Abomination of the Secret Mass* (1525), in *WA* xviii. 22–36, and *LW* xxxvi. 309–28; on these see Clark, *Eucharistic Sacrifice and the Reformation*, 99–101.
34. S and S iii. 100; Clark, *Eucharistic Sacrifice and the Reformation*, 101–9; Stephens, *Zwingli*, 219–27.
35. *Melanchthon*, ed. Manschreck, 221–30; cf. *Inst.* IV. xviii. 12–18.
36. Bornkamm, *Mid-Career*, 506 and refs.; Stephens, *Zwingli*, 223; *Melanchthon*, ed. Manschreck, 220; *Inst.* IV. xvii. 35–7; Thirty-nine Articles, Art. XXVIII.
37. *WA* vi. 506–7; *LW* xxxvi. 27; Stephens, *Zwingli*, 218–19; *Inst.* IV. xvii. 47–50.
38. See Ch. 6. 3. n. 63.
39. *WA* vi. 508 ff.; *LW* xxxvi. 28 ff.; *Z* iv. 794 ff.; *Inst.* IV. xviii. 13–15; Stephens, *Zwingli*, 220–1, 223, *et. seq.*; Wright (ed.), *Common Places of ... Bucer*, 362–3.

40. *WA* vi. 515; *LW* xxxvi. 40.
41. *Melanchthon*, ed. Manschreck, 218; cf. *MWA* ii. i. 156.
42. *Inst.* iv. xvii. 1.
43. S and S iv. 54.
44. A. E. McGrath, *Reformation Thought* (Oxford, 1988), 128 and refs.; E. Cameron, 'The "Godly Community" in the Theory and Practice of the European Reformation', in W. J. Sheils and D. Wood (eds.), *Voluntary Religion, SCH* 23 (Oxford, 1986), 134–5 and refs.; *Inst.* iv. xvii. 44–6.
45. *WA* vi. 508–12; *LW* xxxvi. 28–35.
46. Althaus, *Luther*, 375–403; for the development of Luther's thought see also R. W. Quere, 'Changes and Constants: Structure in Luther's Understanding of the Real Presence in the 1520s', *Sixteenth Century Journal*, 16. 1 (1985), 45 ff.
47. The authoritative study on this topic is that of W. Köhler, *Zwingli und Luther. Ihr Streit über das Abendmahl nach seinen politischen und religiösen Beziehungen*, 2 vols. (Leipzig and Gütersloh, 1934–53).
48. See Ch. 15. 1.
49. Bornkamm, *Mid-Career*, 507–8; Rupp, *Patterns*, 141–8; R. J. Sider, *Andreas Bodenstein von Karlstadt: The Development of his Thought 1517–1525*, *SMRT* 11 (Leiden, 1974), 293–9.
50. The text is found in *Z* iv. 505–19, and trans. in Oberman, *Forerunners*, 268–78.
51. *Z* iii. 322–54; Köhler, *Zwingli und Luther*, i. 61–117.
52. *Z* iv. 841–58; S and S iv. 11–15, 51–6, 58; Stephens, *Zwingli*, 228 ff.
53. Zwingli's *Commentary on True and False Religion* is ed. in *Z* iii. 590 ff., *An Addition or Summary on the Eucharist* in *Z* iii. 327 ff., and *The Lord's Supper* in *Z* iv. 773–862.
54. Wright (ed.), *Common Places of . . . Bucer*, 315–36; Köhler, *Zwingli und Luther*, i. 117 ff.
55. Luther's *The Sacrament of the Body and Blood of Christ, against the Fanatics* is ed. in *WA* xix. 482–523, and *LW* xxxvi. 331–61; *That these Words . . . Still Stand Firm against the Fanatics* in *WA* xxiii. 64–283 and *LW* xxxvii. 3–150; and *Confession Concerning Christ's Supper* in *WA* xxvi. 261–509, and *LW* xxxvii. 153–372. See Bornkamm, *Mid-Career*, 513 ff.; G. R. Potter, *Zwingli* (Cambridge, 1976), 287 ff.; Köhler, *Zwingli und Luther*, i. 462–729; see also id., *Das Marburger Religionsgespräch 1529: Versuch einer Rekonstruktion* (Leipzig, 1929).
56. Köhler, *Zwingli und Luther*, ii. 66–163; Bornkamm, *Mid-Career*, 631–52; Potter, *Zwingli*, 316 ff.; Kidd, *Documents*, 247–55; further texts on the Marburg colloquy are in S and S iv. 173–204.
57. Wright (ed.), *Common Places of . . . Bucer*, 355–79; on the Wittenberg accord see also the sources cited in Ch. 19 n. 15.
58. *Inst.* iv. xvii. 5–10.
59. Ibid. 12–15, 21–34; cf. Wendel, *Calvin*, 329–55.
60. E. Jacobs, *Die Sakramentslehre Wilhelm Farels* (Zürich, 1978), esp. 162 ff.; G. Berthoud, *Antoine Marcourt: réformateur et pamphlétaire du 'Livre des Marchands' aux Placards de 1534* (Geneva, 1973), 223 ff., and esp. 231.
61. As e.g. in 1557 when on a mission to Württemberg: see E. Cameron, *The Reformation of the Heretics* (Oxford, 1984), 197–8 and refs.
62. C. L. Manschreck, *Melanchthon, the Quiet Reformer* (New York, 1958), 229–49; *Inst.* iv. xvii. 16–31; Wendel, *Calvin*, 223–4, 345–50, attributes belief in the ubiquity of Christ's body to Luther himself.

63. *WA* vi. 56 ff.; *LW* xxxvi. 109; cf. *COD* 541 ff.; *DThC*, 'Sacrements', xiv, cols. 536ff., 553ff.; see *Inst.*, as ed. McNeill and Battles, iv. xix. 1–3, 1449.
64. See Chs. 8. 6 and 11. 2.
65. *WA* vi. 543 ff.; *LW* xxxvi. 81 ff.; *Melanchthon*, ed. Manschreck, 237 ff.; *Inst.* iv. xix. 14–17.
66. *WA* vi. 549–50, 560ff., 567ff.; *LW* xxxvi. 91–2, 106ff., 117ff.; *Inst.* iv. xix. 4ff., 19ff., 22ff.
67. *Inst.* iv. 22.
68. 1 Thess. 5: 2.
69. *Inst.* iv. xix. 34; cf. *WA* vi. 550–3; *LW* xxxvi. 92–6.
70. *WA* vi. 546ff., 553ff.; *LW* xxxvi. 86ff., 96ff.; *Inst.* iv. xix. 35–7.

12. The Conversions of the Reformers

1. This topic is fully explored by H. Boehmer, *Martin Luther* (Philadelphia, 1946), 3–163; R. H. Fife, *The Revolt of Martin Luther* (New York, 1957), 1–178; M. Brecht, *Martin Luther: His Road to Reformation* (Philadelphia, 1985), 15–105. A classic literary survey of this period can also be found in R. H. Bainton, *Here I Stand: A Life of Martin Luther* (New York, 1950), 15–51. This chapter deliberately does not discuss the psychoanalytical theories of some writers who have tried to explain Luther's development and later career in terms of his childhood experiences (as far as these can be inferred). The evidence about Luther's early influences of which he *was* aware is quite complex enough without speculating about influences in his subconscious. However, see Ozment, *Reform*, 223–31, and J. Delumeau, *Naissance et affirmation de la réforme* (3rd edn., Paris, 1973), 287–93, for discussions.
2. The various texts of the *Psalms* lectures are found in *WA* iii, and iv. 1–462; *LW* x–xi; those of *Romans* in *WA* lvi; *LW* xxv; *Hebrews* in *WA* lvii/iii. 1–238; *LW* xxix. 109–241; the ensuing debate among the older Luther scholars about Luther's development is surveyed by W. D. J. Cargill Thompson, 'The Problem of Luther's "Tower-Experience" and its place in his Intellectual Development', in his *Studies in the Reformation: Luther to Hooker*, ed. C. W. Dugmore (London, 1980), 60–80, and esp. 60–6; see also the other authors cited below.
3. See Ch. 6. 2, and N. Paulus, *Der Augustiner Bartholomaeus Arnoldi von Usingen, Luthers Lehrer und Gegner: Ein Lebensbild* (Strasbourg/Freiburg-im-Breisgau, 1893), esp. 1–27.
4. For Luther's opinions of Occam see Scheel, *Dokumente*, 86, 87, 94, 110, 144, 162, 175.
5. Above all by H. A. Oberman, 'Headwaters of the Reformation: *Initia Lutheri—Initia Reformationis*', in H. A. Oberman (ed.), *Luther and the Dawn of the Modern Era: Papers of the Fourth International Congress of Luther Research* (Leiden, 1974), esp. 69–82; cf. the summary in D. C. Steinmetz, *Luther and Staupitz* (Durham, NC, 1980), 23–7, and in H. A. Oberman, *Luther: Mensch zwischen Gott und Teufel* (Berlin, 1982), 126ff.
6. Most forcefully by Steinmetz, *Luther and Staupitz*, 27–34; see also A. E. McGrath, *Luther's Theology of the Cross* (Oxford, 1985), 63–71, and id., *Intellectual Origins of the European Reformation* (Oxford, 1987), 108–16.
7. Steinmetz, *Luther and Staupitz*, 78–92; McGrath, *Luther's Theology of the Cross*, 72–93, 100–28; cf. Scheel, *Dokumente*, 247–58.
8. *WA* lvi. 269–72; *LW* xxv. 258–60; cf. Scheel, *Dokumente*, 272–4. The [different] earlier

and later meanings of these stock phrases of Luther are discussed in L. C. Green, *How Melanchthon helped Luther discover the Gospel* (Fallbrook, Calif., 1980), 171 ff.

9. McGrath, *Luther's Theology of the Cross*, 133 ff; cf. Scheel, *Dokumente*, 263–5.

10. Scheel, *Dokumente*, 284, 287, 291–2.

11. *WA* i. 221–8; *LW* xxxi. 5–16; and L. Grane, *Contra Gabrielem: Luthers Auseinandersetzung mit Gabriel Biel in der Disputatio contra scholasticam theologiam, 1517* (Copenhagen, 1962).

12. e.g. in *WA* viii. 96–7; *LW* xxxii. 213–14.

13. See Cargill Thompson, 'Problem of Luther's "Tower-Experience"', 65–7; this was suggested by U. Saarnivaara, *Luther discovers the Gospel* (St Louis, 1951); by E. Bizer, *Fides ex Auditu: Eine Untersuchung über die Entdeckung der Gerechtigkeit Gottes durch Martin Luther* (2nd edn., Neukirchen, 1961), 124 ff.; more recently by Brecht, *Martin Luther. His Road*, 221 ff., and M. J. Harran, *Luther on Conversion* (Ithaca, NY, 1983), 151–73. Cf. also G. W. Locher, *Zwingli's Thought* (Leiden, 1981), 252. This position is cautiously endorsed by Dickens, *German Nation*, 85–7 and nn.

14. *WA* ii. 143–52; *LW* xxxi. 295–306; cf. Scheel, *Dokumente*, 313, and Ch. 8. 1. Different scholars place the emergence of the mature doctrine at different periods: Saarnivaara in the sermon 'On threefold righteousness' of 1518 (*WA* ii. 41–7); Brecht (*Martin Luther: His Road*, 223 ff., and also id., 'Iustitia Christi: Die Entdeckung Martin Luthers', in *Zeitschrift für Theologie und Kirche*, 74 (1977), 179–223), in the sermon 'On twofold righteousness', as above; E. Bizer, *Fides ex Auditu* (2nd edn., Neukirchen, 1961), 12 ff., cites the *Exposition of the Lord's Prayer* (*WA* ix. 124–59); Green, *How Melanchthon helped*, 137–80, offers some highly provocative suggestions about the possible contributions made by Luther's younger colleague.

15. See Ch. 8 n. 62.

16. Scheel, *Dokumente*, 91, 148, 162, 166–7, 172–3, 177–8.

17. Ibid. 186–92; trans. of parts in E. G. Rupp and B. J. Drewery (eds.), *Martin Luther* (London, 1970), 5–7; see discussions by Cargill Thompson, 'Problem of Luther's "Tower-Experience"', 60–1; Bizer, *Fides ex Auditu*, 165 ff.; Oberman, *Luther: Mensch zwischen Gott und Teufel*, 163–84; Harran, *Luther on Conversion*, 174–88; and McGrath, *Luther's Theology of the Cross*, 95–8.

18. Professor Ozment, as is remarked by T. A. Brady, *Ruling Class, Regime and Reformation at Strasbourg, 1520–1555*, *SMRT* 22 (Leiden, 1978), 9; see Ch. 17. 3.

19. See the authors discussed by Cargill Thompson, 'Problem of Luther's "Tower-Experience"', 63–4.

20. Cf. H. A. Oberman, '"*Iustitia Christi*" and "*Iustitia Dei*": Luther and the Scholastic Doctrines of Justification', in id., *The Dawn of the Reformation* (Edinburgh, 1986), 109–13.

21. McGrath, *Luther's Theology of the Cross*, 141–7; see also his *Reformation Thought* (Oxford, 1988), 73–5.

22. See the remarks of E. Iserloh in IGJ 39 f.

23. As emerges from the experiences and attitudes of some of the Italian figures discussed in Ch. 13. 2; see also the suggestions of J. Atkinson, *Martin Luther: Prophet to the Church Catholic* (London, 1983), regarding Luther's position relative to modern-day catholicism.

24. McGrath, *Luther's Theology of the Cross*, 48–50; Oberman, 'Headwaters of the Reformation', in Oberman (ed.), *Luther and the Dawn of the Modern Era*, 45–6;

M. Grossmann, *Humanism at Wittenberg 1485–1517* (Nieuwkoop, 1975), 83–5; S. E. Ozment, 'Humanism, Scholasticism and the Intellectual Origins of the Reformation', in F. F. Church and T. George (eds.), *Continuity and Discontinuity in Church History* (Leiden, 1979), 133–49 and esp. 141 ff.; M. Greschat, 'Humanistische Selbstbewusstsein und reformatorische Theologie', in *L'Humanisme allemand (1480–1540): 18ᵉ colloque international de Tours* (Munich and Paris, 1979), 379 ff.; J. H. Overfield, *Humanism and Scholasticism in Late Medieval Germany* (Princeton, NJ, 1984), 299–304.

25. Dickens, *German Nation*, 79–83; B. Gerrish, *Grace and Reason: A Study in the Theology of Luther* (Oxford, 1962), esp. 43 ff.; Oberman, 'Headwaters of the Reformation', in id. (ed.), *Luther and the Dawn of the Modern Era*, 54–69 and refs.; Boehmer, *Martin Luther: Road*, 140–2.

26. Steinmetz, *Luther and Staupitz, passim*; McGrath, *Intellectual Origins*, 86–93.

27. See S. E. Ozment, *Mysticism and Dissent: Religious Ideologies and Social Protest in the Sixteenth Century* (New Haven, Conn., 1973), 16–24; Boehmer, *Martin Luther: Road*, 143 ff.; H. A. Oberman, '*Simul Gemitus et Raptus*: Luther and Mysticism', in id., *The Dawn of the Reformation* (Edinburgh, 1986), 126–54; see also id., *Luther: Mensch zwischen Gott und Teufel*, 190–7.

28. See McGrath, *Intellectual Origins*, 59–68; id., *Luther's Theology of the Cross*, 27–32, 52; H. Junghans, *Der junge Luther und die Humanisten* (Göttingen, 1985), esp. chs. 2 and 3; id., 'Der Einfluss des Humanismus auf Luthers Entwicklung bis 1518', *Luther-Jahrbuch*, 37 (1970); Dickens, *German Nation*, 49–71, and id., 'Luther and the Humanists', in P. Mack and M. C. Jacobs (eds.), *Politics and Culture in Early Modern Europe* (Cambridge, 1987), 199–213. On the background see M. Grossmann, *Humanism at Wittenberg*, esp. 55–77.

29. *WA. B* i. 93; cited by *LW* xiv, pp. ix–x, and Fife, *Revolt of Martin Luther*, 236 ff.

30. Oberman, *Mensch zwischen Gott und Teufel*, 223 ff., 260 ff.

31. As cited, Ch. 7 n. 27.

32. See sect. 12. 4 below.

33. On Karlstadt see Rupp, *Patterns*, 49–153; R. J. Sider, *Andreas Bodenstein von Karlstadt*, *SMRT* 11 (Leiden, 1974), *passim*; Bornkamm, *Mid-Career*, 23 ff., 58 ff.; see also H. Barge, *Andreas Bodenstein von Karlstadt*, 2 vols. (Leipzig, 1905), and K. Müller, *Luther und Karlstadt* (Tübingen, 1907). On Zell see M. U. Chrisman, *Strasbourg and the Reform* (New Haven, Conn., 1967), 91 ff.; P. A. Russell, *Lay Theology in the Reformation* (Cambridge, 1986), 186, 204 ff.; P. E. Lehr, *M. Zell le premier pasteur évangélique de Strasbourg (1477–1548) et sa femme Catherine Schutz: Étude biographique et historique* (Paris, 1861). On Farel there are two symposia, [Comité Farel], *Guillaume Farel, biographie nouvelle* (Neuchâtel and Paris, 1930), and P. Barthel, R. Scheurer, and R. Stauffer (eds.), *Actes du colloque Guillaume Farel*, 2 vols. (Geneva, 1983); see also P. G. J. M. Imbart de la Tour, *Les Origines de la réforme* (Paris and Melun, 1914–48), iii. 456 ff.

34. W. S. Stafford, *Domesticating the Clergy: The Inception of the Reformation in Strasbourg 1522–1524* (Missoula, Mont., 1976), 7, and 243 n. 1 for sources.

35. Rupp, *Patterns*, 56–7; Chrisman, *Strasbourg*, 91 ff.; for Farel's family see E. Cameron, *The Reformation of the Heretics* (Oxford, 1984), 168–70, and sources cited there.

36. McGrath, *Luther's Theology of the Cross*, 28 ff.; Grossmann, *Humanism at Wittenberg*, 60 ff.

37. Rupp, *Patterns*, 50–1.
38. *Guillaume Farel*, 98ff.; Cameron, *Reformation of the Heretics*, 170.
39. See most recently D. McEwan, *Das Wirken des Vorarlberger Reformators Bartholomäus Bernhardi: Der Lutherfreund und einer der ersten verheirateten priester der Lutheraner kommt zu Wort* (Dornbirn, 1986), 17–22.
40. Rupp, *Patterns*, 56–7 as above; Sider, *Andreas Bodenstein von Karlstadt*, 17–44.
41. Bornkamm, *Mid-Career*, 277 and ref.
42. Sider, *Andreas Bodenstein von Karlstadt*, 59ff., 70ff., 146–7, 302–3.
43. E. J. D. Douglass, *Justification in Late Medieval Preaching* (Leiden, 1966), 112ff., 134ff., as in Ch. 6 n. 37.
44. Chrisman, *Strasbourg*, 100ff.; Stafford, *Domesticating the Clergy*, 7–46, for the context and a summary of Zell's tract.
45. *Guillaume Farel*, 105; compare this with Luther's rhetorically misleading statement 'I have [learned] nothing from Erasmus; everything I received from Doctor Staupitz': Scheel, *Dokumente*, 86.
46. *Guillaume Farel*, 104–10.
47. Ibid. 111–24; for some significant corrections to Farel's early biography see J. J. Hemardinquer, 'Les Protestants de Grenoble au xvi⁰ siecle d'apres des etudes récentes', *Bulletin de la Société d'Histoire du Protestantisme Français*, 111 (1965), 15–22; Eire, *Idols*, 185–9, based on H. Meylan, 'Les Étapes de la conversion de Farel', in *Colloque de Tours: l'humanisme français au début de la renaissance* (Paris, 1973), 253ff.
48. See Ch. 15. 1.
49. As below, sect. 12. 4, and Ch. 15. 2.
50. See above all H. A. Enno van Gelder, *The Two Reformations in the Sixteenth Century: A Study of the Religious Aspects and Consequences of Renaissance and Humanism*, trans. J. F. Finlay and A. Hanham (The Hague, 1961); for a more moderate version see Léonard, *Protestantism*, i. 129; this distinction forms the main framework for Dr McGrath's *Intellectual Origins* and *Reformation Thought*.
51. See Locher, *ZR* 55ff.; H. Eells, *Martin Bucer* (New Haven, Conn., and London, 1931), 1–2; J. M. Kittelson, *Wolfgang Capito: From Humanist to Reformer*, *SMRT* 17 (Leiden, 1975), 9f.; H.-M. Maurer and K. Ulshöfer, *Johannes Brenz und die Reformation in Württemberg* (Stuttgart, 1973), 13; Rupp, *Patterns*, 359ff.; W. Näf, *Vadian und seine Stadt St Gallen*, 2 vols. (St Gallen, 1944–57), i. 129ff.; W. Delius, *Lehre und Leben, Justus Jonas 1493–1555* (Gütersloh, 1952), 5; H. J. Grimm, *Lazarus Spengler, a Lay Leader of the Reformation* (Columbus, Ohio, 1978), 4.
52. See Overfield, *Humanism and Scholasticism*, 102ff., 208ff., 298ff.
53. On Heidelberg see Eells, *Bucer*, 3ff.; Rupp, *Patterns*, 3–5; W. Maurer, *Der junge Melanchthon zwischen Humanismus und Reformation*, 2 vols. (Göttingen, 1967–9), i. 75ff., as cited by Oberman, *Masters*, 19–20, 56–7; Maurer and Ulshöfer, *Johannes Brenz*, 14ff.; on Vienna see C. Bonorand, *Vadians Weg vom Humanismus zur Reformation* (St Gallen, 1962), 50–5; on Erfurt, L. W. Spitz, *Religious Renaissance of the German Humanists* (Cambridge, Mass., 1963), 132ff., and Delius, *Justus Jonas*, 6f.; on Nuremberg see Grimm, *Lazarus Spengler*, 20–36.
54. On Oecolampadius see Rupp, *Patterns*, 15–17; on Linck, Grimm, *Lazarus Spengler*, 32–3; on Blarer see Oberman, *Masters*, 125ff.
55. This list derives partly from Kidd, *Documents*, 164; cf. a similar list in Léonard, *Protestantism*, i. 91; some obscurer names on these lists have been omitted.

56. See L. W. Spitz, 'The Third Generation of German Renaissance Humanists', in id. (ed.), *The Reformation: Basic Interpretations* (2nd edn., Lexington, Mass., 1972), 51 ff.; Moeller, *Imperial Cities*, 32–3.

57. *Melanchthon*, ed. Manschreck, viii–xi; Bornkamm, *Mid-Career*, 264–8 and refs.; Oberman, *Masters*, 57–61.

58. On Melanchthon see besides the above: Maurer, *Der junge Melanchthon*, *passim*; C. L. Manschreck, *Melanchthon, the Quiet Reformer* (New York, 1958), 30 ff.; R. Stupperich, *Melanchthon*, trans. R. H. Fischer (London, 1966), 19 ff.; E. Bizer, *Theologie der Verheissung: Studien zur theologischen Entwicklung des jungen Melanchthon, 1519–24* (Neukirchen, 1964).

59. Bornkamm, *Mid-Career*, 270–3 and refs.; Spitz, 'Third Generation', 56–7.

60. Delius, *Justus Jonas*, 5–25; Bornkamm, *Mid-Career*, 278 f.; Spitz, 'Third Generation', 54. See also G. Kawerau (ed.), *Der Briefwechsel des Justus Jonas*, 2 vols. (Halle, 1884–5).

61. For Jonas's conversion see *EE* iv. 486–93 (no. 1202), and v. 409 f. (no. 1425); Bornkamm, *Mid-Career*, 279 and refs.

62. Grimm, *Lazarus Spengler*, 25–43; J. Lorz, *Das reformatorische Wirke Dr. Wenzeslaus Lincks in Altenburg und Nürnberg* (Nuremberg, 1978), covers Linck's biography from 1523 onwards.

63. See Ch. 8. 3.

64. Locher, *Zwingli's Thought*, 152, esp. n. 28; cf. Locher, *ZR* 68–78.

65. Locher, *Zwingli's Thought*, 156–60; the original text is ed. in *Z* i. 256–63.

66. Locher, *ZR* 75–6 and n. 122.

67. Luther to M. Stifel, 4 May 1527, in *WA.B* iv. 199, as cited by Locher, *ZR* 87.

68. Locher, *ZR* 87–90.

69. Claims documented by W. Neuser, *Die reformatorische Wende bei Zwingli* (Neukirchen, 1977), based (e.g. ch. 1.3.*a*) on verbal similarities between *Z* ii. 131 and *WA* vi. 514; discussions in Locher, *ZR* 87 nn.; but cf. U. Gäbler, 'Huldrych Zwinglis "reformatorische Wende"', in *ZKG* 89 (1978), 120–35.

70. The possibility is discussed by P. Blickle, *Die Reformation im Reich* (Ulm, 1985), 62 n. 1, 129–33.

71. See Stephens, *Zwingli*, 21–8, for a fuller discussion of the whole question.

72. Eells, *Bucer*, 4–32; Chrisman, *Strasbourg and the Reform*, 83–8.

73. Oberman, *Masters*, 123.

74. See the very detailed analysis in Kittelson, *Wolfgang Capito*, esp. 12–111.

75. T. Schiess (ed.), *Briefwechsel der Brüder Ambrosius und Thomas Blarer (1509–1567)*, 3 vols. (Freiburg, 1908–12), i. 47–9; see the discussion in Oberman, *Masters*, 124–7.

76. Moeller, *Imperial Cities*, 24–30; Spitz, 'Third Generation', 48.

77. See Dickens, *German Nation*, 63, 150.

78. Moeller, *Imperial Cities*, 30–5.

79. A. Ganoczy, *The Young Calvin*, trans. D. Foxgrover and W. Provo (Edinburgh, 1987), 57–102; F. Wendel, *Calvin* (London, 1963), 16–37.

80. The text occurs in the preface to Calvin's *Commentary on the Psalms* of 1557, in *CO* 32, 22.

81. See Ch. 16. 5.

82. Ganoczy, *Young Calvin*, ch. 25, 241–66; Wendel, *Calvin*, 37–45; these authors provide refs. to the abundant other works on this topic.

13. *Rejections of Reform*

1. L. W. Spitz, 'The Third Generation of German Renaissance Humanists', in id. (ed.), *The Reformation: Basic Interpretations* (2nd edn., Lexington, Mass., 1972), 51–2.
2. L. W. Spitz, *Religious Renaissance of the German Humanists* (Cambridge, Mass., 1963), 58ff., 76ff., 192ff.; the pattern was much less clear in the case of the northern Swiss humanists like Wölflin, Anshelm, or Wyttenbach, some of whom later reconciled themselves to the new Church order. See Locher, *ZR* 45ff.
3. Spitz, 'Third Generation', 52.
4. Oberman, *Masters*, 115–24.
5. Rupp, *Patterns*, 75–6 and refs.; R. J. Sider, *Andreas Bodenstein von Karlstadt*, *SMRT* 11 (Leiden, 1974) 81–5; H. Barge, *Andreas Bodenstein von Karlstadt*, 2 vols. (Leipzig, 1905), i. 172ff.
6. e.g. Spitz, *Religious Renaissance*, 150ff.
7. This statement was attributed to both Summenhart and Staupitz: see D. C. Steinmetz, *Misericordia Dei* (Leiden, 1968), 27, 106–7; id., *Luther and Staupitz* (Durham, NC, 1980), 28; Oberman, *Masters*, 222 and nn. 52–3.
8. Ozment, 'Homo Viator: Luther and Late Medieval Theology', in Ozment, *Perspective*, 148–52; cf. also S. Ickert, 'Defending the *Ordo Salutis*', *ARG* 78 (1987), 81–97.
9. See for instance J. M. Headley, 'The Reformation as a Crisis in the Understanding of Tradition', *ARG* 78 (1987), 5–23.
10. See Ch. 4 n. 105.
11. R. H. Bainton, *Erasmus of Christendom* (London, 1972), 218–21.
12. Cited in the early 16th-cent. trans. of Alexander Barclay; see *The Ship of Fools translated by Alexander Barclay*, ed. T. H. Jameson, 2 vols. (Edinburgh, 1874).
13. E. G. Rupp and P. S. Watson (eds.), *Luther and Erasmus: Free Will and Salvation*, *LCC* 17 (London, 1959), 38ff.
14. Bainton, *Erasmus of Christendom*, 216 and refs.
15. *EE* iv. 487–93 (no. 1202).
16. Rupp and Watson (eds.), *Luther and Erasmus*, 54; cf. ibid. 41f., 64, 92ff.
17. Trans. of the first 2 of these texts are provided in Rupp and Watson (eds.), *Luther and Erasmus*; Luther's *De Servo Arbitrio* is ed. in *WA* xviii. 551–99 (introd.), and 600–787 (text); *LW* xxxiii. 15–295. The most recent survey of this topic is M. O'R. Boyle, *Rhetoric and Reform: Erasmus's Civil Dispute with Luther* (Cambridge, Mass., 1983), *passim*.
18. As in Ch. 6. 2.
19. M. O'R. Boyle, 'Erasmus and the "Modern" Question: Was he Semi-Pelagian?, *ARG* 75 (1984), 59–62, 74, 76.
20. Ibid. 73–6; see also C. Trinkaus, 'Erasmus, Augustine, and the Nominalists', *ARG* 67 (1976), 5–32, to similar effect.
21. Bainton, *Erasmus of Christendom*, 245, based on the Leclerc edn. of Erasmus's *Works* (Leiden, 1703ff.), ix. 814–954.
22. Bainton, *Erasmus of Christendom*, 229, based on the Leiden *Works*, x. 1327, 1487, 1528; cf. *EE* vii. 8ff. (no. 1804).
23. Bainton, *Erasmus of Christendom*, 271–337.
24. On the Cassinese see B. Collett, *Italian Benedictine Scholars and the Reformation: The Congregation of Santa Giustina of Padua* (Oxford, 1985), 77ff.; on the Capuchins and

Lateran canons, P. McNair, *Peter Martyr in Italy: An Anatomy of Apostasy* (Oxford, 1967), 33 ff., 70–6, 181–205.

25. Collett, *Italian Benedictine Scholars*, 79–81; D. Fenlon, *Heresy and Obedience in Tridentine Italy: Cardinal Pole and the Counter Reformation* (Cambridge, 1972), 7–21.

26. On Valdés, see J. Longhurst, *Erasmus and the Spanish Inquisition: The Case of Juan de Valdés* (Albuquerque, NM, 1950); J. N. Bakhuizen van den Brink, *Juan de Valdés réformateur en Espagne et en Italie* (Geneva, 1969); J. C. Nieto, *Juan de Valdés and the Origins of the Spanish and Italian Reformation* (Geneva, 1970); P. Lopez, *Il Movimento valdesiano a Napoli* (Naples, 1976); McNair, *Peter Martyr in Italy*, 17–32, 142–79; for Lutheran influence on Valdés see C. Gilly, 'Juan de Valdés: Übersetzer und Bearbeiter von Luthers Schriften in seinem *Dialogo de Doctrina*', *ARG* 74 (1983), 257–305.

27. Collett, *Italian Benedictine Scholars*, 102–10, 119–37.

28. Fenlon, *Heresy and Obedience*, 45–68; P. Matheson, *Cardinal Contarini at Regensburg* (Oxford, 1972); see Ch. 19. 1 n. 20.

29. The analysis of the *Beneficio* in Collett, *Italian Benedictine Scholars*, 157–85, supersedes all previous accounts. See ibid. 157 n. 1, for references to earlier treatments.

30. McNair, *Peter Martyr in Italy*, 206–62; Fenlon, *Heresy and Obedience*, 49 ff.; see also S. Caponetto, *Aonio Paleario (1503–1570) e la riforma protestante in Toscana* (Turin, 1979); M. Welti, *Kleine Geschichte der italienischen Reformation* (Gütersloh, 1985).

31. McNair, *Peter Martyr in Italy*, 263 ff.; 277 ff.

32. Fenlon, *Heresy and Obedience*, 51 ff., 89 ff.

33. Collett, *Italian Benedictine Scholars*, 186–209.

34. Fenlon, *Heresy and Obedience*, 220–50, 269; McNair, *Peter Martyr in Italy*, 15 ff.

35. A useful concise summary of 'double justification' is provided by Collett, *Italian Benedictine Scholars*, 278.

36. See above, Ch. 8 nn. 66–7.

37. Ibid., nn. 8–10, 26–8, 34–43, 78, 81–2; Ch. 9 nn. 2–5; Ch. 10 nn. 2–5; Ch. 11 nn. 3–5.

38. See the discussions in Chs. 17. 3–4 and 21. 2, and the evidence cited there.

14. *Unsuccessful 'Affiliations' to the Reformed Cause*

1. See R. W. Scribner, 'Is there a Social History of the Reformation', *Social History*, 2 (1977), 483–505; also his comment in his unpublished lecture 'Urban Culture and Religious Reform in Sixteenth Century Germany', Oct. 1985, 'Until the 1960s ... [the Reformation] was studied largely by church historians, who ghettoised themselves by a strict separation from *Profanhistoriker*'. In a slightly different way, the opposite poles of theological and social history still tend to draw historians to one or the other, and not only in Germany: only a few prominent historians in the vast literature since Moeller's *Imperial Cities and the Reformation* have matched his attempt to combine the social and the doctrinal in roughly equal proportions.

2. Cf. J. M. Kittelson's acerbic review of Pelikan, *Dogma*, in *Journal of Modern History*, 58 (1986), 261–3.

3. See the remarks of T. A. Brady, 'Social History', in Ozment, *Guide*, 176: 'When the grand systems of long-dead theologians fall away, when the sixteenth-century mutations of Christianity are seen entirely in historical context, then the Reformation will be regarded as ... Christian and European. Neither confessional nor racial–cultural explanations of the place of the Reformation in European history have survived the

fire of historical criticism. Perhaps the social-historical explanation will.' See also the debate between B. Moeller, 'Stadt und Buch. Bemerkungen zur Struktur der reformatorischen Bewegung in Deutschland', in *Stadtbürgertum und Adel*, 25–39, and T. A. Brady, '"The Social History of the Reformation" between "Romantic Idealism" and "Sociologism"': A Reply', ibid. 40–3; and the comments of S. E. Ozment, ibid. 46ff.

4. See Ch. 17. 1.
5. H. Holborn, *Ulrich von Hutten and the German Reformation*, trans. R. H. Bainton (New Haven, Conn., 1937), 16ff.; T. A. Brady, *Turning Swiss: Cities and Empire, 1450–1550* (Cambridge, 1985), 52–4; H. J. Grimm, 'Social Forces in the German Reformation', in L. W. Spitz (ed.), *The Reformation: Basic Interpretations* (2nd edn., Lexington, Mass., 1972), 90–1; see also H. Rössler (ed.), *Der deutsche Adel 1430–1555* (Darmstadt, 1965), esp. 48–56, and articles by H. H. Hofmann, 'Der Adel in Franken' (95–126) and H. Gensicke, 'Der Adel in Mittelrheingebiet' (127–52); V. Press, *Kaiser Karl V, König Ferdinand und die Enstehung der Reichsritterschaft* (Wiesbaden, 1976), 17ff.
6. Holborn, *Ulrich von Hutten*, 18f., 154f.; Strauss, *Manifestations*, 202–7 and cf. 172ff.; see also W. R. Hitchcock, *The Background of the Knights' Revolt 1522–1523* (Berkeley, Calif., 1958), 1 17.
7. H. Wiesflecker, *Kaiser Maximilian I*, 5 vols. (Munich, 1971–86), v. 54–9.
8. Strauss, *Manifestations*, 179ff.; Hitchcock, *Background*, 17ff.
9. Holborn, *Ulrich von Hutten*, 173–87, 200–2; Hitchcock, *Background*, 42 56; Press, *Kaiser Karl V. ... und die Entstehung der Reichsritterschaft*, 22ff.; P. Blickle, *Die Reformation im Reich* (Ulm, 1985), 70ff. For the aftermath of this episode in the later 16th-cent. history of the knights, see V. Press, 'Adel, Reich und Reformation', in *Stadtbürgertum und Adel*, 330–83.
10. Brady, *Turning Swiss*, 132.
11. On humanism, H. Rössler, 'Adelsethik und Humanismus' in Rössler (ed.), *Der deutsche Adel*, 234 50; on the early Reformation, Press, 'Adel, Reich und Reformation', 343ff.
12. R. W. Scribner, *For the Sake of Simple Folk* (Cambridge, 1981), 34–5.
13. See *Die Schriften Hartmuths von Cronberg*, ed. E. Kück, *NDL*, 154–6 (Halle, 1899) for tracts written *c*.1521–2; see also Hitchcock, *Background*, 78–110; Dickens, *German Nation*, 117; Grimm, 'Social Forces', in Spitz (ed.), *The Reformation: Basic Interpretations*, 91.
14. P. Blickle, 'Peasant Revolts in the German Empire in the Late Middle Ages', in *Social History*, 4 (1979), 223–31.
15. Ibid. 234–9; id., 'The "Peasant War" as the Revolution of the Common Man', in R. W. Scribner and G. Benecke (eds.), *The German Peasant War of 1525: New Viewpoints* (London, 1979), 19–22; see also G. Franz, *Quellen zur Geschichte des Bauernkrieges* (Munich, 1963), 9–58; T. Scott, 'The Peasants' War: A Historiographical Review', *Historical Journal*, 22 (1979), 695ff.
16. Blickle, 'Peasant Revolts', 234–9.
17. See Ch. 4. 3, n. 45.
18. The classic narrative of the Peasants' War is that of G. Franz, *Der Deutsche Bauernkrieg* (cited in the 11th edn., Darmstadt, 1977); an English narrative is found in the intro. to P. Blickle, *The Revolution of 1525*, ed. and trans. T. A. Brady and H. C. E. Midelfort (2nd edn., Baltimore, 1985); an account in some ways complementary to the latter is

in A. F. Pollard, 'Social Revolution and Catholic Reaction in Germany', *The Cambridge Modern History*, ii. *The Reformation*, ed. A. W. Ward, G. W. Prothero, and S. Leathes (Cambridge, 1904), 174–94. The literature up to *c*.1981 is succinctly described and analysed by R. W. Scribner, 'The German Peasants' War', in Ozment, *Guide*, 107–33; see also Scott, 'Historiographical Review', 693–720, 953–74.

19. On this see Williams, 64–6; T. Scott, 'Reformation and Peasants' War in Waldshut and Environs: A Structural Analysis', *ARG* 69 (1978), 82–102, and 70 (1979), 140–68.

20. Franz, *Deutsche Bauernkrieg*, 98–112; Strauss, *Manifestations*, 153–66.

21. See T. Scott, *Freiburg and the Breisgau* (Oxford, 1986), 190–228, esp. 199ff.

22. Franz, *Deutsche Bauernkrieg*, 134–40; T. Scott, *Thomas Müntzer: Theology and Revolution in the German Reformation* (London, 1989), 129–41; for further discussion of Müntzer see Ch. 18. and nn. 4–9.

23. The text of the articles is analysed and ed. in Blickle, *Revolution of 1525*, 25–67, 195–205.

24. For fuller details on Swabia see Franz, *Deutsche Bauernkrieg*, 113–34; id., *Quellen*, 124–223.

25. For Franconia, see Franz, *Deutsche Bauernkrieg*, 176–212; id., *Quellen*, 315–409; on Heilbronn, see T. Sea, 'The Reformation and the Restoration of Civic Authority in Heilbronn, 1525–32', *Central European History*, 19 (1986), 235–61.

26. On Thuringia, see Franz, *Deutsche Bauernkrieg*, 238–76; and id., *Quellen*, 462–546; Williams, 68ff.; Scott, *Thomas Müntzer*, 141–75; and id., 'The "Volksreformation" of Thomas Müntzer in Allstedt and Mühlhausen', *JEH* 34 (1983), 194ff.

27. W. Klaassen, *Michael Gaismair: Revolutionary and Reformer* (Leiden, 1978), *passim*; Franz, *Deutsche Bauernkrieg*, 153–76; id., *Quellen*, 270–314.

28. On these last see references cited below, n. 36. On the Peasants' War in other districts see Franz, *Deutsche Bauernkrieg*, 148ff., 212ff., 227ff., 276ff.

29. For some selected interpretations see Scribner and Benecke (eds.), *German Peasant War*; J. Bak (ed.), *The German Peasant War of 1525* (London, 1975); K. C. Sessions (ed.), *Reformation and Authority: The Meaning of the Peasants' Revolt* (Lexington, Mass., 1968).

30. Luther's *Admonition to Peace: A Reply to the Articles of the Peasants in Swabia* is ed. in *WA* xviii. 291–334, and *LW* xlvi. 5–43; *Against the Robbing and Murdering Hordes* in *WA* xviii. 357–61, and *LW* xlvi. 47–55; cf. Bornkamm, *Mid-Career*, 355–87; M. U. Edwards, *Luther and the False Brethren* (Stanford, Calif., 1975), 60–82.

31. Bornkamm, *Mid-Career*, 389ff., 408ff.

32. See R. Kolb, 'The Theologians and the Peasants', *ARG* 69 (1978), 103–30; also K. C. Sessions, 'Christian Humanism and the Freedom of a Christian: Johann Eberlin von Günzburg to the Peasants', in L. P. Buck and J. W. Zophy (eds.), *The Social History of the Reformation* (Columbus, Ohio, 1972), 137–55.

33. See D. Demandt and H.-C. Rublack, *Stadt und Kirche in Kitzingen: Darstellung und Quellen zu Spätmittelalter und Reformation* (Stuttgart, 1978), 70ff. and refs.

34. At least until Ch. 18.

35. On Rothenburg see Williams, 68ff.; Rupp, *Patterns*, 148; on Schappeler see P. A. Russell, *Lay Theology in the Reformation* (Cambridge, 1986), 83–9; on Schaffhausen, Locher, *ZR* 373ff. and refs.; see also Bak (ed.), *German Peasant War*, 14.

36. See P. Blickle, *Gemeindereformation: Die Menschen des 16. Jahrhunderts auf dem Weg*

zum Heil (Munich, 1985), 38ff., 50ff., 110ff.; id., *Revolution of 1525*, 158–61. Blickle's thesis is controversial: see comments by H.-C. Rublack, 'Is there a "New History" of the Urban Reformation?', in E. I. Kouri and T. Scott (eds.), *Politics and Society in Reformation Europe* (London, 1987), 125ff. and nn., and by Scott, 'Historiographical Review', esp. 965ff.; and R. W. Scribner's so far unpublished conference paper of 1986, 'Paradigms of Urban Reform: Gemeindereformation or Erastian Reformation', kindly communicated to me by Dr Scribner. For a more cautious assessment see e.g. H. J. Hillerbrand, 'The German Reformation and the Peasants' War', in Buck and Zophy (eds.), *Social History*, 106–36.

37. See F. Conrad, *Reformation in der bäuerlichen Gesellschaft: Zur Rezeption reformatorischer Theologie in Elsass* (Wiesbaden, 1984), 93ff., 107ff., 116ff.

38. The 'Waldensian' protestant communities in the Alps and Provence (see Ch. 5. 2 and Ch. 16. 4) were exceptional as centres of rural village protestantism within hostile territorial states. Those of the Alps owed their survival to exceptional military tenacity, the relative weakness of state power, and the disproportionately great interest taken by Geneva in their fate. See E. Cameron, *The Reformation of the Heretics* (Oxford, 1984), 129–263.

15. *Self-Governing Towns and Cities*

1. Dickens, *German Nation*, 182; the full phrase is 'the German Reformation was an urban event at once literary, technological and oratorical'. To take the words 'urban event' thus out of context is therefore misleading. But see H.-C. Rublack, 'Forschungsbericht Stadt und Reformation', in B. Moeller (ed.), *Stadt und Kirche im 16. Jahrhundert* (Gütersloh, 1978), 9; B. Moeller, 'Stadt und Buch', in *Stadtbürgertum und Adel*, 26; H.-C. Rublack, 'Reformatorische Bewegung und städtische Kirchenpolitik in Esslingen', in *Städtische Gesellschaft*, 193; P. Blickle, *Die Reformation im Reich* (Ulm, 1985), 73; H.-J. Goertz, *Pfaffenhass und gross Geschrei: Die reformatorischen Bewegungen in Deutschland 1517–1529* (Munich, 1987), 119; these are only a few of the discussions of this expression.

2. Guidance through the vast literature on this subject is essential. It is provided by R. W. Scribner, *The German Reformation* (London, 1986); H.-C. Rublack, 'Is there a "New History" of the Urban Reformation?', in E. I. Kouri and T. Scott (eds.), *Politics and Society in Reformation Europe* (London, 1987), 121–41 (esp. the refs.); T. A. Brady, 'Social History', in Ozment, *Guide*, 161–81; in German, see H.-C. Rublack, 'Forschungsbericht Stadt und Reformation', in Moeller (ed.), *Stadt und Kirche*, 9–26; K. von Greyerz, 'Stadt und Reformation: Stand und Aufgaben der Forschung', *ARG* 76 (1985), 6–64. R. Wohlfeil, *Einführung in die Geschichte der deutschen Reformation* (Munich, 1982), 118ff. and bibl., may also help.

3. Cf. *WA* vi. 427ff., and esp. 450ff., 465ff.,; *LW* xliv. 156ff., and esp. 189ff., 212ff. Notwithstanding H.-C. Rublack who, in 'Martin Luther and the Urban Social Experience', *The Sixteenth Century Journal*, 16 (1985), 16–32, argues that Luther's 'understanding' of the specific religious and social qualities of city life as shown in his writings was 'nothing short of disappointing' (18). That conclusion, even if correct, does not affect the applicability of his basic prescriptions, and rather reflects contemporary historians' seeking after categories.

4. As was the central contention of Moeller, *Imperial Cities*, 85ff., much debated since: see Ch. 17. 2.

5. But see Ch. 21 for some ways in which such differences in priorities did emerge.
6. Dickens, *German Nation*, 177ff.; Blickle, *Reformation im Reich*, 74–5.
7. On these see R. W. Scribner, 'Civic Unity and the Reformation in Erfurt', *P and P* 66 (1975), 29–60; S. C. Karant-Nunn, *Zwickau in Transition 1500–1547: The Reformation as an Agent of Change* (Columbus, Ohio, 1987); D. Demandt and H.-C. Rublack, *Stadt und Kirche in Kitzingen* (Stuttgart, 1978).
8. See sect. 15. 2, and Ch. 19. 1.
9. R. W. Scribner, 'The Reformation as a Social Movement', in Scribner, *PC and PM*, 145–9; N. Müller, *Die Wittenberger Bewegung 1521 und 1522* (Leipzig, 1911), *passim*; also published as articles in *ARG* 6 (1909), 161–226, 261–325, 385–469; Bornkamm, *Mid-Career*, 24ff., 51ff.
10. Sehling, i, pt. 1, 697f.
11. The sermon texts ed. in *WA* x/iii. 1–64; *LW* li. 69–100; excerpts in E. G. Rupp and B. J. Drewery (eds.), *Martin Luther* (London, 1970), 100ff.; Bornkamm, *Mid-Career*, 69–79.
12. Sehling, i, pt. 1, 698–700; the Latin *Formula Missae* ed. in *WA* xii. 197–220, and Sehling, i, pt. 1, 3–9; the *Deutsche Messe* in *WA* xix. 44–113, and Sehling, i, pt. 1, 10–16; see Bornkamm, *Mid-Career*, 109ff., 134f., 474ff.
13. The catechisms are ed. in *BSLK*, 501–27, 545–733.
14. For narratives and documents relating to these developments see Sehling, i, pt. 1, *passim*.
15. For more details on the visitations see Chs. 16. 1 and 21.
16. On Erfurt see R. W. Scribner, 'Civic Unity and the Reformation in Erfurt', *P and P* 66 (1975), 29–60; also in Scribner, *PC and PM*, 185–216. On Naumburg see Sehling, i, pt. 2, 59ff.
17. See Ch. 7. 3.
18. For documents on Nuremberg see Sehling, xi. 11–284; for the literature see H. von Schubert, *Lazarus Spengler und die Einführung der Reformation in Nürnberg* (Leipzig, 1934); P. E. Kalkoff, *Die Reformation in der Reichsstadt Nürnberg nach den Flugschriften ihres Ratsschreibers Lazarus Spengler* (Halle, 1926); G. Müller, *Reformation und Stadt: Zur Rezeption der evangelischen Verkündigung* (Akademie der Wissenschaften und der Literatur, Mainz, 1981), esp. 19–35; G. Seebass, 'The Reformation in Nürnberg', in L. P. Buck and J. W. Zophy (eds.), *The Social History of the Reformation: In Honor of Harold J. Grimm* (Columbus, Ohio, 1972), 17–40; G. Seebass, 'Stadt und Kirche in Nürnberg im Zeitalter der Reformation', in B. Moeller (ed.), *Stadt und Kirche im 16. Jahrhundert* (Gütersloh, 1978), 66–86; G. Strauss, *Nuremberg in the Sixteenth Century* (New York, 1966), 154–86; G. Vogler, *Nürnberg 1524/25. Studien zur Geschichte der reformatorischen und sozialen Bewegung in der Reichsstadt* (Berlin, 1982); id., 'Imperial City Nuremberg, 1524–1525: The Reform Movement in Transition', in R. Po-Chia Hsia (ed.), *The German People and the Reformation* (Ithaca and London, 1989), 32–49; and in H.-R. Schmidt, *Reichsstädte, Reich und Reformation: Korporative Religionspolitik 1521–1529/30* (Stuttgart, 1986), 30ff., 45ff., 51ff., 130ff., 152ff., 274ff.; also Dickens, *German Nation*, 135–46.
19. On these see Sehling, xi. 559–678; Locher, *ZR* 481f., 495ff., and refs.
20. For a general account of this period see L and B 59–61 and refs.; for documents, Sehling, vi, *passim*. See the discussion of the politics of the Baltic and Hanseatic cities in sect. 15. 5 below for fuller references.

21. For narrative and analysis of the Strasbourg Reformation see (especially, but by no means exclusively) M. U. Chrisman, *Strasbourg and the Reform* (New Haven, Conn., 1967), 131–76; L. J. Abray, *The People's Reformation* (Oxford, 1985), 39ff.; T. A. Brady, *Ruling Class, Regime and Reformation at Strasbourg, 1520–1555, SMRT* 22 (Leiden, 1978); W. S. Stafford, *Domesticating the Clergy: The Inception of the Reformation in Strasbourg 1522–1524* (Missoula, Mont., 1976); and in Schmidt, *Reichsstädte, Reich und Reformation*, 33ff., 48ff., 57ff., 180ff., 284ff.; Dickens, *German Nation*, 146–55.

22. For the tetrapolitan cities other than Strasbourg see Locher, *ZR* 459ff., 473ff. and refs.; on Constance see esp. B. Moeller, *Johannes Zwick und die Reformation in Konstanz* (Gütersloh, 1961); H. Buck, *Die Anfänge der Konstanzer Reformationsprozesse 1510–31* (Tübingen, 1964); H.-C. Rublack, *Die Einführung der Reformation in Konstanz* (Gütersloh, 1971).

23. For narratives and documents on the Swabian cities see Sehling, xii, *passim*; Locher, *ZR* 469–99.

24. On Augsburg see Schling, xii. 15–85; F. Roth, *Augsburgs Reformationsgeschichte*, 4 vols. (Munich 1901–11), i. 197ff., 289–354; ii. 1–370; see also P. Broadhead, 'Politics and Expediency in the Augsburg Reformation', in P. N. Brooks (ed.), *Reformation Principle and Practice: Essays in Honour of Arthur Geoffrey Dickens* (London, 1980), 53–70; id., 'Popular Pressure for Reform in Augsburg, 1524–34', in *Stadtbürgertum und Adel*, 80–7.

25. See Ch. 7. 3.

26. For a narrative of the Zürich Reformation see Locher, *ZR* 123–73; G. R. Potter, *Zwingli* (Cambridge, 1976), 126ff.; W. Köhler, *Huldrych Zwingli* (2nd edn., Stuttgart, 1952), 103ff.

27. Locher, *ZR* 257–82, 366f.; also R. Dellsperger, 'Zehn Jahre bernischer Reformationsgeschichte (1522–32)', in *450 Jahre Berner Reformation: Beiträge zur Geschichte der Berner Reformation und zu Niklaus Manuel* (Berne, 1980), 25–59.

28. Locher, *ZR* 367ff. and refs.; H. R. Guggisberg, *Basel in the Sixteenth Century* (St Louis, 1982), 19–35; the classic account is that of R. Wackernagel, *Geschichte der Stadt Basel*, 3 vols. in 4 (Basle, 1907–24).

29. See Ch. 7. 3.

30. W. Näf, *Vadian und seine Stadt St Gallen*, 2 vols. (St Gallen, 1944–57), ii. 180–313; also Locher, *ZR* 365f.

31. Locher, *ZR* 373ff.; J. Wipf, *Reformationsgeschichte der Stadt und Landschaft Schaffhausen* (Zürich, 1929).

32. Locher, *ZR* 442ff. and full refs. esp. to works of E. Camenisch and O. Vasella cited there.

33. On the Baden disputation see E. Staehelin (ed.), *Briefe und Akten zum Leben Oekolampads*, 2 vols. (Leipzig, 1927–34), i. 484–545; id., *Das theologische Lebenswerk Johannes Oekolampads* (Leipzig, 1939), 331–76.

34. Locher, *ZR* 344ff.; Potter, *Zwingli*, 225ff.

35. Locher, *ZR*, 354ff., 502–37; Potter, *Zwingli*, 343ff..

36. On his origins see Ch. 12. 2.

37. H. Vuilleumier, *Histoire de l'église réformée du Pays de Vaud sous la régime bernois*, 4 vols. (Lausanne 1927–33), i. 31–88. See also Kidd, *Documents*, 478ff., and Locher, *ZR* 413ff.; Léonard, *Protestantism*, i. 315ff. For a revision of the old picture of Farel's

political relationship with Berne see L.-E. Roulet, 'Farel, agent bernois? (1528–1536)', in P. Barthel, R. Scheurer, and R. Stauffer (eds.), *Actes du colloque Guillaume Farel*, 2 vols. (Geneva, 1983), i. 99–105; see also R. Scheurer, 'Farel et les Neuchâtelois, de juillet à septembre 1530', ibid. i. 83–7.

38. Vuilleumier, *Pays de Vaud*, i. 122–222, 251ff.; Léonard, *Protestantism*, i. 320ff.

39. On Geneva's politics to 1536 see Eire, *Idols*, 123–5 and refs.; Kidd, *Documents*, 496ff.; E. W. Monter, *Calvin's Geneva* (New York, 1967), 29–59.

40. Eire, *Idols*, 125–51; also Kidd, *Documents*, 500–21; Monter, *Calvin's Geneva*, 49–56.

41. For Calvin's background and conversion, see Ch. 12. 4.

42. See Kidd, *Documents*, 544–88; F. Wendel, *Calvin* (London, 1963), 46–68; Léonard, *Protestantism*, i. 322–6; J. T. McNeill, *The History and Character of Calvinism* (New York, 1954), 137–58; Monter, *Calvin's Geneva*, 64–71.

43. The various texts (draft and approved) of the *Ordonnances* are edited in *CO* x (a) 15–30 and nn., 91ff.; and one version in Kidd, *Documents*, 589–602.

44. See discussion in Kidd, *Documents*, 629–31; Wendel, *Calvin*, 70–107; Léonard, *Protestantism*, i. 331ff.; McNeill, *History and Character of Calvinism*, 159–78; Monter, *Calvin's Geneva*, 71–89; R. Stauffer, 'Calvin', in Prestwich, *Int. Calv.* 22ff.; G. Lewis, 'Calvinism in Geneva in the time of Calvin and Beza (1541–1608)', ibid., esp. 41–51.

45. See Ch. 17.

46. For such hostilities see Ch. 4.

47. See D. Demandt, 'Konflikt um die geistlichen Standesprivilegien im spätmittelalterlichen Colmar', in *Städtische Gesellschaft*, 136–54; and R. Kiessling, 'Stadt und Kloster: Zum Geflecht herrschaftlicher und wirtschaftlicher Beziehungen im Raum Memmingen im 15. und in der 1. Halfte des 16. Jahrhunderts', ibid. 155–90, esp. 185ff.

48. For pamphlet printing see esp. R. G. Cole, 'Reformation Pamphlet and Communication Process', in H.-J. Köhler (ed.), *Flugschriften als Massenmedium der Reformationszeit* (Stuttgart, 1981), esp. 146–52; id., 'The Dynamics of Printing in the Sixteenth Century', in Buck and Zophy (eds.), *Social History of the Reformation*, 93–105; Russell, *Lay Theology in the Reformation*, 7–10.

49. On the book trade see R. Hirsch, *Printing, Selling and Reading 1450–1550* (Wiesbaden, 1974), 61–77; for the Frankfurt book fairs, see F. Kapp, *Geschichte des deutschen Buchhandels bis in das 17. Jahrhundert* (Leipzig, 1886), Chs. 8 and 10; B. Recke, *Die Frankfurter Büchermesse 1462–1792* (Frankfurt, 1951); for page numbers of pamphlets see Cole, 'Reformation Pamphlet and Communication Process', 158; on the circulation of books by travelling pedlars see e.g. R. Mandrou, *De la culture populaire aux 17ᵉ et 18ᵉ siècles: la bibliothèque bleue de Troyes* (Paris, 1964); an instance of a *colporteur* of protestant literature can be found in E. Cameron, *The Reformation of the Heretics* (Oxford, 1984), 161.

50. R. W. Scribner, 'How Many Could Read? Comments on Bernd Moeller's "Stadt und Buch"', in *Stadtbürgertum und Adel*, 44–5; id., 'Flugblatt und Analphabetentum. Wie kam der gemeine Mann zu reformatorischen Ideen?', in Köhler (ed.), *Flugschriften als Massenmedium*, 65–7; also (in more detail) M. Rössing-Hager, 'Wie stark findet der nicht-lesekundige Rezipient Berücksichtigung in den Flugschriften', ibid. 77–137; on communication difficulties see Cole, 'Reformation Pamphlet and Communication Process', 144–6.

51. See R. W. Scribner, *For the Sake of Simple Folk* (Cambridge, 1981), 244–9, esp. 245 n. 44.

52. See Ch. 13. 1.
53. G. Farel, *Summaire et briefue declarations daulcuns lieux fort necessaires a ung chascun chrestien pour mettre sa confiance en dieu at ayder son prochain* (n.p., 1525); *Martin Butzers an ein christlichen Rath und Gemeyn der statt Weissenburg Summary seiner Predig daselbst gethon* (Strasbourg, 1523); 'H. Bodius', *Unio dissidentium in sacris literis locorum* (Cologne, 1531; Lyons, 1532; Basle, 1557, and subsequently); see P. Chaix, *Recherches sur l'imprimerie à Genève de 1550 à 1564* (Geneva, 1954), 90; but cf. D. F. Wright (ed.), *Common Places of Martin Bucer* (Abingdon, 1972), 39; R. Peters, 'Who Compiled the Sixteenth-Century Patristic Handbook *Unio Dissidentium*', in G. J. Cuming (ed.), *SCH* 2 (London, 1965), 237–50.
54. On *The Old and the New God* (now no longer attributed to Vadian by most scholars) see H.-G. Hofacker, '"Vom alten und nüen Gott, Glauben und Ler"': Untersuchungen zum Geschichtsverständnis und Epochenbewusstsein einer anonymen reformatorischen Flugschrift', in J. Nolte (ed.), *Kontinuität und Umbruch* (Stuttgart, 1978), 145–77; also H. Scheible, 'Das reformatorische Schriftsverständnis in der Flugschrift "Vom alten und nüen Gott"', ibid. 178–88; text ed. as 'Judas Nazarei', *Vom alten und neuen Gott, Glauben und Lehre*, ed. E. Kück, *NDL* 142–3 (Halle, 1896); on the *Karsthans* und its uuuuuuuur uuu Diukunn, *German Nation*, 118 so; [M. Bucer], *Gesprechbiechlin neüw Karsthans*, ed. E. Lehmann, *NDL* 282–4 (Halle, 1930); on the context see M. Gravier, *Luther et l'opinion publique: essai sur la littérature satirique et polémique en langue allemande pendant les années décisives de la réforme (1520–1530)* (Paris, 1942), esp. 50ff.
55. Ozment, *Cities*, 47–120, discusses these and c.50 Reformation pamphlets for their core lessons; on Eberlin see also Rössing-Hager, 'Wie stark findet'; see also M. A. Pegg, *A Catalogue of German Reformation Pamphlets 1516–1546, in Libraries of Great Britain and Ireland* (Baden-Baden, 1973); id., 'Short Title Catalogues: Notes on Identity of Texts', in Köhler (ed.), *Flugschriften*, 29–41.
56. Ozment, *Cities*, 74–9, H. J. Grimm, *Lazarus Spengler* (Columbus, Ohio, 1978), 36–7, 59–60, 87–90.
57. L. W. Spitz, *The Religious Renaissance of the German Humanists* (Cambridge, Mass., 1963), 178ff.; but see also N. Holzberg, *Willibald Pirckheimer: Griechischer Humanismus in Deutschland* (Munich 1981), 191–5.
58. Dickens, *German Nation*, 142–3; P. A. Russell, *Lay Theology in the Reformation* (Cambridge, 1986), 165–81; see H. Sachs, *Werke*, ed. A. von Keller and E. Goetze (Hildesheim, 1964–); also F. H. Ellis, *Hans Sachs Studies*, i. *Das Walt got: A Meisterlied* (Bloomington, Ind., c.1940), 36ff.; and for an early version of the 'Wittenberg Nightingale', ibid. 41–7.
59. On Jörg Vögeli, see A. Vögeli (ed.), *Jörg Vögeli: Schriften zur Reformation in Konstanz 1519–1538*, 2 vols. (Tübingen, 1972–3); B. Hamm, 'Laientheologie zwischen Luther und Zwingli: Das reformatorische Anliegen des Konstanzer Stadtsschreibers Jörg Vögeli aufgrund seiner Schriften von 1523/4', in Nolte (ed.), *Kontinuität und Umbruch*, 222–95; on Niklaus Manuel, Ozment, *Cities*, 111–16; M. U. Chrisman, 'Lay Response to the Protestant Reformation in Germany, 1520–1528', in Brooks (ed.), *Reformation Principle and Practice*, 39–41; *450 Jahre Berner Reformation: Beiträge zur Geschichte der Berner Reformation und zu Niklaus Manuel* (Berne, 1980), esp. 104ff., 289–438.
60. Chrisman, 'Lay Response', 33–51; Russell, *Lay Theology in the Reformation*, 80–211.

61. Chrisman, 'Lay Response', 51 f.; Russell, *Lay Theology in the Reformation*, 214ff..
62. cf. Dickens, *German Nation*, 129–34.
63. Scribner, *For the Sake of Simple Folk*, Chs. 2–7.
64. See Ch. 12.
65. See Ch. 16. 2.
66. See Ch. 16. 3.
67. See Ch. 16. 5 and Ch. 21. 1.
68. See sect. 15. 2.
69. See Ch. 18. 1.
70. On Bugenhagen, see Sehling, v. 488ff.; vi. 334ff.; on Blarer, Locher, *ZR* 461–2.
71. See Ch. 7. 3.
72. See Ch. 13. 1.
73. See Abray, *People's Reformation*, 30–1.
74. For More's polemics see his *Dialogue Concerning Heresies* in *Complete works*, vi (1981), and his *Confutation of Tyndale's Answer*, ibid. viii, pt. 2, and esp. the editors' introd. to the latter; on other anti-Lutheran polemics see Dickens, *German Nation*, 121–4, and R. Rex, 'The English Campaign against Luther in the 1520s', *Transactions of the Royal Historical Society*, 5th ser. 39 (1989), 85–106.
75. The theological faculties of Louvain and Cologne were amongst the first to condemn Luther; the University of Rostock gave no aid to the Reformation movement there.
76. See sect. 15. 5.
77. Dickens, *German Nation*, 148–51; Chrisman, *Strasbourg and the Reform*, 98–130.
78. Scribner, 'Reformation as a Social Movement', in Scribner, *PC and PM*, 159–61.
79. Russell, *Lay Theology in the Reformation*, 86.
80. Scribner, 'Reformation as a Social Movement', 153; Karant-Nunn, *Zwickau in Transition*, 98–103; T. Scott, *Thomas Müntzer: Theology and Revolution in the German Reformation* (London, 1989), 17–28; E. W. Gritsch, *Thomas Müntzer: A Tragedy of Errors* (Minneapolis, 1989), 19–32.
81. Eire, *Idols*, 130–5.
82. Locher, *ZR* 464ff., 479ff.; Broadhead, 'Popular Pressure for Reform', in *Stadt-bürgertum und Adel*, 82–3; for the varied response to the preachers see Moeller, *Imperial Cities*, 93–5 and refs.
83. For St Gallen, Rupp, *Patterns*, 371–2, and for Augsburg, Moeller, *Imperial Cities*, 93–5; cf. the case of Clemens Ziegler at Strasbourg, as in Ch. 18. 1.
84. From the Constance delegation: see Locher, *ZR* 460, based on H.-C. Rublack, *Die Einführung der Reformation in Konstanz* (Gütersloh, 1971), 31.
85. R. W. Scribner, 'Ritual and Reformation', in Scribner, *PC and PM*, 104, 108–9; id., 'The Reformation as a Social Movement', ibid. 146–8; for Memmingen, see Russell, *Lay Theology in the Reformation*, 86.
86. R. W. Scribner, 'Reformation, Carnival and the World Turned Upside-Down', in Scribner, *PC and PM*, 72–8; id., 'The Reformation as a Social Movement', 154. These incidents were not confined to the cities nor to the earliest years of the Reformation: see the similar episode in the Queyras in 1574, in Cameron, *Reformation of the Heretics*, 226–7.
87. Scribner, 'Ritual and Reformation', 103ff.; Eire, *Idols*, 138.
88. See the definition of this phrase in Scribner, 'The Reformation as a Social Movement', 149–51; also in the discussion in his *The German Reformation*, 25ff.

89. Oberman, *Masters*, 227–31, based on *Z* i. 508 ff.; see also Kidd, *Documents*, 417–19; cf. the cases of Friar Guy Furbiti at Geneva in 1534 (Eire, *Idols*, 134), and Conrad Treger at Strasbourg (Stafford, *Domesticating the Clergy*, 172–3).

90. Dickens, *German Nation*, 148–9; Locher, *ZR* 473; Ozment, *Cities*, 148; Seebass, 'Reformation in Nürnberg', in Buck and Zophy (eds.), *Social History of the Reformation*, 24–7.

91. Besides the sources cited above, see Locher, *ZR* 469, for Konrad Sam.

92. Locher, *ZR* 93 ff., 272 ff.; Schmidt, *Reichsstädte, Reich und Reformation*, 123 and refs.

93. The list has been compiled from the following sources, several of which also discuss the phenomenon: Schmidt, *Reichsstädte, Reich und Reformation*, 122–3; P. Blickle, *Gemeindereformation* (Munich 1985), 90 ff. and refs., T. A. Brady, *Turning Swiss: Cities and Empire, 1450–1550* (Cambridge, 1985), 157–8; Locher, *ZR* 495–6; G. Franz (ed.), *Quellen zur Geschichte des Bauernkrieges* (Munich, 1963), 510–11 (for Stolberg); Stafford, *Domesticating the Clergy*, 146, 160; H.-C. Rublack, 'Reformatorische Bewegung und städtische Kirchenpolitik', in *Städtische Gesellschaft*, 212 and nn.; see also B. Moeller, 'L'Édit strasbourgeois sur la prédication du 1.12.1523 dans son contexte historique', in G. Livet and F. Rapp (eds.), *Strasbourg au coeur religieux du xvie siècle* (Strasbourg 1977), 51–61; and cf. the edicts for Brandenburg-Ansbach in 1524–6, in Sehling, xi. 80, 89.

94. Ozment, *Cities*, 145–51.

95. But see the exceptional cases of ecclesiastical states, as in Blickle, *Gemeindereformation*, 91 and refs.: see sect. 15. 8 and nn.

96. R. W. Scribner, 'Civic Unity and the Reformation in Erfurt', in Scribner, *PC and PM*, 197–211; Stafford, *Domesticating the Clergy*, 145.

97. Locher, *ZR* 272–3.

98. Kidd, *Documents*, 112.

99. Ibid. 121; note Luther's hostile response to the Nuremberg edict, as in *WA* xii. 58–67, cited by Schmidt, *Reichsstädte, Reich und Reformation*, 125.

100. Strauss, *Manifestations*, 143: 'the council should instruct the preachers of the four regular orders to preach nothing but the true word of God and to utter no lies or fables, rather to be silent altogether and say nothing'; cf. the reference to 'all fables, useless little things, and matters of dispute' in the Constance mandate: see Ozment, *Cities*, 149, and Rublack, *Einführung der Reformation in Konstanz*, 35 ff.

101. Locher, *ZR* 114–15, 94–5; Ozment, *Cities*, 146–8.

102. Schmidt, *Reichsstädte, Reich und Reformation*, 125–8; Oberman, *Masters*, 194–204; Brady, *Turning Swiss*, 156–8; Blickle, *Gemeindereformation*, 91–4.

103. Locher, *ZR* 95.

104. e.g. Luther's disputation for his student Bartholomäus Bernhardi, Zwingli's versus François Lambert, or Oecolampadius's at Basle: D. McEwan, *Das Wirken des Vorarlberger Reformators Bartholomäus Bernhardi* (Dornbirn, 1986), 17–22; Oberman, *Masters*, 212–14, 197–8; Rupp, *Patterns*, 19–20.

105. Oberman, *Masters*, 228 f., 234–7. For the debate on the status of the Jan. 1523 disputation see Locher, *ZR* 110–15; Oberman, *Masters*, 190–239; Ozment, *Reform*, 327–8.

106. Russell, *Lay Theology in the Reformation*, 86; Locher, *ZR* 473.

107. Eire, *Idols*, 134; Kidd, *Documents*, 152–64.

108. Compare the instances of open disputations in Piedmont, Locarno in the northern

Milanese, the Valtelline, and the Grisons cited in Cameron, *Reformation of the Heretics*, 163, 174–5, 257–8 and refs.

109. See Ozment, *Cities*, 125, 145; and cf. Oberman *Masters*, 191 n. 7.

110. P. N. Bebb, 'The Lawyers, Dr Christoph Scheurl, and the Reformation in Nürnberg', in Buck and Zophy (eds.), *Social History of the Reformation*, 68; Seebass, 'Reformation in Nürnberg', ibid. 29–30.

111. Oberman, *Masters*, 235–6.

112. Locher, *ZR* 276–80, 558–9.

113. Oberman, *Masters*, 237; Locher, *ZR* 182ff., 432ff.

114. Stafford, *Domesticating the Clergy*, 150.

115. See Ozment, *Cities*, 131, and in general 121–31; R. W. Scribner, 'Paradigms of Urban Reform', and id., 'Social Control and the Possibility of an Urban Reformation', in Scribner, *PC and PM*, 175–84; also the very pertinent remarks of T. A. Brady, 'In Search of the Godly City: The Domestication of Religion in the German Urban Reformation', in R. Po-Chia Hsia (ed.), *The German People and the Reformation* (Ithaca, NY, and London, 1988), 14–31 and esp. 26ff.

116. L and B 59–61; Dickens, *German Nation*, 156–68 (with refs. to earlier works); J. J. Schildauer, *Soziale, politische und religiöse Auseinandersetzungen in den Hansestädten Stralsund, Rostock und Wismar im ersten Drittel der 16. Jahrhunderts* (Weimar, 1959), esp. 117–205; R. Postel, 'Bürgerausschüsse und Reformation in Hamburg', in W. Ehbrecht (ed.), *Städtische Führungsgruppen und Gemeinde in der werdenden Neuzeit* (Cologne and Vienna, 1980), 369–83; H. Schilling, 'The Reformation in the Hanseatic Cities', *Sixteenth Century Journal*, 14/4 (1983), 443–56; also id., 'Die politische Elite nordwestdeutscher Städte', in *Stadtbürgertum und Adel*, 235–308; and id., *Konfessionskonflikt und Staatsbildung: Eine Fallstudie über das Verhältnis von religiösen und sozialen Wandel in der Frühneuzeit am Beispiel der Grafschaft Lippe* (Gütersloh, 1981), 73–106; O. Mörke, *Rat und Bürger in der Reformation: Sozialen Gruppen und kirchlicher Wandel in den welfischen Hansestädten Lüneburg, Braunschweig und Göttingen* (Hildesheim, 1983); for a slightly different case in the same region, see S. Müller, *Stadt, Kirche und Reformation: Das Beispiel der Landstadt Hannover* (Hanover, 1987).

117. Scribner, 'Civic Unity and the Reformation in Erfurt', in Scribner, *PC and PM*, esp. 201ff.; Blickle, *Gemeindereformation*, 78–82.

118. Blickle, *Gemeindereformation*, 82–5; I. Bátori, 'Ratsherren und Aufrührer. Soziale und ökonomische Verhältnisse in der Stadt Kitzingen zur Zeit des Bauernkrieges und der Reformation', in *Stadtbürgertum und Adel*, 149–214; see also I. Bátori and E. Weyrauch, *Die bürgerliche Elite der Stadt Kitzingen: Studien zur Sozial- und Wirtschaftsgeschichte einer landesherrlichen Stadt im 16. Jahrhundert* (Stuttgart, 1979), and Demandt and Rublack, *Stadt und Kirche in Kitzingen*.

119. On Memmingen, see Russell, *Lay Theology in the Reformation*, 86ff. as above; Locher, *ZR* 373ff., 473ff.; on Rothenburg, Williams, 68ff.; see also P. Schattenmann, *Die Einführung der Reformation in der ehemaligen Reichsstadt Rothenburg ob der Tauber* (Munich, 1928); for Würzburg, H.-C. Rublack, *Gescheiterte Reformation: Frühreformatorische und protestantische Bewegungen in süd- und westdeutschen geistlichen Residenzen* (Stuttgart, 1978), 42ff., and id., 'Die Stadt Würzburg im Bauernkrieg', *ARG* 67 (1976), 76–100; on Heilbronn, T. Sea, 'The Reformation and the Restoration of Civic Authority in Heilbronn, 1525–32', *Central European History*, 19 (1986), 235–61.

120. Scribner, 'Social Control and the Possibility of an Urban Reformation', in Scribner, *PC and PM*, 180; Guggisberg, *Basel in the Sixteenth Century*, 29–30; Blickle, *Gemeindereformation*, 85–90.

121. Moeller, *Imperial Cities*, 58–68; Ozment, *Cities*, 121–31.

122. Brady, *Turning Swiss*, 165–6.

123. Moeller, *Imperial Cities*, 41; Dickens, *German Nation*, 177–81.

124. E. Naujoks, *Obrigkeitsgedanke, Zunftverfassung und Reformation: Studien zur Verfassungsgeschichte von Ulm, Esslingen und Schwäbisch Gmünd* (Stuttgart, 1958), 64ff., 73ff., 87ff.; Rublack, 'Reformatorische Bewegung und städtische Kirchenpolitik in Esslingen', in *Städtische Gesellschaft*, 212–17.

125. F. Roth, *Augsburgs Reformationsgeschichte* (Munich, 1901–11), ii. 100–25, 145–64, 175–99; P. Warmbrunn, *Zwei Konfessionen in einer Stadt: Das Zusammenleben von Katholiken und Protestanten in den paritätischen Reichsstädten Augsburg, Biberach, Ravensburg und Dinkelsbühl von 1548–1648* (Wiesbaden, 1983), 49ff.

126. Blickle, *Gemeindereformation*, 107; Scribner, 'Social Control and the Possibility of an Urban Reformation', in Scribner, *PC and PM*, 182; Dickens, *German Nation*, 187–8; Ozment, *Cities*, 128, 211.

127. See the formulation in Brady, *Turning Swiss*, 165.

128. See Kidd, *Documents*, 110–11, 184; Schmidt, *Reichsstädte, Reich und Reformation*, 332.

129. T. A. Brady, *Ruling Class, Regime and Reformation at Strasbourg, 1520–1555* (Leiden, 1978), 163–96.

130. Ibid. 202–15, 236–45. This explanation cites Professor Brady's evidence in order to disagree with his favoured thesis (which is discussed in Ch. 17).

131. Seebass, 'Reformation in Nürnberg', in Buck and Zophy (eds.), *Social History of the Reformation*, 21–30; Bebb, 'The Lawyers, Dr. Christoph Scheurl . . .', ibid. 53–68; Grimm, *Lazarus Spengler*, 45ff.

132. Seebass, 'Reformation in Nürnberg', 27–8; id., 'Stadt und Kirche in Nürnberg', in Moeller (ed.), *Stadt und Kirche im 16. Jahrhundert*, 73–8; Vogler, *Nürnberg 1524/25*, and his article, 'Imperial City Nuremberg, 1524–1525: The Reform Movement in Transition', in Hsia (ed.), *The German People and the Reformation*, 32–49 and esp. 37ff.

133. Karant-Nunn, *Zwickau in Transition*, 109–24, 172–4.

134. Moeller, *Imperial Cities*, 92–5; Brady, *Turning Swiss*, 199–202.

135. R. C. Walton, *Zwingli's Theocracy* (Toronto, 1967), *passim*, but esp. 49, 53–4, 103, 221–3; cf. N. Birnbaum, 'The Zwinglian Reformation in Zurich', *P and P* 15 (1959), 27ff., but esp. 37–40.

136. Locher, *ZR* 174–7.

137. Karant-Nunn, *Zwickau in Transition*, 245–6; Warmbrunn, *Zwei Konfessionen in einer Stadt*, 60ff.; K. von Greyerz, *The Late City Reformation in Germany: The Case of Colmar, 1522–1628* (Wiesbaden, 1980), 111–23; E. Weyrauch, 'Die politische Führungsgruppe in Colmar', in *Stadtbürgertum und Adel*, 215–34.

138. Rublack, *Einführung der Reformation in Konstanz*, 45–6; Moeller, *Johanes Zwick*, 86ff.; Locher, *ZR* 450–2.

139. On these see Ch. 2 n. 32.

140. Scribner, 'Civic Unity and the Reformation in Erfurt', in Scribner, *PC and PM*, 196.

141. Karant-Nunn, *Zwickau in Transition*, 131ff.; Seebass, 'Reformation in Nürnberg', in Buck and Zophy (eds.), *Social History of the Reformation*, 33.

142. Stafford, *Domesticating the Clergy*, 124–38; Locher, *ZR* 462ff.; Blickle, *Gemeindereformation*, 95–6; B. Moeller, 'Kleriker als Bürger', in *Festschrift für Hermann Heimpel zu 70. Geburtstag am 19.9.1971*, 2 vols. (Göttingen, 1971–2), ii. 210–17 (for Strasbourg), 217–22 (for elsewhere).

143. R. W. Scribner, 'Ritual and Popular Religion', in Scribner, *PC and PM*, 21ff.

144. See Ch. 8. 6.

145. Kidd, *Documents*, 121–2.

146. Karant-Nunn, *Zwickau in Transition*, 134; Seebass, 'Reformation in Nürnberg', 37; Kidd, *Documents*, 167–9: For Reutlingen, Locher, *ZR* 495–6. Further instances of liturgical conservatism in Lutheran lands are discussed by Scribner, 'Ritual and Popular Religion', 46–7.

147. Luther to Zwilling, 7 Mar. 1528, *WA.B* iv. 404–5, as cited in Locher, *ZR* 279.

148. Texts in *Z* ii. 552–608, 617–625, 664–803; Kidd, *Documents*, 424–5, 431–8, 440–1.

149. Locher, *ZR* 142–6; Kidd, *Documents*, 441–4.

150. Schmidt, *Reichsstädte, Reich und Reformation*, 195–8; Abray, *People's Reformation*, 118; R. Bornert, *La Réforme protestante du culte à Strasbourg au xvie siècle (1523–1598): approche sociologique et interprétation théologique*, *SMRT* 28 (Leiden, 1981), 101–3, 131–41.

151. Rublack, *Einführung der Reformation in Konstanz*, 73–4; Locher, *ZR* 365–73.

152. Sources in Müller, 'Wittenberger Bewegung', *ARG* 6 (1909), 424ff.; Sehling, i, pt. 1, 697–8; Scribner, 'Reformation as a Social Movement', in Scribner, *PC and PM*, 146–9; Eire, *Idols*, 62–4; C. C. Christensen, *Art and the Reformation in Germany* (Athens, Ohio, 1979), 23ff., 35–41; also Rupp, *Patterns*, 90–111.

153. M. U. Edwards, *Luther and the False Brethren* (Stanford, Calif., 1975), 6–33; Eire, *Idols*, 65–73 and refs.; Oberman, *Masters*, 292–3.

154. Sehling, v. 513; vi. 358.

155. Seebass, 'Reformation in Nürnberg', in Buck and Zophy (eds.), *Social History of the Reformation*, 36; Christensen, *Art and the Reformation*, 66–78; Karant-Nunn, *Zwickau in Transition*, 134.

156. See Ch. 20. 2.

157. Cf. the more complex analysis of types of iconoclasm in Eire, *Idols*, 151–5.

158. Eire, *Idols*, 79–83, 92–3; *Z* iv. 150–2; Locher, *ZR* 143–5, 463, 470; Rublack, *Einführung der Reformation in Konstanz*, 74–5; Warmbrunn, *Zwei Konfessionen in einer Stadt*, 49–65; Christensen, *Art and the Reformation*, 79–92; Bornert, *Réforme protestante du culte*, 11–13, 103, 133–4.

159. Eire, *Idols*, 108–19 and refs.; Christensen, *Art and the Reformation*, 93–102.

160. See P. Mack Crew, *Calvinist Preaching and Iconoclasm in the Netherlands, 1544–1569* (Cambridge, 1978), esp. 5–38.

161. For England, see R. Hutton, 'The Local Impact of the Tudor Reformations', in C. Haigh (ed.), *The English Reformation Revised* (Cambridge, 1987), 114–38; for Germany's 'second Reformation' see Ch. 20. 2 and refs.

162. For Scandinavia (Norway especially) see the sources cited in Ch. 16. 2. In Scotland some churches which were too large for congregational worship were either subdivided into several 'parish' buildings by the raising of internal walls (as in Dundee or Aberdeen) or abandoned and pillaged for building stone (as in the cathedral of St Andrews).

163. Bornkamm, *Mid-Career*, 253ff., 411ff.

164. On St Gallen's struggles with its abbey, see Näf, *Vadian und seine Stadt*, ii. 286ff., 302ff.; on Weingarten, Warmbrunn, *Zwei Konfessionen in einer Stadt*, 57ff.; on Grunhain, Karant-Nunn, *Zwickau in Transition*, 124–9.
165. See for instance Moeller, *Johannes Zwick*, 94ff., for Constance.
166. Seebass, 'Reformation in Nürnberg', in Buck and Zophy (eds.), *Social History of the Reformation*, 35; Warmbrunn, *Zwei Konfessionen in einer Stadt*, 54ff.
167. Text in Kidd, *Documents*, 259–89.
168. On the *Tetrapolitana* see Bornert, *Réforme protestante du culte*, 284–9, and trans. in A. C. Cochrane, *Reformed Confessions of the 16th Century* (London, 1966), 54–88; Zwingli's *Fidei Ratio* in S and S iv. 3–18.
169. For its origins see L and B 80–3, 120, 127–30, trans. in Cochrane, *Reformed Confessions*, 97–111.
170. Sehling, vi 84–7, 128–34.
171. Ibid. i, pt. 1, 151ff.; xi. 141–71.
172. See discussion in Ch. 21. 2.
173. Sehling, xi. 119, 206–79; Locher, *ZR* 377–8; H. Höpfl, *The Christian Polity of John Calvin* (Cambridge, 1982), 57, 67–76. *CO* xxii. 33–74, 85–96.
174. Sehling, i, pt. 1, 18ff., 21ff.; xi. 33ff.; Locher, *ZR* 129 and refs.; Bornert, *Réforme protestante du culte*, 142–3.
175. Sehling, i. pt. 1, 2–16.
176. Ibid. xii. 285–8.
177. For Allstedt, see Sehling, i, pt. 1, 472ff., 497ff., 504ff.; for Nuremberg, ibid. xi. 39ff., 46ff., 51ff., 56ff.; for Coburg ibid. i, pt. 1, 542ff.; for Erfurt ibid., pt. 2, 375ff.; Seebass, 'Reformation in Nürnberg', in Buck and Zophy (eds.), *Social History of the Reformation*, 36.
178. Bornert, *Réforme protestante du culte*, 110–21, 143–7.
179. Locher, *ZR* 145–8; text in *Z* iv. 1–24.
180. Sehling, v. 515ff., 347ff.
181. Ibid. xi. 657ff., 481–553.
182. Bornert, *Réforme protestante du culte*, 172–5.
183. Sehling, i, pt. 1, 8–9; *WA* xii. 218; *LW* liii. 36ff.
184. Bornkamm, *Mid-Career*, 460–5; Luther's liturgical works are ed. in *WA* xxxv; *LW* liii; see also H. Robinson-Hammerstein, 'The Lutheran Reformation and its Music', in id. (ed.), *The Transmission of Ideas in the Lutheran Reformation* (Dublin, 1989), 141–71.
185. *WA.B* v. 639; *LW* xlix. 426–9; trans. in Rupp and Drewery (eds.), *Martin Luther*, 143f.
186. See Scott, *Thomas Müntzer*, 53–6; Gritsch, *Thomas Müntzer*, 48ff.; the Allstedt service order is ed. in Sehling, i, pt. 1, 472–97.
187. Wendel, *Calvin*, 53, 60; M. Prestwich, 'Calvinism in France, 1555–1629', in Prestwich, *Int. Calv.* 75; Léonard, *Protestantism*, ii. 172f. On Marot see most recently G. Joseph, *Clément Marot* (Boston, 1985).
188. See Ch. 2 nn. 6–8; G. Strauss, *Luther's House of Learning: Indoctrination of the Young in the German Reformation* (Baltimore, 1978), 19.
189. The Leisnig order is ed. in *WA* xii. 1–30; Sehling, i, pt. 1, 598ff.; partial trans. in Kidd, *Documents*, 122ff. and Rupp and Drewery (eds.), *Martin Luther*, 102ff. S. C. Karant-Nunn, 'Luther's Pastors: the Reformation in the Ernestine Countryside',

Transactions of the American Philosophical Society, 69/8 (1979), 43, points out that the Leisnig order did not actually take effect until 1529.

190. Strauss, *Luther's House of Learning*, 13.

191. Sehling, v. 495–500, 339–47.

192. See e.g. Melanchthon's *Instructions to the Visitors in Saxony*, in Sehling, i, pt. 1, 171 ff. Cf. a typical programme of school provision as set out in the Scottish *First Book of Discipline* of 1560, as ed. J. K. Cameron (Edinburgh, 1972), 54 ff., 129 ff.

193. Strauss, *Luther's House of Learning*, 14 ff.

194. Sehling, xi. 23 ff., 72 ff., 674 ff.; for later developments see H. Liermann, 'Protestant Endowment Law in the Franconian Church Ordinances of the Sixteenth Century', in Buck and Zophy (eds.), *Social History of the Reformation*, 340–54.

195. Sehling, i, pt. 1, 601 ff. (Leisnig); i, pt. 2, 449 ff. (Magdeburg); Karant-Nunn, *Zwickau in Transition*, 131 ff., and esp. 133.

196. Braunschweig trans. in Kidd, *Documents*, 231–3; Hamburg ed. in Sehling, v. 531 ff.; Lübeck, ibid. 359 ff.

197. *Inst.* IV. iv. 5–9; R. M. Kingdon, 'John Calvin's Contribution to Representative Government', in P. Mack and M. C. Jacob (eds.), *Politics and Culture in Early Modern Europe* (Cambridge, 1987), 188–90; E. W. Monter, *Calvin's Geneva* (New York, 1967), 139.

198. See J.-P. Gutton, *La Société et les pauvres en Europe (xvie–xviiie siècles)* (Paris, 1974), 97 ff.; B. Pullan, *Rich and Poor in Renaissance Venice* (Oxford, 1971); P. Bonenfant, 'Les Origines et la caractère de la réforme de la bienfaisance publique aux Pays-Bas sous le règne de Charles Quint', *Revue Belge de philologie et d'histoire*, 5 (1926), 887–904, and 6 (1927), 207–30.

199. This antithesis is a deliberate caricature: the active lay life was praised by medieval authors like Guillaume de St-Amour or Jehan de Meung, as well as by Aristotle. However, Renaissance writers may have made the value-system more popular without necessarily inventing it. See Gutton, *Société et les pauvres*, 101–2.

200. Ibid. 104 ff.

201. M. Todd, *Christian Humanism and the Puritan Social Order* (Cambridge, 1987), 145 n. 107 and refs.

202. Ibid. 137–47; P. Slack, *Poverty and Policy in Tudor and Stuart England* (London, 1988), 8 ff.

203. *WA* vi, esp. 450 ff., 465 ff.; *LW* xliv, esp. 189 ff., 212 ff. See H. J. Grimm, 'Luther's Contribution to Sixteenth-Century Organization of Poor Relief', *ARG* 61 (1970), 222–34.

204. See Ch. 17. 1.

205. R. Kiessling, *Bürgerliche Gesellschaft und Kirche in Augsburg im Spätmittelalter* (Augsburg, 1971), 216 ff.; J. Chiffoleau, *La Comptabilité de l'au-delà* (Rome, 1980), 321 ff.

206. The Zürich *Ehegerichtordnung* of May 1525 ed. in *Z* iv. 176–87; Locher, *ZR* 154 ff., 191–6; Walton, *Zwingli's Theocracy*, 209 ff. The classic survey of this topic is W. Köhler, *Zürcher Ehegericht und Genfer Konsistorium*, 2 vols. (Leipzig, 1932–42), esp. i.

207. On Strasbourg, see Köhler, *Zürcher Ehegericht*, ii. 349–504; Bornert, *Réforme protestante du culte*, 216–17, 408–17; F. Wendel, *L'Église de Strasbourg, sa constitution et son organisation 1532–1535* (Paris, 1942); Abray, *People's Reformation*, 47 ff., 159 ff.; E. Cameron, 'The "Godly Community" in the Theory and Practice of the European

Reformation', in W. J. Sheils and D. Wood (eds.), *Voluntary Religion, SCH* 23 (Oxford, 1986), 136–9, 142–4 and refs. On the south German cities and their marriage court legislation see Köhler, *Zürcher Ehegericht*, ii. 1–232; for later 16th-cent. comparisons see T. M. Safley, *Let No Man Put Asunder: The Control of Marriage in the German Southwest: A Comparative Study, 1550–1600* (Kirksville, Mo., 1984).

208. On Geneva, see Köhler, *Zürcher Ehegericht*, ii. 505–652; Monter, *Calvin's Geneva*, 136–9; R. M. Kingdon, 'The Control of Morals in Calvin's Geneva', in Buck and Zophy (eds.), *Social History of the Reformation*, 3–16; Höpfl, *Christian Polity*, 188–206; on Augsburg, see Köhler, *Zürcher Ehegericht*, ii. 280–322; Warmbrunn, *Zwei Konfessionen in einer Stadt*, 49ff.

209. *WA* xix. 75 (text also in Sehling, i, pt. 1, 12); Sehling, xi. 186–8; v. 542; and, on the Wittenberg consistory, i, pt. 1, 200ff.; on the latter see also Karant-Nunn, 'Luther's Pastors', 69ff.

210. Naujoks, *Obrigkeitsgedanke, Zunftverfassung und Reformation*, 96–103; Locher, *ZR* 485–6.

211. Scribner, 'The Reformation as a Social Movement', in Scribner, *PC and PM*, 159–72.

212. R. W. Scribner, 'Why was there no Reformation in Cologne?', in Scribner, *PC and PM*, 217–34.

213. Dickens, *German Nation*, 161f.; Rublack, *Gescheiterte Reformation*, 42ff., 76ff.; id., 'Reformatorische Bewegungen in Würzburg und Bamberg', in Moeller (ed.), *Stadt und Kirche im 16. Jahrhundert*, 109–24; Scribner, 'Why was there no Reformation in Cologne?', 234–41.

214. H. R. Guggisberg, 'The Problem of "Failure" in the Swiss Reformation: Some Preliminary Reflections', in E. I. Kouri and T. Scott (eds.), *Politics and Society in Reformation Europe* (London, 1987), 193–9; Locher, *ZR* 421–31.

215. Guggisberg, 'Problem of "Failure"', 199–201; Locher, *ZR* 432–6.

216. Cf. the community of Italian exiles in the Valtelline village of Morbegno in the late 1580s, attested in F. Ninguarda, *Atti della visita pastorale diocesana*, Società Storica Comense (Como, 1892–4), i. 269f.

217. Here I am indebted to Dr R. W. Scribner's unpublished paper 'Paradigms of Urban Reform: *Gemeindereformation* or Erastian Reformation', 3.

16. *Principalities and Kingdoms*

1. Bornkamm, *Mid-Career*, 481–90.

2. Ibid. 490–2; Sehling, i, pt. 1, 142–8.

3. Bornkamm, *Mid-Career*, 492–500; Sehling, i, pt. 1, 149–74.

4. Ibid. i, pt. 1, 200–9; for further details see S. C. Karant-Nunn, 'Luther's Pastors', *Transactions of the American Philosophical Society*, 69/8 (1979), 60–70, and I. Höss, 'The Lutheran Church of the Reformation: Problems of its Formation and Organization in the Middle and North German Territories', in L. P. Buck and J. W. Zophy (eds.), *The Social History of the Reformation* (Columbus, Ohio, 1972), 317–39 and esp. 317–27.

5. The table is based on material in Sehling, and also in Kidd, *Documents*; useful evidence on the unfashionable theme of the princely Reformations is supplied by IGJ 208ff.; and more can still be gleaned from the older narrative histories, e.g. J. Lortz, *The*

Reformation in Germany, trans. R. Walls, 2 vols. (London, 1968), ii. 3–91.

6. W. Hubatsch, *Albrecht von Brandenburg-Ansbach, Deutschordens-Hochmeister und Herzog in Preussen 1490–1568* (Heidelberg, 1960), 114–44; id., *Geschichte der evangelischen Kirche Ostpreussens*, 3 vols. (Göttingen, 1968), i. 1–63; Bornkamm, *Mid-Career*, 321–3, 333–6; Höss, 'Lutheran Church', 332 ff.; H. Cohn, 'Church Property in the German Protestant Principalities', in E. I. Kouri and T. Scott (eds.), *Politics and Society in Reformation Europe* (London, 1987), 164–5.

7. L and B 108–11.

8. Ibid., 175–6; the territory was re-catholicized in 1548 and re-protestantized under Duke Julius in 1568: see G. Strauss, *Luther's House of Learning* (Baltimore, 1978), 277.

9. L and B 55–9.

10. Ibid. 77; Kidd, *Documents*, 133–4, 141–51, 181.

11. E. Fabian, *Die Entstehung des schmalkaldischen Bundes und seiner Verfassung 1529–1531/3* (Tübingen, 1956), 8–11. For the members see Table 16.2.

12. L and B 77–8.

13. On which see Ch. 11. 3.

14. L and B 77–80. See Table 16.2.

15. See details in Ch. 19. 1.

16. Fabian, *Entstehung des schmalkaldischen Bundes*, 63 ff.

17. L and B 80–3; Fabian, *Entstehung des schmalkaldischen Bundes*, 101–12, 128 ff.; lists of members can be found in IGJ 266–8.

18. See Ch. 19. 1 for Saxony; for the Palatinate, see N. G. Parker (ed.), *The Thirty Years' War* (London, 1984), 64–7, 118 ff.

19. Kidd, *Documents*, 306.

20. For the fate of some of the spiritual estates in northern Germany see Sehling, i, pt. 2, 3–9, 42–3, 53–9, 92–4, 397 ff., 473 ff.

21. This narrative is largely based on E. H. Dunkley, *The Reformation in Denmark* (London, 1949); Kidd, *Documents*, 233 ff.; N. K. Andersen, 'The Reformation in Scandinavia and the Baltic', in *The New Cambridge Modern History*, ii. *The Reformation 1520–1559*, ed. G. R. Elton (Cambridge, 1958), 134–46; IGJ 302–6. See the forthcoming article by O. Grell, 'The Reformation in Scandinavia', in A. Pettegree (ed.), *The Early Reformation in Europe*; L. Grane and K. Hørby (eds.), *Die dänische Reformation vor ihrem internationalen Hintergrund* (Göttingen, 1990); and also E. L. Petersen and K. J. V. Jespersen, 'Two Revolutions in Early Modern Denmark', in Kouri and Scott (eds.), *Politics and Society in Reformation Europe*, 473–501, esp. 475 ff.; and T. B. Willson, *History of the Church and State in Norway* (London, 1903).

22. The fullest modern account in English of Sweden in this period is that of M. Roberts, *The Early Vasas: A History of Sweden, 1523–1611* (Cambridge, 1968), besides which see Kidd, *Documents*, 151 ff., 233 ff.; Andersen, 'The Reformation in Scandinavia', 146–56; IGJ 306–11; Grell's forthcoming chapter; S. Lundkvist, 'The European Powers and Sweden in the Reign of Gustav Vasa', in Kouri and Scott (eds.), *Politics and Society in Reformation Europe*, 502–15; C. J. I. Bergendoff, *Olavus Petri and the Ecclesiastical Transformation in Sweden, 1521–1552* (New York, 1928); J. G. H. Hoffmann, *La Réforme en Suède 1523–1572 et la succession apostolique* (Neuchâtel and Paris, 1945).

23. Poland's Reformation history is described in W. F. Reddaway *et al.*, *The Cambridge History of Poland to 1696*, (Cambridge, 1950), 322 ff.; N. Davies, *God's Playground:*

A History of Poland, 2 vols. (Oxford, 1982), i. 144–55, 177–90; IGJ 317–21;
E. M. Wilbur, *A History of Unitarianism: Socinianism and its Antecedents* (Cambridge,
Mass., 1946), 265–81; Williams, 404–7, 639–46; see also O. Bartel, *Jan Łaski* (Warsaw,
1955); B. Stasiewski, *Reformation und Gegenreformation in Polen* (Münster, 1960);
G. Schramm, *Der polnische Adel und die Reformation* (Wiesbaden, 1965). For the
background see also J. K. Fedorowicz, M. Bogucka, and H. Samsonowicz (eds.), *A
Republic of Nobles: Studies in Polish History to 1864* (Cambridge, 1982), esp. chs. 4, 5,
and 10.

24. See I. Białostocki, 'Borrowing and Originality in the East-Central European Renaissance', in A. Mączak, H. Samsonowicz, and P. Burke (eds.), *East-Central Europe in
Transition from the Fourteenth to the Seventeenth Century* (Cambridge, 1985), 153ff.

25. For Danzig see Sehling, iv. 160ff.; for Elbing and Thorn, ibid. 222ff.; for Poznań,
ibid. 246ff.

26. Davies, *God's Playground*, i. 191, argues that this may have been a case of relapse to
Judaism rather than protestant heresy.

27. For the political background see A. Wyczanski, 'The System of Power in Poland,
1370–1648', in Mączak, Samsonowicz, and Burke (eds.), *East-Central Europe in
Transition*, 140ff., esp. 145–51.

28. Specialist histories of Hungarian protestantism include M. Bucsay, *Geschichte des
Protestantismus in Ungarn* (Stuttgart, 1959), of which see esp. 20–64; and id., *Der
Protestantismus in Ungarn 1521–1978*, 2 vols. (Vienna 1977–9), of which see esp. i. 36–
161; W. Toth, 'Highlights of the Hungarian Reformation', *Church History*, 9 (1940),
141–56; see also E. Pamlényi (ed.), *A History of Hungary* (Budapest, 1973), 119–32,
140–2; Williams, 708–15; IGJ 321–7; R. J. W. Evans, 'Calvinism in East Central
Europe: Hungary and her Neighbours, 1540–1700', in Prestwich, *Int. Calv.* 167–
96. On Transylvania, see L. Makkai, *Histoire de Transylvanie* (Paris, 1946), 162ff.;
O. Wittstock, *Johannes Honter, der siebenbürger Humanist und Reformator* (Göttingen,
1970), E. Roth, *Die Geschichte des Gottesdienstes der siebenbürger Sachsen* (Göttingen,
1954), esp. 69–121; id., *Die Reformation in Siebenbürgen*, 2 vols. (Cologne, 1962–4);
K. Reinerth, *Die Reformation der siebenbürgisch-sächsischen Kirche* (Gütersloh, 1956).

29. At the time of writing (early 1990) no single account of the English Reformation is at
once both fully comprehensive and up to date. The older surveys, above all
A. G. Dickens's classic *The English Reformation* (London, 1963) and C. Cross, *Church
and People 1450–1660* (London, 1976), [neither cited in detail below] may be sup-
plemented by the brief account in W. J. Sheils, *The English Reformation 1530–1570*
(London, 1989), and the articles in C. Haigh (ed.), *The English Reformation Revised*
(Cambridge, 1987). Accounts in general histories such as G. R. Elton, *Reform and
Reformation: England 1509–1558* (London, 1977), and most recently J. Guy, *Tudor
England* (Oxford, 1988), are of value above all on the background in secular politics.
The literature up to the 1970s is reviewed by C. Haigh, 'Some Aspects of the Recent
Historiography of the English Reformation', in *Stadtbürgertum und Adel*, 88–106; and
by P. Seaver, 'The English Reformation', in Ozment, *Guide*, 271–96.

30. Guy, *Tudor England*, 118–22; also id., *The Public Career of Sir Thomas More* (Brighton,
1980), 13, 103ff.; see also W. A. Clebsch, *England's Earliest Protestants 1520–1535*
(New Haven, Conn., 1964).

31. On details of the marriage-suit see G. Bedouelle et al. (eds.), *Le 'Divorce' d'Henry VIII
d'Angleterre* (Geneva, 1987).

32. J. A. Guy, 'Henry VIII and the *Praemunire* Manoeuvres of 1530–1531', *EHR* 97 (1982), 481–503; cf. G. W. Bernard, 'The Pardon of the Clergy Reconsidered', *JEH* 37 (1986), 258–82.

33. Texts of the Tudor acts may be found in G. R. Elton (ed.), *The Tudor Constitution: Documents and Commentary* (2nd edn., Cambridge, 1982); see Guy, *Public Career of Sir Thomas More*, 141–201; id., *Tudor England*, 130–1.

34. See above all G. R. Elton, *Policy and Police: The Enforcement of the Reformation in the Age of Thomas Cromwell* (Cambridge, 1972), esp. 171 ff.

35. On the monasteries see D. Knowles, *The Religious Orders in England*, 3 vols. (Cambridge, 1948–59), iii; J. Youings, *The Dissolution of the Monasteries* (London, 1971); on the Ten Articles see A. G. Dickens and D. Carr (eds.), *The Reformation in England to the Accession of Elizabeth I* (London, 1967), 74 ff.; on Cromwell's religious allegiances see S. Brigden, 'Thomas Cromwell and the Brethren', in C. Cross, D. Loades, and J. J. Scarisbrick (eds.), *Law and Government under the Tudors; Essays presented to Sir Geoffrey Elton* (Cambridge, 1988), 31–49.

36. J. Guy, 'The Privy Council: Revolution or Evolution?', in C. Coleman and D. R. Starkey (eds.), *Revolution Reassessed: Revisions in the History of Tudor Government and Administration* (Oxford, 1986), 59–85; also id., *Tudor England*, 159–64.

37. See G. Redworth, 'A Study in the Formulation of Policy: The Genesis and Evolution of the Act of Six Articles', *JEH* 37 (1986), 42–67.

38. For this see J. J. Scarisbrick, *Henry VIII* (London, 1968), 659–60.

39. Guy, *Tudor England*, 193–6.

40. M. L. Bush, *The Government Policy of Protector Somerset* (London, 1975), 100–26; R. Hutton, 'The Local Impact of the Tudor Reformations', in Haigh (ed.), *The English Reformation Revised*, 114–38; Guy, *Tudor England*, 203–7.

41. On Northumberland's protestantism see Guy, *Tudor England*, 219–24; B. L. Beer, *Northumberland* (Kent, Ohio, 1973), 140–3; on Bucer's impact in England see *Common Places of Martin Bucer*, ed. and trans. D. F. Wright (Abingdon, 1972), 24–9 and refs.; for some local responses to visible liturgical change see A. G. Dickens, 'Robert Parkyn's Narrative of the Reformation', *EHR* 62 (1947), 58–63.

42. Guy, *Tudor England*, 224–5; D. E. Hoak, *The King's Council in the Reign of Edward VI* (Cambridge, 1976), 174 ff., 213 ff., 242 ff.

43. On aspects of Mary's religious policy see D. M. Loades, *The Reign of Mary Tudor: Politics, Government and Religion in England, 1553–1558* (London, 1979), 37 ff., 148 ff., 324 ff., 428 ff.; Guy, *Tudor England*, 233–40; R. H. Pogson, 'Revival and Reform in Mary Tudor's Church: A Question of Money', in Haigh (ed.), *English Reformation Revised*, 139–56; id., 'Reginald Pole and the Priorities of Government in Mary Tudor's Church', *Historical Journal*, 18 (1975), 3–20.

44. G. Alexander, 'Bonner and the Marian Persecutions', in Haigh (ed.), *English Reformation Revised*, 157–75 (also in *History*, 60 (1975), 374–92); Loades, *Reign of Mary Tudor*, 333 ff.; also id., *The Oxford Martyrs* (London, 1970); the classic study of the exiles is C. H. Garrett, *The Marian Exiles* (Cambridge, 1938).

45. On the Meaux circle see Eire, *Idols*, 177–85 and refs.; H. M. Vose, 'A Sixteenth-Century Assessment of the French Church in the Years 1521–4 by Bishop Guillaume Briçonnet of Meaux', *JEH* 39 (1988), 509–19, and refs.; M. Veissière, 'Guillaume Briçonnet, évêque de Meaux, et la réforme de son clergé', *Revue d'histoire ecclésiastique*, 84 (1989), 657–72; R. J. Knecht, *Francis I* (Cambridge, 1982), 143 ff.; J. H. M. Salmon,

Society in Crisis: France in the Sixteenth Century (London, 1975), 85ff.; Léonard, *Protestantism*, i. 224ff.; M. Greengrass, *The French Reformation* (Oxford, 1987), 14ff. and refs. Full references to recent accessible literature are provided by Dr Greengrass's book.

46. Knecht, *Francis I*, 145, 390ff.
47. Ibid. 180ff., 202ff., 244ff.; Greengrass, *French Reformation*, 9ff.; Léonard, *Protestantism*, i. 228ff.; N. M. Sutherland, *The Huguenot Struggle for Recognition* (New Haven, Conn., and London, 1980), 17–28.
48. Knecht, *Francis I*, 249–52; G. Berthoud, *Antoine Marcourt* (Geneva, 1973), 157–222; and on the Placards, R. Hari, 'Les Placards de 1534', in G. Berthoud *et al.*, *Aspects de la propagande religieuse* (Geneva, 1957), 79–142; Fire, *Idols*, 189–93; Greengrass, *French Reformation*, 24ff.
49. Knecht, *Francis I*, 390–7; Léonard, *Protestantism*, i. 234ff.; Sutherland, *Huguenot Struggle*, 30–3; E. Cameron, *The Reformation of the Heretics* (Oxford, 1984), 144–7 and refs.
50. Knecht, *Francis I*, 397ff.; Sutherland, *Huguenot Struggle*, 33ff.; G. Audisio, *Les Vaudois du Luberon: une minorité en Provence, 1460–1560* (Mérindol, 1984), 296–407; Cameron, *Reformation of the Heretics*, 147–55.
51. Greengrass, *French Reformation*, 32ff. and refs.; Sutherland, *Huguenot Struggle*, 40–61; R. Weiss, *La Chambre ardente: étude sur la liberté de conscience en France sous François Ier et Henri II (1540–1550)* (Paris, 1889; repr. Geneva, 1970), pp. lxiiiff.; Salmon, *Society in Crisis*, 87ff.
52. Léonard, *Protestantism*, ii. 95–100; H. Heller, *The Conquest of Poverty: The Calvinist Revolt in Sixteenth-Century France* (Leiden, 1985), 27–69.
53. On Calvin's intervention see Heller, *Conquest of Poverty*, 111–41; Léonard, *Protestantism*, ii. 100–4.
54. Léonard, *Protestantism*, ii. 104–9; Greengrass, *French Reformation*, 38ff. and refs.
55. G. Donaldson, *The Scottish Reformation* (Cambridge, 1960), 29ff.; I. B. Cowan, *The Scottish Reformation: Church and Society in Sixteenth-Century Scotland* (New York, 1982), 93ff.; J. Wormald, *Court, Kirk, and Community* (London, 1981), 102ff.; J. K. Cameron, 'Aspects of the Lutheran Contribution to the Scottish Reformation', *Records of the Scottish Church History Society*, 22/1 (1984), 1–12; id., 'John Johnsone's *An Confortable Exhortation of our mooste Holy Christen Faith and her Frutes*: An Early Example of Scots Lutheran Piety', in D. Baker (ed.), *Reform and Reformation: England and the Continent, c. 1500–c. 1750*, SCH Subsidia 2 (Oxford, 1979), 133–47.
56. Donaldson, *Scottish Reformation*, 37ff.; Cowan, *The Scottish Reformation*, 96ff.; Wormald, *Court, Kirk, and Community*, 96ff.
57. Donaldson, *Scottish Reformation*, 30ff.; Cowan, *The Scottish Reformation*, 99ff.; Wormald, *Court, Kirk, and Community*, 105ff.
58. Donaldson, *Scottish Reformation*, 33ff.; Cowan, *The Scottish Reformation*, 77ff.; Wormald, *Court, Kirk, and Community*, 92ff.; J. K. Cameron, '"Catholic Reform" in Germany and the pre-1560 Church in Scotland', *Records of the Scottish Church History Society*, 20 (1979), 105–17.

17. *Motives for Establishing the Reformation?*

1. See Ch. 15.5.
2. H. Cohn, 'Church Property in the German Protestant Principalities', in E. I. Kouri

and T. Scott (eds.), *Politics and Society in Reformation Europe* (London, 1987), 164, 179, and refs.

3. T. A. Brady, *Ruling Class, Regime and Reformation at Strasbourg 1520–1555* (Leiden, 1978), 215 ff., note that Professor Brady uses this point in support of the argument discussed below, n. 25.

4. Cohn, 'Church Property', 166–70.

5. Ibid. 167–72 and refs.; S. C. Karant-Nunn, 'Luther's Pastors: The Reformation in the Ernestine Countryside', *Transactions of the American Philosophical Society*, 69/8 (1979), 45 and n., gives the figures. For Hesse see also H. C. E. Midelfort, 'A Protestant Monastery in Hesse', in P. N. Brooks (ed.), *Reformation Principle and Practice: Essays in Honour of A. G. Dickens* (London, 1980), 75 and n. 15.

6. J. Guy, *Tudor England* (Oxford, 1988), 144–5 and refs.

7. F. Heal, *Of Prelates and Princes: A Study in the Economic and Social Position of the Tudor Episcopate* (Cambridge, 1980), 117 ff. N. L. Jones, 'Profiting from Religious Reform: The Land Rush of 1559', *Historical Journal*, 22 (1979), 279–94.

8. See Midelfort, 'Protestant Monastery', 71–93; Cohn, 'Church Property', 166–7.

9. Cohn, 'Church Property', 173–6.

10. J. J. Scarisbrick, *The Reformation and the English People* (Oxford, 1984), 112 ff., 124 ff.

11. Cohn, 'Church Property', 167–9.

12. Guy, *Tudor England*, 145 and n. 55.

13. On the connection between financial difficulties and the expectation of an aggressively protestant foreign policy in England, see C. Russell, *Parliaments and English Politics 1621–1629* (Oxford, 1979), 88 ff., 124 ff., 148 ff.

14. E. H. Dunkley, *The Reformation in Denmark* (London, 1949), 55 ff.

15. J. Wormald, *Court, Kirk, and Community* (London, 1981), 96–8.

16. F. L. Carsten, *Princes and Parliaments in Germany from the Fifteenth to the Eighteenth Century* (Oxford, 1959), 373 ff.; on Church–State relations in Bavaria see also M. Spindler (ed.), *Handbuch der bayerischen Geschichte*, ii (Munich, 1971), 626–31.

17. See Ch. 4. 3.

18. B. Moeller, 'Kleriker als Bürger', in *Festschrift für Hermann Heimpel zu 70. Geburtstag am 19.9.1971*, 2 vols. (Göttingen, 1971–2), ii. 210 ff.; on the thesis in general, see H.-C. Rublack, 'Reformatorische Bewegung und städtische Kirchenpolitik', in *Städtische Gesellschaft*, 194, with ref. to A. Schultze, *Stadtgemeinde und Reformation* (Leipzig, 1918).

19. S. C. Karant-Nunn, *Zwickau in Transition 1500–1547* (Columbus, Ohio, 1987), ch. 1.

20. See A. Fox and J. Guy, *Reassessing the Henrician Age: Humanism, Politics and Reform 1500–1550* (Oxford, 1986), esp. 151 ff.

21. Dickens, *German Nation*, 181, quoting the work of Franz Lau.

22. Ozment, *Cities*, 124, citing Moeller, *Imperial Cities*, 61; cf. G. Seebass, 'Reformation in Nürnberg', in L. P. Buck and J. W. Zophy (eds.), *The Social History of the Reformation* (Columbus, Ohio, 1972), 30.

23. See the sources cited by Brady, *Ruling Class, Regime and Reformation*, 34–6.

24. See Ch. 15. 5.

25. T. A. Brady, '"The Social History of the Reformation" between "Romantic Idealism" and "Sociologism": A Reply', in *Stadtbürgertum und Adel*, 40; with ref. to id., *Ruling Class, Regime and Reformation*, 234–5.

26. H. Schilling, 'Die politische Elite nordwestdeutscher Städte in den religiösen Auseinandersetzungen des 16. Jahrhunderts', in *Stadtbürgertum und Adel*, 307–8; cf. the theses of Schildauer and others as discussed in Ch. 15 n. 116.

27. See Ch. 15 nn. 121–6; discussions in H.-C. Rublack, 'Reformatorische Bewegung und städtische Kirchenpolitik in Esslingen', in *Städtische Gesellschaft*, 194–5; H.-J. Goertz, *Pfaffenhass und Gross Geschrei* (Munich, 1987), 120–1.

28. See the discussion in P. Blickle, *Die Reformation im Reich* (Ulm, 1985), 122–33; R. Wohlfeil (ed.), *Reformation oder frühbürgerlicher Revolution?* (Munich, 1972).

29. D. Demandt, 'Konflikt um die geistlichen Standesprivilegien in spätmittelalterlichen Colmar', in *Städtische Gesellschaft*, 136–54; E. Naujoks, *Obrigkeitsgedanke, Zunftverfassung und Reformation* (Stuttgart, 1958), 96ff.

30. Compare Rapp, *Réformes*, 467ff: 'La révolte des laïcs préparée, puis déclenchée par les clercs.'

31. See Ch. 10. 3, and esp. Ch. 21.

32. Cf. W. S. Stafford, *Domesticating the Clergy* (Missoula, Mont., 1976), 108–114.

33. A. G. Dickens, 'Intellectual and Social Forces in the German Reformation', in *Stadtbürgertum und Adel*, 22.

34. Cohn, 'Church Property', 164–5.

35. See Chs. 15. 8 and 16. 1.

36. See Ch. 8. 1.

37. G. Strauss, 'Protestant Dogma and City Government: The Case of Nuremberg', *P and P* 36 (1967), 38–58; also id., *Luther's House of Learning: Indoctrination of the Young in the German Reformation* (Baltimore, 1978), 10–11.

38. Ozment, *Cities*, 11–12.

39. See Ch. 10. 3 and n. 34.

40. See the sources cited above for these regions.

41. See W. J. Wright, *Capitalism, the State, and the Lutheran Reformation: Sixteenth Century Hesse* (Columbus, Ohio, 1987).

42. See G. Strauss, *Nuremberg in the Sixteenth Century* (New York, 1966), 160–2; H. J. Grimm, *Lazarus Spengler* (Columbus, Ohio, 1978); but cf. H.-C Rublack, 'Is there a "New History" of the Urban Reformation?', in Kouri and Scott (eds.), *Politics and Society in Reformation Europe*, 128–9, based on B. Hamm, 'Stadt und Kirche unter dem Wort Gottes', in L. Grenzmann and K. Stackmann (eds.), *Literatur und Laienbildung im Spätmittelalter und in der Reformationszeit: Symposion Wolfenbüttel* (Stuttgart, 1982), 710–29, which finds Spengler's piety heavily infused with civic priorities and attitudes.

43. See details in Ch. 20. 2 and sources cited there.

44. L. Febvre, 'Une question mal posée: les origines de la réforme française', in id., *Au coeur religieux du xvie siècle* (Paris, 1957), 1–70; also in *Revue Historique*, 161 (1929).

45. H. Heller, *The Conquest of Poverty* (Leiden, 1985), e.g. 174–5, 234ff., 256ff.

46. M. Weber, *The Protestant Ethic and the Spirit of Capitalism*, ed. and trans. C. T. Parsons (London, 1967); Heller, *Conquest of Poverty*, 257.

47. For the literature on the Weber thesis see A. Biéler, *La Pensée économique et sociale de Calvin* (Geneva, 1959), 477–514; J. Delumeau, *Naissance et affirmation de la réforme* (Paris, 1973), 299ff.; G. Marshall, *In Search of the Spirit of Capitalism: Max Weber and the Protestant Ethic Thesis* (London, 1982); A. Giddens, *Politics and Sociology in the Thought of Max Weber* (London, 1972); W. J. Mommsen

and J. Osterhammel (eds.), *Max Weber and his Contemporaries* (London, 1987).

48. P. Collinson, *The Religion of Protestants: The Church in English Society 1559–1625* (Oxford, 1982), 182ff.; Heller, *Conquest of Poverty*, 70ff., 164ff., 193ff.

49. See Ch. 15. 5; and Brady, *Ruling Class, Regime and Reformation*, 238–9; but one should bear in mind that late medieval extravaganzas like the shrine of the *Schöne Maria* at Regensburg or the parish churches of East Anglia may have given a vested interest in the old order to more people than just a tiny civic oligarchy.

50. As in Ch. 15. 3, and nn. 85–7.

51. Exactly this simple social structure is portrayed by Brady, *Ruling Class, Regime and Reformation*, 26–33.

52. Ibid. 234–5.

53. S. Ozment, 'Pamphlets as a Source: Comments on Bernd Moeller's "Stadt und Buch"', in *Stadtbürgertum und Adel*, 46–7.

54. N. Z. Davis, 'Strikes and Salvation at Lyons', *ARG* 56 (1965), 48–64; also in id., *Society and Culture in Early Modern France* (London, 1975), 1–16.

55. Rublack, 'Is there a "New History"?', 123 and n. 7: 'What is misleading is to conceive of the relationship between ideas and social interests as strictly reciprocally determined.'

56. Moeller, *Imperial Cities, passim*, and 103 for the quotation.

57. Ozment, *Cities*, 7–8 and nn.

58. G. Swanson, *Religion and Regime: A Sociological Account of the Reformation* (Ann Arbor, 1967); see discussion in Ozment, *Cities*, 9–11, and in *Journal of Interdisciplinary History*, 1 (1970/1), 380ff.

59. See M. Fulbrook, *Piety and Politics: Religion and the Rise of Absolutism in England, Württemberg, and Prussia* (Cambridge, 1983).

60. As suggested in Ch. 8. 6.

61. See Ch. 1. 1.

62. See Ch. 1. 2.

63. Ozment, *Cities*, 22–32, and id., *Reform*, 216ff., are the main statements of the thesis; see J. Geffcken, *Der Bildercatechismus des fünfzehnten Jahrhunderts und die catechetischen Hauptstücke in dieser Zeit bis auf Luther*, i. *Die zehn Gebote* (Leipzig, 1855), esp. 103ff., for some of the background to Ozment's thesis. See the discussion in Ch. 6. 1 and n. 11.

64. As remarked by L. G. Duggan, 'Fear and Confession on the Eve of the Reformation', *ARG* 75 (1984), 155; Brady, *Ruling Class, Regime and Reformation*, 9.

65. Ozment, *Reform*, 222–3.

66. e.g. a mini-version of the thesis may be found in S. E. Ozment, 'The Social History of the Reformation: What can we learn from Pamphlets?', in H.-J. Köhler (ed.), *Flugschriften als Massenmedium der Reformationszeit* (Stuttgart, 1981), 171–203, esp. 172ff.

67. Ozment, 'Pamphlets as a source', in *Stadtbürgertum und Adel*, 47: 'The social impact of the Reformation lay in effectively displacing so many of the beliefs, practices, and institutions that had organized daily life and given it security and meaning for the greater part of a millenium.' Cf. Ch. 6. 1.

68. Ozment, *Cities*, 176 n. 50.

69. T. N. Tentler, *Sin and Confession on the Eve of the Reformation* (Princeton, NJ, 1977), 103, 131, 148, 349; cf. the comments of Ozment, *Reform*, 218–19 and n. 70.

70. See Duggan, 'Fear and Confession', and Ch. 6. 1 nn. 12–15.
71. Ibid., n. 16.
72. Though even that may be hard to sustain. See Duggan, 'Fear and Confession', 154.
73. e.g. Scheel, *Dokumente*, 74, 98–9, 104–5, 117, 132, 185f., etc.
74. See Ch. 12. 1.
75. Duggan, 'Fear and Confession', 155 (italics added).
76. See Ch. 8. 6 and texts cited there; cf. Tentler, *Sin and Confession*, 349–62.
77. See Ch. 15. 7 n. 209.
78. Ozment, *Cities*, 51–5; Ozment describes Strauss's *Ein neüw wunderbarlich Beycht-beüchlin* of 1523 as 'one of the great unrecognized tours de force of the early Reformation'.
79. P. A. Russell, *Lay Theology in the Reformation* (Cambridge, 1986), 45–7, 182–3, 223–4; the pamphlets studied by Russell provide *some* support for this thesis (cf. 99, 125, 127), but not enough to bear the weight imposed on it by Ozment.
80. In some ways this is the oldest explanation: E. Gothein, *Politische und religiöse Volksbewegungen vor der Reformation* (Breslau, 1878), remarked that the preaching of the Lutheran doctrine of grace 'satisfied a yearning in the hearts of men': for this and other such ecstatic remarks see Karant-Nunn, 'Luther's Pastors', 52–3 and nn.
81. See Scribner, 'Ritual and Popular Belief in Catholic Germany at the Time of the Reformation', in Scribner, *PC and PM*, 17ff.; but cf. Karant-Nunn, *Zwickau in Transition*, 203ff., on possible differences between town and country.
82. R. W. Scribner, *For the Sake of Simple Folk* (Cambridge, 1981), 190–228.
83. The phrase used by Brady, as in n. 25 above.
84. Cf. the remarks of T. A. Brady, reviewing L. W. Spitz, *The Protestant Reformation, 1517–1559: The Rise of Modern Europe* (New York, 1985), in *Sixteenth Century Journal*, 16 (1985), 410–12.
85. L and B, 40–1; B. Moeller, 'Was wurde in der Frühzeit der Reformation in den deutschen Städten gepredigt?', *ARG* 75 (1984), 177.
86. H.-J. Goertz, 'Aufstand gegen den Priester', in P. Blickle (ed.), *Bauer, Reich und Reformation: Festschrift für Günther Franz* (Stuttgart, 1982), 182–209; id., *Pfaffenhass und gross Geschrei* (Munich, 1987), *passim*.
87. Moeller, 'Was wurde . . . gepredigt?', 177–83.
88. Ibid. 183–91.
89. Dickens, *German Nation*, 132–3; note that Dickens was here objecting to those writers of the early 20th-cent. 'Luther Renaissance' whose linguistic and theological subtleties often exceeded those of Luther, let alone those of most 16th-cent. observers.
90. Russell, *Lay Theology in the Reformation*, esp. 105, 140, 162, 200.
91. Eire, *Idols*, 94–103.
92. H.-R. Schmidt, *Reichsstädte, Reich und Reformation* (Stuttgart, 1986), 196 and refs., 330.
93. See its significance as discussed in Ch. 15. 6.
94. Russell, *Lay Theology in the Reformation*, 165–80; Dickens, *German Nation*, 142–3, 133 n. 20; see also Ch. 15 n. 58.
95. Delumeau, *Naissance et affirmation de la réforme*, 76–7.
96. As is almost, but not quite, implied by Dickens, *German Nation*, 134.
97. Cf. R. Gawthrop and G. Strauss, 'Protestantism and Literacy in Early Modern Germany', *P and P* 104 (1984), 31–55.

98. See Ch. 15 n. 77.
99. Scribner, *For the Sake of Simple Folk*, 229–39.
100. Cf. the cases of Fabri and Treger discussed in Ch. 15 n. 89 and refs.
101. For instance Mazzolini's *Dialogus de potestate Papae* of 1517, excerpted in Kidd, *Documents*, 31 f. For further ref. to such propaganda see Ch. 15 n. 74.
102. See Ch. 2.
103. See Ch. 6. 4.
104. Cf. the ch., 'Images of Luther 1519–25', in Scribner, *For the Sake of Simple Folk*, 14–36; also 'Incombustible Luther', in Scribner, *PC and PM*, esp. 332 ff.
105. As for instance in Luther's *To the Christian Nobility*, or Zwingli's position at the Jan. 1523 disputation in Zürich.
106. Cf. Ch. 15. 8.
107. Bornkamm, *Mid-Career*, 363 n. 25 and refs.
108. Dickens, *German Nation*, 118–20; R. W. Scribner, *The German Reformation* (London, 1986), 19; M. Gravier, *Luther et l'opinion publique* (Paris, 1942), 51 ff.
109. Ozment, *Cities*, 66–7 and refs; D. Demandt and H.-C. Rublack, *Stadt und Kirche in Kitzingen: Darstellungen und Quellen zu Spätmittelalter und Reformation* (Stuttgart, 1978), 68–73; R. W. Scribner, 'Practice and Principle in the German Towns: Preachers and People', in P. N. Brooks (ed.), *Reformation Principle and Practice: Essays in Honour of A. G. Dickens* (London, 1980), 99 and n. 5; Russell, *Lay Theology in the Reformation*, 52–3.
110. Ozment, *Cities*, 86–9 and refs.
111. An interesting contrast to the reformers' customary idealizing of the common people is provided by Sebastian Franck: see Strauss, *Manifestations*, 227 ff., and indeed by the later Luther: G. Strauss, *Luther's House of Learning* (Baltimore, 1978), 43.
112. Strauss, *Luther's House of Learning*, 4 ff.; on this as on so many other issues, however, Luther's emphases were inconsistent.
113. Oberman, *Masters*, 237; cf. id., 'The Impact of the Reformation: Problems and Perspectives', in Kouri and Scott (eds.), *Politics and Society in Reformation Europe*, 6–7.

18. *The Sects Reject the 'Coalition'*

1. See L and B 40–1 on the absence of a clear distinction between mainstream reformers and sectarians in the early years.
2. Hence the title of G. H. Williams, *The Radical Reformation* (London, 1962). See his typology of sectarianism ibid., pp. xxiv ff. For some comments on the recent historiography of this attitude see K. Deppermann, *Melchior Hoffman: Social Unrest and Apocalyptic Visions in the Age of Reformation*, trans. M. Wren (Edinburgh, 1987), 1 ff.
3. For guidance on the literature see J. M. Stayer, 'The Anabaptists', in Ozment, *Guide*, 135–59; also the bibliographies to U. Gastaldi, *Storia dell'Anabattismo*, 2 vols. (Turin, 1972–81).
4. See Ch. 15 n. 80; Rupp, *Patterns*, 163 ff.
5. T. Scott, *Thomas Müntzer* (London, 1989), 28–45; E. Gritsch, *Thomas Müntzer: A Tragedy of Errors* (Minneapolis, 1989), 33–46; Müntzer's writings may now be studied in P. Matheson (ed.), *The Collected Works of Thomas Muentzer* (Edinburgh, 1988); see also W. Elliger, *Thomas Müntzer: Leben und Werke* (3rd edn., Göttingen,

1976); K. Ebert, *Thomas Müntzer: Von Eigensinn und Widerspruch* (Frankfurt, 1987); Rupp, *Patterns*, 169 ff.

6. The Allstedt service orders are printed in Sehling, i, pt. 1, 472 ff.

7. See Rupp, *Patterns*, 185 ff., 305 ff.; T. Scott, 'The "Volksreformation" of Thomas Müntzer in Allstedt and Mühlhausen', *JEH* 34 (1983), 194–213; id., *Thomas Müntzer*, 57–95; Gritsch, *Thomas Müntzer*, 47–83. Müntzer's 'Sermon before the Princes' is trans. in G. H. Williams (ed.), *Spiritual and Anabaptist Writers: Documents Illustrative of the Radical Reformation*, LCC 25 (London 1957), 49 ff.

8. Scott, *Thomas Müntzer*, 97–125; Gritsch, *Thomas Müntzer*, 83–91; also Ch. 14. 2; Rupp, *Patterns*, 221–50; H.-J. Goertz, *Pfaffenhass und gross Geschrei* (Munich, 1987), 14 ff., 186 ff.

9. Rupp, *Patterns*, 249–50; Scott, *Thomas Müntzer*, 181 ff.; Williams, 435 ff.; Deppermann, *Melchior Hoffman*, 9.

10. F. Blanke, *Brothers in Christ: The History of the Oldest Anabaptist Congregation, Zollikon, near Zurich, Switzerland*, trans. J. Nordenhaug (Scottdale, Pa., 1961), 9–13; Williams, 85 ff.; Williams (ed.), *Spiritual and Anabaptist Writers*, 41 ff.; K. Deppermann, 'The Anabaptists and the State Churches', in K. von Greyerz (ed.), *Religion and Society in Early Modern Europe* (London, 1984), 98–9; H. S. Bender, *Conrad Grebel, c. 1498–1526, the Founder of the Swiss Brethren, Sometimes called Anabaptists* (Goschen, Ind., 1950), 89–162; G. R. Potter, *Zwingli* (Cambridge, 1976) 160 ff.; Locher, *ZR* 235 ff.; C.-P. Clasen, *Anabaptism: A Social History, 1525–1618* (London, 1972), 1–14; Kidd, *Documents*, 451 ff.

11. Blanke, *Brothers in Christ*, 19–55; Williams, 118 ff.; Potter, *Zwingli*, 182 ff.; Locher, *ZR* 245 ff.

12. Williams, 181 ff.; Williams (ed.), *Spiritual and Anabaptist Writers*, 138 ff.; Deppermann, 'Anabaptists and the State Churches', 100–1.

13. Williams, 149 ff.; on Denck see Williams (ed.), *Spiritual and Anabaptist Writers*, 88 ff.; G. Seebass, 'Müntzers Erbe: Werk, Leben und Theologie des Hans Hut', Diss. (Erlangen, 1972).

14. Williams, 176 ff.

15. Ibid. 204 ff., 417 ff.; Clasen, *Anabaptism*, 210–12.

16. Williams, 241 ff.; M. U. Chrisman, *Strasbourg and the Reform* (New Haven, Conn., 1967), 177–90; Deppermann, *Melchior Hoffman*, 167–203.

17. Williams, 254 ff.; R. E. McLaughlin, *Caspar Schwenckfeld, Reluctant Radical: His Life to 1540* (New Haven, Conn., and London, 1986), 125–59; Deppermann, *Melchior Hoffman*, 203–19. Hoffmann's *The Ordinance of God* is trans. in Williams (ed.), *Spiritual and Anabaptist Writers*, 184 ff.

18. Williams, 273–98; Chrisman, *Strasbourg and the Reform*, 190–200; Deppermann, *Melchior Hoffman*, 268–311.

19. Williams, 341 ff.; Deppermann, *Melchior Hoffman*, 312–42.

20. Williams, 362 ff.; R. Po-Chia Hsia, 'Münster and the Anabaptists', in R. Po-Chia Hsia (ed.), *The German People and the Reformation* (Ithaca, NY, and London, 1988), 51–7, and for a social analysis, 57–69; for a further social analysis of the population of the city see K.-H. Kirchhoff, *Die Täufer in Münster 1534–1535: Untersuchungen zum Umfang und zur Sozialstruktur der Bewegung* (Münster, 1973), esp. 78–88; for the aftermath in Münster itself see R. Po-Chia Hsia, *Society and Religion in Münster, 1535–1618* (New Haven, Conn., 1984).

21. Gastaldi, *Storia dell'Anabattismo*, ii. 7ff., 17ff., 34–47; Williams 381ff.; Deppermann, *Melchior Hoffman*, 358ff.
22. Gastaldi, *Storia dell'Anabattismo*, ii. 24ff., 48ff.; Williams, 387ff.
23. Gastaldi, *Storia dell'Anabattismo*, ii. 69–97; Williams, 477ff., 764ff.
24. L. Gross, *The Golden Years of the Hutterites: The Witness and Communal Thought of the Communal Moravian Anabaptists during the Walpot Era, 1565–78* (Scottdale, Pa., 1980), *passim*; Gastaldi, *Storia dell'Anabattismo*, ii. 473–520; Williams, 417ff.; 670ff.; Clasen, *Anabaptism*, 212–43; Williams (ed.), *Spiritual and Anabaptist Writers*, 274–84.
25. Gastaldi, *Storia dell'Anabattismo*, ii. 520–9.
26. Clasen, *Anabaptism*, 394ff.; Gastaldi, *Storia dell'Anabattismo*, ii. 221–62.
27. Williams, 453ff.; for editions of Marpeck's writings see Gastaldi, *Storia dell'Anabattismo*, ii. 290 n. 2, with refs. to *Quellen zur Geschichte der Täufer in der Schweiz*, ii. *Ostschweiz*, ed. L. Muralt and H. Fast (Zürich, 1974); *Glaubenszeugnisse oberdeutscher Taufgesinnter*, iv. *Das Kunstbuch und andere Schriften aus dem Marpeckhkreis* (planned), and W. and W. Klaassen (eds.), *The Writing of Pilgram Marpeck* (Scottdale. Pa., 1978).
28. Gastaldi, *Storia dell'Anabattismo*, ii. 289–361.
29. Ibid. 363–400 (for Zürich), 401–27 (for the rest of Switzerland).
30. E. M. Wilbur, *A History of Unitarianism: Socinianism and its Antecedents* (Cambridge, Mass., 1946), 285ff.; see also L. Szczucki, *Marcin Czechowić 1532–1613* (Warsaw, 1964, with English summary); Williams, 647ff.
31. Wilbur, *History of Unitarianism*, 297ff.; on the Italians see D. Caccamo, *Eretici italiani in Moravia, Polonia, Transilvania (1558–1611): studi e documenti* (Florence, 1970), *passim*; see also L. Szczucki et al. (eds.), *Socinianism and its Role in the Culture of the Sixteenth and Seventeenth Centuries* (Warsaw, 1983), 7–67; Williams, 653ff.
32. Wilbur, *History of Unitarianism*, 302ff.; Williams, 658ff.
33. Wilbur, *History of Unitarianism*, 310ff.
34. Ibid. 314ff.; Williams, 664ff.
35. Wilbur, *History of Unitarianism*, 326ff.; Williams, 686ff.
36. Wilbur, *History of Unitarianism*, 356ff.; on Raków see S. Kot, *Socinianism in Poland: the Social and Political Ideas of the Polish Antitrinitarians*, trans. E. M. Wilbur (Boston, 1957); Williams, 698ff.
37. Wilbur, *History of Unitarianism*, 396ff.; Williams, 733ff.
38. Williams, 708–18.
39. Ibid. 718–25.
40. Ibid. 725–32.
41. Deppermann, 'Anabaptists and the State Churches', 95.
42. Ibid. 95–7, points out the evolving character of anabaptist thought, and that the peaceful, moderate groups only came to be regarded as 'essentially' anabaptist with hindsight. However, these later groups, close as they were to the mainstream reformers, were sufficiently different to support the present argument without citing the extremists' ideas. See also the introduction to Deppermann, *Melchior Hoffman*, as cited above, n. 2.
43. See e.g. Bender, *Conrad Grebel*, 206.
44. See Ch. 8.
45. Bender, *Conrad Grebel*, 206.
46. W. E. Keeney, *The Development of Dutch Anabaptist Thought and Practice from 1539 to 1564* (Nieuwkoop, 1968), 114ff.

47. Williams, 305; cf. Rupp, *Patterns*, 325 ff.
48. Deppermann, 'Anabaptists and the State Churches', 101, 104; Deppermann, *Melchior Hoffman*, 229; cf. Hubmaier's *On Free Will*, in Williams (ed.), *Spiritual and Anabaptist Writers*, 114 ff., 120 ff., 124 ff., 131 ff.; and see D. C. Steinmetz, *Luther in Context* (Bloomington, Ind., 1986), 59–71. Evidently a rehabilitation of free will undermines the entire logic of the Reformation critique of medieval piety.
49. See Chs. 8. 3 and 8. 4; cf. Keeney, *Dutch Anabaptist Thought*, 120. The implications of this conclusion are discussed by Deppermann, *Melchior Hoffman*, 6–8.
50. Bender, *Conrad Grebel*, 206–7; Keeney, *Dutch Anabaptist Thought*, 117–20.
51. Keeney, *Dutch Anabaptist Thought*, 119–20; cf. Deppermann, *Melchior Hoffman*, 233 ff.; 385 ff.
52. Deppermann, 'Anabaptists and the State Churches', 97, shows how this issue only gradually came to the forefront, but cf. H.-J. Goertz, *Die Täufer: Geschichte und Deutung* (Munich, 1980), 77–97: 'Taufe als öffentliches Bekenntnis'.
53. Cf. Williams, 300 ff.; 473 ff.
54. *Z* iv. 253, as cited in Ch. 8 n. 124; Williams, *Radical Reformation*, 300 ff.
55. Williams, *Radical Reformation*, 304 ff.; Clasen, *Anabaptism*, 99 ff.; Deppermnann, *Melchior Hoffman*, 230–1.
56. Bender, *Conrad Grebel*, 207.
57. Keeney, *Dutch Anabaptist Thought*, 78 ff.
58. Bender, *Conrad Grebel*, 204–5.
59. Keeney, *Dutch Anabaptist Thought*, 149 ff.
60. Ibid. 153.
61. Bender, *Conrad Grebel*, 205 and refs.; cf. Keeney, *Dutch Anabaptist Thought*, 130 ff., 155–6; Goertz, *Die Täufer*, 20 ff.; J. M. Stayer, *Anabaptists and the Sword* (Lawrence, Kan., 1972), 335.
62. For a trans. of the Schleitheim Confession see J. C. Wenger, 'The Schleitheim Confession of Faith', *Mennonite Quarterly Review*, 19 (1945), 243–53; also J. H. Yoder, *The Schleitheim Confession* (Scottdale, 1973).
63. Keeney, *Dutch Anabaptist Thought*, 123–8 and refs.; cf. Waldensian heretics, as in E. Cameron, *Reformation of the Heretics* (Oxford, 1984), 105–6.
64. On the social organization of the Hutterites see Gastaldi, *Storia dell' Anabattismo*, ii. 504 ff.; Clasen, *Anabaptism*, 243–97.
65. This was precisely the purpose of the Schleitheim Confession itself, intended to mark off Sattler's peaceful followers from violent extremists.
66. Bender, *Conrad Grebel*, 204–5; Keeney, *Dutch Anabaptist Thought*, 160–2; Clasen, *Anabaptism*, 106 ff.
67. Keeney, *Dutch Anabaptist Thought*, 162–8; cf. Menno Simons's *On the Ban* of 1550, trans. in Williams (ed.), *Spiritual and Anabaptist Writers*, 263 ff.
68. Bender, *Conrad Grebel*, 205 and refs.
69. Ibid., and Keeney, *Dutch Anabaptist Thought*, 130–1; cf. Clasen, *Anabaptism*, 172 ff.
70. But cf. with the very positive estimate of a secular magistracy in the thought of Hubmaier: see Stayer, *Anabaptists and the Sword*, 141–6.
71. Keeney, *Dutch Anabaptist Thought*, 132 ff. This principle was diluted later in the 16th cent., and was not held by Melchior Hoffmann (see Deppermann, 'Anabaptists and the State Churches', 103, and id., *Melchior Hoffman*, 388–9); on this issue see Stayer, *Anabaptists and the Sword, passim*.

72. See Stayer, *Anabaptists and the Sword*, 74ff., 167ff., 216ff.
73. See n. 10 above; cf. Deppermann, 'Anabaptists and the State Churches', 105.
74. See n. 64 above.
75. McLaughlin, *Caspar Schwenckfeld*, 106ff.; see n. 2 above.

19. Crisis, Survival, and Compromise in Politics

1. L. von Ranke, *History of the Reformation in Germany*, partial trans. by S. Austin, ed. R. A. Johnson, 2 vols. (1905, repr. New York, 1966), esp. bks. III–VI.
2. See H. Baron, 'Religion and Politics in the German Imperial Cities during the Reformation', *EHR* 52 (1937), 405–27, 614–33; H.-R. Schmidt, *Reichsstädte, Reich und Reformation* (Stuttgart, 1986), esp. 34ff., 75ff., 130ff., 243ff., 268ff.; for narratives see also J. Lortz, *The Reformation in Germany*, trans. R. Walls, 2 vols. (London, 1968), ii. 3–91, 275–329.
3. L and B 73ff.; Kidd, *Documents*, 105ff.
4. Kidd, *Documents*, 133ff.; IGJ 208ff.
5. As discussed in Ch. 16. 1.
6. L and B 77; IGJ 211–13.
7. See esp. S. A. Fischer-Galati, *Ottoman Imperialism and German Protestantism* (Cambridge, Mass., 1959), 13–31.
8. See Ch. 16. 1.
9. L and B 78–9.
10. IGJ 242–5; the 1529 protesters are listed in Ch. 16. 1, Table 16. 2.
11. The text of the Augsburg Confession is ed. in *BSLK* 44–137, and Melanchthon's *Apology* ibid. 141–404; also Kidd, *Documents*, 259–89; the *Tetrapolitana* trans. in A. C. Cochrane, *Reformed Confessions of the Sixteenth Century* (London, 1966), 54–88; cf. L and B 80ff.; IGJ 253–65.
12. On these edicts see Kidd, *Documents*, 289–300.
13. See Ch. 16. 1 n. 17.
14. L and B 85; IGJ 268; A. F. Pollard, 'Conflict of Creeds and Parties in Germany', *Cambridge Modern History*, ii (1904), 221–2.
15. L and B 108–22; IGJ 269ff.; on the Wittenberg Accord see also W. Köhler, *Zwingli und Luther*, 2 vols. (Leipzig and Gütersloh, 1934–53), ii. 320–525; E. Bizer, *Studien zur Geschichte des Abendmahlsstreits im 16. Jahrhundert* (Darmstadt, 1972), 65ff.; M. U. Edwards, *Luther and the False Brethren* (Stanford, Calif., 1975), 127–55.
16. L and B 123–31; IGJ 270ff.
17. L and B 141–7; IGJ 273ff.; Fischer-Galati, *Ottoman Imperialism*, 66–75.
18. L and B 153–7; on the origins of catholic moderatism see H. Rabe, *Reichsbund und Interim: Die Verfassungs- und Religionspolitik Karls V und der Reichstag zu Augsburg 1546/48* (Cologne, 1971), 92–117.
19. L and B 161–5; IGJ 274ff.
20. L and B 165–71; for the Italians' reactions see Ch. 13. 2.
21. L and B 178–80, 187–9, 193, 197, 200; IGJ 283; for further sources for the Cologne experiment see J. K. Cameron, 'The Cologne Reformation and the Church of Scotland', *JEH* 30 (1979), 41 and nn.
22. L and B 172–5.
23. Ibid. 157–60.
24. Ibid. 183–4.

25. See Ch. 16. 1 n. 8.
26. L and B 175–8; IGJ 281–2.
27. L and B 189ff.
28. Ibid. 190–6; on this period see also F. Hartung, *Karl V und die deutschen Reichsstände von 1546–1555* (Darmstadt, 1971).
29. See K. Repgen, 'What is a "Religious War"?', in E. I. Kouri and T. Scott (eds.), *Politics and Society in Reformation Europe* (London, 1987), 311–28, esp. 318ff., for a subtle analysis of Charles's presentation of his case.
30. L and B 201–7; IGJ 284–8; F. L. Carsten, *Princes and Parliaments in Germany from the Fifteenth to the Eighteenth Century* (Oxford, 1959), 211–13.
31. Cf. Rabe, *Reichsbund und Interim*, 69ff.
32. On the *Reichstag* see Ibid., 195ff.; on the *Interim*, ibid. 407ff.; see also L and B 208–13, IGJ 288–94; cap. 26 of the *Interim*, on the Sacraments, is ed. in Kidd, *Documents*, 359–62.
33. L and B 213–19; Rabe, *Reichsbund und Interim*, 443ff.; documents in E. Naujoks, *Kaiser Karl V und die Zunftverfassung: Ausgewählte Aktenstücke zu den Verfassungsänderungen in den oberdeutschen Reichsstädten (1547–1556)* (Stuttgart, 1985), but see also 1–31, 335ff.; T. A. Brady, *Turning Swiss* (Cambridge, 1985), 221 and refs.
34. L and B 224–9; IGJ 294–5.
35. On religious 'parity' in the cities up to and after 1555 see E. Naujoks, *Obrigkeitsgedanke, Zunftverfassung und Reformation* (Stuttgart, 1958), 162ff.; P. Warmbrunn, *Zwei Konfessionen in einer Stadt* (Wiesbaden, 1983), 69–130; see also H. Tüchle, 'The Peace of Augsburg: New Order or Lull in the Fighting', in H. J. Cohn (ed.), *Government in Reformation Europe 1520–1560* (London, 1971), 145–60.
36. L and B 232–9; IGJ 295–300; Tüchle, 'Peace of Augsburg', 160–5; partial trans. of Augsburg peace in Kidd, *Documents*, 362–4.
37. *Of Good Works* (1520) is ed. in *WA* vi. 196–276; *LW* xliv. 17–114; *Secular Authority: To What Extent it should be Obeyed* (1523), in *WA* xi. 245–80; *LW* xlv. 77–129.
38. W. D. J. Cargill Thompson, *The Political Thought of Martin Luther* (London, 1984), 91–5; Skinner, *Foundations*, ii. 14ff. On Luther see also G. Müller, 'Martin Luther and the Political World of his Time', in Kouri and Scott (eds.), *Politics and Society in Reformation Europe*, 35–50.
39. See the discussion of Church and State relations in Ch. 10. 3; Cargill Thompson, *Political Thought of Martin Luther*, 98–9.
40. This was the famous jurists' dispute between 'Azo and Lothair': see Skinner, *Foundations*, ii. 127–8.
41. *WA.B* ii. 454–7; *LW* xlviii. 388–93; also trans. in E. G. Rupp and B. J. Drewery (eds.), *Martin Luther* (London, 1970), 80–2; see Cargill Thompson, *Political Thought of Martin Luther*, 96.
42. *WA.B* v. 209–11; *LW* xlix. 254–60; see Skinner, *Foundations*, ii. 196–7.
43. Skinner, *Foundations*, ii. 66–71.
44. *Inst.* IV. xx. 23; Skinner, *Foundations*, ii. 191–4; Eire, *Idols*, 288; M.-E. Chenevière, *La Pensée politique de Calvin* (repr., Geneva, 1970), esp. 308ff.
45. S and S iv. 59–60; cf. Stephens, *Zwingli*, 295–309; on Zwingli see also J. Rogge, 'Staatstheorie und Widerstandrecht bei Zwingli', in P. Blickle *et al.* (eds.), *Zwingli und Europa: Referate und Protokoll des internationalen Kongresses aus Anlass des 500.*

Geburtstages von Huldrych Zwingli, 1984 (Zürich, 1985), 183–98; W. Schulze, 'Zwingli, lutherischen Widerstandsdenken, monarchomachischer Widerstand', ibid. 199–216.

46. Cf. Eire, *Idols*, 289.
47. See above, n. 41.
48. Cargill Thompson, *Political Thought of Martin Luther*, 96 ff.
49. Skinner, *Foundations*, ii. 191–4; Eire, *Idols*, 288 f.
50. Cf. Cargill Thompson, *Political Thought of Martin Luther*, 98; or J. W. Allen, *A History of Political Thought in the Sixteenth Century* (London, 1957), 15 ff., 52 ff., 125 ff.
51. On these see Ch. 4. 1.
52. Skinner, *Foundations*, ii. 114–17; and see works cited in Ch. 4. 1.
53. Skinner, *Foundations*, ii. 131–4.
54. This was the theme of the Azo–Lothair debate as above, n. 40.
55. See e.g. K. S. Bader, 'Approaches to Imperial Reform at the end of the Fifteenth Century', in Strauss, *Pre-Ref. Germany*, esp. 142 ff.
56. Skinner, *Foundations*, ii. 127–31.
57. Ibid. 123–7.
58. Cf. Skinner, *Foundations*, which explores the structure of the arguments from the ideological rather than historical perspective.
59. H. Scheible, *Das Widerstandrecht als Problem der deutschen Protestanten, 1523–46* (Gütersloh, 1969), 20 ff.
60. Ibid. 25–9; Skinner, *Foundations*, ii. 199; Eire, *Idols*, 295–6; C. G. Shoenberger, 'The Development of the Lutheran Theory of Resistance: 1523–1530', *Sixteenth Century Journal*, 8 (1977), 61–76, and esp. 65 ff. on Bugenhagen.
61. For Luther's reluctance see *WA.B* iv. 448–50, 465; *WA.B* v. 76–7, 101–2, 181–3, 203–4, 209–11, 258–61, 319–20; *LW* xlix. 189–96, 221–31, 244–60, 272–80, 295–9; Cargill Thompson, *Political Thought of Martin Luther*, 103–5; Skinner, *Foundations*, ii. 194–7.
62. Skinner, *Foundations*, ii. 197–9.
63. *WA.B* v. 662; *LW* xlix. 429–33; Scheible, *Widerstandrecht als Problem*, 67–8; Müller, 'Martin Luther and the Political World', 45 ff.
64. Cargill Thompson, *Political Thought of Martin Luther*, 105 ff.; Skinner, *Foundations*, ii. 200 ff.; Shoenberger, 'Development of the Lutheran Theory', 67–74.
65. Scheible, *Widerstandrecht als Problem*, 89–92; Cargill Thompson, *Political Thought of Martin Luther*, 106 ff.; Eire, *Idols*, 286.
66. See Ch. 10. 3.
67. Scheible, *Widerstandrecht als Problem*, 94–8, based on *WA* xxxix/ii. 34–91, esp. 88; see also W. D. J. Cargill Thompson, *The Political Thought of Martin Luther*, ed. P. Broadhead (Brighton, 1984), 108–11; and id., 'Luther and the Right of Resistance to the Emperor', in his *Studies in the Reformation*, ed. C. W. Dugmore (London, 1980), 3–41.
68. As in the case of Osiander or Bucer: see Skinner, *Foundations*, ii. 201 ff., 204 ff.; Eire, *Idols*, 287 f.
69. Skinner, *Foundations*, ii. 207–9; O. K. Olson, 'Theology of Revolution: Magdeburg, 1550–1551', *Sixteenth Century Journal*, 3 (1972), 56–79; on Melanchthon's views in 1547, see L. D. Peterson, 'Melanchthon on Resisting the Emperor: The *Von der*

Notwehr Unterrichte of 1547', in J. Friedman (ed.), *Regnum, Religio et Ratio: Essays Presented to Robert M. Kingdon* (Kirksville, Mo., 1987), 133–44.

70. Cargill Thompson, *Political Thought of Martin Luther*, 111; Skinner, *Foundations*, ii. 321; id., 'The Origins of the Calvinist Theory of Revolution', in B. C. Malament (ed.), *After the Reformation: Essays in Honor of J. H. Hexter* (Philadelphia, 1980), 309–30.

71. Eire, *Idols*, 297, 304–10.

72. See Chs. 20. 3 and 20. 4.

73. Shoenberger, 'Development of the Lutheran Theory', 75–6.

74. *Inst.* IV. xx. 31; Eire, *Idols*, 289; Skinner, *Foundations*, ii. 231–4 and refs.; cf. ibid. 214.

75. Skinner, *Foundations*, ii. 220 and refs.

76. *Inst.* IV. xx. 32; Skinner, *Foundations*, ii. 219 f.; on Viret, see R. D. Linder, *The Political Ideas of Pierre Viret* (Geneva, 1964), 127–42, and esp. 136 ff.: active resistance was allowed to those rescuing the victims of persecution from prison, or to magistrates 'rescuing' a monarch from wicked advisers. Cf. Eire, *Idols*, 289–95, and esp. 294 n. 72.

77. Skinner, *Foundations*, ii. 227–30; Eire, *Idols*, 298 ff., and see also the bibl. note on 301. See esp. R. E. Giesey, 'The Monarchomach Triumvirs: Hotman, Beza, and Mornay', *Bibliothèque d'humanisme et renaissance*, 32 (1970), 41–56; D. R. Kelley, *The Beginning of Ideology* (Cambridge, 1981).

78. Eire, *Idols*, 296–8; Skinner, *Foundations*, ii. 309 ff.

79. For the political thought of the league see Ch. 20 n. 42 and sources cited there.

80. Bornkamm, *Mid-Career*, 100–2; G. Parker, *The Dutch Revolt* (London, 1977), 37.

81. See Chs. 16. 4 and 16. 5.

82. See Ch. 16. 5; also the exhaustive study by G. Audisio, *Les Vaudois de Luberon* (Mérindol, 1984), and E. Cameron, *The Reformation of the Heretics* (Oxford, 1984), 147–55.

83. See the evidence (including comparison with similar protestant areas not peopled by former heretics) in Cameron, *Reformation of the Heretics*, 220 ff., 258–62.

84. For the statistics see Audisio, *Vaudois de Luberon*, 386–99.

85. J. Crespin, *Le Livre des martyrs* ([Geneva], 1554); the story of the 1545 Waldensian massacre was continually republished, e.g. in id., *Actes des martyrs* (n.p., 1565), 189–217, and id., *Histoire des martyrs* (1619), 141ʳ–155ᵛ; and as a separate book, *Histoire mémorable de la persecution et saccagement du peuple de Mérindol et Cabrières et autres circonvoisins, appelez Vaudois* (n.p., 1556). On the martyrology see J.-F. Gilmont, *Jean Crespin: un éditeur réformé du xviᵉ siècle* (Geneva, 1981), 165 ff.

86. For numerous other authors, including some moderate catholics, who recopied the story of the massacres in Provence, see Cameron, *Reformation of the Heretics*, 237–41.

87. See the sources cited in Ch. 2 n. 14.

88. N. M. Sutherland, *The Huguenot Struggle for Recognition* (New Haven, Conn., and London, 1980), 35 ff.

89. See the *Histoire ecclésiastique des églises réformées au royaume de France*, sometimes attrib. to Théodore de Bèze ('Anvers', 1580), i. 23.

90. L. Rabus, *Historien der ... Martyren*, 8 vols. (Strasbourg, 1554–7); see A. G. Dickens and J. M. Tonkin, *The Reformation in Historical Thought* (Oxford, 1986), 51–2.

91. M. Flacius Illyricus, *Catalogus Testium Veritatis qui ante nostram aetatem reclamarunt papae* (Basle, 1556); on some martyrological elements see Cameron, *Reformation of the Heretics*, 238.

92. H. Pantaleon, *Martyrum Historia* (Basle, 1563), introd. sect. entitled 'Pacis commendatio'.

93. Dickens and Tonkin, *Reformation in Historical Thought*, 49–51.

94. J. Foxe, *Actes and Monuments of these latter and perillous dayes, touching matters of the Church* (London, 1563); for accounts and analyses of Foxe's work see Dickens and Tonkin, *Reformation in Historical Thought*, 44–9 and refs.

95. Cameron, *Reformation of the Heretics*, 162–4 and sources cited there.

96. *Histoire mémorable de la guerre faite par le duc de Savoye contre ses subjectz des vallées* (1561); modern edn. by E. Balmas and V. Diena (Turin, 1972); *Histoire des persecutions et guerres faites despuis l'an 1555 jusques en l'an 1561 contre le peuple appelé vaudois* (1562), modern edn. by E. Balmas and C. A. Theiller (Turin, 1975); Crespin, *Histoire des martyrs* (1619), 583ᵛ–600ʳ; for use of these texts by others see Cameron, *Reformation of the Heretics*, 237ff.

97. Cameron, *Reformation of the Heretics*, 222 and refs.

98. Cf. n. 67.

99. Cameron *Reformation of the Heretics*, 223.

100. J. Sleidanus, *De Statu Religionis et Reipublicae, Carolo Quinto Caesare, Commentarii* (Strasbourg, 1556); Dickens and Tonkin, *Reformation in Historical Thought*, 10–19.

101. For examples of such advocacy see Cameron, *Reformation of the Heretics*, 188–91, 196–9, and refs. cited there.

102. For the role of Strasbourg in the early French protestant movement see e.g. M. Greengrass, *The French Reformation* (Oxford, 1987), 21ff.

103. See for instance A. Pettegree, *Foreign Protestant Communities in Sixteenth-Century London* (Oxford, 1986).

104. See C. H. Garrett, *The Marian Exiles* (Cambridge, 1938), as in Ch. 16 n. 44.

105. On Italian exiles see e.g. A. Pascal, 'La Colonia piemontese a Ginevra nel secolo xvi', in *Ginevra e l'Italia* [collected essays] (Florence, 1959), 64–110; Cameron, *Reformation of the Heretics*, 259 and refs.

20. *Reformers at Odds: The 'Confessional' Reformation*

1. See Ch. 19 n. 30.

2. R. Kolb, *Nikolaus von Amsdorf (1483–1565): Popular Polemics in the Preservation of Luther's Legacy* (Nieuwkoop, 1978), 69–112; id., *Andreae and the Formula of Concord: Six Sermons on the Way to Lutheran Unity* (St Louis, Mo., 1977), 20–6; IGJ 350ff.; R. Stupperich, *Melanchthon* (London, 1966), 122ff.; *Melanchthon*, ed. Manschreck, 280–302; also R. Kolb, 'Dynamics of Party conflict in the Saxon Late Reformation: Gnesio Lutherans vs. Philippists', *JMH* 49 (1977), D1289–1305.

3. Kolb, *Nikolaus von Amsdorf*, 123–71, and for the statement that good works may be harmful, ibid. 158ff.; id., *Andreae and the Formula of Concord*, 26–7; see also IGJ 347ff.; R. Kolb, 'Good Works are detrimental to Salvation: Amsdorf's use of Luther's Words in Controversy', *Renaissance and Reformation*, 4 (1980), 136–51; id., 'Georg Major as Controversialist: Polemics in the Late Reformation', *Church History*, 45 (1976), 455–68.

4. Kolb, *Nikolaus von Amsdorf*, 181–224; id., *Andreae and the Formula of Concord*, 27–

31; IGJ 344 ff.; see also E. Muehlenberg, '*Synergia* and Justification by Faith', in L. W. Spitz and W. Lohff (eds.), *Discord, Dialogue and Concord: Studies in the Formula of Concord* (Philadelphia, 1977), 15 ff.

5. See R. W. Quere, 'Melanchthonian Motifs in the Formula's Eucharistic Christology', in Spitz and Lohff (eds.), *Discord, Dialogue and Concord*, 58 ff.; Kolb, *Andreae and the Formula of Concord*, 36–9; IGJ 356 ff.

6. M. Stupperich, *Osiander in Preussen* (Berlin, 1973), *passim*, but esp. 110 ff.; W. Hubatsch, *Geschichte der evangelischen Kirche Ostpreussens*, 3 vols. (Göttingen, 1968), i. 79–86; id., *Albrecht von Brandenburg-Ansbach* (Heidelberg, 1960), 167–83; Kolb, *Andreae and the Formula of Concord*, 34–6; IGJ 352–5 and refs; *Inst.* III. xi. 5–12.

7. Kolb, *Andreae and the Formula of Concord*, 39 48; on Andreae's early efforts see also T. R. Jungkuntz, *Formulators of the Formula of Concord: Four Architects of Lutheran Unity* (St Louis, Mo., 1977), 34 ff.

8. Kolb, *Andreae and the Formula of Concord*, 48–56; on Saxony in the 1570s see E. Koch, 'Der kursächsische Philippismus und seine Krise in den 1560er und 1570er Jahren', in H. Schilling (ed.), *Die reformierte Konfessionalisierung in Deutschland: Das Problem der 'zweiten Reformation'* (Gütersloh, 1987), 60–77; R. Po-Chia Hsia, *Social Discipline in the Reformation: Central Europe 1550–1750* (London, 1989), 28–30.

9. The text of the Formula of Concord is available in *BSLK*, 739–66 (preface), 767–827 (*Epitome*), and 829–1100 (*Solida Declaratio*); on its formulation see L. W. Spitz, 'The Formula of Concord: Then and Now', in Spitz and Lohff (eds.), *Discord, Dialogue and Concord*, 5 ff.; also Jungkuntz, *Formulators*, *passim*; Léonard, *Protestantism*, ii. 23–33.

10. For the semantic point see H. J. Cohn, 'The Territorial Princes in Germany's Second Reformation, 1559–1622', in M. Prestwich (ed.), *International Calvinism* (Oxford, 1985), 135–66, and esp. 141 n. 8; for the question of a 'second' or 'continuing' Reformation see Schilling (ed.), *Die reformierte Konfessionalisierung in Deutschland*, esp. the articles by W. H. Neuser (379 ff.) and H. Schilling (387 ff.). For a definition of 'confessionalization' in the German context see Hsia, *Social Discipline in the Reformation*, 2–9.

11. See J. F. G. Goeters, 'Genesis, Formen und Hauptthemen des reformierten Bekenntnisses in Deutschland: Eine Übersicht', in Schilling (ed.), *Die reformierte Konfessionalisierung in Deutschland*, 44–59; also M. Heckel, *Deutschland im konfessionellen Zeitalter* (Göttingen, 1983); and Hsia, *Social Discipline in the Reformation*, 26–8, 31–8.

12. See sect. 20. 3.

13. IGJ 402–4.

14. On the Palatinate in general see V. Press, 'Die "zweite Reformation" in der Kurpfalz', in Schilling (ed.), *Die reformierte Konfessionalisierung in Deutschland*, 104–29; also V. Press, *Calvinismus und Territorialstaat: Regierung und Zentralbehörden der Kurpfalz, 1559–1619* (Stuttgart, 1970), *passim*; C.-P. Clasen, *The Palatinate in European History, 1555–1660* (Oxford, 1963); on the princely 'Second Reformations' in general see IGJ 404–10.

15. Cohn, 'Germany's Second Reformation', 140.

16. See above n. 5.

17. Press, *Calvinismus und Territorialstaat*, 181–229; IGJ 405 ff.; Léonard, *Protestantism*, ii. 12 ff.

18. Press, *Calvinismus und Territorialstaat*, 229 ff.; C. Burchill, 'On the Consolation of a

Christian Scholar: Zacharias Ursinus (1534–83) and the Reformation in Heidelberg', *JEH* 37 (1986), 565ff.

19. The text of the Heidelberg catechism is trans. in A. C. Cochrane, *Reformed Confessions of the Sixteenth Century* (London, 1966), 305–31, and summarized in Léonard, *Protestantism*, ii. 13–16; see also Burchill, 'Zacharias Ursinus', 570ff., on its drafting and promulgation.

20. Press, *Calvinismus und Territorialstaat*, 267–515.

21. On Nassau-Dillenburg see P. Münch, *Zucht und Ordnung: Reformierte Kirchenverfassung im 16. und 17. Jahrhundert (Nassau-Dillenburg, Kurpfalz, Hessen-Kassel)* (Stuttgart, 1978); on the Johannea see G. Menk, *Die hohe Schule Herborn in ihrer Frühzeit (1584–1660): Ein Beitrag zum Hochschulwesen des deutschen Kalvinismus im Zeitalter der Reformation* (Wiesbaden, 1981).

22. See G. Schmidt, 'Die "zweite Reformation" im Gebiet des Wetterauer Grafvereins', in Schilling (ed.), *Die reformierte Konfessionalisierung in Deutschland*, 184–213; H. Klueting, 'Die reformierte Konfessions- und Kirchenbildung in den Westfälischen Grafschaften des 16. und 17. Jahrhunderts', ibid. 214–32.

23. On Lippe see above all H. Schilling, *Konfessionskonflikt und Staatsbildung: Eine Fallstudie über das Verhältnis von religiösen und sozialen Wandel in der Frühneuzeit am Beispiel der Grafschaft Lippe* (Gütersloh, 1981), esp. 151–204; id., 'Between the Territorial State and Urban Liberty: Lutheranism and Calvinism in the County of Lippe', in R. Po-Chia Hsia (ed.), *The German People and the Reformation* (Ithaca and London, 1988), 262–83.

24. See G. Menk, 'Die "zweite Reformation" in Hessen-Kassel: Landgraf Moritz und die Einführung der Verbesserungspunkte', in Schilling (ed.), *Die reformierte Konfessionalisierung in Deutschland*, 154–83; Hsia, *Social Discipline in the Reformation*, 35ff.

25. On Anhalt see IGJ 409–10; Cohn, 'Germany's Second Reformation', 138ff.

26. Schilling, *Konfessionskonflikt und Staatsbildung*, 25f., 176ff., 350ff., 365ff.; Cohn, 'Germany's Second Reformation', 156.

27. See K.-H. Blaschke, 'Religion und Politik in Kursachsen 1586–91', in Schilling (ed.), *Die reformierte Konfessionalisierung in Deutschland*, 79–97; T. Klein, *Der Kampf um die zweite Reformation in Kursachsen 1586–1591* (Cologne, 1962); F. L. Carsten, *Princes and Parliaments in Germany from the Fifteenth to the Eighteenth Century* (Oxford, 1959), 225–7; Hsia, *Social Discipline in the Reformation*, 30–1.

28. On Brandenburg see R. von Thadden, 'Die Fortsetzung des "Reformationswerks" in Brandenburg-Preussen', in Schilling (ed.), *Die reformierte Konfessionalisierung in Deutschland*, 233–50; B. Nischan, 'The Second Reformation in Brandenburg: Aims and Goals', *Sixteenth Century Journal*, 14 (1983), 173–87.

29. Cohn, 'Germany's Second Reformation', 150.

30. See above nn. 2ff.

31. On Maximilian II's response see Léonard, *Protestantism*, ii. 21ff.; N. G. Parker (ed.), *The Thirty Years' War* (London, 1984), 19ff., 25ff.

32. On France in general during this period see M. Greengrass, *The French Reformation* (Oxford, 1987), 38–80 and refs.; Léonard, *Protestantism*, ii. 109–71; J. H. M. Salmon, *Society in Crisis: France in the Sixteenth Century* (London, 1975), esp. 117ff.; M. Prestwich, 'Calvinism in France, 1555–1629', in Prestwich, *Int. Calv.* 71–107; N. M. Sutherland, *The Huguenot Struggle for Recognition* (New Haven, Conn., and London, 1980), 62ff.

33. See Ch. 16 nn. 53–4 and sources cited there.

34. Prestwich, 'Calvinism in France, 1555–1629', 71 ff., 84 ff., 90 ff.; see also S. Mours, *Les Églises réformées de France* (Paris, 1958); id., *Le Protestantisme en France au xvie siècle* (Paris, 1959), 101–85; Greengrass, *French Reformation*, 42–7.

35. Léonard, *Protestantism*, ii. 111–20; Greengrass, *French Reformation*, 47–54; Sutherland, *Huguenot Struggle*, 63–73.

36. Léonard, *Protestantism*, ii. 121–8; Sutherland, *Huguenot Struggle*, 73–136.

37. Léonard, *Protestantism*, ii. 128–32, 151 ff.; Salmon, *Society in Crisis*, 146–51, 169–77, 196–9; Sutherland, *Huguenot Struggle*, 137–231.

38. Léonard, *Protestantism*, ii. 142–4; Salmon, *Society in Crisis*, 183–7; N. M. Sutherland, *The Massacre of St. Bartholomew and the European Conflict 1559 1572* (London, 1973); J. Estèbe, *Tocsin pour un massacre: la saison des Saint-Barthélemy* (Paris, 1968); P. Benedict, 'The Saint Bartholomew's Massacre in the Provinces', *Historical Journal*, 21 (1978), 205–25; Prestwich, 'Calvinism in France, 1555–1629', 91 ff.; Greengrass, *French Reformation*, 78 ff.

39. Salmon, *Society in Crisis*, 187–9; R. E. Giesey, 'The Monarchomach Triumvirs: Hotman, Beza, and Mornay', *Bibliothèque d'humanisme et renaissance*, 32 (1970), 41–56; Skinner, *Foundations*, ii. 304 ff., as in the previous chapter.

40. Léonard, *Protestantism*, ii. 146–50; Prestwich, 'Calvinism in France, 1555–1629', 98–100; Salmon, *Society in Crisis*, 191–3.

41. Léonard, *Protestantism*, ii. 133–42; Salmon, *Society in Crisis*, 179–81; J. Garrisson-Estèbe, *Protestants du midi 1559–1598* (Toulouse, 1980), 142–3; detailed discussion in R. M. Kingdon, *Geneva and the Consolidation of the French Protestant Movement 1564–1572* (Geneva, 1967), 43–137; also in T. Maruyama, *The Ecclesiology of Theodore Beza* (Geneva, 1978), 80–105.

42. Léonard, *Protestantism*, ii. 153 ff.; Salmon, *Society in Crisis*, 234–73; Sutherland, *Huguenot Struggle*, 232–78; for the League's political ideas see F. J. Baumgartner, *Radical Reactionaries: The Political Thought of the French Catholic League* (Geneva, 1976); Skinner, *Foundations*, ii. 345 ff.

43. Léonard, *Protestantism*, ii. 159–71; Prestwich, 'Calvinism in France, 1555–1629', 100 ff.; Salmon, *Society in Crisis*, 291 ff.; Sutherland, *Huguenot Struggle*, 278–332; M. Greengrass, *France in the Age of Henri IV: The Struggle for Stability* (London, 1984), 1–87.

44. G. Parker, *The Dutch Revolt* (London, 1977), 30.

45. Ibid. 30–6.

46. A. Duke, 'Salvation by Coercion: The Controversy surrounding the "Inquisition" in the Low Countries on the Eve of the Revolt', in P. N. Brooks (ed.), *Reformation Principle and Practice: Essays in Honour of A. G. Dickens* (London, 1980), 140–51; id., 'Dissident Voices in a Conformist Town: The Early Reformation in Gouda', in S. Groenveld, M. E. H. Mout, and I. Schöffer (eds.), *Bestwurdes en geleerden ... aangeborden aan Prof. dr. J. J. Woltjer* (Dieren, 1985), 23 ff.; Léonard, *Protestantism*, ii. 77–8, 47; Parker, *Dutch Revolt*, 36–7.

47. A. Duke, 'The Ambivalent Face of Calvinism in the Netherlands, 1561–1618', in Prestwich, *Int. Calv.* 117–23; Léonard, *Protestantism*, ii. 78–80.

48. See E. M. Braekman, *Guy de Brès*, i. *Sa vie* (Brussels, 1960), esp. 122 ff.; Léonard, *Protestantism*, ii. 82–4; P. Mack Crew, *Calvinist Preaching and Iconoclasm in the Netherlands 1544–1569* (Cambridge, 1978), 51–82, points out that the Calvinist

effort was neither homogeneous nor the only form of protestantism in the region.

49. Léonard, *Protestantism*, ii. 81–2.

50. Duke, 'Salvation by Coercion', 137f., 152–6; Léonard, *Protestantism*, ii. 84ff.; Parker, *Dutch Revolt*, 41–72.

51. Mack Crew, *Calvinist Preaching and Iconoclasm*, 5–38; Léonard, *Protestantism*, ii. 88–9; Parker, *Dutch Revolt*, 72–117.

52. Duke, 'Ambivalent Face of Calvinism', 109–13; Parker, *Dutch Revolt*, 121–68.

53. Léonard, *Protestantism*, ii. 92–4; Parker, *Dutch Revolt*, 169–224.

54. Duke, 'Ambivalent Face of Calvinism', 128ff.

55. J. Guy, *Tudor England* (Oxford, 1988), 258ff.

56. For the post-1950s orthodoxy see J. E. Neale, *Elizabeth I and her Parliaments*, 2 vols. (London, 1953–7), i. 51–84; for the more recent version see N. L. Jones, *Faith by Statute: Parliament and the Settlement of Religion 1559* (London, 1982); W. S. Hudson, *The Cambridge Connection and the Elizabethan Settlement of 1559* (Durham, NC, 1980); see summaries in G. R. Elton, *The Parliament of England 1559–1581* (Cambridge, 1986), 199; Guy, *Tudor England*, 260–4, and W. J. Sheils, *The English Reformation 1530–1570* (London, 1989), 51–60.

57. N. L. Jones, 'Profiting from Religious Reform: The Land Rush of 1559', *Historical Journal* 22 (1979), 279–94; Elton, *Parliament of England*, 203f.; R. Houlbrooke, *Church Courts and the People during the English Reformation* (Oxford, 1979), 16ff.

58. P. Collinson, *The Elizabethan Puritan Movement* (London, 1967), 29ff.

59. For surprising insights into Parker's relations with Elizabeth see P. Collinson, *The Religion of Protestants: The Church in English Society 1559–1625* (Oxford, 1982), 35; on Grindal see P. Collinson, *Archbishop Grindal 1519–1583: The Struggle for a Reformed Church* (London, 1979), 217ff., and on 'exercises', 233ff.; also Collinson, *Elizabethan Puritan Movement*, 168–207; on Whitgift, ibid. 243ff.

60. C. Cross, *Church and People 1450–1660: The Triumph of the Laity in the English Church* (London, 1976), 137ff.; Collinson, *Elizabethan Puritan Movement*, 35ff., 68–83; Collinson, *Religion of Protestants*, 32ff.

61. Neale, *Elizabeth I and her Parliaments*, i. 165ff., 191ff., 291ff., 346ff., and ii. 58ff., 145ff., 216ff.; cf. Elton, *Parliament of England*, 205–16; M. A. R. Graves, *Elizabethan Parliaments 1559–1601* (London, 1987), 35ff., 47ff.; for detailed modifications attempted officially or unofficially to church worship, see Collinson, *Elizabethan Puritan Movement*, 360ff.

62. For full details on the 'Admonition Controversy' see P. Lake, *Anglicans and Puritans: Presbyterian and English Conformist Thought from Whitgift to Hooker* (London, 1988); Cross, *Church and People*, 141ff.; Collinson, *Elizabethan Puritan Movement*, 101–55.

63. Cross, *Church and People*, 148ff.; Collinson, *Elizabethan Puritan Movement*, 208–39, 333–467.

64. See above n. 61.

65. Cross, *Church and People*, 157ff.; Collinson, *Religion of Protestants*, 172–7.

66. Most spectacularly in London in 1625: see Cross, *Church and People*, 184–5.

67. Collinson, *Religion of Protestants*, 258f.; id., *Elizabethan Puritan Movement*, 372–82.

68. Cross, *Church and People*, 171ff.; Collinson, *Religion of Protestants*, 45ff.

69. J. Wormald, *Court, Kirk, and Community* (London, 1981), 110–15; G. Donaldson, *The Scottish Reformation* (Cambridge, 1960), 49–52; I. B. Cowan, *The Scottish Reformation*

(New York, 1982), 110–14; J. Kirk, *Patterns of Reform: Continuity and Change in the Reformation Kirk* (Edinburgh, 1989), 1–15.

70. Wormald, *Court, Kirk, and Community*, 115–17; Donaldson, *Scottish Reformation*, 53; Cowan, *The Scottish Reformation*, 115–20.

71. Wormald, *Court, Kirk, and Community*, 117–27; Donaldson, *Scottish Reformation*, 53–75; Cowan, *The Scottish Reformation*, 120ff.; J. K. Cameron, *The First Book of Discipline* (Edinburgh, 1972), *passim*. On the 'Calvinist' character of the settlement see Kirk, *Patterns of Reform*, 70–95; on 'superintendents', ibid. 154–231.

72. Donaldson, *Scottish Reformation*, 102–182; Cowan, *The Scottish Reformation*, 122ff.

73. Donaldson, *Scottish Reformation*, 183ff.; for the debate on the origins of the 'presbyterian' movement in the post-Reformation Scottish Church see e.g. Kirk, *Patterns of Reform*, 352ff.; G. Donaldson, *Scottish Church History* (Edinburgh, 1985), 92ff., 120ff., 178ff.

74. Wormald, *Court, Kirk, and Community*, 128ff.; Donaldson, *Scottish Reformation*, 203ff.; Cowan, *The Scottish Reformation*, 128ff.; J. Kirk (ed.), *The Second Book of Discipline* (Edinburgh, 1980), *passim*. The detailed emphasis to be laid on any particular event or actor in this drama is a topic of controversy whose ramifications cannot be developed here.

21. Reformers and Laymen: A Conflict of Priorities

1. See Ch. 15 nn. 206ff.

2. See e.g. H. Meylan, 'Le Recrutement et la formation des pasteurs dans les églises réformées du xvie siècle', in id., *D'Érasme à Théodore de Bèze* (Geneva, 1976), 248; S. C. Karant-Nunn, 'Luther's Pastors: The Reformation in the Ernestine Countryside', *Transactions of the American Philosophical Society*, 69/8 (1979), 8–10.

3. Meylan, 'Recrutement et la formation des pasteurs', 248, and see also Ch. 20.

4. See Ch. 2.

5. See Ch. 10. 2.

6. See the comments to this effect of G. Strauss, *Luther's House of Learning: Indoctrination of the Young in the German Reformation* (Baltimore, 1978), 306.

7. For England see e.g. R. O'Day, *The English Clergy: Emergence and Consolidation of a Profession, 1558–1642* (Leicester, 1979), 33ff.; for the reasons behind that development see Ch. 20 n. 57.

8. Karant-Nunn, 'Luther's Pastors', 13; but cf. R. W. Scribner, 'Practice and Principle in the German Towns: Preachers and People', in P. N. Brooks (ed.), *Reformation Principle and Practice: Essays in Honour of A. G. Dickens* (London, 1980), 106; Meylan, 'Recrutement et la formation des pasteurs', 252.

9. Scribner, 'Practice and Principle', 100.

10. Ibid. 103–4; cf. B. Vogler, 'Recrutement et carrière des pasteurs strasbourgeois au xvie siècle', *Revue d'histoire et de philosophie religieuses*, 48 (1968), 151–74.

11. Scriber, 'Practice and Principle', 105–6. Cf. these conclusions with B. Klaus, 'Soziale Herkunft und theologische Bildung lutherischer Pfarrer der reformatorischen Frühzeit', *Zeitschrift für Kirchengeschichte*, 80/1 (1969), 22–49.

12. Karant-Nunn, 'Luther's Pastors', 13. See also R. Po-Chia Hsia, *Social Discipline in the Reformation: Central Europe 1550–1750* (London, 1989), 14–19; and compare the post-Reformation Genevan Clergy, as in R. M. Kingdon, 'Calvin and the Government of Geneva', in W. H. Neuser (ed.), *Calvinus Ecclesiae Genevensis Custos: Die Referate*

des Congrès Internationale des Recherches Calviniennes [1982] (Frankfurt, 1984), 53ff.

13. Karant-Nunn, 'Luther's Pastors', 8–13.

14. See H. Kamen, *European Society 1500–1700* (London, 1984), 134, for one parent's attitude to a legal career; B. Vogler, *Le Clergé protestant rhénan au siècle de la réforme* (Paris, 1976), 18–19, 23, 26; Meylan, 'Recrutement et la formation des pasteurs', 252–5.

15. Vogler, *Clergé protestant rhénan*, 18, 21–3 and n. 26; Meylan, 'Recrutement et la formation des pasteurs', 255.

16. P. Collinson, *The Religion of Protestants* (Oxford, 1982), 115–17.

17. On Rhineland pastors' incomes see Vogler, *Clergé protestant rhénan*, 149–89; on their (continued) recourse to farming in rural areas, ibid. 191–226, and Hsia, *Social Discipline*, 17.

18. On common chests see Ch. 15. 7; on pastors' stipends Karant-Nunn, 'Luther's Pastors', 42–3; id., 'The Economic Position of Lutheran Pastors in Ernestine Thuringia, 1521–1555', *ARG* 63 (1972), 94–113; M. Brecht, 'Herkunft und Ausbildung der protestantischen Geistlichen des Herzogtums Württemberg im 16. Jahrhundert', *Zeitschrift für Kirchengeschichte*, 80/2 (1969), 163–75; compare Strauss, *Luther's House of Learning*, 374 n. 2.

19. Karant-Nunn, 'Luther's Pastors', 43–52.

20. On the Valtelline see E. Cameron, *The Reformation of the Heretics* (Oxford, 1984), 258 and n. 30.

21. O'Day, *The English Clergy*, 172–89; see also C. Cross, 'The Incomes of Provincial Urban Clergy, 1520–1645', in F. Heal and R. O'Day (eds.), *Princes and Paupers in the English Church 1500–1800* (Leicester, 1981), 65–89; M. Zell, 'Economic Problems of the Parochial Clergy in the sixteenth century', ibid. 32–41.

22. Cf. O'Day, *The English Clergy*, 159–60.

23. See Ch. 10 nn. 16–18.

24. Karant-Nunn, 'Luther's Pastors', 21–31.

25. Locher, *ZR* 161ff.; Stephens, *Zwingli*, 39–40; Meylan, 'Recrutement et la formation des pasteurs', 238.

26. O'Day, *The English Clergy*, 166–71; Collinson, *The Religion of Protestants*, 128–40 and refs.

27. I owe this example to the paper by Dr Mark Byford, 'What Price Rural Reformation? The Career of William Sheppard, Rector of Heydon 1541–1586', presented to the 1988 Reformation Studies Colloquium at Sheffield.

28. Karant-Nunn, 'Luther's Pastors', 11–12 and refs.

29. Vogler, *Clergé protestant rhénan*, 58ff., 66ff.

30. Meylan, 'Recrutement et la formation des pasteurs', 237, 240–1; Collinson, *The Religion of Protestants*, 94–5; O'Day, *The English Clergy*, 49–65, 132ff.; on Marburg see W. Falckenheimer, *Personen- und Ortsregister zu der Matrikel und den Annalen der Universität Marburg 1527–1652* (Marburg, 1904); on the Scottish case see J. K. Cameron, *The First Book of Discipline* (Edinburgh, 1972), 58–62, 137–55 and nn.

31. See L. Junod and H. Meylan, *L'Académie de Lausanne au xvi* siècle: Leges Scholae Lausannensis 1547* (Lausanne, 1947), 13.

32. On the Strasbourg *Gymnasium* see esp. A. Schindling, *Humanistische Hochschule und freie Reichsstadt: Gymnasium und Akademie in Strassburg, 1538–1621* (Wiesbaden, 1977); Junod and Meylan, *L'Académie de Lausanne*, 11–17.

33. On these projects of academic reform see E. Gailleur, *Histoire du collège de Guyenne* (Paris, 1874); M.-J. Gaufrès, *Claude Baduel et la réforme des études au xvie siècle* (Paris, 1880); J. Le Coultre, *Maturin Cordier et les origines de la pédagogie protestante dans les pays de langue française* (Neuchâtel, 1926).

34. On Lausanne see Junod and Meylan, *L'Académie de Lausanne*, *passim*; Meylan, 'Recrutement et la formation des pasteurs', 238; id., *La Haute École de Lausanne, 1537–1937* (2nd edn., Lausanne, 1986); H. Vuilleumier, *Histoire de l'église réformée du Pays de Vaud sous la régime bernois*, 4 vols. (Lausanne, 1927–33), i. 397–427.

35. On the Genevan academy see P.-F. Geisendorf, *L'Université de Genève 1559–1959: quatre siècles d'histoire* (Geneva, 1959), 19–87; S. and S. Stelling-Michaud (eds.), *Le Livre du recteur de l'académie de Genève* (Geneva, 1959–66), Léonard, *Protestantism*, i. 345–6, ii. 4–7; Meylan, 'Recrutement et la formation des pasteurs', 239; G. Lewis, 'Calvinism in Geneva in the Time of Calvin and of Beza (1541–1605)', in Prestwich, *Int. Calv.* 63ff.; also P. Fraenkel, *De l'écriture à la dispute, le cas de l'académie de Genève sous Théodore de Bèze* (Lausanne, 1977); C. Borgeaud, *Histoire de l'université de Genève*, i. *L'académie de Calvin 1559–1798* (Geneva, 1900); P.-D. Bourchenin, *Études sur les académies protestantes en France au xvie et au xviie siècles* (Paris, 1882), 86ff.

36. Bourchenin, *Études sur les académies protestantes en France*, 97–147; Meylan, 'Recrutement et la formation des pasteurs', 239; H. Meylan, 'Collèges et académies protestantes en France au xvie siècle', in id., *D'Érasme à Théodore de Bèze* (Geneva, 1976), 191–9.

37. See Ch. 20 n. 21.

38. V. Press, *Calvinismus und Territorialstaat: Regierung und Zentralbehörden der Kurpfalz 1559–1619* (Stuttgart, 1970), 320–1.

39. Vogler, *Clergé protestant rhénan*, 54–6.

40. Karant-Nunn, 'Luther's Pastors', 12.

41. M. Prestwich, 'Calvinism in France, 1555–1629', in id., *Int. Calv.* 86 and refs.

42. Karant-Nunn, 'Luther's Pastors', 52–6; Collinson, *The Religion of Protestants*, 100–14 and refs.

43. Cf. Collinson, *The Religion of Protestants*, 96–100.

44. See Ch. 7 n. 27.

45. See Ch. 8. 2.

46. As observed by Moeller, *Imperial Cities*, 93–5, for the case of Augsburg.

47. Karant-Nunn, 'Luther's Pastors', 22; *BSLK* 500–1, and cf. Luther's letters to Spalatin about that time, in *WA.B* iv. 605 and v. 46–7.

48. Karant-Nunn, 'Luther's Pastors', 52–4; *BSLK* 503–6; G. Strauss, 'Reformation and Pedagogy: Educational Thought and Practice in the Lutheran Reformation', in T and O *Holiness*, 280–1; Strauss, *Manifestations*, 227–31.

49. See Ch. 15. 3.

50. For the late medieval meaning of the term see J. Geffcken, *Der Bildercatechismus*, i. *Die zehn Gebote* (Leipzig, 1855), 16–22; for the 1520s alone see the collection ed. by F. Cohrs, *Die evangelischen Katechismusversuche vor Luthers Enchiridion*, 2 vols. (Berlin, 1900–2; repr. Hildesheim, 1978).

51. Edns. in *BSLK* 500–41, 545–73.

52. J. Brenz, *Catechismus Deutsch . . . für die Jugendt zu Schwebischen Hall . . .* (Nuremberg, 1550); id., *Catechismus pia et utili explicatione illustratus* (Frankfurt, 1551); W. Capito,

Kinder bericht und fragstuck, von gemeynen puncten Christlichs glaubens (Strasbourg, 1527).

53. Text in Sehling, xi. 206ff.; and in G. Müller and G. Seebass (eds.), *Osiander: Gesamtausgabe* (Gütersloh, 1975–), ii. 182ff. (text on 197–334).

54. *CO* 22. 85–96.

55. F. Wendel, *Calvin*, trans. P. Mairet (London, 1963), 52, 78–81; *CO* 6. 1–160.

56. Strauss, *Luther's House of Learning*, 164–5 and refs.

57. See Ch. 20. 2; text in A. C. Cochrane, *Reformed Confessions of the Sixteenth Century*. (London, 1966), 305–31. For England see T. Cranmer's translation of Justus Jonas's text: *A Catechism*, ed. D. G. Selwyn (Abingdon, 1976); see also *The Catechism of Thomas Becon S. T. P.*, ed. J. Ayre, Parker Society (Cambridge, 1844).

58. See Strauss, *Luther's House of Learning*, 161–2; cf. L. W. Spitz, 'Further Lines of Inquiry for the Study of "Reformation and Pedagogy"', in T and O *Holiness*, 302.

59. As for instance in the Heidelberg catechism.

60. *BSLK* 504; cf. Strauss, *Luther's House of Learning*, 169–75; also Strauss, 'Reformation and Pedagogy', 275 and refs.

61. e.g. the Heidelberg catechism is divided into 129 questions in groups for each of the 52 weeks in the year.

62. G. Strauss, 'The Mental World of a Saxon Pastor', in Brooks (ed.), *Reformation Principle and Practice*, 162–3.

63. Ibid. 164–5; Cameron, *Reformation of the Heretics*, 194–5, based on Bodleian Library, Oxford, MS Barlow 8. 513–20.

64. *BSLK* 505; Strauss, *Luther's House of Learning*, 165–8; cf. Collinson, *The Religion of Protestants*, 232–4.

65. Strauss, *Luther's House of Learning*, 168.

66. E. Cameron, 'The "Godly Community" in the Theory and Practice of the European Reformation', in W. J. Sheils and D. Woods (eds.), *Voluntary Religion*, *SCH* 23 (Oxford, 1986), 137–9, 142–6 and nn.; cf. G. Hammann, *Entre la secte et la cité: le projet d'église du réformateur Martin Bucer, 1491–1551* (Geneva, 1984).

67. Collinson, *The Religion of Protestants*, 242–73; id., 'The English Conventicle', in Sheils and Wood (eds.), *Voluntary Religion*, 223–59, and esp. 240ff.

68. See Ch. 8. 6.

69. Strauss, *Luther's House of Learning*, 214–22, 235–6.

70. Ibid. 203–14, 235–6; cf. Spitz, 'Further Lines of Inquiry', 295–8.

71. *BSLK* 504–5; Cameron, 'The "Godly Community"', 131f.

72. Strauss, *Luther's House of Learning*, 170–4; Strauss, 'Reformation and Pedagogy', 279; for a different estimate of the possible impact of Reformation catechising see S. E. Ozment, *When Fathers Ruled: Family Life in Reformation Europe* (Cambridge, Mass., 1983), 172ff.

73. Cameron, *Reformation of the Heretics*, 124ff.

74. On 'acculturation', see the debate between R. Muchembled and J. Wirth in von Greyerz, *Rel. and Soc.* 56–78.

75. See Ch. 8. 4.

76. As Erasmus (for one) had pointed out in *On the Freedom of the Will*: see E. G. Rupp and P. S. Watson (eds.), *Luther and Erasmus*, *LCC* 17 (London, 1959), 41f.

77. Sehling, i. 153; cf. 161–3.

78. Strauss, *Luther's House of Learning*, 236–8.

79. Ibid. 239; but cf. Vives's view of the ideal housewife, as in I. Maclean, *The Renaissance Notion of Woman: A Study in the Fortunes of Scholasticism and Medical Science in European Intellectual Life* (Cambridge, 1980), 59.

80. Strauss, *Luther's House of Learning*, 245–6.

81. T. N. Tentler, *Sin and Confession on the Eve of the Reformation* (Princeton, NJ, 1977), 229.

82. Cf. Ch. 8. 1.

83. e.g. Sehling, i. 153; Cameron, *Reformation of the Heretics*, 207.

84. Trinity College, Dublin, MS 259. 15–21, 59–61, as analysed in Cameron, *Reformation of the Heretics*, 205.

85. Strauss, *Luther's House of Learning*, 242 and refs.

86. An introduction to the subject is provided by M. Wiesner, 'Women's Response to the Reformation', in R. Po-Chia Hsia (ed.), *The German People and the Reformation* (Ithaca and London, 1988), 148–71. For a general discussion of the literature see J. Irwin, 'Society and the Sexes', in Ozment, *Guide*, 343–59.

87. P. A. Russell, *Lay Theology in the Reformation* (Cambridge, 1986), 186ff.; C. Bynum, *Jesus as Mother: Studies in the Spirituality of the High Middle Ages* (Berkeley, Calif., 1982), 172, 250; D. Herlihy, *Medieval Households* (Cambridge, Mass., 1985), 113ff.

88. Eileen Power, *Medieval Women*, ed. M. M. Postan (Cambridge, 1975), 89–99; E. McLaughlin, 'Equality of Souls, Inequality of Sexes: Women in Medieval Theology', in R. R. Ruether (ed.), *Religion and Sexism: Images of Woman in the Jewish and Christian Traditions* (New York, 1974), 213–66, esp. 236–45.

89. Ozment, *When Fathers Ruled*, 9–16; cf. the accusations of Erasmus cited in Ch. 4 n. 87.

90. Ozment, *When Fathers Ruled*, 16ff.; Bornkamm, *Mid-Career*, 258ff.

91. See Ch. 15 n. 166; however, it is hard to understand the mentality which made Katharine Bulkeley, abbess of Godstow, reassure Thomas Cromwell in 1538 that 'there is neither pope, purgatory, images nor pilgrimages nor praying to dead saints used amongst us': see L. B. Smith, *Tudor Prelates and Politics 1536–1558* (Princeton, NJ, 1953), 168.

92. Russell, *Lay Theology*, 204ff.; see also M. Chrisman, 'Women and the Reformation in Strasbourg 1490–1530', *ARG* 63 (1972), 143–68; R. H. Bainton, *Women of the Reformation in Germany and Italy* (Minneapolis, 1971), 55f.

93. N. L. Roelker, 'The Appeal of Calvinism to French Noblewomen in the Sixteenth Century', *Journal of Interdisciplinary History*, 2 (1971/2), 391–418; id., 'The Role of Noblewomen in the French Reformation', *ARG* 63 (1972), 168–95; J. H. M. Salmon, *Society in Crisis* (London, 1975), 120–1.

94. P. McNair, *Peter Martyr in Italy* (Oxford, 1967), 28–32; see Valdés's *Alfabeto Cristiano*, written in the form of a dialogue between the author and Giulia Gonzaga, in G. H. Williams (ed.), *Spiritual and Anabaptist Writers*, LCC 25 (London, 1957), 357ff. See also Bainton, *Women of the Reformation in Germany and Italy*.

95. Williams, 466ff.

96. R. A. Houlbrooke, *The English Family 1450–1700* (London, 1984), 111ff.; S. Heller Mendelson, *The Mental World of Stuart Women: Three Studies* (Brighton, 1987), esp. 80ff.

97. *The Catechism of Thomas Becon, S. T. P.*, ed. J. Ayre, Parker Society (Cambridge, 1844), 375ff.; see also Ch. 15 n. 189.

98. *Catechism of Thomas Becon*, 339.
99. Ibid. 87, 340, 357 ff.; cf. Ch. 19. 2.
100. See M. Todd, *Christian Humanism and the Puritan Social Order* (Cambridge, 1987).
101. See Ch. 15 nn. 206 ff.
102. Hsia, *Social Discipline*, 144 ff. for an intro. See also L. Roper, 'Going to Church and Street: Weddings in Reformation Augsburg', *P and P* 106 (1985), 62–101; id., *The Holy Household: Religion, Morals, and Order in Reformation Augsburg* (Oxford, 1989); M. E. Wiesner, 'Frail, Weak, and Helpless; Women's Legal Position in Theory and Reality', in J. Friedman (ed.), *Regnum, Religio et Ratio: Essays presented to Robert M. Kingdon* (Kirksville, Mo., 1987), 161–9; Ozment, *When Fathers Ruled*, 25 ff.; T. M. Safley, 'Civic Morality and the Domestic Economy', in Hsia (ed.), *The German People and the Reformation*, 172–92; see also T. Robisheaux, 'Peasants and Pastors: Rural Youth Control and the Reformation in Hohenlohe, 1540–1680', *Social History*, 6 (1981), 281–300.
103. See for instance L. B. Alberti, *The Family in Renaissance Florence*, ed. and trans. R. N. Watkins (Columbia, SC, 1969), esp. 155 ff.; Skinner, *Foundations*, i. 98–9 and refs.
104. On this topic see L. K. Little, *Religious Poverty and the Profit Economy in Medieval Europe* (London, 1978).
105. See Spitz, 'Further Lines of Inquiry', 304.
106. Strauss, *Luther's House of Learning*, 242–5.
107. See J. T. Noonan, *The Scholastic Analysis of Usury* (Cambridge, Mass., 1957), for the intricate casuistry on lending at interest in the late Middle Ages; note that great merchant families like the Fuggers of Augsburg were as committed investors in the old religious order as they were in the Habsburg dynasty.
108. A. Biéler, *La Pensée économique et sociale de Calvin* (Geneva, 1959), esp. 306 ff., 378 ff.; see the discussion in J. Delumeau, *Naissance et affirmation de la réforme* (3rd edn., Paris 1973), 299–314.
109. See for instance R. Houlbrooke, *Church Courts and the People during the English Reformation 1520–1570* (Oxford, 1979), 7 ff., 86 ff.
110. As in Tentler, *Sin and Confession*, 16 ff.
111. A classic (perhaps unfair) complaint of the feebleness of medieval penance was that of P. Stubbes, *The Anatomie of Abuses* (London, 1583), as cited by P. Hair, *Before the Bawdy Court: Selections from Church Court and other Records relating to the Correction of Moral Offences in England, Scotland and New England, 1300–1800* (London, 1972), 57; but cf. M. Ingram, *Church Courts, Sex and Marriage in England, 1570–1640* (Cambridge, 1987), 334 ff. and refs.
112. Houlbrooke, *Church Courts and the People*, 16–20; on 'godly' discipline see K. Wrightson and D. Levine, *Poverty and Piety in an English Village: Terling, 1525–1700* (London, 1979); and from a different viewpoint M. Ingram, 'Religion, Communities and Moral Discipline in Late Sixteenth- and Early Seventeenth-Century England: Case Studies', in von Greyerz, *Rel. and Soc.* 177–93; id., *Church Courts, Sex and Marriage*, 92 ff.
113. Sehling, i. 165–6, 204–7.
114. See Ch. 15 n. 206.
115. R. M. Kingdon, 'The Control of Morals in Calvin's Geneva', in L. P. Buck and J. W. Zophy (eds.), *The Social History of the Reformation* (Columbus, Ohio, 1972), 4.

116. On the workings of Genevan moral censure see W. Köhler, *Zürcher Ehegericht und Genfer Konsistorium* (Leipzig, 1932–42), ii. 568–626; Kingdon, 'Control of Morals', 12–16 and refs.; E. W. Monter, 'The Consistory of Geneva, 1559–1569', *Bulletin d'humanisme et renaissance*, 38 (1976), 467–84, estimates the average level of excommunication as 5 per week in the 1560s, though most cases ended in a reconciliation.

117. G. Lewis, 'Calvinism in Geneva in the Time of Calvin and Beza, 1541–1608', in Prestwich, *Int. Calv.* 48–52 and refs.; Monter, 'Consistory of Geneva', 483ff.

118. Ingram, *Church Courts, Sex and Marriage*, 278ff.; id., 'Religion, Communities and Moral Discipline', 184ff., 188ff.; Collinson, *The Religion of Protestants*; 227f.

119. See Ch. 1. 1.

120. See for instance *Inst.* IV. xii. 15–21.

121. See J. Delumeau, 'Les Réformateurs et la "superstition"', in Société de l'histoire du protestantisme français (ed.), *Actes du colloque l'Amiral de Coligny et son temps (Paris, 24–28 octobre 1972)* (Paris, 1974), 451–87 and esp. 459ff. For the treatment of superstition by the Genevan consistory see Monter, 'Consistory of Geneva', 475, 479–80; for that in Germany see R. W. Scribner, 'Ritual and Popular Religion in Catholic Germany at the Time of the Reformation', in Scribner, *PC and PM* 45ff.; cf. K. Thomas, *Religion and the Decline of Magic* (London, 1971), 58ff.

122. Strauss, *Luther's House of Learning*, 302–5 and refs.

123. Thomas, *Religion and the Decline of Magic*, 80–5.

124. Ibid. 74ff.; on the association between religious feasts and over-indulgence see for instance the English Proclamation of 1536 in A. G. Dickens and D. Carr (eds.), *The Reformation in England to the Accession of Elizabeth I* (London, 1967), 73–4. On hardening 'puritan' attitudes to theatre see P. Collinson, *The Birthpangs of Protestant England: Religious and Cultural Change in the Sixteenth and Seventeenth Centuries* (London, 1988), 99–106, 112–15.

125. R. W. Scribner, 'Reformation, Carnival, and the World Turned Upside-Down', in Scribner, PC and PM, and 73, 95 and refs.

126. Cameron, *Reformation of the Heretics*, 195–6 and refs.

127. e.g. Collinson, *The Religion of Protestants*, 224ff.; see also K. L. Parker, *The English Sabbath: A Study of Doctrine and Discipline from the Reformation to the Civil War* (Cambridge, 1988), esp. 41–138.

128. Cameron, *Reformation of the Heretics*, 179.

129. Cameron, 'The "Godly Community"', 138–9; *Martin Bucers deutsche Schriften*, ed. R. Stupperich, xvii (Gütersloh, 1981), 327–8; cf. J. M. Kittelson, 'Successes and Failures in the German Reformation: The Report from Strasbourg', *ARG* 73 (1982), 160, 167.

130. Collinson, *The Religion of Protestants*, 146–7, 221–4.

131. See sect. 21. 4.

132. Cf. Thomas, *Religion and the Decline of Magic*, 88–9.

133. *WA.B* v. 652; cf. vi. 346–8, 513; vii. 47–8; viii. 97–8; xi. 119–20; Strauss, *Luther's House of Learning*, 268ff.

134. Kittelson, 'Successes and Failures', 159.

135. Meylan, 'Recrutement et la formation des pasteurs', 255 and refs.

136. Karant-Nunn, 'Luther's Pastors', 54–5 and refs.; Cameron, *Reformation of the Heretics*, 258 and refs.

137. Strauss, *Luther's House of Learning*, 268–99; cf. id., 'Success and Failure in the

German Reformation', *P and P* 67 (1975), 30–63; and his defence of the argument in id., 'The Reformation and its Public in an Age of Orthodoxy', in Hsia (ed.), *The German People and the Reformation*, 194–214.

138. Collinson, *The Religion of Protestants*, 201–2, based on C. Haigh, 'Puritan Evangelism in the Reign of Elizabeth I', *EHR* 92 (1977), 48.

139. Cameron, *Reformation of the Heretics*, 179–80, 193–4, 232, based on Bodleian MS Barlow 8. 483, 491–511.

140. Kittelson, 'Successes and Failures', 158ff., 165ff.

141. B. Vogler, *Vie religieuse en pays rhénan dans la second moitié du xvi⁰ siècle (1556–1619)* (Lille, 1974), 650–743; Cameron, 'The "Godly Community"', 147f. and refs.

142. Ingram, *Church Courts, Sex and Marriage*, 116, 123, and 85–124 in general.

143. Cf. Kittelson, 'Successes and Failures', 155; and the comments of P. Laslett and M. Spufford cited in Collinson, *The Religion of Protestants*, 198. For a moderate position see B. Vogler, 'Die Entstehung der protestantischen Volksfrömmigkeit in der rhenischen Pfalz zwischen 1555 und 1619', *ARG* 72 (1981), 158–96.

144. Sehling, i. 12; *WA* xix. 75; Cameron, 'The "Godly Community"', 134–5; cf. Zwingli's observations of how few people of Zürich in 1523 were actually committed supporters of the reforming pastors, as in *Z* iii. 381ff., 405ff.

145. See above n. 66.

146. Cameron, 'The "Godly Community"', 143–6 and refs.

147. Collinson, *The Religion of Protestants*, 230–1.

148. See ibid., 239ff., and the numerous local studies cited there; for the accusation of sponsoring schism and division, see e.g. A. Peel (ed.), *The Seconde Parte of a Register*, 2 vols. (Cambridge, 1915), i. 231ff., 238ff.

149. Cf. the minimal evidence of such social division found by Ingram, *Church Courts, Sex and Marriage*, 94–5, 118–23.

150. Cf. the vision of 'puritanism' offered by such authorities as C. Hill, *Society and Puritanism in Pre-Revolutionary England* (London, 1964); and by M. Walzer, *The Revolution of the Saints: A Study in the Origins of Radical Politics* (London, 1966).

151. On the original 'Erastianism' see Léonard, *Protestantism*, ii. 23–4 and refs.; V. Press, *Calvinismus und Territorialstaat* (Stuttgart, 1970), 245–54; Cohn, 'Germany's Second Reformation', in Prestwich, *Int. Calv.* 159–60; C. Burchill, 'On the Consolation of a Christian Scholar: Zacharias Ursinus (1534–83) and the Reformation in Heidelberg', *JEH* 37 (1986), 573f.

Suggestions for Further Reading

A comprehensive bibliography of the European Reformation, even if it were confined to works published in the last quarter-century, would be considerably longer than the present book. Even a simple alphabetical list of all items cited in the references above would produce an indigestible and unhelpful catalogue of books and articles. Therefore these suggestions have the more modest aim of setting out a small, personal, and at times no doubt highly arbitrary selection of some of the tools, texts, and studies which have been found useful in preparing the present book, and which may guide a reader who wishes to follow the themes of this work further. They are grouped in sections approximately corresponding to the structure of the text, though inevitably some works will relate to more than one section. As in the references, works in English are given preference; English translations of works published in other languages are usually cited rather than their originals; foreign-language works are listed where these are basic to the topics concerned. Full-length books are in general cited in preference to specialized articles where appropriate. The suggestions are grouped under the following headings:

1. *Bibliographies and Guides*

1.1. *On the Reformation in general*

Archiv für Reformationsgeschichte: Literaturbericht [annual thematic survey of research publications].

OZMENT, S. E. (ed.), *Reformation Europe: A Guide to Research* (St Louis, Mo., 1982) [a series of wide-ranging bibliographical essays on research up to *c*.1980].

for some works published 1940–70, see:

Commission internationale d'histoire ecclésiastique comparée, *Bibliographie de la réforme, 1450–1648: ouvrages parus de 1940 à 1955* (Leiden, 1958–).

BAKER, D. (ed.) (for the British Subcommission of CIHEC as above) *The Bibliography of the Reform 1450–1648 relating to the United Kingdom and Ireland for the years 1955–70* (Oxford, 1975).

See also the bibliographical sections in:

DELUMEAU, J., *Naissance et affirmation de la réforme* (3rd edn., Paris, 1973).

LÉONARD, E. G., *A History of Protestantism*, ed. H. H. Rowley and trans. J. M. H. Reid and R. M. Bethell, 2 vols. (London, 1965–7) [the trans. is fuller and more accurate in this respect than the French original].

SCRIBNER, R. W., *The German Reformation* (London, 1986).

1.2. *Bibliographies, reviews, and guides to particular aspects*

ALAND, K., *Hilfsbuch zum Lutherstudium* (3rd rev. edn., Witten, 1970).

ATKINSON, J., 'Luther Studies', *JEH* 23 (1972), 69–77.

BENZING, J., *Lutherbibliographie: Verzeichnis der gedruckten Schriften Martin Luthers bis zu dessen Tod* (Baden-Baden, 1966).

BIGANE, J., and HAGEN, K., *Annotated Bibliography of Luther Studies, 1967–1976* (St Louis, Mo., 1977).

BURCHILL, C. J., 'The Urban Reformation and its Fate: Problems and Perspectives in the Consolidation of the German Protestant Movement', *Historical Journal*, 27 (1984), 997–1010.

FRAENKEL, P., and GRESCHAT, M., *Zwanzig Jahre Melanchthonsstudium: Sechs Literaturberichte (1945–1965)* (Geneva, 1967).

GÄBLER, U., *Huldrych Zwingli im 20. Jahrhundert* (Zürich, 1975).

GREEN, L. C., 'Luther Research in English-Speaking Countries since 1971', *Lutherjahrbuch*, 44 (1977), 105–26.

GREYERZ, K. VON, 'Stadt und Reformation: Stand und Aufgaben der Forschung', *ARG* 76 (1985), 6–64.

HSIA, R. PO-CHIA (ed.), *The German People and the Reformation* (Ithaca, NY, and London, 1988), 285–94.

——*Social Discipline in the Reformation: Central Europe 1550–1750* (London, 1989), 188–212.

KEMPFF, D., *A Bibliography of Calviniana 1959–1974*, *SMRT* 15 (Leiden, 1975).

McGRATH, A. E., *Reformation Thought: An Introduction* (Oxford, 1988), apps. 2 6 and bibl. (162–79, 184–207).

NIESEL, W., *Calvin-Bibliographie, 1901–1959* (Munich, 1961).

PIPKIN, H. W., *A Zwingli Bibliography* (Pittsburgh, 1972).

ROBBERT, G. S. (ed.), 'A Checklist of Luther's Writings in English', *Concordia Theological Monthly*, 36 (1965), 772–92, and 41 (1970), 214–20; *Concordia Journal*, 4 (1978), 73–7.

RUBLACK, H.-C., 'Forschungsbericht Stadt und Reformation', in B. Moeller (ed.), *Stadt und Kirche im 16. Jahrhundert* (Gütersloh, 1978), 9–26.

SCOTT, T., 'The Peasants' War: A Historiographical Review', *Historical Journal*, 22 (1979), 693–720, 953–74.

2. Sources

2.1 Editions of individual authors (including letters)

BLARER, A., and BLARER, T., *Briefwechsel der Brüder Ambrosius und Thomas Blarer (1509–1567)*, ed. T. Schiess, 3 vols. (Freiburg, 1908–12).

BUCER, M., *Martin Bucer: résumé sommaire de la doctrine chrétienne*, ed. F. Wendel (Paris, 1951).

——*Martini Buceri Opera Omnia*, ed. F. Wendel, E. Staehelin, R. Stupperich, J. Rott, and R. Peter (Gütersloh and Paris, 1960–) [separate German and Latin sequences].

——*Common Places of Martin Bucer*, ed. and trans. D. F. Wright (Abingdon, 1972).

——*Correspondance de M. Bucer*, ed. J. Rott, *SMRT* 25 (Leiden, 1979).

BUGENHAGEN, J., *Dr Johannes Bugenhagens Briefwechsel*, ed. O. Vogt (Stettin, 1888).

BULLINGER, H., *The Decades of Henry Bullinger*, trans. 'H.I.' and ed. T. Harding, 4 vols., Parker Society (Cambridge, 1849–52).

CALVIN, J., *Joannis Calvini Opera Quae Supersunt Omnia*, ed. G. Baum, E. Cunitz, and E. Reuss, *CR* 29–87 (Braunschweig and Berlin, 1853–1900).

Erasmi Epistolae, ed. P. S. and H. M. Allen, 12 vols. (Oxford, 1906–58).

LUTHER, M., *M. Luther, Werke: Kritische Gesamtausgabe*, 58 vols. [many sub-divided] (Weimar, 1883–1948) [in addition, there are separate sequences for the letters: *Briefwechsel*, 12 vols. (Weimar, 1930–67); the German Bible: *Die Deutsche Bibel* (Weimar, 1906–); the 'Table Talk': *Tischreden*, 6 vols. (Weimar, 1912–21).

—— *Luther's Works*, American edition, ed. J. Pelikan and H. T. Lehmann, 55 vols. (Philadelphia and St Louis, Mo., 1955–) [the largest series in English trans. of selected works by Luther].

—— *Martin Luther*, ed. E. G. Rupp and B. J. Drewery (London, 1970).

MELANCHTHON, P., *Philippi Melanchthonis Opera Quae Supersunt Omnia*, ed. C. G. Bretschneider *et al.*, *CR* 1–28 (Halle, 1834–60); also the *Supplementa Melanchthoniana*, 4 vols. (Leipzig, 1910–29) [works omitted from the *CR* edition].

—— *Melanchthons Werke in Auswahl*, ed. R. Stupperich (Gütersloh, 1951–).

—— *Melanchthon on Christian Doctrine: Loci Communes 1555*, ed. and trans. C. L. Manschreck (New York, 1965).

—— *Melanchthons Briefwechsel: Kritische und kommentierte Gesamtausgabe*, ed. H. Scheible (Stuttgart, 1977–).

MÜNTZER, T., *The Collected Works of Thomas Müntzer*, ed. and trans. P. Matheson (Edinburgh, 1988).

OECOLAMPADIUS, J., *Briefe und Akten zum Leben Oekolampads*, ed. E. Staehelin, 2 vols. (Leipzig, 1927–34).

OSIANDER, A., *Andreas Osiander: Gesamtausgabe*, ed. G. Müller and G. Seebass, 8 vols. (Gütersloh, 1975–).

POTTER, G. R., and GREENGRASS, M. (eds.), *John Calvin* (London, 1983).

ZWINGLI, H., *Huldreich Zwinglis Werke*, ed. M. Schuler and J. Schulthess, 8 vols. (Zürich, 1828–42).

—— *Huldreich Zwinglis sämtliche Werke*, ed. E. Egli *et al.*, *CR* 88 *et seq.* (Berlin, Leipzig, and Zürich, 1905–).

In addition, helpful translations of major reformers' works may be consulted in vols. 15–26 of the *Library of Christian Classics* series, covering Luther (vols. 15–18), Melanchthon's 1521 *Common Places* and Bucer's *Of the Kingdom of Christ* (vol. 19), Calvin (vols. 20–3), Zwingli and Bullinger (vol. 24), spiritualists and anabaptists (vol. 25), and English reformers (vol. 26).

2.2. *Collections of documents*

Die Bekenntnisschriften der evangelisch-Lutherischen Kirche, herausgegeben im Gedenkjahr der Augsburgischen Konfession 1930 (repr. Göttingen, 1976) [includes Melanchthon's *Augsburg Confession* and *Apology*, Luther's *Catechisms*, and the *Formula of Concord*].

COCHRANE, A. C., *Reformed Confessions of the Sixteenth Century* (London, 1966).

COHRS, F., *Die evangelischen Katechismusversuche vor Luthers Enchiridion*, 2 vols. (Berlin, 1900–2; repr. Hildesheim, 1978).

Conciliorum Oecumenicorum Decreta, ed. J. Alberigo *et al.* (3rd edn., Bologna, 1973).

DICKENS, A. G., and CARR, D. (eds.), *The Reformation in England to the Accession of Elizabeth I* (London, 1967).

FRANZ, G. (ed.), *Quellen zur Geschichte des Bauernkrieges* (Munich, 1963).

KIDD, B. J. (ed.), *Documents Illustrative of the Continental Reformation* (Oxford, 1911) [edns. of Latin and French texts, trans. of extracts in German].

Patrologia Latina, ed. J.-P. Migne, 221 vols. (Paris, 1844–90).

SCHEEL, O. (ed.), *Dokumente zu Luthers Entwicklung (bis 1519)* (2nd edn., Tübingen, 1929).

SEHLING, E. (ed.), *Die evangelischen Kirchenordnungen des XVI. Jahrhunderts*, i–v, (Leipzig, 1902–13); vi–viii, xi–xiii (Tübingen, 1955–).

3. *Textbooks, Surveys, Essays, and Symposia*

Many of the most important contributions to Reformation history in recent years have been in the form of collections of essays and articles. To save space contributions to such collections will not be cited individually in this bibliography. References to them are found in detail in the notes.

BÁTORI, I. (ed.), *Städtische Gesellschaft und Reformation* (Stuttgart, 1980)

BLICKLE, P., *Die Reformation im Reich* (Ulm, 1985).

——(ed.), *Revolte und Revolution in Europa: Referate und Protokolle der internationalen Symposiums zur Erinnerung an den Bauernkrieg 1525 (Memmingen, 24–27 März 1975), Historische Zeitschrift*, Neue Folge Beiheft 4 (1975).

——(ed.), *Bauer, Reich und Reformation: Festschrift für G. Franz* (Stuttgart, 1982).

——(ed.), *Zwingli und Europa: Referate und Protokoll des internationalen Kongresses aus Anlass des 500. Geburtstages von Huldrych Zwingli, 1984* (Zürich, 1985).

BOSSY, J., *Christianity in the West 1400–1700* (Oxford, 1985).

BROOKS, P. N. (ed.), *Reformation Principle and Practice: Essays in Honour of Arthur Geoffrey Dickens* (London, 1980).

BUCK, L. P., and ZOPHY, J. W. (eds.), *The Social History of the Reformation (in honor of H. J. Grimm)* (Columbus, Ohio, 1972).

CARGILL THOMPSON, W. D. J., *Studies in the Reformation: Luther to Hooker*, ed. C. W. Dugmore (London, 1980).

CHAUNU, P. (ed.) *The Reformation*, trans. V. Acland *et al.* (Gloucester, 1989).

DAVIS, N. Z., *Society and Culture in Early Modern France* (London, 1975).

DELUMEAU, J., *Naissance et affirmation de la réforme* (3rd edn., Paris, 1973).

DICKENS, A. G., *The German Nation and Martin Luther* (London, 1974).

FEBVRE, L., *Au coeur religieux du xvie siècle* (Paris, 1957).

FRIEDMAN, J. (ed.), *Regnum, Religio et Ratio: Essays Presented to Robert M. Kingdon* (Kirksville, Mo., 1987).

GREYERZ, K. VON (ed.), *Religion and Society in Early Modern Europe 1500–1800* (London, 1984).

HSIA, R. PO-CHIA (ed.), *The German People and the Reformation* (Ithaca, NY, and London, 1988).

ISERLOH, E., GLAZIK, J., and JEDIN, H., *Reformation and Counter Reformation*, trans. A. Biggs and P. W. Becker, vol. v of *History of the Church*, ed. H. Jedin and J. Dolan (London, 1980).

KÖHLER, H.-J. (ed.), *Flugschriften als Massenmedium der Reformationszeit: Beiträge zum Tübinger Symposium 1980* (Stuttgart, 1981).

KOURI, E. I., and SCOTT, T. (eds.), *Politics and Society in Reformation Europe: Essays for Sir Geoffrey Elton on his Sixty-Fifth Birthday* (London, 1987).

LAU, F., and BIZER, E., *A History of the Reformation in Germany to 1555*, trans. B. A. Hardy (London, 1969).

LÉONARD, E. G., *A History of Protestantism*, ed. H. H. Rowley and trans. J. M. H. Reid and R. M. Bethell, 2 vols. (London, 1965–7).

MOELLER, B., *Deutschland im Zeitalter der Reformation* (3rd edn., Göttingen, 1988).

—— (ed.), *Stadt und Kirche im 16. Jahrhundert* (Gütersloh, 1978).

MOMMSEN, W. J., ALTER, P., and SCRIBNER, R. W. (eds.), *Stadtbürgertum und Adel in der Reformation: Studien zur Sozialgeschichte der Reformation in England und Deutschland* (Stuttgart, 1979).

OBERMAN, H. A., *The Dawn of the Reformation* (Edinburgh, 1986).

—— (ed.), *Luther and the Dawn of the Modern Era: Papers of the 4th International Congress of Luther Research*, SMRT 8 (Leiden, 1974).

OLIN, J. C., SMART, D. S., and MCNALLY, R. E. (eds.), *Luther, Erasmus and the Reformation* (New York, 1969).

OZMENT, S. E., *The Age of Reform 1250–1550: An Intellectual and Religious History of Late Medieval and Reformation Europe* (New Haven, Conn., and London, 1980).

—— (ed.), *The Reformation in Medieval Perspective* (Chicago, 1971).

PRESTWICH, M. (ed.), *International Calvinism 1541–1715* (Oxford, 1985).

ROBINSON-HAMMERSTEIN, H. (ed.), *The Transmission of Ideas in the Lutheran Reformation* (Dublin, 1989).

SCRIBNER, R. W., *Popular Culture and Popular Movements in Reformation Germany* (London, 1987).

SKINNER, Q., *The Foundations of Modern Political Thought*, 2 vols. (Cambridge, 1978).

SPITZ, L. W., *The Protestant Reformation 1517–1559* (New York, 1986).

—— (ed.), *The Reformation: Basic Interpretations* (2nd edn., Lexington, Mass., 1972).

WOHLFEIL, R., *Einführung in die Geschichte der deutschen Reformation* (Munich, 1982).

In addition, use may still be made of older syntheses and textbooks such as those of R. H. Bainton, O. Chadwick. A. G. Dickens, H. J. Grimm, or H. Hillerbrand, to name but a few.

4. Works on Late Medieval and Renaissance Religion

4.1. General

AUBENAS, R., and RICARD, P., *L'Église et la renaissance (1449–1517)*, vol. xv of *Histoire de l'église*, ed. A. Fliche, V. Martin, and E. Jarry (Paris, 1951).

DELARUELLE, E., LABANDE, E. R., and OURLIAC, P., *L'Église au temps du grand schisme et de la crise conciliaire (1378–1449)*, vol. xiv of *Histoire de l'église*, ed. A. Fliche, V. Martin, and E. Jarry, 1 vol. in 2 pts. (Paris, 1962–4).

DOBSON, R. B. (ed.), *Church, Politics, and Patronage in the Fifteenth Century* (Gloucester, 1984).

HARPER-BILL, C., *The Pre-Reformation Church in England 1400–1530* (London, 1989).

OAKLEY, F., *The Western Church in the Later Middle Ages* (Ithaca, NY, and London, 1979).

RAPP, F., *L'Église et la vie religieuse en occident à la fin du moyen âge* (Paris, 1971).

SOUTHERN, R. W., *Western Society and the Church in the Middle Ages* (Harmondsworth, 1970), esp. 44ff., 133ff., 331ff.

SWANSON, R. N., *Church and Society in Late Medieval England* (Oxford, 1989).

4.2. Religion and the people (including heresy)

ADAM, P., *La Vie paroissiale en France au xive siècle* (Paris, 1964).

AUDISIO, G., *Les Vaudois du Luberon: une minorité en Provence (1460–1560)* (Mérindol, 1984).

BARTOS, F. M., *The Hussite Revolution 1424–1437*, trans. J. M. Klassen (New York, 1986).

CAMERON, E., *The Reformation of the Heretics: The Waldenses of the Alps 1480–1580* (Oxford, 1984), esp. 1–126.

CHIFFOLEAU, J., *La Comptabilité de l'au-delà: les hommes, la mort et la religion dans la région avignonnaise à la fin du moyen âge (1320–1480)* (Rome, 1980).

DUGGAN, L. G., 'Fear and Confession on the Eve of the Reformation', *ARG* 75 (1984), 153–75.

GALPERN, A. N., *The Religions of the People in Sixteenth-Century Champagne* (Cambridge, Mass., 1976).

HUDSON, A., *The Premature Reformation: Wycliffite Texts and Lollard History* (Oxford, 1988).

KAMINSKY, H., *A History of the Hussite Revolution* (Berkeley, Calif., 1967).

KIESSLING, R., *Bürgerliche Gesellschaft und Kirche in Augsburg im Spätmittelalter: Ein Beitrag zur Strukturanalyse der oberdeutschen Reichsstadt* (Augsburg, 1971).

MOELLER, B., 'Religious Life in Germany on the Eve of the Reformation', in G. Strauss (ed.), *Pre-Reformation Germany* (London, 1972), 13–42.

MONTER, E. W., *Ritual, Myth and Magic in Early Modern Europe* (Brighton, 1983).

MUCHEMBLED, R., *Popular Culture and Elite Culture in France 1400–1750*, trans. L. Cochrane (Baton Rouge, La., 1985).

OBELKEVICH, J. (ed.), *Religion and the People, 800–1700* (Chapel Hill, 1979).
O'NEIL, M., 'Magical Healing. Love Magic and the Inquisition in Late Sixteenth-Century Modena', in S. Haliczer (ed.), *Inquisition and Society in Early Modern Europe* (London, 1987), 88–114.
POST, R. R., *The Modern Devotion: Confrontation with Reformation and Humanism, SMRT* 3 (Leiden, 1968).
RAPP, F., *Réformes et réformation à Strasbourg: église et société dans le diocèse de Strasbourg (1450–1525)* (Paris, 1974).
SMAHEL, F., *La Révolution hussite, un anomalie historique* (Paris, 1985).
STRAUSS, G. (ed.), *Manifestations of Discontent in Germany on the Eve of the Reformation* (Bloomington, Ind., 1972).
TENTLER, T. N., *Sin and Confession on the Eve of the Reformation* (Princeton, NJ, 1977).
THOMAS, K., *Religion and the Decline of Magic: Studies in Popular Beliefs in Sixteenth- and Seventeenth-Century England* (London, 1971), esp. 3–89.
TOUSSAERT, J., *Le Sentiment religieux en Flandre à la fin du moyen-âge* (Paris, 1963).
TRINKAUS, C., and OBERMAN, H. A. (eds.), *The Pursuit of Holiness in Late Medieval and Renaissance Religion, SMRT* 10 (Leiden, 1974).

4.3. *The Church, its administration and personnel*

BLACK, A., *Council and Commune: The Conciliar Movement and the Fifteenth-Century Heritage* (London, 1979).
BOWKER, M., *The Secular Clergy in the Diocese of Lincoln 1495–1520* (Cambridge, 1968).
—— *The Henrician Reformation: The Diocese of Lincoln under John Longland 1521–47* (Cambridge, 1981).
GAZZANIGA, J.-L., *L'Église du midi à la fin du règne de Charles VII d'après la jurisprudence du parlement de Toulouse* (Paris, 1976).
HAMILTON THOMPSON, A., *The English Clergy and their Organization in the Later Middle Ages* (Oxford, 1947).
HAY, D., *The Church in Italy in the Fifteenth Century: The Birkbeck Lectures, 1971* (Cambridge, 1977).
HEATH, P., *The English Parish Clergy on the Eve of the Reformation* (London, 1969).
THOMSON, J. A. F., *Popes and Princes 1417–1517: Politics and Piety in the Late Medieval Church* (London, 1980).

4.4. *Dogma and theology*

BROWN, D. C., *Pastor and Laity in the Theology of Jean Gerson* (Cambridge, 1987).
DOUGLASS, E. J. D., *Justification in Late Medieval Preaching: A Study of John Geiler of Kaysersberg, SMRT* 1 (Leiden, 1966).

HAMM, B., *Frömmigkeitstheologie am Anfang des 16. Jahrhunderts: Studien zu Johannes von Paltz und seinem Umkreis* (Tübingen, 1982).

MCGRATH, A. E., *Intellectual Origins of the European Reformation* (Oxford, 1987).

OBERMAN, H. A., *The Harvest of Medieval Theology: Gabriel Biel and Late Medieval Nominalism* (Cambridge, Mass., 1963).

—— *Forerunners of the Reformation: The Shape of late Medieval Thought Illustrated by Key Documents* (2nd edn., Philadelphia, 1981).

—— *Masters of the Reformation: The Emergence of a New Intellectual Climate in Europe*, trans. D. Martin (Cambridge, 1981).

O'MALLEY, J. W., *Giles of Viterbo on Church and Reform: A Study in Renaissance Thought SMRT* 5 (Leiden, 1968).

OZMENT, S. E., *Homo Spiritualis: A Comparative Study of the Anthropology of Johannes Tauler, Jean Gerson, and Martin Luther (1509–16) in the Context of their Theological Thought, SMRT* 6 (Leiden, 1969).

PASCOE, L. B., *Jean Gerson: Principles of Church Reform, SMRT* 7 (Leiden, 1973).

PELIKAN, J. J., *Reformation of Church and Dogma (1300–1700), vol. iv of The Christian Tradition* (Chicago, 1984).

STEINMETZ, D. C., *Misericordia Dei: The Theology of Johannes von Staupitz in its Late Medieval Setting, SMRT* 4 (Leiden, 1968).

—— 'Libertas Christiana: Studies in the Theology of John Pupper of Goch (d. 1475)', *HThR* 65 (1972), 191–230.

ULLMANN, K. H., *Reformers before the Reformation*, trans. R. Menzies, 2 vols. (Edinburgh, 1855) [remains useful for extended extracts from primary sources despite obsolete line of argument].

4.5. The Renaissance and humanism

BOYLE, M. O'R., *Rhetoric and Reform: Erasmus's Civil Dispute with Luther* (Cambridge, Mass., 1983).

—— 'Erasmus and the "Modern" Question: Was he Semi-Pelagian?', *ARG* 75 (1984), 59–72.

GROSSMANN, M., *Humanism at Wittenberg 1485–1517* (Nieuwkoop, 1975).

L'Humanisme allemand 1480–1540: 18ᵉ colloque international de Tours (Munich and Paris, 1979).

MURPHY, J. (ed.), *Renaissance Eloquence: Studies in the Theory and Practice of Renaissance Rhetoric* (Berkeley, Calif., 1983).

OVERFIELD, J. H., *Humanism and Scholasticism in Late Medieval Germany* (Princeton, NJ, 1984).

RENAUDET, A., *Préréforme et humanisme à Paris pendant les premières guerres d'Italie (1494–1517)* (2nd edn., Paris, 1953).

SPITZ, L. W., *The Religious Renaissance of the German Humanists* (Cambridge, Mass., 1963).

TRINKAUS, C., *The Scope of Renaissance Humanism* (Ann Arbor, Mich., 1983).

5. *Works on the Reformers and their Teachings*

5.1. *Comprehensive surveys of doctrine as a whole*

McGRATH, A. E., *Reformation Thought: An Introduction* (Oxford, 1988).

REARDON, B. M. G., *Religious Thought in the Reformation* (London, 1981).

STROHL, H., *La Pensée de la réforme* (Neuchâtel and Paris, 1951).

5.2. *Studies of a particular individual's life and teachings*

5.2.1. *Luther*

ALTHAUS, P., *The Theology of Martin Luther*, trans. R. C. Schultz (Philadelphia, 1966).

BAINTON, R. H., *Here I Stand: A Life of Martin Luther* (New York, 1950).

BIZER, E., *Fides ex Auditu: Eine Untersuchung über die Entdeckung der Gerechtigkeit Gottes durch Martin Luther* (2nd edn., Neukirchen, 1961).

BOEHMER, H., *Martin Luther: Road to Reformation*, trans. J. W. Doberstein and T. G. Tappert (Philadelphia, 1946).

BORNKAMM, H., *Luther in Mid-Career 1521–1530*, ed. K. Bornkamm and trans. E. T. Bachmann (London, 1983).

BRECHT, M., *Martin Luther: His Road to Reformation 1483–1521*, trans. J. L. Schaaf (Philadelphia, 1985).

EBELING, G., *Luther: An Introduction to his Thought*, trans. R. A. Wilson (London, 1970).

EDWARDS, M. U., *Luther and the False Brethren* (Stanford, Calif., 1975).

—— *Luther's Last Battles* (Leiden, 1983).

FIFE, R. H., *The Revolt of Martin Luther* (New York, 1957).

GERRISH, B. A., *Grace and Reason: A Study in the Theology of Luther* (Oxford, 1962).

GREEN, L. C., *How Melanchthon helped Luther discover the Gospel* (Fallbrook, Calif., 1980).

HARRAN, M. J., *Luther on Conversion: The Early Years* (Ithaca, NY, 1983).

LOHSE, B., *Martin Luther: An Introduction to his Life and Thought* (Edinburgh, 1987).

McGRATH, A. E., *Luther's Theology of the Cross: Martin Luther's Theological Breakthrough* (Oxford, 1985).

OBERMAN, H. A., *Luther: Mensch zwischen Gott und Teufel* (Berlin, 1982).

SIGGINS, I. D. K., *Martin Luther's Doctrine of Christ* (New Haven, Conn., 1970).

STEINMETZ, D. C., *Luther and Staupitz: An Essay in the Intellectual Origins of the Protestant Reformation* (Durham, NC, 1980).

—— *Luther in Context* (Bloomington, Ind., 1986).

5.2.2. *Other reformers*

BARTHEL, P., SCHEURER, R., and STAUFFER, R. (eds.), *Actes du colloque Guillaume Farel*, 2 vols. (Geneva, 1983).

BONORAND, C., *Vadians Weg vom Humanismus zur Reformation* (St Gallen, 1962).

DELIUS, W., *Lehre und Leben, Justus Jonas 1493–1555* (Gütersloh, 1952).

DUFFIELD, G. (ed.), *John Calvin* (Abingdon, 1966).

EELLS, H., *Martin Bucer* (New Haven, Conn., and London, 1931).

EIRE, C. M. N., *War Against the Idols: The Reformation of Worship from Erasmus to Calvin* (Cambridge, 1986).

[Comité Farel], *Guillaume Farel, biographie nouvelle* (Neuchâtel and Paris, 1930).

GANOCZY A., *The Young Calvin*, trans. D. Foxgrover and W. Provo (Edinburgh, 1987).

GRIMM, H. J., *Lazarus Spengler, A Lay Leader of the Reformation* (Columbus, Ohio, 1978).

HILDEBRANDT, F., *Melanchthon: Alien or Ally?* (Cambridge, 1946).

HÖPFL, H., *The Christian Polity of John Calvin* (Cambridge, 1982).

JACOBS, E., *Die Sakramentslehre Wilhelm Farels* (Zürich, 1978).

KENDALL, R. T., *Calvin and English Calvinism to 1649* (Oxford, 1979).

KITTELSON, J. M., *Wolfgang Capito: From Humanist to Reformer*, SMRT 17 (Leiden, 1975).

KÖHLER, W., *Huldrych Zwingli* (2nd edn., Stuttgart, 1952).

LOCHER, G. W., *Die Zwinglische Reformation im Rahmen der europäischen Kirchengeschichte* (Göttingen and Zürich, 1979), esp. 55–363, 502–53.

——*Zwingli's Thought: New Perspectives*, Studies in the History of Christian Thought, 25 (Leiden, 1981).

McNAIR, P., *Peter Martyr in Italy: An Anatomy of Apostasy* (Oxford, 1967).

MANSCHRECK, C. L., *Melanchthon, the Quiet Reformer* (New York, 1958).

MAURER, W., *Der junge Melanchthon zwischen Humanismus und Reformation*, 2 vols. (Göttingen, 1967–9).

NÄF, W., *Vadian und seine Stadt St Gallen*, 2 vols. (St Gallen, 1944–57).

NIESEL, W., *The Theology of Calvin*, trans. H. Knight (Philadelphia, 1956).

PARKER, T. H. L., *John Calvin* (London, 1975).

POTTER, G. R., *Zwingli* (Cambridge, 1976).

RUPP, G., *Patterns of Reformation* (London, 1969) [biographical essays on Oecolampadius, Karlstadt, Müntzer, and Vadianus].

SIDER, R. J., *Andreas Bodenstein von Karlstadt: The Development of his Thought 1517–1525*, SMRT 11 (Leiden, 1974).

STAEHELIN, E., *Das theologische Lebenswerk Johannes Oekolampads* (Leipzig, 1939).

STEPHENS, W. P., *The Holy Spirit in the Theology of Martin Bucer* (Cambridge, 1970).

——*The Theology of Huldrych Zwingli* (Oxford, 1986).

STUPPERICH, R., *Melanchthon*, trans. R. Fischer (London, 1966).

WENDEL, F., *Calvin: The Origins and Development of his Religious Thought*, trans. P. Mairet (London, 1963).

6. Works on the Political Background and Establishment of the Reformation

6.1. The German knights

HITCHCOCK, W. R., *The Background of the Knights' Revolt 1522–1523* (Berkeley, Calif., 1958).

HOLBORN, H., *Ulrich von Hutten and the German Reformation*, trans. R. H. Bainton (New Haven, Conn., 1937).

PRESS, V., *Kaiser Karl V, König Ferdinand und die Entstehung der Reichsritterschaft* (Wiesbaden, 1976).

RÖSSLER, H. (ed.), *Der deutsche Adel 1430–1555* (Darmstadt, 1965).

6.2. The Peasants' War

BAK, J. (ed.), *The German Peasant War of 1525* (London, 1975).

BLICKLE, P., 'Peasant Revolts in the German Empire in the Late Middle Ages', *Social History*, 4 (1979), 223–39.

—— *The Revolution of 1525*, ed. and trans. T. A. Brady and H. C. E. Midelfort (2nd edn., Baltimore, 1985).

—— *Gemeindereformation: Die Menschen des 16. Jahrhunderts auf dem Weg zum Heil* (Munich, 1985).

CONRAD, F., *Reformation in der bäuerlichen Gesellschaft: Zur Rezeption reformatorischer Theologie in Elsass* (Wiesbaden, 1984).

FRANZ, G., *Der deutsche Bauernkrieg* (11th edn., Darmstadt, 1977).

KOLB, R., 'The Theologians and the Peasants', *ARG* 69 (1978), 103–30.

SCOTT, T., 'Reformation and Peasants' War in Waldshut and Environs: A Structural Analysis', *ARG* 69 (1978), 82–102, and 70 (1979) 140–68.

—— *Freiburg and the Breisgau: Town–Country Relations in the Age of Reformation and Peasants' War* (Oxford, 1986).

SCRIBNER, R. W., and BENECKE, G. (eds.), *The German Peasant War of 1525: New Viewpoints* (London, 1979).

SESSIONS, K. C. (ed.), *Reformation and Authority: The Meaning of the Peasants' Revolt* (Lexington, Mass., 1968).

6.3. Free cities and city-states

ABRAY, L. J., *The People's Reformation: Magistrates, Clergy and Commons in Strasbourg 1500–1598* (Oxford, 1985).

BARON, H., 'Religion and Politics in the German Imperial Cities during the Reformation', *EHR* 52 (1937), 405–27, 614–33.

450 Jahre Berner Reformation: Beiträge zur Geschichte der berner Reformation und zu Niklaus Manuel (Berne, 1980).

BIRNBAUM, N., 'The Zwinglian Reformation in Zurich', *P and P* 15 (1959), 27–47.

BORNERT, R., *La Réforme protestante du culte à Strasbourg au xvie siècle (1523–1598): approche sociologique et interprétation théologique*, *SMRT* 28 (Leiden, 1981).

BRADY, T. A., *Ruling Class, Regime and Reformation at Strasbourg, 1520–1555*, *SMRT* 22 (Leiden, 1978).

——— *Turning Swiss: Cities and Empire, 1450–1550* (Cambridge, 1985).

CHRISMAN, M. U., *Strasbourg and the Reform: A Study in the Process of Change* (New Haven, Conn., 1967).

DEMANDT, D., and RUBLACK, H.-C., *Stadt und Kirche in Kitzingen: Darstellungen und Quellen zu Spätmittelalter und Reformation* (Stuttgart, 1978)

GOERTZ, H.-J., *Pfaffenhass und gross Geschrei: Die reformatorischen Bewegungen in Deutschland 1517–1529* (Munich, 1987).

GREYERZ, K. VON, *The Late City Reformation in Germany: The Case of Colmar, 1522–1628* (Wiesbaden, 1980).

GUGGISBERG, H. R., *Basel in the Sixteenth Century* (St Louis, Mo., 1982).

HALL, B., 'The Reformation City', *Bulletin of the John Rylands Library*, 54 (1971), 103–48.

HOFACKER, H.-G., 'Die Reformation in der Reichsstadt Ravensburg', *Zeitschrift für Württembergische Landesgeschichte*, 29 (1970), 71–125.

KARANT-NUNN, S. C., *Zwickau in Transition 1500–1547: The Reformation as an Agent of Change* (Columbus, Ohio, 1987).

LOCHER, G. W., *Die Zwinglische Reformation im Rahmen der europäischen Kirchengeschichte* (Göttingen and Zürich, 1979), esp. 364–499.

MOELLER, B., *Johannes Zwick und die Reformation in Konstanz* (Gütersloh, 1961).

——— 'Zwinglis Disputationen: Studien zu den Anfangen der Kirchenbildung und des Synodalwesens im Protestantismus', *Zeitschrift der Savigny-Stiftung für Rechtsgeschichte*, Kanonistische Abteilung 56 (1970), 275–324; 60 (1974), 213–364.

——— 'Kleriker als Bürger', in *Festschrift für Hermann Heimpel zu 70. Geburtstag am 19.9.1971*, 2 vols. (Göttingen, 1971–2), ii. 195–224.

——— *Imperial Cities and the Reformation: Three Essays*, ed. and trans. H. C. E. Midelfort and M. U. Edwards (Philadelphia, 1972).

MONTER, E. W., *Calvin's Geneva* (New York, 1967).

MÖRKE, O., *Rat und Bürger in der Reformation: Sozialen Gruppen und kirchlicher Wandel in den welfischen Hansestädten Lüneburg, Braunschweig und Göttingen* (Hildesheim, 1983).

MÜLLER, G., *Reformation und Stadt: Zur Rezeption der evangelischen Verkündigung*, Akademie der Wissenschaften und der Literatur (Mainz, 1981).

NAEF, H., *Les Origines de la réforme à Genève*, 2 vols. (Geneva, 1968).

NÄF, W., *Vadian und seine Stadt St Gallen*, 2 vols. (St Gallen, 1944–57).

NAUJOKS, E., *Obrigkeitsgedanke, Zunftverfassung und Reformation: Studien zur*

Verfassungsgeschichte von Ulm, Esslingen und Schwäbisch Gmünd (Stuttgart, 1958).

—— *Kaiser Karl V und die Zunftverfassung: Ausgewählte Aktenstücke zu den Verfassungsänderungen in den oberdeutschen Reichsstädten (1547–1555)* (Stuttgart, 1985).

OZMENT, S. E., *The Reformation in the Cities: The Appeal of Protestantism to Sixteenth-Century Germany and Switzerland* (New Haven, Conn., and London, 1975).

ROTH, F., *Augsburgs Reformationsgeschichte*, 4 vols. (Munich, 1901–11).

RUBLACK, H.-C., *Die Einführung der Reformation in Konstanz* (Gütersloh, 1971).

—— 'Die Stadt Würzburg im Bauerknkrieg', *ARG* 67 (1976), 76–100.

—— *Gescheiterte Reformation: Frühreformatorische und protestantische Bewegungen in süd- und westdeutschen geistlichen Residenzen* (Stuttgart, 1978).

—— 'Nördlingen zwischen Kaiser und Reformation', *ARG* 71 (1980), 113–33.

SCHILDAUER, J. J., *Soziale, politische und religiöse Auseinandersetzungen in den Hansestädten Stralsund, Rostock und Wismar im ersten Drittel der 16. Jahrhunderts* (Weimar, 1959).

SCHILLING, H., 'The Reformation in the Hanseatic Cities', *Sixteenth Century Journal*, 14 (1983), 443–56.

SCHMIDT, H.-R., *Reichsstädte, Reich und Reformation: Korporative Religionspolitik 1521–1529/30* (Stuttgart, 1986).

STAFFORD, W. S., *Domesticating the Clergy: The Inception of the Reformation in Strasbourg 1522–1524* (Missoula, Mont., 1976).

STRAUSS, G., *Nuremberg in the Sixteenth Century* (New York, 1966), esp. 154–86.

TÜCHLE, H., 'Die oberschwäbischen Reichsstädte Leutkirch, Isny und Wangen im Jahrhundert der Reformation', *Zeitschrift für Württembergische Landesgeschichte*, 29 (1970), 53–70.

VOGLER, G., *Nürnberg 1524/25: Studien zur Geschichte der reformatorischen und sozialen Bewegung in der Reichsstadt* (Berlin, 1982).

VUILLEUMIER, H., *Histoire de l'église réformée du Pays de Vaud sous la régime bernois*, 4 vols. (Lausanne, 1927–33).

WALTON, R. C., *Zwingli's Theocracy* (Toronto, 1967).

WARMBRUNN, P., *Zwei Konfessionen in einer Stadt: Das Zusammenleben von Katholiken und Protestanten in den paritätischen Reichsstädten Augsburg, Biberach, Ravensburg und Dinkelsbühl von 1546–1648* (Wiesbaden, 1983).

WHALEY, J., *Religious Toleration and Social Change in Hamburg* (Cambridge, 1985).

6.4. *Principalities and kingdoms*

ANGERMEIER, H., *Die Reichsreform 1410–1555: Die Staatsproblematik in Deutschland zwischen Mittelalter und Gegenwart* (Munich, 1984).

BUCSAY, M., *Geschichte des Protestantismus in Ungarn* (Stuttgart, 1959).

—— *Der Protestantismus in Ungarn 1521–1978*, 2 vols. (Vienna, 1977–9).

CARSTEN, F. L., *Princes and Parliaments in Germany from the Fifteenth to the Eighteenth Century* (Oxford, 1959).

COHN, H. J. (ed.), *Government in Reformation Europe 1520–1560* (London, 1971).

COWAN, I. B., *The Scottish Reformation: Church and Society in Sixteenth-Century Scotland* (New York, 1982).

CROSS, C., *Church and People 1450–1660* (London, 1976).

DAVIES, N., *God's Playground: A History of Poland*, 2 vols. (Oxford, 1982).

DICKENS, A. G., *The English Reformation* (London, 1963).

DONALDSON, G., *The Scottish Reformation* (Cambridge, 1960).

DUNKLEY, E. H., *The Reformation in Denmark* (London, 1949).

ELTON, G. R., *Policy and Police: The Enforcement of the Reformation in the Age of Thomas Cromwell* (Cambridge, 1972).

FABIAN, E., *Die Enstehung des schmalkaldischen Bundes und seiner Verfassung 1529–1531/3* (Tübingen, 1956).

FEDERORWICZ, J. K., BOGUCKA, M, and SAMSONOWICZ, H. (eds.), *A Republic of Nobles: Studies in Polish History to 1864* (Cambridge, 1982).

FISHER-GALATI, S. A., *Ottoman Imperialism and German Protestantism* (Cambridge, Mass., 1959).

GREENGRASS, M., *The French Reformation* (Oxford, 1987).

GUY, J., *Tudor England* (Oxford, 1988).

HAIGH, C. (ed.), *The English Reformation Revised* (Cambridge, 1987).

HARTUNG, F., *Karl V und die deutschen Reichsstände von 1546–1555* (Darmstadt, 1971).

HELLER, H., *The Conquest of Poverty: The Calvinist Revolt in Sixteenth-Century France* (Leiden, 1985).

HUBATSCH, W., Albrecht von Brandenburg-Ansbach, Deutschordens-Hochmeister und Herzog in Preussen 1490–1568 (Heidelberg, 1960)

——*Geschichte der evangelischen Kirche Ostpreussens*, 3 vols. (Göttingen, 1968).

KNECHT, R. J., *Francis I* (Cambridge, 1982).

MĄCZAK, A., SAMSONOWICZ, H., and BURKE, P. (eds.), *East-Central Europe in Transition from the Fourteenth to the Seventeenth Century* (Cambridge, 1985).

MAKKAI, L., *Histoire de Transylvanie* (Paris, 1946).

RABE, H., *Reichsbund und Interim: Die Verfassungs- und Religionspolitik Karls V und der Reichstag zu Augsburg 1546/48* (Cologne, 1971).

REDDAWAY, W. F., et al., *The Cambridge History of Poland to 1696* (Cambridge, 1950).

ROBERTS, M., *The Early Vasas: A History of Sweden, 1523–1611* (Cambridge, 1968).

ROTH, E., *Die Geschichte des Gottesdienstes der siebenbürger Sachsen* (Göttingen, 1954).

SALMON, J. H. M., *Society in Crisis: France in the Sixteenth Century* (London, 1975).

SCARISBRICK, J. J., *The Reformation and the English People* (Oxford, 1984).

SHEILS, W. J., *The English Reformation 1530–1570* (London, 1989).

SUTHERLAND, N. M., *The Huguenot Struggle for Recognition* (New Haven, Conn., 1980).

WIESFLECKER, H., *Kaiser Maximilian I: Das Reich, Österreich und Europa an der Wende der Neuzeit*, 5 vols. (Munich, 1971–86).

WORMALD, J., *Court, Kirk and Community: Scotland 1470–1625* (London, 1981).

6.5. Communication, propaganda, and persuasion

BERTHOUD, G., *et al.*, *Aspects de la propagande religieuse* (Geneva, 1957).

CHRISMAN, M. U., *Lay Culture, Learned Culture: Books and Social Change in Strasbourg, 1480–1599* (New Haven, Conn., 1982).

DICKENS, A. G., and TONKIN, J. M. *The Reformation in Historical Thought* (Oxford, 1986).

EISENSTEIN, E., *The Printing Press as an Agent of Change*, 2 vols. (Cambridge, 1979).

FEBVRE, L., and MARTIN, H.-J., *The Coming of the Book*, trans. D. Gerard (London, 1976).

GAWTHROP, R., and STRAUSS, G., 'Protestantism and Literacy in Early Modern Germany', *P and P* 104 (1984), 31–55.

GILMONT, J.-F., *Jean Crespin: un éditeur réformé du xvie siècle* (Geneva, 1981).

HIRSCH, R., *Printing, Selling and Reading 1450–1550* (Wiesbaden, 1974).

MOELLER, B., 'Was wurde in der Frühzeit der Reformation in den deutschen Städten gepredigt?', *ARG* 75 (1984), 176–93.

RUSSELL, P. A., *Lay Theology in the Reformation: Popular Pamphleteers in Southwest Germany 1521–1525* (Cambridge, 1986).

SCRIBNER, R. W., *For the Sake of Simple Folk: Popular Propaganda for the German Reformation* (Cambridge, 1981).

7. Anabaptist and Sectarian Movements

BENDER, H. S., *Conrad Grebel, c.1498–1526, the founder of the Swiss Brethren, Sometimes called Anabaptists* (Goschen, Ind., 1950).

BLANKE, F., *Brothers in Christ: The History of the Oldest Anabaptist Congregation, Zollikon, near Zurich, Switzerland*, trans. J. Nordenhaug (Scottdale, Pa., 1961).

CLASEN, C.-P., *Anabaptism: A Social History, 1525–1618* (London, 1972).

DEPPERMANN, K., *Melchior Hoffman: Social Unrest and Apocalyptic Visions in the Age of Reformation*, trans. M. Wren and ed. B. J. Drewery (Edinburgh, 1987).

EBERT, K., *Thomas Müntzer: Von Eigensinn und Widerspruch* (Frankfurt, 1987).

ELLIGER, W., *Thomas Müntzer: Leben und Werke* (3rd edn., Göttingen, 1976).

GASTALDI, U., *Storia dell'Anabattismo*, 2 vols. (Turin, 1972–81).

GOERTZ, H.-J., *Die Täufer: Geschichte und Deutung* (Munich, 1980).

——(ed.), *Umstrittenes Täufertum, 1525–1975: Neue Forschungen* (Göttingen, 1975).

GRITSCH, E., *Reformer without a Church: The Life and Thought of Thomas Müntzer* (Philadelphia, 1967).
—— *Thomas Müntzer: A Tragedy of Errors* (Minneapolis, 1989).
GROSS, T. L., *The Golden Years of the Hutterites: The Witness and Communal Thought of the Communal Moravian Anabaptists during the Walpot Era, 1565–78* (Scottdale, Pa., 1980).
KEENEY, W. E., *The Development of Dutch Anabaptist Thought and Practice from 1539 to 1564* (Nieuwkoop, 1968).
KOT, S., *Socinianism in Poland: The Social and Political Ideas of the Polish Antitrinitarians*, trans. E. M. Wilbur (Boston, 1957).
LIENHARD, M. (ed.), *The Origins and Characteristics of Anabaptism* (The Hague, 1977).
McLAUGHLIN, R. E., *Caspar Schwenckfeld, Reluctant Radical: His Life to 1540* (New Haven, Conn., and London, 1986).
SCOTT, T., *Thomas Müntzer: Theology and Revolution in the German Reformation* (London, 1989).
STAYER, J. M., *Anabaptists and the Sword* (Lawrence, Kan., 1972).
WILBUR, E. M., *A History of Unitarianism: Socinianism and its Antecedents* (Cambridge, Mass., 1946).
WILLIAMS, G. H., *The Radical Reformation* (London, 1962).

8. Political Thought

BIÉLER, A., *La Pensée économique et sociale de Calvin* (Geneva, 1959).
CARGILL THOMPSON, W. D. J., *The Political Thought of Martin Luther*, ed. P. Broadhead (Brighton, 1984).
CHENEVIÈRE, M.-E., *La Pensée politique de Calvin* (repr. Geneva, 1970).
EIRE, C. M. N., *War Against the Idols: The Reformation of Worship from Erasmus to Calvin* (Cambridge, 1986), esp. 276ff.
GIESEY, R. E., 'The Monarchomach Triumvirs: Hotman, Beza and Mornay', *Bibliothèque d'humanisme et renaissance*, 32 (1970), 41–56.
KELLEY, D. R., *The Beginning of Ideology: Consciousness and Society in the French Reformation* (Cambridge, 1982).
LINDER, R. D., *The Political Ideas of Pierre Viret* (Geneva, 1964).
OLSON, O. K., 'Theology of Revolution: Magdeburg, 1550–1551', *Sixteenth Century Journal*, 3 (1972), 56–79.
SCHEIBLE, H., *Das Widerstandrecht als Problem der deutschen Protestanten, 1523–46* (Gütersloh, 1969).
SHOENBERGER, C. G., 'The Development of the Lutheran Theory of Resistance, 1523–1530', *Sixteenth Century Journal*, 8 (1977), 61–76.
SKINNER, Q., *The Foundations of Modern Political Thought*, 2 vols. (Cambridge, 1978).

9. *The Later Sixteenth-Century 'Confessional' Period*

9.1. *Germany*

BURCHILL, C., 'On the Consolation of a Christian Scholar: Zacharias Ursinus (1534–83) and the Reformation in Heidelberg', *JEH*, 37 (1986), 565–83.

CLASEN, C.-P., *The Palatinate in European History 1559–1660* (Oxford, 1963).

HECKEL, M., *Deutschland im konfessionellen Zeitalter* (Göttingen, 1983).

JUNGKUNTZ, T. R., *Formulators of the Formula of Concord: Four Architects of Lutheran Unity* (St Louis, Mo., 1977).

KLEIN, T., *Der Kampf um die zweite Reformation in Kursachsen 1586–1591* (Cologne, 1962).

KOLB, R., *Andreae and the Formula of Concord: Six Sermons on the Way to Lutheran Unity* (St Louis, Mo., 1977).

——*Nikolaus von Amsdorf (1483–1565): Popular Polemics in the Preservation of Luther's Legacy* (Nieuwkoop, 1978).

NISCHAN, B., 'The Second Reformation in Brandenburg: Aims and Goals', *Sixteenth Century Journal*, 14 (1983), 173–87.

PRESS, V., *Calvinismus und Territorialstaat: Regierung und Zentralbehörden der Kurpfalz, 1559–1619* (Stuttgart, 1970).

SCHILLING, H., *Konfessionskonflikt und Staatsbildung: Eine Fallstudie über das Verhältnis von religiösen und sozialen Wandel in der Frühneuzeit am Beispiel der Grafschaft Lippe* (Gütersloh, 1981).

——(ed.), *Die reformierte Konfessionalisierung in Deutschland: Das Problem der 'zweiten Reformation'* (Gütersloh, 1987).

SPITZ, L. W., and LOHFF, W. (eds.), *Discord, Dialogue and Concord: Studies in the Formula of Concord* (Philadelphia, 1977).

9.2. *Other European countries*

CAMERON, J. K., *The First Book of Discipline* (Edinburgh, 1972).

COLLINSON, P., *The Elizabethan Puritan Movement* (London, 1967).

——*Archbishop Grindal 1519–1583: The Struggle for a Reformed Church* (London, 1979).

COWAN, I. B., *The Scottish Reformation: Church and Society in Sixteenth-Century Scotland* (New York, 1982), esp. 110ff.

CREW, P. M., *Calvinist Preaching and Iconoclasm in the Netherlands, 1544–1569* (Cambridge, 1978).

CROSS, C., *Church and People 1450–1660: The Triumph of the Laity in the English Church* (London, 1976), esp. 124ff.

DONALDSON, G., *The Scottish Reformation* (Cambridge, 1960), esp. 49ff.

GREENGRASS, M., *France in the Age of Henri IV: The Struggle for Stability* (London, 1984), esp. 1–87.

——*The French Reformation* (Oxford, 1987), esp. 38ff.

HUDSON, W. S., *The Cambridge Connection and the Elizabethan Settlement of 1559* (Durham, NC, 1980).

JONES, N. L., *Faith by Statute: Parliament and the Settlement of Religion 1559* (London, 1982).

KINGDON, R. M., *Geneva and the Coming of the Wars of Religion in France 1555–1563* (Geneva, 1956).

——*Geneva and the Consolidation of the French Protestant Movement 1564–1572* (Geneva, 1967).

KIRK, J., *The Second Book of Discipline* (Edinburgh, 1980).

——*Patterns of Reform: Continuity and Change in the Reformation Kirk* (Edinburgh, 1989).

MOURS, S., *Les Églises Réformées de France* (Paris, 1958).

——*Le Protestantisme en France au xvie siècle* (Paris, 1959).

PARKER, G. *The Dutch Revolt* (London, 1977).

SALMON, J. H. M., *Society in Crisis: France in the Sixteenth Century* (London, 1975), esp. 117 ff.

SHEILS, W. J., *The English Reformation 1530–1570* (London, 1989), esp. 51 ff.

SUTHERLAND, N. M., *The Massacre of St Bartholomew and the European Conflict 1559–1572* (London, 1973).

——*The Huguenot Struggle for Recognition* (New Haven, Conn., and London, 1980), esp. 62 ff.

WORMALD, J., *Court, Kirk and Community: Scotland 1470–1625* (London, 1981), esp. 110 ff.

10. Pastors and People in the Developing Reformation

BAINTON, R. H., *Women of the Reformation in Germany and Italy* (Minneapolis, 1971).

——*Women of the Reformation in France and England* (Minneapolis, 1973).

——*Women of the Reformation from Spain to Scandinavia* (Minneapolis, 1977).

BELLARDI, W., *Die Geschichte der 'christlichen Gemeinschaft' in Strassburg 1546/1550, der Versuch einer 'zweiten Reformation'* (Leipzig, 1934).

BOURCHENIN, P.-D., *Études sur les académies protestantes en France au xvie et au xviie siècles* (Paris, 1882).

CAMERON, E., 'The "Godly Community" in the Theory and Practice of the European Reformation', in W. J. Sheils and D. Wood (eds.), *Voluntary Religion, SCH* 23 (Oxford, 1986), 131–53.

COLLINSON, P., *The Religion of Protestants: The Church in English Society 1559–1625* (Oxford, 1982).

——*The Birthpangs of Protestant England: Religious and Cultural Change in the Sixteenth and Seventeenth Centuries* (London, 1988).

DELUMEAU, J., 'Les Réformateurs et la "superstition"', in Société de l'histoire du protestantisme français, *Actes du colloque l'Amiral de Coligny et son temps (Paris, 24–28 octobre 1972)* (Paris, 1974), 451–87.

HOULBROOKE, R., *Church Courts and the People during the English Reformation 1520–1570* (Oxford, 1979).

HSIA, R. PO-CHIA, *Social Discipline in the Reformation: Central Europe 1550–1750* (London, 1989).

INGRAM, M., *Church Courts, Sex and Marriage in England, 1570–1640* (Cambridge, 1987).

JUNOD, L., and MEYLAN, H., *L'Académie de Lausanne au xvi᷎ siècle: Leges Scholae Lausannensis 1547* (Lausanne, 1947).

KARANT-NUNN, S. C., 'The Economic Position of Pastors in Ernestine Thuringia, 1521–1555', *ARG* 63 (1972), 94–113.

——'Luther's Pastors: The Reformation in the Ernestine Countryside', *Transactions of the American Philosophical Society*, 69/8 (1979).

KITTELSON, J. M., 'Successes and Failures in the German Reformation: The Report from Strasbourg', *ARG* 73 (1982), 153–74.

KÖHLER, W., *Zürcher Ehegericht und Genfer Konsistorium*, 2 vols. (Leipzig, 1932–42).

MEYLAN, H., 'Le Recrutement et la formation des pasteurs dans les églises réformées du xvi᷎ siècle', in id., *D'Érasme à Théodore de Bèze* (Geneva, 1976), 235–58.

MONTER, E. W., 'The Consistory of Geneva, 1559–1569', *Bibliothèque d'humanisme et renaissance*, 38 (1976), 467–84.

O'DAY, R., *The English Clergy: Emergence and Consolidation of a Profession, 1558–1642* (Leicester, 1979).

OZMENT, S. E., *When Fathers Ruled: Family Life in Reformation Europe* (Cambridge, Mass., 1983).

ROPER, L., *The Holy Household: Religion, Morals, and Order in Reformation Augsburg* (Oxford, 1989).

STRAUSS, G., *Luther's House of Learning: Indoctrination of the Young in the German Reformation* (Baltimore, 1978).

VOGLER, B., 'Recrutement et carrière des pasteurs strasbourgeois au xvi᷎ siècle', *Revue d'histoire et de philosophie religieuses*, 48 (1968), 151–74.

—— *Vie religieuse en pays rhénan dans la seconde moitié du xvi᷎ siècle (1556–1619)* (Lille, 1974).

—— *Le Clergé protestant rhénan au siècle de la réforme* (Paris, 1976).

Index